Breaking the Rules

The Intimate Diary of Ross Terrill

Edited and with an Introduction by Philip Gambone

ROSS TERRILL

RATTLING GOOD YARNS
PRESS

Rattling Good Yarns Press
33490 Date Palm Drive 3065
Cathedral City CA 92235
USA
www.rattlinggoodyarns.com
Library of Congress Control Number: 2023941581
ISBN: 978-1-955826-18-1
First Edition

For all the people who have touched and enriched
my life in many ways...

"The man is a success who has lived well, loved much, and laughed often."

—Robert Louis Stevenson

"It is the first duty of every individual to develop all his faculties of body, mind and spirit as completely and harmoniously as possible."

—Frank Harris

"If 'confession' can add even a little to our knowledge of the vagaries of human personality, one might as well confess."

—Michael Davidson

Contents

Introduction

"Life is horrible—at the level of logic. Life is wonderful—at the level of imagination." So wrote Ross Terrill in the pages of his private Diary (always capitalized by him), a journal he has been keeping for well over sixty years. At the time he wrote those words, Ross was forty-six years old and at the peak of his professional career—"in the process," he added, "of moving from the basement of the first realm to the penthouse of the second."

Ross's Diary is an intimate and candid record of a life lived at the penthouse level of imagination, an imagination nourished by meticulous scholarship, keen powers of observation, love of travel, athletic and culinary gusto, and an almost unbridled delight in sex. Calling himself a "born sensualist," he has lived a life—exuberantly, passionately, sometimes even recklessly—that bears full witness to that moniker. In all the ways that one might appraise a person of imaginative intensity, Ross fits the description.

To begin with, Ross has distinguished himself as one of the sharpest and most well-regarded China watchers of our era. A first-class academic, historian, and journalist, he has written numerous books and articles—each one a model of scholarly rigor—about the People's Republic of China and his native land, Australia. His astute, firsthand knowledge of the ins and outs of the Chinese political world, under Mao and after Mao, has won him serious critical attention and a large readership. To take but one example, his *Atlantic Monthly* articles on China were the first pieces that Henry Kissinger gave to Richard Nixon as the president was preparing for his historic trip to Beijing.

Ross has delivered lectures and addresses all over the world. The list of political leaders, scholars, writers, and other luminaries whom he has known, corresponded with, advised, and befriended constitutes a virtual Who's Who in international relations. Among reporters looking to get an insider's perspective on contemporary China, he became, as one of them once told him, "a household word." His TV commentaries on Nixon's China visit "cut through the fog with succinct answers to specific questions," *Newsweek* noted. Among the many awards and recognitions that Ross has received over the years are the Curtin-MacArthur Leadership Award; the *Los Angeles Times* Book Prize; the National Magazine Award for Reporting Excellence; and George Polk Memorial Award for Outstanding Magazine Reporting.

But the public side of this acclaimed China watcher is only one half of the imaginative life Ross has led. The other half was his sex life, "a wild beast that can spring surprises," he wrote in the Diary. Conducted in a mostly private and discreet manner, it was a life often lived precariously on the edge, at times even threatening, as he put it, "to play too large a role in one's overall life." Ross's life as a gay man spanned the pre- and post-Stonewall years. While his professional life was never under the same kind of vicious surveillance as was, for example, Frank Kameny's, nevertheless, Ross had to be secretive. He lived in a society where his sexual orientation could get him into a lot of trouble. On a few occasions, it came close to doing that. Aside from the frequency and variety of his sexual liaisons, what is most remarkable is how well—how cheerfully, enthusiastically, and usually levelheadedly—Ross made his own way as a happy homosexual.

◆◆◆

Born in 1938, Ross grew up in Bruthen, a small town in the southeastern Australian bush country. His parents, he noted many years later, "did not seem to love each other." In the Diary, he describes his upbringing as "narrow petty bourgeois." His father always told him to keep away from Black people, even though it was exactly the opposite that Ross wanted to do. As a teenager, he yearned "to go with the big boys, to take off [my] clothes as they did, get muddy too like them, swear like them." But his mother, who, he wrote, "hated to see me come alive sexually," forbade such behavior. Her restrictions left him "closeted, half-baked," and full of "sexual jealousy."

When he was twelve, the family moved to Melbourne, where he enrolled at Wesley College, an independent boys' school. There he rose to become Dux, the student with the highest academic standing. During these years, he began to cultivate a "contrarian streak," an attitude that left him with "a taste for difference." He favored Asians over Westerners, boys over girls. Drafted into the Army for his nine-month National Service—a casualty of the "birthday ballot"—he was appalled by the racism of his commanding officers.

At Melbourne University, among the first Australian students to attend classes with non-whites, Ross majored in history and political science. Influenced by his professors, he traveled to India in 1960, the first Australian participant in the Experiment in International Living. "I could see that India as well as China was going to be important in Australia's future," he later wrote. "Yet, when my teachers lionized India as the democratic path, I wondered if China's authoritarian path might be more effective. This was the seed of my interest in seeing China."

Ross first came to the US in 1963. At the time, as a Christian and a social democrat, he participated in, as he later described it to me, "an idealistic international solidarity attempt" for young students, which took him to various college campuses. The experience whetted his interest in the United States. Two years later, he was back, this time to begin graduate school at Harvard, but also for "freedom and privacy," he later noted. The young, 27-year-old scholar soon encountered the so-called "new awakening." It was the Harvard—and the America—of "blue jeans, loud music, drugs, the sport of Frisbee, and organic food grown in communal gardens," he wrote. The euphoria of the counter culture, so foreign to this bookish Australian, seemed revolutionary. Years later, he would confide in the Diary: "Only in the US do I *see* what I really want."

During those graduate school years, students "were meant to play only with papers and books, nothing else," he wrote. But even the austerities of graduate school—"my dorm room was the size of a large shoebox"—could not quell Ross's ardent extracurricular interests. Feeling that he "could be freer sexually in the U.S. than in Australia," he began exploring his homosexuality with ever greater abandon. He became quite adept at the art of the gay pick-up and began to perfect what became a lifelong, two-pronged policy: "Work hard. Play with indulgence."

Ross enjoyed an impressive early teaching career at Harvard. He also grew increasingly comfortable with life in America—"an offense," he noted in his Diary, "in the eyes of Australian intellectuals." "My sense of identity—scholarly, journalistic, erotic, religious—all largely spring from my [first] five years in the United States." But there were aspects to his professional life at Harvard that did not suit him. As his homosexual life blossomed, he had to face a critical choice: "Was I going to let Harvard shape me, or was I going to let the sexual come through?" It was, he later told me, a matter of love: "how you get it and what do you sacrifice along the way."

When Harvard did not award him tenure, Ross turned toward a career as an independent scholar. The books came out at a rapid clip. First was his big biography of Mao, which was translated into several European languages and, in its Chinese-language edition, sold over 1.5 million copies. He followed that triumph with *White-Boned Demon* (1984), a biography of Madame Mao, which Harrison Salisbury, a veteran writer on foreign affairs for the *New York Times*, called "a magnificent display of investigative reporting, research and reconstruction."

In 1979, Ross became an American citizen. Reflecting on that occasion, he wrote in the Diary, "Americans give the new arrival space to blossom." And, indeed, it was in America that he blossomed, both intellectually and sexually. *White-Boned Demon* was followed by *The Australians* (1987); *China in Our Time* (1992); *The Australians: The Way We Live Now* (2000); and *The New Chinese Empire* (2003). Independent professionally, Ross also became "more open as a gay." He began to see his sexual activity as something more than just sex, as, in fact, "an expression of personality." He had "jumped on board and signed on for the duration."

I first met Ross in the spring of 1996. Introduced by a mutual writer friend, we met for coffee so that I could pick his brain about China. I was about to take a semester-long teaching job in Beijing and was particularly keen to know what the scoop was about gay life in the People's Republic. Ross was not encouraging. He could only suggest a beach several hours from the capital and a hotel where, he had "heard," I might be able to find some gay men in the hotel's nightclub. As it turned out, gay life in Beijing, as clandestine as it was over twenty-five years ago, was hardly moribund. Still, Ross's discouraging advice was not ill-conceived. The one gay bar I found in Beijing that autumn was sometimes raided by the police.

When I returned to Boston, Ross and I went on to become friends. Coffees and dinners together were delightful occasions full of good conversation about writing, China, and, increasingly as we became more comfortable with each other, our boyfriends and lovers. Ross's warm personality, wry humor, utmost courtesy, and carefully measured opinions (often delivered with a gleam in his eye) remain, for me, the hallmarks of his personality.

Soon I was being invited to Ross's annual Christmas party. Given in his large, open-space condominium, which was lined, floor-to-ceiling, with books and papers, those gatherings became the highlight of my holiday season. The room was packed with gay men from all walks of life, including several who were or had been Ross's lovers. As the early winter sunset glowed outside his windows, lively conversation and delicious food were served up in festive, hearty proportions.

In 2007, I interviewed Ross for *Travels in a Gay Nation*, a book of profiles I was writing about prominent LGBTQ Americans. (Unfortunately, my publisher cut a number of profiles from the finished manuscript; Ross was one of the casualties.) During our interview, he told me that he was working on a memoir. That memoir, *Australian Bush to Tiananmen Square*, was subsequently published in 2021. As with all of Ross's books, I found it engaging, informative, and fascinating, especially about his years in China, including an eye-witness account of the Tiananmen Square uprising.

But *Australian Bush* is scrupulously discreet with regard to Ross's sexual life. I knew he was holding back, because over the years, he had told me many "juicy" (his word) stories of his "bold sexual adventures" and "crusades of lust." I kept thinking about what he had told me during the interview: "My memoir excludes the personal entirely."

When, years earlier, one of Ross's good friends remarked to him, "What would be fascinating is if you wrote about your homosexuality," her words stayed with him. "Diary bits maybe," he mused, "efforts to answer certain questions, some utopian dreaming, confession, portraits of certain people. The sensibility behind such a book would be my moon-struck awe at the experience of being a homosexual. The saturating impact of it on one's life. The continual excitement of it. There would be no need to drink while writing this book. It would be Ross facing up to Ross." But he worried that "people would object to the sex." How, he wondered, could he pull off such a book so as "to get away with a bit of lurid sex"?

Ross knew that he had the skills to carry out such a risky project: "The difference between the writer on the one hand, and the drunk and prostitute on the other, is only that the latter two never record their experience." His decision to bring out his Diary owes something to another memoir by another gay Harvard professor, Roger Brown's *Against My Better Judgment*. When he read it, Ross noted that Brown "throws down the compartment walls of his life," juxtaposing accounts of his sex life against his professional life. "God, what if I wrote of my life with Pan, Edward, Harry like this?" he opined.

The Diary is more than just a Don Giovanni-like tally of trysts. Ross's descriptions of his sexual activities are candid, lively, ribald, sometimes funny, sometimes wry, occasionally wince-inducing. One assignation will leave him waxing rhapsodic; another ironically amused. Unlike many of his sex partners, about whom he wrote that "experience just slides off them," Ross was intent on "mulling everything over." The Diary is a manifestation of how thoroughly he kept mulling over his life in all its many moments.

◆◆◆

There was, for a while, a girlfriend, a woman named Rachel, who, Ross reports in one Diary entry, was "interested in sex...with anyone." When she got married in the late

1960s, Ross felt released to explore male-on-male liaisons more ardently and purposefully. From then on, the Diary is replete with stories and vignettes of hook-ups, sex binges, and love affairs, some fleeting, other of longer duration. He threw himself passionately into these homosexual liaisons, and wrote about them with remarkable candor, detail, and insight. His tastes ranged from "romantic dallying" to "animal sexuality." Often, he confessed, he could not distinguish the one from the other.

By the time he was in his mid-40s, the "veneer," as he called it, of his schooling in Australia, had started to fall off. He became "less afraid of what other people think, less concerned to fulfill the demands that other people (whether in the literary world or the personal world) make upon me." Ross was enjoying not only great professional success but a parade of bold sexual adventures that left him both exhilarated and (occasionally) craving the respite of an evening alone at home. As an enormously busy scholar—with "the mentality of an insurance clerk, yet the hedonism of a sunbaked youth"—he found he had to negotiate "the tension between the hedonistic life and the monk-like life of the writer." It was, he wrote, "a dualism [that] crossed every aspect of my life, a dualism of gayness and all the forces and pressures arrayed against it."

At times, Ross felt like "an unguided missile" in his quest for sexual pleasure. And occasionally in the Diary, he would confess to some misgivings: "Perhaps," he wrote in 1987, "at the back of my mind is a lack of full acceptance of sex. Because it was at first presented to me as forbidden fruit, I feel an overly strong push to win that fruit." Another time, he wrote, "I am insecure because as a child I sensed—with a working mother—abandonment always just around the corner." But for the most part, he pursued his sex life with joyous abandon.

The frequency and range of Ross's sexual and amorous liaisons are, to say the least, staggering. At one point, he considered it "a minimum" to have sex with five different guys in a week. In his early fifties, he tallied up that he had enjoyed "56 incidents of sex with men more than 3 times" in the past half year. With his Rock Hudson good looks and gym-toned body, he was able to attract and hook up with men everywhere: at the gym, on the street, in bars and on the beaches, at conferences in the U.S. and abroad, and in other, far more louche venues. Acutely and enthusiastically aware of the "colossal power of sex," he noted that he "could not do without it." Orgasms left him "trembling." His loins would "not stay quiet."

Sex was for Ross never a shameful experience. It provided too much pleasure, exuberance, and joy for him to think of it as a guilt-inducing activity. He thought ninety percent of the world's guilt was "unnecessary."

"I think of times of sexual experience as among the very best times of my life," he wrote when he was forty-six. "Some will say that is selfish, but nothing could be more wrong. My memories of sexual pleasure are as much of giving as receiving. I think I have given more joy to others through sex than through writing, teaching, friendship, or conversation." Maybe, he speculated a few years later, friends "with sex added" would become the pattern of the future.

Who exactly were these partners—these bedmates, boyfriends, tricks, lovers, "half affairs," dalliances, fuck buddies? Generally, he was attracted to younger guys—what he called his "bond with youthfulness." And younger guys, who so often initiated the cruising, seem to have been quite attracted to him. He loved young men who combined "intelligence, sexiness, and a penchant for loyalty and domesticity," though he hardly ever passed up a chance for a casual romp.

"The perfect pattern for me," he noted, "is to make love in the afternoon, go to a movie, have a reasonably early dinner, then relax by walking the streets or sitting in a bar, knowing that the evening is winding down rather than building up toward lovemaking." He did not always adhere to this schedule.

Ross was not particularly exercised about sex roles—bottom vs. top, dominant vs. submissive. What truly mattered was that his sexual life be "life at its most intense." To one lover, he quoted Camus' words: "Don't walk in front of me, I may not follow. Don't walk behind me, I may not lead. Walk beside me and just be my friend." Ross was, above all, keen on friendship—friendly relations with his tricks and lovers, deeper friendship with a few.

He was careful to give his lovers leeway to make their own lives. A letter he wrote to one such lover in 1985 beautifully sums up Ross's "philosophy": "We can be original and find our own path. I expect for years to know you, and when you are married to see you, and your family. That itself may seem complex—but is it necessary to let complexity worry us? I suppose your life is going to have, as it already does, original patterns—maybe the time to pioneer them and get experience of them is now."

As he neared his fiftieth birthday, Ross reflected on the possibility of a gay partnership: "Sexually I'm full of curiosity. But I'm not desirous of really giving myself to anyone." He felt he was ready to accept his "irrevocable separateness and thus avoid super-romantic oneness with another." He no longer felt the urge, as he had with earlier long-term sex partners, "to merge myself with the other person, share everything with him."

Nevertheless, the Diary recounts several deep, lasting relationships. (In some cases, Ross has resorted to pseudonyms to protect their privacy.) One of the most poignant of these enduring love affairs was with a young Thai graduate student, Pan, who later succumbed to AIDS. Another was Edward, a young bisexual Black man with whom Ross conducted a long and sometimes unsettled affair. A third is Abdul—we meet him only briefly at the end of Volume 1—who remains a significant person in Ross's life. Juggling these more intense relationships with the tricks that came and went was often hard to manage—"an apples and bananas situation," he called it.

There are many amusing episodes where Ross had to choreograph, like a character in a Feydeau farce, the comings and goings of two or more sex partners within the space of an evening. No sooner had one lover flown off to Hong Kong than another one was in his bed. "Keeping two over-sexed Chinese happy takes its toll," he wrote. "With boyfriends as with dentures it is wise to have a spare. Something can always happen to Number One." Several boyfriends and regular tricks seem to have had keys to his apartment. Others would ring his bell at all hours of the night.

Ross's array of lovers exposed him to interesting and telling cultural differences. When he brings a former Chinese lover to a gay bar in Boston, the man asks, "Won't we be arrested?" Then there's the hilarious story of the Black evangelical preacher—"not totally otherworldly"—who, while they are making love, insists on playing a tape of his singing gospel jazz, and announcing "the biblical text that the song was based on." In another entry, written during a return trip to his homeland, he worries that he's lost the technique for getting guys in Australia. One Australian student invites him to tea. "But what a tortuous route that would be to getting into bed with him." Ross concludes: "If an erotic environment isn't there, lust doesn't arise the way it normally does. And in this situation, an orgasm tends to be mediocre. In time you could almost come to the dreadful conclusion that you didn't need or want one! The more you get the more you want (Boston) and the less you get you less you want (Melbourne)."

By the middle of the 80s, Ross had to confront the risk of contracting HIV, which, in those days, was tantamount to a death sentence. Often, but not always, he took precautions to protect himself. Nevertheless, as he wrote in March 1987, "I have a yearning for perfect unity & harmony, and not being able to thrill to getting fucked is a detraction." The ever-present specter of AIDS put him into darkly reflective moods: "AIDS is a metaphor for the basic helplessness of the human condition. What people do with each other in bed defies prudence, reason, certainly science." He worried about his partners who liked to get fucked without a condom. Ross never contracted the disease, but several of his friends and bedpartners did.

There are, as well, many lighthearted moments in the Diary, lovely instances of Ross's wry humor. About Japanese lovers, he noted that they are "quiet and effective in achieving their goals. Like Japan in trade policy." When one regular sex partner noticed the new clothes in Ross's closet and quipped, "You're into trendy," Ross confided to his Diary, "I don't think he realized they are not all mine." Another time, finding himself in a gay pub in Manchester, England, he inquired if any Chinese men were to be found in the city. The bartender shook his head but said he could give Ross the name of a good Chinese restaurant. That night, Ross wrote, "You ask the English about love; they tell you about food."

◆◆◆

Was he a "sex maniac," as one of his lovers once accused him of being? On occasion, even Ross wondered about that. If so, he opined, the cause might be his early experiences with his parents—a father who molested him as a child, a mother whom he felt had abandoned him. There was, he said, "something in me that just does not know when to stop." Was it "some silly wish to prove something" that made him want to fuck every day, he wondered. In the end, his answer was always, "No, it's just the pleasure of it." Nevertheless, as he approached his fifties, Ross began to consider that "sex two times a week, rather than five" might be prudent. "If I can calm down, do things step by step, think things through, listen to people, heed signals and realities around me, and not be too self-oriented, then my Golden Age is ahead."

In his late fifties, Ross recorded his qualms about getting old. "An ageing homosexual is seldom a pretty accomplishment—it is unlikely that I will be an exception," he wrote in 1998. From time to time, he experienced "tornado-like" assaults on his self-esteem: a novel that for years he'd tried to bring out never found a publisher. He fretted whether, professionally, he was merely "an ornament to the Sinological profession." Neuralgic illnesses beset him. There was an ongoing dispute with his brother over his mother's will, and "a general sense of old age's encroachment." All told, these turns seemed "like a tide against which it is difficult to remain standing."

The awareness of ageing began to dominate his life. "Quite often," he wrote when he was sixty-one, "the orgasm marks the feeling that it is time to stop—and go eat, or do something else. Sex is often surpassingly pleasurable, to be sure. But there is also the element of wanting to perform. Of needing to assure myself that I can still bring it off." He saw that he must "find a balance between striving and acceptance of reality as it presses in on us."

◆ ◆ ◆

As important as sex has been to him, Ross always saw his sexual life as but "part of a complex bundle of aspects" that defined him. Early on, he noted that "the gay part is not the whole of me, because sexuality is not the whole. Tennessee Williams is right in Memoirs to say that 'putting work first' is terribly important."

Consequently, the Diary contains a lot more than just accounts of sexual capers and romantic adventures. Ross took great delight in athletic competition and won several state championships in squash, his sport of choice. Dining out was another activity he keenly enjoyed. We read much, as well, about "the mad cantor of book-writing": the business of film options, publicity people, serial timing, royalties, good and bad reviews, the disappointment of books not garnering more sales or positive reviews, the missing pages of corrections faxed to a publisher, and "how little agents, even good ones, understand the writer's craft."

There are, too, occasional musings about how his life might have turned out had he not been gay. In 1984, on a return trip to Australia, Ross wrote, "If I had been straight, I may well now be a minister in the Hawke cabinet. Yet I do not regret the course of events." A few years later, he speculated that perhaps his cock had "derailed my ambition."

Some may be surprised to follow the course of what Ross calls his "political transformation," from Labor Party supporter of the sixties to the Reaganite of the eighties, or as he wrote in another Diary entry, "from the left-leaning *800,000,000* to the anti-communist *White-Boned Demon*." By the early 90s, he began to feel that the "liberal consensus among Cambridge intellectuals [had] squelched out original thinking on most public issues." He wondered whether he could ever have been a "long-haul leftist" because he sensed that by nature he was "aloof" and "elitist." Ross's turn from the left is yet another example of his fiercely independent spirit, his insistence on not toeing anyone's ideological line but his own. He has always been a champion of "the individual with his quirky and changeable ways."

◆ ◆ ◆

Ross once wrote, "It's not enough to write a superlative book; the higher task is to write an arresting book." There is no question that *Breaking the Rules* is an arresting book. The Ross Terrill who presents himself in this Diary is an engaging, witty, and scrupulously honest self-portraitist. Comparing himself to Madame Mao—"a (straight) willful conformist"—he calls himself "a (gay) willful conformist." Well, perhaps. But the conformist in Ross—a meticulous academic and latter-day conservative voter—is overshadowed by his wonderfully outré amatory life. "I hate a boring life"—a sentence he once inscribed in the Diary—could stand as his rallying cry.

A few days after his fortieth birthday, vacationing in San Juan, he wrote, "I am part vagabond and part citizen with a pinch of the bourgeois; in what proportions, it is not easy ... to say." It would not be inaccurate to observe that Ross has spent his entire extraordinary life calibrating again and again the proportions of that life formula. Each reader of the Diary will have to come to their own conclusion about who Ross is: sexual vagabond, scholarly citizen, self-possessed bourgeois, or some combination thereof.

For me, Ross has found an impressive balance between his life and his art, logic and imagination. He's never compromised on any of it. Early on—before he even reached his thirtieth birthday—he wrote, "What endures finally is integrity." As candid, hedonistic, and outrageous as Ross's Diary is, what most shines through is his brave pursuit of a life of freedom and integrity.

Frank Harris, another sexual memoirist, once wrote, "It is the first duty of every individual to develop all his faculties of body, mind and spirit as completely and harmoniously as possible." Ross's life, as told in his candid Diary, is a witness to that duty bravely realized.

◆◆◆

A word about the actual physical diary. Ross began his Diary sometime in the late 1950s, when he was in college. At first, he wrote it by hand, sometimes in journals and sometimes on loose sheets of paper. By the late 80s, he had switched to writing on a Kaypro, an early "luggable" personal computer. As the years went on, he kept upgrading to more powerful and sophisticated machines.

When he eventually decided to publish excerpts from his Diary, Ross began the laborious task of transcribing the handwritten diaries and downloading the information contained on his old floppy disks onto his newer model computer. He printed out these documents, but in a rather helter-skelter fashion, ending up with piles of transcripts that were not necessarily in chronological order. The process of sorting through all this material, putting the pages in order, verifying dates, correcting mistakes, and eliminating duplicate entries was a long, sometimes exciting, sometimes frustrating task, a task that we worked on together for more than a year. "The originals"—the early handwritten journals and the printouts of the computer-written entries—are currently stored in a storage vault in the basement of Ross's condominium building.

This volume of *Breaking the Rules* brings the Diary up to the late summer of 1989, when Ross, having returned from a harrowing few weeks in Beijing during the Tiananmen protests, meets Harry, who will become an important relationship in his life. As for the next thirty-four years of his life, stay tuned for Volume 2.

1963

Terrill began his Diary sometime in the late 1950s when he was in college. Those early entries record his observations of classes, professors, politics. Two years after he graduated from Melbourne University, he came to the United States for the first time, a delegate at an international gathering of young Christians. The twenty-five-year-old social democrat was greatly surprised, challenged, and "immensely stimulated" by the cultural and academic scene in which he found himself.

September 14, 1963, Princeton

I have been a very slow learner in the lessons of love, but I understand more than a year ago. I see that love is unconditional. To live this way, one has to respond to Christ, rather than to men. As Garrett says in *Crux*,[1] *the free man is one who lives as one who has been loved*. That way is the only Christianity I can see which releases one to love unconditionally.

On the plane coming over, I read the *Carnets* of Camus.[2] He dwells a lot on awareness, and isn't it a key word for Christians? I am horrified sometimes—I was today—at the ease with which I slip out of this realization and live where life becomes fear. It is because of the importance of awareness that prayer is now basic to me: it is the way I keep myself aware and open.

Fall, 1963

I feel shock encountering American society: money-crazed, practical, insular yet dynamic, practical yet wildly vibrant, friendly but violent. Rich, yet it seems 38 million out of 200 million live without money for necessities. If you fall in the great race for wealth here, no one stops to pick you up. So, I am told. I was excited by the Negro communities in SF and Chicago. Everyone talks about a racial revolution, but haven't they had a revolution already?

November 22, 1963, Princeton

During lunch in a Nassau Street restaurant with students of Princeton University, many talking about Cuba, a woman beside me grabbed my arm, a finger to her lips. "Blood was visible on the President's face," said the TV screen. "He has been taken to Parkland Hospital. It is not known whether he is dead or alive," a shaky voice on the TV screen whispers. Horror froze us in ours. A waitress fainted, and her tray clattered to the floor. Another girl carrying soup vomited.

Short of nuclear war, I did not think anything could bring the shock of this moment. The leader of the Western World in a hospital bed, death hovering, his blood-splattered

---

[1] *Crux,* an Australian journal of Christian thought and opinion.
[2] Carnets 1942-1951: *Camus' Diary and Working Notebooks.*

wife at his side. She had cried out, "Oh no, my God, they've killed my husband," as pandemonium followed the attack. Supreme power became supreme affliction.

Across Nassau Street, on Princeton's campus, students clustered around transistor radios. At the student center, heads rested on folded arms at cafeteria tables. From Washington an official croaked, "President Kennedy is dead." Helpless, some brimming with anger, others weeping, the Student Center rose for "The Star-Spangled Banner." One TV anchor groped for context by recalling that three other US presidents—Lincoln, Garfield, and McKinley—had been murdered in office. During the grey, timeless afternoon, churches opened, bells tinkled, organs began to play. The Princeton library prepared to close, as did most businesses.

Brand new to the USA, I marveled that guns could be bought more or less by post. In the evening, I ask myself what the next act of world-shaking criminality might be. In an age of H-bombs that seems alarming. Has the Bomb brought us to the end of the road?

Any Christian or social democrat (I am both) must feel the spiritual world and the working-class world are both without direction. Our God is too small, a god-of-the-gaps. First the geologists evicted God from their realm. Then the biologists did. Now the social scientists. We don't after all know what it means that "all things cohere in Jesus Christ."

November 25, 1963, Washington

Two Australians and I drive almost in silence for The Funeral. We stand two blocks from the Catholic Cathedral, where the crowds in black resemble a flock of birds. In wintry gloom, towering over the kings, prime ministers, and presidents was lofty, ramrod straight President Charles de Gaulle, striding nobly, almost as if in personal denial of death. But JFK is no more.

1964

1964, Athens, Ohio

I am the Australian delegate to a Christian conference of 3400 youth. "For the Life of the World" is the theme. Left-wing politics tugs daily against church theology. Outside the windows lies the beautiful valley of Athens. The food we kids eat is better than the stuff my parents eat in Melbourne.

A Texas girlfriend's account of her group's bus ride from Dallas to Athens jolts me. Each time the bus stopped for a meal, service was refused *unless* whites sat in one room and Blacks in another. The Texans declined and stayed hungry.

Between sessions today an Ohio student and I fell for each other. Only the third or fourth time I've had sex with a Black man. I have to learn new tricks. We take a risk as there are roommates with keys. Easily worth it.

After the conference, Terrill was keen to visit China, but entry into the PRC was difficult. "Beijing guarded visas for people from non-Communist countries like precious jewels," he later recalled.

His summer travels began in Europe, where he was, after many attempts, successful in obtaining a visa to China. Years later, in recollecting that odyssey, he wrote, "I missed so many opportunities in those years—including one day when a Brazilian, sitting on his bed at the Foyer John Knox [in Geneva], had a lovely hardon and smiled at me as I looked at it. In those days, I was one to study all the time. And I was one to agonize over moral questions. I suppose the only good thing about my abstinence during the 1960s was that, had I plunged in then, I might have gone to the extreme—as RT has been known to do—and undermined health and career alike."

July 1964, Prague

Hitchhiking through Europe, I knock on the carved wood-and-brass doors of Beijing's embassies in East Europe (few exist in West Europe), saying I would like to see the New China. I previously obtained permission from the Australian government to travel to China (a necessity). In Budapest, Belgrade, and Prague I am crisply told to wait two weeks for an answer. But I have to take a train or hitchhike to the next capital on my list before a reply comes at the previous Chinese embassy. This 25-year-old Australian with little cash is in a revolving door, a Chinese visa always just out of reach.

July 1964, Budapest

Budapest has many surprises: a beautiful place, quite lively, independent, and politically outspoken. After an absence of four years, I find it the most open and buoyant of the Communist capitals. The great thing is that Hungary is becoming part of Europe again. It is out of date to think of Europe as NATO and the Warsaw Pact, two blocs with an iron curtain between them.

July 1964, Warsaw

Warsaw is my last stop in East Europe. At the PRC embassy on Bonifraterska Street, I drop my humble approach and ask to see the ambassador to debate whether or not it is a good thing for Australian youth to understand China. A senior diplomat twice my age emerges, smiling slightly. Cups of tea appear before us; I make my case. Within 24 hours, a phone call to my room at the Bristol Hotel tells me a Chinese visa is waiting.

July 1964, Moscow

Impressive to see Russian women and men working together on road repairs, chatting and taking lunch together. Must tell my girlfriend Rachel in Melbourne. I have never seen such strong women or been served cold fish and vodka for breakfast. Much is gigantic, including the GUM department store that lasts a block.

At a collective farm a sign hangs on the school auditorium wall: "The Present Generation of Soviet People Will Live Under Communism." I politely tell a teacher that in Australia rural schools are small and we have no collective farms. "But you will have them in the future!" she cries in triumph.

July 22, 1964, Moscow

I am suspicious of the cult of personality. The Palace of Pioneers for youth looks like an exhibition of Lenin's life. Lenin is all over the bloody place. This is not how leaders are produced. A real Lenin could never emerge from a Pioneers Palace.

At Lenin State Library, holding 21 million volumes, I tell a blond female librarian I am en route to China. She warns me, like a doctor criticizing a poor diet: "Remember, the present government of China is just a dictatorship of one man, the chauvinist Mao Zedong. It is not a government of the people—and it is bent upon war."

1964, Tomsk, Soviet Union

An Aeroflot turboprop boards for Omsk. Two Hungarians struggle aboard with huge melons in four over-stuffed string bags. A Finnish business woman, on her sixth trip to China, is going to buy textiles at a trade fare in Shanghai. Albanian commercial officials plan a vacation in the imagined fleshpots of North Korea. Omsk looks like Alaska or the far north of Japan.

1964, Irkutsk

An Intourist guide leads me to a breakfast of buns and apricots. As we eat, a worn Chinese (CCAC) airliner that will fly me to Beijing rolls up outside the window, modest as a neighbor's truck. The cabin smells of bamboo fans and fragrant tea. Small Chinese hostesses bring chewing-gum, cigarettes, and plastic envelopes for fountain pens. When a male steward squeezes by, I move my elbow against the front of his pants; he beams. We fly over Lake Baikal, the barren ginger waste of the Gobi Desert, and North China's yellow streams and velvety hills. Siberia is huge; can Moscow hang onto it forever?

At Peking's[3] little airport a guide from the China Travel Service peers across the tarmac in my direction. Even a wandering Australian student cannot arrive in Mao's China unmet.

August 1964, Peking

A huge mass of Chinese in white shirts and blue pants fill Tiananmen Square protesting President Johnson's attack on North Vietnamese vessels in the Gulf of Tonkin, close to Chinese territory.

No high-rise or international chain hotels exist in this city, nor does any foreign airline but Aeroflot fly regularly to China. Drivers of the few cars, imports from Russia and Poland, with tired Chevrolets from "imperialist" days, make constant use of the

---

[3] Peking, the old-style Romanization of the capital of China, subsequently spelled Beijing in the Maoist pinyin system. Terrill used both spellings in the Diary, as he does with other Chinese cities as well.

horn, sending boys scurrying and old men hauling wagons lurching. My taxi dashes at fifty miles an hour for half a mile, then coasts at fifteen—to save gasoline, I'm told.

I check in at the Russian-style Xin Qiao Hotel, a rectangular cement block in the old Legation Quarter. I cannot make a phone call without first giving the hotel operator details of who I am calling and why, just as in Moscow and East Europe.

The Xin Qiao Hotel's guests include Laotian dancers and Cambodian table tennis players. Africans on trips of "Goodwill" come in and out of the lobby; in 1964 one-third of China's forty-eight embassies are located in Africa. Except for three Western resident journalists (UK, France, Canada), the main foreigners in the city are a scattering of French visitors. They stride in the terrible August heat in Parisian clothes, feeling proud that France, under de Gaulle, has led the way to diplomatic ties with the PRC.

I have never seen a pedicab before. Patched all over, perhaps being phased out as an imperialist relic? I like them because of the open-air ride, absence of a tooting horn, and leisured pace that permits sight-seeing. The drawback is the precarious seat and guilt that it might be "un-socialist" for a Westerner in his 20s to be pedaled by a middle-aged Chinese worker.

To my room at the Xin Qiao an attendant brings an English edition of the *New China News* Agency bulletin. The main theme of its hysterical reports on world events is anti-colonialism. One morning during breakfast, four Africans from my flight to Beijing from USSR come into the restaurant. They approach my table, and we shake hands and chat. The hotel staff erupt in oohs and ahs. I do not understand why, but soon see the point. To Chinese, schooled in Marxist orthodoxy about imperialism and national liberation forces, human warmth between a white person and Third World brothers is a shock.

No longer an abstraction, here is China as steel plants, crying babies, 3000-year old tombs, soldiers with fixed bayonets, bookstores selling Marxist pamphlets and the social realist works in Chinese of Jack London and Mark Twain.

The hotel dining room staff use bread as magic to keep Westerners content. These cheerful youths are convinced no European can eat a meal that does not include slices of dense, dry bread. A culture needs pigeon holes for other cultures; for Chinese, bread is The West (as, for Westerners, rice means Eastern civilization). If I order a meal that does not include bread, the waiter looks at me, "Haven't you forgotten something?" flashes a knowing smile, and writes the Chinese characters for bread on his docket as I press the back of my hand against his trousers in gratitude.

I know little of China, nothing of its language, and my eyes are my only tool. But I see first-hand the CCP repressing Buddhists and Christians. Religion seems a test of China's new society. I ask to see a Protestant pastor, Zhao Fusan, head of the Beijing Research Institute of Theology, and he receives me at Beijing's Rice Market Church. I know of Zhao from church contacts in Europe, since he represented China at international Christian gatherings before the Cold War put an end to Chinese participation.

Zhao wants to talk about socialist China, not about theology. He puts everything in a framework of imperialism, which my education makes me inclined to accept. "There is little light for us in Western theology," he complains. But I get little light from Zhao about Chinese theology. I ask him: "Which parts of the Bible do you turn to most often?" Looking impassive, he replies, "All parts of the Bible have appeared in a new light to us since 1949." Zhao does not seem a free agent. I am a persistent Christian believer, my liking for Chinese young men being my one deviation ("sin").

I visit the Beijing Library with its six million books and the head librarian, who learns English and German in his spare time, leads me through airy reading rooms and a rare book room. I ask what sections of the library were the most popular. "The one on Marxism-Leninism," he replies like a recording. I look up the English name C. Wright Mills, whose left-wing sociology books I read at Melbourne University, and find four English titles. I am startled when he answers my question about rules for borrowing: "Generally speaking, only organizations may borrow books—not individuals."

August 1964, Peking

The Chinese ultra-leftists are correct to say that a lot of "old crap" remains in China. The Tian Qiao folk entertainment area, south of Qian Men gate, attracts happy crowds with painted magicians, gesticulating storytellers, and double-jointed acrobats. It isn't forbidden to consult the writings of Confucius and Taoist philosopher Lao Zi, enjoy the symphonies of Mozart and Beethoven, go dressed in a colorful skirt to a dance on Saturday night and prepare at a hair salon. Not everyone yet realizes—or can say out loud—that the new crap (Soviet socialist realism) is not necessarily better than the old.

I sense an old-fashioned world. My room at the Xin Qiao is equipped with a chamber pot and a steel-nibbed pen beside a bottle of ink. In a nearby park, older Chinese men play tennis in long white flannels, gravely inching their way through a baseline game. My room has no shades and sun streams in upon the bed at 4:30 AM, as outside my window cicadas sing in millions. In the hotel courtyard, the bushes, although lush, exude heat. Beside them, old men and women do rhythmic snakelike *tai ji quan* exercises as dawn rises.

September 1964, Canton[4]

Ready to leave Beijing, I report to the CCAC air office near the Beijing Hotel. The small colonial building is deserted. "There is a storm over south China," an official says with a shrug. "No flight to Guangzhou until it's over. Try again in two hours." There are but a dozen flights out of Beijing to anywhere all day.

Returning to Australia, Terrill felt "spurred to serious study of China by an impression that China was Asia's center." He wrote a series of pieces for a new journal, The Australian, founded by a young newspaper mogul named Rupert Murdoch.

---

[4] Old-style spelling of the Chinese city Guangzhou.

1965

February 1965, Melbourne, Australia

Rupert Murdoch edits with a blue pencil a series of six articles on my trip to China. They go in his brand-new Canberra newspaper, with many pictures. He pays me in pounds rather than guineas (the British affectation still common in Australia). He says on the phone *The Australian* is losing money so he can only afford 30 pounds for the six pieces.

When the *New Zealand Herald* reprints the series without permission Murdoch, who's only in his 30s, goes after the Auckland daily, exacts money, and writes to me: "I hope the enclosed check for twenty pounds will make you feel happier."

With these six newspaper articles in *The Australian*, the nation's first-ever national daily, I felt China may have launched me on a journey. I wrote at the end of my sixth article for Rupert in February 1965: "All around the world, from Singapore to San Francisco, you see pockets of Chinese society. But only in China do you find the civilization in its power and its old and beautiful setting. Only in China do you realize what the Chinese as a race and a nation must increasingly mean. Just as once in the past, long before the present barren era of clashing ideologies and wrenching divisions, China was the greatest power on earth, so in the future she may become so again."[5]

August 1965, Melbourne

Gough Whitlam,[6] deputy leader of the Labor Party, is jacking up his fight with the leftwing Victorian party establishment over "unity tickets." I am a junior helper. Today, at Gough's suggestion I put my six ounces into the fray by resigning as vice-chairman of the foreign affairs committee of Victorian branch. Reporting this, *Bulletin* magazine calls me "Victorian Labor intellectual Ross Terrill." That's a first! I thought I was just a student. I want to study China at a world-class university.

The London School of Economics and Harvard have both offered me a fellowship to do a PhD Goodness, the little boy from Bruthen as a Doctor of Philosophy! Hard to imagine. Having read Professor John Fairbank's[7] *Trade and Diplomacy on the China Coast* inclines me to choose Harvard, where he teaches. I also have a hunch that life in the U.S. might suit my temperament better than life in "Mother England," as my grandmother calls Britain.

Harvard's offer was the Frank Knox Fellowship, which goes to the best graduate student applicant from "the British Commonwealth of Nations." Knox, in FDR's cabinet as Navy Secretary, was an Anglophile. The Knox apparently is hard to turn down—and I didn't want to.

---

[5] "China Face to Face," *The Australian*, March 22-27, 1965.
[6] Gough Whitlam (1916-2014) went on to become Prime Minister of Australia from 1972 to 1975.
[7] John King Fairbank (1907-1991), American historian of China. Often abbreviated in the Diary as JKF.

September 9, 1965, Melbourne

But the prickly China issue in U.S. politics almost cancels my plans for Harvard. As I pack, American officials in Melbourne deny me a visa because I oppose the Vietnam War, favor recognition of Beijing and favor nuclear disarmament. "Your views are incompatible with the American national purpose," wrote Consul Lin Roork, as precise as a surgeon telling me I belonged to the wrong blood group.

Carrying her letter of denial, I take a green Melbourne tram to the U.S. Consulate-General, pondering the phrase "American national purpose." Miss Roork asks if I've been to China, and I admit to this offense. She pushes a stapled sheaf of papers across the desk. "Is that your signature on a petition to the United States government protesting our testing of nuclear weapons?" Yes. "Do you see who signed the petition next after you?" I recognize the name of a well-known Melbourne Communist. Miss Roork is not impressed when I say you never know who might sign a petition after you.

The Leader of the Opposition, Arthur Calwell, wrote to the American ambassador in Canberra saying I was a social democrat with no Communist connections. Miss Roork backed down graciously and gave me a visa.

In the fall of 1965, Terrill returned to the US to begin his graduate studies at Harvard.

September 21, 1965, Tokyo to San Francisco

Some months ago, it seemed exciting to study in the United States. It's dynamic and culturally marvelous. But tonight, waiting at Tokyo International Airport for a Northwest flight, I am flat. Since leaving Australia 12 days ago, for stops in Asia, Americans have often horrified me. They trample upon Asia. They do not listen. They know only the way of dominance. In Singapore, they try to manipulate Lee Kuan Yew[8] through the CIA. In Saigon their huge machines bungle before Ho Chi Minh's soldiers. Japan they still view as a tamed colony. In Hong Kong, they strut as if to buy and sell the globe. Perhaps they almost can. Am I too harsh? Anyway, it's a funny mood to begin a career as a graduate student at Harvard.

September 1965, Cambridge

Arriving in Boston with just a few hours to register at Harvard and find accommodation, I see a notice on a bulletin board. "Mr. J. Vincent offers a room in his house for rent." Unaware of what lies ahead, I spend my first night in Massachusetts under the roof of a celebrated victim of the American "Loss of China" in 1949. "Mr. J. Vincent" was John Carter Vincent, formerly of the State Department and posts all over China, before being dismissed by John Foster Dulles.

Sitting in front of Professor Fairbank's desk, I propose a PhD thesis on the 19th-century political philosopher Kang Youwei. "How is your Classical Chinese?" Fairbank shoots back, poker-faced. Having just begun modern Chinese language class, I realize I

---

[8] Lee Kwan Yew (1923-2015), Prime Minister of Singapore, 1959-1990.

must wait years to read Kang in old Chinese. But a shiver of delight runs down my spine at meeting the man who virtually founded the study of Chinese history in the U.S.

From my rented room in John Carter Vincent's house, I trudge to my classes in Chinese from a Taiwan teacher, Chinese history from Fairbank, and political philosophy from famous scholars. I feel small and alone in the vast world of Harvard. I doubt I can succeed given its fierce competition and high standards.

Amazing is the Taiwan-orientation of China studies here. In Australia few take notice of Taiwan, but Cambridge is different. I don't think Chiang Kai-shek's regime in Taiwan is China, but the U.S. government and many Americans do.

As one of the few people at Harvard who had visited the People's Republic, Terrill was "viewed as a kind of messenger from China." Churches in Boston asked him to speak, and the Harvard student travel guide, Let's Go, commissioned him to write a piece on "Travel to Red China. During that first year as a graduate student, he wrote a four-part series on China for The New Republic. He was criticized from both the right—who thought he had been deceived by "the exotica of a revolutionary mass society"—and by the left, who saw the miracle of the "New Man" forming in the PRC. The summer after his first year at Harvard, Terrill traveled again to Europe.

1966

Warsaw, July 1966

Our Trade Mission is throwing a reception to celebrate a Poland-Australia Trade Agreement. I walk in. Poles are talking to Poles; Australians yarn to Australians; Italians, French and others form a third cluster. Fortunately, the tables are laden and the wine flows.

Jack McEwen, Deputy Prime Minister of Australia, nods gravely as a Silesian boasts of Polish chickens and hams. The head of the Department of Trade moves from guest to guest and from vodka to vodka. The Australian Trade man from Vienna, in Warsaw to make arrangements, is occupied with two attractive Australian secretaries. The Australian group approach Warsaw gingerly, astonished that people walk on two legs and cars run on four wheels. "I didn't expect nice hotels," one secretary says, her glass at forty-five degrees.

A Polish official corners me on hams. "You know why our hams are so good? Because our farms are small, and the pigs get a variety of food. In the West your farms are big, and the food is monotonous. All the world buys our hams." Then comes the barb, "The world buys our hams, without any fuss, but Australia obstructs this trade with sanitary regulations. As if our hams are not clean."

Our man from Vienna tries to calculate the cost of the banquet—which Australia is paying for—with a portly Polish caterer who fumes as the Australian fumbles, spewing traveler's checks left and right. The caterer has his mind on the bill; the Australian is tipsy. "I have given for them three receptions," says the sweating Pole, "and every time he is like this when the time is arrived to pay the bill." I say, see the funny side—not every day do Australian boys hit Warsaw.

September 2, 1966, London

Peggy Duff,[9] plump and talkative, is just back from a disarmament meeting in Japan where she and her leftist cronies tackled the Russians on the need to make clear, as Jean-Paul Sartre urges, that they will intervene if China is attacked. The possibility arises that in a land war between U.S. and China, China would do well, yet U.S. will not escalate to the nuclear level because the Russians will come in. In this way the Russians could play a crucial role. So says genial Peggy Duff, broaching Doomsday as she downs a hearty lunch.

September 1966, Cambridge

It is strange to be returning from an overseas trip, yet not to Melbourne. I am back, yet not really, and don't know whether to feel at home. As usual, the first re-contact with Americans is abrasive. Crude, naive, and loud. After a while you find that they are not all like that; I suppose I will grow accustomed.

I am filled with memories of just one year ago when I flew in from Tokyo, and on to Harvard—then a completely unknown quantity to me. This time I know the ropes; I'm in my dorm room an hour after touching down at Boston. I already envisage the smiles and frowns of my professors. But I do start to belong here.

September 1966, Cambridge

Dinner with a fellow political science student Chai, a Thai Buddhist. I understand Thailand better after glimpsing, in him, the calm of the Siamese. Chai's pattern after work is to play golf, promenade, drink at a night club. Chinese and other northern Asians at Harvard don't do that. Chai believes he can't find happiness "in this life." He is rare among my classmates in asking what is worthwhile and acting on his values.

September 1966, Cambridge

Tonight, is tense, for as I write the Australian Labor Party is electing a new leader. Nick Whitlam, son of Gough, and an undergraduate here at Harvard, has been on the phone half the day, and of course is even more anxious than me. I think Gough will get it, maybe easily. If he does, I hope left-winger Jim Cairns is Deputy. Then a new era would begin for our beleaguered party, not through the Victorian left's string-pulling, but by Gough's choice of a leftist top colleague.

Late September 1966, Cambridge

The place looks beautiful, very green and the weather is the best of the year. Yesterday, John Wong, a Hong Kong friend from London, called on his way to take up a job at Singapore. We spent the day in Plymouth, where the Pilgrims first landed in 1620, and at night in Chinatown.

---

[9] Peggy Duff (1910-1981), British political activist and organizer of the Campaign for Nuclear Disarmament.

I like the Chinese; they are humorous and subtle; two qualities Americans are seldom strong on.

November 1966, Cambridge

Our long Indian summer is passing; a chill is in the air. But the trees are still aflame, a glory in New England. The nation is almost in revolt in many places, caused either by Vietnam or race injustice.

Rachel from Montreal writes tortured letters about the struggles. At first, she was very anti-American, but I have opened her eyes to admirable aspects. The proof of America's appeal is that people come here, and millions more clamor to come. America as a magnet draws me and countless others. They call it voting with your feet.

Late Fall, 1966, New York City

With Alice Hageman to the *Battle of Algiers*. A good film, striking to see in the midst of the Vietnam War. The French tried the same impossible things as the U.S. now tries disregard of powerful nationalist feelings; futile militarism amidst a struggle that is political; even use of torture. Ten years later, even conservative Frenchmen look back on the Algerian War as pointless. At the time, they thought the Algerian National Liberation Front were "bandits," just as U.S. conservatives now consider the Vietnam NLF "bandits."

There is a dramatic stiffening of opposition to the war here. Real courage among draft resisters. For once, American leftists are doing more than talk; they are joined by thousands of mainstream political types.

The War could ruin this great country, if it is not stopped. What the four deserters from US forces said on Moscow TV last week is true: "The war is simply mass murder." (The US protested at Moscow "harbouring" the deserters; but what about the Open Arms program in South Vietnam, where our side does exactly the same?)

December 14, 1966, Cambridge

A dramatic stiffening of opposition to the War. Real courage among draft-resisters. For once American leftists are doing more than talk; they are joined by thousands of "mainstream" political types.

The War could ruin this great country, if it is not stopped. I get information from Vietnam, through Julie Sipiere in Singapore, who has one brother in Saigon, one in Hanoi, and a third fighting with the NLF. What the four deserters from U.S. forces said on Moscow TV last week is true: "The War is simply mass murder." (The U.S. protested at Moscow "harboring" the deserters; but what about the "Open Arms" program in South Vietnam where our side does the same?)

1967

January 21, 1967, Boston

Lunch with Rachel at Dew Hung in Chinatown, and what a week it ends. I have been sick as a dog, but perhaps the illness began (and will end) with Rachel. The shock of her marriage, straight after our warm time together in Cleveland, struck a blow which my busy-ness with a Montreal Conference fails to cover up. I did not oppose the marriage, I could not. Yet it makes me sad and lonely. Rachel who was so open is now closed. I thought she loved me.

Physically it has been one of the worst weeks of my life. Weakness all over, pain in limbs, eyes bad, a sore cock. Is there something wrong inside? Tuesday's tests will show.

PhD general exams have receded, and the future must be faced. Are the old crises coming back? What does life mean, what do I do with myself, as Margaret Bearlin[10] used to ask, helplessly, in Melbourne. To Shanghai to teach English for a year? Back to Australia, despite all? Just now, I would like to go to a village in Andorra and think everything out, helped by the rays of a sun I have ceased to believe exists in Boston. The finishing of the thesis and its hoped-for publication will probably reduce my frustrations.

Maroh 1967, Cambridge

As a spin-off from being in Vincent's house as a tenant, I tackle an essay on him in *The Atlantic Monthly*. It's to be called "When America Lost China: The Case of John Carter Vincent." Subject to Bob Manning's[11] editing, the piece will say, with exaggeration: "Just as Mao Zedong conjured up the myth of Liu Shaoqi's apostasy in the 1960s to guard the image of his own leadership as correct, so certain mandarins in Washington a decade earlier conjured up a myth of the China Hands' apostasy in order to guard their image of American leadership as omni-competent. It proved more satisfying to say that America could have stopped Mao if China Hands like Vincent had not betrayed their country, than to admit that the world was a very complicated place, diverse in culture, polycentric in power, in which prudence might be worth as much as zeal."

April 1967, Cambridge

A department store in Hartford, Connecticut, asks me to enlighten its customers about "this Mao Zedong." Even Fairbank asks me questions about my 1964 experience in China.

Fairbank is tall and benign, often in a bow tie, quick to give a slight smile. A kind and single-minded professor, he offers total attention to a person talking with him. He

---

[10] Margaret L. Bearlin (1930 -), Australian educator, feminist and social activist.
[11] Robert Manning (1919-2012), editor-in-chief of *The Atlantic Monthly*.

strides across the Harvard campus, head down, mentally drafting a letter demanding a job for a graduate student or seeking funds for China studies from the Ford Foundation. Amazing dedication, unwavering belief in education.

May 5, 1967, Madrid Airport

Hills in Latin shapes, olive groves, meticulously tiled roofs, a bleaching sun bathing all. Having been in East Europe, I see today the contrast between Slav and Latin. The Slav is intense, rather than sparkling; he conducts himself more quietly than the Latin; probably he has known more suffering. The Slav walks humbly, the Latin walks in self-assertion. More public display in Madrid—smiling, arguing, waving, staring—than in Prague and Warsaw. Perhaps Stalin's shadow inhibits this in Prague and other East European cities.

May 9, 1967, Madrid

I sit in the Plaza de Celebes, with magazines, newspapers and a sweet vermouth, watching the Spaniards stroll by. Fewer beautiful men in the streets than I expected; but when good, they are very good. And the personalities shine; beyond physique, they are fine lovers.

In the Prado Museum, I saw a work by Murillo that the guide proudly announced had been returned to Spain by Petain in 1941. "He was a good man, who liked Spain," she said of the French traitor. For a tour of the museum, I join the French group; our guide is soon making cracks against Americans. Sorry to say, everything goes better when I am not taken for an American.

In the heart of Madrid, a strange pang shot through me when I came upon Christopher Columbus Square, with the caption that this man discovered America.

Sunday is still a day apart here, even more than in Poland. But the priests in rich satins did not appeal. In the shops, clothes are superb in color and design, but I decide to wait for Hong Kong, where things are made to fit.

At a bullfight, the matadors look wonderful in their iridescent, floppy pajamas, their cocks as prominent as the design of glittering costumes make possible. At first there was little action. Then death came near. A matador slipped and fell in front of a bull. Seconds later the poor wounded beast managed to knock over the horse, exposing its rider to attack. Both happened close to the rails, so disaster was avoided. Was the crowd happy or disappointed? I will never know.

The real dialectic, I guess, is between bullfighter and spectators. Mixed together are lust for excitement, pride in a Spanish art, fear of death, belief in oneself. Perhaps bullfighting expresses "after empire" Spain. It is a subtle, if cruel sport; primitive, yet rich in "glory"—a substitute for imperial conquest.

May 11, 1967, Madrid to New York

Americans beside me in the TWA plane cast a blanket of Philistinism around them. Yet I begin to feel at ease living in the USA—in my selected USA. In any country, one selects. At Harvard, I have found in eighteen months a dynamic and welcoming environment.

As happened during my trip to Europe last summer, the War got worse during the summer. The history of the Suez crisis of 1956, vivid to me as an Australian teenager, offers two lessons relevant to Vietnam. Eden mistook a sideshow for a new Munich. And the British misread the nature of the opposition. We—the US and its allies—overweigh Vietnam, under-weigh China, and are at sea with Asian nationalism.

In the summer of 1967, Terrill received approval for a second visit to China. He intended to go via Japan and Hong Kong, where he was to pick up his visa. But by the time he reached the British Crown Colony, a message was waiting for him: "We regret that your idea of visiting China during 1967 has to be abandoned." The gyrations of the Cultural Revolution had made his visit "inconvenient."

Summer, 1967, Tokyo

Japan, half the Orient, half not. Their writing binds Japanese to the East, but when you see that writing on super-express trains and advanced electronic equipment, you feel Japan escapes our categories.

Japanese seem suspicious of foreigners—underneath their marvelous politeness. "We are less cosmopolitan than the Chinese," says my YMCA friend Ken Shiuzuki, explaining why Japanese did not pour into Southeast Asia as the Chinese did. "Japanese always want to come home again." There is no big "Japan town" in the whole of Southeast Asia, Ken says, though scores of Chinatowns.

Summer, 1967, Tokyo

If there are no Japanese who drive me crazy with sexual desire, thousands are acceptable. Are they fairly flat in shape (limbs, heads, bums, breasts) because they have been sleeping on the floor for 2000 years? Probably a silly question.

July 1967, Tokyo

I find among Japanese scholars a love of form, of taxonomy, of ordered progression of argument. Max Weber is popular here, because many Japanese want an explanation of things that does not rely largely on economics. Since World War II, for many intellectuals, Weber has replaced Marx as chief social theorist. Some say interest in Marxism is declining among Japanese students. Others say interest in all philosophies is low. The smooth society? They would like my friend Dan Bell's book, *End of Ideology*.

September 1967, Canberra

A good day in "my nation's capital." By chance, Gough Whitlam, now Leader of the Opposition, was arriving from Sydney as I came in from Melbourne. He invited me to drive with him to Parliament House.

"What should my son do?" he asked me of Nick, still an undergrad at Harvard. I replied that he seemed to want to go into politics. "But I wonder if that would be wise," the Leader of the Opposition said. "Perhaps the public service would be better." He added pensively: "It's four years since I had a good talk with him—but I like him." It being budget day, the photographers were after him; as we reached the steps of Parliament House, he straightened his tie and said to me, "Well, here we go—all the networks are waiting for us!"

September 1967, Cambridge

Lunch with Judith Shklar,[12] one of my professors, European-born, at the Harvard Faculty Club. She flutters like a bird. "Half of my family was killed by Nazis and half by Soviet Russians," she says between mouthfuls of Boston scrod. A survivor, she prefers, now, to attach herself to the insignificant, tossing interchangeable political theory concepts high in the air like a juggler playing with random colored balls. Give it to her, she is one of the truly brilliant members of our department; she really believes in the world of the intellect.

September 1967, Cambridge

Today I read *Ordeal by Slander*. I like the way Owen Lattimore recognizes the moral dubiousness of vindicating himself against McCarthy by one-sided testimonies and proof texts. Read seventeen years after it was written, *Ordeal* leaves me with a question: what is a loyal American? If Lattimore had been more involved with the Reds than he was, he could not have made the (effective) anti-Red defense he did—but would he have been a less loyal American for that?

November 4, 1967, Cambridge

At the Government Department party Sam Huntington comes up and grates, "Congratulations. You're the top man, this time, you did very well [in the general exams]." I asked the chairman if we will be seeing his Vietnam report. "All scholars like to publish their stuff—some of it will come out." He evidently knows of my *New Republic* writing on the war and on China, which are not in agreement with his views.

Sam Beer[13] has changed his opinion on the war, but doesn't sound convincing ("It hasn't worked out"). Explained his toughness in my PhD oral exam with the comment, "Our good students have to be given something to wrestle with."

Peter Gourevitch, a teaching fellow, gave me the dismal news that *Public Policy*, which has accepted my essay "The Deputy Leadership of the British Labor Party," does not pay for articles. He managed to visit Paris three times in the last year; these teaching

---

[12] Judith N. Shklar (1928-1992) was Professor of Government at Harvard.
[13] Samuel Hutchison Beer (1911-2009), American political scientist and professor at Harvard. Terrill deemed him "my mentor."

assistantships are not bad, apparently. I would like one. Stanley Hoffman[14] sails up to say in France only the journalists, not the scholars, have got fresh stuff on China. Ed Epstein urged me to see his editor at *New Yorker* some time—Aron A "He is left-wing and likes your stuff."

December 12, 1967, New York

Lunch with FC of the Polish mission—from Christians to Communists!—who is more cordial than ever. My *New Republic* article from Warsaw has gone down well—it was translated into Polish—and he wants to "keep closer in touch." But his idea of me "writing a document on Vietnam" is puzzling. Write a document for the Polish Communist government? No.

He was scornful of the Russians, "so eager to imitate the Americans." "Poles are too European to like this," he added. He conceded some Chinese positions and said they are "the only power in the world really opposed to the USA." He cited Germans telling him the allied bombing of Germany helped Hitler by bolstering German morale; thus will U.S. bombing in Vietnam backfire. He said, political views apart, "we Europeans are amazed at the foolishness of the U.S. on Vietnam."

December 18, 1967, Cambridge

Cocktails at the Vincents'. The usual pattern: Scotch, crackers smeared with anchovy paste, exchange of news; the topic of China as liquor sets in. JC served in Changsha and other posts in China from the 1920s and Morocco and Switzerland later. So many stories, such an array of colleagues.

John Carter is a different breed from other ex-ambassadors I've so far met at Harvard—John Kenneth Galbraith[15] and Edwin O. Reischauer[16] being the main ones. He reminds me of an America at once refreshing and hard to credit. What did this man in? The system? McCarthy's one-man crusade? The Soviet Union showing its teeth? Of course, Vincent was fired, a humbling experience, unlike Galbraith and Reischauer whose careers soared after their ambassadorship.

Who runs US society, where does power really lie? I do not yet know. Was Wright Mills correct in identifying a power elite? Perhaps it's just that US society is a headless monster, like so many entities that at first appear to have personality and unity.

John Carter pointed out that Fairbank and EOR did not know Southeast Asia, only China and Japan, respectively, so they were unprepared for Vietnam. In the 30s and 40s, Americans neglected the rest of Asia, he explained, because it was in "dirty colonial hands" (France, UK).

---

[14] Stanley Hoffman (1928-2015), at the time Terrill was writing, was C. Douglas Dillon Professor of the Civilization of France at Harvard.
[15] John Kenneth Galbraith (1908-2006), Canadian-American economist, diplomat, advisor to five Democratic presidents and popular Harvard professor, who authored almost fifty books.
[16] Edwin O. Reischauer (1910-1990), American diplomat, scholar, and professor. He served as Ambassador to Japan from 1961 to 1966, and was the founding director of the Japan Institute at Harvard.

Interesting by-product of this: in FDR's time, the Far Eastern and European divisions disagreed on colonialism. John Carter, head of the former, lost out against George Kennan and others in the latter, who said the U.S. must compromise with the Europeans out of global considerations. The turning point, John Carter says, was when "certain generals" got the upper hand in advising FDR. John Carter and Betty, like Jack Service and John Paton Davies, knew China; they clashed with those who created a China out of their own psyche and/or ideology.

Growing old is terrible; how to avoid its worst aspects? What endures finally is integrity.

December 20, 1967, Cambridge

I begin to feel, since the PhD general exams have finished, that I should do the thesis quickly and then go "out into the world."

December 1967, Cambridge

Christmas party at John and Wilma Fairbank's house, with Ben Schwartz,[17] inscrutable, of course, Ezra Vogel,[18] a rising star in sociology, and others. Met Eddie Chen and his wife, who are renting in Vogel's house while Eddie researches Vogel's book on Canton. With pleasure and astonishment, the Chen's realize as non-Americans we three are kindred spirits. They open up! "Vogel treats me like a child," Eddie complains.

Later, Ezra says, amazingly, to me. "I'm not sure what we are going to do with Eddie, now he is no longer much use to us." Toss him away like a used Kleenex? That seems to be Ezra's way. One day he may do it to me if he can. But Fairbank was very encouraging about my future plans.

1968

Despite the frustrations of still being a graduate student and living in cramped and Spartan quarters, Terrill traveled a good deal during 1968: to Czechoslovakia for a Peace Assembly and research on a piece for The New Republic; then a summer based in Paris and London, interspersed with events in Sweden and Finland for the World Christian Student Federation; and finally another trip to Paris, mainly for the working committee of the Peace Conference, with a Casablanca mini-holiday on the way home.

March 5, 1968, New York

My Czech diplomat friends are in excellent form, and helpful about my trip to Prague this month. Cognac in the morning they coped with better than I. By the time I left—

---

[17] Benjamin I. Schwartz (1916-1999) taught at Harvard from 1950 until his retirement in 1987. He was also director of the Fairbank Center for Chinese studies. In the Diary, Terrill frequently abbreviates his name as BIS.
[18] Ezra Vogel (1930-2020), the Henry Ford II Professor of the Social Sciences at Harvard.

late—to lunch with the Soviet diplomat Kuzmin[19] at the UN, I was swaying. Kuzmin was agitated, and not only by my lateness. Perhaps the departure of his wonderful boss Fedorenko[20] has left him less secure in his China work. He insisted on us both drinking whisky sours throughout the meal.

I ask Kuzmin why Moscow is embracing Delhi. "Lenin said Russia, India, and China would decide the future of the world." I ask about the famous pro-USA UN vote on Korea in 1950 for which Moscow's Malik was unaccountably absent. "We don't know why," Kuzmin said a little wearily. "Instructions, instructions...." Evidently not mere chance.

Later: Prague

I met my Hungarian friend Karoly Toth in the lobby of the Park Hotel, where our council will meet, and he asked my view of recent Czechoslovakia events. Of course, he is haunted by the memory of 1956. "Remember," he says, "Hungary is very close to here."

Within hours of arriving, I sense a relaxation of atmosphere: in the friendly officials at the airport; uninhibited street scenes; a buzzing in the lobby of key hotels; a keenness to read the papers and tune in to radio and TV.

Spring, 1968, Cambridge

At my former landlord John Carter Vincent's dinner party, wife Betty produces a petition lambasting bull-fighting. "If you've ever seen a bullfight, you'll sign this." Stalling for time, I remark to Stanley Hoffman, a French-born political scientist, that it seems the sport of an "after-empire" country. If the young Spaniards were abroad seeking natural glory, like their ancestors in South America, or young Brits recently in India, they wouldn't be in bull rings.

Betty tells the dinner table that the woman sponsoring the petition, the RI environmentalist activist Mrs. Pell, widow of a former US senator and ambassador to Portugal, has published a version of the Bible with all the "cruel parts" cut out.

"Is the crucifixion out?" I ask.

"Oh no, only cruelty to animals," Betty says.

Spring, 1968, Cambridge

In the crisis atmosphere over Vietnam, we troop to 2 Divinity Ave,[21] past the stone lions that announce Asia, for an "East Asian Studies" caucus on what we should do. I am amazed as an Australian at the bold challenges from students to teachers—and how the teachers accept this reversal of fortunes. One kid gets up and says Ed Reischauer, Kennedy's ambassador to Tokyo, is a coward not to speak up against the war. Reischauer listens gravely and says little.

---

[19] Aleksandr Ivanonich Kuzmin (1941-2022), Russian diplomat.
[20] Nikolai Trofimovich Fedorenko (1912-2000), Soviet ambassador to the UN (1963-68).
[21] Address of the Harvard-Yenching Library, the university's Asian Studies library.

Our liberal professors are privately nervous. "Kids have got to learn the limits that must be enforced," said one at a party. The radicals "are pushing the liberals too far," said another professor the same evening. "The students don't have a prayer against the University." A third cynic quipped, "Everything will settle down when the [leftist] SDS kids turn 30."

Later, April 1968

Stirred up, I need a change; happily, it arrives. On a lovely evening I walk by Langdell Hall at the Law School. A Black student of medium height and perfect build approached. Our eyes met; that was it. My dorm room nearby was the size of a large shoe-box. We students were meant to play only with papers and books, nothing else. Doug and I tore each other's clothes to the floor. It was the first time I swallowed cum to the last drop. Doug will soon start law school in that same Langdell Hall. If he shows the precision and command I saw and felt, law courts will give him many victories.

June 12, 1968, Paris

Not the best place to try and recover from the horror of last week's assassination of Robert Kennedy. The French liked him in their way but have little appreciation of what a loss his death is right now to the US. Parisian journalists say: "Oh well, that's America." Putting things down simply to "America," they are unable to sense the tragedy, or triumph, of any particular event in America.

Besides, they are pre-occupied with their own affairs. De Gaulle has (for the moment) dropped his gaze from lecturing the planet to contemplating his own shabby backyard. I watched two students nearly killed by police near the Pont St. Michel tonight.

June 16, 1968, London

Read Bertrand Russell's second volume of autobiography today. Not as good as the first. It has less passionate wrestling with life and struggle for truth, more about making money in order to live and keep a family. He does not glitter the way he did up to 1914. But he is still marvellously concerned to discover the truth about life, even if less sure that he will do so.

Desolate in body and spirit these last days. Which is cause and which effect? The diet of Paris has certainly not done me any good, and already leaving New York I was tired and depressed by the RFK disaster. But a larger problem exists: what is there really to live for, and how to avoid the rat race that is almost universal? Live in Asia? Write about matters other than politics?

Certainly I still take myself too seriously and am too vain.

June 20, 1968, London

The English have let their hair down; they clasp incoming tastes and fashions to their bosom. The empire disposed of (as children are ejected from a household they grew up in), ex-imperialists open a bottle of sherry—no kids to notice now—and simply enjoy themselves. Let foreigners come to them, instead of themselves going to the ends of the earth, establishing colonies, trading, preaching, educating. *New Statesman* editor Kingsley Martin says the English have changed from Romans into Italians.

June 21, 1968, London

Basil has the punch of a Jamaican, yet pathos, too. What happened to the West Indians; they seem beaten down in spirit? Eight years in London, yet Basil still feels a stranger, more so than me after a few weeks. Maybe he misses swaying palms, bananas, and baking sunshine?

Still, a good evening of lovemaking, considering my ten days of unfamiliar food, too much drink, irregular hours, and the strain of interviewing for my Harvard thesis. Basil sucked hungrily and I tried to match him. But how hard to do more than one thing at once. I have to do something single-mindedly or not at all.

June 29, 1968, London

A sign of the particularism in world politics recently, upon which I have dwelled in my Czech piece in *Christianity and Crisis*: the terms of political degree have lost their universality. "Liberal," "Conservative," "Left," "Radical"—all can now be used only with reference to a particular context. Leftists in Prague are called conservatives, both there and in the West, while rightists are called radicals. How far away are the years of international ideology! How fragmented world politics has become!

July 14, 1968, London

Hearing Donald Soper preach at the citadel of Methodism, Kingsway Hall, I feel nostalgia. How much is autobiographical—a battered Christian looking back on more orthodox days? How much is historical—watching the end of the phase of British Christianity when notable preachers had great influence?

July 1968, Stockholm

Youths' hair has lengthened. "Jesus figures" are everywhere. Smooth, clean lines abound. God, what beautiful limbs at the swimming pool; golden, supple, relaxed.

The smell of the *bastu*[22]—wood, sweat, humanity. The glistening copper skin of back and legs, sharply contrasting with white loins. The human freedom of this bathhouse.

I catch up with the movie *I Am Curious*. Some good sex scenes: a superb fellatio, as a guy comes across a girl in the garden, grabs her, sits her back, with a jab unzips her, then plunges his head at her loins, his tongue lashing and writhing, thrust deep into a red hot cunt. Then with hungry lips, she kisses, licks, gum-licks, and mooches his cock,

---

[22] *Bastu*, Swedish sauna.

her lips, and his weapon about equally in view. Later a fucking scene, the pair sitting facing each other on a parapet outside the Royal Palace.

Sweden reminds me of Australia. Repression (Protestant) and hedonism together. Spaciousness. Dullness. Privatism. Good housing and many cars. Unsophistication and practical freedom amidst affluence.

In the sauna, every male in our WSCF team—me excepted—puts a towel over their sex throughout the process.

August 5, 1968, Manchester, UK

In the gay Rockingham Club, I ask a bartender if any Chinese men are to be found in the city. He shakes his head. Then he brightens and says he could give me the name of a good Chinese restaurant. You ask the English about love; they tell you about food.

September 10, 1968, London

I strolled around Chelsea. This neighborhood has grown loud and psychedelic. The streets are still brown and solid, but the Beautiful People have sprouted. The gay wine of their free-flowing existence has filled the solid Chelsea bottles. You need dark glasses to navigate the Brompton Road, and X-ray vision to know how to address these pretty creatures of indeterminate sex.

October 1968, Near Paris

The moment of truth on Czechoslovakia seems to have come at this first Working Committee meeting of the Christian Peace Conference since Soviet tanks rolled into Prague. The Russians in their black robes are grave. Bulgarians sit in solidarity beside them, but Poles and Hungarians distribute themselves among the various non-Bloc nationalities.

Why do people talk of a terrible danger of US-Soviet war? Nothing seems more distant at present. The Czech crisis has not harmed Moscow-Washington relations one bit! LBJ didn't lift a finger to help Prague. We face a crisis of socialism and a human tragedy, but certainly not a US-Soviet crisis.

Georges Casalis[23] very earnestly brings the French évènements into relation with Czechoslovakia and declares that the world is in revolt against "imperialism in whatever form." I really don't agree. In most of Asia and Africa they are building not rebelling.

Last morning: The Russians have changed gears today. Conciliatory and even reasonably good-humoured. They have accepted, I think, that they will have to stomach a resolution that criticises the invasion of Prague. They've decided to pay this (slight) price asked of them and are relieved it is not higher (withdrawals by West and Third World people from our peace movement).

---

[23] Georges Casalis (1917-1987), French pastor and theologian.

October 12, 1968, Casablanca

The airport cannot be much different from in the Bogart film. Fog, palms, Arabic music. Loitering, dozing officers; a faint air of eroticism and mystery; the long glass-walled terminal, facing onto a wavily-uneven tarmac. In town, you still find the Café des Negociants, and the Café de France, much as they must have been for Bogart.

October 13, 1968, Casablanca

The "salt sea smother," in Masefield's phrase, takes me over as I swim for hours in the Atlantic. From the beach, I go with Mustapha to his home in the casbah. After winding through tiny lanes, we suddenly stop. In the half-light a curtain faces us. With a skip, Mustapha pushes it aside, crouches low, and slips in; his sister and I follow. Inside are several children, some in the care of grandfather. One puffs a bellows at a little fire under a kettle; she beams as I admire her handiwork. In the thick-walled living room a couch is piled high with velvet rugs. It is here that Mustapha and I make love, while his wife prepares a dinner of couscous for us all to eat when passion is spent.

October 14, 1968, Casablanca

In the Ain Diab-to-Casablanca bus, a young Arab is seated and a young French couple are standing. Frenchman taps Arab on the shoulder, tells him to give up his seat to the French wife. Arab does so, moves to the back of the bus. French wife sits sullenly, as if resenting that she must move among people as unkempt as Morocco's Moroccans.

November 13, 1968, Cambridge

Drinks at the John Carter Vincent's. For the first time ever, he did not this year vote for the Democratic candidate for President, but for the Socialist. Thus behaves a former State Department minister in this year of horrors.

December 17, 1968, Cambridge

Christmas dinner and a play at Kirkland House.[24] I've seldom seen anything as bawdy in public. The famous political philosopher Louis Hartz[25] from my department was lapping it up. He roared at a line to the effect that Alice (our House Secretary, who is the lover of poet Elizabeth Bishop) "serves under the Master."

I found Louis interested in Tawney, the topic of my thesis. What a boon. But a man from the Superintendent's Office slapped Hartz on the back warmly and said, "How now, do you remember me? I certainly remember you." Broad grin. "You're from the

---

[24] Kirkland House, one of the residential "colleges" at Harvard. Terrill was a member of Kirkland House's Senior Common Room, an informal group of distinguished professors and others associated with the House.
[25] Louis Hartz (1919-1986), American political scientist best known for his book *The Liberal Tradition in America* (1955). Hartz was a professor of government at Harvard from 1956-1974.

kitchens." Louis looked nonplussed and the fellow corrected himself. "Oh, not the kitchens, You're the Procurer! I knew it was to do with food."

"The wrong man."

"The wrong job perhaps, but not the wrong man. How could I forget you?"

Louis said as if changing the level of the conversation: "I am a Professor of Government" and turned away. I went to get another drink. I wouldn't be surprised if the great Louis is indeed sexually mixed.

December 21, 1968, Cambridge

My first-ever book galleys arrive from Friendship Press. What a strange and impressive metamorphosis a book goes through between the typescript stage and its identity as a book in galleys!

A cocktail dinner at my history classmate Edwin Moise's place. Full of mathematicians, including Tom Lehrer,[26] a mathematician before music claimed him. Lehrer, in a fresh velvety voice offers clever lines on the muddled state of the world, accompanying himself on the piano, showy and brilliant.

At night, I went to see Dallas upstairs at Kirkland House. Black, smooth-skinned, and affectionate. A wonderful orgasm. I felt part of me was tearing away, giving forth without end. My eyes felt melted into my head, losing their separate identity.

December 22, 1968, Cambridge

I run hot and cold on the question of interest in Australia, and its politics, these days. I am very interested in what I am doing here, my graduate studies, etc., and yet I am certainly going to go back and have a crack at politics before very much longer.

1969

January 1, 1969, Cambridge

Another year gone. For the world at large, not a good one. More of Vietnam; the invasion of Prague; Middle East trouble; a general sense of drift in the West; little progress against encroaching world poverty. How many more evils can we adjust to without losing our hope altogether? And the other, quite different problem is that my academic superiors may well take an ambiguous view of all my non-scholarly literary activity.

January 2, 1969, Wellesley

Party and overnight with the Australian-born Clem Green and his bouncy wife. Clem says to me: "I am fascinated by the mixture in you of the international man and the homespun attachment to the Australian soil."

---

[26] Tom Lehrer (1928-), a popular mathematician and singer-song-writer.

January 9, 1969, Cambridge

Saw John Kenneth Galbraith about my study of Tawney. Rather offhand. Very quick method with a visitor; in interviewing him you face the danger of being unready for your next question.

At the end, I went to shake hands, but he had not intended to do so. I doubt that he was very impressed with me, or really understood what I am trying to get at in my study of Tawney. Why should he bother with a little fish like me? His ante-office walls are lined with copies of his own books in myriad tongues and editions.

January 20, 1969, Boston

TV brings us the Inaugural Ball of Richard Nixon. It is like watching a children's party. Bejeweled denizens rush to a camera to chirp for the viewers. Little sophistication: no tradition to soften the crudeness of it.

February 20, 1969, Warsaw

At an opulent government reception, a Polish Vice-Minister speaks. Four Peace Conference figures then speak. Unexpectedly the Vice-Minister rises once more, thanks three of the four preceding speakers—omitting Ondra, the Czech who is General Secretary—and ends with a blunt warning that acts, not words, count. "Your Christian Peace Conference must not be a mere debating society."

Tonight, brings the end of the Working Committee session. It also brings the end of my involvement with the Peace Conference. And the end, for the present, of my links with East Europe. Neither can survive Moscow's invasion of Czechoslovakia.

February 21, 1969, Warsaw

Moeskewicz, a Warsaw journalist friend of Lithuanian origin, comes to see me at the Bristol Hotel, but he is tense and apprehensive. His main reflection on Czechoslovakia is a general but arresting one: "Our great hope in Poland has been that Russia would join Europe. Last August set back that hope."[27]

But the impish joyfulness of this Lithuanian aristocrat and Polish patriot flashes to the surface when I tell him of the contrast between the billboards outside the airports of East Berlin and Warsaw. The Germans have put up: "Reunify the Motherland." The Poles chose: "Eat Polish Strawberries."

Moeskewicz thinks worry about China is the number one issue in the Kremlin. It strengthens the hands of the military. "I hope you are not a Maoist," he says firmly.

---

[27] On August 21, 1968, the Soviet Union invaded Czechoslovakia to suppress the reforms made during the so-called "Prague Spring."

March 1, 1969, Cambridge

How shabby things seem on return to Boston. Is this not dynamic America? Well, only for some. The inner cities in the USA are not dynamic. They have a gloom nowadays. I got back to find a back log of examining and other teaching-fellow work. I sit at it while outside the windows the students, or an energetic segment of them, demonstrate that they do not care a fig for university studies and procedures as the world has hitherto known them.

May 21, 1969, Cambridge

Dinner with Chuck Bahmueller,[28] during which I amused him by saying cheekily of his heroine Hannah Arendt, "She's the farting rhinoceros of the Western intellectual world." About nine they asked us to leave the Faculty Club, as CFB was roaring with ribald laughter, and I was drinking from a bottle of Beaujolais in a way that someone felt looked like fellatio.

During the spring of 1969, anti-war unrest at Harvard reached a fevered pitch, culminating in the take-over of University Hall by a group of student protestors on the night of April 8-9. City and state police ejected the students and over 100 were arrested. In the aftermath, the faculty elected a special "Committee of Fifteen" to deal with those who had participated in the occupation.

May 24, 1969, Cambridge

We've have had a lively time on campus with war protests. I think by and large some good was done; certainly, more good than harm. But that was only possible because there were a lot of people who took initiatives and did a lot of work, from a position left of center, but not as far left as the SDS.

May 26, 1969, Cambridge

Cocks vary.

Summer 1969, Cambridge

We should be grateful for the Hippies in Harvard Square. It brightens the life of the street immeasurably that some people, instead of bustling around on their way making money, should sit and talk and dream and kiss. What irony that the police, far from thanking them, are intolerably infuriated by this display of humanity. Why is capitalism so reluctant to let life sprout naturally?

---

[28] Author of, among other books, The National Charity Company: Jeremy Bentham's Silent Revolution.

August 13, 1969, Cambridge

Drinks at the Vincents' with Milton Katz [29] and the delightful Maxine up from Washington. Milton says that Ben Schwartz as a member of the "Committee of 15" dealing with the student crisis, is strong precisely because he's an ethicist. When someone seems wrong, he just won't approve; the more political professors' compromise. I think Ben just sits on the fence because he likes to. Milton argues that because 40% of the college age kids in the U.S. are at college, it is obligatory to accept college students—and their current views—as representative of the nation's future.

August 18, 1969, Cambridge

The Prague journalist Igor Hajek came up from New York for dinner last night. Naturally he is very shaken up about the whole Czechoslovakia crisis, and mournful about his own prospects. "I would not survive if I went back there to live," he declared.

August 23, 1969, Cambridge

In *Power*, Bertrand Russell gives a memorable description of Mussolini, as a pilot, reveling in the Abyssinian horror. It is often said particular nations toss up men like Mussolini or Hitler. The point is, rather, that only in certain nations do such men become head of government. Every country has bastards, idiots, twisted spirits. Political science should be able to tell us why, in some societies and some circumstances, these unworthy ones get to the top.

September 8, 1969, Cambridge

A number of US Secretaries of State have been poor; hence certain military decisions have, by default, become crucial to the course of US foreign policy in the East. Dewey in Manila Bay committed the US to colonial rule over the Philippines. McArthur's sabre-rattling led to Chinese intervention in Korea. Military requirements led to the embrace of Taiwan in the summer of 1950 (that even today binds Washington in a straitjacket of immobility vis-a-vis China). Gun leading the mind might be happening again in Vietnam.

September 18, 1969, Cambridge

The honeymoon period of the Nixon administration is drawing to a close, and I think by the time the students come back late this month, he will come under strong attack that will cease only when he puts an end to the war.

I have bad news from friends in Washington who tell me of generals absolutely refusing to accept the realities of the Vietnam situation, and wanting to press on for victory now that Ho Chi Minh is dead.

---

[29] Milton Katz (1907-1995), professor of international law at Harvard Law School.

October 1969, Buckow, East Germany

The DDR Regional Committee took us far away from the complications of Berlin to the isolation of the beautiful hills of Buckow. We were perched on a mountainside of golden foliage with a lake below us. It was very quiet; a bicycle now and then, hens, birds, very rarely a car, and the air was pure.

There seems to be a period of greater fluidity emerging internationally. Compared with the immediate postwar years when at Yalta, Potsdam, etc., the great powers planned the future, none of the great powers today find it easy to work their will upon smaller countries; furthermore, all three great powers are considerably pre-occupied with internal questions. Here is an opportunity for diplomacy by the middle powers; also for regional groupings. We should encourage these tendencies, as an opportunity to move away from great power hegemony, and the politics of blocs.

Naturally the CPC has moved somewhat away from its single-minded concentration on the Bomb in recent years and confronted wider political problems, but we should not go too far in the other direction; the disarmament questions are vital. Terrible weapons hang like a cloud on the mood of the younger generation. Their cost is tragic. In particular we should stress two lines of approach: opposition to trade in armaments whereby big powers keep alive wars in smaller countries (e.g., Nigeria); and, second, the menace of chemical and bacteriological war.

Also, we cannot analyze the international scene without considering the relation of peace and war to the quest for social change and social justice. We have to analyse the meaning of socialism; the problems of authoritarianism; and raise our sights to think of politics in terms of the entire quality of social life.

October 24, 1969, Berlin

Left Bucknow, the pretty East German village where the Peace Conference was meeting, after breakfast.

The Hospiz, our depot in Berlin, was full of solid evangelical "squares" up from the provinces for a look at the capital. After some quick but quite good shopping (leather, wood, toys), I passed through checkpoint Charlie and on to Tempelhof for a plane to London.

Returning to the West brings a good feeling; the world starts to move again. I find that Willy Brandt has been elected FRG Chancellor and that the Lebanese government is tottering.

In the East you have equality without freedom. In the West you have freedom inside a jungle.

October 25, 1969, London

The solid decency of London. Tonight, it is crisp and beautiful, a diversity of buildings in winding streets of gray-purple hue. The layout is less that of a city than of a swollen small town.

Yet today's Londoners have little to do either with the city core or with the countryside surrounding London, through which the steam trains puff. They live in the rather awful suburbs of London, which visitors from abroad rarely set eyes on.

Two trademarks of the inhabitants of this old nag of a city: their pathetic gratitude when nature tosses them a morsel of sun or warmth. "Lovely weather" or "magnificent weather," they chortle all day when a shaky ray of lukewarm sunshine grudgingly breaks the grey oppression.

And their splendid public spirit. The BBC requests them (with a high expectation of compliance) to "use electricity lightly this evening" as the power system is "very slightly overloaded."

October 30, 1969, Cambridge

Back in Boston, the first thing I hear on the radio is a war report from Vietnam. Comes as such a shock when you have just been in Europe. Are the Americans still at it? The senselessness of the war is so taken for granted in Paris and London that it is a mental effort to have to confront the whole grisly business again as a daily topic.

November 3, 1969, Cambridge

Nixon's much-awaited speech on Vietnam was depressing. Just an appeal for patience while he tries more of the same. Not even a small new troop withdrawal announcement. Of course, there are good reasons why not; I wrote about them last May in the *Atlantic*. Vietnamization, or de-Americanization as it was then called, will not work. To pull out is indeed to hand the country over to the communists. Nixon is now snared by that reality.

November 7, 1969

In the Faculty Club these days, everyone is talking about the "university crisis." Documents about it are on every second table and strewn throughout the lounge. There in one corner is Talcott Parsons[30] looking and sounding like a Romanoff on the eve of 1917, discussing student revolt. Is it not all a trifle immature?

November 24, 1969, Cambridge

At Holyoke Center[31] the "problem" is "immoral hippies" congregating at the Plaza in various states of dress; even, it is whispered, making love. A syrupy blonde is with a handsome, half-naked Black. As they embrace, her pearly hands hold his great cock as nonchalantly as a bunch of keys. The sight makes Melbourne seem like a Sunday Bible Class.

---

[30] Talcott Parsons (1902-1979), American sociologist who established the Department of Social Relations at Harvard.
[31] Holyoke Center, an administrative office and student center building at Harvard.

In John Stuart Mills' terms these hippies are doing no harm to others. But they bother the spirit of others—notably the police. So, they are swept away like smelly rubbish. A "bomb scare" comes at Holyoke Centre. The bombs should not entirely surprise us. Society had already rejected these "immoral" people.

December 23, 1969, Cambridge

To follow the inner fire. To do, as Gide insists in *Fruits of the Flesh*, what only you can do. Why be afraid; what is there to be afraid of?

December 31, 1969, Cambridge

New Year's Eve dinner with Rachel at Chez Jean. She shyly presents me with the Taizé Book and the Book of Common Prayer; I was moved and gave her Kingsley Martin's autobiography, *Editor*. In my dorm room, we drank white wine, a candle burning, and discussed the sixties, which we both like for different reasons. Later we relaxed. But when she started talking about husband Wade (and broached phoning him), it was time to take her home to Jack's.

1970

The beginning of the new decade found Terrill with an appointment to the Harvard faculty, thoughts about entering Australian politics, and increasing candor about his sexual interest in men. The Christianity of his youth was giving way to another kind of doctrine. As he wrote in the Diary, "the physical has its own spirituality, and also knows reverence."

January 2, 1970, Cambridge

Everything has gone well recently, and the difficult thing is trying to summon the ambition to return to Australia and go into politics, when the alternatives here are so attractive.

January 31, 1970, Cambridge

Harvard offered me an appointment on the Faculty of the Department of Government, and I accepted the same day. Though the other places which had been in touch with me offered more pay, the prestige and the advantages of colleagues and facilities at Harvard seemed to outweigh that. Apparently, I will be the first Australian to teach political science on the Faculty at Harvard.

Now I can feel that, as a political scientist, I have got high recognition; but that doesn't mean I will be a political scientist ten years from now!

February 3, 1970, London

Today, England seems soft and gentle, and a bit quaint. But the grimy chimneypots and other relics of ancient industry are a reminder of the England that was the first nation to industrialize and the natural home of the aggressive businessman. The vigor, ambition, and ruthlessness has burnt itself out after many generations and much war.

At London House, where I stay—still on my Tawney work—the rooms are not numbered consecutively. I am 402, and a few doors away, still on the fourth floor, are several in the 700s and several in the 330s!

February 1970, London

I upset a cab driver by hopping into his cab before receiving his word of assent to do so. Inside, I announced my destination, but the driver sat silent and did not begin the journey. Eventually, he recovered enough to tell me in a wounded tone that I should first have caught his eye, got his nod, then entered the cab. "This is Britain," he said with finality.

London's differences from America are sometimes in its favor. Life is less of a strain. People are more polite in ordinary contact, though not always as immediately friendly in leisure-time contact. There is a sense of public probity, settled order, established standards. The English, in the present age, are surely the least violent of people. Of course, they are not efficient. They fill in a form, stamp it, take it to someone to sign, consult two colleagues—all over a matter that a machine would do in a jiffy in America.

February 22, 1970, London

The Vietnamese are simple men, as I discovered in talking with them in Paris. Independence for Vietnam is their main aim. We were right to go into the streets in Melbourne against this war on the ground that it was a colonial war. Their aim is independence. United States can never thwart that aim, by definition, unless it stays in Vietnam. And by now, the main guardians of that aim, on behalf of the people of Vietnam, are Communists. You cannot fight a colonial war with a stated war aim of withdrawal.

March 1, 1970, Cambridge, MA

Quoi faire? Seldom have I been so deeply unsure of an erotic situation. He has given many positive hints. And there is a suggestive interpretation of things which paints him as a profound guy and also keen on me. But it's not the only one. Maybe largesse rather than passion. What is to be lost by a declaration? From the point of view of discretion, more or less nothing. Immediate embarrassment? Can be coped with. Must get a "decision" tonight.

March 22, 1970, Cambridge

My attitude to communism has two strands. I am "soft" in that I see communism historically rather than ideologically; it performs a modernizing task in lagging countries. I am "hard" on the question of power. The rules of Power do not exempt Communists. So politically, communism, because it is wrong about human nature, elevating "class" in its place, goes seriously wrong indeed.

May 18, 1970, Cambridge

Rachel is down again from Montreal for the weekend. She is outrageous yet lovable. Born in the wrong epoch, UK in the 18ᵗʰ century would have suited her. She was created to write letters, drink champagne, go to parties, and care for friends. She said of her marriage with Wade: "I always said I'd never go steady with anyone; and I never have, even since my marriage." (Tossed off as she lay on my bed, listening to Brahms' double concerto.)

May 22, 1970, Cambridge

I have been awarded the Government Department's top thesis prize for 1970, the Sumner Prize. A $1200 check nestles against my thigh. Even better, I am hopelessly in love with Joseph from Taiwan. Eyes hold me for a minute on end. His vibrant voice seems to come from the stomach. Look of a south China "urchin" melts me. In my room, he fingered my bound PhD thesis lovingly, his golden hands sliding up and down the black binding. When will the urchin finger me?

June 5, 1970, New York

Does the Bomb make any difference? We tossed that around, drinking smoky tea. How to encompass, even intellectually, this monstrous factor of our current situation!

June 12, 1970, Cambridge

It would be hard to over-estimate the national unease at the Cambodian gaffe.[32] People who know what is going on accept that the war will get worse before it gets better. The most depressing thing is that some at least in the Administration, notably in the Pentagon, really do believe in Vietnamization. Last year I thought it was a smokescreen for a dignified and slow withdrawal; and as such it seems a reasonable ploy. However, if they really believe it can work (Rogers does not, but he is isolated), they are making for themselves a string of future crises, for the central problem is still that Saigon will not stand up politically unless propped up by the United States.

June 15, 1970, Cambridge

Boston to Lisbon through the night, on Pan Am, which lacks frills but is effective. Waiting at the Lisbon terminal for my Sabena flight to Morocco, I observe the sleepy amiability of the Portuguese.

June 17, 1970, Ain Diab, Morocco

A little rest (and recreation) at this small coastal town south of Casablanca—a spot fit for the angels. Warm days, cool nights. Arab men by day, French cuisine in the evening,

---

[32] In the spring of 1970, US military troops, accompanied by the South Vietnamese Army, invaded Cambodia under the pretext of disrupting the North Vietnamese supply lines.

then a promenade along the boulevards, where the air is alive with the smell of jasmine and grilled lamb.

I needed to get away from America. Ambition, competition, minute calculation of time, excessive concern for appearances—let them go for a while. Here in Morocco, you do not have to pretend things are more important than they are. For lunch, a bouillabaisse at an Alsacien spot on the Boulevard de la Corniche. As I eat, I watch the glistening Atlantic Ocean and the French blondes promenading alongside it.

June 19, 1970, Ain Diab, Morocco

Moroccan music and dance are the same as their lovemaking: devoted, single-minded, relentless. I eat a brochette, and afterwards couscous au poulet. As a Moroccan waiter tends the table, the Australian man across the aisle says to his wife, "They're well-trained, aren't they, these native waiters?" Hostility to Australia, even to the white race, surges within me.

June 30, 1970, Stockholm

I am won anew by the slumbering countryside that Bergman has conveyed in his films. White pine trunks and white rocks, set against the greens. The straw-like hair of a farm boy working placidly under a sky that seems higher than anywhere in the world.

Buildings going up on all sides. Recklessly, without flinching, the Swedes make all things new. Yet the old town is as charming as Warsaw's. Hippies lounge in the Kurgstaadgrad now. Young men's hair in general is six inches longer than during my last visit to Sweden in 1968.

Today I spent mostly at Vanadinbadet; a day of sensual, concrete things. Alternating in the bastu and the swimming pool, I preened the body and rejoiced in a growing sense of physical well-being. What another world from the WSCF, in the coils of whose rhetoric and self-inflated abstractions I wrestled in Switzerland last week! It emerges from my day in the bastu and the pool, that the physical has its own spirituality, and also knows its own reverence.

July 2, 1970, Stockholm

Odd to be hunting for pornography amidst the stately beauty of the Old Town. Prices are too high. But I do like the furniture and the glassware.

July 4, 1970, Stockholm

Just back from cruising and dancing at the City Club. Eerie white light—it is 3 AM. Young Swedes wander home, many drunk. Some buy sausages, soaked in catsup, as they go. The faces inside the City Club are wan, sexless, without charm. Nice bodies, but heads take away the appeal. With R, I feel I am dancing with a turnip. S is better, a talkative original. "Homosexuality is a fashion in Sweden," he tells me. "I am neither for girls nor for boys—because I am an egoist." On this he may be correct; egoism does cut across the categories of sexual love. And across the moral rules of sexual love.

July 6, 1970, Moscow

An Aeroflot plane from Stockholm—it is like moving from the garden to the boxroom. A weighty hostess serves bananas. But after visits to the sex shops of Gamla Stan, I cannot look at someone eating a banana and fail to see a cock being sucked.

Six years since I was here in Moscow airport. Russia has a different meaning for me now, for August 1968 stands in between. I have begun to think of the Soviet Union as a shabby bureaucratic state, capable of pretty much the same evil as any other Big Power.

July 10, 1970, Shinjuku, Japan

After tonight with Ko, I abandon my negative view of Japanese as lovers. An impromptu, frenetic half-hour at Club Mako brought Ko into my arms. He and a waiter set upon me like smiling octopuses. As Ko ravished my cock, the waiter sucked each nipple alternately. Others watched from low-slung couches beneath colored lights making flashing shades of their faces. I was glad in the end to be alone with Ko. All night in my hotel bed we caressed, sighed, thrusted.

July 11, 1970, Tokyo

At small, crowded Regent Bar, I meet a basketball enthusiast, and later at La Cave, a handsome, serene guy who seems to like me, but did not jump. After I waited, however, he invited me to come to Club Mako. Mako was full of butterflies, but Shinje did not join in. A little while after showing me round, he left, smooching my hand first. I went into the streets of Shinjuku, confronting the approaching dawn, in grey and blue over a ribbon of neon. Shinje will meet me later, he said.

With both Shinje and Chake, the action began with few preliminary words and no preliminary "agreements." Yet they got their way on sex techniques. They were quiet and effective in achieving their goals. Like Japan in trade policy, in lovemaking (and other realms), the Japanese don't fix the procedures beforehand, as Americans insist on doing. An American couple often discuss sex techniques before agreeing to go to bed together. Less often do Japanese.

July 14, 1970, Tokyo

Why do I feel more at home in East Asia than in Europe? Many reasons, but ultimately a taste for difference.

In lovemaking (as perhaps in other realms) the Japanese don't go out of their way to fix the procedures beforehand, as Americans insist on doing. An American couple may well discuss the sex techniques to be used before agreeing to go to bed together. Less often Japanese.

In fact, both Shinje and Chake have been just the opposite. The action began with very few preliminary words and no preliminary "agreements." Yet I notice that they got their way on the issue of sex techniques. They were quiet, effective in achieving their goals. Is this the Japanese way?

July 21, 1970, Akasaka, Japan

RK and I prowl through this night district where Tokyo Establishment types keep their second and third wives and come for extracurricular pastimes. Along the narrow lanes, black sedans with clean white covers over the seats are drawn up, like dark fish resting in the weeds. The drivers wait patiently, consoled to glimpse now and then a powdered beauty, lips crimson and hair jet black, shuffling along the dusty sidewalk. Dawn comes, superb in gentle grey and finds them still waiting. Inside the low brown and grey buildings, RK tells me, bankers, industrialists, Liberal-Democratic politicians are at play; tables laden; steaming baths; beds behind every door.

July 28, 1970, Kyoto, Japan

The pace is slower here. In cafes, and on trams, companions look into each other's face and eyes for lengthy periods and find delight in looking; do many Americans still do that?

Walking down a fairyland of streets, wearing loose robes and red sandals, RK and I see a car parked inside the front of a shop for the night. I gape at this sign of intensive use of space, but RK says: "It is not polite to look into other peoples' houses."

Kyoto-ites are proud and do not often praise Tokyo. The former Imperial Palace here is called "Imperial Palace" and the Imperial Palace in Tokyo is called "Temporary Imperial Palace." A city of beauty and culture, the ancient capital slightly disdains the present capital, which is bigger and the hub of commerce and communications. Kyoto sees Tokyo the way Krakow sees Warsaw, the way Hue sees Saigon.

July 29, 1970, Tokyo

Young Japanese flock at night to coffee shops, where they perch gracefully on stools and sip sodas or coffee as Western classical music plays. There is a quiet charm to these places, different from the sad-subdued mood or obliterating noise of youth spots in the U.S.

Japanese coffee-shops are clean with superb service. Patrons are neat and well-polished; girls have Dresden shoulders and flawless complexions. Their "alienation" seems milder than that of urban American youth. Whatever they reject, oppose, or despise, they most certainly do not, like many American counterparts, hate their own country. They seem to have fewer doubts about their worth as Japanese than those now in their thirties and forties shaped during the American Occupation.

I am struck by the pride in being Japanese; the deeply felt, if presently muted, nationalism of this country that on the surface is so ready to please.

July 30, 1970, Haneda, Japan

As I leave Japan, I realize that I will never be able to neglect this amazing country.

August 1, 1970, Taipei

Orgasm is not the goal of lovemaking. Better to allow the culminating passion to stalk as it wills while intimate communion continues as the end in itself. Loving is a relationship which the orgasm punctuates.

August 1970, Hong Kong

Chopsticks and knife and fork present an interesting contrast. The fork is explicit, as is the knife; its purpose is to spear the food, and it is built accordingly. The purpose of the knife is to cut the food, and it is built accordingly. But the function of chopsticks is not written on their face. They have a multitude of uses—you can cut and lift and spear and separate—but the source of the differentiation lies only in the movement of the hand. So with Chinese thought, and sometimes with Chinese foreign policy. The differentiations are not explicit, and therefore they can be missed if one is used to Western ways.

September 7, 1970, Melbourne

I feel hope is with the young people in Australia. I think the older generation could go and there would be very little to regret. One's hope can only be with the young. The whole paraphernalia of knighthoods and privileges here is just an empty form waiting to be condemned. But with the young there is hope.

September 14, 1970, Melbourne

I gave two broadcasts over the Australian Broadcasting Commission this afternoon. For the News Commentary, I chose the topic "USA-China Relations." It went alright, though I do not like speaking at the rat-a-tat speed that the host thinks appropriate.

Then John Cassidy interviewed me on *Law and Order*. He is a "new type." You don't fix on a clear topic well in advance; the broadcast is a kind of happening, a blending of souls. We talked for a while; suddenly he turned on the machines and the interview began. Though I did not like the method, what I said was probably better than if I had written a script.

September 15, 1970, Nandi, Fiji

Charming people living sleepily in healthy circumstances: that is Fiji. I went to New Town Beach, not far from my Sky Lodge. Hardly a soul, just coconut palms, white sand, and shimmering blue water. I meet youths who cane-cut in the morning, fish in the afternoon. The youths invite me to share their lunch. One asks, "Is New York in America or New Zealand?" Another, "Is Australia closer to Fiji than to England?"

September 16, 1970, Fiji

This afternoon around Nandi takes me back to my origins in Bruthen and the languid calm of Australian aboriginal life. A sleepy town with one main street, wide verandas, people in bare feet, taxi men dozing beside their dusty cars. The air after lunch hangs with eroticism. Shapely young girls lack bras and shoes. But Fijian cocks bear no comparison to American Blacks.

September 26, 1970, Cambridge

Chinese have taught me how to go to bed. They turn off as the day recedes. I have been the opposite: Going to bed casually; grabbing a book, hardly bothering to undress, let alone put on pajamas. Drifting from the waking, reading state toward a kind of sleep. Too often carrying the day's worries into the night. Watching Chinese go to bed in Taiwan, I may never be the same. They (or some I observed close-up) respect the ending of the day. Yielding to the night, they respect themselves.

October 31, 1970, Cambridge

I was coming past Harkness Commons Graduate Center after squash, with the thought of calling in to see Joseph, when there he was, hand in hand with an American girl, going off, it seemed, to eat supper. She was a blond in a bright yellow dress and coat. I was shaken to the foundations. Almost choking, I managed to say, "Hello, Joe," in a voice that tried to be easy and gay. But if gaiety was on my lips, death was in my stomach. Tears welled up. I walked away to Harvard Square in a trance.

Another hand holding Joe's. Another pair of lips pressing that sensuous mouth. Another breast feeling the warmth of this golden son of China, looking into those searing, liquid eyes. How could it be? Reality has rent my dream as fire ends the life of a newspaper.

December 17, 1970, Cambridge

At a party for my graduate students in Government 219, one long-haired type, the brightest man in the seminar, says he went to a Colloquium for first-year graduate students, at which Prof. Judith Shklar said the purpose of political theory is to clear our minds of prejudice and ideology.

My student dissented and said political theory is important because political science has given rise to war criminals! When asked by Judith what kind of people he had in mind, he said Sam Huntington, chairman of our department. There were sparks and lashing of tongues. I wonder how much longer this sort of exchange will be heard in America.

December 20, 1970, Cambridge

Betty Vincent added points to her longstanding list of Chinese-Japanese differences. Chinese do not get drunk as much as Japanese, she said, and Chinese, unlike Japanese, have a sense of humor.

1971

January 25, 1971, London

In Old Brompton Road the English are at play. They have a pattern for their homosexual bars. La Casserole's ground floor has a restaurant, lit up and advertised. In the basement, the same people run an intimate bar for homosexuals. The establishment can switch its mien to suit the people. All are catered for, the customer is always right, no one goes out on a limb. A trio of Cambridge snobs at dinner in La Casserole. Said one, "Did you ever go over to Oxford? I did once, and the dress was jeans and T-shirts. Well, I mean, that sort of thing is all right for one term, but after that..." Their bill comes and another of the Cambridge trio, with pointed nose and straight hair, a cross between a human being and swordfish, says, "My God, eleven pounds, and without service. I'll be glad when decimal currency comes!"

The third one from Cambridge grabs the bill and says, "Look here, Pepper, I'm going to check this bill. You have to, you know. It's not that they cheat, they just make mistakes every time." I'd be interested to see these charmed ones on a Chinese commune.

January 27, 1971, London

Darryl comes around and we make gentle love. He said he's been thinking of me for two days. I am fond of him in the same way I am fond of Ch'eng far off in Hong Kong. A Black from South Africa, a Chinese from south China. I like the purity of these young men; they represent something lost from my own past.

April 13, 1971, Bangkok

"Thai International" Singapore to Bangkok. Girls offer glistening silver boxes of cigarettes and light one for each smoker. Sweet girls pipe up with announcements; better to term them "suggestions," so soft and wistful is the tone. The flight recalled a teen-age party, full of grave-faced boys and giggling girls, all very good-looking.

In Don Muong airport terminal, a notice in English at the men's toilet door: "Please do not remove your precious belongings here; you may forget them."

In Bangkok, despite the late hour, I did not go to bed but to Sea-Hag bar. I saw "JJ" chatting with an American buffoon. Dark, husky eyes and brown, sensual hands. A message asking him if he'd give up the American for me, brought a positive reply. Soon we were melded on the dance floor. I felt a deep belonging, more than I have ever felt to a man in Australia. Is my attachment to travel and its stimuli becoming almost equal to my attachment to any one country—other than Australia?

April 15, 1971, Bangkok

In Singapore, Julie remarked that Laotians are "slow." The Thais, like the Vietnamese, do have a strength that both Cambodians and Laotians lack. Thai strength is their self-assurance. Passive, flexible as they are, their goals are clear. To sleep with a Thai is to meet strength—not only, as with a Lao, the charm of a clinging vine. Thai affection is not dependent; exciting without being sentimental.

April 18, 1971, San Francisco

Being near the sea, the city reminds me of Sydney. So do the bridges and hills and sudden views of the bay from everywhere. People don't snap; they smile during the simple dealings of life. The climate allows you to step outdoors, meet and greet people; you are not condemned 24 hours a day to be either inside four walls or in a motorcar.

April 20, 1971, San Francisco to Boston

Coming back to the United States feels like coming home. My work is here. Many friends are here. I know the country a bit. My sense of identity—scholarly, journalistic, erotic, religious—all largely spring from my five years in the United States. American handsome young men are a daily delight. A limitation is acute: how long can I stay in USA? Immigration law breathes at my shoulder.

Appointed by Robert Manning as the youngest contributing editor to The Atlantic Monthly, Terrill was commissioned to write a series of articles on the "new China." More and more, he was becoming respected as a specialist who could help the West in its dealings with the PRC.

April 21, 1971, Boston

I feel the "work ethic" again. In the haze of Bangkok, I cared not a fig to write an *Atlantic Monthly* piece, or talk to a scholarly colleague. Back here, impossible to discount these things. One must go one step further, be praised for today, not yesterday, watch out for money. Finishing my book comes next. Only a dog and two cats will read it, alas.

April 30, 1971, New York

Our China meeting adjourned for the day, I went to the apartment of Rick and Aoki, where I was to stay the night. I'd not met Aoki before; he's attractive, if not handsome. Rick was his urbane self. He smoothly changes gears from living with an American woman to living with a Japanese man.

We went to Willie's, a nice place near 82nd Street with flashing lights and a dance floor. Aoki was hot as a furnace and very eager. I am not sure whether Rick minded my dancing with him. I asked him first and he said Okay. Rick seldom betrays his feelings.

About a third of the guys were Black, which displeased Aoki, but not me. Rick prefers Japanese but there were none. Suddenly a good-looking brown guy smiled. I thought he was Indian. He had a walking stick, black shirt and the complexion of an Indian. Tony turned out to be Latin. He was off to night shift, but we arranged to meet next morning. Back at Rick's, the three of us had coffee. I toyed with the idea of getting Aoki, but realized Rick might mind, so I went solo to bed.

May 1, 1971, New York

Very late last night, Aoki crept in just in his shorts and hovered over me. But I still felt Rick's possible feelings were an obstacle. I thought Aoki "wanted" the night before, but his English is limited so it's hard to tell. The sight of him reminded me of Shunje at La Cave in Tokyo, especially without clothes on.

When the day's China seminar ended, I went from 89th and Broadway to look for Tony, the Latin of last night. He was at the appointed spot, drinking coffee in the corner store, and we went to his place. A Cuban, he lives with an Irishman on 89th Street in a basement lit by brilliant-colored lights. There are a mountain of cushions and, alas, a dog. Tony is studying at a community college and will go on to psychiatry school.

We began on the couch; by the first orgasm we were halfway across the room under a table. But the dog kept looking; it was almost a threesome. Nothing is better than to have a roll in the hay after a long day sitting round a table at a conference. By 7:00 I had to rush to get my bag and say goodbye to Rick and Aoki. Delightfully, they had bought me a copy of *Confessions of a Mask*, inscribed from the two of them on May Day. On the plane to Chicago, I read Mishima's book; powerful, subtle.

May 2, 1971, Chicago

This city resembles a gigantic country town. Only in numbers and wealth is it a city. Palpably, it's inland, wide streets, much space, and a railroad city—though now with few trains. The city information center says Chicago is the crossroads of the world; inland cities go for grandiosity.

My speeches at the Rockefeller Chapel and the International Centre seemed to go OK. Nice to speak in a stately building like the vaulting Rockefeller Chapel. At the continuing education center restaurant, a menu the size of *The New York Times*, chock-a-block with phrases like "enhance your dining pleasure with wine." The waiters have zero knowledge of the food let alone wine. They are unable to connect what they see in the kitchen with what appears on the menu.

May 2, 1971, Chicago, Later

From a boring meeting to Nightlife, full of weary businessmen. They sat with blondes, hair piled high, twirled into a sphere, body and head of equal size. All the ladies were painted as for a war dance. Fur coats hung loosely on their shoulders. Below each coat you saw a stool on which a blonde perched like a hen on a fence. I gulp an orange juice and escape into the night. Back at the CCE, I find a Chinese boy, but he does not seem inclined to things of the flesh.

May 3, 1971, Boston

In from Chicago at 11 AM. The plane could not land at first try. By the time the pilot sighted the airport, there was no time to descend. Up we swooped. The pilot said cheerfully, "Well, we'll have another go."

It's sweet, unreal, mischievous to return to Boston in the morning. My bed at Kirkland House is made up. No routine for the day engulfs me. The cake of Harvard life has been cut a fresh way. I ask myself, as others scurry off to work, and a cleaning lady ambles alone nearby, what is the point of our routines? Why not sex at 11 AM, food at 3 PM, sleep at 6 PM? Do we erect routines to hide from ourselves? At night our Government Department Faculty meet. I feel "secure" once more; but no longer do I see life with the clarity of the morning.

May 4, 1971, Boston

Bessie[33] said two of his colleagues had read my Tawney, and they wouldn't want it for the House. Then Bessie hands me the card of Mark Carroll, head of Harvard University Press, and suggests that I go and talk to him about the Tawney manuscript. After lunch we saw Carroll in the lobby. Once Bessie introduced me, the first thing Carroll said was, "We are publishing your manuscript on Tawney." Bessie, stunned, later remarked, "He must have done his homework between 10 last night and this afternoon."

"I suppose you want three things, in your life," Mike said as we took a drink before he flew back to NY: "To get at the truth of things; to address the public; and to take some role in political affairs." Not a bad analysis.

May 5, 1971, Cambridge

Ellen comes in for drinks—a masterful, willful woman. Like the star of the Chinese drama Ye Mei Gui,[34] she is too ardent, scheming, and ambitious for her husband. She likes me and wants me, but after dinner in the bare-bones dining room of Kirkland House, I farewell her; she purrs off in her green sports car.

May 11, 1971, Cambridge

An exciting cable tonight from Gough Whitlam in Canberra which reads: "Eureka. We Won." Peking has invited us to send a Labor Party delegation to China. My contacts are in good shape, after all. I feel a bit scared because Whitlam, now opposition leader, has said China will not buy one more grain of Australian wheat until Australia has a Labor Party government that recognizes the PRC.

The editor of *The Atlantic Monthly* urged me to return to China, and now he's commissioned articles and paid a little money. I will also observe China's reactivated foreign policy for a course I am starting (the first-ever) at Harvard.

---

[33] Simon Michael Bessie (1916-2008), senior editor at Harper & Row.

[34] Ye Mei Gui (野玫瑰), "Wild Rose": A Chinese play and silent film from 1932 about the love affair between a country girl and an artist.

Memorial Day, 1971, Cambridge

The Chinese Embassy in Ottawa not only told me I had a visa to China but said "you should come for it immediately because Peking thinks it would be good for you to arrive two weeks before Mr. Whitlam."

May 12, 1971, Cambridge

In summer, I am unafraid, and a sweet ache enters my cock, wheedling for release. A distracting awareness takes over. In the lovely warmth of the evening, I get a headache simply trying to go to sleep.

I take my new friend Atsuko Hirai[35] to a Government Department party at the Busch Reisinger Museum. Then we go to an Australian Club meeting, where I give a speech on "America, China, and Australia." An Australian audience is sharper, yet less informed than an American one. Afterwards, at dinner, I learn much about Atsuko. Inside this bland Japanese exterior are coiled up secrets. How can I deal with her, for I take our relationship less seriously than she does?

May 24, 1971, Cambridge

To appear on "The Advocates" or not? Senator Buckley of New York, Bob Scalapino at Berkeley, and Admiral Sharp in Washington won't be the easiest of debating opponents. I say I'm too busy.

Morning coffee in Jerry Cohen's garden with Ted Kennedy[36] to talk about China. Kennedy looks young and relaxed; he has put on weight since I saw him last. When you talk, he looks at you. "To gather poise," he has taken up painting, he says. He just sold one of his works for $3000, the money to benefit the Kennedy Library fund.

I tell him about the dramatic Australian experience with China over the last two months. Some colleagues suggest getting a bi-partisan group of senators to go to China, but I say no. I think Kennedy ought to go all out to embarrass this Washington government, get to China, and stake a claim to the presidency in which he would be an improvement over Nixon and Johnson.

In June 1971, Terrill flew to China, accompanying Gough Whitlam, at the time the Leader of the Opposition Party (Labor), who met with Premier Zhou Enlai. It was a "magic summer," he recalled. "I let China flow over me like ripples of a brook."

July 14, 1971, Beijing

I am excited to meet Premier Zhou Enlai, to whom I am introduced by Ma Yuzhen (later ambassador to the UK). Zhou warmly welcomes us to the East Chamber—high ceilings, leaping murals, crimson carpets. Present also are Ji Pengfei, foreign minister,

---

[35] Atsuko Hirai (1936-2014), eminent historian of modern Japan. She and Terrill met when they were doctoral students at Harvard.
[36] Edward ("Ted") Moore Kennedy (1932-2009), Democratic senator from Massachusetts from 1962-2009.

and Bai Xiangguo, trade minister, whom we both met in previous days. Zhou Enlai asks me with a smile, "Where did you study Chinese?"

"In America," I reply, a little surprised the premier understood my poor Chinese, with its Australian accent.

Zhou remarks: "That is a fine thing, for you, an Australian, to learn Chinese in America!"

Zhou Enlai is a slight, handsome man with expressive hands and a theatrical manner. He is dressed in gray except for a red "Serve the People" badge, black socks inside his sandals, and black hairs amidst the gray ones.

July 25, 1971, Shanghai

Shengde[37] looked as lovely as ever though my first sight of him brought alarm. I went to his house and asked the neighborhood telephone office for Shengde, as you must. The lady said she didn't know him, looking at me with eyes unable to conceal her lie. I cursed, went up the rickety stairs, and burst in on the family. Seeing me, Sheng looked the color of the green sweater his mother was knitting. He grabbed me and hauled us downstairs and under a stairwell. I flashed a quick smile to family members and went with him.

Shengde is a construction worker of 23 who leaves home at six-thirty for his ride to work, gets back at five, and has no paid vacation for the year beyond national holidays.

He pushed me into a dark doorway, made me face away from the traffic so people couldn't see I was a foreigner. Last month he had a visit from the Public Security people because he was an acquaintance, apparently, of one or two who were arrested in the current crackdown. They also said: "You have a foreign friend, don't you"!

We found a rough restaurant that put us at a huge back table that could have held fifteen people. We sat side by side with a red centerpiece containing fried noodles, dumplings with meat inside, hot and sour soup, and chicken with peanuts. The mediocre meal was washed down with three large bottles of beer, which didn't make Shengde as pink as I expected. He said he wouldn't go into the Peace Hotel, or the Jingjiang or any hotel. I said, "Take a minute to change your clothes and catch your breath me and I'll meet you in half an hour."

He's become obsessed with getting out of the country. In a month, he's learned a few English words. Just going to evening classes a couple of times a week. He thinks now that the marriage route is the best. Can I throw some women into his path? Foreign women, preferably *hua qiao*,[38] who might then agree to a marriage of convenience. Of course, it's difficult; two big barriers are that his English is minuscule and he doesn't have relatives abroad. Also, he doesn't realize the danger to himself of me being a writer.

---

[37] A young Chinese whom Terrill had first cruised in the street. Their relationship went on for several years as Shengde tried to get into the United States.

[38] *Huá qiáo* (華僑), overseas Chinese.

Full of beer and noodles, we found minutes alone in a shower of a swimming pool near the restaurant. He said to me, smiling but with pity, "A fat man cannot understand a thin man."

July 30, 1971, Bangkok

The Oriental Hotel is splendid with lawns *à l'Anglaise*; cuisine *à la Française*; Viennese music at meals—the customer always comes first. Fantastic Thai service always.

I sit at the waterfront nursing a late-afternoon beer. At six, a boy appears with smoking boxes, an anti-mosquito plan. At seven, another boy comes with a tray of flickering candles for the pool-side restaurant tables. His timing is good. I am reading Francis Hsu's *Americans and Chinese* and the light can't catch the fine print of footnotes.

July 31, 1971, Bangkok

Underrated physical pleasures: a glass of cold water on a hot afternoon; exercise which makes you sweat; breeze off the waves; crisp warm toast with butter (and Vegemite, if I'm in Australia).

August 1, 1971, Bangkok

The political side of me, which stems from Christian religion ("Man is Fallen") conflicts with an aesthetic side, which may owe something to homosexuality. A moral compulsion, a sense of duty, characterizes the political instinct just as it did the religious. But my aesthetic side questions both politics and religious faith.

August 11, 1971, Papeete, Tahiti

Tahiti is French exactly as Fiji is Anglo-Saxon. France without pressure and pollution. You see robed curés, gendarmes, Gitanes cigarettes. Papeete could be a sleepy, provincial French town. Except there are hills, valleys, beaches, sensuous people. At the Post Office, a boy sends a letter to apply for a scholarship in Paris; a French military wife posts a parcel. In the water-front bars, tourists from the *S.S. Fairsea* eat, drink and take pictures.

August 12, 1971, Papeete, Tahiti

To Lafayette, a recommended gay spot, miles away. It is closed; my taxi has gone. I am stranded. After walking a mile, I come across a cluster of boys. Grinning, they tell me there is no bus. One older guy with the picturesque name of Flores, has a motorbike and offers to take me back. The warm air caresses our faces. My eager hands grip Flores' strong warm thighs. The only way to hang on to the hurtling motorbike, I told myself.

At the Hotel Tahiti, we have a glass of wine and Flores tells me about his wife. Like other Tahitians I've met, he appears to be offering his wife on a bed of love. In Diderot, this happens to a French priest who travels to Tahiti. Flores comes into my bedroom, his eyes flashing with the spirit of the South Seas. Forget the wife, I thought. Flores is my first time in Tahiti. A Gargantuan explosion; from hunger to satiety.

August 13, 1971, Papeete, Tahiti

The seafront is cozy, intimate, dotted with pot plants. The *S.S. Himalaya* is in port and passengers line its decks to look at our proud town. The *Himalaya* is a British ship, symbol of the empire. But now the empire is but a memory of empire; the voyagers re-enacting the memory are not rulers, colonizing, but petty bourgeoisie, holidaying.

Three boys enter the Café Vaima. When the curvaceous bar maid, breasts pressing against a thin cotton dress, is not looking, one boy leans over the counter and takes three bottles of orange soda. Returning, the bar maid notices the loss and asks for the money. He will not pay. A certain playfulness is in the air. This youngest boy, very handsome, leads the woman on. Looking into her eyes, he toys with the flower in her hair, and touches her arm. He produces the money and puts it down the front of his tiny shorts. "Why don't you reach over and take it?" In the bar maid's eyes, professional fury blends with lust for the beautiful youth, whose cock announces itself in his flimsy pants. In his eyes, an amoral reckoning, with only $5 at stake, battles sexual electricity.

August 15, 1971, Papeete, Tahiti

In the Café Vaima two girls, one Australian, the other American. They smooch. The American is idealist, a college graduate, visiting Tahiti. The Australian is simple and homely; she works for Qantas Airways in Tahiti.

"It's an education being here," she says. The American is frustrated: "my husband is a lot older than me." They talk about holidays and leisure hours. The Australian says of life in Tahiti: "We do the God-damnest things and see the God-damnest people." Australians are square, yet they are part of the South Pacific. The mentality of an insurance clerk, yet the hedonism of a sunbaked youth. Both aspects are in me.

August 16, 1971, Tahiti to LA

With Flores and me and everyone, there are two different settings for morality. One, before you get into bed; the other, after you get there. Some people are obsessed with morality in the former, and yet are monsters when it comes to the latter. Yet the latter counts more. How he/she conducts himself/herself in lovemaking is more important ethically than whether or not she/should make love, or with a man or a woman.

August 28, 1971, Cambridge

With some political men, you wonder if they wouldn't rather not be in Parliament, but doing something else—writing in the study, surfing, yarning in the bar, in bed with a girl or boy on the side. You know there's a cock in those trousers, a tanned arm within that well-tailored sleeve. You can see at times that he's scared; you imagine him feeling that if you got into trouble, he'd help. If I go into Australian politics, I want to be a politician of this kind.

1972

January 1, 1972, Cambridge

The Formosan Club invited me to their annual dinner and New Year's party, a friendly affair, held on the 29th floor of an MIT building. I was asked to speak, which I did like a cat walking on broken glass, trying to give impressions of China, and answer questions on Taiwan, without endorsing or flatly opposing Taiwan independence.

I took an immediate liking to a guy called Ho; even while lecturing, I could not take my eyes off the silky skin, rustic curves, earthy sexiness. Then as Tom Engelhardt drove me home, he told me Ho is a KMT agent, planted to spy on the Formosans and list those keen for independence.

On February 21, 1972, President Nixon flew to Beijing, kicking off his historic eight-day diplomatic visit. Terrill was on hand at the CBS studio in New York to provide commentary. "I tried to keep my commentary sober and balanced, but I am not sure I succeeded," he wrote in his diary. In fact, he did. Newsweek hailed his reporting: "A bright young scholar named Ross Terrill cut through the fog with succinct answers to specific questions."

February 1972, New York

During Zhou Enlai's banquet for Nixon in the Great Hall of the People, Cronkite,[39] from his chair on a balcony above the head table asked me in the CBS studio in New York, "Why have the Chinese hosts served Nixon a plate of Jell-O for dessert?" When I looked into the screen beside me, I saw before each guest a white plate holding a brilliantly-colored tangerine. "Is it Jell-O, Walter?" I murmured, "or are those tangerines?" A heavy silence came from Cronkite in Beijing.

It is new in the U.S. for China to be a topic of daily conversation. An athlete phones the CBS studio to ask if I could help him run across the top of the Great Wall. Cleveland Museum of Art seeks assistance to set up cultural exchanges with museums in Chinese cities. A professor in North Carolina cables to seek a cassette of "Red Detachment of Women" for his next class on Chinese culture. Most to the point, a professor at the University of Massachusetts [Eric Einhorn, a classmate of mine as graduate students at Harvard, later a specialist in Scandinavian politics], who knew of my immigration struggles as an Australian trying to get a green card in the U.S. wrote: "I hope Immigration Department officials watch CBS!"

Nixon eventually said his trip added up to "a week that changed the world." As summit meetings go, the trip did so. China emerged with a flourish from the Cultural Revolution, triangular diplomacy was born, the Russians were agitated like ants on a hot stove, and most of the domestic critics of both Zhou Enlai and Nixon were (for the moment) silenced.

---

[39] Walter Cronkite (1916-2009), anchor for CBS News from 1962 to 1981.

February 1972, New York

Late at night, after an Italian dinner on West 57th, I did the late-evening CBS China program. Talked with Cronkite at the Great Wall, and added comments, at Collingwood's bidding, some trivial, some grand.

With Ernie Leiser, my producer, and Charlie Collingwood, we went to the Holiday Inn for a farewell drink, against a background of loud music; thence to Willie's where the marvelous Michael fell into my arms and China was forgotten.

In March, Terrill's book 800,000,000: The Real China was published. It was the beginning of a decade-long outpouring of books. "A kind of paradise for writing and publishing," he later remarked about the 1970s. To celebrate, he took himself to San Juan, Puerto Rico, the first of many R & R trips to the island.

April 4, 1972, San Juan

A thrill as 85-degree temperature hits me at the airport. The name "Atlantic Beach" is apt, for my hotel room towers over the sea, and in 100 seconds I go from my bed to crashing waves. When I come back, would-be lovers gaze up from the sand to my window.

April 6, 1972, San Juan

Within the radical democracy of the beach, the high are not superior and the low can be princes of the earth. Especially when nearly naked. An early-teenager on the beach near the Sands Hotel wears brief shorts inscribed, "SEX RELIEVES TENSION." You see a guy and categorize him as a hustler, but in San Juan what is a hustler? These Puerto Rican "hustlers" sometimes turn out to be students, musicians, 9-to-5ers!

April 8, 1972, San Juan

To counter the brick wall between homosexuality and heterosexuality, just make love *à trois*, one man partner and one woman partner. Sometimes the brick wall isn't there after all.

An obstacle in front of straights who toy with trying a gay experience is they don't know the techniques. Mostly, if they knew the variety of possibilities, and if they knew the gay guy would be willing to do most of them, 95 percent of their hesitations would melt away. The trouble is they have a vision of being fucked and raped and losing control of the whole experience. A sad misjudgment.

After getting nicely warmed in the sun, I came back to the old town and dined at El Mesón Vasco on San Sebastian Square. The proprietor is a portly, beady-eyed Spaniard. His chief waiter is a total contrast, thin where his boss is stout, nonchalant where his boss is twitching with nervous energy, not with beady but large and vacant eyes.

San Sebastian Square is beautiful by night. An air of sensuality, of hunting, of availability. Two or three couples take the opportunity to make love on the benches.

One pair is sitting astride a bench facing each other and through the shadows, I see that he manages to make her in that position.

After dinner, I walked back to El Convento. Racing down Cristo Street is a tiny boy on roller skates. He is so skilled that he can get up the velocity of about twenty miles per hour and still stop himself by some subtle twist of his ankles. Two T-shirts have slogans that stick in the mind. "President McGovern 1972;" "I have slept on a virgin isle."

In the evening, some work on my Hangchow chapter and then to the Lion's Den, where there is a friendly crowd. I meet one nice guy who has a beard and a very charming and soft manner. In a warm vibrating voice, he kept whispering in my ear. "I would like to fuck you. I would like to fuck you."

1972, New York

Association for Asian Studies conference for the first time. I met Frank Ching[40] and got a chance to tell Dorothy Borg from Columbia how much I like her books on history. Wilma Fairbank introduced me to John Melby, bright but less mellow than Wilma. Li-li Ch'en[41] took the opportunity to slap my face as a "male chauvinist."

May 13, 1972, San Francisco

Overnight at Dave's Bathhouse and met enticing Blacks, Latinos and others. A slim Latin came in ahead of me. As usual—a mistake—I did not look directly at him, but waited. Soon in the steam room I saw a tableau which made blood rush to my head. The Latin was reclining on a bench, his cock, large and beautiful, stretched to the right, as another young beau obeyed the Biblical injunction, "This is my flesh, take and eat."

Spellbound, I could not leave the steam-room. What next unfolded was new to my eyes. A third man got with the Latin's partner! Impelled by jealousy as well as desire, I moved toward the Latin's legs. The partner's peach-like lips were pulling and twisting at the head of the Latin's hot dick. Kneeling before a step in the steam room, I put my tongue on the back mid-section of this lovely cock, slithered downwards, and reached the silky balls. The Latin groaned, his face contorted.

The third guy withdrew. The Latin leaned over and grabbed my cock, and I pawed at his jet-black curls as he played with me like a piece of dough. Parallel with John Donne's lines, a steam-room of love was the universe itself. One night, a lifetime.

June 18, 1972, Singapore

On a beautiful warm evening, B and I, for history's sake, eat dinner at the Raffles Hotel. It has changed, with a new wing and spiffy refurbishment, but it is still colonial, stately, and spacious. The waiters are numerous and deferential. You never sense rushing or a crowd. The food is superb, as in the cherries jubilee and the miraculously fresh salmon.

---

[40] Frank Ching, *New York Times* journalist and writer. He would later open *The Wall Street Journal*'s bureau in Beijing.

[41] Li-li Ch'en, professor of Chinese language and literature at Tufts University, 1972-1994.

The courtyard is now lit up with colored lights. A new bar has cane chairs with tangerine cushions. Afterwards, B and I wander in the park surrounding the monument to victims of Japanese occupation, then to my room. Smooth Asian skin delights me after weeks without it.

When Queen Elizabeth came here, Julie's lovely little son Freddie noticed pot plants along the route she would follow from the airport. The pot plants stopped at a point at which the Queen would turn off that road. Freddie wondered what would happen if the Queen said she'd like to continue along the road instead of turning off. The tiny boy said, "I suppose the driver would say, 'I'm sorry, Queen, we can't do that because Singapore has no more plants.'"

June 22, 1972, Hong Kong

I discover the Chinese bathhouse. A taximan who drives me to the Yuk Tak in Prince Edward Road, smiles and says with pity, "We Cantonese do not have such bathhouses. We wash ourselves; only the northern Chinese do it that way."

Inside the door of Yuk Tak sit a roomful of grinning, dark-eyed boys, some of whom are bath boys, some callboys. A bath boy scrubs you like a potato for the pot. You plunge into a warm pool like a Japanese ofuro.[42] The bath boy rinses you by pouring buckets of water over your head, and swathes you in towels. You stagger upstairs to a cubicle for a massage.

When I went upstairs, a little marvel finds his way to my towel-draped cubicle. His face is angular and square for a Cantonese, almost like a Szechuanese. The mouth is masculine and sensuous. He started with my toes and though it was pleasant, I wondered whether I was going to get aroused—so many orgasms within recent days.

But proof came that it's all in the power of attractiveness, rather than an objective measure of energy. The bath boy ran his hands up and down my back, and on to the slippery mountains. He brushed my cock, now red hot, and I grabbed him round the thighs. Suddenly he leaned over me. His hands still applied with a masseur's touch to my stomach, he kissed me long and warmly. From then on, the whole session was an erotic express.

He kept saying, "There's people there, there's people there." I would say in Chinese, "Nobody's there" or "It doesn't matter."

June 25, 1972, Hong Kong

Lai washed and soaped me, and my cock soared like an elephant's trunk. Then Lee came up with his busy fingers. He was small and beautiful, with liquid eyes, a winning smile, and sensuous lips that glided up and down my cock. But Chung!; I craved him.

Something drew me to Chung, beyond his boyish toughness. I found out that he was recently from China, which explained part. No sooner were we in bed at the Mandarin Hotel than he began to tug at my cock in the business-like Cantonese manner. I had to restrain him, for I could have come within seconds.

---

[42] Ofuro (お風呂), Japanese bath.

I found his "weakness": suck his tits and he swoons. This I alternated with licking his ears, long drawn-out kisses, and a slow assault on his legs, thighs, balls, and pert and chunky shaft. He panted and uttered phrases in Mandarin (practice for me). The climax, as often with Chinese, was no less delightful than the preliminaries. We lay back and smoked and he told me his life story.

1972, San Francisco

I love the trees that remind me of Australia. And the hills, visible from all points of the University of California and San Francisco, for they qualify the routine of city life with open-endedness and vision. There is nostalgia, too, for nine years ago when I met America and its handsome men in Berkeley and San Francisco. I have regarded it as a center of my Emotional World ever since.

August 17, 1972, Cambridge

Rachel has left after four days of excitement that leaves me exhausted as well as enriched. I still cannot work her out, especially how interested in sex she is, with anyone. Since we first became intimate, she is more sensual and more physically attracted to me. Yet is the capture more important to her than enjoyment of the captured? She stayed here last night, and the scene was domestic. I forgot entirely that she's married to Wade. How insecure she is, just like me, and how good it is to fill up each other's weaknesses by affection and kindness.

Discussing whether or not I should go back to Canberra in the event of a Labor government, she weighs it up and says, "But remember, your enemies make you a personal target when you are in government." There are streaks of naivety in Rachel; but shrewdness too. I realize she is devoted to me, yet she does not greatly admire me. The distinction poses problems about feminine ambivalence, and the extreme difficulty of a woman being honest toward a man.

August 19, 1972, Cambridge

My sailor friend Maurice, on his way from Denver to the Navy base at Newport, came by and passed the night. Something about his personality and body clicks with me. It became a case of two people marveling at each other for hour after hour.

Born in Mississippi of a very large family, Maurice is earthy, with a rural father like me, and we stimulated each other by tales of boyhood experiences. Delightfully, if falsely, he kept saying, "I am a novice; you'll have to teach me."

In sexual relations with women, he was far from a novice; he broke off an engagement with a white girl two weeks ago—and I suppose I caught him on the pent-up rebound. In some technicalities he was inexperienced; but how nice to re-steer a sensual and practiced guy into slightly new paths. He kept saying, "Oh, that feels so good!"

Dawn came; I had hardly slept. Maurice had dozed a few times; in between he would wake up and our mad cantor would restart. I'd put a mirror alongside the bed—a good idea, given the beauty of his body.

After having had two long orgasms, I woke from a short doze—this must have been about 6:00 AM—and looked down from my pillow to this superb form and a hand beginning to play around with his cock. I gazed at this for about a minute, which fired me up totally; 20 minutes later I had come for the third time and he for the second.

August 21, 1972, Cambridge

If you come to believe less in an afterlife, other things subtly but profoundly change. The truths you can touch, sensual things, become more precious; they are one's new path to the transcendental.

If Anthony Burgess is correct in saying imagination and sensuality are the twin redeemers of thought, our thinking is lent wings by uncertainty about an afterlife. A new pathos enters, a new sense of mortality is accompanied by a new poignancy; things and passing moments, being perishable, seem infinitely tender.

August 29, 1972, Cambridge

Li-li is in good form tonight and more detached about her passion for me than before. I am going to Europe tomorrow to give speeches in Holland and London. "Impress those people," she said, "impress the hell out of them."

September 7, 1972, Cambridge

Li and I go for an evening of eating and bar hopping. I told her about my nights with Somchai in Bangkok, and she murmured: "How fascinating is the gay world." When she goes with a Chinese man she behaves more conservatively, as if in a throwback to her rigid Chinese upbringing, than when she goes with a non-Chinese man.

October 1972, Cambridge

Phannarong ("Pan") has come into my life like a spring blossom. We met in the Coop book shop, started talking. It turned out he knew quite a bit about me. He was in Government 117 when I lectured. He's a friend of Martin G and knew my telephone number. I said: "Let's get together. I am busy for a few days, but in one week I will be less so."

Exactly one week later the phone rang. It was Pan and we arranged to meet at five. He came around, dashing with his gleaming black hair, liquid eyes and firm, pink lips. I still didn't know whether he was physically available or not. If I had to guess as he walked in the door, I would have guessed not. But he mentioned a Moroccan student called Ramos, and when I realized this was the guy in the white hat whom Mark G had introduced me to, I began to wonder. On the other hand, he'd never heard of any of the Bangkok bars whose names I mentioned. He glanced at a book of photos of Japanese male nudes; his bland reaction was a good sign.

Then he clinched it. "I saw you also on June the fifth," he said, "near the news agent in Harvard Square and Cardullo's Delicatessen." He was looking at me, he said, and I looked back. Frankly, I don't remember this. He said, "Look it up in your Diary to verify" if it could have been me or not.

After this I said, "Just as you saw me on June fifth, I saw you this morning walking up Bow Street in a pair of smart blue-jeans, carrying an umbrella." I added: "When I saw this Thai young man this morning, I thought how much I would like to go to bed with him." He smiled faintly. I said, "I wonder what his reaction would have been had he known." Eventually Pan said quietly, "I think that question was settled when I telephoned you." Ten minutes later we were wrapped hot and naked on my sheep skin rug. Afterwards we dined at Grendel's Den.

A few days later we met again and had a feeling already of attachment. The first night he had not come but this time he did. I also fucked him. I did not expect to, but he said he wanted me to but thought it would not possible. But for a while we lay there, and I got my finger up him with Vaseline on it, and soon I was inside very slowly, and eventually I fucked him uproariously and he said he loved it.

Then we went to Central Square post office to pick up my passport from the Japanese Consulate in New York. We had a bite at La Crêpe. Back at my room, I packed for departure to San Francisco and Tokyo the next morning. Then we went to bed, entwined like amorous snakes.

The next morning, I rose early for an enormous day, but before I left, we managed to meet again at my office. He brought me two superb pictures of himself taken at the family house in Bangkok. We kissed fondly and he went to class.

1973

February 7, 1973, Cambridge

Galenovich from the UN, back from many trips to China, says regional officials want their interests represented in Peking, but they themselves don't like to leave the region and go and work in Peking. Different from Soviet Union. At the end, he presented me with a bottle of vodka and told me to have a nice weekend. There is something very homely about Russians.

May 4, 1973, Washington

A magical quality to Pennsylvania Ave at dusk on a summer evening. Warm and bright. People stroll in the square opposite the White House. Everything is green and clean and prosperous.

I come out of Winston Lord's office.[43] My taxi drives along the side street. Suddenly I see Nixon get into his helicopter in the Rose Garden. The machine roars, and in a moment the loud, buzzing beast takes off and swoops over the park behind the White

---

[43] Winston Lord (1937-), at the time was a member of the National Security Council planning staff. He had accompanied Nixon to Beijing in 1972.

House. It keeps to a low trajectory; President Nixon is out on a spin to view his capital on a sparkling evening.

Terrill was to be part of a delegation of Harvard Sinologists slated to visit China in 1973. But Beijing canceled the invitation. Instead, he went to Japan via Honolulu and Hong Kong.

October 8, 1973, Honolulu

Yukio Mishima's *Sun and Steel* fills the four hours flying from San Francisco to Honolulu. A kind of liberation lurks, yet it does not quite claim me. Is it because his central theme, death, so far means nothing to me? Is it that he became anti-intellectual when he decided to pursue words through the body, and not the body through words, and I am not anti-intellectual (yet)?

But I sense what Mishima feels. He despises the separation of a man from his body. He delights in the washing away of every-day emotions through extreme exhaustion. Maybe Mishima is right even about death; anyone who walks the homosexual-narcissistic path finds perfection of the physical self leads only to the last threshold of death.

October 27, 1973, Hong Kong

Living on my nerves. A dark dream last night about trouble because I was gay, even trouble with the law. And to make it far worse, Pan abandoned me in the middle of the ordeal. I woke up stiff as a board.

I wonder if the life of the mind has to rescue the personality of R.T. The life of the mind is worthwhile for its own sake. And for the good, when it sometimes enriches the world around us. But it can also have a big effect on a person's psyche. After some heavy sex or even cruising, turning to a book, taking a draft and editing it—these things steady me.

I can only go to China with Gough if I have a role in the talks; not to go just as an ornament. And it is embarrassing to get out of the conference in Japan that I came to attend (air fare from Boston to Japan paid by the conference).

October 30, 1973, Tokyo

Reception at the embassy after the Whitlam-Ohira press conference. The press conference had 100-odd journalists. Each leader gave an opening statement. What Ohira said seemed a mind at work; Whitlam's was mere phrase making. Ohira made his point by saying, "We note that the Australian policy of economic nationalism is selective; secondly we notice that there has been a promise that Japan will not be discriminated against; thirdly, we assume that once Australia has supplied its own needs it will be able to sell the rest to other people." In this delicate way he got his points across.

John H, the doctor who looked after my troubled insides in Canberra, was there, looking after Gough, and said he was glad I had the barium enema because this covered the one possibility that he hadn't been able to check while I was under his care. During the party, he was getting along famously with two of the prettiest girls in the garden. One of them, introduced to me, fluttered and chuckled and said she thought I'd be "more serious, more formal." In Canberra she only saw me naked. How can you seem formal with zero garments?

The Japanese Prime Minister came up with Ambassador Freeth introducing him. Tanaka is small, modest, not handsome, and walks with a slight waddle. One could have taken him for a driver or security man. But he has a nice open smile and engaging manner.

October 31, 1973, Tokyo

A couple of hours at Sanpo, publishers of my *800,000,000*. Serialization probably did not affect one way or the other the sales of the book. Sanpo received a lot of reader letters, which they sample and translate for me, and the comments were similar to other countries. Most readers appeared to be teachers, students, traders, or people long interested in China.

They printed 15,000 copies and they have sold half that number. They think it will go on selling steadily. First, they sent out 13,000 and the returns were 70 percent after several months—not good. There are 10,000 bookshops in Japan but most of them are tiny, where things other than books are sold. And the number that take books non-returnable is only six. The number of major stores that sell essentially only books is 1500.

The "fourth printing" is partly a subterfuge practiced by Japanese publishers. When the returns come back, they insert a new page, putting a new date in to make the book look more recent. This they have done three times, so there is indeed, now, an edition of my book that is a "fourth printing." Of course, it is a lie. With a certain embarrassment, they explain, "this is the way things are done in Japan."

Wednesday, October 31, 1973, Hakone, by Mount Fuji

George Ball[44] says Nixon will not be president a month from now.[45] Watergate will come to a climax when the Republican leadership goes to the White House and tells Nixon they are hurting too much.

An editorial in the *Wall Street Journal* two days ago calling for Nixon's resignation is, in George's view, a straw in the wind. I am not convinced Nixon cannot hang on, especially if he invokes an international crisis.

A main point today is that in this part of the world there are essentially four over-arching powers. The fact that only America and Russia have massive nuclear deterrents is balanced by the non-military ways in which Japan and China have influence. It is unlikely that any two of the four will tie themselves up intimately with one of the others.

---

[44] George Ball (1909-1994), American diplomat and briefly Ambassador to the U.N.
[45] The break-in of the DNC headquarters at the Watergate Office Building on June 17, 1972 set off a huge scandal for the Nixon administration that continued for two years. Eight weeks after Terrill wrote this Diary entry, a grand jury indicted seven former aides of Nixon. Facing impeachment, Nixon resigned on August 8, 1974.

The pressure is on Russia and China to be less mutually hostile, because they face the most hostile nation among the four countries, and it is a weakening factor for both.

November 2, 1973, Hakone

The first wave of Asian reaction to Watergate was courtesy mixed with its frequent companion, hypocrisy. Later, especially in Indonesia and countries in similar positions, there was alarm.

Asia is a moralistic region compared with other regions of the world, though the moralism varies among China, Japan, the Moslem world. The Christian parts are the least moralistic.

When I hear Harlan Cleveland[46] talk about the need for a new creation, I tremble. He feels, just as Dean Acheson felt he was present at the creation of the post-war world order after WWII, that we are on the threshold of a new creation. Of course, Cleveland says it has to be different: post-Vietnam, post-Watergate, post-nuclear, post-nationalistic, and post-regional grouping. But I am uneasy because the values, political and moral, which would lie behind such a new creation are not shared sufficiently across the globe.

There was a fascinating debate between Koko and Tanaka[47] on the issue of whether freedom and democracy mean anything. Ironically, Tanaka took the positive side. He delivered an eloquent speech which ended up by saying that he stood in hope for the Thai people and their possession of freedom and democracy.

Koko (an Indonesian) said this is not the choice. You cannot make an abstract choice about freedom or authoritarianism. You have to evolve a system inch by inch as you tackle concrete problems. Implicitly, Koko denied that the value choice Thai students make against militarism-authoritarianism is valid. He really threw cold water on the Thais, saying to get power is one thing, to run a country is another.

November 2, 1973, Tokyo, evening

One has to decide what one judges important. In this Greg was helpful. He said, "You're an authority on China, if you can be in those talks it's a great thing." And he was right, and I would like that, but to just be an ornament, as Greg put it, to be at the banquets, well, that would have been acceptable I think, only if I had not accepted for the Rockefeller conference.

Greg has contempt for political circles, but I don't. This crowd is a better Australian government than we've ever had before. And all governments, when you look closely, take you aback. I'm not sure I'd be much better, on the issues Greg mentions, if I were in their shoes in Canberra.

---

[46] Harlan Cleveland (1918-2008), American diplomat, educator and author of twelve books. At the time of his talk, he was the President of the University of Hawaii.
[47] Soedjatmoko Mangoendiningrat (1922-1989), known as "Bung Koko," was an Indonesian politician, intellectual and diplomat. Kakuei Tanaka (1918-1993) was prime minister of Japan from 1972-1974.

November 3, 1973, Hakone to Tokyo

On the bus back to Tokyo, George Ball recalls a Security Council debate when Ignatiev of Canada, like Ball, both ambassadors at the UN, was sick and tired of Baraudy, the Saudi Arabian delegate, who would talk endlessly and pointlessly. When Baraudy began to speak, Ignatiev told his assistant to wake him up when Baraudy finished, and the vote was taken. However, halfway through, the French ambassador came over to consult Ignatiev, and laid a hand on his shoulder. Ignatiev suddenly woke up, shot his hand into the air and said, "Mr. President, I abstain." The chamber broke up.

Koko and I are much less sanguine than George about the prospect of three years of Gerald Ford as president. It is all very well for George, who is a Democrat, and hates Nixon. He thinks Ford would simply be a caretaker. I don't think that is certain, and I am not sure that George has foreseen all the effects of a three-year Ford presidency.

November 3, 1973, Tokyo

Breakfast with John Rockefeller,[48] wise and thoughtful, and Bob Barnett, a longtime diplomat with a focus on Asia. Bob names three points which make the Williamsburg Asia-Pacific Seminar unique. First, people are not dealing with their specialty, so there is an absence of jargon. Second, people are of some eminence, yet they know others are also of eminence, so they don't put on airs. Third, the topic is such that while no one is directly on his specialty, everyone feels at some point that there is something he knows and can say. All correct. I think (or hope) there is a fourth point: people speak only for themselves.

Rockefeller was very critical of *The New York Times*, which he baldly called a Jewish paper. He went on about how he thought Barbara Tuchman's *Stilwell* was good, but Bob Barnett said it wasn't, because it was too harsh on Chiang Kai-shek; which it is. Barnett is a decent man, almost too decent. Rockefeller, on the other hand, is like an elderly missionary, and indeed his attitude towards the Asia Society reminds me of the attitude of Margaret Flory to her Christian flock. You cannot but feel this American paternalistic idealism is declining as older True Believers bow out.

I gave an interview to Yoshimura of the *Tokyo Shimbun* while a photographer takes at least 200 pictures and then Ito and I have a glass at the Sinko and later coffee at one of these synthetic little shops like a wedding parlor. He said he was very pessimistic about Japan's international future, because of the American retreat and the possibility of a Sino-Soviet rapprochement. Also, because Japan is a middle-class society (which means strong driving leadership is not easy), guilt from the war, the lack of natural resources, and Japan is deeply divided politically. So he talks about an internal left pressure meeting an external left pressure.

I feel it was unduly pessimistic, first because it is not clear how far the American retreat will go, second, because Japan is not just a passive factor in the situation. The three great over-arching questions are, "How far will the American retreat go?", "Will

---

[48] John Davison Rockefeller III (1906 - 1978), American philanthropist.

there be a Russia-China rapprochement?", and "What course will Japan take?" I would go so far as to say that the second might hinge to some extent on the third.

On Chinese internal politics, he makes the analogy too readily between Stalin and Mao, saying policies don't count, it is who is on top. I think Mao is more a man of ideas than Stalin, and that Chou Enlai himself does not know what this brooding, constantly thinking man above him will think next Monday about policy.

There is an article in the *People's Daily* about how cheating in exams is not a bad thing. Ito of the *Tokyo Daily* takes this very seriously as a sign of the power of the left.

November 4, 1973, Tokyo

After dinner with Ito, I went to Regent and at once met Shozo, sexy clock clerk in a Tokyo company. Medium height, handsome, solid. He reminded me of the photos of Japanese nude men Pan looked at in Kirkland House, in the picture book from Los Angeles.

I asked Shozo about Pal, the new bar which I have heard is a favorite of Japanese workers. He'd never been there, but suggested we go. Pal was extremely crowded, with fewer foreigners than the Regent. We drank sake. He planned to go to bed alone.

We sat on stools at the bar and every new arrival had to squeeze past us at the back. This meant brushing and gentle pushing, which I reciprocated as another man squeezed past. Shozo became alarmed in a friendly way. From Pal, we took a cab to the Okura; he'd changed his mind.

Shozo was a nice lover in pragmatic, virile Japanese fashion. After making love we went to sleep in separate beds and then made love again in the morning. He inspected me inch by inch, as if he were a physician, but you get used to this in Japan. After one inspection he announced that foreigners' legs are longer, slimmer, and shapelier than Japanese legs.

He has a lover, off and on, who teaches at a university in the States and runs some kind of a business on the side. Lately though, the lover has been too busy to see Shozo. That proved to be my opportunity.

November 22, 1973, Cambridge

Quiet Thanksgiving dinner with Charlotte. She prefaced the turkey with a lovely fresh salmon, and stuffed the turkey with chestnuts and liver. We talk about Nigel Nicholson's book about his parents[49] and she says," Nigel himself thinks fidelity is not crucial to marriage, but he really shows a way in marriage other than possessiveness. His parents loved each other without the need to possess each other."

---

[49] Nigel Nicholson (1917-2004), English writer, publisher and politician. The book Terrill discussed with Charlotte is *Portrait of a Marriage: Vita Sackville-West and Harold Nicolson* (1973) about his bi-sexual parents.

November 25, 1973, Cambridge

Jim T comes in for drinks. "I think I'd better have Scotch," he says, and I remember with horror the last time he was here. A martini is what he likes and surely would have liked tonight. But on that previous occasion (Diana and also the Spences from Yale were here) I had bungled the martini, putting far too much vermouth in it. Hence his gentle, "I think I'd better..."!

December 1, 1973, Cambridge

Dinner with the Suns in Watertown, and Ruxiang[50] comes with me. A Mongolian barbecue *à la table*. We seem to be eating an enormous amount, but the slices of raw chicken, beef, fish are so thin that this may not be so. We talk about Taiwan where Sun's father is a retired general, weighing up whether or not to seek a return to Peking, which he loves and knows like the palm of his hand. I see photos of him—as a commander in Peking—receiving the Japanese surrender in 1945.

Long is relaxed. "Why don't you return to Australia?" she enquired; then as I hemmed and hawed, she murmured, "You may as readily ask me why I do not return to live in China."

December 4, 1973, Cambridge

When I was a child, my parents did not seem to love each other...

December 6, 1973, Cambridge

As this job issue trauma subsides for the moment, the muddy truth dawns upon me. What a Harvard University department is really asking when they look over a candidate for promotion is, "This guy, is he one of us?"

December 16, 1973, Cambridge

Dinner with Charlotte at Peking Gardens in Lexington and she translates for me the latest batch of German language reviews of my *800,000,000*. They say I talk about the people rather than the system. Two, I have a basis of comparison from 1964. Three, I was able to use the Chinese language. Four, I declare my values as a democratic socialist. Five, as a Westerner, I do not pretend that one can get into the soul of the Chinese. All these reviews, like the 40 or 50 Dirk translated for me, add up to an extremely favorable reception in Germany, Austria, and the German-speaking part of Switzerland.

December 26, 1973, Cambridge

Dinner with Ruxiang. Alarmed at the prospect of me going back to Australia, she becomes emotional, then sullen, then quietly persistent, and says that I really should not go back. It was the first time a Chinese had told me not to go back to my own

---

[50] Chinese friend of Terrill's and a language coach at the Fairbank Center.

country. I said we ought to go to China together and she took me up like a flash. When I eventually asked whether I or she should take it up with the Chinese government, she said she would. What reason could she give, she asked me. I felt her beauty tonight as never before, and indeed she made it clear as never before. She even discussed marriage and said she did not believe in it, either in its US form or in its form in China today.

December 28, 1973, Cambridge

A late-night rendezvous with Pan at his room in Leverett House, which he has made a sanctuary of Thailand. I caught him just stepping out of the shower with a towel around him. As we lay in bed, he told me about our first "meeting."

When I gave a lecture to BIS's course on Chinese government, Pan was a member of the class. As soon as I walked in the room and went to the podium, he said to himself, "I'd like to go to bed with that man." Throughout the lecture, he took hardly any notes. Later he looked back at his notebook and saw there was no lecture at Harvard for which he had fewer notes. All he can remember is I started out by saying there would be four points. From that moment, he said, he was gripped with sex fantasies. All this is eighteen months ago and I was thirty.

He loves it when he lies back on the cushion, and I work my tongue up his legs and suck his balls. I watch him tossing his head around in ecstasy with his black hair glinting in the moonlight. And while I've got his cock in my mouth, I gently put my finger up his ass and he starts to cry out; our crusade of lust has begun.

December 30, 1973, Cambridge

America and China. The set-up is entirely different, the people are a *bit* different.

1974

January 4, 1974, Cambridge

In the Square at midday, I wondered: if you were not born in USA, can you ever trust your instincts, walk the paving-stones with confidence? I think not with the same raw assertiveness that I find possible for myself in Australia. I simply do not feel and care about the background here as I do in my own land.

This means I may not be able to write about America. But it does not mean I cannot write about Australia—for a world audience. In fact, it may be easier to do so while breathing the wider challenges of life outside Australia. Thus, my roots are irreplaceable, yes; but need not be limiting for my life in the USA, and can be a literary richness for it.

January 7, 1974, Cambridge

Read Virginia Wolf's *Writers Diary*, gripping though Leonard has cut out all the personal stuff. "Virginia Woolf was not only a tormented spirit, but her writing and thinking style have a reckless and stretched character. For all her fame, she was sensitive to criticism and ten nice reviews were never enough to balance in her mind the weight of one bad one."

Writing became an addiction for her so that though one book tortured her, it no sooner would be finished than she would lust toward the next. I cannot consider her a fine writer; to read the journal of Gide at the same time puts Virginia Woolf in a lower category as a craftsman of words. There is a poignant naiveté, as when she goes shopping for hats and shoes and clothes and people stare at her because of her strange ways and she wonders why. Coming home, she remarks, "Where is my paper knife? I must cut Lord Byron."

She is a snob about working people and yet, we have in common a contempt for honors. When a university asks her to come and receive an honorary doctorate, she notes, "I need not emerge from my fiction in July to have a tuft of fur put on my head." After an evening with GBS [George Bernard Shaw], she quotes the old man about his trip to the Orient: "The tropics are the place. The people are the original human beings. We are smudged copies. I caught the Chinese looking at us with horror—that we should be human beings!"

January 12, 1974, Cambridge

Finished the *Journals* of Andre Gide. I bought the book in Canberra while I was in the hospital and read it in bed between visitors. It is an unforgettable journal, if too introspective. He is so honest with himself that even when he is pathetic, there is much to be learned: on youth; on Christianity's relation to communism; on his contemporaries in French literature; on the mutual relation of love of men and love of women; on how the literary is related to the social.

January 25, 1974, Cambridge

Lunch with Senator Lowell Weicker[51] at the Faculty Club. Weicker believes Dean's[52] testimony is correct in all substantial respects and there is no possible conclusion other than that Weicker believes Nixon to be guilty of crimes. He also assured us that Goldwater is as firm as ever in his anti-Nixon line. Incredibly, he has not talked to the President since early 1971.

January 28, 1974

Martin Kilson[53] phones to congratulate me on the promotion to associate professor and to express a couple of barbs. "There was a bit of shit," he said, "because of a few jealous people, who are interested in political thought but never write anything on the subject which has any relevance to anything. "You know who I mean." I do: Shklar and

---

[51] Lowell Palmer Weicker Jr. (1931 -), U.S. Senator from Connecticut, 1971-1989.

[52] John Dean (1938 -), served as White House Counsel for President Nixon from July 1970 to April 1973. In June 1973, he testified before the Senate Watergate Committee, disclosing that Nixon had been directly involved in the Watergate coverup, an allegation that Nixon denied.

[53] Martin Luther Kilson Jr. (1931-2019), Professor of Government (1988-1999) at Harvard. He was the first fully tenured Black professor at the University.

Walzer.[54] Judith Shklar outside the classroom resembles a clever suburban housewife. That she is indeed extremely clever does not make her less suburban.

February 1, 1974, Cambridge

Dr. Arbatov[55] comes to the Center for International Affairs to talk about US-Soviet relations, hinging on the question of criticism of each other's society and the boundary between this and interference. He said we must accept that there will be important things about each other's societies that we cannot accept. The important thing is that we do not make our criticisms a part of national policy.

This distinction is more difficult to uphold in America because the government cannot neglect a pressure group that feels strongly about a moral issue. China can do it, but not the us.

BIS asked what sounded like a good question. "Why do you expel newsmen from Russia? Are they not engaging merely in criticism? Arbatov said, "If we expelled anyone for criticism, there would only be one correspondent left in Moscow instead of 240—the one from the *Daily Worker*."

In fact, the correspondent to which Schwartz referred was expelled for having distributed a questionnaire to certain dissidents. The first question was "Why don't the dissidents organize public demonstrations?" Second was "Why don't the persecuted Jews in the Soviet Union organize public demonstrations?"

February 4, 1974, Cambridge

At the department meeting Karl Deutsch[56] says "Your promotion is a victory for civilization." No other promotion in the department "has enabled me to offer congratulations with as much enthusiasm as yours."

During the business session, there were curious and revealing references to languages, which tell one a little about our department. Barrington Moore had written in a letter about a new course he is giving—two new courses, in fact—one about German Labor history and one about post-revolutionary regimes in Russia and China. In describing the first, he commented that German would be required and that he greatly laments that this elementary tool is not possessed by many students. Yet he blandly is offering a course on Russian and Chinese society when he cannot read a word of Chinese.

February 6, 1974, Cambridge

Bob Manning is interested in two pieces. One is about what China is likely to do in Asia after the Vietnam cease-fire; this he would like to do by April 1 for the June issue. The other is the notebook about North Africa.

---

[54] Michael Laban Walzer (1935 -), Professor of Government (1966-1980) at Harvard.
[55] Georgy Arkadyevich Arbatov (1923-2010), Soviet political scientist.
[56] Karl Wolfgang Deutsch (1912-1992), was the Stanfield Professor of International Peace at Harvard.

February 16, 1974, San Juan

It takes a few hours to switch from New England precision to the sense of timelessness in this Latin outpost. Once you get used to the idea that things won't be done, that people won't arrive on time, it doesn't matter in the slightest.

The Eastern Airlines flight was three hours late, so there was no question of going to the beach in the afternoon. I settled in at El Convento, did a little work and walked around town feeling the sensuality of cobbled lanes and balconies. I saw the Roman noses and the substantial asses on the smallest of Puerto Rican boys, the heaving half-covered breasts of very fuckable Puerto Rican women.

The Lion's Den was lively, and I spent a pleasant half-hour with one of the dancers, a new boy, small and beautiful who speaks little English but eloquent body language. In matters of love, the Latins do not stint.

February 18, 1974, San Juan

We eyed each other off and on for half an hour or so and then I became aware that next to him on a deck chair was an attractive man, who was his father. In the father's arms was a very young son and I suppose the mother was at home today. I found the father as magnetic as the son. I lay there in the sun and invented fantasies of having sex now with the boy, now with the father, now both together, and of watching the two of them in the process of this orgy discovering each other in an explicit sexual way.

There were moments in the real situation when one of them would look up my body, which was arranged to make it easy for them to be enticed, and the other would notice him, and the first would become aware of this and turn away. Moments later the process would be reversed.

February 25, 1974, San Juan

It's beautiful to get out of bed at El Convento and walk to the window and overlook the old town with the sun streaming through the trees in the Square. I had a late breakfast at Las Meridas and later went to the gay beach.

That evening I met Francesco at El Convento. We had run into each other last night outside the Small World Bar. He's a tall Black guy from the south of the Island with a small beard, a very small beard, thank God. I liked him immediately and even though he spoke very little English, we got along and arranged to meet tonight. He came and we quickly went upstairs and went to bed.

He was hot and earnest and he wanted to come about one minute after we got into bed. This stimulated me and when he said he wanted me to fuck him, I was hardly inside before I had to come also. So we were dressed and downstairs again all within about twenty minutes of going inside.

I dined alone at La Mallorquina, which is lovely in its decor of marble floors, bath mirrors, and old wooden furniture. The service is also good. But the food is mediocre. I ordered a sea food stewed in wine, which was mostly green peas and shells. After dinner, I walked around the streets, but I did not go to any bars.

March 4, 1974, Cambridge

Department meeting tonight and an epic but quite civilized debate over the appointment of a new Assistant Professor in political theory. On one side, a traditional, rather narrow theorist. On the other, a man who tries to bring theory into relation with the rest of political science. Of course, the theorists on the faculty were vehemently for the former guy.

Afterwards at dinner, Bob B, Don P, Adam, Harvey, and I sit and talk about Mr. Nixon. Harvey is pretty silent as we discuss it all and, when I turn to him and ask his opinion, he said, "Mr. Nixon has done nothing impeachable." And Bob said, "What would be an impeachable offence in your opinion?" And Harvey said, "For instance, a unilateral withdraw of troops from Indochina would be impeachable." Harvey went on to say that the break-in into the office of Ellsberg's psychologist was justified. "He was entitled to find out anything he could find out from that expedition."

March 13, 1974, Cambridge

Dinner at the home of Francis, who has a writer on Cuba there—rather shallow. I ask if there are interesting Marxists in Cuba and he says, "Yes, just listen to the speeches of Castro and of the leaders of the young communist movement."

Dan Bell[57] is there with his second wife, Pearl, and we have a talk about the state of political science and sociology. Dan dares me to make a prediction about the future of China after Mao and I took up his challenge. I am to send him in a sealed envelope a half page about the major developments one might expect. He will not open it until after the death of Mao, though we have not yet agreed what length of time should elapse between the passing of Mao and the opening of the envelope.

March 20, 1974, Cambridge

Shall I write this to the *NYR*? "I am grateful to Mr. Cameron[58] for pointing out several misprints in my book; it is a pity that a mind so sharp as to detect these did not also apply itself to one or two of the book's themes or arguments."

March 26, 1974, New York

A talk with Scott Meredith,[59] who turns out unlike what I'd expected, not a man of taste to judge by his room, his tie, or anything he said, yet impressive in his way, typified by his remark that he doesn't drink, and he never eats lunch and that when he goes to Los Angeles, he often never leaves the airport. But he might just be the thing for me.

He would handle everything in the written realms, apart from British Commonwealth where he would respect the arrangement with Charlotte. He would

---

[57] Daniel Bell (1919-2011), professor of sociology at Harvard, described as "one of the leading American intellectuals of the postwar era."

[58] J. M. Cameron had reviewed Terrill's book *R.H. Tawney and His Times: Socialism as Fellowship* in the March 21, 1974 issue of *The New York Review*.

[59] Scott Meredith (1923-1993), American literary agent.

advise and dip into the question of what the writer is doing as much as he can, as much as the writer would allow him. He would personally be involved in negotiation with every one of his authors. I left the chapter on Hangchow with him, and the outline and we are going to talk on Friday.

March 28, 1974, Washington, DC

An hour and a half with Hsieh at the Chinese Liaison Office in Washington. A rather dour and narrow man, who said they had heard about me for a long time, and they would like me to call in anytime I am in Washington.

I asked him what he thought of the Irv Drasnin film on Shanghai.[60] He said it was basically a bad film and later he reiterated "a bad film" over against my remark that it wasn't a hostile film but perhaps a superficial film. The motive of it was bad, to suggest that "communism was a passing phase in China and later on it would be transformed into something else." This means ultimate defeat for China. I didn't point out that it could be viewed another way, that China will endure even if Mao doesn't.

He made a big speech about Confucius—somewhat convincing. Even in the countryside, peasants who have never read Confucius are influenced by Confucianism—the position of women, the worship of ancestors, blind obedience of young to old, disrespect of manual labor. He liked my idea that the anti-Confucius drive is just carrying forward the May 4th movement.

I think the question they ask every time—"Did you come specially?" or "What did you come down for?"—is very interesting. It may mean their effort to clear their minds against any doubt that the visitor has a double purpose. If he came specially, they might feel anxious on that, but if they know that he was in New York or Washington or wherever on other business, they seem to feel a little easier that he has maybe just dropped in.

March 28, 1974, Washington, DC

Leaving town from Washington airport, I go to snack in the appalling dining room where the cutlery is stained, the table-clothes filthy and the service non-existent. In trundle a group of East Europeans, Bulgarians I guess, and they order a hearty meal washed down with extraordinary quantities of beer. The fat waitress waddles up and down in answer to their requests, and as the orders for beer come thick and fast, she suddenly puts her hands on her hips and says, "Sir, in Virginia we can only leave one beer at a time."

March 29, 1974

Rachel may be right when she says the book on China is brilliant in its genre; the book on Tawney is a very good book indeed, yet with flaws.

---

[60] Irv Drasnin (1934 -), American journalist and documentary filmmaker. The film Terrill mentions is *Shanghai* (1974).

April 2, 1974, Boston

I take Charlie N to the Union Oyster House for lunch because we wanted to follow up a reference I made to him yesterday about the current state of the Taiwan question, and in particular something that Premier Chou is reported to have said to the Algerians last month.

He feels there is a great problem, in China, of internal communication of the issues of foreign relations. The level of sophistication, education, and knowledge of the world is so various as between the inland peasant masses and the foreign policy elite, that the presentation of issues of detente and imperialism has not been easy.

Slightly to my surprise, he really accepts the point about impeachment politics. He doesn't think there is an identifiable Kuomintang[61] lobby in the Senate, but he thinks the general question of keeping conservatives on side in order to preserve those 34 votes will predominate until the House has voted to impeach as most of Washington thinks it will, and the Senate has voted on the matter. This could be this calendar year, but there won't be any give until then.

April 8, 1974, Cambridge

Dinner with I.F. Stone[62] and I find him a moralist, not an ideologue. Before, there had been a Government Department meeting with a discussion of how to supervise PhD theses and then at dinner I sat with Dick Neustadt who bet me a $100 that Nixon would still be in office at the end of 1975.

The I.F. Stone dinner atmosphere was something else again. Franker, more restrained, less sharp, yet at the same time perhaps more likely to throw up an insight for our times. Stone's discourse reminded me of the chapter in Kingsley Martin's memoirs where he looks back on the 1930s and says, "We overestimated nurture and underestimated nature."

He was speaking like an American Tawney—it's the principles that count. He has a kind of serenity which is surprising. He says the *New York Review* is a piddling thing. He is thinking, he says, about fundamental questions of the human condition, but I bet he won't write a great book because, the genius of Stone lies in the talent which can be reflected by the remark "Publishing a newspaper is like making love, you pull out your cock and you start to do it. You can't teach anyone that. Unless an editor has a fire in the belly, he is nothing."

And in a way, now that Izzy no longer has a fire in his belly, he is nothing—although he is a more lovable and, in some ways, more interesting human being than ever. Much of the I.F. Stone of today boils down to the fact that he is a Jew. He hates the Russian system for this reason, he has a sense of the need to start with the individual and his

---

[61] The Kuomintang or Guomindang (GMD) was the Chinese Nationalist Party, a major political party in the Republic of China.

[62] Isidor Feinstein "I. F." Stone (1907-1989), politically progressive American journalist and author; best known as the editor of the newsletter *I. F. Stone's Weekly* (1953-1971) and winner of numerous awards for journalism.

courage and his talent and his imagination—these are marks of the Jew. The hope of the radical left in the breast of I.F. Stone died with the Russian experiment.

April 13, 1974, Belmont

Dinner of the Australian Club at the house of David Hawkins.[63] I give a speech on Australia in Asia, especially on the foreign policy of the Labor Government. General impression is of a more sympathetic audience than I expected, though also an audience with a low level of knowledge about international affairs.

David's house is an old mansion with oak panels—he needs it with seven young children.

When I got home, I found myself thinking back to sexual adventures in Melbourne. The gathering among Australian people had the effect of reviving passions of a kind that are apparently different in Australia than anywhere else—memories that one had thought no longer resided in the mind.

April 18, 1974, Cambridge

Lunch with Anthony Lewis and a few Niemans.[64] Tony is quite revealing about himself in recounting incidents at *The New York Times*. Reston chose Tom Wicker over Tony to be Washington bureau chief saying Wicker got on better with people than did Lewis

He argued that the *Times* is a marginal paper economically, that there are a dozen papers in the US that make more money than the *Times*. Its income is enormous, but its expenditure is also enormous.

Tony told the story of the night that Woodward and Bernstein launched their greatest Watergate story and he said, "What did Ben Bradlee say as he walked through the newsroom that night? Nothing about history of Nixon, but Abe will eat his heart out."

April 20, 1974, Cambridge

At the Signet Society dinner, Robert Lowell[65] reads two poems whose theme does not excite, but whose word play is that of a master.

---

[63] David Hawkins (1934-2020), Australian-born professor at the Harvard Business School, author of 16 books and monographs.
[64] The Nieman Group, an annual "class" of two dozen seasoned journalists awarded fellowships to study at Harvard.
[65] Robert Lowell (1917-1977), American poet. In 1974, Lowell had just won his second Pulitzer Prize.

April 26, 1974, Cambridge

Jim Thomson's[66] forum on China reporting was a pleasant evening, with Harrison Salisbury,[67] Richard Dudman,[68] Stan Karnow,[69] Irv Drasnin, and myself speaking on the panel. Harrison told a story of Joseph Alsop[70] calling him up at the end of Alsop's trip to China in '72 and saying: "Well, Harry, I guess you and I were the only ones that were right about China all along."

Richard's Midwest perspective was interesting: "I went there to find out why things worked".

I told Harrison that I didn't agree with the line of argument in his book *War Between Russia and China*. His reply was that both the Chinese and the Russians thought it was correct, and one day the Chinese even marched into the border talks with a copy of his book under their arms and used it as evidence, in a complaining voice, that the Russians think him so friendly to the Chinese that they keep pestering him for information on what is the Chinese view on this and on that. All unappetizing if true.

May 7, 1974, Cambridge

Helmut Sonnenfeldt[71] is up from Washington to chat about American-Russian relations.

When discussing nuclear weapons, he said in a casual aside: "Of course, the Russians have three more potential nuclear enemies than we do, Britain, France, and China." Overall, the most interesting thing was his firm conviction that Russian power is on the rise, that in the relatively long term the US will have to accept a slippage in its power relative to Russia, that Russia now thinks of its interests as global for the first time in Russian history. This is the striking thing, and Stanley says Henry thinks the same way.

May 26, 1974, Cambridge

Francis has the composer, Randall Thompson, for dinner. He certainly has seen a lot of musical history having taught Leonard Bernstein as well as having his own symphonies performed by Bernstein and other leading conductors.

Thompson thinks music is going to the dogs. He said no one, not even Bernstein, cares a damn whether he writes any more music or not. Nor do they care whether any American composer, even Samuel Barber or Aaron Copland, writes another word of music or not. "In such an atmosphere," he laments, "how can there be a continuing surge of composition?" English music, he feels, is flawed by the snobbishness of the English and it is hopelessly insular.

---

[66] James C. Thomson (1931-2002), curator of the Nieman Foundation (1972-1984), which awards year-long fellowships at Harvard for mid-career journalists.

[67] Harrison Salisbury (1908-1993), American journalist who wrote 29 books, including several on China.

[68] Richard Beebe Dudman (1918-2017), American journalist and author.

[69] Stanley Abram Karnow (1925-2013), American journalist and historian.

[70] Joseph Alsop (1920-1989), American journalist.

[71] Helmut Sonnenfeldt (1926-2012), American foreign policy expert. At the time of his talk, he was a special advisor and consultant to the Secretary of State in the Nixon and Ford administrations.

June 10, 1974, Cambridge

I talked with Lois Snow at Betty's. When Lois approached the Chinese about scattering part of Ed's ashes in China, they quickly suggested the Babaoshan Cemetery of Revolutionary Martyrs. Lois said no; Ed was neither revolutionary nor a martyr; he was a teacher and he wanted to be with young people. So she suggested Peking University, and the Chinese government agreed.

On the day of the ceremony, it happened that a crew from ABC TV was in Peking and they came out to film it. One photographer was Black and as Chou En-Lai walked with Lois, he noticed this Black guy, went up to him and said: "Congratulations, you have stood up." On her first arrival in Peking on this 1973 trip, Chou and his wife came to her room at the guest house. They talked for an hour, Chou entirely in English.

When she met Mao in 1970, Ed introduced them atop Tiananmen. Mao looked at her very hard. Lois said she had the impression that through his mind went the thought: my she has changed. The previous time Mao had seen Ed with his wife, it was a different wife! She said the 1960 episode with *Look* went this way. They arranged for three pieces; printed one, then no more. Ed believes the White House itself pressured against parts 2 and 3. The 1970 trip, she explained, was paid by Italians.

June 13, 1974, Cambridge

Feeling groggy from the stomach upset last night, but less overheated this morning when the phone rings and a voice says it's a special agent from the State Department. At first, I thought he was after me ("Have you had illicit relations with an enemy of the American people?"), but it turned out he was enquiring after one of my students, Mary Ahern, whom I got a job at the SD. "Do you have any reason to question her loyalty to the United States?" the voice asks.

Well it all seems a bit ironic, since I have no such loyalty myself (not to speak of the fact that I do not understand the meaning of the term loyalty to one's country). But I told the voice that her family was a pillar of Lake Forest which seemed to assure him a great deal (LF is a very rich and Republican bedroom suburb of Chicago).

Late in the afternoon, I went over to Ken Galbraith's champagne party, one of the nicest events of the year. Everyone is there. I chat with Henry Kissinger's first wife, Ann, and realize as I watch her and her new husband together, how totally unable to rise with Henry she would have been. I give Tom Winship, editor of the *Globe*, the tidbit that Nixon is planning a trip to Peking in September, and he jumps like a man bitten.

Derek Bok[72] is more relaxed than usual; tells me Vogt must be a good man since he takes students with him each year on his research trips to Mexico. Krister Stendhal[73] tells me about his recent trip to Australia. Looking either firmly at the ground or high into the sky, he said he gave a series on "Jesus as Ever" to mixed crowds of Catholics and Protestants.

---

[72] Derek Bok (1930-), President of Harvard University, 1971-1991.
[73] Krister Olofson Stendahl (1921-2008), dean of the Harvard Divinity School and later Lutheran Bishop of Stockholm.

June 16, 1974, Cambridge

I am restored to health after the tummy upset at Betty's party. Feel fresher than before, no doubt because of the break in routine. Wrote three pages this morning; then spent most of the afternoon with Ruxiang. She is going to Hong Kong tomorrow, and wanted a briefing on some US issues, before facing the "comrades" to whom she reports.

June 22, 1974, Cambridge

Went to see a film from Peking last night; called *Fiery Years*, it is about the steel industry in Tientsin in the 1950s. It's about the struggle between two lines. Correct one was self-reliance, following the mass line in work, opposition to bureaucratism. Lee Choumin was there and introduced me to a Korean-Chinese friend of his, who I cruised with my foot and leg during the movie. He pressed against me hotly; but when the lights went up, he turned to his girlfriend on the right, and left with her.

June 22, 1974, Cambridge

Difficulties this morning with the latter portion of my Shanghai chapter. Not quite sure where to go; pondering, but no writing done for two days now.

June 24, 1974, Cambridge

Horrible weather; rain and wind like March at its worst. But my chapter flows again. One more week and the draft will be done—then I may flee to San Juan for a few days.

June 28, 1974, Cambridge

Long and envious faces at the East Asian Research Center this morning. One more of our "group" is going to visit China under separate arrangements, which makes other members of the group sad and grumpy. Senator Henry Jackson[74] is making a trip to Peking; Dwight will be one of the entourage. In cases like this, the National Committee on US-China Relations recommends a scholar to the politician concerned. It seems less and less likely that Peking will invite the EARC group—a little outrageous after making an invitation (then withdrawing it). Ben Schwartz, who has never been to China, sighs with depression. Meanwhile, China's courtship of Jackson is one more sign of their obsession with Russia. Jackson's only mark of distinction is anti-Sovietism.

July 14, 1974, Cambridge

The Alumni College seminar on China kicked off today with a party in the Kirkland House courtyard. John runs it; I come in for a couple of lectures. I find the small-talk with these middle-aged, middle class American tedious. Why live in this country, I sometimes ask myself, when the average middle-class person is so lacking in sparkle and

---

[74] Henry Martin "Scoop" Jackson (1912-1983), U.S. Senator from the State of Washington, 1953-1983.

attractiveness? Imagine a group of 60 or 70 Chinese, or Thai, or Kenyans. How much more stimulating they would be.

July 15, 1974, Cambridge

I rummage at a second-hand book sale in Brattle Street. Titles are going at 90% discount. All very merry, and yet I walk out sadly. First, at the thought that no author gets any royalty at all from this disposal of books; second, at the stark evidence that thousands of worthless or un-demanded books are published year by year.

July 28, 1974, Cambridge

So, the House Judiciary Committee has voted the first article of impeachment. Is it all over: No, it is not all over. There are the following twists in the path toward conviction:

(1) The timing of the cumbersome impeachment process is hazardous in the light of the November elections. No-one can foresee just how the oncoming of the election, the holding of the election, the result of the election, and the influx of new members will affect the impeachment process if it is still going on by the end of the year, and the White House certainly has the capacity to delay things if it sees a possible profit in the resulting complexity of timing.

(2) There is a tendency to assume that Nixon is a fixed quantity, a passive factor—the same next month as last month. Of course, that is an illusion. The president is a live actor in the situation who could make key decisions. He could decide to face things in a quite different way from that which he has chosen in the past. All kinds of differences in attitude on his part from a personal breakdown to a sentimental appeal to the public, to a sudden act of great contrition, a speech that lays himself bare and says he was guilty and let's now bind up the wounds of the country.

(3) A sudden serious international crisis, whether brought on by the White House itself or a bolt out of the blue from abroad, could stay the hand of a crucial number of members of Congress.

(4) Even a national crisis, if of sufficient dimensions—whether natural or social—could take enough of the wind out of the sails of action in the House or Senate to save Mr. Nixon by a narrow margin.

August 4, 1974, Cambridge

Yesterday afternoon I was coming back from the office when I saw Pan carrying a lot of shopping and I rushed up behind to give him a surprise and called out, "Sir! could I help you with your parcels?" I was a bit excited because I was anxious to ask him about last night. He had seen Bobby for the second time. As we came in the gate, he happened to say something which turned out a bomb shell: they had been together to Sporters, a gay club in Boston.

I knew he was going to go to be with Bobby for the second time and I didn't mind that. We have an agreement that occasionally going with someone else is alright. But this going to a gay club caught me. Well, we came inside and I threw myself on the bed.

Later he came and lay down. We had several hours of alternate silence, crying, and intense conversation. There was never any recrimination, but we both faced some issues that maybe we had not faced, certainly which we had not talked about. He said he was sorry and I said as long as his fundamental feeling for me is the same then we could quickly forget about this incident.

However, we plunged a little deeper than that because he said he was worried at the change that had come over him. He's starting to want to make sexual conquests outside our bedroom. This is what I already do. Until his trip to Bangkok in June, he never wanted to do it. Now he does and he said, "I think I'm becoming a whore." No one less like a whore than Pan can I imagine. His loyalty and fidelity to me has taught me the meaning of those terms. But I can see that he has changed.

When we first met, I realized that because he was so inexperienced, his very ready avowal of love had to be taken cautiously both by him and by me. At the same time, yesterday, I could not but furtively ask myself whether his reason for throwing himself into my arms ten months ago had not broken down. On the one hand, he said he was in love with me; on the other hand, he said he was confused. Where did the emphasis lie?

Pan talked a lot about our months together and he said we have shared so much, the room, the decorations, etc., and we have done so many things together. I felt very moved because this weeping afternoon on the bed brought home to me just how close we have become. It also brought home to me, for the first time in my life, how important the non-sex aspects are in a relationship like ours. Pan has taught me a lot about that. And it made me realize that the similarity of our interests as members of Harvard, though we take it utterly for granted, is quite important.

We recovered somewhat and he told me from now on he wanted to apply no rules to me. This meant he withdrew the one remaining rule about not going with another Oriental if I could possibly avoid it. I then told him that whether he saw Bobby again and how often, was up to him, that I didn't mind, that I trusted in our fundamental relationship, and I trusted therefore that he would keep his contact with Bobby in proportion to that. Then we went and had dinner. I never knew Pan to talk so much as at this dinner. He was tremendously excited and, on every topic, he made lively discourse. After dinner we went to see the film 'State of Siege' in the Science Center.

During our session on the bed, Pan said, at one point, "Why am I gay?" It's not a question which I was able to answer. I told him that the same kind of tangled emotions occur with straight situations, which I firmly believe. On the other hand, he is probably going through an experience which I had forgotten that he had not already gone through.

Someone who had had as few sexual experiences as he had when he came to live with me, is hardly into the gay life. The tensions that arise from social milieu have until recently not been part of his experience. And those that are linked to career and social position will not face him for years yet to come.

August 9, 1974, Cambridge

Sometimes a voice within me says, Strip away the growth that comes from the past, and the packaging designed for impressing others, and the props that are a tribute to the power of fear, and the essential things you care about are three:

A healthy and attractive body. You take for granted that your body can meet the demands put on it, but look around and you see that for many people this soon ceases to be so. Even more frighteningly does the body lose its attractiveness when not cared for.

Second, the use of a lucid mind. You must be able to weigh up what can be observed in the world and make judgments about it. To decide what is just and throw one's puny strength on that side. To follow one's curiosity and learn more about man and what he has made for himself on the earth. To pace oneself through life, not too eager and yet on the other hand, not too tardy and complacent.

Thirdly, enough money to live in comfort, to be able to afford the services that you have grown accustomed to, and to feel secure against small or medium misfortunes.

Fourthly (and starting the minor list), I need to live in a big city. I like my independence, I need often to be alone, but do not like to feel in isolation at a remote spot. Not good at planning well ahead, I need everything around me. Prone to the zigzag of subjective mood, I need stimulus at hand without having to decide I need it and make a big step to reach it.

Fifthly, accepting institutional responsibilities is an anxiety for me. I'm not wholly against it; I can generally perform them with credit; yet they cause me a lot of bother and I am much happier without them. It may be by temperament that I like to evade responsibility. It may be the more exalted point that my mind and pen work best in a vacuum of responsibility. From a psychological point of view, this point and the previous one mean that I like a cafeteria pattern of life.

December 14. 1974, Cambridge

Rachel went back to Montreal this morning and as I walk back through the Square, the beauty seems overcast with bleakness. She is impossible, yet also marvelous and she brings into the calculus of academic life a fresh breeze of whim and recklessness.

She remarked how bourgeois the Cambridge and Harvard mentality is, and her point hinges on a distinction between manners and behavior. About manners, these liberal intellectuals are not strict or finicky. About behavior, they are extremely so, and it goes back to the Massachusetts traditions—of the law officers coming in and whipping up the blankets to see what was going on underneath. Even behavioralism in political science may have got its momentum from this moralistic concern about a set of norms for behavior.

In England, of course, it is the opposite. Manners are all; behavior does not matter so much. The parents of Nigel [Nicholson] had the right manners. They were born correctly, and on this basis, they were able to behave in what a lot of people would count to be outrageous ways. We talked on throughout the afternoon and drank a bottle of champagne between us even after the enormous lunch, and then it got dark and there was a great peace.

1975

Terrill went back to China in 1975. He was, he wrote, "moved to see American diplomates in Beijing. One remembers the Korean War. One remembers the Vietnam War. The movies on American TV about the millions of red ants in China.... And here in the big new building of the Liaison office, Americans and Chinese bustle around, cooperating with each other in happy routine."

On his way home via Canada, American officials asked where he had been. When Terrill said China, he was told he had broken the laws of the United States. As a resident alien, he was required to seek permission before visiting "hostile" countries. His green card was confiscated, but he was allowed to continue on to Boston "on parole." He was given one month to leave the U.S. for good. Terrill was allowed an appeal, for which he sought the help of Senator Ted Kennedy. His appeal was granted. "I did not have to resign from the Harvard faculty and return to Australia."

September 10, 1975, Vancouver

A beautiful city in a beautiful setting. It recalls Scandinavia—clean, nature close by, crisp air, polite and undemonstrative people. Coming from the airport, the bus driver farewells us at our hotel with, "God bless you."

September 11, 1975, Vancouver

Last night to the Taurus Bathhouse in Hornby Street and the first guy I meet is a well-built Black hustler from Montreal—he came west because the cops are turning on the heat. I'm enticed, though, by a lithe, smooth, well-hung Italian-Canadian youth. Nice to have a white body in my arms. More rapport at the body level than with an Oriental, even with a Black.

September 19, 1975, Cambridge

A long quiet dinner with Pan's friend Thurlow, an agreeable, well organized pale fellow. Turns out he has never talked to Pan about us. Just back from Dallas, he had a greeting from gorgeous Joseph. In Boston, Joseph and I could hardly keep our hands off each other. Thurlow told Joseph he'd be seeing me in Cambridge; Joseph sent a special hello. This was in front of his wife; Thurlow said she is a very understanding wife.

When I first got back to Cambridge I was thrilled, but that has changed. Cambridge is fine, yes, but my feelings about my link with Harvard, and indeed my feelings about my link with Bob and The Atlantic are apparently not inwardly firm. It is probably freedom from the tie of ambiguous duties for which I hanker.

First time in two years that I have spent time in Cambridge without Pan. I learn that to link up with someone as we have done is to change one's self. So, when you are suddenly without the partner, you realize that, having adjusted to being with him, you are not resourceful without him as you used to be alone.

September 23, 1975, Cambridge

Why do senior professors like to come to Kirkland House, giving up time they treasure for more substantive purposes? They are expressing a loss they feel in being encased in a nuclear family, and the yearning to be with the young and in a broader group that is trusting and anonymous.

It was difficult to explain to Thurlow just what I meant between the gap I feel between the academic establishment I'm involved in and personal visions I have. I caught myself being more wrapped up in the ways of academia than I pretend to be.

My first claim to distinction is use of the English language (thanks Melbourne). My second is interpreting China to an English-speaking public. Alongside these two, the flotsam and jetsam of a university can't amount to much.

September 24, 1975, Cambridge

An obstacle facing straights who toy with the idea of a gay experience is they don't know the techniques. Most of the time, if they knew the possibilities, 95 percent of their hesitations would melt away. They have a vision of being fucked and raped and of losing control of the whole experience. Yet they might love to be sucked.

In Lamont Library, I looked through the last weeks of *Publishers Weekly* and to my delight found a most enthusiastic review of *Flowers on an Iron Tree* in the issue of August 18. I stayed on browsing among a score of magazines.

October 19, 1975, Tokyo

On a drenched Saturday night, my British friend D and I go to a Love Hotel, or "Businessman's Club" as they are called, on the fringes of Shinjuku. Young men are sincere, modest, and gentle; no less lustful for that.

There are bedrooms in the Japanese manner, with a tatami bed covering the floor, sliding doors, and a bathroom. Japanese guys are resting, coupling, or engaged in mass orgies. There is neither conversation nor background music. Everyone is dressed with dignity in a kimono complete with belt. Here are office boys, insurance salesmen, students. One guy smiled, lay down, and pulled me down on top of him. We made love for an hour. Zero rush. No world weariness. Three others came in on the act. Eventually I was sucked off by one of these, while kissing my main partner and having my left nipple almost eaten by a dark shadow from a pile of eiderdowns.

There is a custom of coming up and looking into your face to see whether you are suitable. At first, I found it rude, but I now think getting a relation between faces and eyes is preferable to American bathhouses that focuses on chest and cock. Mineo is a student, slight of figure, with an angelic face. The beauty of our time together was that it was a meeting of two people—despite the language barrier—almost an hour before I touched his cock. In the end, he sucked me off beautifully.

The environment contributed to our lovemaking. An older guy was talking to a young man of twenty called Yasakawa. When he saw Mineo and me together, he mustered a few words of English and said: "You have a nice boy of twenty-one, and here is another nice boy of twenty. Take them both and make love with them together." This I did. Yasakawa was delightful, quite different from Mineo. Mineo was shy, Yasakawa was polished.

The slight guilt I felt toward Mineo was reduced when I looked down and saw a new person had entered the room and was jerking Mineo off with mechanical ferocity. After the storm was over, Mineo and I lay together cuddling and caressing and chuckling for 40 minutes, and strange to say, this was almost the nicest part of a lovely evening. During this time, he said just three words: "I love you."

October 31, 1975. Hong Kong

Reaching Kai Tak, on a delayed JAL flight that made a time-consuming stop in Osaka, I feel a delicious sense of non-responsibility. To come to a hotel where the mail has been sent on, but where there are no appointments. To come to a city where I know many people, but none know I'm here unless I choose to call them. To enter a period of several weeks where the daily pattern is up to myself alone.

I find an electronic misprint of genius in a popular straight bar not far from my Astor Hotel. The "p" is blacked out in the illuminated phrase "Playboy," so that the sign screams out across Tsimshatsui: "San Francisco Lay Boy Bar."

November 9, 1975, Hong Kong

China has no freedom; Hong Kong has no friendship. Where are the hearts of these Cantonese? You are almost driven to the conclusion that the Chinese care more for money than anything else—certainly more than for freedom.

November 10, 1975, Hong Kong

Here is a lower key, a gentler spirit, a life with more curves than life in Japan. Japanese journalist friend Ito says he is amazed the way Chinese can live under oppression and the way they can live under any system—including this colonial British arrangement in Hong Kong. He contrasted them with Japanese. The Japanese would constantly oppose such a colonial set-up. The Chinese way is to live with it and gradually rise up within it and eventually take it over by indirection. Our mutual friend Kojima tells him he was asked to give advice to the Komei Party leaders before their 1971 visit to China. He told them not to take notes during the conversations, nor to carry cameras into the Great Hall.

The Chinese in China, adds this thoughtful Japanese journalist, have lived very satisfactorily, if with hidden hearts, under the dictatorship of Mao, but they could easily arise if circumstances made it possible.

November 12, 1975, Hong Kong

At Shanghai Happy Bathhouse, I am washed by a Cantonese peasant who left a commune 50 miles from Canton a year ago. He is as gay as a New Orleans mardi gras, without being effeminate. Obligingly he took out his cock from his blue cotton underwear so I could play with it with my foot as he did his massage. I soon got the red-hot weapon into my mouth, but he was abruptly called off to eat supper.

A Tokyo guy goes into raptures; a Hong Kong guy methodically gets out his cock and arranges his body in the best position. He does not care for style and appearance; he does not throw himself on you with gasps and sighs. While the Japanese guy glides around in a graceful kimono, the Chinese is casual in a tee shirt and black pants.

Chinese differ from both Japanese and Thai in not being turned on by the hair on a Western body. The guy in Tokyo, and in Bangkok, but not in China or Hong Kong, likes to feel your hair and seems to revel in the contrast with his own smoothness. Or does he just take pleasure in foreign things?

November 15, 1975, Hong Kong

At the Businessmen's Club of the YMCA, I was sitting in the TV room when in came a guy in black suit and flowered shirt, medium height and handsome, fiery eyes and sensual mouth. As soon as I set eyes on him, I wanted him.

We sat opposite each other in the TV room with only hot towels on. When I got a hardon, he watched and started to feel his cock. In the steam room, I tried to talk to him, but he spoke virtually no Mandarin and only one English word "crocodile."

But he put a hand on my forearm and drew me into one a bathroom cubicle. His cock was hard, and his big tough hands were in control. He had it worked out: he squatted at the back of the toilet bowl and had me sit in the normal position. This way my feet alone were visible outside.

He then kissed me. Our mouths bolted together, tongues deep into each other's throats. The guy who had hardly wanted to say a word or glance back was now a tiger who would not let me go. While we kissed, he started to jerk me off with one hand and feel my body up and down with the other. A bit later, the second hand started to play with my ass.

God damn it, someone came into the next cubicle. I decided to leave. Later I would explain to him that I had a safe place to go—the Astor Hotel. It was clear that he was mad with desire. But little did I understand the mind of a gay Chinese. Toilet or nothing.

Oh, the Chinese! When they give, they give all and with heat. When they hold back, there is no colder people on earth.

What would happen if I did cross the threshold and enter the world of the Chinese? My own personality is formed in a Western social mold. Could it ever fit into the social cage of the Chinese way? Would my love for a Chinese man be deep enough to stand the buffeting and heartbreak?

Many of the great loves in Chinese literature are platonic out of failure to make things connect in the real world—as in the marvellous chantefable of the 12th century which Ch'en Li-li has translated. The hero is likely to go to a brothel and satisfy himself with a nameless one furtively, keeping his unfulfilled love like a liqueur set aside for perfect occasions.

Later I wrote Crocodile a note in Chinese saying I had a good place to go that was quiet and secure and comfortable, and could we not go there now? He said: "Mei you yong." This phrase "Unworkable" was one of few Mandarin words he uttered. I planned to catch him as he came out, but he hurried into the Saturday night.

I stood in Nathan Road and cried for ten minutes. It was not a question of lust for someone who did not return the feelings. He had grabbed me and kissed me and caressed me with a master's touch. But then a void of feeling. The strong brown hands, that kiss, those eyes, the practiced, fond way in which he handled my cock. I shall never see him again; I shall always remember him as a symbol of the prisoner which is the Chinese gay. There was not a single thing that was not genuine about the guy.

The experience with Crocodile recalls what Tennessee Williams once said: "People who care the most for me are women. Perhaps that's always been true."

November 17, 1975, Bangkok

Pan was waiting for me at the airport and looks better than I expected—given his strains—and beautiful as always. Ga-ga took us directly to the Narai Hotel, where Pan had reserved a room for me.

He had not received my letters since I left China, or the long letter from Cambridge giving an account of my doings and feelings. Did the U.S. authorities make mischief? Was it the floods here? Did Lisa send the cassette by sea mail instead of by air? Pan thinks the most likely explanation is that they all reached his household, but not him. What a mother!

The illness of his father is sad and a strain on the mother. This makes her moody and, in turn, creates problems for the two sons. She does not like to sleep alone, and the younger brother must share her bedroom. Pan was asked to do this, but at the age of twenty-three declined.

In our hotel bed, Pan utters a phrase which echoes over two years. "Can I slide up Ross's back?" A few minutes later, a question I have never heard before: "Is there anyone else in the world who likes to slide as Pan does?" Why does Pan like to "play doctor" when we go to bed? It was a marvelous bit of Cambridge far from home when he did both in our bed at the Narai Hotel.

We went shopping in Silom Road, where he bought me a pale blue silk tie and handkerchief and I bought a length of Thai silk for my mother and a T-shirt each for Pan and me. We hit upon the tailor from whom I had bought shirts two years ago and ordered a casual suit for me, designed by Pan.

We came back to the hotel and made love. He was hot as fire and came in gushes. He had planned this rendezvous at the Narai ever since we spoke on the phone between Hong Kong and Bangkok on Friday.

We had a French lunch and talked about Pan's graduate study plans. He has taken care, at last, with applications, and he will be coming back to the United States. At the earliest, he will get news in December and come to the U.S. in January. He has three favored places: Harvard, Stanford, and Chicago.

One feature of the superb French buffet was prunes in Armagnac and Pan loved these. While he took a nap—after being weakened by yet another seminal loss and made a bit dizzy by the Armagnac—I went down to the swimming pool to cruise and think for an hour.

I wonder which gap is the greater: race or gay/straight? Last night I was sure the second is the real fence. And yet when you think about the reasons why people have sex or decline to have sex, even when they are attracted to someone, you often reach the door of culture and race.

November 19, 1975, Bangkok

I don't think anything has changed between Pan and me after four months of separation. I think Greg was right in New York: "There is not much doubt about the love from Pan's side." If Pan has any caution, it is as a reaction to a fear that I might want to revert to independence.

November 21, 1975, Bangkok

"I saw you this afternoon," said a smiling middle-aged man at the bar.

"Who was I with?"

"With a girl." I said he must be mistaken because I was with my boyfriend all afternoon.

He smiled and said, "You are gay then." I said of course I am gay. "Don't be irritated," he said. "I am the owner of this bar, and I was only being friendly and giving you a welcome." He had another duty in mind: he thought I might be straight and had wandered into the wrong bar by mistake. I admired his indirect method and charm.

Whereas Hong Kong has got brash and commercial, Bangkok is softer, more deeply Asian, pleasantly unaware of any need to join the modern world in spirit. During dinner I took a liking to the boy who filled our glasses with water. As I gazed at him Pan said, "Don't trade a jewel for a petal."

In Thailand, I kept to Pan's "wish"—as he put it—except for the quick visit to Somsat and the first night with Somchai, which was before Pan announced his wishes. "I don't see the need for you to have Thai boys," he said, "while I am seeing you."

At the airport I told him no matter how big the distance that separates us, no matter even if there should be big difficulties, I would always treasure him. "I have only you, Pan," I said to him in remembrance of how last year in Cambridge, he said to me, "I have only you, Ross."

November 23, 1975, Hong Kong

The massage guy at the sauna in the YMCA seemed pleasant. I was just about to hand over the massage ticket when I noticed he was reading an enormous Morocco-bound copy of the Bible; the bookmark was a colored photo of grinning Billy Graham. My hopes were dashed. But I remembered something from a talk in Japan: ideology can roll on and off the Chinese. This includes religion as well as the thought of Mao, so I went ahead with the massage and was not disappointed.

November 25, 1975, Hong Kong

The last session with Somsat. left me with a pure feeling. But I think I was right not to press sex on him more than I did. He will ripen and after another six months, I'll check again.

As a half apology when we parted, he said he is conservative on social matters. He said it is the influence of having spent his whole life in the PRC. I said there are good points about that too. He gets his sense of responsibility from that upbringing.

Sitting in my Universities Service Center office on the last morning, I ponder one more approach, this time directly physical. Drop down on my knees in front of him and put my face to his cock? Something stops me; all things are not, after all, possible. Gore Vidal says you should always push to the limits and beyond the limits, but he must mean you do this as a writer. You cannot do it in life.

Innocent young boys can resemble mature lovers. The way they hold arms and hands is just the same as gay lovers do. It is as if nature makes a universal proposal, which, among adults, only gays take up.

Since I left Bangkok, I have tired of bathhouses in Hong Kong. Is it because of the magic days with Pan? Or is there something false about my whole relationship to people at these places. I wonder if Stephen and the others miss me any more than I miss them.

December 9, 1975, Taipei

A straight guy in my hotel sauna makes jokes with his friends about gays who sidle close to him in the hot box. Yet he displays himself to me, wants me to think his body is fine. He can't have it both ways. Knock us, or join us, but not both.

December 13, 1975, Honolulu

Surf Baths was full of a nice crowd, white Americans the most numerous, followed by Japanese, Black Americans, and Hawaiians. Satisfying to get one's arms around a Caucasian after months in Asia. Bodies understand each other unerringly; you meet yourself. Second was a handsome, slim Black army man. Wish I had been less tired and could have done justice to him. Third was a Japanese from Kyoto, who works as a "cook man" in a tea shop and is on a group tour to Hawaii. He fucked me with grace and rhythm and then jerked me off with my cock pointing at his smooth golden neck.

December 15, 1975, Honolulu

Any nationality that gets affluent and does widespread international travel produces its own parallel to the Ugly American. It's a functional issue. This Ala Moana Hotel is half full of Japanese. They are subject to the fallibilities of all mortals who travel long distances; they get tired and grumpy and doze off to unedifying sleep in public places. And, like any people of high visibility, they are scrutinized to the point where their flaws are not secret. Away from home, the Japanese lose a bit of balance—so do the citizens of Germany and all other Tourist Powers. One day it will happen to the Chinese.

Future of Honolulu? It will come under increasing Japanese, and later Chinese influence. The USA may well hold onto it politically. But in way of life, culture, and spirit, it will ebb toward the East.

December 17, 1975, Cambridge

One day back and the strangeness seeps away. Jim helped. My first friend—Pan apart—on the new big bed at 395 [Broadway]. Good to get my arms around those muscles again. He asked to fuck me, and did it with such delicacy and consideration that it hurt little. Then I came on his chest like the Fountain of Peace in Geneva.

What a contrast to Pan. A peasant where Pan is a patrician. Not handsome but sexy, while Pan is beautiful but not sexy. Both are well-built, but whereas Pan's complexion is peachy, and his movements are graceful, Jim is darker, rougher.

Unhappiness is far more real than happiness. But the latter does exist. I think it has about 10% the vividness that unhappiness has. So, avoiding unhappiness is basically the aim of life.

The pressure has rolled off from committees and letters and telephone. I can hold in mind the memory of summer's existence; I know spring will come once more; I think of potential joys all around me, of friends over neighbouring hills. I savour how even tonight will bring refreshing sleep.

December 20, 1975, Cambridge

We enter an apolitical era, a sharp break from the Political Age of the 20th Century up till Vietnam. In the coming era many of us ex-politicals will retreat to an inner world. Supreme will be economics and psychology. I will probably write a novel.

December 21, 1975, Cambridge

"I Need Your Love," says a song on the radio. Nice to stop and listen; it is a favorite of Pan's and reminds me of him. But how wrong is its message: anyone who needs the love of another is not really worth loving.

Boston suits a person who is a sensual internationalist yet also a Puritan who works hard. The Americans are open; they go for the short term; they can be persuaded of things. I must write about my adopted land before I get so used to the comfort of her lap that I forget I came from somewhere else. Other countries may be best for serving causes, for holidays, for retirement, or for purity. But for living, America is the greatest country on earth.

December 22, 1975, Cambridge

Who should phone tonight but Don Butterfield[75] of the Kirkland House Senior Common Room? He has, it seems, found out from Howard Spendelow[76] that I am one of the redeemed. Will I not come dine with him one night at the new Japanese restaurant (his friend Kazu works there)? Won't I come for Christmas Dinner? I have just read *The Best Little Boy in the World,* and Don doubts the book is based scrupulously on fact. He recommends highly *The Homosexual Matrix.*[77] "It knocks over the Freudian stuff in style."

Li-li came over to Broadway with a handsome silver Christmas tree and a bottle of *bai gan jiu,* a fiery drink! We dined at Colleen's, where I told her about the cloud that has come over the tie between D and me. She said I ought not be surprised; I am too trusting; she had warned me to be wary of D. But she does not know him well. Better I talk to Hsiao who does. I think it is wrong to examine a cloud separately from the sun it rests nearby.

December 25, 1975, Cambridge

I can't escape a twinge of loneliness when alone on this particular day of the year, fighting off syrupy Christmas music from the radio.

Picked up a copy of *The Advocate* and *QQ* in the Square. A gay magazine fills a gap in the circle of consciousness, helps one to be clearer as to who one is, makes the world seem warmer. *The Advocate* has an interview with Christopher Isherwood: "I don't think a long-term relationship exists, it hasn't been tested, until exposed to—what's a polite word?—screwing around." On his existence as a gay and a writer Isherwood says: "Being gay has given me an oblique angle of vision on the world. Without it I might never have been a writer."

December 27, 1975, Cambridge

On the stroke of midnight, I finished Tennessee Williams' *Memoirs.* For all its faults, it is moving—and little is more valuable in a memoir. I cried when poor Frankie died and Tennessee felt he could not go on down life's crazy, cruel path. My mother's love for me has been as mixed as Tennessee thinks his mother's love for him had been.

---

[75] Donald Butterfield (1932-2022), Boston physician, researcher, and amateur astronomer.

[76] Howard Randall Spendelow III, at the time a PhD candidate in History and East Asian Languages and Literature at Harvard.

[77] *The Best Little Boy in the World* (1973) by Andrew Tobias, a memoir about growing up closeted and gay; *The Homosexual Matrix* (1975) by C. Arthur Tripp, a critique of the standard, Freudian explanations for homosexuality.

But many things are different. Behind the dissipation there is in Williams a Southern sense of style, a *noblesse oblige*. As a boy sprung from the Australian soil, I lack that, though we Australians share the earthiness present in Southerners.

The gay part is not the whole of me, because sexuality is not the whole. Tennessee Williams is right in *Memoirs* to say that "putting work first" is terribly important. He waded out into the deep. I salute his courage in kicking off restraints. I need a way of life where juices flow richly, if not out of control like Tennessee's juices. If only Pan and I could do what Tennessee and Frankie did when they lunched with Hollywood's Warner, and Warner turned to Frankie and said: "What do you do, young man?" and Frankie replied: "I sleep with Mr Williams."

1976

January 3, 1976, Cambridge

Mishima's *Sun and Steel* still eludes me. Self-consciousness is overcome and he feels one with the blue sky and infinite things, the world of physical beauty and strength. But he does not make a convincing link between beauty of the body and death. His is a personal drama, not a universal one. Mishima cannot become one with beautiful men by writing *Sun and Steel*. Athletes are mute, giving us only their present physical moments, no writings. By writing this book Mishima shows us, among other things, that he remains an imprisoned intellectual.

January 10, 1976, Boston

Channel 7 for a TV program on U.S. relations with China. The interviewer, a Hawaiian, knows nothing of the subject. She begins with an absurd slip of the tongue: "This morning Dr. Ross Terrill is with us to discuss relations between China and Peking."

She had not read my article on Zhou Enlai in yesterday's *Boston Globe* (though she is producing a Boston TV program on the subject of this front-page piece!). On air, she began with an elaborate compliment to this *Globe* article, "extraordinarily good!" Much TV news and culture are useless.

January 11, 1976, Cambridge

Mark leaves a trail of debris and a good feeling in my gut. He's complex and I warmed to his very contradictions. Devout Catholic upbringing, but a born sensualist. A case of homophobia, but part-gay himself. Middle-class in *mœurs* but since the split between his parents, destitute economically.

Everything had to be discussed in advance. "Ross, excuse me asking, you're not a homo, are you?" I could only murmur "Partly." To which he rejoined buoyantly: "Partway, I can cope with that."

Nervous, he masked his desire in a poor man's anthropology: "We are just two people, right? I like you as a guy, you really zip and dazzle me. I think two people can get together and just be natural, don't you?" He drank a great deal of Scotch—with

Coke added. When he finally plucked up the courage to join me in bed, he was hot and, in the end, almost insatiable. The hang-ups continued to pour out of him like clichés from a Harvard professor: "I wish my cock was big like yours."

"Ross, if I take off my trousers, you won't stick you cock up me, will you?" But these hang-ups were a bagatelle alongside his passion.

January 24, 1976, Cambridge

People ask do I prefer to return to Australia or to go on living in the USA. It is like asking which is more delicious, a pear or a banana. America has taken away my beliefs. It has done this to generations of immigrants, and I should not have expected to be an exception. My religion and my socialism have both been weakened by living in a society whose only "ism" is Americanism. Words come to mind from Hu Shih, the Chinese philosopher who came as a student to the USA after World War One: "America will not have a social revolution because America is in the middle of a social revolution every day."

January 22, 1976, Cambridge

Snowstorm last night and coming to work along Cambridge Street this morning, I see two people slip and fall. The first is a Japanese—he chuckles as he picks himself up. The second is a burly white American—he curses.

A letter from Henry Kissinger[78] today, thanking me for sending him a copy of *Flowers*, which he has "heard is excellent," and ending, "With warm regards."

January 23, 1976, Boston

Good sex is a matter of habit. You forget how glorious it can be. You hardly credit that making love can shake the heavens and rock the earth. I was out of the habit tonight, at La Grange bathhouse; did not expect enough so did not give enough. Vision shrinks with even a short spell of absence.

March 9, 1976, Washington

Chat with Mark F at his basement apartment in Georgetown. That he referred to his Vietnamese lover as his "chum" slightly put me off. But the Vietnamese himself, an artist, is appealing; features fine and smile winning.

Mark is thinking of leaving the newspaper, in the vague way I am thinking of leaving academia. Is there something in the gay temperament that can't stand the harness of an institution? We pine for the moon at the very moment we doubt we want to reach the moon!

---

[78] Henry Kissinger (1923-) was, at the time, Secretary of State under President Gerald Ford.

March 14, 1976, Cambridge

I may need something to restrain me—an allegiance, pressure to keep to a line—or else I might wobble all over the shop. This is a subtler version of the "need for structure" that comes up when you leave an institutional haven. Mental categories, as much as organizational ones, give us our bearings. There may not (yet) be enough inner poise to enable me to navigate the world of ideas and values with success.

March 16, 1976, Cambridge

A large segment of the East Asia visiting committee turns up at my Government 177 lecture this morning. Intimidated, I stumble over words in my nervousness. But the session, on the Russia-China split, seems to go well. I draw Phil Talbot and others into the question period.

Later, Howard Spendelow tells me Mrs. Robert McNamara said to him at the students' lunch: "I went to an excellent lecture this morning, by Mr. Terrill; he speaks in complete sentences." On reflection, one or two of my colleagues do not always do that.

March 25, 1976, Cambridge

A curious incident at Yenching restaurant with Li. The scientist Paul Doty and a young woman are there, at a table not far from ours. Generally, their conversation cannot be heard, but at one point, Paul's voice rises markedly and he says "Oh, Tom Lehrer, you know, he's become a homosexual, has turned from liking women to liking men. Pity—he's a bright guy." Then Paul's voice resumes its lower pitch. Li-li was as struck as I was by this sudden attempt to say something we could not fail to overhear.

March 26, 1976, Cambridge

It is like a lovely dream to have Pan back. Saturday, I had just come from buying a ticket to San Juan at Crimson Travel when Western Union called with a cable from Pan that said he was on the way to Cambridge.

I went out to the airport just one and a half hours away from the first of three lectures for the day, and there he was, done up in white linen in splendid disregard of the Boston winter, just as if he'd stepped off a yacht at Monte Carlo, despite having flown without overnight stop from Tokyo. He was like an image cut clean in quartz.

I found Pan hasn't changed a bit. Still an oasis of peace, trusting, straightforward, an ornament for our sordid times. Nor has his extravagance ebbed.

March 31, 1976, San Juan

I left Pan installed at Chicago, and now Puerto Rico thaws me marvelously. Am staying for the first time at the YMCA. Fine location in Old San Juan with the lovely public library next door; a sauna and exercise room, not otherwise available in San Juan. Weather has been good and Puerto Rican youth superb.

Watched young guys flirt longingly with schoolgirls. I see Catholicism still has immense power. It is the only effective dike against the torrent of sensuality. Cocks versus the Pope. But for Catholicism, San Juan would make Sodom and Gomorrah seem tame. Yet it may be the taunting half-resistance of the women that makes the men as sexually obsessed as they are.

April 2, 1976, San Juan

Breakfast of Spanish omelet and *New York Times* at my favorite café near the bottom of Calle de San Justo. Then two hours in Biblioteca Carnegie writing a letter to Pan in Chicago and reading the March issue of *Red Flag*. This Chinese-language magazine has a disgusting article by Jiang Qing's literary fig leaf, which lambasts excellent policies of Teng Hsiao-ping [Deng Xiaoping].[79]

Flirtation with a straight guy on the beach. A good sign was his request to anoint his back with suntan oil. We moved to the parapet beyond the Hyatt. He was pretty warmed up now, so I dropped to my knees and ferreted out his cock with my tongue. Damn it if at that moment a construction worker nearby didn't drop a hammer—probably we were visible from the shorefront buildings. This guy reckless in big things—three marriages, knife wounds and bullet marks from fights—decides it's "too risky" to make it right there. We part with the muted cheerfulness of those who have just buttoned up.

April 3, 1976, San Juan

After five days, I pass the natural limit for plunge-in debauchery. Two other things start to interest me: simple rest; and the pursuit of friendships with Puerto Ricans. Today I spent the afternoon with two straight youths—for the charm of their company, and the challenge of trying to get them both to bed with me. That I failed in the latter was partly due to having lost my edge after the mad first four days. But unconsummated hours can be sweet.

April 16, 1976, Chicago

A butterfly of a plane brings me from Bloomington, Indiana to O'Hare Airport, where we flutter down to the tarmac in between whizzing jets. I came to spend the weekend with Pan, and have a talk with Professor Tang Tsou, his teacher.

Bloomington and my lecture fade into the background: being a pundit, thinking of three things at once, looking in the mirror to adjust my tie—all past. The happy drift of spending time with Pan takes over.

Chicago is wind, space, prosperity, appealing unsophistication. The immense pleasures of Chicago are a skeleton in the cupboard of an eastern establishment man. A lamp shop is called "De-lights." We go to a combination nightclub-and-fun parlor

---

[79] Deng Xiaoping (1904-1997), leader of the People's Republic of China, 1978-1989. At the time Terrill was writing, Deng, a reformer, was under severe criticism by Madame Mao and the Gang of Four.

called "Crystal Pistol." At a good European Restaurant called "The Bakery," a motto at the top of the menu reads: "Make love at home, eat here."

April 18, 1976, Chicago

In snack bars and restaurants, the look on faces and the way people tackle food inclines me to think that hunger is an expression of discontent. To want food is to be unsatisfied in a vague but powerful way. The desire for food is less on the part of a person who, at any given moment, is contented.

April 19, 1976, Cambridge

There were so many happy moments during the weekend with Pan that it comes as a shock that there also were knots of anxiety. I am apparently a butterfly. Pan seems to compare himself to every guy I happen to look at. Pan eventually said gently: "I will forgive you if you will forgive me."

The calm happiness of Sunday morning and lunch at the French Quarter was lovely. We had slept well and woke like birds aware of the spring. We played on the bed; we pottered in Lincoln Park; coffee at a neighborhood food shop. At lunch I was so relaxed that I ate dessert for the first time in months.

April 22, 1976, Cambridge

All agree the *Times* is a unique paper. Yet Abe Rosenthal's[80] manner as we talk at Harvard is almost intolerable; he speaks like Moses on the hill with the tablets of stone—as I whispered to Bob Manning, editor of *The Atlantic*. Agreeing with my impression, Bob said the reason is that Abe adores the *Times*, thinks it is the last word in greatness. There is certainly more enthusiasm and sense of authority in Abe Rosenthal than among Harvard professors.

April 26, 1976, Cambridge

The gay watches a scene at a gym, feels a swelling in his cock, and ends up jerking off as he watches sweating bodies. The straight steals into the girls' dormitory at Radcliffe and feels the same excitement and jerks off amidst the giggles and pale soft flesh.

Anatomically, the same thing has occurred. The bond of cock and balls ties the gay and the straight together. For the gay, it's his secret reminder that underlying gay and straight is nature's own foundation of sensuality. For the straight, the shadow of the curse of gay existence that can fall upon him.

April 27, 1976, Boston

Dollar Night at Regency Baths and a young Black guy, either shy or inexperienced, enveloped me for an hour. When I emerged into Otis Street, I felt so peaceful that even

---

[80] A. M. Rosenthal (1922-2006), managing editor of *The New York Times* and to become its executive editor.

when the taxi got lost and drove me around Boston for fifty minutes, I sat back in silence and watched the view.

April 29, 1976

A tender evening with Ray in his (once more) fresh apartment. He grills steak and cooks vegetables wrapped in silver foil with immense care and about 11:00 PM we finally sit down to eat it. He is troubled about his relation with John. In part, it is because he is troubled with his own identity as gay. I can understand it if John feels that Ray may not be giving all of himself; Ray is not comfortable with all of himself. When we talked about Pan, Ray unexpectedly remarked: "You and Pan have humor, but in our relationship, there seems to be no humor."

Coming home, the taxi driver has a notice on his windshield: "Of all my relations, I like the sexual ones the best."

April 30, 1976, Cambridge

For a Japan Forum on the Lockheed bribe scandal, I arrive late and, in the crowd, have to stand by the door in a stifling spring-rain atmosphere. Soon I become aware of a handsome guy behind me—Japanese or Korean—who brushes me from time to time. I reciprocate and soon my hands, clasped behind my back, are caressing his fiery cock.

May 6, 1976, Cambridge

The most exciting and stretching moments of one's life come when from outside of oneself: there is an intimation that on a particular issue one's feelings or conduct were wrong.

May 7, 1976, Cambridge

The pain of separation. Yet there may be a love that goes beyond the bond of coupling, a kind of love that can even outlast separation, where love of mankind and a sense of oneness with the universe overcome love as an ego trip or a family's self-protection. I feel I will never cease to love Pan for his quality, even if we should have to part or choose to part.

May 18, 1976, Washington

I hate to leave and go back to Cambridge. The weekend plunged me into a happier world. Pan came from Chicago and we stayed in a big warm bed at Van Lung's house.[81] Bobby—who has been 13 years with Van—was there with his boyish charm.

Van met us at National Airport, and we dined in his Alexandria restaurant; such a generous man. Fascinating to watch Van and Pan size each other up. Adam and Gordon

---

[81] S. Van Long (1926-1991) founder of Yenching Palace, a popular D.C. restaurant that advertised it "entertained more diplomats daily than the White House." Van was the son of a leading general who switched sides from Nationalist to Communist.

arrived. "I like your tie," said Gordon as he looked at my mauve and blue silk tie. "I like my Thai too," I replied, laughing and pointing to Pan. This broke the ice and the evening took off. Hours later it ended in a dim neighborhood bar on Connecticut Avenue.

May 30, 1976, San Juan

Why is P.R. such a gay paradise? So many guys are handsome; beauty after all cuts its own cabbages. Climate releases the body. Economic backwardness takes away busy-ness, ambition, and self-importance, which obstruct sensuality.

June 1, 1976, San Juan

Emilio, a slim attractive guy, chatted as we rode the waves. "Would you like to fuck me?" I asked him when I established that no girlfriend was panting for him on the beach. "I'd love to fuck you," he shot back immediately with a broad grin. "But I don't know if I can stay hard under the water like this." He could; he did. After a while in the water, I said let's go to the beach and lay a blanket on top so you can give me the last couple of inches of that marvelous dick.

June 3, 1976, San Juan

Some people wouldn't know me down here. Drinking beer, eating pizza, going to Howard Johnson's for a sundae, talking to people all morning—will I carry these habits back to Boston?

Every country seems, from the outside, a bundle of contradictions. A Puerto Rican will show the marks of a strict Catholic upbringing, then pull out his cock, as if the pent-up repression suddenly gives way. I can imagine a Hispanic saying of Australians: one minute they seem egalitarian frontiersmen, the next like stuffy British.

June 4, 1976, Cambridge

Funny to walk on brick pavements again instead of San Juan's ivory sand. To pass little wooden cottages instead of Hispanic arches and cornices. You feel something in the air inducing you toward work that lacks in the sensuous air of Puerto Rico. Maybe it's just that the phone may ring—a sound I haven't heard for days. At my desk, Lucian Pye's biography of Mao,[82] which I am reviewing for *The New Republic*.

June 7, 1976, Cambridge

Pan on the phone tells me about a Jamaican he made love with in Chicago who had a cock that was "one inch when soft and ten inches when hard." He sighs with fatigue at the ordeal of the exams he has completed, then announces that tonight, five days before his return to our nest at Boston, he has begun packing.

---

[82] Mao Tse-Tung: The Man in The Leader. New York (Basic Books, 1976).

June 27, 1976, Cambridge

It seems an aeon since Pan arrived from Chicago. We have settled into a domestic routine, after the Spring Term ended, with its commencement fatuities. Some friends are coming in for cocktails and they will be received by a triangle of Pan, Li-li and myself. That will confuse the gossip-mongers.

June 28, 1976, Cambridge

"Why are you studying Chinese, Pan?"

"I am going to master many little-known Chinese documents on the Zhuang people [cousins of the Thai], and translate them into Thai. If in the future, China attacks Thailand, I will go to our government and turn over secret materials to arouse the Thai people to defend our country. These documents show what awful things the Chinese did to the peaceful Zhuang."

June 28, 1976, Cambridge

More than sixty people swarmed into my modest Broadway apartment for a party to celebrate the coming of summer. John Fairbank drank orange juice while Wilma put down five gin and tonics and each of them devoured half of one of Li-li's succulent ducks.

July 4, 1976, Boston

Pan and I joined 400,000 people at the Esplanade to salute America's 200th birthday. Arthur Fiedler conducted an orchestra in middle-brow bits and pieces that New England loves. 1200 fireworks shot high over the Charles River and people applauded them as if they were living creatures. I was moved when the throng began spontaneously to sing "Happy Birthday, Dear America." There is something gentle and infinitely resilient about the United States.

I remember ten years ago when I was still feeling my way into this friendly but puzzling society. That memory evokes Vietnam; I had been to Saigon a few months before. I still believe the Vietnam War was as American (in its moment) as apple pie but a perilous mistake. What cannot be overlooked tonight is how quickly Vietnam has vanished from the national mind. Here is the resiliency. Here also the lack of historical sense, the existential here-we-go spirit of America that scares me a bit.

President Ford makes a wooden speech in Philadelphia. Sailors jerk off high on the masts of their ships upon the Hudson River. In Florida, the oldest citizen in the land celebrates his 134th birthday by recalling that he came to the USA on a slave ship from Liberia and was sold from an auction block in New Orleans at age 12.

It would have been a contradiction in terms for the USA to stage a smooth and consistent Bicentennial party. She is the sum of her sparring, litigious parts.

In America you jump on board and find you have signed on for the duration. With a crew whose great virtue is its lack of complacency. America always thinks it possible that a better idea might come up. It tries to give any new thing a space to be born.

Cambridge, Signet Society Dinner[88]

Everyone was there. Ed Weeks[84] enthused about Ronald Steel's biography of Lippman[85] he is editing, and about Peter Ustinov's memoir which is next. Deane Lord[86] looked at me with those five-sided eyes and asked me how old I am. After making her guess—she put me 6 years younger than I am—she said she is doing a book with a photographer friend on people in their thirties—their feelings on getting older. Would I "sit" for them?

Speeches mixed. John Updike was superb with poems about his recent life as an ex-spouse living in rooms in central Boston. John Findley was rasping and garrulous—like a Rossini overture that went on too long. He is the victim of didacticism brought on by 60 years of lecturing to captive undergraduates.

Barney Frank[87] told of a conservative legislator who rose to interrupt a Barney speech about liberties: "He's for homosexuality, prostitution, pornography, marijuana—when will the man stop?" Barney replied: "When I've found something the honourable gentleman likes to do."

Next to me at dinner was chairman of the Republican Party in the State, John Sears. His lack of rabidness was expressed in the remark that Republicans are for character, Democrats for compassion—and 90% of the issues of public policy require a blend of the two.

July 28, 1976, Cambridge

At Massachusetts Hall, Prime Minister Fraser[88] arrived and no one was ready. I saw the cars pull up outside and Fraser stride toward the front door. But Henry Rosovsky[89] was not by the door, or even in the corridor. I flew to Bok's office and called out loudly, "They're here" to Henry and Bok, who were closeted together. Henry emerged just in time to be in the corridor after I had saved a minute by greeting the Australian leader myself—I'd never met him before.

August 1, 1976, Cambridge

Take a stud or a hustler to a good restaurant and he melts like butter in the sun. The tough pro of the streets becomes a timid babe before a strutting *maitre d'hôtel*.

---

[83] Signet Society, primarily an undergraduate club at Harvard, whose members are involved in arts and letters.

[84] Edward A Weeks (1898-1989), former editor of *The Atlantic Monthly* from 1938 to 1966.

[85] Ronald Steel, *Walter Lippmann and the American Century* (1980).

[86] Deane Lord, director of the Harvard News Office, known as the "godmother of Cambridge."

[87] Barney Frank, member of the U.S. House of Representatives (Massachusetts) from 1981 to 2013.

[88] John Malcolm Fraser (1930-2015), twenty-second prime minister of Australia, 1975-1983.

[89] Henry Rosovsky (1927-2022), at the time, Dean of the Faculty of Arts and Science at Harvard.

August 2, 1976, Cambridge

A handsome Black guy is promoting a religious sect at Harvard Square. He proffers a leaflet, but I turn away. "Young man," he says with a slight smile beneath his big white eyes, "won't you say a word to a brother." Indeed, one should say a word to a brother. But if we spoke and he proselytized me, I might return the compliment and constrain him to some gay fun. Would he still be in favour of engaging with a brother?

August 4, 1976, Cambridge

Why does youth exert immutable appeal? Because with youth, there is always hope; and the possibility of beauty.

August 5, 1976, Cambridge

In his essay "Childlike Mind," the Ming dynasty philosopher Li Chih criticizes teachers and argues that morality cannot be taught. "The teachers of today: one day absent the office and their disciples abandon them; one day without funds and their followers scatter." How contemporary!

August 9, 1976, Cambridge

In the movie *Swept Away*, a voice rings out: "Everyone has to die once, in order to understand. Better that it happens young, since it is easier to recover from the blow then."

August 23, 1976, Cambridge

I come across a passage in Wang Ken, philosopher of the Ming dynasty, with a truth about love and respect for the self. "If others do not love me, I should realise that it is not because of others' inhumanity but because of my own, and if others do not respect me, it is not that others are disrespectful, but that I am."

September 1976, Paris

French have good relations with the Chinese. They have in common a sense of two countries with great civilizations, an insistence on independence, and a Mandarin tradition. At the same time, France knows the Soviet Union has more muscle than China; and since France also likes to think it has a special relation with the Soviet Union, there is a limit to how rich the France-China relationship can be.

At a bathhouse, a middle-aged guy thinks a foot put on my thigh is enough to catch me, but it is not. I expect a little romanticism from the French.

On September 9, 1976, Mao Zedong died. Terrill was in Morocco at the time. He then flew on to London.

September 10, 1976, Moroooo

Was Mao a great man of China alone, or can parts of Mao transfer elsewhere? Some aspects, I think. His early idea of rooting thought in observed reality. Of a leader keeping his compass on ordinary people's needs. Of taking the long view. Of holding a poet's whimsy amidst grinding struggle."

London

Heathrow Airport is thick with South Asians. I spot the new phenomenon of "EEC" passports; what will happen to Little England? After Morocco and France, talking English seems strange; like getting out of pointy shoes and into carpet slippers.

I see automobiles as a threat to cities comparable to that posed by weapons of war to nations.

On the news, much about Africa. The British seem delighted that one of "their" topics, Africa, is the focus of American and indeed world attention.

September 23, 1976, London

A London comedy, *Bed Before Yesterday*, about class, money, and sex-as-naughtiness. The audience for this entertaining play is the homely, dusty part of the middle class, plus noisy American tourists. At intermission, flustered females sell drinks at the speed of sound. Imbibing them are tweedy gents and women in black dresses and pearl necklaces.

I visit Piers Burnett at André Deutsch.[90] Arriving, I seek a proper mental orientation; to Piers I am an author of a book on Tawney and English socialism, not a China Hand. Piers looked thin and stooped as if sheltering his cigarette. He said the firm's links in Australia have improved, and they also have good Hong Kong links which can make it worthwhile to publish for the Hong Kong market alone. Dick Hughes's *Borrowed Time, Borrowed Place* is a recent case.

September 28, 1976, Cambridge

Details filter my way about the media's efforts to reach me in Morocco when Mao died. The *LA Times*, Dan Yergin[91] says, tracked down my travel agent in case he knew what hotel I was at in El Jadida. CBS were prepared to fly me back to New York—if they could locate me anywhere in the world. Of course, it's a one-day wonder; there can be no sustained interest in China on the part of TV.

October 2, 1976, Cambridge

An excellent idea for Harvard to hold a Reception for Minority Students; I go between office hours and squash at the YMCA. Nice to see an equal blend of Blacks and

---

[90] British publishing house.
[91] Daniel Howard Yergin (1947-). American author best known for *The Prize: The Epic Quest for Oil, Money, and Power*.

Orientals at the party; the two groups even cooperated closely, I was told, in planning it.

First person I run into at the bar is Dean Henry Rosovsky, who is Jewish. I am about to make a joke to him (is he the Number One Minority Person Taking the Establishment Road?) when Harvard's boss, Derek Bok, greets me. He is also cordial; just back from a trip to the Greek islands. "I thought you didn't like travel," I said. "Going to the Far East for the University," he replied, "staggering tired off a flight of 15 hours, speaking through interpreters—all that's one thing. A holiday in Greece is quite another." The friendliness of dean and president seemed to prove the old adage: publicity as a powerful weapon nearly always outweighs publicity as an embarrassment.

October 4, 1976, Cambridge

The very bright people are nearly always philosophical materialists. The truly great people are nearly always philosophical idealists.

October 6, 1976, Cambridge

Many letters from strangers over the tenure reverse. A touching moment this morning as I arrived at my office. The big, genial janitor approached me a bit diffidently: "They've been knocking you about, eh?"

"Well, yes," I said.

"Is it, maybe, that you don't wear a necktie to work?" I love him.

October 14, 1976, Cambridge

Back from Washington, and news of the downfall of Mrs. Mao and her extremist friends. Ron Gollobin comes from Channel 5 for an interview on my front lawn by Broadway, with neighbours gawking. Next night a similar thing at Channel 4 studio, where I distinguished myself by walking in front of a live camera after ending my appearance. A good session for National Public Radio with bright and charming Susan Stamburg.

October 21, 1976, Boston

Bob Manning pops a question as we stroll to the Tavern Club for lunch. Would I do a biography of Mao? I just might. Are there no other books, other authors? But Mao is a great subject; why leave him to Han Suyin (popular bootlicker) and Stuart Schram (dry academic)? Sometimes I need a publishing friend to put a subject on my plate. This may be one of those moments.

October 24, 1976, Washington

A long weekend with Pan at Van's and Bobby's in Washington. Many delights but three days is enough. Cars, food, drink, confusion about arrangements; it is a whirlwind. I need time to read and space to be quiet. I cannot be content without daily exercise and tossing ideas around with informed people. I would rather stroll a block to eat pizza than drive 20 miles for Peking duck. But Van and I always have much on China to chat about.

November 3, 1976, Cambridge

I was glad, on balance, that Carter won. One could not hope for the victory of a man as mediocre as Ford. Especially, one prefers the entourage that Democrats bring into those that Republicans typically bring in.

Many at Harvard do not care passionately about this election. Rachel and I went to three election night "watching parties" and they were all parties first, watching—well, now & then. Rachel made the slip of assuming Jonathan Moore was, like nearly everyone else at Harvard, a Democrat, which led Jonathan to say tactfully that he was an "unusual Republican."

At Quincy House Common Room, the main students' watching post, couples lolled on the floor looking into each other's eyes more than at the mammoth TV screen. Rachel and I finished the evening at DH's, where the same situation obtained, except that most couples were gay.

The election stirred Pan a great deal. He stayed up till 4 AM, which was more than I did (true I had to spend the next day lecturing at Amherst). The Carters he finds stylistically "grotesque." Mrs. C "cares nothing for clothes." Jimmy "smiles mechanically." The sons are "ugly to an unreasonable degree."

A wrench will come as Pan soon goes back to Bangkok to be a diplomat for at least 2 ½ years (a bonded period equal to half the time the Thai government supported him as a student). We are both conscious of this dark cloud ahead.

November 6, 1976, Chicago

Pan came out to O'Hare to meet me. We followed a good plan, taking a room at a hotel right next to TWA baggage claim, spending most of my 5-hour stopover in bed, broken by lunch at the "Seven Continents" overlooking the tarmac. Dear Pan had prepared drawings for the overcoat, shirts, and gabardine trousers which I casually remarked in Washington I would try to have made in Hong Kong after my Penang conference. After we made love with especial passion, I finalized an article for *Foreign Affairs*, and posted it to Bill Bundy as Pan farewelled me for a United flight to Honolulu. I think our deep joy in each other's company has seldom been greater.

November 19, 1976, Songkhla

Southern Thailand is something else. No monuments, no traces of foreign rule, no bowing to external standards. The very clock might as well not exist.

The innocence of the men is almost Chinese, yet once the ice is broken, a naturalism takes over not found among northern Chinese. Man, the waiter, had, I think, been sucked off before, but maybe friend Tila had not. I went with Man only out of courtesy to Tila who'd brought him along, but I enjoyed Tila immensely as I sucked him and he jerked me off.

To my slight disappointment they were both regular Thais, not Moslems, and uncut. At one point a knock on the door announced the maids (who had certainly seen the two guys come in). But all the smiling beauties wanted was to offer extra towels!

To my astonishment, a lady sits at a stall selling and smoking marijuana. I buy a little plastic bag-full for twenty-five cents, and she rolls a few cigarettes for me as an extra. Tila turns to me and says with a grin, "Oh, how drunk you will get with that bag."

Thais must be the calmest of all Asians in accepting a Westerner in their midst. The only people who stare at me are those sexually interested in me. Nor do Tila and Man seem to feel embarrassed at having a foreigner in tow. The contrast with China is staggering.

I come home in a tuk-tuk, a small motor bus. It must be the friendliest form of transport on earth, since you crouch with fellow passengers like mates over a campfire. We swished through the sheets of water, just missing passers-by, emitting terrible fumes and sounding like a speedboat.

November 22, 1976, Bangkok

Former foreign minister Pote Sarasin[92] admits he was wrong in opposing recognition of China in days gone by, for now he sees that the Chinese embassy here has not tried to stir up the Chinese community. He spoke of the setback in 1975 to the Dusit Thani Hotel beside his house, with waiters swimming naked in the hotel pool, in full view of the dining room, as a way of embarrassing the management.

November 28, 1976, Tokyo

A pleasant lunch party with a Tokyo diplomat. Two Frenchmen join us for Italian wine and Chinese duck. Michel Guy, until recently French Minister of Culture, is marvelous fun, and Thierry, Cultural Counsellor at Paris's embassy here, tells stories.

I asked Michel about the phrase Tennessee Williams uses in his memoirs for crabs, "papillons d'amour." He drew himself up to Ministerial height and commented, "As a Frenchman for forty-nine years, gay for thirty-one years, Minister of Culture for three, I declare that the phrase does not exist in the French language." Thierry demurred and said the phrase was so good it ought to exist.

We discussed the phenomenon of writers who are also politicians. Michel was eloquent on Lamartine and Hugo, Thierry recalled the boys of Manila and Bali (where Michel will spend Christmas). To our mutual amusement, we discovered that the two Frenchmen and myself had all been in the Shibuya Inn last night and even in the same room!

I asked Michel if he may go back into government. "No, why slave for sixteen hours a day, when you have the feeling, you are actually becoming more stupid by that way of

---

[92] Pote Sarasin (1905-2000), was Thai foreign minister from 1949-1950.

life. Now I plan for a while to cultivate my private life." With that, he inquired about night spots in Singapore.

Japanese guys are earnest yet polite, persistent even when courtly, clean to a fault. If Americans, who are clean, put cleanliness only below Godliness, I would say that Japanese put it somewhere above. Each time I shoot, one of the guys I have been entangled with reaches for the roll of paper tissue that is supplied at the head of each mattress and wipes me as dry as the Sahara.

December 21, 1976, San Juan

Suddenly we are out of the snow and into the sun. If Boston is bleakly handsome under its coat of ice, San Juan is unbuttoned in its golden rays. At dinner in Carlos and Charlie's restaurant, Pan is talkative and assertive. Now he likes only bathhouses and bars with a dark room—all other places for meeting sex partners threaten to waste his precious study time. He plans to flail out tonight and go straight to Lion's Den—a place he used to despise.

He talked about his youth in Bangkok. The two themes were his early steps in sex and the image he developed as an academic high-achiever. One link in his mind is that, in Thailand's rigid educational system, to be a good student resulted in timidity in every other department of life. But he feels an exhilaration now that he's left timidity behind: "In the Gay Yearbook they will soon have my birthday recorded," he said in a burst of self-confidence.

December 23, 1976, San Juan

Unfortunately, Pan is tonight plunged into gloom, convinced he is unattractive, not only, as before, because he is Oriental in an Occidental world, but because he is "no good at sex." Well, it is a great exaggeration, yet while it lasts, it makes him morose. He says I am "lucky" in sex and also that I am "strong" in handling erotic situations. That is not the most of it. Sex simply matters a lot to me; the will snaps into line with lust.

1977

January 16, 1977, NY to Casablanca

As Royal Air Maroc heads across the Atlantic, I am reading Bob Lifton's book about Mao, *Revolutionary Immortality*. People feel a powerful need, he writes, to transcend mortality. Suddenly the plane begins to buck like a wild horse. Thoughts of death dart into my mind soon joined by thoughts about "post-death."

My colleagues in Cambridge think I'm flying in a rush to London to broadcast for the BBC. But if my plane crashes they will find out that I detoured to Agadir, and wasn't that rushed. This thought appalled me. Dead I would be, but my own pride cares about what people think of me even after I have passed into oblivion.

January 17, 1977, Agadir

The town center is sparse and dripping with architectural styles; how architects must love earthquakes as big as Agadir's.[93] Like the new towns Saudi Arabia is building in the desert, hiring the Middle East's most expensive designers and architects.

In a street near the hotel where Pan and I choose to stay, an old man sells a cornucopia of hats and scarves. Locals say he only knows one word of English, pineapple: he repeats it all afternoon.

I sucked a lovely youth on the hotel bathroom floor. We were expecting room service to bring a snack, so Abdul waited in a corner for the food to arrive. After the sandwiches, we moved to the bed. I came with my swollen cock clenched against his. I wondered if Abdul was too spent to have Pan, so I jumped on top of Pan as he lay face down on Abdul's electric body. Abdul soon took my place and came within a minute. We all lay calmly and smoked. Later I have a sore throat. Is it Abdul's black dog or the French cigarettes?

I wonder if Abdul goes after European girls. "Almost impossible." I then ask whether he desires a white girl greatly more than a white man. Silence.

January 31, 1977, Marrakesh

Ahmed, as we prepare to make love among cushions in his brother's apartment: "Take off your trousers, leave your shirt on—but, oh, take out those two pens from the shirt pocket, they would be uncomfortable."

Ahmed is a stunning Black Berber. Unfortunately, the setting had its problems. Ahmed speaks virtually no French and, in the souks, where we met, a tough young companion of his acted as intermediary. Ahmed's companion wanted to make love with me also. This was solved, and Ahmed and I got down on those velvet cushions.

Second problem was that Ahmed's brother burst in. His technique was to frown darkly on the situation as a tactic to achieve his aim of joining in himself. But by now I was unsettled about the whole business. The tough young companion saw a chance of retrieving his fortunes and proposed a foursome. In different circumstances I would have done it—Ahmed and his brother were both handsome—but I'd only met them an hour before. I had my passport and my money with me, and I wondered just what I could do if the worst happened and two of them held me down and robbed me while the third fucked me with a cock the size of a marrow.

January 30, 1977, Marrakesh

Being in love is indeed a rose garden of sweetness. Yet best of all about it is not being not in love.

---

[93] Morocco's largest-ever earthquake in 1960 levelled much of Agadir and killed 12,000 people.

February 2, 1977, Marrakesh

At dinner in the marble dining room of Hotel Mamounia, I notice an elegant Frenchman and his wife. A Paris banker, I would guess. Tight mouth, silk tie, gold cuff-links, the appetite of a sparrow, a sentence to his wife every ten minutes.

I exchanged glances with a waiter who was especially handsome. He managed to come to my table to bring more butter and we fleetingly arranged to meet in the Bar du Soleil after I left the dining room. Half an hour later, I was in this cozy bar, now closed and deserted, kneeling before the magnificent torso of the waiter who'd plied me with butter.

Suddenly, something made me glance through the shadows to the far end of the bar. Mon Dieu! There was another Moroccan waiter standing against the green marble wall, trousers undone, face contorted in pleasure. And kneeling before him, with lips now far more aroused than at dinner, was the French banker!

February 7, 1977, London-to-Boston

Work hard. Play with indulgence. But in sticking to this "two-pronged policy," I must exclude the pale, non-intensive activities that gather like vultures after famine: committees; speeches to do-good rallies; reviewing books for journals that only a man and a dog read; ploughing through long-winded and pretentious essays written by students who are aping their teacher.

February 1977, Cambridge

The head of Summit Books, Mr. Silverman, has left the business side of publishing to go back to editing and talking with authors. He's very happy, he tells *The New York Times*. "If you're with an established publishing house, some things come to you simply because you exist. When you're on your own, things come because you're energetic. I haven't had this much fun in years."

February 11, 1977, Cambridge

Here he is again this morning. Sitting in his shabby car opposite my front window on Broadway. I noticed him and stared down smiling. As always, he starts his car within a minute and drives off. No passenger came out to his car in the meantime. What was he waiting for, why does he stop there when he does not visit or know anyone in the street?

Over dinner with Rachel, I propose coq au vin. Says she with a questioning look: "Cock oh Who?"

March 23, 1977, San Juan

A deep peace comes on seeing Pan again with time for each other. He finished his semester a day ago and came down before me. The sun helps, and the salty waves, and the forthright colors of the Caribbean. Still, I don't leave work totally behind me, and maybe I couldn't. On the plane, I polished a column on Carter's human rights policies, and sent it off to Tom Winship of the *Globe* (who asked for it), and to five other papers (who didn't).

High on the bluff, a Black guy is sitting on a rock looking for a girl. Already scantily clad, I sit beside him and make my clothes even more scanty. A mound rises in his cut-off jeans. We talk. He is a middleweight boxer. His English is little, but he manages to convey that "my dick is for sale." I had the thrill of seeing him pull it out for my inspection. And the pleasure of conversation with a very handsome stud. I said goodbye and went down to watch a baseball game by the fun fair.

There I caught sight of a young guy who aroused me. Sensuality in his big eyes, thighs more mature than shoulders. When I left the baseball game for the lovely park on the hill, he followed. Just to see him saunter turned me on so much that I sat down on a parapet and fondled my red-hot cock. He threw stones at dogs, hit trees with a stick, perched on top of statues.

I was torn. I half-decided that if I could get him on the deserted beach between San Juan and the Hilton, why not have a go? We maneuvered down toward the Reserve Officers' compound, still without a word spoken or a glance exchanged. Eventually, he set out on the high coast road. I followed casually.

The sun was going down, but I kept my eye on those blue jeans. He's already followed me doggedly for forty-five minutes. I haven't given clear encouragement. So, I headed down a path from the road to the beach below. Would he come down too? He did. Even better than coming down, he chose an abrupt slope not visible from the road and climbed halfway down. I joined him. I perched beside him and with no more than "hello," slid my hand to his crotch.

He was hot and big and he smiled beautifully. The rocky slope was anything but comfortable, so we shifted to beneath a frangipani tree at the edge of the sand. There were ants, but so what.

His cock was so big that his body seemed ridiculously thin and weak by comparison. As it swayed out in front of him, it wrenched his entire gut toward itself. I sucked it endlessly, like a dog with a tasty bone. Meanwhile, he jerked me off. As he did so, this guy repeated as a refrain, "Gee, your cock is a small one."

It was dark when we left the beach. Waves crashed noisily through the gloom. I dragged myself up the grassy slope. Clothes were soaked with cum, but the cops outside the Capital gave me not a second glance. I rejoined Pan.

March 27, 1977, San Juan

A lady comes knocking at the door of Lion's Den. She asks for the manager, brow furrowed, voice urgent. When he comes out, she says her son is in here. She announces with comic superfluity that he's "doing things with other men" and she wants to reclaim him. You want to take him home, lady, but can you really offer him anything as good as this?

April 3, 1977, Cambridge

I have achieved a deep peace today, only six days after coming back from San Juan. Of course, there is no peace in the merry-go-round of the academy. But equally true, there is no enduring peace in the sex binge Pan and I pursued in Puerto Rico.

Under the sun and on top of the waves there is a passing peace. But lust gives its charges little true peace. Now, back in my study, lounging and browsing, without a mountain of specific tasks, I have found myself again.

My brown body is a photographic record of last week's hedonism. As such, a mere memory. But that skin is me, linked with my mind, writing and teaching. So, it's just as real as the three-dimensional "me" that pulled his pants off in San Juan.

April 7, 1977, Cambridge

What is real in my life? Identity as a professor? Reputation as a writer? Sex life? I think none of these but rather my partnership with Pan. Our world, even though some may frown, is the core of my existence.

April 17, 1977, New York

Have left behind professionalism and do-goodism and enjoyed myself. Long lunch at Antica Roma with Li-li. She is fresh from her triumphs in winning the National Book Award[94] and the National Magazine Award. We wandered through the West Village and then to her suite at the St. Regis to take a nap.

The evening I spent with Gregory. Much talk in his apartment, Chinese dinner, drinks at the Last Call, more talk at his apartment before turning in (but in separate beds, which slightly surprised me).

I am hardly back in Boston before Charlotte whisks me off to a party to celebrate the visit of our dear friend Felix from Geneva. He thinks Europe "has no future" and insists that America is "not only dirty but ugly."

April 25, 1977, Cambridge

Martin Peretz[95] talks about his magazine like a king newly installed on the throne. He certainly "possesses" it as a child might clutch a toy. But his conversation at the Nieman group leaves me wondering how long *The New Republic* will last under Marty. He frankly says he has a readership bent on nostalgia and that this is awful. He also says that one aim for the magazine is to lead the Gentile world to a fair judgment of Israel.

But his large vision of society, he said, comes from R.H. Tawney's Equality. I am startled at this because until now his conversation had been that of a rich playboy; now he says the inspiration of it all is an austere English socialist. He speaks quite movingly of Tawney. In the end it may be that *The New Republic*'s future will be a pitched battle

---

[94] Ch'en had won the 1977 National Book Award for Translation for *Master Tung's Western Chamber Romance*.
[95] Martin H. Peretz (1938-) was, at the time, the editor of *The New Republic*.

between Tawney and Zionism: progressive social vision versus a narrow issue that is the hobbyhorse of the magazine's owner.

May 9, 1977, Cambridge

It's not enough to write a superlative book; the higher task is to write an arresting book—otherwise few will read what you sweat to produce. Roxanne Witke's book on Jiang Qing[96] is not distinguished, but it gets off the ground by virtue of its topic & circumstances. Without that chance, few know or care whether your work is good or bad.

May 18, 1977

When it comes to dealing with a publisher, what does the author know by comparison with the publisher, on matters vital to both of them? Virtually nothing. Each of a writer's arrangements with a publisher is a blind date with time.

May 19, 1977, Boston

My quarterly check-up at Boston's VD clinic. A piss-arrogant doctor bids me to "spread my cheeks." OK, I know what he means; I am happy to do it. But he is pompous. He grabs my ass like a butcher with lamb chops. Talks to me as if I am a shoe-shine boy.

May 29, 1977, Cambridge

Students do their exam for my course this morning and never do they seem so appealing. The attractive ones seem incredibly seductive. I'm supposed to be at the exam room for a few minutes at the start. When I see Bruce, toiling away in the front row, I stay half an hour. I return earlier than required. By now his shirt is wide open, his hair tousled, sweat on his hands. I stare at the brown chest, thrilled yet sad at the complexity of a teacher and a student being friends.

June 7, 1977, New York

Teddy White[97] gave me advice on the freelance life in his East Side apartment. He first sought to dissuade me: "The streets of Manhattan are white with the bones of writers." Then came the advice: "Do the Mao book for your reputation, and the novel for the money."[98]

---

[96] Jiang Qing (1914-1991), "Madame Mao." She was to become the subject of Terrill's biography, *The White-Boned Demon* (1984).

[97] Theodore Harold White (1915-1986) was a political journalist and historian, who, during World War II, reported from China. Most noted for his four *Making of the President* books, the first of which earned him a Pulitzer Prize in 1962.

[98] Terrill's novel, entitled *Only One Moon,* remains, to date, unpublished.

It seemed to work out that way for him. When he left *Collier's* (or it left him by collapsing in 1956)—his last salary job—he turned to fiction for the money. When he made some, he resumed his true love of political writing.

He wrote four pages this morning, is pleased with himself, so permits himself a martini. The pages will then "marinate" for six weeks; he is never sure when he writes something whether it's any good or not, has to wait.

At a neighbouring Irish pub over lunch, Teddy lambasts "high-brow" reviewers who love to criticise a book for being "low-brow." He (and his wife Beatrice, who joined us for broiled halibut and martinis) think the world of John Fairbank, and Teddy was horrified when I told him that John was scrounging for funds to pay a post-retirement secretary. He reached for his pen and on the spot wrote a note to Vogel about the matter. After his second martini, Teddy announced that he wanted to go to Harvard Commencement. Beatrice was not keen, but Teddy burst out: "You see, I LOVE Harvard."

July 1977, Peking

Ruth and Frank Coe[99] are relaxed at their marvelous old house near the Drum Tower. Ruth was asked to translate a story on the life of Peng Dehuai[100] with facts changed for political reasons. She told colleagues the world would laugh their heads off and they must change it. They did.

Both Frank and Ruth get worked up at Chinese "stay at home" mentality; they won't go to the frontiers as Americans do. On Hainan Island there are fields that are called waste; but they're not hopeless from the point of view of cultivation. It's just that they're less good than some other land, and Chinese people won't go down there.

I phoned in Chinese to call a taxi and the guy asked my nationality. Ruth said. "They always do that because they won't come for Chinese. Chinese are very rude to other Chinese." The other day her daughter, who is bilingual and speaks just like a Pekinese, called the airport on what time a plane was arriving. The voice snarled at her and said, What do you want to know for? She riposted, "Is this meant to be an international airport? Do you know who you're talking to?" Once the voice realized Ruth's daughter was a foreigner, the whole picture changed.

August 18, 1977, Beijing

At the bathhouse in WFQ,[101] near me were two guys in their 30s, both in spectacles, and I think gay. Both were attractive so I asked for help with my Peking map. I spread it out near one's chair; the two of us sat naked side by side and searched for streets.

The showers come on when you stand on a wire rack underneath each shower. A pleasant and attractive old guy rubbed my back with a pot cleaning cloth and drenched

---

[99] Frank Coe (1907-1980), former Treasury Department official accused of being part of a Soviet spy network. He and his wife Ruth moved to Beijing in 1958, where he worked a research fellow at the Academy of Social Sciences.
[100] Peng Dehuai (1898-1974), Chinese Communist military leader.
[101] Wangfujing, major shopping street in Beijing.

me. I went into the cooler pool alongside a handsome guy with enormous muscles and watched him take his shower. A young guy soaked himself endlessly on a stone slab inches from my face. These bathhouses could not exist but for a compromise between the principles of the Party and the reality of demand from below.

A guy in the pool addresses me in English. Jie is a post-graduate student in pharmacology from Tianjin. "You have blue eyes and a prominent nose," he ventures. He asked why I didn't take a bath in the hotel, and I said I found the scene here more interesting—"especially I find Chinese men interesting." Jie laughed and said, "Yes, we are."

August 21, 1977, Beijing Airport

Hookup with a pilot, quite moving. We had only five minutes before he had to fly a plane to Wuhan. We were giving each other addresses, when his co-pilot swept him off.

However, at Wuhan, which was my destination and his stop-over, I kept my eyes open. Sure enough, the pilot walks toward the men's room. I follow. Our meeting this time is intense, though there was someone in one of the cubicles four feet away. I told him I'd be at the Dong Fang Hotel in Canton, but he said it's almost impossible for a Chinese to visit. I'll never forget his brilliant eyes as we buttoned up our trousers. He went to his plane and I went among the anonymous masses of Wuhan—and soon to Hong Kong and the West where gay love is comparatively a matter of course.

August 26, 1977, San Francisco

I am weary from jetlag, and Professor Franz Schurmann and Sandy are puffing and panting from putting out the week's Pacific News Service. As always Franz is finicky about arrangements. Hates the phone. Won't let Sandy park by herself—though she was driving. Fusses that I may not know exactly where the restaurant is located (I did).

We dine Italian-style and broach the world. Franz has a great mind and much learning. Two things I do not follow him on. He believes Washington will determine the future of the world. Curious that this almost-Renaissance man should be blindly ethnocentric. The other thing is Franz's fetish for special information. He is not as bad as historian D. F. Fleming with his weakness for newspaper clippings. But it is the same. He finds a new fact and swings from it like a monkey on a freshly-discovered chandelier. Sandy has passion and charm. She is a spaniel for F. Her big tits heave in devotion to his fastidious spirit.

August 27, 1977, San Francisco

Damned near impossible to buy a *New York Times*. If I lived here, the bookstores would frustrate me, too. Fiction, yes. Cookbooks, SF lore, Eastern religions—all in abundance. But few stores even have a section devoted to politics or current affairs. A glance of pity meets my request for any book in these fields.

August 28, 1977, San Francisco

Where else but in SF do you find charm all day. A notice on the hotel-room door: "The lark is up to meet the sun, the bee is on the wing, the ant its labor has begun, the brooklet gaily sings... So, PLEASE MAID MAKE UP THIS ROOM EARLY."

Like a lizard in the sun, I crawl from rock to grassy patch. A meal here, a drink there, a fuck at the next place. A notice at a bar on Polk Street says: "Minors Allowed."

The YMCA is not as in Boston. More swinging, more friendly, more healthy-looking. Glances are less furtive. Yet they are not crude boring stares; often straightforward pleasurable observations, accompanied by a quick smile.

I knew SF is cosmopolitan but here are even a group of Arabs. They try to hide their nakedness (in the Moslem way). But these lovely truncheons cannot be confined by wet underpants. If these guys are straight, it is passing strange they get a half-hardon in the steam room.

Blacks walk around the locker-room with no apparent coil of tension inside them. They eye the world evenly. Their heavy cocks swing free and proud. When you speak with them, they don't look at you as if they expect a lofty attitude from you. Nothing apologetic, nothing wounded.

Castro Street on a Sunday morning. A burning sun dapples the wooden porches and ignites the colored billboards. Types are less smart than on Polk. In the cafés, couples come in to eat enormous breakfasts served by gay guys who sing at their counters. Great piles of pancakes with fresh strawberries on top. Steak attended by three eggs. And in SF, champagne for breakfast! Only one irritation. SF is still a no newspaper town. The *SF Chronicle* is thin. Hard to buy anything else.

September 8, 1977, Cambridge

Pan is delightful, but utterly self-centered. He takes no erotic initiative. This becomes demoralizing after a while. I don't think lovers can go on that way. Yet I cannot raise it with him. If I do, he will fall on me and start to make love. But this is almost as bad as his passivity. It's by request. There's no future in that. One moment Pan burns for sex; the next he is repulsed by sex—hostile to sex, scornful of sex.

September 28-29, 1977, Washington

What is the purpose of these House of Representatives hearings I am here to enlighten? They seem ill-timed—Vance and Carter are not going to do anything on China until Panama is tied up. Thank God I don't work in government. I don't have the stamina. These trips to DC wear me to a frazzle. I get back at noon, teach my seminar on Mao from 2 till 4, and am spent.

October 4, 1977, Cambridge

Very bright people are nearly always philosophical materialists. Truly great people are nearly always philosophical idealists.

October 27, 1977, Cambridge

I put my mind into nothing but my work. Most people are more even-handed. They amaze me with their knowledge of a hundred realms. I turn off my mind—but not my sensibility—when I go to the theater or the beach or a relaxed dinner party.

November 1, 1977, Cambridge

Has Harvard let me go because I'm gay? Not really. They have fired me because I'm me. It is one aspect of me—but part of a complex bundle of aspects—that I am gay.

November 4, 1977, Cambridge

William Morris is correct on what makes us happy. Working hard at things we want to do, savouring the rest and satisfaction that follows, making something beautiful for friends. Feeling useful in a worthy cause.

Morris has been called a visionary, but he was no escapist. You have to work, and you have to take care of yourself in this world, and Morris insisted we live at full-tilt and meet things head on. "Take trouble," he said, "and turn your trouble into pleasure: that I shall always hold is the key to a happy life."

December 27, 1977, San Juan

Sometimes ideas are pearls that may be strung to produce a new reality. At other times they seem arbitrary, and the entire intellectual realm seems a ragbag in which anything may be stuffed and nothing is better than anything else.

December 29, 1977, San Juan

The guy is handsome and has dreamy eyes. He is Columbian. He went to high school here, where his father works as a mechanical engineer, and is out of work in the usual manner of PR youth. With him was a Hawaiian. I was smitten with the Columbian. All four of us got together at the Y. There was hardly a language in common, but gestures were enough. Pan felt comfortable taking the Hawaiian up to the roof. I stayed downstairs and addressed the Columbian.

His cock grew until it was PR size. I sucked it, but the fire came when I intimated he fuck me. This he did, in a variety of positions, gurgling and straining. It hurt but delight at feeling this brown flower-child's loins grinding at me from behind was fiercer. When he was spent, he jerked me off forever.

December 30, 1977, San Juan

I sat on the rooftop of the Y and felt content. It has taken days: to drain myself of tension, to shake off busyness, the vague feeling of anxiety. I was able to waste time blissfully, without guilt, and feel no desire other than to sit under blazing sun and watch the ships sail by in San Juan harbor.

I worry about the evolution of my writing style. The Dell-book style is probably successful, for what is attempted. Crisp, lively nonfiction prose. But Mao presents a bigger challenge; the political scientist has to shake off his old skin. At times I feel I've found a sparse yet vivid style; at other times I seem to be striking poses and overwriting.

My relations with the PRC seem to have gone down-hill. My views on Russia have got something to do with it. Tant pis. I cannot change tack to please Peking. My probable next two books don't hinge on access to the PRC: nonfiction for the Asia Society, and the Hong Kong novel.

I have drifted from Australia, and the re-election of Fraser and retirement of Whitlam accelerate it. This is a decisive step toward seeking United States citizenship. With Mum's health poor, and my tie with brother Peter bloodless, the Australian chapter of my life may be nearly done.

Independent professionally, I become more open as a gay. It's true of my friendships, my phone conversations, the things in my house, even my clothes. Anyone I have worked with at Harvard would not need to be excessively poky to see my tie with Pan. "Ross and Pan" continue to flourish, though sex is less the summation. He means more to me now, I think, than he ever has. It's a partnership that seems part of the natural order, like rays of the sun or a tree in the garden.

December 31, 1977, San Juan

Today was suckling pig day (lechon as the Hispanics call it). Pan and I had a few delicious pieces left over from last night and I ate it for breakfast. For lunch we ate the Palm Beach Restaurant version; again, very good. Coming home tonight, we could not resist buying a pound at the little store opposite, Tapia Theatre, and nibbling it as an early supper. Every bit of food that has passed our lips so far today (it's 9 pm) has been lechon. At midnight we will dine at San Francisco Inn—a nice place to bring in 1978.

1978

January 1, 1978, San Juan

New Year was a quiet Pan-and-Ross occasion. The city of San Juan is always near-deserted on this evening—at least till after midnight—so one makes a private world within its purple and silver streets. We had a drink on the rooftop of La Vista. Robert and Jobert were there and two Italian stewards from a boat—both took Pan's eye—and drinks flowed at half-price. Then we dined at San Francisco Inn. Just before our steak arrived, dinner became a candle-light occasion. A strike threatened all weekend, materialised and all power went off. Flickering shadows did not stop our low-key fun. On the stroke of midnight, kissing became obligatory, even the owner Jack did the rounds. Pan and I looked on 1977 with gratitude and forward to 1978 with immense hope though a twinge of apprehension as to external arrangements—by next New Year's we will probably be separated by thousands of miles.

Pan has a nasty dream, following a day when he felt spurned on all sides. In the dream, he pursues a handsome blond but is turned down. He then takes a towel—

shades of the intra-mural scene here at the Y—and strangles the blond. "With the towel around his neck," Pan said, "I swung his whole body against a wall, just like I do at home when crushing ice in a cloth."

January 3, 1978, Cambridge

Three weeks with Pan have ended. I am suddenly alone, my work staring me in the face. Pan is like a drug. He keeps me going; I spend the whole day in awareness of him, planning everything around him, living in expectation of his responses, his treacly voice, his conquering smile. From today, it must be different. He becomes again the graduate student in Chicago, and I the Harvard professor in Boston.

January 4, 1978, Cambridge

D. H. Lawrence wrote ungenerously of travel: "It only excites the outside. The inside it leaves more isolated and stoic than ever. It is all a form of running away from oneself and great problems."

January 19, 1978, Tokyo

A glass of Australian wine once more, a piece of Australian cheese. These are pleasures at a lunch given me by John Menadue, Ambassador for Australia, here. He brings four or five of his staff. These earnest, bright-eyed young diplomats call me "Dr. Terrill" with silly solemnity.

They all ply me with questions, mainly of an economic kind; I suppose serving in Japan makes that inevitable. What kind of industrial pattern will China have—South Korean kind, Japanese, European? They are sceptical of the advantages to the United States of completing normalization with China. Who have they been listening to?

Later, to the gym at the national stadium to recover. I noticed a guy in the sauna whom I took to be a ballet dancer. He did not seem to notice me, but later while I was watching sumo wrestling in the TV room, he entered and sat down close. Eventually, I smiled, and he smiled; to my good fortune he spoke some English.

"Are you dancing tonight?" I asked him. He was pleased that I had guessed he was a dancer. There was little time to meet, because it was my last night in Tokyo, and I had a dinner appointment. But he agreed to come to the hotel at ten-thirty that evening. Tada is slim, strong and sensual; his face angular and full of character. We made love quickly—he was a hot potato—and then went to Shinjuku for a drink at one or two clubs.

Tada and I got on better than with anyone met casually for a long time. He drank beer and I drank sake and we explored each other's feelings. I found him astonishingly attractive, and he kept saying I was "funny" and "very sexy." He was briefly a dancer in Philadelphia, and has fond memories of America. I hope he visits me in Boston.

January 26, 1978, Melbourne

When I look at an Asian in a cruising way, a basic misunderstanding occurs. I am expressing sexual interest, but he thinks I am merely expressing the racial fascination of the awestruck, isolationist Aussie. My country's reputation has erected a barrier against simple erotic communication.

January 30, 1978, Melbourne

No one should say Australians look the same as Americans. Quite distinctive. Big jaws; eyes half closed; a manner part-arrogant and part-humble. Eyes are seldom fully open, when they ARE open there is a steadiness to the gaze, almost defiance. No country so blends innocence and guilt.

A Malaysian student at a party says that Australia is a good place to study though a dull place to live. We both agree it's a free place (he has in his pocket a copy of *The Seventies*, the Chinese-language left wing magazine published in Hong Kong; it is banned in Malaysia).

Australian political atmosphere reminds me at times of China's. In both places politics does not seem to matter. Yet the explanation is different in the two cases. In China, political polemic is pervasive to the point where it cancels itself out. In affluent, bare-minded Australia, politics is simply a mental absentee; life is fine without it. The result in both cases is that social bonds matter a hundred times more than affairs of state, in the daily life of the people.

The Australian male—is he crude? Well, not quite. He is blunt, calculating, yet also soft in manner. I notice it in taxi-drivers, a gentleness of style that is almost effeminate; appreciated by someone who lives in Boston, where to step into a cab is to risk insult.

January 31, 1978, En Route Australia to USA

Sydney to Honolulu, I met a blond surfer from Bondi. He was with three companions. Yet a logistical detail set him apart from them—and near to me. The plane was a 747. "Surfie" was in a centre seat, his friends in the three side seats to his left, and I was in the aisle seat of the center block to Surfie's right. Two empty seats between us.

Out of Sydney, dinner was served and soon a movie. You twist and turn; put your knees up; fold them; rearrange the pathetic pincushion that passes for a pillow; still, you ache. So, I suggested to Surfie—who was shifting about as I was—that we use the four seats we spanned in a more rational manner: each stretch out, head to toe, sharing the width of the four seats.

With that flicker of a smile accompanied by a soft grunt that is the Australian way of acquiescing, he took off his shoes, hoisted his legs onto the seats, and lay down as firm as a log. The next couple of hours were a stark improvement. We touched limbs, pushed our asses together, tucked our feet into armpits; and so on.

Before landing in Honolulu, I had shot the biggest load in months. As the stewards brought breakfast, Surfie looked his calm, even bored self. He talked with his three friends. I read a book. We ignored each other. The communication of the night needed no footnotes.

February 6, 1978, Cambridge

Boston Globe last night said, "Brace For It," and how right they were. It is mid-afternoon and we've had 24 inches of snow. Winds scream. Snow drifts cover cars outside my condo building. The sidewalks are hills. Anyone who tries to drive a car—save in demonstrable emergency—gets arrested. Schools, banks, shops, every institution is shut down. Our homes are retreats. But if society closed for more than a couple of days, they would become prisons. The fragmentation would drive people crazy. The white hegemony notwithstanding, I reached Yenching restaurant to celebrate the coming of the Year of the Horse with Lung (brother of Van) and friends. Jerry Cohen[102] was there, just back from a trip to China and Japan with Ted Kennedy.

At a banquet in Beijing, a senior Chinese host said to Ted Kennedy: "You know, Senator, United States-China relations would be much better if it were not for the so-called China experts." Ted's response, five minutes later, was to ask Jerry to propose a toast on behalf of his delegation.

March 1978, Cambridge

To Seattle and nearby points to give lectures. The city is marvellous: reminiscent of Scandinavia; more like British Columbia than California. I gave speeches till I got sick of the sound of my own voice.

Stopped a night in Chicago with Pan on the way out. We dined at Jovan's, which must be one of America's best restaurants—but coming back I had to rush straight through. Ted Kennedy is going to China next month, and he and wife Joan asked me to dine at the faculty club and talk about people to meet.

April 2, 1978, Cambridge

A dinner meeting atop Holyoke Centre of the East Asian Visiting Committee. Much of it was about money. Joseph Buttinger[103] does not stop talking about his own virtue in giving 9000 Vietnamese books to our library. At dinner I was seated opposite Margaret McNamara.[104] I told the story of Richard Pfeffer[105] (pro-war) and me (against) clashing over Vietnam in 1966, with a fist fight at Boylston Hall. Margaret leaned across the table and said, "I hope you won."

---

[102] Jerome A. Cohen (1930-), Professor and Co-Director of the US-Asia Law Institute at NYU School of Law and Adjunct Senior Fellow for Asia at the Council on Foreign Relations.

[103] Joseph Buttinger (1906-1992), author of several books on East Asia, particularly Vietnam, and co-founder of the American Friends of Vietnam, a lobbying group.

[104] Margaret Craig McNamara (1915-1981), wife of U.S. Secretary of Defense Robert McNamara.

[105] Author of *No More Vietnams? The War and the Future of American Foreign Policy* (1968).

I remember the visit of her husband, then Secretary of Defence, probably 1967. He defended the war right down the line. Something has happened to his views, or Margaret never shared her husband's sense of mission about crushing Reds in Vietnam.

Spring, 1978, Miami

You'd hardly know you were in the USA. Spanish is spoken, Cuban dishes are served, skins are mostly non-white. As an urban area, the city is a pleasant surprise; no decayed look like San Juan and half a dozen Mainland cities.

Spring, 1978, Fort Lauderdale

At the Riverside Motel pool, a guy of 25 says to friends: "You know what I'm gonna do when I get home? Fill my car up with gas and just drive around town for the hell of it until the tank runs dry." We wait—at least I do—for an explanation. "I am going *crazy* down here without my car. I'm not *me* without it." At the Greyhound Bus station in Fort Lauderdale, a framed notice on the bright wall: "THANKS FOR TAKING THE BUS AND SAVING ENERGY - JIMMY CARTER."

May 6, 1978, Cambridge

Society is an organised conspiracy to hide abnormality. The deeper you see into the lives of people around you, the more unusual "normalcy" seems. Yet we uphold it. We live in vague consciousness of the gap between what's "right" and what is practised. Our institutions become pincers of hypocrisy.

May 10, 1978, Cambridge

You mustn't smoke, you mustn't drink, VD may grab you. But it's no good keeping the body from breaking if the heart is going to break first.

May 12, 1978, Cambridge

Non-intensive activities recede—Committee meetings, advising a student on God knows what, anxiety over an intra-university struggle. These things go. Instead, Brahms, squash, sex at dusk. These things matter.

Write about yourself yesterday, from the vantage point of yourself today. Preferring the former; dwelling with the earlier Ross, celebrating him, taking refuge within him.

May 28, 1978, Cambridge

If that man outside my window at 395 Broadway[106] is an FBI agent spying on me, the least I can do is turn my stereo up to highest point loud to inconvenience (or entertain) him.

June 1, 1978, Cambridge

Grading exams for the last time at Harvard and I hope in my life. A Japanese student answers on China's foreign policy: "They [the Peking leaders] must realize that military suppression of other people is destined to fail. As for natural resources, it is much cheaper to buy them." Did I teach him anything? Not much, but he teaches me about Japan.

June 5, 1978, New York

Dinner at Rupert Murdoch's on Fifth Avenue. Australian PM Malcolm Fraser is there, a bit warmer than when we met last year. The food was superb, catered by "Windows on the World" atop the World Trade Centre. Shop talk is interspersed with friendly competition over who has flown the Concorde most often.

Rupert's wife Anna seats me next to her—a surprise, why isn't she next to Malcolm? She speaks of her Catholicism as does the actress Geraldine Fitzgerald on the other side of me. After several glasses of champagne, I discreetly tell this "Irish Piaf" I am gay. She'd said many people read Tennessee William's *Memoirs* mainly for the exotic element of his gayness. I said I wasn't sure. After all, I am gay myself, and there were other themes—such as life in the South—that gripped me equally.

PM Fraser says that in two interviews given after his resignation, Whitlam showed that his thinking is really much more left wing that he'd ever let on before. "But Hayden's going down the same path."

I asked Fraser about the Indian Ocean? "I now see the Russian problem in a wider context." He says he tried last year, and will try again, to persuade Carter to take the Chinese more seriously. Hua he liked. "You could get him off the ideology stuff." Tammy said that only once on the China trip—in Canton—was she able to talk to anyone. "It's so superficial," she said of traveling as the Prime Minister's wife.

July 2, 1978, Cambridge

Don Butterfield dines with me at nearby Autre Chose. When he was six, his mother died, and his father soon remarried. Never enjoyed love from his father. Now he's built up a loving community of gay people around him in Boston—quite an achievement. As a doctor, has had to settle for lower goals than a decade ago. "A kind of a cop-out," he

---

[106] Terrill's apartment in Cambridge, often referred to in the Diary as "395." He later moved to 200 St. Botolph Street in Boston's Back Bay neighborhood. His FBI report, begun in 1975 when he traveled, without permission, to China on only a green card, ended with Cambridge.

says. "Some people have the intensity to stand the strain of striving all the time. Others don't." Is it one more proof that gays in general don't?

Certainly, after today's *New York Times* review of FOC,[107] some people may believe that Ross Terrill is in decline. Harvard University denies him tenure; *New York Times* notes that his new book is less good than his previous ones.

July 6, 1978, Cambridge

The barium enema is less of an ordeal than the sigmoidoscopy. Dr. Brookes, as he pokes the plastic stick up my ass, observes that some people are built differently from others. Being interpreted, this means that I am hard to penetrate. "I have had two in a row just the same," he says. I recalled Tony's last effort to fuck me.

But once the Doctor was really at work, any attempt to think gorgeous sex visions turned out counter-productive; pain was simply too close to the spot where pleasure was supposed to be.

August 27, 1978, San Juan

On this planet, there are three types. The first is the citizen. He cares for the public realm, loses himself in large causes, has a sense of the state, and knows the individual could not live without organized society. His moods rise and fall with the tempo of the times. This man is rare.

The second type is the bourgeois. Private concerns largely consume him. He is a family man. He has a function within his household, and a function within a unit that pays him a wage, daily bread for the household. The world is a far-off environ for him, a Saturday and Sunday object for his attention, if then. The family, in suburban confinement, is his world. He has a sense of propriety. He may well sacrifice himself for his children, if not for his wife. He counts his pennies because his dollars are not unlimited. He would not sacrifice himself for anything connected with the public weal. This man is extremely common.

Third type is the vagabond. He has some empathy for the citizen. He knows where the citizen "is at," but doesn't feel the citizen's imperatives. He is congenitally divertible. He sees the concrete, the particular, while the citizen focuses on the general. He has the urge to dally; the citizen feels the whip of duty or catches a beckoning finger of opportunity. With all that, the contrast with the bourgeois is sharper.

Vagabond and citizen make the world go round. The bourgeois is dependent on both. His dependence on the citizen is clear; but his dependence on the vagabond is just as great. What does the bourgeois look up to?

I am part vagabond and part citizen with a pinch of the bourgeois; in what proportions, it is not easy in 1978 to say.

That fall, Terrill—"citizen, vagabond, and bourgeois"—travelled to Thailand on his way to Australia.

---

[107] The Future of China: After Mao.

October 25, 1978, Pattaya

After the first evening of Williamsburg 8,[108] Thanat Khoman[109] asked me for a drink to his elegant suite, big enough for twenty people. He's going to Peking on Monday—his first ever visit to North China, though he was in South China during the war. He wondered what he should ask to see.

Here in Thailand, he urges the government not to get too close to China, and to balance it with Russia. He points out with disapproval that no ministers turned up at the Russian National Day. By contrast a whole array of generals turned up at the August 1 celebration of PLA Day, not to speak of October 1. On the occasion of the Prime Minister's death, the Peking ambassador was one of only two (the other was from Singapore) who went to the bathing ceremony.

Khoman laughs when I raise the topic of Burma. "They are just like the Cambodians, except they are not so aggressive. A strange country, a child-like people," he says. He doubts Thailand would do much if Vietnam took the Cambodian capital. But he thinks it's unlikely that Vietnam would try a change of regime in Phnom Penh—rather than actually trying to occupy the country. The big question is what would China do.

I don't think they need fear the Russians coming in because I doubt that China would itself get into a full-scale war with Vietnam over a change of government in Cambodia. Nor are the Russians crazy, though they are clumsy; they would be reluctant to get involved in a two-front conflict with China, in the south as well as subsequent hostilities along the long northern border.

October 26, 1978, Pattaya

Dick Holbrooke says the dollar and yen question has given him the biggest education of any issue since he has been in his present job. The statement by Deng yesterday in Tokyo crystallizes the flexibility on Taiwan that I discovered in Peking four weeks ago. Last night Dick said that the Taiwan question may not be resolvable, but today he says that the United States intends to normalize. Why? Because everyone is waiting on President Carter. Dick said—contrasting the situation to the Japan problem—that the China question is pre-eminently one for presidential leadership.

Two important things happened after Dr. Press's visit to Peking. A readiness to have government-to-government scientific and technical relations even before normalization; and the effective setting aside of Peking's self-reliance philosophy. After that visit, "Mike Oksenburg and Roger Sullivan[110] were jumping up and down." Dick said he discounts this with Mike because he's always jumping up and down, but Roger's judgment is sober.

---

[108] 8th Session of John D. Rockefeller IV's Asia-Pacific Seminar. Terrill to editor: "It was very private and very influential."

[109] Thanat Khoman (1914-2016), Thai diplomat and politician.

[110] Michel Charles Oksenberg (1938-2001), American political scientist and China watcher; Roger Sullivan (1929-), Deputy Assistant Secretary, East Asian and Pacific Affairs.

The question of a visit by the secretary of state to Taiwan, which I put to him, mildly interests him. It does seem as if the Americans have discussed US visits to Taiwan after normalization with Peking, but certainly not visits at the level of secretary of state— Winston Lord was struck with the point I made to him that United States official visits after normalization would differ from the Japan and Australian formulas.

At a private meeting in Washington, Doak Barnett[111] and others urged Dick Holbrooke not to normalize with Vietnam before doing so with China, apparently on the ground that the Chinese would be upset, and I said this was nonsense, and that it may even make the Chinese more forthcoming to the United States if the United States moved first with Hanoi.

October 1978, Pattaya

Alex's wife told me she and Chairman Mao discussed philosophy of life, and Mao said to her, "Be careful, when you get into a high position, people start to throw stones at you." Imelda Marcos has become an enthusiast for Peking. Her idea of the green revolution came from China. She came back with some ideas about applying the thoughts in the Little Red Book to Philippine problems, and some people, like the head of UP, became her willing followers in this task.

October 1978, Pattaya

A Japanese delegate at our conference declares: since it's the American way to start a speech with a joke, and the Japanese way to start a speech with an apology, the culturally internationally thing for a Japanese to do is to start a speech with an apology that he has no joke.

October 1978, Bangkok

The Australian ambassador sees Thailand as Asia's front line country. Here communism in Asia will stop and in a very Thai fashion, different from the way anyone else would do it. He esteems their diplomatic skill, derived from their culture, and takes a sanguine view of the new Thai links with China—all made possible by the Russia-China split.

November 1978, Perth, Australia

I saw him at a bus stop in St George's Terrace. Typical Cantonese, round-faced, with a shapely ass, and a firm nut-brown body. I asked directions for getting to William Street (where, according to *Campaign* magazine, there is an "adult bookstore"). To hear his reply, I sat down beside him at the bus stop. We talked. I gave him my phone number at the hotel.

---

[111] A. Doak Barnett (1921-1999), American journalist and author of more than 20 books on US relations with China.

As we undressed to go to bed, nothing explicit was said by either of us. Once between the sheets we talked for a while. Soon I began to caress him.

"What are you doing to me, Mate?" (This spoken in a Cantonese accent packs a cultural punch). And then: "My nipple is all wet, have you been licking it?" I took this same low road of indirection.

"Really, how could your nipple have got wet?" Soon he said: "I am gay." He wanted to get this clear before we made love. "How many times do you come in a night of lovemaking?" he asked before beginning to arouse me again toward dawn. I don't think he lost his hardon from the time we went to bed until breakfast-time. From the start, he planned to stay all night.

December 10, 1978, Canberra

Freelance writers think about one topic more than any other: money. It's logical; the person who becomes a freelance writer does so out of a passion to be free. And money is one of the surest guarantors of freedom.

1979

January 6, 1979, Cambridge

Seymour Hersh[112] tells me a story about Pham Van Dong's[113] visit to Mao in late 1971. There'd been a certain amount of discussion as to whether Pham should meet Kissinger, but the Vietnamese side, and perhaps their Chinese friends, in the end thought it better to wait until after Nixon's visit to China. Pham Van Dong came and saw Mao and early in the conversation Mao said to him: "We have a Chinese saying that if there's a spider in the closet and your broom is too short to reach it, you have to leave the spider there. Maybe Taiwan is our spider, and maybe Thieu is your spider." According to the Vietnamese sources which told Hersh the story, Pham Van Dong was simply enraged by Mao's parable.

January 18, 1979, Boston

Going to the VD clinic is humbling and warming. These fragile bodies of ours; how odd, how complex they are. But everyone is afflicted/blessed with one. My cock hurts, but there's always 50 other cocks in the clinic that are hurting more. The walls exude sympathy for anyone who has been jolted from passion to pain.

Going back over 1971-72 files to find some documents EGW has asked me for, I realize something odd about my career. A little burst of fame came upon me before I understood it. Even today I am hardly conscious that it occurred. Yet many other people are—and they see that coloration of notoriety on me. In a sense, it never goes.

---

[112] Seymour Myron "Sy" Hersh (1937 -), American journalist and author. He received the Pulitzer Prize in 1970 for investigative reporting.
[113] Phạm Văn Đồng (1906-2000), Prime Minister of North Vietnam from 1955-1976, and Prime Minister of the reunified Vietnam from 1976 to 1987.

February 22, 1979

In a profile of Irving Lazar, a remarkable literary agent, in *The New York Times*: "The clue to longevity and happiness is primarily your work," he said. "It comes before your wife, before everything."

"It's a challenge, it's me against the world, and I've beaten them at it," he went on. "If you keep moving, they ain't going to get you. You won't get hit with a hunk of pie with a brick in it. If you stop, somebody is going to get you. I like people in action," he said. "People who stand still are liable to get run over by people like me." He does not intend to be run over by a man like Irving Lazar.

March 4, 1979, Boston

I may be the only person in the Chinese field who writes "popular" books that are in fact not very popular.

April 1979, Cambridge

Nice to have Whitlam here. He dove into our libraries with an eager-beaver spirit unheard of for an ex-prime minister. Came back one night with a story of a Greek book he'd found; it spelled out the punishment for certain sexual crimes: radishes and other vegetables were pushed into the anus.

I had a small cocktail party one evening for the Galbraiths, the Mannings, the Yergins, Mike Janeway[114] and our inimitable Australian pair. Quite pleasant but few intellectual sparks. I took Gough and Margaret to Autre Chose later, where Gough ate like a horse. Someone asked Whitlam why he didn't appoint me his ambassador to China. I froze. Gough said: "Well, he was not on the spot." It was a reasonable answer. Later, on reflection, I am not unhappy that Jim asked the question.

1979, Cambridge

This from *The New York Times* is pretty true of writing: "I could do with less self-pity, less dollar-a-word complaining about the lonely craft and how hell is a blank sheet of paper. We weren't drafted, we volunteered. And even as I suspected in high school, you do set your own hours. You can go fishing when you feel like it. My father, a failed scrap dealer, worked a lot harder than I do without anything like the satisfactions. On bad days, it's good to remember that.

I staggered through the engagement at Coca Cola, but even to look at a new person scared me. When it was all over, I sank into my seat in the plane and felt desperately tired.

---

[114] Michael Charles Janeway (1940-2014), an American journalist. At the time, he was editor of the Boston Globe.

Terrill "took the step," as he put in in his memoir, Australian Bush to Tiananmen Square, and became a U.S. citizen at a ceremony in Boston's historic Faneuil Hall. "I was no longer a guest who made suggestions" he wrote, "but a voter and taxpayer".

August 31, 1979, Port-au-Prince

The first time I've used my United States passport. "Nationality," the form asked, and to my astonishment, I wrote "American."

The Grand Hotel Olufsen is a swirling pile of verandas and turrets, set in a vast tropical garden on a hillside overlooking the city. I have got to know it well for Hurricane David has tormented us for two days. Not yet by its arrival, but by its potential arrival. We had to sleep in the lobby lest landslides hit our rooms.

Catholic churches everywhere. A curiosity at the white man that reminds me of China. A people who at first glance disappoint. They have grace of movement; friendliness; rather good bodies. But I was surprised by limbs that look undernourished; eyes have a tell-tale effect of poor diet. The other disappointment is that the Haitian guy is not, it seems, nearly as open in showing his feelings as, say, a Puerto Rican or a Moroccan.

December 20, 1979, Melbourne

A visit with Rachel before she goes to the Peninsula for a holiday with Wade. It's the same old Rachel: she asks about Pan, and all my affairs and emotions, but not until the end, after quite a deal of silky Australian white wine, does it become possible to pry anything out of her.

1980

In his memoir, Australian Bush to Tiananmen Square, *Terrill wrote that in US-China relations, "the 1980s were the decade of Ronald Reagan and Deng Xiaoping. A long climb up for the movie actor; a stunning recovery for the chain-smoking Cultural Revolution victim."*

February 12, 1980, Bucharest

An atmosphere of lust is created by thousands of Arab students studying in Romania who hang around the Intercontinental Hotel. There are 11,000 foreign students in Romania and judging by what I saw, they spend their time fucking Romanian women in return for Kent cigarettes.

March 1, 1980, Hong Kong

Hong Kong is getting tougher and rougher. On the Cathay Pacific plane, hostesses just about threw the food at us. The girl next to me, who was sick, took little, but the staff, hostile at her refusal, dumped trays in front of her. At one point, they clumsily poured her a glass of white wine that she didn't want.

In Nathan Road, once an Elderado for foreign shoppers, I ask a shoeshine boy what the cost is before he starts, and he spits out: five. No smile, no bargaining, no thank you at the end.

Two worlds, two ways of conceiving reality, pass the other like ships in the night. On one hand, a view that politics are supreme, elections are worth it, the press is powerful, conventional morality counts, there is a Western Alliance and a Third World, embassies are valid, schools are the key to a young persons' future, etc.

Another view is that social change skews political categories, issues cut across ideological dividing lines, countries which advance do so by quiet strides, saying nothing, the "Third World" is as avaricious and commercially-minded as any imperial power has ever been, ordinary people of the Western World get left behind, and race becomes not less but more important as modernization proceeds. Some say one view is the past and one the future.

March, 1980, Boston

After this trip, I have a different attitude to money: a sense that the little I have is eroding fast, and a readiness to spend it before the apocalypse. In the subway an elderly lady is handing out leaflets headed "What must I do to be saved ?" Two young men pass and she dutifully gives them a sheet each. Politely the Boston boys take them. One gazes at the sheet and says to his friend, "That's a good question.

People who work for an institution say after lunch or a coffee break, "I must get back to my work!" Once you've become freelance you realize 80% of the time they really mean, "I must get back to my work place."

March 5, 1980, Cambridge

Coming back, I ask : "What holds America together?" The answer is an anti-climax: there's nothing strong to pull us apart (as pulls apart many nations).

March 31, 1980, Cambridge

Ben Bradlee[115] talks at lunch about the work of the *Washington Post* and trends in the world. Last night, he and a few others met President Carter to discuss Iran. Ben said the Administration "thought it had a deal." *WP* asked Harrison Salisbury to take over the job of ombudsman, but *The New York Times*, from which he is retired, said they would view it as a hostile act and they would stop his pension.

Ben's wife, Sally Quinn, talked about the Brzezinski[116] drama, and I feel his love life was not a suitable one for her article. How would she and Ben like the assessment of themselves as journalists to be based on their private ways? All she was addressing was

---

[115] Benjamin Crowninshield Bradlee (1921-2014), executive editor at *The Washington Post*, from 1965 to 1991.
[116] Zbigniew Kazimierz Brzeziński (1928-2017), National Security Advisor from 1977 to 1981 under Jimmy Carter.

the accuracy of her story—in the end it turned out inaccurate, thanks to a stupid person who was her source.

I suppose it is interesting to know that Brzezinski goes in for innuendo as a social tactic. It was also incredible that he asked Sally to stay in his house, his wife being absent abroad, when she was pressing him for an interview.

April 4, 1980, Cambridge

I'm only going to drink as a means to an end: an extra paragraph on the morning's writing; enliven an evening with friends; help ease the path into bed with that Adonis; go to sleep at the end of the day.

April 6, 1980, Cambridge

Why this peace today? Some work completed. The body tuned up. Beyond those—or it is through them—a reduced vulnerability; a surge of hope in my own ability?

April 7, 1980, Cambridge

Gradually people are coming round to realizing—including Ross Terrill?—that Terrill is an ornament to the Sinological profession.

June 1, 1980, Peking

In the Friendship Store, Michael Armacost and Nicholas Platt[117] enter the winter garment section just as I am buying a pair of gloves. They have that mixture of languor and self-importance which marks the traveling government official.

"When I came with Brzezinski in the spring of 1978, I certainly did not expect that the US Secretary of Defense would be in Peking within 18 months."

A morning tour with SS and EF starting at the Catholic Cathedral, crowded with some 800 people, probably two-thirds Chinese. Mass was said inaudibly. A collection taken up in a red satin bag held on the end of a fishing line. Some fifteen times as many people there as when I attended church in late 1978.

In SYS Park,[118] folk taking photos of each other, many against the background of cars placed, like post-industrial stegosauruses, among the garden bushes and rockeries, adding modernity to the portraits.

Sunshades. Skirts above the knee. Brightly dressed children. I was reminded of the morning at Osaka Castle in Japan. Soon it's going to look like a park in Hong Kong. The consumerism of it, an end to tranquility.

We viewed an exhibition of Asian women in honor of International Women's Year photographs. But many bodies look Western; the Chinese feel more comfortable using

---

[117] Michael Armacost (1937 -), U.S. Ambassador to Japan, 1989-1993; Nicholas Platt (1936 -), another high-level diplomat. Both were in the early stages of their careers at the time of the Peking encounter.
[118] Sun Yat-Sen Park, named after the first (provisional) president of the Republic of China (1912) and the first premier of the Nationalist Party of China (1919-1925).

foreign rather than Chinese bodies, just as the Japanese seem to prefer Catholic nuns over Buddhist figures in films with rape or orgy scenes.

June 24, 1980, Peking

Talk with Frank Ching, joined for a while by Janet Wang, my former student who later worked for *Book Digest* in New York. Frank is still living in the Peking Hotel, not because his apartment isn't ready, but because his furniture hasn't arrived.

Frank met Deng Xiaoping's daughter, who paints pictures. She was entering the Peking Hotel, and Frank asked her if she signed in. She said, touching her clothes, "Oh no, it wasn't necessary, I'm not dressed like ordinary people." Chen Yun's son is delayed for a year in coming to Boston because his father was nervous about the privilege of it. It was some kind of compromise that delayed the son for a year.

"Reference Material" comes out twice a day, every recipient's name on his copy, and copies are to be returned. This means the government does not trust the rank and file.

June 25, 1980, Peking

Two and a half hours with Zhang Wenjin, Vice Minister for Foreign Affairs, together with Mr. Yao and Mr. Zhu, at the International Club. Always pleased to see me, Zhang Wenjin says. Also to receive a copy of *The China Difference*.[119] He said, "It's very good to have this informal exchange of views, and for you to tell us what's going on in America." When I said, in response to his question, that I like the absence of an overall political campaign in China at the moment, he said, "So do we."

Why is it that China can handle Pakistan when so many others fail? Zhang Wenjin said we must give a good deal of the credit to India. He got quite worked up about India, clearly under the influence of the old view from the sixties.

I reminded him of his fears about Carter in America. He responded, "Well, we know Carter, we don't know Reagan." He was clearly worried about the idea in America that China might get too close to the Soviet Union.

He said China will not be able to give military assistance, as donations, as in the past. He said you have to take the measurement, and look at the price, and look at the stature, and look at the work of who's being fitted for the garment.

He remarked that lots of people didn't pay the bills for foreign aid. He said that China would probably have to charge for military assistance in the future. Egypt did not pay the Soviet Union, and we even encouraged Egypt not to pay the Soviet Union the bills for the military aid. At this point, he laughed a great deal.

July 26, 1980, Cambridge

The Olympic Games are people-to-people international relationships—immensely more important than the shuttling back and forth of government leaders and their gray officials. Athletics do far more to knit together the array of peoples. Yet foreign ministers take note of the Games only as an arena in which they are tempted to project

---

[119] An anthology of essays by sixteen experts on China, edited by Terrill.

government squabbles. Instead, they should build bridges between the level of formal diplomacy and the international intercourse of peoples.

August 27, 1980, San Francisco

The freedom of gays in parts of SF is an umbrella—others gather beneath. Straights contribute to the spirit of the boulevard. But they are not typical straights. They have come to escape conformity. A rich WASP girl in love with a Black stud. Artist couple who value the expressive ways of the place. Leftwingers who reject the acquisitiveness of suburbs they were brought up in. They are all leaning on the foundation of the gays. They piggyback on the gays.

Case Two: a couple dining at the next table in La Piazza. I am close enough to hear the conversation. The gist is that the guy is a bi-sexual trying to go straight. The girl—face like a battle-axe—is trying to keep him on the straight and narrow (she may have Lesbian tendencies herself). He glances a lot at gay guys throughout the restaurant. But he is hers this evening. He is trying hard. And Polk St. seems to be helping him.

As a new American citizen, Terrill voted for the first time in the November 1980 presidential election. "It was almost automatic for Harvard folk to vote Democratic. But I decided to vote Republican. Absurd inflation with interest rates of nearly 20% shook me, as did Carter's failure to recover hostages from Iran. Telling no one, I went alone to the high school [voting station near Harvard]. In the booth, my hands trembling, I pulled the lever for Reagan. Still a registered Democrat, I was a ripple in the tide of 'Reagan Democrats.'"

November 8, 1980, Boston

Michael Ng-Quinn introduces me to Chen Ming-ming,[120] who is at Tufts for a year of study, on leave from the Foreign Ministry in Peking. An attractive and interesting man. He said that since he left China in August, he has been amazed and very pleased to read so much in the Chinese newspapers about bureaucracy.

A TV program focused on the cars outside the WFC department store, filming the people getting in and out of the cars unknown to them. The image was quite clearly one of bureaucrats using government cars on private business. It was such a popular show that it was shown again and again, and the result was that most of the long row of cars outside the department store disappeared.

November 1980, Cambridge

Food is not integral to life in America as it is in China. For the Chinese the meals are rituals, they divide the day. The very definition of well-being is having eaten.

---

[120] Chen Mingming (1950 -), was, at the time of their meeting, a Deputy Division Director in the Ministry of Foreign Affairs in Beijing. By the early 2000s, he had risen to Ambassador.

November 1980, Columbus, Ohio

Gregory and I come away together for the first time and how pleasant it has been. I had an engagement to speak at Denison University and Gregory announced he wanted to come with me. The school is in a small town modeled after one of the same name in New England, 25 miles from Columbus, in Ohio. Rural, with social ways that are slow and courtly, students who are also a bit slow to the eye of a visitor.

We stayed together in the campus guesthouse, which is a beautiful mansion set on a hill, at present wreathed in autumn leaves. The president of the university gave a dinner and I took Gregory. He reveled in it. And I felt entirely at home in having him there. He is quite brilliant on these occasions, socially adept as well as able to discuss very intelligently anything that should come up.

Afterwards we joined a few students and the chairman of my meeting for a few drinks at an extraordinary New England type tavern called "The Buxton." Gregory and I talked a long time about the house in Cambridge among other things. He said that he had enjoyed himself enormously that evening.

"You always made a separation between this aspect of you and your friendship with me." I explained that it was not really very deliberate. At any rate he had taken the initiative to cross over that dividing line, and it did cement our relationship.

He said he felt my speech was very polished; I think he had seen for the first time a professional, even calculating side of me.

The day after we came to Columbus, we went walking around the Ohio State University campus. Vast, well-equipped, but architecturally undistinguished. These mid-western towns give you a sense of space. Also the vibrancy of that white middle-class America which—it is easy to forget—is actually the backbone of USA.

November 1980, Cambridge

There is a sweet pleasure in coming back to town on a Saturday morning and having no appointments for the weekend. At the same time, these concentrated trips away are so exhausting that the first day back is a dead loss.

November 1980, Cambridge

After speaking at the New England seminar on Wednesday night, apparently successfully, I took an early morning plane to Washington to address a gathering called the "All Saints Book and Author Review." You could hardly believe you were in America. Episcopalian ladies with flinty faces, strong principles, enduring traditions. I spoke in a church, signed fifty copies of *Mao* in a parlor, and then had a sandwich lunch with a group of people who could have stepped out of the pages of a Victorian novel.

"You have no idea what your visit to us has meant," said the charming Dorothy Echols, who had alarmed me, after I met her at the airport and judged her to be some eighty years old, by driving at breakneck speed in a tiny car from National Airport to Chevy Chase.

New York:

This bathroom seems far better than "Barracks." Friendliness, sincerity, both more in evidence. Also a great cosmopolitanism of clientele. Three charming Black guys in the hot dry room all go at me. The next morning, before returning to the real world, the lovely guy who is the staff member in charge of the third floor consented to come into my room and "say goodbye" before his night shift ended.

In the evening, the dinner in honor of Margaret Flory[121] at Riverside Church turned out to be moving, somehow more than the sum of the individuals who were there. She has created a community that seems to have an almost mystical power to make its members act above themselves. I'm reluctant to attribute this to Margaret's religion and yet there is something remarkable about the power of her life to uplift others.

Unfortunately, these religious people destroy the language. "Her presence will be here in other ways," says someone who could not make it. The Lord does this. The Lord does that. The Lord does whatever I select him to do. Dick Shaull[122] strikes the note that Margaret paid a price for all her work on behalf of others. Yes, and perhaps only she knows how much it was. We went out of the hall, I think, wondering if any of us could be as unselfish as Margaret in her fundamental motives.

Flying back to Boston in the middle of the night, it struck me that Endymion Wilkinson[123] was right when he said that I lost tenure at the Government Department at Harvard because of Pan; I could never see that when I was in the midst of the situation. What I can also see, now, is that I lost Pan largely because of writing *Mao*. It is almost a religion to write a long book, and one does become—I become—a difficult monk.

November 18, 1980, Cape Cod

Justin Kaplan[124] and I drive down to Falmouth at the Cape to talk to a book-and-author forum. He remarks in his talk that writing a biography is not mainly a question of putting the facts together, but of finding a literary and narrative strategy with which to make your own creation. He also gives a lovely quotation from Coleridge: "There are fountains everywhere, even in the desert." Justin says that Walt Whitman's life was a love story; can one's life be made into a love story? If so, it is over and above all questions of sex, and must be related to creative acts.

November 20, 1980, New York

Jim Brown[125] took me to a favorite fish restaurant not far from his house in the pleasantly mixed neighborhood of East 69th Street. He would like to have me as one of

---

[121] Margaret Flory (1914-2009), founder of the Office for Student Work for the Presbyterian Board of Missions among many other international and student-oriented programs.

[122] Millard Richard Shaull (1919-2002), an American Presbyterian theologian.

[123] Wilkinson wrote the indispensable *Chinese History: A Manual* (Harvard), was EU ambassador in Beijing, and eventually retired to Thailand.

[124] Justin Kaplan (1925-2014), author of several biographies, including one on Walt Whitman.

[125] New York literary agent.

his authors; I told him I am reassessing matters and will not make any decisions until I come back from Australia.

He is an old-world figure. There is a great charm to that. On the other hand, you wonder if he has kept up with the new pace and toughness in the industry. "I've known him for a hundred years," he keeps saying of various people. He talks almost like an outsider about the image-making that has attended Mailer and Capote.

Once, years ago, he was going to a party in the Village at which Mailer was the leading guest. He took a taxi but couldn't remember the exact address. He told the taxi driver he was going to a party for Mailer. "Oh, the guy who stabbed his wife," said the driver, who knew where the party was.

"I am a drug addict, an alcoholic, and a homosexual," says Capote to Jim, and off he sails on that. He knows enough of what this means to write to Lonnie in Savannah that without jumping into this maelstrom he cannot expect his books to make much impact; and yet he does not really like it.

Jim had a copy of *Mao* on his table and I inscribed it "affectionately" for him. In the days when he was growing up, and then attending the Annapolis Academy and later law school at Harvard, conventionality simply required that you went the route of getting married, having children, and so on almost as automatically as you got a job. He had virtually no other experience. And even since he's divorced his wife, I don't think he's had much. He looked at me intently with those large liquid eyes and said: "I know that the more liberated way of life gives you some anxieties, but I still envy you for it."

There's a certain excitement to Jim, for all his slowness and courtliness. We are talking about the case of Herbert Gold v Random House[126] when the phone rings and it's Hank calling from San Francisco. "I love him," Jim says as he returns from the phone. But he does not approve of multi-book contracts of the kind that brought all the trouble in that case. There's pressure from authors for them, and also sometimes from publishers, but as an agent he thinks they are troublesome—unless the deal is really big.

November 30, 1980, Honolulu

Four hours on the beach and have become a different creature. Is it just the sun? Perhaps it is the delicious irresponsibility of travel. There is no phone in my simple but large room at the Armed Services YMCA. No one is going to ask anything of me this weekend. And I had a long sleep last night, after virtually weeks of short and troubled nights.

A graffiti at the beach pavilion in Honolulu: "Sex is like snow: you never know how many inches you're going to get, or how long it will last." I think the veneer of Wesley College, and then Melbourne University, has started falling off now that I'm forty, and that in the end the personality that was clear even in childhood reasserts itself to join other influences.

---

[126] Random House had contracted with Gold for a four-book deal, which, after publishing two of Gold's books, it sought to terminate. In 1979, the U.S. District Court in New York found in favor of Gold for advances paid on the two published books, but ruled that he had no claim on advances paid for the books Random House had canceled.

After San Francisco, the city is remarkably clean; to keep Waikiki as tidy as they do is a miracle. It's a convenient place. To stop here a day or two before leaving the US is a good idea. You need a few extra things, you can buy them here. You need to send back some messages, you can still send a postcard quickly with the stamps you have left in your wallet. At the last minute, I left my little tape recorder home, but here at a discount store I was able to buy an excellent General Electric radio and cassette recorder for $70, which is no more than you'd pay in so-called duty-free airports around the world.

Japanese department stores have moved into Honolulu. I welcome them, for their style, their cleanliness, and the new range of products that they bring. I have the impression that they are much cheaper than in Tokyo, certainly that they go in for sales much more, enabling me to buy a small portable Sanyo shaver this morning for a mere $8.

One strange, recurring feature about leaving Cambridge. As I tidy up my papers, and pack my luggage, and clear the decks in general, I have this ridiculous feeling that the process in itself obviates the need to go away. At last, I feel, I can resume; I can work again. Perhaps it is an illusion; perhaps the preparations are really part of the actual going away and cannot be thought of as a separate act that can substitute for going away. At any rate, it is nice to feel the renewing possibility that still exists within one.

I should not overlook the possibility in my rethinking next month, to do articles on China, but books on other subjects, might be a wise pattern. The commentary on China is always interesting to me and there will be an increasing appetite for it. Yet books on China remain a ghetto industry.

November 30, 1980, Sydney

My God, it seems I have to be nostalgic; this is as difficult and as bad as having to act all the time in the United States. I am caught between nostalgia and playing a role. Sydney presents itself as a vast expanse of blue tiled roofs interspersed with green trees, set on rolling hills around a sprawling harbor.

The voices! They say ye-es very slowly as they look at you and wait for elaboration, expressing their passivity and somehow their apathy.

Here right close to the Sydney airport are gum trees, dust, and the space of a country town. Warwick is there to meet me, suppressing his excitement as Australians always do, but still so glad to see me that he can hardly stop talking about the Chinese man he's bringing from Peking and Caesar, too, from Manila.

December 2, 1980, Sydney

The first day in Sydney goes better than expected. I had not expected much, given what I knew of Harper and Row in Australia, and given the fact that communication with them from so far away was necessarily difficult. But it was quite worthwhile.

From the pleasant Strata Motor Inn in Cremorne, Sue Blackwell picked me up and we went to Channel 7 for the live morning program "11 AM," where the interviewer was Ann-Maria. Jim Cunningham from *Sydney Morning Herald* joined us there and did an interview in the car as we drove toward the city. He is intelligent, charming; an

Irish-born Australian. I only feared that he stuck too close to politics rather than drawing a broader profile.

Lunch with BW and Harry, his salesman, and Sue. Publishers and author are always at cross purposes, but I found it particularly irritating when they dismissed the fact that the *Sydney Morning Herald* and the *Age* had given the excerpt material—free—to the *Courier Mail* in Brisbane and to the *Advertiser* in Adelaide, as if the rights they had from Harper & Row were for publication anywhere and everywhere in Australia.

Harry, the sales manager, simply smiles and says it doesn't matter because it's always good publicity. I begin to boil. Are an author's writings simply to be given away by a publisher because it's some kind of supposed good publicity? I don't think he even understood the point when I went ahead to press him on how many good bookstores there actually were in Brisbane and Adelaide, and found out that there's probably a total of about twenty books in the stores of each city. In other words, the point that what the author can get out of Adelaide and Brisbane should be more than from the first serial seemed to be entirely lost on these three pleasant publishing folk.

After lunch we went back to the Harper Offices and I phoned a few people, and then back to the Australian Broadcasting Corporation for another interview with David, this time on Ronald Reagan's relations with China. It was all very tiring, just a day after arriving from Boston, but probably worthwhile. Tomorrow I have a similar program. Headline in the *Sydney Morning Herald* today: "A Light Rosé to Wash Down the Fat Christmas Goose."

December 3, 1980, Sydney

I entered another world by shifting to the Albury Hotel in the gay district. It's an old-fashioned Australian pub. The friendliness almost makes me feel ashamed of having lost the sense of the Australian mateship.

I pay the lady for the first night's "rent," as she calls it, with a fifty-dollar note which is all I have. She doesn't have the thirty dollars available to give me back, and says she'll give it to me later. For a moment I think I should not leave it hanging—but there was no problem, the cook brought it to me late at night.

Warwick and I dined at the Cricketer's Arms Hotel, in their upstairs dining room called Stumps. Few people, and only a reasonable dinner; the dining room at the Albury is better. But an excellent talk, again with someone who is not only in this other world of Australia, so far from my own, but enormously different from me. He is trying to bring Caesar from Manila and his attitude to Caesar is an extraordinarily flexible one. He simply doesn't know how Caesar will behave emotionally when he reaches Sydney; he cares less about that than I would.

After dinner, he took me on a quick tour of some of the gay clubs. Caps, Flo's, which I thought very nice, and Palms, where we watched a first-rate series of guys performing as girls in cabaret acts. Then, to the Midnight Shift, where I was not admitted because I had a shirt with a flowered pattern. Warwick laughed: "You have to dress down here," he said. I must say, though I have been excluded from places before this, I've never before got a "No" for the pattern in my shirt being too elaborate. The guy at the door, however, was nice; he announced the rejection with a lovely smile, and said that I could take off the shirt because it was quite acceptable to be in the bar naked from the waist up.

What struck me at all these places was how young the people were. I wonder if it is because liberation has rather recently and suddenly come to Australia and it's caught a generation, as it were, just as its late arrival left a previous generation in a more timid and scattered state.

In the Palms there is a machine like a bull, and you are dared to sit on it and then it shakes and rolls, and if you fall off it you fall into a double bed. Australia is changing.

December 5, 1980, Melbourne

The problem to be faced during this retreat is myself. The areas which I would like to improve seem interconnected. Getting rid of compulsive behavior. Taking reverses with more tranquility. Reducing the intensity of my impact on less intense people. Taking the day's work a step at a time, and more philosophically, so that nothing will be allowed to ruffle me. All these things, and so many more, require me to renovate my own view of myself.

My brother asks me at dinner, a couple of nights after I make love with a Chinese guy and get a love bite on the neck, what on earth has happened to my neck. He asks this in front of his wife and children; he simply does not know what a love bite is. What kind of sex exists within heterosexual marriages?

December 7, 1980, Melbourne

In Australia, natural selection operates just as relentlessly as in the poor countries; here it is stupid accidents and excessive obesity that weeds people out, just as it is hunger and disease that does so in the Third World.

December 10, 1980, Melbourne

The account which Bruce Grant[127] gives of the arrival of Vietnamese boat people in Australia is riveting. Some of them sailed down as far as Singapore, for instance, and the authorities then pushed them away from the shore while handing them maps. "Go on down to Australia; look here's a map, you can see where it is, you just have to keep going south."

Bruce said that when some of them arrived, they had in their possession maps in the form of a page torn out of a geography textbook. It's almost as if the old idea of the Menzies era turned out to have a modicum of truth. Those maps—I forget whether they were literal or just figurative—showing arrows pointing from Asia south to Australia, implying that by force of gravity, if for no other reason, we lived in danger of being joined by Asian people.

---

[127] Bruce Grant (1925 -), Australian writer journalist, foreign correspondent, and diplomat.

I can hardly believe my eyes to see in a Swanston Street bakery, in the middle of staid old Melbourne, a loaf of bread in the shape of a man's genitals; a rigid cut near the "long end" to mark a circumcision, some pine leaves stuck on the "round parts" to mark pubic hair.

December 15, 1980, Melbourne

Lunch with Stuart Sayers, the literary editor of *The Age*, at the Naval Military Club. He's awfully nice, but I'm left with the impression at the end of a long lunch of cold cuts and white wine that his mind does not exist. You sally, and he retreats. You try to pin him down, and he giggles. A faceless editor with a military background, Australian style. It's like dealing with a bowl of jello.

December 17, 1980, Melbourne

Sinking back in the Australian scene, I realize that when in the USA I am always acting to a degree. Here in Melbourne the pain and the danger are different The past is a burden when I am in Australia; in America I have no past, so each moment is clay in my hands.

December 26, 1980

Australian officials are hopeful about India at the moment, in part because of one of those trivial incidents that seem important to diplomats. During the Prime Ministers' conference in India, Mrs. Ghandi was assembled with the other leaders in an anteroom just before dinner. Who would she walk into dinner with? She chose Mr. Fraser, much to the ecstasy of Australian officials.

Alan Marshall, the Australian author, now quite old, looks back in today's *Age*: "So much of my love for life was given to me by the bush. I'm bewitched by the trees and the birds and the stillness. The she-oak sings her sad song, and to look at the stamen and pollen of the black boys and running postmen, milkmaids and black eye susans, is to see right into their hearts. When you need comfort, wrap your arms around a gum tree and all the strength of that tree will flow into you."

I feel enough of that to be moved by what Alan says; yet I have drifted away to a degree from that anchor in the soil—and am poorer for it.

December 27, 1980, Melbourne

An interesting, low-key party at the home of Rick and Patti in Brunswick. People sit around and talk to each other in a sustained way; this is a nice aspect of the Australian languor. Rick's parents drop in for an hour—a more readily manageable event than I can imagine it being in the States. Chris O[128] introduced me to the hosts. Again, I was bewitched by him, but I haven't time in the few days remaining to get to know him as I

---

[128] Chinese-Malaysian friend of Terrill's.

would like to. "I have satisfied my sexual curiosity about you," he says. Was that his main aim?

December 29, 1980, Melbourne

Rachel asks me about submitting some of my articles for the Australian China Council journalistic award, and after we discuss it with excitement for a few minutes, I remember I am now an American citizen—no longer eligible.

1981

January 3, 1981, Melbourne

A visit with Rachel before she goes to the Peninsula for a holiday with Wade. It's the same old Rachel: she asks about Pan, and all my affairs and emotions. Most of her men friends seem to be gay. She explains this by saying that she was brought up in Australia when men were unimpressive, always her intellectual inferiors and so on.

Bill Emmerton, the Australian long-distance runner, still has not given up his hope of running along the Great Wall of China. A few years ago when Lawrence McIntyre was ambassador at the UN, Bill contacted me through Lawrence to ask assistance in arranging this feat. I pointed out that quite apart from the political difficulties, there is the physical difficulty: that the wall is broken and uneven and could not be run upon for more than small stretches at a time. Bill was not convinced by my letter. Now he and Bobby Riggs have set up a challenge to race against each other, in fifty mile stretches and for a prize of $25,000, along this intermittent heap of stones which is fancifully called the Great Wall of China.

January 8, 1981, Cambridge

Fragmentary thoughts on returning from Australia. Can I live without Chris O; on the other hand, could Chris and I live together? A few weeks when you are a visitor is one thing, living together—even living in the same city—is another thing. As I freeze here, I think of Chris opening his front door in Melbourne and saying with a smile: "Come in quickly," in order that not too much air from the temperature of 110 degrees would rush into his cool, old apartment!

A good result from the trip: I seem to have become more calm, less given to impulse, more realistic about the need to acknowledge and build upon roots, less afraid of what other people think, less concerned to fulfill the demands that other people (whether in the literary or the personal world) make upon me. But will it last? Returning to Cambridge from Melbourne, I enter a world that is less comfortable, more challenging and productive of anxiety, yet filled with more opportunity.

January 10, 1981, Cambridge

One thing I have learned from six weeks in Australia is to be aware of, and eschew, my mother's failings: not listening; jumping from issue to issue; self-preoccupation; confronting others instead of facing yourself.

January 14, 1981, New York

What do I really want and value? The creative excitement that I felt each day in writing *Mao* and other books; the searing pleasure I felt last night with the nameless Black guy who ravaged me and took my cock at Man's Country. Those two things especially. Only in the US do I *see* what I really want.

"Is the House on Fire?" Pan used to say when he saw me with a cigarette in my mouth. I miss his impishness and his correcting smile.

Run into Osborn Elliott[129] at the Harvard Club after coming back from talking with Morrow about Jiang Qing. He worries that the Kennedy School at Harvard might get the grant for seminars on the media and public affairs that *he* wants to get for the Columbia Journalism School. I say I will take an interest. I told him about the new editor, Bill Whitworth, at the *Atlantic Monthly*, and the increase in fees. He quizzed me with unaccustomed thoroughness on the topic of my proposed article. When I said Bill had offered me four thousand dollars, he said, "Ask him for more."

January 15, 1981, Cambridge

The PEN forum on the "Blockbuster" does not give us anything new. Richard Marek, the publisher, seems glib. At one point he says the conglomerates never interfere with their tiny publishing components; a few minutes later he's talking about "one of the fights I had with them" (in his case MCA).

John Irving, the novelist, is the most impressive, and it is his pessimism that bothers me the most. He said he no longer feels able to say what he always said to writing students: if you write something very good it will be published.

The chairperson, a novelist, said it is bizarre and unnecessary that writers should feel wounded at the level of self-esteem if they do not become famous and very well off.

The answer to many of the questions raised from the floor is that publishers are gamblers; they throw a hundred seeds on the ground in the hope that a few will take root and flourish, but they have no idea which few it will be. Does Richard Marek[130] sometimes feel guilty when a book does not do well? "Sometimes, I think, I could have had more lunches. So that book club people and paperback editors would have heard of my enthusiasm for the book." Does this not merely underline the blockbuster

---

[129] Osborn Elliott (1924-2008) was the editor of *Newsweek* magazine from 1961-1976. At the time Terrill ran into him at the Harvard Club, Elliott was the dean of the Columbia University Graduate School of Journalism. Inger McCabe Elliott was his second wife.

[130] Richard Marek (1933-2020), writer, editor, and publisher. A few years after his appearance at the PEN forum, Marek published a novel, *Works of Genius* (1987), which concerned the inner workings of the publishing industry.

syndrome? For book clubs are only going to take a few books. The paperback giants are only going to select the commercial cream. Marek was not giving us a philosophy for the health of publishing as a rational industry that publishes the worthwhile, medium-level book. No one on the panel was. There's no way to expect it in the present era of decline of rationality in the publishing industry.

January 26, 1981, Delhi

My Indian host takes me to a squash club. Alas, I find waiting for me none other than Anil, once on Harvard's top team.[131] On the court, I am simply no match for him. I have one good game against a medium player, and then when I am quite tired, a venerable old man looks up and says I am now to play his grandson.

The grandson is a very good player, with a beautiful ass, which I can hardly stop looking at, and eyes to make you melt on the spot. But soon I am fighting for my life to keep up with him, we win one game each, and then, as I tire, this beautiful child beats me in the third game!

After a large dinner at the Tanjore in Bombay, I rose early to fly to Bangalore. I felt shaky. But it seemed the consequence of too much wine and beer. Arriving at the hotel in Bangalore, I was taken by the program manager to meet Mr. Fry, the program director. Then my upper stomach began to give me pains; when I breathed in, I felt constriction in the stomach. I went upstairs to lie down, in the middle of what was meant to be lunch.

Taking off my clothes, I found to my horror that I was covered in a rash, the skin rising up in welts. The pain was consuming me like a fire. I rushed across the enormous suite to a telephone and asked the reception to get me a doctor. It turned out to be an allergy, the doctor said it was possible the stomach instability might be quite separate.

Some injections took the goddamned allergy away as quickly as it had come, both the heat and every mark on my skin disappeared within two hours. It was a transformation, I felt like celebrating my body again, and called up the swimming pool to send for a masseur. Abdul came, and delighted at meeting a Muslim at last, I sucked him off as he massaged me, and then he jerked me off and I came with a force that climaxed the day. As I sat in a daze, spent with the sex, reduced by an Indian virus, the doctor rang. Informed about the stomach, he said I must eat only soup.

January 1981, Madras

Being in India is like living each day with a large sack of wheat on your back; India's size and heat and noise weigh down.

The room boy at the Chola Hotel was a good performer in bed. But, my God, cultures do vary. I think the guy is gay, but since he has little experience, he (happily) lacks any sense of himself as gay or straight. "Is my cock big enough to do it with a lady," he says as I'm holding it in my hands and him in my arms. Stopping, I assure him that

---

[131] Most likely Anil Nayar, U.S. National Squash Championship. In 1969, the *Harvard Crimson* called him "perhaps the best individual performer in any sport Harvard has ever had."

it is. A moment later as he is gripping my cock with his steel-like fingers, he inquires earnestly, "So big, how did you make yours so big?"

January 1981, Calcutta

Calcutta looks like Shanghai, and the chaos, color, & jungle-like nature of the city remind one of pre-1949 Shanghai. My attitude to beggars has changed since I first came to India 20 years ago. Then my heart bled. Now I am callous when a legless boy tugs terrifyingly at my just-cleaned trousers.

Ordinary Indians are subservient, unlike ordinary Chinese, who deal with you as an equal. Calcutta is filthy and everyone grasps for money; Calcutta is a city of words; people say sentences at you with no thought behind them. Marxist phrases fly around (the state government is Communist) and young people who beam at me, looking like shoeshine boys, are in fact university students, 500% Stalinist. In contrast, Chinese no longer choose to talk about politics, of any kind.

February 24, 1981, New York

I would not have accepted the invitation to the *Firing Line* celebratory reception, if my debate with William Buckley[132] had been more recent. The march of time reduces partisan feelings; in the end I could agree with Alistair Cooke's remark—after saying he himself was somewhere to the left of Vice President Bush—that Buckley did over the years draw a vast number of diverse people into conversation. Buckley greeted me warmly as a long-lost friend and was gracious enough to say it was a tribute to my tolerance that I was there.

The New York Yacht Club is mellow and comfortable. It seemed that a Who's Who of New York had come to sip a drink and eat the succulent clams and shrimps. Mayor Koch told me he has made one great mistake as a mayor. Reading William Buckley's book about what he would do if *he* had been elected mayor in 1965, Koch came across the idea of bicycles on Second Avenue; alas, he made a mistake in 1980, in his choice of avenue, authorizing them for Sixth.

Stephen Solarz[133] said he wants to hold hearings on China policy this spring. I urged him to think twice; is public discussion of the Taiwan issue going to do anything else than make Taipei's power to influence events even more pregnant than it has been since November 4? Shouldn't we wait until the administration makes its mind up on a few points? Stephen said no, he wants to help them make up their minds. This time he

---

[132] William Frank Buckley Jr. (1925-2008) was a conservative political commentator and the host of the public affairs television program Firing Line (1966–1999). His debate with Terrill, entitled "The Meaning of China," was broadcast on February 29, 1972. During the debate, which occasionally turned into a clash, Buckley had questioned what, at the time, was Terrill's social democratic stance. Terrill fired back: "I want people to think about their own society at the same time as they think about China. In the past, we've looked at China as a kind of exotic area—as if, indeed, it were another planet—without thinking that there were points, problems with points, about our own country as well."

[133] Stephen Joshua Solarz (1940-2010) was a Democratic member of the U.S. House of Representatives from New York from 1975-1993. At the time of the conversation with Terrill, Solarz was a member of the New York State Assembly.

would like to get some people with impeccable conservative credentials. I suggested that it wouldn't be easy in the China field but that he should get people with a broader approach to China policy—as one facet of a larger policy.

Among the doves, Harrison Salisbury, looking fresh and young as ever, asked me "how things are going with our friends over there," meaning in Beijing, and made the obligatory points against the Reagan administration. Bill Bundy [134] thinks Henry Kissinger now has a difficult role to play, because feelings between him and Al Haig[135] are not good.

Bill Bundy [136] thinks Henry Kissinger now has a difficult role to play, because feelings between him and Al Haig[137] are not good. Vernon Jordan[138] looked smart and prosperous in a pale grey suit, and astonishingly fit and well for someone who'd been shot nearly to death a year or so ago. He's not very hopeful for the Reagan government. On the other hand, "I do have access to them." Oh, this false god of access.

Mayor Koch [139] is basically an entertainer, and one interesting thing about the Reagan presidency will be whether he turns out to be essentially that, too. Being an entertainer is an aspect of being a politician; in some it is subdued, in others prominent, in a few it can be almost the whole person.

Governor Jerry Brown [140] is a startling fulfillment of his reputation. Absolutely without pretention, quoting the classics and the theologians, listening to ideas from whatever quarter, despite the growing hubbub in the Club. He didn't leave early as most of the other politicians did, but stayed to the end, drinking nothing at all, taking things in like a vacuum cleaner.

"What brings you to New York?" I ask.

"To have dinner with President Reagan and come here and talk to people like you."

I think he is shy; when you begin to establish a relation with him his eyes come out of the dark tunnels in which they seem to be placed, and his lips take on a reality they didn't possess before.

Teddy White says to Brown, "The ideas in your campaign were the highlight of 1980, but somehow it was not managed well." Brown said that he and Teddy must "talk

---

[134] William Putnam Bundy (1917-2000) had served as a foreign affairs advisor to presidents Kennedy and Johnson. At the time of the conversation with Terrill, Bundy was a professor at Princeton University and editor of *Foreign Affairs*.

[135] Retired US Army general Alexander Meigs Haig Jr. (1924-2010) was the US Secretary of State under President Ronald Reagan and White House Chief of Staff under presidents Nixon and Ford.

[136] William Putnam Bundy (1917-2000) had served as a foreign affairs advisor to presidents Kennedy and Johnson. At the time of the conversation with Terrill, Bundy was a professor at Princeton University and editor of *Foreign Affairs*.

[137] Retired US Army general Alexander Meigs Haig Jr. (1924-2010) was the US Secretary of State under President Ronald Reagan and White House Chief of Staff under presidents Nixon and Ford.

[138] Vernon Jordan (1935-2021) American businessman and political activist. He subsequently became an advisor to President Bill Clinton. On May 29, 1980, Jordan was shot and seriously wounded in Fort Wayne, Indiana, by Joseph Paul Franklin.

[139] Edward Irving Koch (1924-2013) was mayor of New York from 1978 to 1989.

[140] Edmund Gerald Brown Jr. (1938 -), governor of California from 1975-1983 and 2011-2019.

about that some time." He kept saying to everyone, "Come and see me in my office, we'll talk about ideas, right, not about business, come and see me any time."

At Barracks Bathhouse, a placard in the office: WE LIKE ALL OUR VISITORS—SOME WHEN THEY COME, SOME WHEN THEY GO.

February 24, 1981, Cambridge, Later

The seasons of life are all delightful, but they rush by and each is so partial. The young have energy and idealism; yet they do not know much. The older person has experience and knowledge; yet he can be set in his ways and less pure in his choices. The pity is having to choose before you are ready, and being passed the moment for an honest choice just when you are finally equipped to choose.

March 7, 1981, Eugene, Oregon

After a beautiful day yesterday the drizzling rain has come. It is one more respect in which Oregon is reminiscent of New Zealand. More positively, the freshness, openness, and monolithically European stock remind me of Auckland or Christchurch.

A large number of people came to my lecture, and Deanna, my host at the University of Oregon, turned out to be a charming person, as natural and trustworthy as an Oregon tree. Alas, she wanted to spend endless days talking with me & showing me things, and it is in the nature of these lecture visits that you fly in and soon must fly out again.

At the motel last night, a large group of high school debaters arrive for a tournament at the University of Oregon. Extremely noisy. Yet the presence of this shoal of youth had its compensations. This morning, after a breakfast meeting with two journalists, and then a genteel, inconsequential session with the president of the university (desperately worried about budget cuts), I went back to the sports complex at the hotel—impressively, it has squash courts as well as a jacuzzi.

March 8, 1981, Portland, Oregon

It is a rather dull drive from Eugene to Portland, but more restful than an airplane ride. The Portland Hilton is clean and sumptuous, at the outstanding bargain price of twenty-two dollars a day. My room has a panoramic view of the center of the city.

As is quite usual in these semi-professional affairs, the relation with the press has been bungled. Naturally the main papers are not terribly interested. But Jane Larson has made the mistake of filling up my program with marginal freelancers. I have to meet them before the reception and the dinner, and it is terribly tiring, and entirely counterproductive to the real aim of the organizers, which should be focused on the after-dinner speech. One of the freelancers uses his time with me to introduce his own work and gently inquire if I could help him get some kind of visiting position at an eastern university!

The speech went particularly well. I concentrated on Mao, his life as well as his thought; it produced a wonderful crop of questions. We sold eleven books at the door, thanks in part to the enthusiastic salesmanship of Jane's assistant.

Portland is not cosmopolitan, but it is cozy, feeling pleased that my two Oregon engagements were successfully done.

March 9, 1981, San Francisco

The flight from Portland this morning was beautiful. White-capped mountains on our left for much of the trip; the San Francisco bay glistening under a brilliant sun as we arrived. The World Affairs Council put me in the Cartwright Hotel, small, expensive, centrally located.

I ate too much, and was lazy, but in the evening had a wonderful reunion with Matthew. He came up from Sacramento and we dined together at a fish restaurant in Polk Street. We talked about each other's lives and the issues that arise in them more fully than we had ever done lying in bed. He's spending more time on his music, and trying his hand at writing—I'm not sure that will go anywhere. Will he come back to Boston? I'm very fond of him.

The meeting at the World Affairs Council was predictable—a bit too much so. The audience is so liberal that you feel you are speaking unnecessarily. And being older, most of them are fixed in their ways. They could not imagine anything good coming from Reagan. They have a fixed notion that China must be good because we did it some injustices in the past.

It is very hard to shake these attitudes, and I just didn't have the appetite to try tonight. Won't General Haig invade Taiwan? asked one lady, and I don't think she believed me one little bit when I said he wouldn't. Won't Reagan's attitude to the Third World upset the Chinese? asked a man, oblivious to the fact that China, since its split with Russia, has been at least as conservative in its attitude toward the Third World (e.g., Chile) as the US has been.

But it is a civilized place, the San Francisco Council, and one enjoys performing there, one sips a glass of wine, and listens to people reinforcing each other's prejudices. I met the head of the Swedish firm Volvo, who was on his way back from Peking; he held the usual double attitude of public approbation of Peking and private exasperation with Peking.

March 10, 1981, Orange County

It could be Sydney, with the eucalyptus trees, wide open spaces, glare of sunlight, and a cheery, bland approach to life. Quite a difference in the atmosphere of my audience here tonight as compared with the lunchtime speech in LA—where the center of gravity seemed quite liberal. Orange County is full of right-wing Republicans. The dinner meeting began with the Pledge of the Allegiance to the Flag. (Fortunately, I was not facing the audience. I turned to face the flag, so they probably did not notice that I mumbled in attempting to recall the pledge's exact words.)

Instead of being asked, as one is in a liberal town, how much better things might have been between America and China if Truman had reined in General MacArthur, I was asked tonight whether we shouldn't have gone across the Yalu River and knocked the Chinese out while they were still, as it were, a baby in the cradle. And there were several angry questions about Tibet. Many of these people—of middle age and above—have doubts about Japan. An insistent strand in the questions was whether Japan might one day go marauding again and get itself into tension with China.

March 11, 1981, Orange County

When you pack as much in a day as I did yesterday, on the next day a few hours become a luxurious expanse of time that goes on and on. You are newly aware of the preciousness of a single hour. There are some charming Mexicans on the staff of this Saddleback Inn in Santa Ana, but I think they're all too well supplied with eager, bland Californian girls to be temptable.

March 13, 1981, Riverside-San Diego

A pity to be so busy giving talks that the delights of this part of the country are merely pieces of scenery glimpsed through windows. Was I justified in getting furious at Pomona College? I thought I was going to Riverside only to talk to the World Affairs Council. Laid on was a whole extra day's program at the college. Even the beauty of the campus and the pleasantness of the gentle students did not eliminate my irritation.

The most interesting place on this trip is San Diego. You cannot but feel that someday the Hispanic population will predominate here. Much local sentiment seems to be in favor of an open border. A man in a store tells me that tomatoes would be twelve dollars a pound if it were not for the illegal Mexicans who are working in the valleys at picking and packing.

A lot of people ask me about Australia. A taxi driver had been down there while in the Navy. "I saw all the cities they had there." He could not remember any of the names. "I went to a big town—what's the big town down there?"

The Club Baths[141] at San Diego has a unique atmosphere. Unfortunately, the theme of violence was too prominent for a timid, pale-skinned New Englander. Not only were the decorations on the walls of a frontier kind with guns prominent, but there was a special room set aside for people interested in S&M—and a gallery for others to watch. People's conversation was peppered with references—who knows how serious?—to weapons and violence. "He'd shoot me if he knew," said a lovely guy from Samoa with a red-hot prick (which he gave to me) of his policeman friend, who was due to arrive at the club at any moment. People stood around in a pose that left it ambiguous whether they had a gun in their pocket or just a tempting erection. I was not tempted.

---

[141] A chain of gay bathhouses in business from the 1960s to the 1990s.

Spring, 1981, Cambridge

Hubert Ling from Nanking comes to see me in my office at Harvard. Like many other people visiting from the PRC these days, he gives the impression of wanting to stay longer in the USA, and of being extremely interested in the material side of life. He was in the department where Edgar Snow[142] taught journalism in Peking. Now he teaches journalism at the University at Nanking. He knew Zhou Enlai and says that in 1957 Zhou tried to keep in contact with America through Luce.

He talks about "the Communists" in a way that is reminiscent of someone from Taiwan: "All these people coming to study here, the sons and daughters of leaders, these are all Communist families—so the impact will be great." Skeptical, I remind him of the observation that Prince Sihanouk[143] once made to me: the Cambodian students whom he sent to Moscow tended to come back anti-communist, and those he sent to France tended to come back Communist.

Ling has a crazy story about there having been an earlier version of the Witke book on Jiang Qing, published but then withdrawn—and replaced by the existing milder version! This is a reflection of the pathetic information vacuum in China and of Chinese ethnocentrism—the notion that because Mao didn't like the way the book was taking shape, changes could somehow be made! The Chinese simply have no idea of the free flow of information that occurs in the USA.

April 1, 1981, New York

A first visit to my new agent Barbara Lowenstein's office on West 57th. On her desk, no manuscripts, just an array of checks and bits of paper with financial additions and subtractions.

April 1981, Cambridge

A long talk on the phone with Chris O. Just as I phoned, he was on the way out of the house carrying a letter for me which he had just finished. "Psychic," he kept calling it. Today he was down in Bourke Street, watching the activities of the Chinese New Year. It made him nostalgic for Penang. He does not think he will ever see Duncan again. He is getting along quite well with John. Luckily, Chris himself answered the phone when I dialed their house from Boston. If it had been John, I was going to give a brief and rather misleading message. As it happened, Chris and I discussed the way to handle such an eventuality and agreed that I would say that it was "Steven" calling from London— Steven, a friend of Chris's sister.

Yes, he did receive my letter in Malaysia; he even gave it to one of his sisters to read—my God. He said he's had enough adventures to last him until he is 25—that is a reference to me. I told him about Michael D, who has been here for the last few days,

---

[142] Edgar Snow (1905-1972), American writer best known for *Red Star Over China* (1937), about the early days of the Chinese Communist movement.

[143] Norodom Sihanouk (1922-2012), known as "King Father," was a Cambodian statesman who served the country as both king and prime minister.

and when I mentioned that he was "not only young, but even younger than you," there was a slight pause on the telephone line from Australia.

I asked him about his extraordinary use of the term "octopus" to address me in the card he sent from Malaysia. Extraordinary, because this is the term that Pan used for me for a long time! Chris said I had never mentioned that Pan used the term. "I called you that because of your long thin limbs."

It gave me a wonderful feeling to sit in my apartment and talk to Chris in his house across all that distance; to reproduce in a new place that relationship which had seemed to be tied strongly to Melbourne-in-summer. He said that he's been thinking of the need to "eliminate bad habits." Sometimes I think *my* whole life is a bad habit.

April 1981, Cambridge

Michael Mao[144] says he feels unloved, and that is why he's smoking five packets of cigarettes a day. Yet the more he says and does such things, the less lovable he becomes. He has the idea that if you meet someone in the course of daily life, as I met Pan, there is a much better chance of the relationship becoming deep and enduring than if you meet the person in a gay club. He looks at me very sternly as he recalls, correctly, that I met Tony at the Regency Club.

May 1, 1981, Cambridge

The memorial service for Holmes Welch[145] at Andover Chapel is brown and gray. You expect it with death, even more with suicide; and it seemed to suit Holmes.

A lot of people were there. Nat, the son of Holmes, told me the essay his father wrote for my book *The China Difference* meant a great deal to him, and he often talked about that piece that he was "doing for Ross." Nat read from a favorite Taoist passage of Holmes to the effect that there can never be meeting without parting, and that life and death are inextricably present everywhere. Ben Schwartz spoke of complexity, as you would expect him to, and said that for all our contact with Holmes, over the years it was not easy to work out his personal relation to these religious systems that fascinated him. Was he a convert to any of them? I do not think so. He was very New England, a scholar, not one to come down from the balcony or really make a commitment—as far as I knew him.

Mrs. Welch, small and shrunken like a walnut, spoke about Holmes's childhood; how he read Arthur Waley at the age of nine, went off to Finland because he wanted to meet Sibelius, and took to Shakespeare even before he got into long pants.

---

[144] Born in Shanghai, Michael Mao, an American dance choreographer, earned an MA degree in Far Eastern Languages at Harvard, where he met Terrill.

[145] Holmes Hinkley Welch (1924-1981), research associate at Harvard's East Asian Research Center. He authored several books on Taoism and Buddhism.

May 2, 1981, Cambridge

Is there some fatal flaw that gay people have? Chris is only 21; what will he want to do when he's 31; and what will he be doing with himself when he's 41?

May 3, 1981, Cambridge

Li-li staunchly defends the proposition that Chinese *do* know what love is. But she has to reach back ten centuries, telling me about a women poetess who was bold enough to remarry after her husband died, then divorce her second husband, and throughout display a commitment to her feelings rather than to her assigned social role. I simply say such individualism is rare in China.

May 13, 1981, Salt Lake City

On the one hand, this city seems awful—the moralism in the air so thick you could cut it in slices, a cultural and racial homogeneity that seems un-American. On the other hand, there is a buoyancy, an unfailing politeness, and a general air of prosperity—the Western part of the United States in general has it—which is very appealing.

Before I give my lecture to Brigham Young University students in a vast and well-equipped hall, a professor steps forward to say a prayer, asking God that I will be a good lecturer. When I'm finished, a student steps forward to offer a benediction; he thanks God that I was a good lecturer.

Behind the campus there are steep rocky hills. "We lose a student about once in three years," said the Vice President as he showed me around. "They try to climb up and don't realize the dangers." Perhaps the confidence in an afterlife makes the Vice President bland as he talks about someone leaving this life. This man is a bishop in the Church of the Latter-day Saints, which has no professional clergy. People come to him for consultation on all kinds of problems. "I help them to avoid moral problems," he says. I asked him as he drove me to the airport for my return flight to Chicago if people ever come to him to talk about homosexuality. For a moment it seems that he does not understand the word. But he recovers himself. He has only ever had one case, "and I was unable to help." It was a young man who "first got into drugs, and from that into homosexuality." The Vice President's position, and that of the Mormon Church, is that homosexuality is a choice, not a difference of condition.

How is the Mormon community able to exist within the United States and yet not become separatist? Spain has its Basque country, the Chinese and the Russians each have their minority groups—going different ways. Many countries have such diversity. And in most cases, it causes enormous problems, recurrent fighting, civil war. Yet here in America something softens the sharpness of the difference; looked at from one angle, the Mormons of Utah are a very ordinary part of the American scene, watching Walter Cronkite at night, flying on United Airlines, eating the same food as I do in Boston.

May 14, 1981, Chicago

Tang Tsou[146] is unaccustomedly frank over lunch at a Greek restaurant near the University of Chicago campus. "I have not been aggressive enough in America," he burst out. "Otherwise I could have gone much further." These are the words of a professor of political science at the University of Chicago and one of the most respected figures in the field of China studies. "I am not known beyond my field," he laments.

June 4, 1981, Cambridge

Ken Galbraith's garden party has the chaos of a spin dryer and yet is wonderful. Joyce Chen[147] says the day the sentencing of Jiang Qing was announced she was so mad it was not a death sentence that she could not work all day.

Helen Caldicott,[148] who gave the address yesterday to the class day meeting on the dangers of nuclear war, remarked, "Whenever I speak to a doctors' group on this question, I have to be careful to avoid emotion—doctors are not convinced by an emotional appeal."

Joe Kraft[149] came up from Washington to deliver tomorrow's class day speech. He thinks my book on Mao "very good indeed." He said Bush should never have made his trip to China last year. Many people in the campaign felt that, he added, "but George has this incredible optimism that his charm and presence can straighten out any problem in the world and he was not to be deterred." In turn, I criticized Kraft for an excessive sensitivity—in some of his columns—to what the Russians might think about this or that aspect of our policy toward China.

July 20, 1981, Cambridge

A while ago, Pan was thrilled at the discovery of a Changsha tomb from the Han dynasty. Why? Because at that time the Thai people were prominent if not dominant in the Changsha area (they called the city Niao). The contents of the tomb gave Pan heart-warming proof that the level of civilization attained by the Thai people was rich and subtle.

August 11, 1981, Cambridge

Vitaly Rubin,[150] small and pale, talks about "Sinology in Russia" to a group of Harvard China specialists. Many swipes against the KGB. No one can blame him. Yet he

---

[146] Tsou Tang (1918-1999), China-born American scholar of contemporary Chinese politics and professor at the University of Chicago 1959-1988.

[147] Joyce Chen (1917-1994), Chinese American chef, restauranteur, and author.

[148] Helen Caldicott (1938 -), Australian-born pediatrician, author, and anti-nuclear activist.

[149] Joseph Kraft (1924-1986), journalist with the *Los Angeles Times*, the *New York Times* and the *Washington Post*. Kraft also authored four books and served as a speechwriter during John F. Kennedy's 1960 presidential campaign.

[150] Vitalii Rubin (1923-1981), professor of Chinese history and a leader in the Jewish emigration movement in the USSR.

displayed no wider vision. I ask him whether his problem in Moscow was his wanting to go to Israel, or what he wrote about China. "Just Israel." I suppose there was one issue: he wanted to be an Israeli, not a Soviet, citizen.

He said Oriental studies in Russia owes much to India. When Nehru visited Moscow, he asked Khrushchev about training Orientalists. Khrushchev was spurred to revamp and expand Russia's whole training system; the African and Asian Institute appeared. In October 1959, however, Sinologists were preparing articles in their fields to mark the 10th anniversary of the PRC in October 1959; suddenly all projects were canceled. It was the first clear sign to Rubin and his friends that relations with China had gone off the rails.

October 27, 1981, Cambridge

I put my mind into nothing but my work. Most people seem more even-handed. They amaze me with their knowledge of a hundred realms. I turn off my mind—but not my sensibility—when I go to the theater or the beach or to a relaxed dinner party.

1982

March 24, 1982, Cambridge

What a lovely smile Bill Leonard[151] has! And despite the usual gripes of a just-retired man, how interesting he was at the Nieman Foundation lunch. He condemned live TV, without saying so; most of the challenges (Why did you announce Jim Brady's death? Why did you say Ford was to be Reagan's running mate?) were met by him saying that such live situations are not normal, "not what we know how to do."

He picked Rather over Mudd as the post-Cronkite anchor,[152] because, beyond the need for the anchorman to be a skilled and experienced professional—which both of these are—he decided to test them on four scores. Ability and stamina in a crisis (Mudd tires easier). Ability and tolerance in network diplomatic situations (Rather doesn't like it but doesn't let this show as much as Mudd does). The market (the other networks wanted Rather). Cosmetic (Rather has edge over Mudd).

In 100 minutes, no mention by anyone of international news.

Interesting was Bill's assumption that the test of TV success is whether it makes good democratic citizens out of the viewers—a more soundly informed electorate. Yet many younger people may think of news as interesting or worthwhile in itself, for reasons that don't have much to do with democracy, just as their concept of news probably includes more non-political news.

---

[151] William Leonard (1916-1994), President of CBS News from 1979 to 1982.
[152] Broadcast journalists Dan Rather (1931 -) and Roger Mudd (1928-2021). "Despite substantial support for Mudd within the ranks of CBS News and an offer to co-host with Dan Rather network management gave the position to Rather after the longtime White House and *60 Minutes* correspondent threatened to leave the network for ABC News" (Wikipedia).

Leonard is not sure that more information makes a better society. I see his point. But he is dealing in nuance. The *basic* answer to the question is found when one looks at communist societies: ignorance is certainly a tool of dictatorship, and information a foe of dictatorship. Energy, ambition, character—in broadcasting as in life, he says, if you have these three, you'll make mistakes, yes, but you'll get ahead.

June 29, 1982, Cambridge

Yang Bingzhang complains that "Harvard University professors are arrogant, without reason to be so." Still he seems to be settling in. I believe his own authoritarian instincts will lead him high or into trouble.

"Have you fallen out of love with China?" Bob Barnett asks me over drinks at 33 Dunster. Over dinner at Yenching Restaurant, I try to respond.

July 4, 1982, Boston

Just finished reading John Fairbank's memoir *Chinabound*. He has kept serene and healthy by not letting anything ruffle him, and at times simply not going into issues deeply.

July 6, 1982, Boston

The start of a novel: "After two days of shopping in Hong Kong, Pamela crossed the bridge at Lo Wu, facing an array of red-and-white signboards with maxims about how one should live."

July 7, 1982, Boston

The fierce joy of summer, it seems almost to unhinge my mind.

July 8, 1982, Cambridge

Many guys get less interested in sex as they settle down within a gay community! (Either with a lover, or in a congenial group). It is almost enough to make you conclude that gays need redefining. Less that they lust for men than that *they don't lust for women.* Once they feel secure against the threat/challenge of women, they subside erotically. I hope it's a minor trend and not a major pattern.

In the fall of 1982, Terrill made the first of what were to be several lecture tours with Pearl Cruise Lines, which specialized in Far Eastern itineraries.

November 6, 1982, Osaka

I called Yasunori but we did not meet. I had the impression that either he's trying to go straight, as he prepares for a business career, or he is living with someone. A student from Kyoto University more than filled the breach. A charming guy, a rare Japanese more interested in the Third World than in Europe or America. He had his special friend with him. At first, he wanted the friend to join in the lovemaking. I wasn't keen; gradually the friend backed away.

Just before leaving for Kobe, I decided on impulse to go to the gym rather than have lunch. It was an excellent idea; Saturday afternoon is peak hour in a Japanese bathhouse. Orgies. A large percentage of guys who are attractive. A sharp line of division between those who like a Westerner and those who do not.

I met a beautifully built guy whose only flaw—a small one—was to talk a lot during our lovemaking. His English was limited, so he would come out with technical terms inappropriate for lovemaking—"Where is your large penis?"

November 9, 1982, Kobe

On board the *Pearl of Scandinavia*, I find the Filipinos charming as staff members, but disappointing erotically. This is because of the psychology that exists between passengers and crew. The passengers are mostly rich, and the Filipinos treat them like kings and queens; it's difficult to convince the Filipinos you just want to be a human being with them. To make it worse, the majority have a wife back home and are unusually dutiful husbands.

November 11, 1982, Pusan

This is a handsome port populated with attractive men. No problem in looking at them; they either look away or look straight back, depending on whether they like you—which is as it should be. In the elevator going up to the tower overlooking the city, I pressed against a guy. He was interested. No barrier of discretion held him back from getting a hardon and pushing it against me.

Korean bathhouses, like Japanese, are equipped with a dry sauna at a fierce temperature. I am scrubbed and washed down with soap by an attractive guy, whose approach is that of the engineer—like the Chinese. But he grabs my cock and "washes" it—the Chinese don't do that.

November 15, 1982, Peking

Driving into Peking from Tianjin was strange. I always come into Peking by air or train.

Our *Pearl* group checked in at the hoary old Qian Men hotel. Handy to the home of Sun.[153] I phoned him at his neighborhood committee phone, which services about seven hundred people. Fortunately, the man who answered the phone knew who he was; Sun's sister came on the line. Although she betrayed the usual Chinese woman's inquisitiveness about why a foreign man is contacting a Chinese man in her family, she did take a message for him.

I was with Shen in my room at the Qian Men when Sun knocked on the door. He looked just as attractive and charming as before. I could hardly restrain myself, but I

---

[153] In a later diary entry (not included in this volume), Terrill described the circumstances his initial encounter with Sun: "It was in a department store that I met Sun, a guide on one of the other busses. Medium height, slim, beautiful face, enticing eyes, sexy lips."

had to. And I had to introduce him to Shen. The two of them sat down, sipping water, looking warily at each other. I had to make the conversation.

I told Shen that Sun and I would arrange a later time to meet—I'd just go downstairs and see Sun off for the moment. We went out into the corridor; neither of us could bear not to embrace. The whole corridor of rooms was vacant, because our tour group was still at the Temple of Heaven. Their bags were in the lobby, not checked in yet; this floor was set aside for them. I said to Sun, "Let's slip into one of these rooms." We became locked in kisses three or four yards inside the door of one room. Some minutes went by. I heard a babble of voices at the other end of the corridor. We had hardly taken our arms from around each other, when the door of the room burst open and two of our tour ladies came in. The ladies let out a small scream. I burst out to Sun, "Oh, this isn't 432 after all."

Amazement covered the ladies' faces. Alas, in my panic I had said just the wrong room number—this *was* room 432. One lady looked at us and said, "*We* are room 432." Moving toward the door, with Sun behind me, I mumbled apologies. Without luggage, I could not have looked like someone just coming into the room. And Sun did not look like a Chinese hotel service personnel: no white jacket, blue jeans, a sweater. As we departed the lady from the tour said heavily, "There must be two room 432s."

November 15, 1982, Evening, Peking

Periodically, as we talked about politics, Shen asked me about "the boy" who had been in my room. Later Sun came back. We watched TV, talked excitedly about what had happened since we met last, compared notes sadly about the cards and letters that never got through, and gradually moved into a fit of physical passion. I still had my doubts about doing it in that bugged room, but after a while I forgot them. Taking it step by step (as one precaution against a sudden intrusion on the part of officials who may have seen us go in), we went about it. It was as if he'd been saving up for all the months since I'd been away. "I cannot live without you," he said.

"Why don't you go with a Chinese man?" I asked. He has done so; he knows of gay people, and places including bathhouses where he could meet others. "But all Chinese men are going to get married and have children," he explained. "You just can't find the individual who will love you, and love you forever. I can play around with someone here, but I don't want that. I only want sex with someone who can be my lover."

November 16, 1982, Peking

Sun came in and we fell on each other. Later, we went to the eastern market area, where my four hundred colleagues from the *Pearl of Scandinavia* were eating lunch. Sun looks more gaunt in the winter chill than he did in the summer—as no doubt I do. Walking in the streets is less pleasant than in the warm months.

Why does Sun have unreliable friends? He is a very impractical man, though not crazy as he sometimes fears. He had one other sex experience since May, with a French friend of a straight American student at Peking University, who knows that Sun is gay.

He presents me with three more books, ancient stories in archaic language I cannot understand. We have lunch at a "masses" restaurant near where the tour group is stationed; I look out the window at the thirteen large busses and watch for the start of the exodus from the tour group's restaurant. Clatter, filth, and rudeness in the restaurant. At our table are three people besides Sun and me. They sit without talking to each other, with wild staring eyes, shoveling food into their mouth, drinking beer from jugs. One of the men was not satisfied with the speed at which he was imbibing the beer from his glass; he took the jug, poked the spout into his mouth, and upturned the jug. Within five seconds it was empty; jug and head came down to the filthy plastic tablecloth.

I looked into the face of the second of the two men at the table. I smiled; he smiled; that wild staring face was transformed into a beautiful face possessed of a winning smile.

Our *Pearl* group took off for Tiananmen Square and the Forbidden City; Sun came with us in the bus. This I arranged with both the *Pearl* authorities and the Chinese. I introduced him to the China International Travel Service people, explaining that he was the relative of friends of mine in Washington and Boston. "Of course, he can come; how nice to have him with us." Soon the Chinese are feeling very proprietorial about having him.

At the Forbidden City the four hundred trooped through the palaces. Sun and I went into Sun Yat-sen Park to be alone. "I can't live without you," he said again. He told me about his first sex experience at age 16. He had a friend in high school whose father used to conduct tutorial lessons in his home to coach them in their courses. This guy, about fifty years of age, was a widower. One day Sun was alone with him in the house after a study session. He started to tell Sun about the gay life, explaining that he was gay, telling Sun what it was like to make love with a man. Soon he touched Sun. Sun didn't resist, and they went to bed. That was his first sex. Was the man attractive? "Terribly ugly," Sun said. Why can't people simply make love with those they are attracted to, and politely decline to make love with others? The world would be a much happier place if that rule applied.

It seems impossible for me to judge anything concerning Sun, and for him to judge anything concerning me. Of course, there are overlapping moralities, and yet they seem outweighed by the separateness.

November 17, 1982, Xingang

Back to the *Pearl of Scandinavia*, glistening white and blue. After an hour on board with the cruise passengers, the gulf between ourselves and China seems immense. Sun's world recedes. Another sucks me in. There was a time when I felt disgust on returning to the West; now I feel pleasure.

A story: a cruise that does not end, but goes on and on. The captain is trying to find a port, any port. Meanwhile the human society on board changes. Its various traits are intensified a hundredfold as if in front of an enlarging mirror. Eventually as a community it erupts in conflict, fear, and despair.

November 18, 1982, Qingdao

For the moment, I am numbed by a glimpse of beauty. We have just come back on board after a day in this German-influenced port. I was impressed with the look of the men. Good-looking faces, fairly square. Many guys have long hair and wear a cap at a rakish angle.

November 19, 1982, Shanghai

It was lunch time at the Peace Hotel. The *Pearl* had arrived in Shanghai a few hours before; I had shaken off the group and felt a delicious freedom as I sat down alone to eat. I ordered a sweet jam soufflé and a bottle of beer—since 1971 I have been unable to resist the soufflés at this hotel.

As I came into the dining room, I caught the glance of a young Chinese man with flashing eyes and a stylish haircut. He was on the short side, with a strong body and a dashing manner. I couldn't guess his profession. He was with a young man and woman. No table near them was free; I went to a window table overlooking the customs house. I began to write postcards. With the beer, the soufflé, and the magnificent view at the window, I momentarily forgot the young man. But when I looked toward him, across six or eight large tables, those brilliant eyes were looking at me. Intermittently, for the next two or three minutes, I glanced at him, until our eyes locked for ten seconds. He quickly gestured with his head to one side of the restaurant. A moment later he left his seat. I followed him to the men's room. Inside, after a quick look around, he grabbed me; soon we were locked in desperate kisses. Ping, as he introduced himself, whispered: "Eight-thirty at the Yellow Banks River."

At eight-thirty, Ping wasn't there, and by nine o'clock I got talking to the son of a doctor and of a mother who teaches Japanese. He was beautifully built, with a baby face. This guy asked me back to his house, saying there were two rooms, and though his mother was sleeping in one, since the father was on duty, we could be undisturbed. I went around the garden again, and Ping was not there. Suddenly the guy said, "I think your friend has come." I looked in amazement at the guy. How on earth did he know? He must have had an eye out to see if anyone was following us, and noticed Ping. I quickly turned around and there indeed at a discreet thirty-yard distance was Ping. The son of the doctor was extremely gracious, saying he understood.

"It's just that I was struck by your beautiful face," he said. "I don't want to take you away from him."

Ping had no plan. I said how about going to the Pu Jiang Hotel, where my four hundred passengers were watching acrobats. Surely, we could sneak in, and at least be inside the hotel. But when we got there, the busses were gone. I liked Ping's candor. I told him I had been in China several times and knew a bit about the situation. "Trust me," I said in Chinese. He replied: "Frankly speaking, I cannot yet trust you."

We went to the Shanghai Mansions. There in various rooms, eventually the men's room, we continued. He was as hot as a furnace. He wanted to kiss so blindly that it was impossible to keep even the side of an eye open for anyone who might come in.

Ping is a singer. He hadn't wanted to walk under the lights on the Bund because he's well-known and some people would recognize him. At length we decided to take a taxi. I would drive him to his home, leave him at a point near his house—not right at it—and then return to the Pearl of Scandinavia. We were hardly in the cab, when he pulled open my trousers, hauled up my shirt, pulled out his own dick, and went to extremes as the Chinese occasionally do. While I was concentrating on not shooting off, he suddenly shot into the back of the front seat of the car, all over my clothes, his own, and the cab. I thought the driver hesitated, but we kept driving. Ping was trembling like a leaf beside me on the back seat.

After we said farewells and he got out, I saw that the top of the front seat, as well as the back part of the front seat, had been splashed with his cum. Every time we went under a streetlight, you could see it. As I began to chat with the driver, I noticed to my horror a big streak of cum on the right shoulder of his uniform. I leaned against the front seat, rubbing my hands into the canvas as I asked the driver a stream of questions about the Shanghai economy. There was nothing I could do about the uniform. When we arrived at the Pearl and the driver turned the lights on in the car, I had my wallet all spread out on the top of the front seat, covering the splashes of Ping's semen. I paid the bill and got the receipt. I did not look back to see what was the driver's reaction to seeing the sticky state of his cab. I did have an explanation up my sleeve—that this Chinese companion of mine had been drinking beer in the cab. Thank God, Shanghai taxi drivers are not capitalist minded, and don't care particularly about the appearance of their cab—they don't own it. One moment Ping was paralyzed with fear, the next he was shooting off into the neck of a taxi driver. Sometimes it seems that the Chinese, in their modernization efforts in a parallel way, oscillate between extremes.

November 20, 1982, Shanghai

I had just left the office of Don Anderson, the American consul-general, when I realized I was close to Shengde's place, so I had Don's driver take me to the address. I'd never been there before. The number turned out to be a shop. Was he a salesclerk? I could not see him. Was there a house above the shop? If so, I couldn't see how to get into it. Then I noticed an alley to one side, with a house that bore the same number as the shop in the boulevard. Up the rickety dark brown stairs I went. At the top of them an old man shooed me away. I stood my ground and repeated the name Shengde. At length he waved me to another side of the rickety balcony.

I knocked on the door and a middle-aged woman came to the door. She was Shengde's mother. Her Shanghai accent was thick, but I gathered it was his day off, he had gone out about an hour ago, and she didn't know where. She phoned to get a friend of his to come and talk to me.

In comes this guy whom I recognized as the one whom I had met with Shengde that unforgettable night in the French club. He said he was Shengde's brother. This I simply couldn't understand, and I was relieved, for the sake of my sanity, when he later on said that he called himself a brother because he was so close. In effect he's a gay friend, called Liu.

He told me—he apparently knows everything about Shengde—that Shengde did get my letter posted from Peking, and he quickly replied to the same address, sending two envelopes, with the inner envelope addressed to me, and enclosing a photo as well as a letter. It never reached me.

Liu said Shengde was out seeing his girlfriend. I took a mental note of that, and reserved judgment. Suddenly the door opened and Shengde walked in. He didn't know that his friend was there, much less that I was. He was absolutely bowled over, ecstatic, confused, struck dumb. His mother retreated into one corner of the room, at one end of which was a double bed, with a baby sleeping. The place was cluttered with half-cabbages, old newspapers, tennis balls, and photos of the family. On one wall hung a certificate congratulating Shengde's father for his output at the factory last year.

Shengde looked magnificent. The same liquid eyes, perfect lips, tidy dress, and dignified bearing. It was time for me to go to an appointment, and he took me down to the bus. We arranged to meet the next day at noon. He said he'd just take the day off from work—"qing jia."[154] He looked at me as I got on the bus and said, "Maybe that overseas Chinese girlfriend of yours did get my reply, but just didn't pass it on to you." Maybe indeed.

November 21, 1982, Shanghai

After breakfast, I found that the *Pearl* was no longer moored at the deck. Those leaving for the all-day tour had gone, and the captain had moved to a buoy. I had dreadful visions of spending the whole day gazing at Shanghai from a window. But fortunately, a little boat came along; I sprang on among chickens and cabbages and reached the dock—in time for a meeting at the American consulate.

Then lunch with Shengde. He looked neat in a pinstriped suit over a colored sweater and gaudy shirt. He's like a piece of silk that flashes two quite different colors according to the angle of vision. At times he looks like the construction worker that he is. At other times he seems gay. This noon he was neutral.

I went inside the Jinjiang Club and chatted with the girl at the front counter. This always helps; she felt she knew me after a few minutes, and when I reentered ten minutes later with Shengde beside me, I gave an ear-to-ear smile as I greeted her with a torrent of polite remarks. By the time I'd finished we were well past her desk. We had lunch in the Chinese dining room, remarkable only for appalling service and the number of times waitresses knocked things over. They brought the food fifteen minutes before the first bottle of beer.

Shengde and I talked about our meetings in the summer. It seems that Liu is not only very close to him, but someone he looks up to. He wants me to try and help Liu get to the USA to study, as a step toward helping him. I'm not sure one follows from the other. I'm even less sure I can help Liu.

After lunch, we toured the Club with its dark wooden panels, lace covered armchairs, electronic games, bowling alley, and chess room. I tried to kiss him in the

[154] Qingjia (請假), ask for a leave.

chess room, but he pulled away and murmured that this was China. He did this again in the amusements room. We went swimming and he opened up like a rose. The pool is an Olympic one, with elegant dressing rooms, attendants and a lifeguard; but at this time of day there were no other customers but us. We were supplied with costumes and towels and soap. We went into the shower room and showered together. This broke down his anxieties, one thing led to another, and it wasn't long before I had come.

We swam a few laps. We floated on big, black rubber tubes. We hurled yellows balls at a target at one end of the pool. The lifeguard gazed at us the whole time, his face, revealing like many Shanghai faces, unable to hide his inquisitive feelings.

We went into the locker room again and resumed our showering and soaping. Soon Shengde came. We slowly dried ourselves, got dressed, and lingered around the Club. We played electronic games, him sitting at the wheel behind a screen which showed the progress of his motor bike in avoiding other bikes coming from front and back. I tried it—the first time in my life I've ever played an electronic game. I managed the head-on traffic, but was blind to bicycles approaching me from behind.

Shengde said the worst of many faults with China is that you don't get anywhere after years of work. His standard of living hasn't changed in the nine years he's been a construction worker. The second worst thing is the stupidity and unfairness of the management in economic enterprises. People take up to ten days a month for so-called sick-leave. Some people don't do any work at all.

Today, in order to see me, he asked for a day off. In my innocence I thought this might mean telling them the day after, or perhaps telephoning them the night before. No—he rose at five, took a bus at five-thirty to his place of work, arriving there ninety minutes later, spent an hour making the application to get the day off, and then took the bus back—a total of four or five hours just asking permission to get the day off!

Shengde never asks for anything. I realized he liked my green velvet jacket. I said, "Do you like the jacket?" He already knew what I had in mind, but declined to say he liked it. I said, "I think you like it, and I want to give it to you." Our taxi was a Red Flag; we set off down the tiny streets in this immense limousine, Shengde with his hand down my trousers and me with mine down his. When we reached his house, I put the jacket into his hand and said in English, "I love you"—the only three words of English he knows. He smiled and then he was gone.

November 22, 1982, South China Sea

After two weeks on the *Pearl*, I feel the bloatedness that comes upon me in Australia in the Christmas season—and the reason is the same. There isn't much to do, you are a captive of the company around you, you mindlessly eat and drink.

Today I overheard someone say they were frightened at the prospect of going to a hotel again, on reaching Hong Kong, after two weeks on the boat. "Here you can talk to anyone, and everyone will say hello to you—a hotel will be so cold." A cruise is a big party with no one left out—that is its great appeal to many people. Also its suffocation to me. These wealthy people are buying companionship. They even buy a meeting with the captain; he holds parties and shakes hands with everyone. The eyes of the matrons and the retired farmers gleam with pleasure when he puts out his hand toward them.

I bungled my time with Lily last night. In the afternoon I desired her sexually. When she said she wouldn't, and gave me only a kiss after that long cocktail party on the Lido deck, I mentally changed gears. In the evening, she sought me out. She still looked beautiful in her red blouse and her black hair, with her chunky body and pearly skin. But I didn't desire her strongly anymore. So I wasn't prepared for endless games of hearing about her children and trying to guess whether she really wanted to be unfaithful to her adored husband. Perhaps the fatigue of the usual day's socializing had got to me. Perhaps it was a mistake from the beginning to make an approach to a woman.

November 23, 1982, Hong Kong

My mind has turned into mashed potatoes. I felt this morning on the deck that if one more person came up to say how much they had enjoyed my lectures, or to ask me how I'd first got interested in China, I would throw them over the railing into the South China Sea. Of course, it's unfair. They don't realize that a hundred and fifty people before them have said the same thing. But the net effect on me is disastrous. I've been out of normal functioning, mental and physical, for weeks. Now I sink into a hotel room and am becalmed.

The Hong Kong Cantonese are getting taller and more solid, and those fierce, hard cocks are getting longer and fatter. Sexual habits are becoming less repressed. I discovered a sauna which is a compromise between the old-style Hong Kong bathhouse and a Japanese outfit. I'd been in the pool five minutes when a guy sidled up to me, moved against me, and wanted me to fuck him there and then under the water. This I did not want to do, but I had enormous pleasure toe-fucking him, as we swirled like mermaids in the green waters. Then I jerked him off under the water. As he was ready to come, he pushed his cock above the water. He shot into my hair and onto my forehead, a tremendous burst.

I took the gleaming new subway over to Kowloon. The smell of air-conditioning, the quickness in the step, the sated foreign tourists, the look of commercial anticipation in almost every face. Just as you begin to think Shanghai and Peking are making strides in the furnishings of life for the traveler, you are reminded that Hong Kong is years ahead.

I arrived at the Yuk Tak Bathhouse. A lovely guy called Xie anointed me with a sweet-smelling oil. At the end he majestically kissed me on the forehead.

November 24, 1982, Hong Kong

I was in a hot pool at the sauna in the Harbour Hotel building when Huang, a dancer, entered the room and jumped into the water. Immediately, I felt electricity between us. Our hands brushed together; soon more than that. Suddenly he cried out in Mandarin, "What's going on?" I was appalled and surprised. I had certainly not been bolder with him than he had been with me. I glided away to another corner of the pool, but I did not leave the pool. In five minutes, he was beside me again. I refused to talk to him or even look at him. Later in the TV room, he again came up to me, and this time we could speak. It turned out that he had never met anyone before, and he expected me to say something to him before the physical contact, minimal as it was, went any further. "Why didn't you tell me you liked me," he said in Mandarin, "and that you wanted to be my friend?"

He is superbly built and has a Cantonese machismo appearance and manner. I asked him if he would like to come to my hotel. No, it was too late, he said. I suggested that he come the next day. He said he would do that, taking a note of my room number.

When the nice massage boy approached me and said would I like his ministrations, I thought why not. But I had reason to regret spending myself in that dark and pleasant room. At two-thirty in the morning, there was a knock on the door. Who on earth could it be in a Hong Kong hotel at that hour? I staggered out of bed and opened the door. There was dancer Huang, with a small bag in his hand. He'd been home to his parents, a long way from Victoria Island, explained to them that he would be away for the night, and come back. "Can I stay with you?"

He was the hottest creature you can imagine, and we made love again and again, ending up at eight o'clock in the morning, before he went off to a rehearsal. He's terribly uptight—said he'd never made love with a man or a woman before. But he was uncontrollably erotic once he began. Before he left, he said, "Why didn't you sleep?" It was true, even in the few hours that were available, while he was sleeping, I did not sleep a wink.

November 25, 1982, Hong Kong

Hong Kong University has a British Empire stamp upon it. Here in the library is a door, "Female Staff Room," and another one, "Library Staff Only. Gentlemen."

I was shocked at Marty's story about police pressure against gays in Hong Kong. Even allowing for a touch of paranoia on his part, the situation is worse than it used to be. He has twice been interviewed by the police, in a bullying way. After the second occasion, when they came to his house and announced in a very threatening way that they had picked up one of his boyfriends and arrested him, he said he sat stunned in his living room for two hours and seriously contemplated suicide. He was going to leave a note that pointed the finger of blame at the reactionary attorney general of the colony. His position is made all the more precarious by his being an American; he has to apply for the renewal of his visa from time to time.

Another night, he was in the Dateline Bar on Wellington Street, dining alone, when in rushed a group of police. They surrounded all the tables and asked everyone for their ID cards, which you have to carry with you at all times in Hong Kong.

It turns out that my darling David—of that wild winter interlude at the Australian Embassy residence in Peking two years ago—is now living with a lawyer named Curt on a small island in the Hong Kong harbor. Michael gets Curt's occasional advice on these alarming police matters. Curt once got a friend to look up the files in the police department and found out that there was a substantial file on him. It came to the chief justice's attention that this bright young lawyer was gay; the chief justice remarked to someone, "I knew that in our profession there were some of these people, but I never thought that he might be one of them. And he's living with a Chinese man. Well, at least they have been together for some years, I understand."

November 26, 1982, Hong Kong

China leads me into the strangest situations. A few weeks ago, I sit at the Sausalito waterfront with two Marin County ladies whom I meet because I am lecturing at Dominican College, at which one of them teaches. There is a proprietary interest in making me happy, in looking after the lecturer.

A week later, standing on a gray concrete Japanese railway platform with Ihara, professor at a girls' college near Osaka. All day I am with him in his office and walking on the surrounding hills. All because of my study of Jiang Qing, on which Ihara has worked for years.

Then, on the *Pearl of Scandinavia*, thrown together with four hundred passengers, ninety percent of whom I would never come across in social life chosen by myself. But China has joined me to them; I am supposed to enlighten them on the subject as they take their painless glimpse of the Middle Kingdom. Sometimes I wonder if these occurrences are not ridiculous, if I am not losing control of my days by being an authority on China.

November 26, 1982, Hong Kong to Honolulu

My back is painful. I am happy to get on the Singapore Airlines flight and be on the way home. It is a pleasant flight, made the more so by the fact that just as I am getting off, one of the stewards, whom I had not noticed until then, came up and propositioned me.

December 23, 1982

My daredevil streak seems to be a settled trait. Leave things until the last moment if you can? Just to see what happens? Dance as near as possible to the brink for the sheer hell of it? Draw extra joy from sex when danger is present? A pity all this gives you such pleasure. But what a threadbare celebration of negative satisfaction.

1983

January 8, 1983, Cambridge

Be happy in what William Morris said makes us happy. Working hard at things we want to do, savoring the rest and satisfaction that follows, making something beautiful for friends. Feeling useful in a worthy cause.

Morris has been called a visionary. But he was no escapist. You have to work, and you have to take care of yourself in this world, and Morris insisted we live at full-tilt and meet things head on. "Take trouble," he said, "and turn your trouble into pleasure: that I shall always hold is the key to a happy life."

During the second half of 1983, Terrill made two long overseas trips: the first to Indonesia and Australia to lecture for the US government; later to Japan and China for another lecture cruise, this time on board the Royal Viking Star.

October 1983, Dalian

A lovely warm October morning. As the seven hundred passengers of the *RVS* went on their tour I walked up Stalin Street and around the town. A notice greeted me at the port. "Cherish the flowers and grass and trees and greenery to beautify the city." A little farther down there was another one: "Discuss cleanliness, discuss public morality, discuss courtesy." A notice in the main street: "For the Four Modernizations, Train the body; For the Motherland, Win Glory." Is this fascism?

I went into a photo shop, decorated with landscapes, potted plants, and slogans about the definition of a good boy; all backdrops to having your picture taken. In the suggestion book, most of the comments seemed to be praise, but there was one curious one from a college student who seemed to be just omitting a cry of triumph: "came here to get my picture taken because I'm going abroad to study and I'm very happy."

A pleasant massage by Mr. Tao in the Dalian Binguan. He had to be coaxed to concentrate on my ass but eventually he did so with a little less timidity than I expected in this city of few foreign visitors. He'd been in Switzerland working as a barber and masseur for the Chinese embassy there for four years. I think I can get him to improve the performance next time.

In Stalin Street a guy in a pajama-like outfit with a baby girl on his shoulder got into an altercation with a woman in street clothes. She was thin, with glasses. He was more solid and plain. I couldn't hear what they were saying because they were really shouting fast. I didn't want to get too close out of embarrassment.

She said, "Why did you hit me then?" and rushed at him and shook her fist without touching him. Soon she was hitting him with a big shopping bag that had something heavy in it. He began to kick her as she still held the baby, and he still held a child. (That was the great difference from a scene which could otherwise have been in any country.) A crowd gathered, including soldiers. For some time, no one physically intervened.

In the square a guy came to talk and announced himself a teacher of politics. I said I suppose that means Marxism and he said yes. Do you agree with it? He said he did; I said I didn't. Economically, I said, it's been a failure. He said what is often lacking is a "deep understanding" of Marxism.

I suggested that at least one member of the G4 that "deep understanding" and how much good was that? He said remember how backward China was. I said after World War II so were Japan and Korea and Singapore and Hong Kong, and look at them all today.

October I, 1983, Xingang, China

It's a beautiful morning as the *Royal Viking Star* pulls into Xingang, though I'm apprehensive about the visa until I actually have the badge with my bus number pinned on. The China Travel Service guides are good. Less awkwardness and self-advertisement than last year. However, they tell a few lies. There is no question of bonus or punishment with family planning, they say. Education is free in China. Medical care is free. Students may choose their own jobs after graduation. My God.

It's a hundred and eighty kilometers to Peking, one chirpy guide announces. "We have the best driver in Tianjin, so we'll be there in a shake of a lamb's tail." Actually, it turns out to take four and a half hours, which is a lengthy shake of any lamb's tail. The chief guide says that the legal marriage age is twenty-two for a man, and twenty for a woman. In general, it's a post-1976, but a pre-December 1978, message.

Can I recapture some of the excitement of my 1964 trip? Passengers ask me about when I first came; I try to think back. It is possible some of the excitement is there—for the first-time visitor. Some of the things that move these people who have just come to China moved me on my first visit, and would move me again if I were in their shoes. Family-mindedness. Conformity. Rectitude. Making do with little. Naivety about the non-Chinese world.

October 1983, Peking

At Tiananmen Square, the same piles of building materials outside the Museum of Chinese History. I never realized just how tawdry are the photographs of the Great Men in the Square. A new one has been added, of Sun Yat-sen, which is interesting, but it's the same makeshift affair on a wooden scaffold. The back of it, fronting onto the Monument of The People's Heroes, is a mass of unpainted wood sticking up in all directions. The portrait looks as makeshift and temporary and unconvincing as Peking's entire set of proposals to Taiwan for "reunification."

A slightly more modest touch from the guides these days: "Tiananmen is one of the biggest squares in the world. Some people say Red Square in Moscow is bigger. Some say that Tiananmen is bigger."

At the Jianguo Hotel, just as last year at the Yanjing, and also at the Qian Men, I am allotted an end room—easier for bugging.

The Chinese people are obedient. I watch the evening TV and read the news and it's all a performance. Where the "news" comes from has no relation to the people below.

Mingming feels he is suffering by being outspoken. On issues of foreign policy, he speaks up at staff meetings. Often others agree with him, but they don't speak up and they advance ahead of him. He's not been given the really top job, which is interpreting in US-China relations. He's been given African work and he's going to India next week for the India-China border problem talks.

What are the issues that he disagrees about within the Ministry? He mentioned the Hu Na case.[155] "It was stupid. Deng is an obstinate man to make an issue of it. He made a collision with the Americans inevitable." I said I thought it might also have been mishandled at the Washington end and he didn't really disagree with that.

He feels that Hu Yaobang and Zhao Ziyang differ from Deng on the Soviet Union because they don't have Deng's personal experience of bitterness with the Russians. So

---

[155] Hu Na (1963-), professional Chinese tennis player who defected to the U.S.

he feels that Deng's passing would produce more openness to the Soviets. He doesn't think it will go far for the moment.

We discussed the Philippines and he said that in China of course no one can say anything about that because the Marcos regime is so important to China. On points like this he sounds like any young foreign service officer frustrated that things aren't more ideal. He agreed with me that perhaps China is more stable than the Philippines or Indonesia.

Curiously enough, on Hong Kong he thinks the Chinese government has gone about as far as it can go. He thinks the present leaders are prepared to leave Hong Kong alone. Later that evening, He gives a critique of my now-famous-in-China *Atlantic Monthly* article.[156] He said, "You criticize things that are actually better now than they were before, and you didn't criticize them before." He said I seemed a bit grudging about saying that the reduced spitting in the streets, and so on, was good. The courtesy campaign is good. Why do I sling off at it?

Mingming urges me to keep on writing about China. Write a letter to Hu Yaobang,[157] he says, and tell him what you think about China's future. Maybe, before, because I was tying my letter to a difficult request, it made Hu less likely to listen. Mingming said that if they wouldn't take notice of you, who understands and is fair to China, who would they take notice of? He asks about Boston. He clearly has part of his heart there. He said his present boss is beginning to think he's too pro-American. I said, well, are these hardcore alligators really any more patriotic than you? Are they serving the Chinese people more than the cosmopolitan Chinese are?

October 1983, Peking

Shen doesn't look any different, but he conveyed more frustration than I expected. He seems desperate to get to the United States and said he is considering desperate methods. Part of this is just that he's not patient enough about Western application procedures. Heavens! If *he* isn't after his years in Australia, imagine how much more difficult it is for those with no taste of anything outside China. His frustration at work has bubbled up again despite the fact that objectively he seems to have made quicker progress than the norm. He sees lazy older men everywhere. He says to get a PhD in China is almost a lifetime affair. And you can sense between the lines all the horrible licking of asses that's involved.

He said he could resign his post but in China that puts you into a terrible limbo. No car, no place to live, nothing. He really thinks that someone like me can help more directly than I am doing now. He quotes an example of a friend of his who was acting as a tour guide and met a professor from Texas and the friend ended up as a graduate student at Austin. Of course, Harvard doesn't work quite that way.

I pushed Shen to ask himself why he wants to go abroad again. He says he wants to fulfill himself and a graduate degree abroad is the best way to do it. I don't think he foresees staying away permanently. He is a patriot. On the other hand, he's possessed of

---

[156] "Trying to Make China Work," *The Atlantic Monthly*, July 1983.
[157] Hu Yaobang (1915-1989), high-ranking official in the PRC.

this stubborn desire for self-fulfillment that puts a strain on his patriotism. He's given up on making a new application to one college because he got angry with them for asking him to send a copy of a term paper he wrote, apparently at Canberra. Truculently he said, "It's my only copy. Are you putting everyone through this kind of procedure, or is this just a special demand upon me?"

Meanwhile, he's a TA to a visiting economics professor at the institute. He's gone beyond language teaching, though he still doesn't have qualifications in economics. He's even going to teach some of the basic economics course. He's got a small room of his own in the city which he can use for lovemaking.

He pulls out thirty yuan and asks me to buy a dozen cassettes in Hong Kong. I'm going to buy the cassettes, but I didn't take the money. He said the cassettes are for him to record the American economics professor's lectures, so that he can listen to them again in preparing to teach the same subject himself. I didn't ask whether the institute should not supply cassettes for that purpose.

"A fat man can't understand the hunger of a thin man," he says. He would have put that in his letter but he didn't want to be so blunt. Of course, he's right. Shen sees individual self-fulfillment as something that is maddeningly elusive to him. When he was complaining about the Western academic application procedures, he said he's had it up to here with the Chinese bureaucracy and he really can't stand having to go through that sort of thing with Western bureaucracy as well.

October 1983, Peking

I found Sun on the Saturday night. First, I got his sister and left a message that I was at the Jianguo Hotel. Next morning, I was sitting down to breakfast at seven o'clock when he appeared at the table. We were both so overcome with the shock and pleasure of seeing each other again that we could eat nothing.

He looks excellent, though he complained a lot about his situation. He worked for a while interpreting for his factory manager but got replaced by a girl. I suppose he could be difficult to get on with in certain circumstances. Also his pronunciation—Chinese as well as English—is sloppy at times.

After breakfast, we went upstairs. I noticed there were uniformed officials near the elevators and they did check one guy who was just ahead of us but they did not check Sun. In the room we fell upon each other and ended up making love in the bathroom. I felt more comfortable there because I was still unable to get out of my mind the possibility that police might burst into the room or come through the window—and if we were in bed together at such a moment God knows what would happen. Sexual tension plus political tension—the combination is extraordinary.

We relaxed in armchairs afterwards. The sexual tension had been released and the political tension, if that's the word for it, was somewhat dissipated by the fact that with our clothes back on and sitting in armchairs, we were not susceptible to any surprise attack by the arm of the state. He was thrilled when I gave him the copy of Van's guarantee letter. I made copies downstairs. He took two and I kept one for myself.

Tonight, I realized that I do want to go back to Peking, and to other parts of China, and that quite a bit of my present revulsion has to do directly or indirectly with the Jiang Qing project. After all, I want to see Shen. I want to see Sun and others. This puts the CET project in a much better light than I felt it to be that tired Monday morning when John and Max and I conferred.

October 18, 1983, Peking

A cold snap, causing high winds delayed us getting into Xingang.[158] I had two badges— one for each group—and I was able to go with the group which, under the emergency plan, was having the one night in Peking. The second group, alas, went up and back from Peking, twelve hours in a bus, and stayed their one night on Chinese soil in Tianjin. A nightmare. As a bonus I shared a room with Richard Chin, an attractive, svelte Hong Kong Chinese who represents Royal Viking Line at the Chinese end.

I phoned the American Embassy and happily they got the Telex. Unhappily they got it late. But Charles Freeman's secretary said it was much better to have got it, even late, and been able to give the protocol department of the Chinese Foreign Ministry an explanation of why I hadn't turned up for vice foreign minister Zhou Nan,[159] than not to have got it. She also had a message for me from Richard Rigby, an Australian diplomat.

There was a message at the American Embassy that Minister Zhou Nan had arranged to see me this morning. Chen Mingming heard about this—one of his colleagues was to come to the Zhou-Terrill session—so there he was as I arrived at the Foreign Ministry. After I finished with Zhou Nan, Mingming was at the gate ready to jump into my car. We drove to Hua Du Hotel for dinner.

Zhou had filled out a bit, but in style he was just the same. "How are you, Ross?" and so on. He didn't like the notion of China being treated only as a regional power, that Schultz expressed in California. I said the idea came from Wolfovitz.[160]

Zhou betrayed not the slightest doubt about Hong Kong. He said that when he was in New York with the foreign minister, he had dinner with Vance and Schlesinger (during the evening Kissinger also popped in). Zhou sat next to Schlesinger, who said— and apparently Vance had the same opinion—that if they were the British, they would accept immediately the terms the Chinese are offering.

Zhou Nan knew about my Jiang Qing book and did not show nervousness. In fact, he insisted that I send him a copy. He and the interpreter both laughed a bit at the title. Zhou Nan said reforms are working in the countryside; implication was now the task is

---

[158] Formally, Tianjin Xingang, i.e., Tianjin New Port, 170 km southeast of Beijing is the largest man-made port in mainland China.

[159] Zhou Nan (1927-), Chinese politician and diplomat, who was First Secretary and Counsellor to the PRC's delegation to the United Nations. At the time of his meeting with Terrill, he had returned to Beijing to engage in preliminary talks with the British government regarding the return of Hong Kong to Chinese rule.

[160] At the time of Terrill's conversation with Zhou Nan, Paul Wolfowitz (1943 -) was Assistant Secretary of State for East Asian and Pacific Affairs.

to tackle industry agriculture. He said that unless there is progress in getting rid of the "offensive" Taiwan Relations Act there will be very serious crises in US-China relations.

Our problem, I told Zhou, is we simply don't know how serious China is about Taiwan (just as people outside America don't know how serious we are about the Russian threat). I said I was more worried about Hong Kong because of the date.

On Hong Kong, Zhou said sovereignty is not negotiable. "We'll leave the economic system unchanged; we'll change the legal system only a little bit." He insisted China will not accept a new unequal treaty with England. I said I wasn't worried about the British, but the five million people in Hong Kong, and the image of China in the world if the thing is mis-handled. I said many Chinese may leave. He said grandly: "If some run away there'll be plenty more to come there."

On the Russian question he said, "Why not trade? You people trade with everyone; our trade with Russia is only a sixth of our trade with you." He doesn't think that relations will get that good. "We've arranged ten students to study in Russia; how many students have you Americans got in Russia? Of course, more than that."

I said, "We've noticed that you don't any longer call Russia a revisionist country or speak of a capitalist restoration there." He said, "Well, we are only interested in their foreign policy, and we don't like that."

I asked about Huang Hua's statement, that "Brezhnev was an outstanding statesman." He said, "That's just politeness on the occasion of a funeral."

In Zhou's talk, there was absolutely no theory. It's all been dropped, whether it's the "three worlds", or the relation of aggression to a social system, or whatever it is.

October 19, 1983, Peking

Mingming says Hong Kong will be ruled essentially by the Hong Kong Chinese. His starting point is the valid one that they are already the real power in the colony. But there are two problems. The umbrella of administration permits those Hong Kong Chinese to be ambiguous in their allegiances, which is just what suits business. Second, if there was a rise of the spirit of self-government and democracy in Hong Kong after British administration ceased, this would be an intolerable cancer within the PRC.

Jealousy and revenge—two big themes in Chinese life. Our driver doesn't want to wait for us in Wang Fu Jing, and then another one doesn't want to go to the Temple of Heaven because he's heading in another direction, and a third one feels it's too close to lunchtime to do any work at all. Sun feels we can't help all this. I get angry, feeling that Sun is putting himself in the position of a supplicant.

He said, "Ah, these are our presidents"—referring to the taxi drivers—"these are the presidents, and you can't do anything with them. They get behind the wheel and they think they're God."

I promised a copy of *White-Boned Demon* to Mingming and to Zhou Nan— extravagant, but I think I'll have to fulfill both. Sun did not want long goodbyes. We sat on the museum steps for a while, I wrote a few postcards, and then we quickly parted.

October 20, 1983, Peking

As soon as Shen came into my hotel room, he noticed that once again I had an end room. He said it gleefully—a connoisseur's fascination with spying—but he also suggested that we go downstairs to talk.

He still pushes me a bit about helping him get to the States but not constantly, and so we just talk about our lives. He was trying to find out if Miss Hu had given any indication in Hong Kong of how much she loves him. Not to me. The pair are probably drifting apart, and they will become "good friends" in the next stage.

December 31, 1983, Boston

Tonight, the uppermost thought is of thankfulness that my health has picked up since New Year's Eve 1982/83. That night was miserable my fever came back, and I was unable to get out of bed to meet Michael and go to the TV studio party. I lay there, hot, lonely, resentful at the world for going ahead in merriment without me. That I am back to a near-normal life would not in any other year be notable, but it is this year. Will my health continue to recover? If a major setback is in store for me, perhaps it will have "declared itself" (to quote my doctor Susan Gordon) by the end of 1984.

Still not able to fill the gap left by Pan. Or is promiscuity my only way? At present, there are two friends who are much more than tricks: Sandy T; Edward T.[161] Apple and banana.

1984

January 1984, Boston

He cannot converse. He is sometimes silent. Other times, he lectures the circle he is in. On yet other occasions, he answers questions as if he were a guest on "Meet the Press." But the equal give and take of conversation is beyond or beneath him. Did Harvard do this to me?

The middle-class washes before lovemaking; the working-class washes after lovemaking.

January 20, 1984, Melbourne.

The *Melbourne Herald* has a sharp quote about the writer Alan Morehead: "Like Sidney Nolan, he is attracted to Australia as a subject home, but he can only reach it in the atmosphere of another world." I also feel this.

---

[161] Edward T, who was bi-sexual and later married a woman whom Terrill only identifies as Arlene, was one of the most significant, long-lasting relationships Terrill had.

January 21, 1984, Melbourne

Saturday morning in Murrumbeena: a high blue sky with satin clouds. One moment January heat, the next, autumnal cool. Gardens, flowers, lawns, neighborly politeness. When you look closer, an almost aggressive complacency. "We like our life here, please don't tell us there is anything wrong with it."

"Have a good day" has crept into Australian usage. I knew Australia had changed as I heard that beer consumption has been going down. I telephoned the International Phone Call Information Service to ask about area codes for the US and for Thailand. "Sorry, there's a work ban on giving out information at the moment." Amazed at this, I asked if that information would be somewhere in the phone book. "I wouldn't know, dear." The voice was not unpleasant, but firm.

On this visit I feel an extraordinary familiarity about everything. The sight of the trees, the feel of the air, meetings with cousins and nephews and nieces. The very phrase "wildflowers" brings on a blaze of memories. Lying in the grass to gaze at a single blossom. The mad chase to find one's favorite variety of marigolds.

L'Express magazine in Paris has just come out with a special issue that declares Australia the country of the future, the Eldorado for our epoch. Perhaps if I can't have Australia, the substitute will be my Australia book that Pat and Barbara in NY very much want me to do.

David, a producer at Australian Broadcasting Corporation says to me of Australian academics and officials: "You unsettle them. And you lack credibility with them. They do not doubt that you can do this and that, but they doubt you want to do these things; they think that the real springs of your being are different from the realms you talk to each other about. It is this which makes you a threat to them."

Lovely Broken Hill is predicted to be a ghost town by 2000, following mining collapse in Kalgoorlie and Mount Isa. Each farmer is responsible for the employment of seventy people, whereas mining is just technology in the desert; Australia is a quarry.

January 23, 1984, Australian National University, Canberra

A job interview—I think the first of my life. The job, for which they flew me here to be inspected, is head of the Contemporary China Center. I spoke for quite a long time. We discussed access to China. I made it clear I thought we should be tough. The fireworks came when Tom Millar asked about scholars trimming their sails in order to get back to China. When I didn't answer it in personal terms, he then brought it around to my case. I said I had not been thus motivated.

Jamie Mackie then took up the point and said it was a question of whether my writing had been geared to the government of the time. I said my books weren't about the government—for the government or against the government; in the case of the book he was mentioning, *Flowers on an Iron Tree*, I said that it was a descriptive book.

Mackie said he was also "worried" about passages in *The White-Boned Demon*, especially direct quotations that may not have been based on sources. I said there was a very firm line here; there are no direct quotations that are not accounted for. I did mention that there was a more difficult line, where I say that she was thinking such and such at a certain point of time. I said I had decided I knew enough to make those assertions in this book. (Actually, it's the first time in my published writing I've done it.)

I got in a few jabs at their lack of knowledge of China and their lack of equipment to head this committee. When I was referring to Wang Jiaxiang,[162] the husband of the source of some information in *The White-Boned Demon*, I said: "Some of you will have heard of Wang." I threw in the observation that people trained in the social sciences have reviewed the book warmly.

The notion that people outside the field, who haven't read your work, bring you halfway around the world supposedly to discuss your work is amazing. The record of the reviews of *Mao* and even *Flowers* (and soon *White-Boned Demon*) is of a large section of the Sinological community praising the books. I said I thought the era of polemics should be over, but the latter part of the discussion proved that in Canberra it is not over. I glanced down at the publications lists, as they droned on about style and minor points in my own six books plus three edited books. Tom Millar has done a current affairs bulletin. Someone else has an article in the *Far Eastern Economic Review*. A distinguished historian has done a memorandum to a committee—these are the publications of the ANU staff.

Jamie never got to the issue of what light has been thrown by *White-Boned Demon*, or what is new in this book; I suppose he couldn't. Only that he was "worried" by the style, or had his "doubts" about the methodology. Isn't it the main point of books to throw new light? Do they care about that issue?

January 24, 1984, Canberra

At dinner in the Bistro, a well-dressed man in a suit is slicing his bread and there are a lot of crumbs on the table. "Sorry," he says to the waiters, "I can't seem to avoid the crumbs." Then he adds, "You should have a competition to see if anyone can cut the bread without crumbs." The waitress brushes up the crumbs. "Oh, never mind," she says. "Anyway, if we had a competition everyone would cheat and try and brush the crumbs away so that I wouldn't be able to see them." Australian backhanded politeness, and with it Australian backhanded self-deprecation.

January 26, 1984, Melbourne

David says to me of Australian academics and officials: "You unsettle them. And you lack credibility with them. They do not doubt that you can do this and that, but they doubt that you want to do these things; they think that the real springs of your being have to do with realms other than those they are talking to you about. It is this which makes you a threat to them."

---

[162] Wang Jiaxiang (1906-1974), an early senior leader of the Chinese Communist Party and China's first ambassador to the Soviet Union.

Australia has aspects of the numb-to-history complacency of South Africa, and yet this place has become the site of a fantastic ethnic mix and experiment. Which will win out?

At Melbourne airport, rose gardens, manicured lawns, the smell of gum trees and the chirping of birds. In America, urban life impinges on rural; in Australia it is the converse. In the suburbs of Melbourne, you can feel yourself in the countryside. The flowering plum trees that line the residential streets; grass everywhere; the sound of birds; the blaze of flowers; and when the cars go by it is with the swish of a car on a country road.

In Australia you still find the butcher shop. Red neon lights against the meat in the window, green fernery, water rushing down the glass. And inside, the smell of sawdust and blood. I buy the chops that have been ordered over the phone, and the butcher presents them to me with hands red from blood.

January 28, 1984, Melbourne

I like the phrase in *The Australian* about the "joyless blanket of Presbyterian socialism that has descended over the garden state [of Victoria]."

One of those Melbourne summer days where it pours with rain one moment, an intense sun burns the next, and a cool breeze replaces the sun five minutes later. The days are long, and at 8:30 PM it is still broad daylight.

I go down to Pokey's in Fitzroy Street, Saint Kilda. Hundreds of gays crowd into the upstairs rooms of the Prince of Wales Hotel. Many are smoking, but among the drinks there is lime and soda and Coke. I like the atmosphere, but almost no one is attractive to me.

There is a new hair style: hair swept up to the top, giving a narrow look, and a look of eternal surprise—is it a copy of David Bowie?

The entertainment guides in Melbourne are adjusting to gay activity. Here is an ad in the *Melbourne Herald* for a program at the Waltzing Matilda Hotel; "It's drag, deviant, dazzling, diabolical, delightful, but never, never dull." At some places where different nights have different clienteles, the gay night is called "Rage Night."

January 30, 1984, Melbourne

At the Richmond station a bill posted on the wall: STOP THE ASIAN INVASION, followed by three points: stop the mass migration of Asians, stop cheap Asian imports, stop Asian-American business firms. How many people feel this way?

February 3, 1984, Melbourne

A Chinese immigrant to Melbourne wonders where all the people are! But he loves the big public gardens, which Hong Kong doesn't have. "When you ask people for directions, they will sometimes take you where you want to go." He's amazed that men give up their seats in trams and trains to women.

He and his family became intoxicated with the Australian dream of a house and a piece of land. Now he looks back to Hong Kong only with nostalgia for making money. "But if you have a Rolls Royce in Hong Kong you have to have a chauffeur. And if you mow your own lawn everyone laughs at you; in Melbourne I mow my own lawn and no one laughs."

February 5, 1984, Melbourne

My old friend Creighton Burns, editor of *The Age*, had dinner with the Prime Minister alone after the 1983 election. They've been close for thirty years since Oxford days. Hawke said although he had kicked the drink problem, he had in no way surmounted his desire to fuck women. Said Creighton to me, "I know if he and [wife] Hazel are in a house for more than a couple of hours there are fireworks."

Top colleague Bill Hayden no longer snipes at Hawke, and in return Hawke seems to have accepted an independent role in foreign affairs for rival Hayden. One day, Bob phoned Creighton, and Creighton quoted Hayden and the Prime Minister said, "Fuck Bill, I don't know what the hell he's up to." This to the editor of a major newspaper about his own Foreign Minister.

A story set in Peking. A China International Service Guide, tired of his set recitations to tour groups, one morning departs from his text. He speaks about agonizing moments in his life, ultimate questions, sex fantasies that most delight him, and asks probing and playful questions to the passengers about these same themes. By lunchtime he is arrested. His friends have never seen him again.

February 7, 1984, Murrumbeena

At Murrumbeena train station I ask for an "inner city ticket." The clerk waits for me to say more. "What kind?" I express my ignorance; he explains the various kinds.

"It's complicated, isn't it?" I said.

"Your bloody oath it is." We laugh. And then he looks at me with a smile and says: "Real bloody progress!"

February 8, 1984, Aboard Pan Am, out of Sydney

As we approach Auckland, Mark Sperling, a schoolmate from Wesley College and our army days, comes to my seat for a chat. He extols the competitiveness of America. Lives in Columbus, Ohio, and says he would never have achieved what he has if he'd stayed in Australia. Most of his talk is about money, houses, swimming pools. He said his memory of me during our time in the army was that I was cynical about the military and perhaps about Australian culture in general. I have no memory of having such an outlook.

On Pan Am 812, an attempt to catch up with Australia. The menu announces for dessert: "Pureed passion fruit in a delicate mousse made with eggs and fresh cream." It arrives; all those words have been expended in order to describe a simple Pavlova!

At Auckland airport, every second man, young or old, looks like a sheepdog. Americans are discussing their visit to Australia. "Canberra's so beautiful, I do hope the people there realize just how beautiful it is."

February 14, 1984, Boston

Edward came in and the world spins again. He said he hadn't been to the gym much and was afraid his body had deteriorated. Grabbing him, I said it had improved. Indeed, his beauty, charm, and rascally personality got at me more than ever.

Meanwhile my "half affair" with Sandy T may be over. With his inimitable sincerity Sandy informs me that after I went away, he put an ad in *Phoenix* for a friend, found one, and now thinks he may have fallen in love for the first time in his life—with a classics-turned-law-student from the South.

February 16, 1984, Boston

I do not want, for the rest of my life, to read *People's Daily*. Or to have to drag my way through *Red Flag, Peking Review* and other turgid rags. Or for the thousandth time to greet a dull, opportunistic delegation visiting from Peking.

March 7, 1984, Boston

Pat calls (while I am in bed with Tim). Thrilled to get my letter about the *Los Angeles Times* review of *White-Boned Demon* and the credit I said was due to Pat for this. "It's the book I take with me, show to people, give to agents I want to impress." She wants to do many books with me. "This is only the start, Ross." Won't I come down to New York and talk with her about the future? So, we fix a dinner for Wednesday.

When I push her on orders and sales, she is not that encouraging. "Frankly, there aren't as many books out there as I would have liked." But she thinks *Demon* will sell over time. "Something happens with this book almost every day."

March 8, 1984, Boston

My agent Barbara Lowenstein[163] calls to say the film option for *Demon* isn't yet closed, but the reason is not bad: a second offer has been received. One is from ITC, apparently a big and good outfit. They want a six-month option for $2500, with two more similar renewals; $75,000 if the show is produced, to include being able to consult me on this & that.

Other offer is from Richard and Esther Shapiro, who did "Dynasty" and "East of Eden." They want a one-year option for $7500. They have in mind a 3-hour show, $100,000 if it's produced, $25,000 of which would be for consulting with me. The pot boils; we'll see in a few days what Barbara and Joel, her sub-agent on the West Coast, decide.

---

[163] Often abbreviated in the Diary as BL.

March 14, 1984, New York

At Pesca, with agent Barbara Lowenstein, Pat is expansive. "So how does it feel, for the professor to make it on to the TV screen with his *Madam Mao*?" She and Barbara seem close. We tackle Pat on publicity timidity but don't go far because Pat says she herself has been "shouting" at Leila and can't get results. The "one thing in life" Pat most wants is a cloth doll Jiang Qing has embroidered in prison.

Afterwards, Barbara and I go for a drink. She wants me to ask Helen Rees[164] about a possible sub-agent deal. She is clearly thinking of giving Morrow world rights for *The Australians* to "get all the money up front." Barbara may have a crush on Helen

She feels my *The Australians* outline is good, but says I don't grasp how outlines should be written; in each chapter outline you must say what is covered; everything should be in full sentences, not notes.

March 15, 1984, New York

Dinner at the Harvard Club with Mike Bessie[165] in good form. As a publisher, he announced, after reading my two outlines—*China on My Mind* and *The Australians*—that he'd like a crack at the second.[166]

March 16, 1984, Boston

Dinner with Edward at Copley's. Whenever a Black waiter appears, the two greet each other with "brother"; I've grown used to it. At the next table is a talkative girl with her parents. Edward can't take his eyes off her, not I think out of attraction, but out of fascinated contempt for how she is carrying on. "She talks too much. You know why, Ross, because she's not getting fucked. That's why."

A little later, as we were eating strawberries and whipped cream, Edward added: "What's probably happened—she's only been fucked by white guys, who just don't know how to do it, and the result is that the poor girl just talks without stopping."

At a lunch party I hold to mark the demise of myself and other writers as Contributing Editors of *The Atlantic*, Bob Manning, our chief editor, tells Ward Just[167] of an incident last week with Gloria Steinem at the Nieman Foundation at Harvard. Jim said to her that he'd heard speculation about her sexual preference; would she comment. I was pouring a drink for Robie [Macauley] and Pam [Painter][168] and got the story mixed up: Gloria asked Jim the question! "What on earth did Jim say?" we all wondered. No reply. Ward nearly fell off his chair with amusement at my inspired mishearing.

---

[164] Helen Rees (1936-2015), leading literary agent in Boston.

[165] Simon Michael Bessie (1916-2008), senior editor at Harper & Row.

[166] *The Australians* was published in 1987. *China on my Mind* was eventually published as *China in Our Time: The Epic Saga of the People's Republic from the Communist Victory to Tiananmen Square and Beyond* (1992).

[167] Ward Just (1935-2019), American novelist, short story writer and war correspondent.

[168] Robie Macauley (1919-1995), an American writer and editor; Pamela Painter, his wife, a short story writer and teacher of fiction.

March 23, 1984, New York

Two days of promotion of *White-Boned Demon*. Very nervous the night before the "Today Show" but fortunately I slept well. Leila picked me up and we went to NBC for that early morning ritual of coffee, makeup, and tension. I wore the yellow tie that Edward bought for me yesterday at Filene's[169] (despite doubts as to its suitability).

Just as Jane Pauley was about to begin my segment, she said that she'd been busy and had not read a single page of the book. What a start; it knocked out *whatever* punch I had in me at 7:30 in the morning. But the millions were watching so I took a deep breath and pretended she hadn't told me that. Leila said I was excellent; the random sample in the waiting room are the best test, she said, and they liked me.

March 25, 1984, New York

The radio shows—Sherrye Henry, Murray Farber, and others—were among the best I've ever done, I think. So much for the TB.[170] Melinda, who escorts me, turns out to be like Diane Muller of Little, Brown, though nicer. "I own land in Vermont." As soon as she said that, I knew I was dealing with one more publicity assistant who is in publishing for the "glamor," doesn't care deeply about the marketing of books.

March 30, 1984, Boston

The New York trip followed by a night with Edward and Hank seemed to do me in. Since then, a kind of anxious ennui has enveloped me. My soul seems to need a new, excellent review of *Demon* every day.

The Chicago *Tribune* review pleased me; *The New Republic* piece was as interesting as could be expected from Merle Goldman. Boston lags. No reviews yet. The Harvard Bookstore doesn't have it in the window, but merely two copies chastely filed in alphabetical order. The two Paperback Booksmiths in Boylston Street do not have it at all—nor does Dalton's in the Prudential Center.

Meanwhile, I am on the Los Angeles Times Best Seller list for the second week in a row, and Barbara phones to say that the *Hollywood Reporter* this week has a story on the Shapiros' having optioned the book for filming.

A fantastic night with Edward. Fucked him and then slept well. For some reason—whether real or tactical—he said next morning that he regretted he could not fuck me. "It's just that it isn't equal." I reminded him that he once remarked that some people like doing it and some like getting it. Moreover, it's a nice balance that he fucks Arlene and I fuck him.

April 4, 1984, Boston

John Fairbank got the bound proofs of *White-Boned Demon* but "didn't write about it" because he felt "the topic went out of his depth." That hasn't stopped him reviewing

---

[169] Filene's was a venerable Boston department store founded in 1881.
[170] Terrill came down with a case of tuberculosis, which was treated during most of 1984.

other comparable books in *New York Review of Books*. Did he suggest Liang & Shapiro to Bob Silvers as the reviewers of the book? He read their piece, he said, when I pushed him on it; he recalled that they felt I had been too creative over dialogue, etc. I told him I had sent a reply. "Good, the more discussion, the better for the state of our field." Is that all he cares about, the state of our benighted field? Not truth, by any chance?

April 5, 1984, Boston

Lunch with Jim Carroll[171] at the Back Bay Bistro. Gail Banks is nearby and Jim introduces us. She reminds me brightly that she was once a student of Asian studies.

Jim's new novel, *The Prince of Peace*, has been bought by New American Library. A substantial sum, though less than they gave for *Family Trade*. Jim is "relieved." How odd that even when the hardback publisher gives a huge advance, and the author is as successful as Jim, there is still a worry on the author's part lest the paperback sale be "too small for the book to make any money."

Barbara Lowenstein phones with a cheery greeting: "More good news." A Japanese first serial sale has been made to *Gendai* magazine of the Kodansha company. She feels that soft tactics toward Morrow and disappointment over their publicity efforts for *White-Boned Demon* are correct; in the very long run she may be right.

Both Anne[172] and Justin Kaplan seem keen about my proposed book on Australia. Is it only that they would be keen on me doing anything other than one more book—China—that holds no interest for them?

April 6, 1984, Cambridge

Farewell party for Jim Thomson as Curator of the Nieman Foundation at the American Academy of Arts and Sciences. Bob Manning is an excellent MC. John Fairbank speaks eloquently of Jim. "I have liked him because he has an office near mine; and I hope in the future he will continue to have one near mine." Jim in return spoke affectionately of his "29 years of harassment" at John's hands.

A bartender looks at me intently, then finding me alone near his table, hisses: "To see someone you have been to bed with talking on the 'Today Show' with Jane Pauley is amusing." He grins, and soon has to turn away to prepare a drink. We did play around once behind the lockers at the YMCA.

April 7, 1984, Boston

I have always been happiest when secure in my own magic garden; in the future I must be faithful to that lesson. On this calm Saturday morning, I love being alone. I savor the prospect of getting into the Australian book—a new magic garden, where for better or for worse, no one will follow.

---

[171] James Carroll (1943 -), Boston-based American novelist and historian.
[172] Anne Bernays, wife of Justin Kaplan and novelist in her own right.

April 13, 1984, Boston

Lunch with Pam Painter at the St. Botolph restaurant. We talked about Edward—the first time I have done so with a straight. She was fascinated and could not leave the subject. "But hasn't he made a commitment to you?" Oh dear, that gap between the straight and gay worlds.

"Have you ever lived with anyone?" She asked the question as if it would be amazing to behold me in domesticity.

She feels that after *White-Boned Demon* the logical next step is not the book on Australia, but the Hong Kong novel. However, unlike Justin and Anne, she hasn't read the outline for the former. And unlike her, I don't have a "husband" to pay the bills while I write just what I like. We were talking about love and attraction and youthfulness, and she said wistfully: "I should stay thin for Robie, but I just don't."

I don't think she understood my point about feeling revolted by being an intellectual. She, being a straight woman, and never deep into academia as I have been, doesn't feel the tension I do between the hedonistic life (represented for me now by Edward) and the monk-like life of the writer.

April 14, 1984, Boston

A wonderful morning of sex with Herbert; I shoot half a cup into his fantastic body. It may be our last, for he confesses to me that he is a prostitute and HIV-positive. That night when we first met on the street, and he came in here and we fell on each other, I had no idea he was a pro. It is true that, despite his fantastic dick, he lacks depth compared with Edward. But I will never forget the joy of this morning, deep inside him, as he twists his body around so that I fuck him in a scissors position, watching his matchless dick and grabbing his balls as he jerked himself off at the same moment as I poured myself into him.

April 15, 1984, Boston

Edward didn't come at the appointed hour. Chris rang the doorbell. I asked him in. We didn't do anything much (and that in the closet off my study, as Chris gets terrified of people seeing him through the windows). But I had it in the back of my mind that when Edward came, I would go ahead with something, all together, should Chris and Edward want. As it happened, Chris said he wasn't interested (though I could see his mind gradually changing). Later Edward said he wondered if Chris's presence had really been accidental. I said it was. But actually, I could have told Chris to go away as soon as he appeared at the door—have done it before—so Edward's guess was partly correct.

Edward dozed off and I went out for a pizza. We ate it upstairs by candlelight. He doesn't want me to feel in competition with Arlene. But a moment later, when we are talking about his "woman lover" and his "man lover" as apples and bananas, he says, can't one prefer one fruit to another? If so, of course I must feel in competition with Arlene.

Each time we make love, which these days means me fucking him, he manages afterwards to make a reference which suggests that there's some kind of inequality involved? And asks when is he going to fuck me. As we munched our pizza and sipped Molson beer, he said he told Reggie at the weekend, "You know, I'm sex crazed."

Several times, in bed and out of bed, he said he loves me. He also said he wants an "unrestricted" relationship with me. He does not seem to feel that love with a man is as encompassing as love with a woman. This is fine, as long as there is a deep trust between us, and the social dimension progresses.

He still longs for a perfect sexual foursome, where everyone likes to do everything. "Fuck, get fucked, suck dick, suck pussy—they're the basics." But I think he now realizes that the prospect of he and I going on that kind of heavy double date is very remote. I adore him, and the orgasm last night, deep inside him, was mind-blowing. After the sex, we lay in the half light, gazing into each other's eyes and chatting quietly.

April 16, 1984, Boston

A Mr. Charles McCarry from the *National Geographic* phones to ask me a nice question.[173] He and his fellow editors have just read my new book, are deeply impressed by it, and wonder if I'd accept an assignment from them to go to Sichuan Province and write a piece? About six weeks there, all expenses plus a "good fee." It's tempting; postpone the next book a year, do this and feel freer for a season, before starting the mad cantor of book-writing. I'll go down to Washington next week and talk it over in detail with them.

April 17, 1984, Boston

I ran into Edward at the YMCA after playing squash. He looked at me intently in the sauna. Only later, as I glanced in the mirror, did I realize why there had been a flicker of a smile on his face: a huge nest of his fresh love-bites (from last night) disfigures the right side of my neck.

Arlene was waiting outside. She complained about Edward. "He knows what to tell everyone else to do, but not how to order his own life. Is he like that with you too?" She thinks the Shawmut Bank job he is applying for would be good for him. I do, too. Certainly there would be more room for promotion than at the IRS where he is now. Perhaps Arlene puts up with him out of the same motivation as drives me—sexual passion. I saw in her eyes what perhaps she sees in mine: a fear that Edward may be captured by the Other One.

April 18, 1984, Boston

A New York woman named Lynn Phillips phones to say she has written a screen play about the Gang of Four and would I read it! I did read it and it is clever, vivid, and funny. The problem with mounting it, she says, is that in today's theater if you use one race

---

[173] Albert Charles McCarry, Jr. (1930-2019), writer and editor-at-large for *National Geographic*. As they became friendly, Terrill referred to him as "Mac."

(whites, in this case) to play another (Asians, in this case) you get sued. Yet audiences "wouldn't go to see Orientals sing and dance all evening."

Melinda and Leila from Morrow both phone with plans for publicity in Washington, California, and Philadelphia. Why the burst of activity? Guilt? Has a third printing been ordered? Has Larry Hughes[174] given a nod on behalf of the book after all? Well, the author is the last to know why publishers do what they do.

April 23, 1984, Cambridge

We decide to eat "formal", so Edward brings round a jacket and tie. First, we make love. Then, sated and relaxed, we dress in our finery and go to Apley's. An excellent meal. Edward cruises one of the waiters. Yet he is far more restrained than I used to be when cruising boys in Pan's company. He can control himself, it seems, so I do not get upset.

We talk about the Mexico crisis (his parents are up in arms that he is planning to go for a holiday with "that man"). To my mind, there is no easy solution. I and his parents haven't met; how could they trust me? And if we did meet, it might become apparent that Edward and I are having an affair. But Edward has made up his mind— he is coming to Mexico regardless of his parents' wishes. Apparently, they think he will arrive back from Acapulco in a plastic bag.

When we have finished breakfast, Edward reads the *Boston Globe* and finds a review of *Demon*. I retreat into the study to shuffle papers. At length, I cannot bear the suspense and so return; dressed in underpants.

"Why did you spend two years on this woman, Jiang Qing? After all, you hate women—why did you do it?" I told him that Jiang Qing, as a (straight) willful conformist, seemed analogous to myself, as a (gay) willful conformist.

April 25, 1984, Cambridge

I go to Edward's, where he and Glen are finishing breakfast. Glen, an old friend of Edward's, is quite different: plain, overweight, slow, alarmingly religious—but no doubt solid and a wonderful friend to the mercurial Edward. "You two are like knives that sharpen each other," Glen said to me.

According to Glen, Edward had a very bad period last year; some people hurt him; since he's met me and Arlene, he's a "new person." How extraordinary that Edward who, like me, loves sex and could not do without it, is closest of friends with this man who apparently never tastes its joys.

Leaving Glen, Edward and I went off to Filene's and Jordan Marsh's[175] for blinds and curtains for my place. What Michael, my mother, and many others failed to do— persuade me to cover some of my windows—Edward has succeeded in doing. He's

---

[174] John Lawrence Hughes (1925-), president and chief executive officer, William Morrow and Company, 1965-1985.
[175] Founded in 1841, Jordan Marsh was, along with Filene's (both located on Washington Street), the other venerable Boston department store.

generous in such things; just as in rushing out to buy me two ties the afternoon before my appearance on the "Today Show."

Suddenly in Jordan Marsh we run into Arlene! She is with a girlfriend, strolling during their lunch break! If she "didn't know" before, seeing Edward and me buying curtains might have pushed her over the brink. Curtains for where, after all?

The ambiguity that arises from Edward's bisexuality can be unnerving. But it is preferable to the total non-ambiguity of the 100% gay. I think I would never trade my occasional insecurity over Edward (caused by my envy of him?) for the self-hatred of the total homosexual.

We walk toward Government Center, where he is to pick up his last check from the IRS and I am to collect money from the sale of Standard of Indiana shares at Stock Cross. He asks if no one else has told me that I walk too close to someone I am accompanying in the street. Rachel, my dear Australian friend, said she'd heard that Australians do this.

April 26, 1984, Cambridge

The Bookshop show goes splendidly. A big crowd, some 40 books signed, and Channel 5 not only turns up but makes a great segment of it for the 11 PM News. Who should be there but Arlene? She comes up with a copy of *Demon* and asks me to sign it.

Joan Colebrook,[176] who is great company at the dinner given for me by Jill and Hong at the Golden Pavilion in Chinatown, says I was quiet. It was out of tiredness—I still find speaking exhausting—and perhaps a touch of sadness at Edward's absence. I am in bed at midnight when Edward phones from Hartford. His cousin has undergone a four-hour brain operation which seems successful.

Idiot Glen told Arlene that Edward could never love her because he is gay, and he fears committing himself to anyone. He feels if he should cast off one of us—Arlene or I—he will cast the two of us off together.

May 7, 1984, In flight to Mexico

Pan Am takes off for New York and Mexico City; our holiday is really on. Edward has brought twice as much luggage as me, though he is dressed in a baseball cap as we check in at Logan. During the flight I realize he is hungry, the unmistakable sign of which is that he gets quiet and grumpy. At Kennedy Airport we have quite an early dinner in the Pan Am terminal, though I content myself with onion soup and white wine.

He has not told his parents that the trip has come about. Arlene knows, however, and yesterday she helped him with shopping for the trip and lent him two towels and a half-used bottle of sun-tan lotion, which Edward said is particularly suitable for Black skins.

---

[176] Joan Colebrook (1910-1991) Australian American writer, author of *A House of Trees: Memoirs of an Australian Girlhood.*

We got out of the plane and bought a magazine called *Forum* for the flight from Houston to Mexico City. It is a somewhat bisexual magazine, ranging from science to pseudo-science to letters about exciting sexual experiences.

One article asks whether Blacks have better sex than whites. We read it together as the L-1011 bumped and waved its way over the Gulf of Mexico. In Boston time it was 2:30 AM when we entered the Maria Isabelle Sheraton Hotel. We unpacked and showered, then made fantastic love. I have fucked Edward many times, but I doubt that the ecstasy has ever been so intense. I apparently screamed out too loud, even though Edward had taken the precaution of putting the television set on, and he brutally clamped a hand over my mouth during the latter stages of our synchronized orgasms.

It was toward 5:00 AM Boston time when it seemed we were going to sleep, but he began again. "I would like to suck Ross off," he announced. Soon we began again, and he asked me to fuck him. As usual, he came by his own hand just as I came inside him. Within a few minutes he was snoring, but I was quite unable to sleep.

Later we resumed, and then when I did come against his dick, he cursed me. "Fuckhead," he said. I've learned to take these things not too seriously. But there is a touch of egoism about him in bed, just as there is a strain of unselfishness at other points. I just excited him to a stage—while we were writhing on the floor—where he could think of nothing else but getting to his orgasm. He said next morning: "After all, you attacked me."

Edward reminded me of Pan in how long he would take to get organized, and how vague he was about time when traveling. Eventually, after breakfast in our room, we walked down toward the Museum of Anthropology. It lives up to its expectation, as far as the exhibit goes; I'm not sure it's "the most beautiful museum building in the world," though the structure is bold in a stark, modern sense.

Edward insisted on dressing up for lunch, and it was an excellent idea. He had on a white jacket, white trousers, and a beautiful see-through white shirt. I wore a white jacket and pale gray pants, and the dining room was extraordinarily elegant, with a piano player. I drank copiously of white wine and we talked about homosexual love.

At one point he asked me again if I would ever get married, and when I explained again the situation he said; "I knew that, but to hear you say it again brings the reality of my situation home." Of course, the ideal to him is that I would get married, he would get married, and we would continue meeting on the side.

At the top of the Latin American Tower, I cruised the elevator boy and even felt him up. Edward was amazed. He looks but almost never acts. I can see that he is indeed quite shy (many Mexicans are shy too, in a different way and for different reasons). If only for this reason, I do not feel the slightest bit jealous when traveling with Edward.

God, how different it is traveling alone from traveling with a lover. The constant feeling of looking out for a man is almost totally absent when I'm traveling with Edward.

At night, Edward asked me many things about the past and I ended up telling him quite a bit about Pan. I also told him the story of David in Cambridge, and the janitor at 1737 Cambridge Street, and of making it on a plane from Beirut to Paris, and on another plane from Manila to Sydney. These things he loved. Actually, his interest in my relating bold sexual adventures had been expressed before, but it was new when he said: "You know I'm getting very interested in this person Pan."

May 8, 1984, Mexico City

Tonight, the idea was for me to rest, but we ended up both going down to the health club in the Sheraton. Later he came up to the room and found that I was not really asleep. We attacked the refrigerator; he had margaritas, I had beer, and we ate peanuts and bags of Doritos and Mexican snacks.

One thing led to another, and soon I attacked him on the floor. This led to a rather strange kind of lovemaking. He was in ecstasy, but he wasn't in a mood to reciprocate very much, or wait for me, and so in the end, although I went up his ass, I did not have time to come before he exploded and collapsed.

May 9, 1984, Mexico City

We decided to fly to Acapulco, rather than take the bus, and thus get onto the beach by mid-afternoon.

We walked in the Zona Rosa, which begins across the road from the Maria Isabelle Sheraton and it reminded me of parts of Paris: boutiques, a slightly Bohemian atmosphere, a pleasant mixture of commercial and residential buildings. Edward became fired up about purchases, produced a pen and notebook, and while I looked around me, mainly window-shopping, had his head down making a list of who he had to buy gifts for, with possible items opposite each name.

The flight to Acapulco was a dream, the crew was pleasant, the aircraft was almost empty, and the flight passed over spectacular scenery.

Acapulco was to produce surprises. The Mexican men at the airport were more attractive than those in Mexico City. Then there was the drive to our hotel, long, rough in the sense that we were in a poorly-sprung station wagon with a number of other passengers, but surpassingly beautiful. We saw Acapulco as we drove in, first the charming village of Puerto Marqués, and then the various beaches until we came to the Zocalo and eventually to the Boca Chica Hotel, where we had reservations.

Within an hour we were on the beach between the Boca Chica and the Hotel Caleta. Edward loves to take a lot of things with him: a blanket, two pairs of sunglasses, various things for the lips and the skin and the hair, and of course the large-toothed comb.

In the evening we dined at a small restaurant in the Zocalo area which the best of the guidebooks had said was very good. Actually, it was medium, but the disturbing thing was that we were the only people there. Seemingly out of some sixth sense, Edward took a disliking to it, sending back his pina colada and changing tables from the one at which we had been put, in a tropical garden with birds and plants, from which beetles fell onto out plates, to another in the front of the restaurant.

We ate a dinner of seafood, which was pleasant enough. Then we went walking in the Old Town, but after a while Edward could not stand the stink. Then he raised the question of a gay club, and soon we were speeding in a taxi toward Peacock Alley. It was the third time in his life that he'd been to a gay place.

Peacock Alley is delightfully decorated, with lights in the form of palm trees, mirrors, and an excellently equipped disco. Edward was in a fantastic mood, and I went on drinking with him, mainly Tequila sunrises. He was utterly unlike he is in Boston, where he would never touch me, or be touched by me, in public. His shirt was open to the waist, he was leaning against me and grabbing me—in a semi-public situation for the first time in our relationship.

A song called "You Make Me Feel Brand New" came on and I told him that it had been a theme song for Pan and me. I could see he wanted to dance to it with me, but after long consideration, he said, "I just could never do a slow dance with a man." A little bit later on—and one black Russian as a follow-up to the Tequila sunrises—he asked me if I would dance with him. A quicker song had now come on, and we danced together. I've seldom seen him so happy.

May 10, 1984, Acapulco

This morning, following a rare sound sleep on my part, I awoke to find Edward looking around the bed. He had momentarily lost his glasses. When he found them on the floor beside the bed, he said "That's problem number two solved." Problem number 1 turned out to be far more serious. He had had diarrhea in the night. It has continued intermittently throughout today and this evening. I had slept so well that I was not even aware of him getting up and going to the bathroom. He ate breakfast, a cheese omelet, which might not have been wise. He should have stuck to liquids and a thing called pan tostada that I bought for him at a corner grocery—but he insisted on the omelet.

We took a boat to La Roqueta, a small island adjacent to the hotel, and there we swam and climbed a mountain and took pictures of each other. But on the way up to the lighthouse, Edward did not seem well, and in the end, he had to sit down halfway up and wait for me to go up alone.

Much of the day was spent in the room, and I took a snack of the various dry objects which I had bought for him. In the late afternoon, he brightened up a bit and we made love, though only I came, not he, and there was no question of adopting our normal methods.

I dined alone on the beautiful terrace of the Boca Chica restaurant, on grilled fish in garlic sauce, preceded by a ceviche, and supplemented by a bottle of Mexican dry white wine.

Unfortunately, Edward had lighted upon an article in a *Playboy* we had with us about AIDS. He became morbid. Of course, it's a morbid subject—but this was not the right day for him to read up on this subject or for the two of us to discuss it.

May 11, 1984, Acapulco

Edward did not feel much better, though he does not have a fever. I prepared to go alone to Condesa Beach. But he decided to come. He managed physically to get through the day.

A Black guy from Bermuda called and with him we parasailed, which is fantastic. You are strapped into a belt attached to a parachute that is in turn tied to a motorboat.

You run a few steps down the beach and then are hauled into the air; you spin around Acapulco Bay high in the air under the extended parachute. Edward went first and I followed him. A photographer took a picture on takeoff and on landing

You would never have thought Edward was sick. After that, he went for a long swim and it was then that I met two boys, who were diving off a boat moored near the shore. I went out to the boat, a perfect place for a bit of secluded activity, and the three of us played around.

Edward had come into the water to hold my hand and even to fool around. Alas, I didn't realize this. Later he was hurt, and thought I'd turned him away because I was busy with the two boys. This impression must have been reinforced when a few moments after I had returned to our things on the beach, the two boys came up and put some tan lotion on my back—as I did on theirs. At this time, Edward was just standing by.

I urged him to come home and rest. He felt that I was tearing him away from something that might have been pleasant, culturally if not erotically. I went off to meet Maxwell alone and we arranged to meet later. When we all met later, he was in a kind and charming mood. He had come dressed in my Chinese shirt, a gift from Tom Gao, which was a gesture to me no doubt. We walked through the Condesa area, window shopping and looking for a place to eat.

Alas, he became ill soon after we sat down at an open-air steak restaurant, wonderfully situated with the ocean just over the railing beside us. We cut it short before we had eaten much and got a cab home. His fever seemed to have risen; his stomach was painful.

May 12, 1984, Acapulco

Edward was physically so miserable that I don't think he realized that it was hardly a coincidence that the friction coincided with the onset of this tourista. And I suppose I was not really able to hide my disappointment that he had got sick, or even my feeling that his own habits may have led to it—having dirty fingernails and sucking them as well as putting them in various other places including my asshole.

On the bus to Condesa in the morning, I met a young guy called Victor, who was on his way to work. The ease of this contact surprised Edward. I asked Victor to call the hotel at 10 PM that evening. But at 10 PM, we were just walking into the restaurant for our abortive festive dinner on the last night in Acapulco. Edward brought some records of his favorite songs, and I would dictate notes and thoughts.

One pity about Edward's being sick is that we had been enjoying the meals tremendously. He is a delightful dinner companion, because he appreciates the food, and is rather easy to please. Most things he finds delicious; he is more adventurous about alien foods than most American Blacks.

How much I envy him his ability to sleep. He is capable—when not ill—of sleeping within minutes of putting his head on the pillow, and this is something I have never been able to do.

When I came down to the pool to dictate, he looked at me with big, wide eyes, streaked with some bloodshot, and asked me what I was going to write about. I said only that the ending would be, "I love him."

The overriding impression of our relationship on the trip: gratified amazement that he can fit in so well to what is essentially the holiday of a pair of gay lovers. You would hardly know, and no one that we have talked to would likely guess, the "other side" of his life. He is certainly among the more complex and extraordinary people I have ever been close to.

May 13, 1984, Boston

To sleep alone last night, for the first time in a week, was delicious. And to read in peace, turn off the light when I wished, simply to be in my own home with its comforts and familiar things—this gave me pleasure. How conservative I am becoming!

May 16, 1984, Boston

My dinner party last night to welcome Joan Kennedy back from China went well. Joan was vivacious as always (she drank no alcohol at all throughout the evening). But she didn't have much to say about her China trip that was new or interesting. The honorary degree next Saturday is the big thing in her life for the moment. She is hoping Ted will attend, but that is not certain.

The Fairbanks were in fairly good form, and cordial, though John talked mostly to Fox; I feel that my book on Madame Mao has brought some cloud between John and myself. Fox said that the English reviews of his book, *China: Alive in the Bitter Sea*, were the best in any country.

May 17, 1984, Boston

This morning I felt depressed. I felt scaringly lonely. After spending a week with Edward in Mexico, I have hated being without him for days. The excitement of giving the dinner party for Joan did not remove this emptiness. In fact, I think Edward's absence from the dinner—I didn't invite him—took the sparkle off my own mood. I was suddenly overwhelmed with non-enthusiasm for my coming trips to Washington, the Far East, and Australia, which are going to separate me from Edward. I cried, which I have not done for a long while.

Edward is anxious at my depression. In the evening, he comes in. Immediately he announces he wants me to come to his place. This is fine with me. I suggest a celebration, for he's just got the news of a permanent job at the bank. Sure, he declares. In fact, at his place the ingredients for a celebration do not exist. Rotten meat; no drinks.

Mexico was dreadful, he says, except for the culture. He will never go anywhere again as my guest. I manipulated him. He wants me to know—what a sledgehammer manner he has at times—that a man can never mean to him what a woman can mean. I guess I am meant to feel ashamed of myself, and ashamed of being gay.

At this point, I should have denounced him and left. But, sad and torn, I sat there and said little nothings. Later he took my hand and led me to bed. There we briefly made love. I did not sleep well. Something seemed wrong—as on the last night in Mexico, lovely as the sex was then—in doing it after an abrasive conversation.

May 18, 1984, Boston

Work on my Washington speeches. God, is it all worth it, these long hours of preparation?

May 19, 1984, Boston

I give a small party for Van Long, who is visiting from Washington. I try to set aside my disappointment that Edward did not want to come. Curt looks ravishing, and his friend Jan, who lives in the same building, is charming. Michael and Ray seem a bit miffed about Edward—both that I am preoccupied with him, and that they have not yet met him. Of course, the latter is largely Edward's doing. Still, racism lurks very near the surface of their resentment at receiving less attention from me than from a Black guy.

I do not have Edward; yet no more do I have the same true relationship with two close friends—because of Edward!

May 20, 1984, Boston

Edward comes in, looking wonderful. It is fantastic to be with him. But bit by bit, he gets on to his "problems." I become unnerved. Eventually I say: "I don't want to be cruel, but I don't care whether you have the party at my place or somewhere else." I was echoing his remark about me going off to meet Maxwell in Acapulco.

"Do you echo me in this way deliberately?" It is deliberate, but quite without any malice. He echoes me, too, I think, in beginning occasionally to say sorry when he does something he regrets, which I often do, but which he never used to do.

Eventually he said he was sorry. "I'll spend the night with you. I'll get up early and leave, so you won't be late for your plane to Philadelphia." We went to dine at Thai Cuisine, after things stabilized themselves. During the meal, he did not go back to the conversation we'd had in my bedroom, though I tried. When we returned to St. Botolph Street,[177] he said will he come up, and I said why not.

May 21, 1984, Boston

It is a golden morning and as I prepare to go to the airport my spirits are quite good. It almost seems a blessing to get away from Boston and try to lose myself in the external world of interviews and meetings. If nothing else, the trip to promote *White-Boned Demon* might be good for my sagging ego.

---

[177] Terrill lived at 200 St. Botolph Street in Boston's South End, not to be confused with the St. Botolph Restaurant, located a few blocks away at 99 St. Botolph Street, where he sometimes dined.

May 21, 1984, train from Philadelphia to Washington

Philadelphia, I loved as always. The narrow, historic streets. A feeling of camaraderie in the air. The beautiful bodies. I did my morning shows, escorted by the pleasant but ignorant Eileen. But I could not take my mind off Edward. By early afternoon, I felt I had to have some relief from the tension of the shows plus the anxiety over Edward.

Pleading to Eileen the excuse to briefly meet an old Harvard friend, I shook her off, went to the Club Baths, and made tempestuous love with a Black guy—the one I could find who most resembled Edward. He sucked me wonderfully, then jerked me off and I shot over his beautiful chest. I hated this even as I enjoyed it. Does Edward understand that he propels me into such situations which are infinitely less preferable to me than devotion to him? Anyway, this helped me take my mind off Edward for most of the rest of the day in Philadelphia.

May 22, 1984, Washington

The city is a riot of green foliage. Howard picks me up at Union Station, after a restful train ride during which I planned my Face-to-Face speech on "Reassessing China." He has a copy of *Spring Moon* in his hand, and his professorial air has grown thicker. With Carl, we dine at a restaurant near their house in Chevy Chase.

It isn't easy to talk about gay matters to both of them together. Only with Carl; for Howard's approach is to pretend that their relationship is simply a marriage, and that the gay world doesn't exist (except perhaps as an intriguing minor strand in history).

All day, I spent in Howard and Carl's apartment preparing my lecture for the evening's face-to-face dinner meeting. My theme was really Jiang Qing and her relation to the Chinese political system. The work paid off; many compliments. The director of the program said I was "candid, witty, and engaging," and that my appearance was "a feather in our cap [at the Carnegie Endowment]."

Going into the Carnegie building, I ran into Dick Solomon,[178] who was in town for "my government stuff." He said the Chinese keep asking him, "Why is it that Ross Terrill has turned from a friend of China's into such a critic?"

In between times, much telephoning to New York over the climax of the negotiations for a contract to write the Australian book. While I am at Howard and Carl's, the matter is decided. I will transfer to Simon & Schuster. Fred Hills will be my editor, the total money will be $75,000, if all goes well with drafting the details of the contract.

Now I'll have to write a difficult letter to Pat, my wonderful editor at Morrow, who wanted the Australian book, but apparently couldn't persuade her boss, Larry Hughes, to back it as much as Hills is prepared to. Still, these days there is not much feeling of guilt about switching from one publisher to another. Moreover, in making the decision for Simon & Schuster, I cannot overlook that Hughes had been lukewarm about *White-*

---

[178] Richard Solomon (1937-2017), American diplomat and scholar. At the time Terrill was writing, he was head of the political science department at the Rand Corporation and had recently published Chinese Negotiating Behavior.

Boned Demon—until it got three book club adoptions. Happily, in this case, feelings between Pat and me should remain good, since *Demon* has done quite well, and Pat is proud of it.

May 23, 1984, Washington

A confirmatory chat on the phone with Hills. He finds the outline "superb." He wants a bit more on culture; urges a narrative approach. He says the whole of Simon & Schuster is "thrilled" to have me on their list.

At night, Van and Mark take me out to dinner at Marrakesh, a lavish and unusual Moroccan restaurant in the seedy downtown area. Eight of us sat around on carpet-covered benches in front of a copper table and ate Moroccan dishes. During the early part of the dinner, I tell stories about sex encounters in Casablanca and Marrakesh, and this loosens up the party. Perhaps until then some of the guys had wondered if I was gay or not.

Later, on the phone I get the bombshell from Edward that he may be going away for the weekend with Arlene. The news cuts me like a knife. He did not come to the party for Van (though he was in town). Sunday night he declined to go to bed with me, saying he had to be fresh for his first day at work the next morning. "But at least I am not going away at the weekend," he said then.

From Van's place, I said to him on the phone pathetically, "I need you. I want you." He rejoined that for me to talk like that was making him feel guilty. Perhaps, but justifiably or unjustifiably?

May 24, 1984, Washington

A speech at the All Saints Book luncheon—everyone is thrilled, and I sell and sign many books. Mrs. Echols says it's the best program the organization has ever had. "You had the audience in the palm of your hand. You simply charmed them out of this world."

Jenny is there, and we reminisce about Australia. Since her divorce, she is living alone and hates it. She asks me if I like it. I can't answer properly, because a straight woman like Jenny can't understand the "twilight" situation of a gay who often has someone sleeping overnight, and has a special friend—with whom he is much closer erotically than are most married partners. It was amazing. One after another, people came up and said it was the best talk they'd ever heard!

I escaped to Van's, took a shower, phoned New York yet again, and prepared for my broadcast with Susan Stamberg on "All Things Considered." She was ill-prepared, unfortunately, but I tried my best to make up for that. While I was in the National Public Radio building, I had a call from *National Geographic*. A warm telex has arrived from Chengdu, saying, "Ross Terrill is welcome to Sichuan," and that my visa will be ready in Hong Kong on June 3. I murmur "Excellent."

In fact, I have mixed feelings. If things go on like this—with me absent half the time—it will be difficult to show Edward that I love him, need him, and want him. Certainly, I can blame only myself—not Edward—for this state of affairs. Perhaps I shall cancel the whole *National Geographic* project, make the quick trip to Taiwan, then come back to Boston?

Mark drives me over to Bob Barnett's, where a small cocktail party in my honor unfolds. Murray McClean from the Australian Embassy is there. Like me, he resists most of Bob's optimistic ideas about how China and Taiwan will smoothly get closer until they unify. Even Nick Lardy seems a bit naive on this question. Nick has the interesting news that Peng Di, who is leaving his post as Xinhua chief here, remarked to him that if the US side "carries through" on technology sales to China, the Chinese side is prepared to keep pretty quiet on the Taiwan question. During the cocktail party, he conveys the information to Don Anderson, head of China Affairs at the State Department, for the US Government's consideration.

Don said the Chinese are pushing to have their trade cases exempt from having to pass through CoCom.[179] So it is that one thing leads to another; declare them a "friendly, non-allied nation" and they draw a logical conclusion from that. You can't blame them.

We go to dine, joined by Nayan Chanda[180] and his wife, both from Delhi, at the Chevy Chase Country Club. A lovely building, poor dinner service, reasonable food.

Happily, Nayan is very bright, and both he and his wife are splendid company. But all I want to do is drink a bit of wine and then go and fuck somebody. I was anxious to get to a phone and talk to Edward, and also to link up with Carl to go and see the club he recommended. After an eternity, I got away and returned to Van's. I dialed Edward. He said he had bad news and good news. The bad was that he and Arlene are going away for the long weekend. The good was that, "I'm going to make this up to you next week. Now I really want to do it—I've made a decision." Despite the second part of the message, I'm afraid I felt like a jelly. I called Carl, having made up my mind that I would have to cope with this by a mindless spree. We drove in Carl's open convertible to "Bachelor's Mill" on Capitol Hill.

I was late meeting Carl at the corner of Porter and Connecticut, but after a bit of silence he forgave me, and we had a good talk about many things. He suggested that it may not be a bad thing that I will have a separation from Edward soon. "Won't it test the relationship?" So easy to say that. So hard to lie in bed alone (or with another), night after night, without the one you think the world of.

Bachelor's Mill is informal, mixed, just as I like it. Not long after midnight Carl goes home. At this stage I go out of the club to phone Edward again, in the quiet of a phone booth in the balmy warmth of the street. Earlier in the evening he'd said there was something else he had to tell me which "you won't like." I said, please go ahead and tell me. But he felt he was "under pressure" and would rather I phoned him again later. Well, the piece of news was that he dropped by my place and made love with Melvin. No big deal. I hope they had a great time.

---

[179] The Coordinating Committee for Multilateral Export Controls (CoCom) was created at the end of World War II to put a trade embargo on Communist countries.
[180] Nayan Chanda (1946-), at the time, a correspondent and editor of the *Far Eastern Economic Review*; co-author of several books on Southeast Asia and globalization.

Back inside the club, I have no intention of going home. First, I am with John, a guy with large sentimental eyes and a conservative manner. I love his wet kisses. By 3 AM, I am with Damion, at home in his bed, within the Episcopal Church where he is a priest. At 4 AM, I am wandering in a large park not far away, still cruising, still fleeing from myself. My mind is full of scorpions; my loins will not stay quiet. By 5 AM, I am at the Greyhound Bus Station in the seedy downtown. It is dawn before I return to Van's and fall into bed for a couple of hours sleep before my final morning's book program in Washington.

May 25, 1984, Washington

Lunch with Ann Bailey,[181] who is charming. I do what I can to help her with her project on Zhou Enlai's widow. Then my book signing appearance at Crown Books, to which Ann drives me. The assistants in the shop are gorgeous. When they hear from my accent that I am from Down Under, they send out for Australian beer to please me. Many people come in for an autograph without any intention of buying a book. This irritates me, but I sign for them if they are good looking.

May 25, 1984, Boston, later

On this Friday night, I am tired and lonely. Memorial Day weekend begins and, expecting to be with Edward, I have contacted no other friends. I drink a bottle of wine and fall into bed.

May 26, 1984, Boston

Not long after breakfast, Suk comes in, takes off his clothes, falls into bed. Throughout the morning we stay there. I give him my best. I receive from him that gift of calmness, that lust for the other, that total union in trust, which I want with Edward.

At night, Hank is at once haughty and affectionate. We discuss my trip to Taiwan, and his eyes gleam. He keeps saying he is exhausted and has to go home—that he just wanted to say hello and kiss me. Eventually, on the landing in front of my apartment door, we fall upon each other. He tears off my towel, which at 1 AM is all that I am clad in. He entices me to stick my dick through the wooden bannisters that lead down to Erwin's apartment. Crouching down a few steps from where I am thrusting myself forward, he sucks me. Soon he rushes up to the top of the landing and whips out his dick, which is even huger than I have ever seen it before. A telegraph pole, brown and hot and rigid.

June 2, 1984, Boston

For three days, Sun, just in from Peking, and I danced a strange pas-de-deux. I suppose the gist of the situation was simple: we both felt guilty. I, that I no longer felt as

---

[181] Ann T. Bailey, co-author with Thomas V. Litzenburg, Jr. of Chinese Export Porcelain in the Reeves Center Collection at Washington and Lee University (2003).

passionately for him as I did in Peking, and before I met Edward. He had not told me about his growing relationship with the Frenchman René. So we maneuvered to see who could blame whom. There was no quarreling. But I tried to elevate the factor of René, and Sun tried to elevate the factor of Edward. Of such are the dealings of lovers and ex-lovers made!

One night I took Sun to Buddies and Chaps.[182] "Won't we be arrested?" he enquired. He was simply amazed that the "government doesn't take any notice of this sort of thing." The dancing fascinated him. He wanted to stand in a dark corner and just watch the dancing. He wouldn't leave. Nor would he come out of the shadows and dance or meet others. He was riveted to the scene, as an observer, hardly more able to join in the scene than would a man from another planet.

Last night, after Edward and I had dined at Newbury's Steakhouse, I took him over to meet Sun.-But we didn't talk much; the mood was not right.

I later learnt that this morning Sun told him that Sun and I had slept together last night! How the Chinese go to extremes—from excessive furtiveness to excessive frankness. My main concern now is that if Sun does indeed leave for France, he probably won't be able to get back into the USA. I told Sun this; does René know—does he care?

June 3, 1984, Boston

I am departing this afternoon for Los Angeles, Taiwan, and China. So much has happened in the past week or so—no time to write much down—that I am now almost trembling with emotion and fatigue.

Edward and I have just said goodbye. Last night, Sun and I said goodbye. The day before, Tim and I said goodbye as he set off for Philadelphia. In all cases, lovemaking was part of the scene. Sometimes I think I am emotionally an unguided missile.

Of course, it is Edward who counts most—perhaps too much. Sun's entire visit has been handled by me within the shadow of Edward. And yet at times I feel that Edward is so unstable about his gay streak that I am in a tight, blind relation with a phantom.

For the umpteenth time, he has changed his mind about his 25th birthday party. As of this morning he is not having it at all, anywhere. We sat in the front room and drank a bottle of champagne. He snapped a picture of me in my Japanese dressing gown. I began to feel I wanted that moment of getting on the plane to come right away...

After Edward leaves, he phones three times, first from his apartment, the next two times from Arlene's. Am I alright? I try to answer. In a way I am, and relieved to be going. But I feel like a jelly. I ask if he will miss me. "Yes, I miss all my friends." The terror of a gay commitment. Really, can I live with it much longer?

June 28, 1984, Chongqing

The guy from near Canton, whom I've been furtively carrying on with in this rambling hotel, comes in this evening. It's difficult to arrange a meeting with Hu,

---

[182] Popular gay bars in Boston's Back Bay neighborhood.

because I am in and out a great deal and he has a roommate who wants to know where he is every moment.

Hu is thin, graceful, good-looking. He seems to be traveling in Sichuan on business for a rural company based in little Shentou, in Guangdong . I noticed him on the balcony one stiflingly-hot evening. He was dressed in a singlet and light blue trousers. I looked at him intently, especially his curved ass, but I didn't realize that he was interested in me. However, when I got back to my room, he was standing on the balcony just outside my door. I invited him in. No sooner was he in the room than he sat down on the bed and eagerly, hotly made himself completely at home.

Unfortunately, on that first occasion, I simply did not have the time or the mental tranquility to do much. My assistant Yang was waiting to go over the day's notes, and I was expecting his knock on the door at any moment. Hu kept murmuring two things. "Too good, too good." And: "It's such a big one, it's such a big one."

Next time, Hu insists on talking in the middle of making love. Are you married? Are there many people like us in your country? I keep telling him not to talk, partly because I don't like a lot of conversation at that stage, and partly out of prudence unless anyone is listening.

He'd like to exchange some money, he announces, "Chinese yuan for either foreign currency or the funny money. I'm saving up to get married, and for us Chinese a motorbike is important as a preparation for getting married." This remark hung in my mind for the rest of the evening.

June 30, 1984, Chongqing

Hu, the Cantonese guy, comes in again as arranged. He is nervous, but elegant in his way. Everything we had agreed to do we did. He wrote down his address and reiterated that when I am visiting Canton, I should write to him first and tell him where I am staying and the dates; then he will come to Canton.

As regards the foreign exchange, he wanted to see the American dollars first. In some countries this would be a slightly risky thing for the traveler to agree to, with a stranger, before the money to be exchanged had been produced. Here, not the slightest problem of that kind. In fact, he had brought a roll of grubby Chinese yuan with him. The amazing thing was that he had no idea of exchange rates, no idea of the function of the funny money, no conception of what an American dollar is worth, or even what it *is*!

When I showed him American money, he said, "How do you turn that into foreign exchange?" I said, "My dear Hu, this is foreign exchange, these are American dollars."

It was not that he did not believe me, but that he seemed unable to conceive of money other than Chinese yuan as being money. I'm reminded of the stories about the PLA soldiers when China was liberated in 1948-49, coming into the cities and lighting their cigarettes with money. They had been used only to a rural and military life and had no conception of the value or use of money, even yuan. Hu had an abstract notion that foreign exchange was valuable for his purposes—that's all. "How much money will this get me?" he asked of the forty American dollars he held in his hand.

With a feeling of helplessness I said, "Look, if you don't understand anything about the money or foreign exchange in general, it might be better for us not to change money." But he wanted to, and he absolutely trusted me, which there was no particular reason for him to do. So, I tried to explain what he could do with the American dollars, and it was just what he had in mind to do. He asked me what it was worth in Chinese yuan and I said 89, but I would take 80 from him. He pulled out the 8 ten-yuan notes and we made a deal.

Before we made love, I wanted to wash hands. But no, the Chinese feel that if they wash themselves once a day that is perfectly fine. A mere foreigner is not going to sway them from the habits of millennia. We got down to business in the usual way. Soon he had to rush off because of potential questions from his roommate. The roommate was taking a bath and Hu could only stay away for the approximate time it took him to have the bath.

"If this guy ever found out what you and I were doing, he would report it to our boss immediately—he's that kind of guy." My goodness, one has to admire Hu for the risk he took with me.

July 1, 1984, Chongqing

It is Communist Party anniversary day and I'm leaving Sichuan for Peking. Until we got to Chongqing University yesterday, there had been nothing these past two weeks to remind me of the Party anniversary. But there at the university, with the professor explaining that people were busy preparing for the Party meeting, and with the fact that all but one of the people who came to talk to us were Party members, we suddenly got a dose of politics.

As we drive to the airport, Yang talks about Hu Ping, a Sichuan man who was elected at Peking University in 1980 or 1981 to a People's Congress, as a spontaneously chosen candidate. His slogan was freedom of speech, a very carefully chosen, limited goal. There were others, says Yang, who chose topics like "Is Mao a Marxist?" for their campaign debates. Hu was more careful, and more effective.

Leaving the US last month, Yang brought a letter from friends in New York to Hu Ping, the gist of which is that if there is anything we can do to help you, either in personal or in larger matters, just let us know. Hu is at the Steel College, married, and is fairly cautious, but a lot of people come to see him. However, these people do not include foreigners. Yang wants me to look up a friend of his in Peking. He is called Chen and has a wife and child in New Jersey. "But he is one of those—how few there are!— who does not want to leave China."

July 4, 1984, Boston

Unreal to be back. Peking one day and St. Botolph Street the next jostles the spirit. Late at night, coming back from a pizza snack in Huntington Ave, I run into a guy called Cornell on the steps of Symphony Hall. He quickly accepts my invitation to come home. Cornell is a student preacher for an evangelical sect. This does not render him totally otherworldly. I put my hand casually on his knee. "If we are going to make love, I must go to the bathroom first." He is in the bathroom before I can open my mouth.

July 5, 1984, Boston

Edward looking wonderful, comes around and we eat at Newbury's Steakhouse. After dinner, we come home, but he doesn't feel like fooling around. He'd been with Arlene during the afternoon; perhaps he was worn out.

Cornell came in a few minutes after Edward left. I had promised to listen to a tape of him singing, and if I liked it, recommend him to people who might help with a recording contract. We went to bed and listened to the tape at the same time. It was really too late to listen to this "gospel jazz" but Cornell insisted. For my part I insisted on staying in bed. One thing led to another and soon we were making love while listening to Cornell's singing.

Regardless of our activity or position at the start of a new song, Cornell would announce to me the biblical text that the song was based on. He sucked my dick, while periodically lifting his mouth off, turning his face toward mine to inform me, for example, that "The Gospel of St John, Chapter 5, Verse 3" is the text for the next song whose lyrics began to crash through the moon-lit room.

July 6, 1984, Boston

Lunch with Curt Anderson[183] at the Bangkok. His eyes are even more beautiful than usual. I am impressed by his practical wisdom. He must have faults, but I cannot see them. He takes it for granted that my affair with Edward won't last. He sees an inherent "instability" in a three-way situation. He doesn't want to see me hurt, he purrs. Of course, he doesn't really know enough to venture such a judgment. Yet he is a shrewder and more detached judge than many—including Michael Mao, who comes to the same conclusion yet without evidence.

At night Chris comes in and we make love. Afterwards, I feel a great peace and we talk for a long time. He gives me back $5 that he says I once lent him. I had no memory of it. He is like an innocent child in all respects except in bed.

July 7, 1984, Boston

I feel bleak. Partly the fatigue of too little sleep and too much sex; partly because I don't know if Edward went to Connecticut and don't know what to expect on his birthday tomorrow.

After going to the gym, I notice at the entrance to the YMCA a tall, good-looking Black guy, coming across the street with a can of Coke in his hand. Dressed only in shorts, without underpants, I perch on the bench within the YMCA lobby. Coming in, this guy stops, then perches on the opposite bench. I get a hardon. He startles me by

---

[183] A successful real estate agent and close friend of Terrill's who lived in the basement apartment at 200 St. Botolph Street.

pointing to it and intimating—as if I didn't know—that my dick was poking out of my shorts. Fortunately, he sweeps away any ambiguity by adding: "It looks great."

In bed at my place, Richard felt wonderful. He is smooth-skinned and affectionate. He soon begged me to screw him, which I did with gusto. He is from Mississippi. At the age of 12, he had an affair with a male cousin. The cousin, aged 19, had a girlfriend. "I was crazily jealous of that girl," said Richard with a smile.

My guts warmed from being inside Richard, I went to bed early but toward midnight the phone awoke me. It was Edward. He hadn't gone to Connecticut. He wasn't with Arlene. He was hibernating. "How are you?" he drawled.

No, he didn't want to come around; he just wanted to talk. This we did for an hour, during which the conversation grew increasingly erotic. Before I knew what was happening, he had me regaling him with tales of Rory, Richard, and others, and then announced that he had just jerked off (it was now his 25th birthday).

July 8, 1984, Boston

Morning Prayer at Trinity Church in Copley Square, where a smooth preacher urged us all to "write our own stories." Edward looked smart, almost preppy, in his summer jacket and good-quality shirt and shoes. "Choose your birthday lunch place," I said. He chose Turner's Fisheries at the Westin Hotel.

At home we made furious love, finishing in time for Edward to go home and straighten himself out for Arlene's arrival at 5:30, to take him off for his birthday dinner. When we kissed, he cried out, "Your eyes are open; when you kiss, you're meant to close the eyes!"

I gave him a Sanyo radio-cassette recorder for his birthday, as well as small items from my trip: a Hong Kong T-shirt, a Chinese track jacket with the two characters for China emblazoned on the chest in white on red, and a key ring obtained on a flight from Chongqing to Peking.

I asked if Arlene might like a simple Chinese fan. Edward was very keen on this idea. "Perhaps I'll bring her round for you to give it to her?" Later the three of us sat on an upstairs couch and drank Dubonnet. I could see Edward's face, but Arlene could not. At one point, Edward gave me a wink. Oh, what will the autumn bring for my crazy, adored man?

July 9, 1984, Boston

Edward comes around dressed in the Hong Kong T-shirt. He asked me: "If you were a girl, or if I were a girl, would you marry me?" I mumbled. Would it be my decision alone? Anyway, the analogy with a straight marriage is less vivid to me than it is for Edward.

July 10, 1984, Boston

Suk phones. Though he never asks a direct question about anything, whenever he phones, he has sex in mind. He arrived in a suit and tie—every inch the dentist—and we made love.

Who was going to fill in whose cavities? The lovemaking was great, until an unaccustomed fumbling on Suk's part marred one or two crucial moments. He begged me to fuck him, but when I did it hurt him too much for me to move; I had to lay still for long stretches, but this meant I lost my hardon.

He never asks questions about my life or my work. I like it that way. He is a charming, tranquil, courteous companion of the bedroom.

July 11, 1984, Boston

Edward is late getting back from work, so instead of going to the movies, which Edward had planned, we strolled to Newbury Street to eat and then came back and watched a TV film on the life of Jessie Owens. Though it was hot upstairs, Edward wanted to watch on the big TV set, so he stripped down to his underpants and draped himself along the black couch, as I nestled between his legs, pretending to be more interested in the TV program than in what was on the black couch.

When the medal-winning young Black athletes at the Mexico City Olympics in 1968 gave the Black Power signal from the podium, Owens was horrified. He was sent by the US Olympic Committee to tell them it was no go. Edward's sympathies were totally with the young guys (he was 11 years old at the time of Mexico).

July 13, 1984, Boston

Restless on a warm Friday night, I decided to go down to the Combat Zone. But at the bus stop, just outside my place, an attractive guy was getting on a bus heading for Dudley Station, so I went that way instead. At Dudley, I went into Roscoe's, an electrifying Black bar. I loved the rugged, frank, sensual atmosphere. Sitting down with a Miller light beer, I was content to watch and muse.

People tried to hide their surprise at the presence of a white. One guy told me that to most people I would seem to be there "either for drugs or as undercover police." Another guy said after he found I was friendly: "I only seen one other white guy in this place—and he never spoke one word to anyone in ten years."

A guy whom I had noticed outside the bar—he had offered to sell me drugs—came by on his way to the bathroom. He was a lithe, loping type, wearing black shorts and an orange T-shirt. I went to the bathroom too. "Black shorts" was just buttoning up, but I saw a shapely, cut dick, smooth and seductive like the rest of his body. We spoke a few words. I said I'd buy $5 worth of grass when I was leaving the bar. Soon after, outside on the steaming sidewalk, we made the transaction. I said how about coming back to my place and fooling around a bit. With a pleased grunt he agreed.

This guy was no innocent. A door scout for Roscoe's, a drug dealer, a street kid—he wasn't going to make love with me for nothing. I was prepared to give him money; and if he tried to rip me off, I was prepared to stop him. Wayne took a shower. He was cheery and relaxed. His plan seemed to be to sip a beer and watch TV; the rest was up to me. Soon we were on the bed, the TV placed just to one side, and I was massaging him with oil.

At Roscoe's, that lean body in shorts had attracted me. Now, naked on my bed, its gleaming black limbs inflamed me, especially the curves and the beautiful smooth complexion. His dick was huge, silky, with a big cut head. His balls were big and round and lovely to the touch of my eager tongue. Wayne's absorption in the TV helped. I was able to ply my ways over a protracted period. He had a pretext for taking no notice of what was going on between his thighs.

I had a finger up his asshole, while my dick ground between his legs. By now he allowed himself to pant and groan. Whenever my cock got near to going inside, he would gently push me aside. I have seldom had so much sexual pleasure over so long a time as during this session of an hour.

He suddenly said: "You want me to come now?" The sight of that Black dick-head getting even larger, the stomach going in and out in spasms of lust, the eyes glazed over, the shiny, greasy balls bobbing up and down! I threw my face into his balls yet one more time. By now he was working my dick as devotedly as I was working his. We shot over each other's bodies at the same time.

Wayne drank a beer, I myself a white wine, and we watched TV. While he was in the bathroom, I looked for my watch, could not find it, then discovered it in the pocket of his black shorts. I removed it and secreted it on a bookshelf. I then discovered that money had gone from the front pocket of the shorts I had been wearing.

I didn't mind the money—the watch as well would have been another thing—but when he left at 3 AM., I felt a touch of relief. Bourgeois relief at the departure of a thief joined forces with working-class "relief" after sexual abandonment. Well, he is a fantastic stud. If the circumstances are OK, I would like to see him again.

July 14, 1984, Boston

Bastille Day, and I awoke feeling warm and happy. I like a summer weekend with time alone in my house, reading and thinking in the air-conditioned cool, making forays into the sensual atmosphere around Symphony Hall and Northeastern University. It's as good as being on holiday—say in San Juan—and one doesn't have to travel to attain it, and one can get work done as well.

After doing my expense list for the Sichuan trip to send to *National Geographic* (I spent more than I had realized), I went to the YMCA to play squash. I saw an Oriental man rubbing sun-oil on his body. Where was he going to sunbake? He explained there is a sun-deck on the roof of the building. We lay side by side in the sun. He turned out to be Chinese, his given name Xue. Having left Shanghai in 1978, he is from a family with branches all over the world, many of its members academics. Now a Harvard undergraduate, he is bright and well-informed, despite being a specialist in the natural sciences. Eventually he guessed my name. For a while he was over-awed. Would he come back to my place? Yes.

At home, Xue seemed to avoid physical contact, but something about him intrigued me. He was not my ideal type physically; nor did I like his endless questions on intellectual subjects. Yet his eagerness and seriousness attracted me. We arranged to meet later.

Being in the Northeastern Library in search of a copy of my reply to Charles Whipple's review of *White-Boned Demon* in the *Boston Globe*, I allowed myself to be diverted. The guy was Black, tall, quiet. I didn't think he was interested. Then I went into the bathroom. As I sat there, someone began peering in upon me, big white eyes glued to the space between the door and the doorway. Who should it be but this same Black guy!

I took off my shirt, leaving myself naked, and began to jerk off. This he could not stand. His pants bulging, he went into the next cubicle. From there, he knelt down and beckoned me to stick my dick under the partition. I did and he began to jerk me off, meanwhile trying to get lower so he could suck my eager pole. I was about to come but didn't want to do it there, in that position. Moreover, he couldn't get himself under the partition at the same time as I was already under. So I whispered, "Can you come to my place?" He said nothing but climbed up and dressed himself.

Five minutes later we were in my bed. He loved sucking my tits, and I loved sucking his. We mutually jerked off, me shooting a huge load over his flat pulsating stomach. His name is Michael. He lives on Tremont Street with room-mates who, like himself, are students at Northeastern. Alas, Wayne took a larger toll than I realized last night: my silver sugar bowl and cream jug are gone from their oval tray!

July 23, 1984, Boston

Yesterday Edward phoned me from work; could we get together the next evening. Tonight, he came dressed in the salmon shirt which, as he knows, is one of my favorites from his wardrobe. We talked about many things but did not directly continue the previous discussion. Soon we fell into each other's arms on the white couch in the front room.

"Why can't we be romantic?" he asked. It was a good question; I am not good at distinguishing romantic dallying and animal sexuality. We went to dine at Bangkok, an excellent meal, including a new chicken dish Edward chose and Thai beer. After dinner, he sat on the couch and the fly of his blue shorts was open. Soon we began one of those bouts of passion that leaves me feeling that at this moment I could be content to die. Sucking his dick, I shoved it far down my throat—last week he mentioned this as being especially desirable.

As I banged my dick inside him, I felt that whatever the difficulties, whatever the price, I must stay with this gorgeous man. We live on a knife-edge, but we have such fun on that knife-edge.

Just after we finished making love, I took a photo of him curled up on the bed, dozing. As usual he didn't want me to take a picture; as usual he liked the result. But he didn't want it copied. So we decided that the photo would be his, but that I would take it to Australia, to warm the cold lonely evenings, and on my return give it to him.

July 25, 1984, New York

A long lunch at excellent La Reserve with Fred Hills, my new editor, a vice-president at Simon & Schuster. At first, he seemed a dry stick, but I warmed to him. He is more cerebral than Pat, and perhaps better organized and better connected in the-house than Pat. But will he have inspiration for the book, as Pat most certainly had for *Demon*?

Into the steamy, asphalt-smelling, erotic jungle of 42nd Street, I plunged, feeling a delicious freedom and anticipation. The first place I entered, a book and film store, seemed pretty straight. After buying a booklet of a Black guy screwing a blonde, I went to another store with an intriguing basement. There were hustlers but gentle and straightforward. The ones I talked with and played with were willing to do things for little money and seemed to enjoy it. One guy kept grabbing my dick, while holding out his own magnificent rod, and saying—after I kept hesitating—that we could jerk each other off for $2. No one tried any tricks.

A "built" guy in a red tank top and white shorts came in. He was hairless and muscled, just as I like. He beckoned me into a booth. He said we could play around for $5. He was so good I ended up giving him $10. We took off all our clothes (there wasn't all that much to take off). I sucked his tits. He began to do the same to me. Before long I had a finger up his ass. The bout had to be constantly interrupted to put quarters into the film machine. If you don't, attendants come and say that you must either watch a film or leave the booth.

Neither of us watched the screen. Eventually he jerked me off—a huge burst that made the whole floor of the booth glisten. The orgasm went on for so long that "red tank top" thought I was starting to come a second time.

I had a second encounter, sweet if swift, before putting my clothes back on and going off to the Parker Meridien Hotel to chat with my agent, Barbara Lowenstein. She unleashed a few unsettling remarks. The deal with Granada in UK for the Australian book is not yet firm after all. "It's a long time since you wrote a book." I stared at her in amazement—it sends a chill down the spine when you get this kind of reminder of how little agents—even good ones, like Barbara, understand the writer's craft.

She urged me to write to Esther Shapiro. "You must type it. Your handwriting is terrible. I'm a patient person, I plough through it—but no one in Hollywood would."

July 26, 1984, Boston

Last night I was hit by one of those cruel darts that Edward cannot help firing from time to time. He's "not sure" we can meet again before I leave for Australia next Saturday. Perhaps he "and Arlene" might drop by together?

July 27, 1984, Boston

Xue is in fine form as we dine on roast beef at Hillary's. I taunt him with the lack of courageous and eloquent dissent in China. After long reflection, he comes back with an interesting answer: "It's because every Chinese is a dissident." I lash out at Chinese culture's stultifications. He says with a half-smile: "You view China, as you view everything at the moment, from the vantage point of the bed."

He insists on walking me home. In the lobby, I kiss him, realizing that he has now decided (but too late!) that he would like to make love with me. What he really prefers is a "romantic" approach. "We Chinese are like that, you know" (that "you know" spoken with Hong Kong cockiness). If only I could have him with me in Australia a month from now!

As I entered the apartment after farewelling Xue, the phone was ringing. I told the caller—Cornell—to come round. He said he was in Copley Square and would arrive in 10 minutes. After the doorbell rang, I stood at my apartment entrance and watched the staircase to see who it was. To my great delight, it was the guy who used to work at Boston Public Library, where we first met (and made love) in an elevator in the spring of 1983.

Before he could get in the door, we fell on each other. Soon his track suit was hanging around his shoes, and my shirt was off, while we were still outside my apartment door. He has "grown up," he announced. He has just turned 20. But to me he is just the same: burning eyes, a slow, catlike smile, a thin and sensual body, a delightful shyness, an unquenchable love of sex. He spent last year as a student at Amherst. "I'll never fail to call you for so long again." I hope not.

In August, Terrill returned to Australia, taking up quarters at the University of Melbourne's Ormond College, the largest of the university's residential colleges. For the next four months—winter and spring Down Under—he did research for his next book, The Australians.

August 15, 1984, Melbourne

Most practical aspects of settling in are going smoothly enough, but I lack motivation and energy after the summer in Boston. I live in an apartment in Ormond College on the campus of University of Melbourne. Fairly old, English-looking buildings. The students are OK, soft and courteous, but they are shy and inarticulate by American standards.

My pleasant office is in the Politics Department, where I once was a student and a tutor. I have rented a computer virtually the same as my own. And certainly better than writing by hand, since many people can hardly read my scrawl. I have started an enormous program of reading on Australia and am beginning to seek out people I want to talk to. At times, though, I wonder if I have the book in me.

August 17, 1984, Melbourne

There are ghosts from the past around Melbourne and I am a person with a great impulse to kick away aspects of my past. I stiffen up in the presence of half-known cousins. I meet church-obsessed friends and feel embarrassed at best. I don't admire what I remember of myself at Melbourne University in undergraduate days. Of course, memory plays tricks, and teenage years bring challenges wherever spent. But I believe I was happier, and more on the right track, after I left Australia for the US, and this colors my view of my Australia.

August 22, 1984, Melbourne

Tonight, my mother took me to dinner for my birthday at Florentino's, a wonderful restaurant like many are in Melbourne. In the course of a long and generally pleasant evening she told me two disturbing things. She nearly had an abortion instead of having me—something to do with economics and my father just having contracted diabetes. The abortion didn't take place because at the last moment a second doctor, my father's specialist in diabetes, exploded and said my father's illness was not reason to abort the birth. So, I arrived after all—an extra guest at a crowded table.

The dear old tigress also said my father, who was a schoolteacher, played around with some schoolgirls in the hot, dry, fruit-growing town of Mildura where we lived and he was the teacher. As my mother related it, the police came to the door to ask questions about these spicy events. Do I want to contemplate such things?

August 25, 1984, Melbourne

Sexual hotness is a matter of the environment that you are in. If an erotic environment isn't there, lust doesn't arise the way it normally does. And in this situation an orgasm tends to be mediocre. In time you could almost come to the dreadful conclusion that you didn't need or want one!

In Boston I have been oriented to sex. Perhaps too much during this past year since I threw off the TB and met Edward—as perhaps too much in the year before coming down with TB. Here in Melbourne sex is virtually absent from my life. I wake up each morning with less excitement toward life than I do at home. All I look forward to is breakfast and then getting down to books.

The more you get, the more you want (Boston) and the less you get you less you want (Melbourne). I hate the life of deprivation, or abstinence, but I begin to understand it. Edward, who has experience of it, and of being able to accept it, has tried without success to make me understand this before).

August 27, 1984, Melbourne

Soon I begin a series of lectures on China—if my lecture notes arrive; they are on the high seas from Hong Kong, where I sent them to myself here. Due to a rail strike—Australia is always full of strikes—cargo sits in Sydney instead of coming down to Melbourne.

I am not relaxed, so I sleep poorly, am half-numb all over and have to force myself to do anything or think any positive thoughts. To keep myself out of depression, I have spent a lot of time on the phone with Edward. He has rented my apartment for eight weeks to two dancers from the musical "42nd Street."

It is nice to talk with him a lot on the phone, but he is not the sort of person with whom a phone conversation across the Pacific is any substitute for having him in the room. I don't want to look for anyone else, yet I face the stark probability that my morale and then my health will go down and down if I don't have "friends." I can't live in a bedroom where virtually no sex takes place—just can't do it.

I recall when I first moved to 200 Saint Botolph St., I looked around and thought, you'll never have fun here as you did in Cambridge; you're too old, you know no-one in this neighborhood, your type of stud won't come into this snazzy place. Well, the anxiety turned out unjustified (though I do now and then get ripped off by tricks who get emboldened by the snazzy apartment).

Several guys in Ormond College are interested in me. One or two of them interest me. But in my present state I've lost the technique for getting guys in Australia—perhaps I never had it here, the way I am reputed to in the USA. It was the USA, after all, that liberated me.

"You must come over for coffee," one guy says with a lovely smile. But what a tortuous route that would be to getting into bed with him. Another one who seems to like me engages me in intellectual discussions at every opportunity. The more we talk, the more my lust subsides. It's all far removed from Black America.

I was reduced to answering an ad in the Melbourne magazine *Outrage*. (I don't know why the magazine has this name; "raging" seems to be a widespread word, amongst straights and gays alike, for having a wild time). The guy I wrote to—his name is Seng—drove over last night. Very Australian; an engineer educated in Adelaide. We had dinner in the Italian quartier around the campus, then went to bed. Low-key, pleasant enough.

August 31, 1984, Melbourne

The past couple of days I did promotion for *White-Boned Demon*; fourteen interviews with radio, TV, or press. Went quite well. The weak point is few books are in the stores; Heinemann in the UK are thinking small about this book.

The Age ran an excerpt, much read, and the same paper reviewed the book respectfully. The British reviewers have been mixed—as I have come to expect from them. In general, they are abstracted from their readers (such readers as there are in Britain).

First serial timing was all out of kilter; it was done by London with scant regard to Australian realities. Heinemann Australia gets furious about this, but the author suffers. No advertising whatsoever. Publicity appearances only in one city—Melbourne. No apparent attention to New Zealand.

September 1, 1984, Melbourne

Last night I went to bed thinking how gentle Australia is. The kids may be pagans, but they are gentle pagans; the politicians may throw mud but there's a softness in their scrapping—they call each other by first names. I went to sleep. At 3:50 AM, I woke. A noise—is that a squirrel at the window just three feet from my pillow? No, two strong arms were trying to pull off the wire screen. I was amazed before I was frightened or able to formulate a strategy. I turned on the bed light. I would rush into the kitchen, pick up a carving knife and from there fly out the front door. But the person ran away. I couldn't go back to sleep; I felt angry at the violation even of this minor crime.

September 4, 1984, Melbourne

Australia is fascinating and I am awash in material. It will take time to get hold of it. I miss Boston a lot and immerse myself in work to transcend that.

September 6, 1984, Melbourne

There is a charming bookshop, old and mellow, managed by an influential woman called Claire Kearney. Today, after signing 30 copies of *The White-Boned Demon*, I took her out to lunch at a gay-run bistro (chosen by her) near her shop. She's Irish, loves books, and seemed relieved to find out that I'm not leftwing.

She brought me up to date on the Australian book scene. Fairly depressing, especially the UK angle—and this is a dominant angle, since nearly all American books come to Australia via their UK edition. The Brits don't know how to market books in Australia—it's time everyone woke up to the fact that Australia is as different from UK as either is from the USA.

Claire can't stand a sight now commonplace in the US. When she was returning some paperbacks, the dealer arrived to get them and instead of bundling them up, tore the covers off, taking these, and leaving the body of the books.

"Fury built up in me at the sight," said Claire. "I told the man to leave my bookshop."

September 10, 1984, Melbourne

My visit to Taiwan in June has borne fruit in regard to *Demon*. A letter today says a magazine has bought serial rights (up to 10% of the book) for $2000. There won't be a contract; they don't do things that way. But it's a step ahead from when the Taiwanese used my stuff without even asking. By raising it first during my visit, I got it done in a professional way.

September 12, 1984, Melbourne

My publisher, John Kerr, took me to an absurdly expensive lunch at the Café Latin. He came scrumptiously dressed; I thought I was lunching only with the Publicity Manager—and I would prefer that he spend his money promoting books rather than wining and dining his authors. After a surly period, things warmed up a bit and he begged me to sign with Heinemann Australia for the Australian rights on the Australia book. I was non-committal, but I listened to him and he made the point that Heinemann Australia, which is apparently separate from Heinemann in UK, at times signs for Australia and NZ rights alone. The problem it would solve is this London-Australia gap that has once again become so evident to me.

I learn to my horror that only 500 books were brought into Australia. Even with Heinemann's feeble efforts these have just about gone and there are no more. Heinemann have no conception of the book as a biography as distinct from a book about China.

September 14, 1984, Melbourne

Shop-keepers in Australia are obliging and polite—up to a point. Yes, the customer is always right, or nearly, in their initial approach. But the pressure tactics you have to use in the US, and which work there, can backfire here. My newspaper has failed to be delivered these past two mornings. The newsagent falls over himself to rectify the situation. A second day it still does not come. In Boston I would rave; had I not paid in advance for a month's supply of papers? That money point is not necessarily decisive in Australia. Anger can have the counter-productive effect of making an Australian shopkeeper withdraw like a shellfish that has been poked.

September 18, 1984, Melbourne

Some reviews of *Demon* think that sex should not come into any discussion of politics. In a similar way there are historians in whose work—even biography—sex is an utter absentee. Yet these writers must know from their own lives that this is nonsense.

September 25, 1984, Melbourne

I am unhappy—and to think that for much of 1983 I kidded myself that if only the TB would leave me, I should certainly be happy! I am gay and also conservative—a tragic combination.

September 30, 1984, Melbourne

A touch of spring in the air. The plum trees come out; the golden Australian wattle smells sweet under my window. My morale will improve as the weather warms up.

Says Steven, a student from Hong Kong whom I met the other day in the showers at the gym: "You are the king." And a little later, when we have finished making love, he asks a question which gives me a surge of nostalgia for Melbourne: "Ro-as, which high school did ya go to?"

I like his company very much. He is no beauty, but he has nice eyes, great sexiness, and utter straightforwardness. These qualities—plus whatever it is he finds in me—are doing the trick and lifting me out of depression.

His candor is disarming. We are in the shower together and as lust rises, he says: "Heh, how about us going to the bed." A few minutes later as we are intertwined, he objects: "Heh, that way hurts my leg—turn over."

October 1, 1984, Melbourne

I prepared the lecture on "China and the Great Powers," played squash, and then met my new Malaysian friend, Cheekun. He wanted to take me to his favorite Chinese restaurant, The Shark's Fin, but it was full, so we went to a nice Australian bistro in the middle of the city. We had pasta and then I had steak and he had lamb. He's a bit of a drinker—unusual for an Oriental—so we tossed back two bottles of Australian vino.

I said what about coming home and he said why not. He likes to kiss so that's how we began. Soon we tore each other's clothes off and went to bed. We weren't sleepy afterwards, so we went into the living room, opened a bottle of champagne, and talked for a couple of hours.

He's got a brother who is a doctor in Oregon (the whole Eastern world wants to go either to America or Australia) and two sisters. None of the four are married—the brother is 31—and Cheekun says his parents keep asking when this one or that one is going to get married.

Cheekun has a girl apartment-mate. He answered her ad for a gay guy to live with. They get on well, and Cheekun's parents think they sleep together.

We went back to bed. Actually, neither of us slept very well; the bed is not as big as I am used to. Perhaps also too much to drink. But I had to get up early, so I tiptoed out leaving him curled up in blissful sleep.

October 2, 1984, Melbourne

Cheekun and I went to the Australian movie *My First Wife*, a torrid account of the breakdown of a marriage. "Sex is a bugger, isn't it?" says the husband at one point. The wife does not dispute the point. I suppose sex made their marriage, and sex also ruined it.

Later that night, as it became clear that the bloom was going off the rose as far as Cheekun and me are concerned, the phrase from the movie leapt back into my mind with a sad, metallic authority. Somehow, as soon we reached his house, we felt strangely uncomfortable with each other. His desire to kiss me had gone.

October 3, 1984, Melbourne

Having kids is a way of being able to extend one's youth and avenge growing older.

October 4, 1984, Melbourne

Steven says at my flat as we shower together, and he grabs my body: "Now I understand; you're strong because you play squash." Then as we get dressed: "I want to ask you a question—do you mind." I didn't. "Are some of your ancestors Chinese?" He thought that, because I speak Chinese, they must be. The Australian environment does not quickly broaden the mind of a guy from Asia.

October 5, 1984, Melbourne

I go to the Xerox machine of the Politics Department, where I'm based, and as I pass the open door of the computer room, I see an attractive Chinese guy sitting at a terminal. He is chunky and masculine. He has nice legs, which his short, thin, pale blue shorts show off well. I said hello and he told me he knew who I was because he attended my lectures last week in Communist Politics. I invited him to drop into my office for a chat later that afternoon.

"You look quite different now from when you lectured to us—20 years younger." I was very attracted to this guy, Henry. I said to him: "You look pretty good yourself." After talking about the situation of Hong Kong for a while we exchanged phone numbers. He is boyish but well-educated and intelligent. He is masculine yet with a touch of the Bohemian. I am eager to see him "unofficially."

October 7, 1984, Melbourne

I phoned Henry and got the impression he was happy I'd called. We had a long talk, during which the name of a mutual friend, known as TJ, a student from Singapore, came up. I explained to Henry that I met him last Tuesday at a party of friends who went to the theater restaurant The Last Laugh.

"What sort of party?" Soon I mentioned in passing that it was more or less a gathering of gay guys. Then I went on to the topic of international affairs. Henry said he wanted to come over some time and discuss international affairs. I looked at my diary and suggested 2 or 3 possible times from the coming week. He chose tomorrow.

October 8, 1984, Melbourne

Lunch with Henry in the Ormond College dining hall. We talk mainly about race issues in Australia, for a time with an Indian scientist who joins us at the long polished wooden "High" table under a vaulted ceiling and stained-glass windows.

Afterwards I invite Henry into my flat to chat. He asks me whether it's tough being a gay. I answer this in a balanced way and then I ask him if he has a girlfriend. He replies that he just broke up with one. More talk of China and then once more he returns to personal matters.

"I too have had fantasies about men." He went on to say that twice he had been to bed with men (I didn't ask if he had done so with the girlfriend). "But I did not enjoy it very much and afterwards I felt bad." He is an evangelical Christian, hot for Jesus if not for his girlfriend.

"Then you shouldn't do it again," I said. Later I told him in passing that I was attracted to him. He said he knew that from the moments by the Xerox machine in the Politics Department. I moved back to the topic of Hong Kong's future.

When 3 PM approached, I looked at my watch and said I should get back to my office. He said he wanted to walk back in that direction, and when we arrived, he just came into the office with me.

"You know, I'm also attracted to you," he burst out. We looked at documents. We moved from the desk to the window. We stood up and we sat down. He sat on the edge of the desk, and at that point I brushed my leg against his. He looked down eagerly at my thighs. He had a hardon as did I. Despairing at all the hesitation, I gently locked my two legs around one of his, me standing and him still sitting on the edge of the desk. We grabbed at each other like drowning men at life-belts.

"Let's go somewhere else," he gasped. Ten minutes later we were back in my flat—which we had just left—pulling our clothes off. Afterwards he said he didn't feel bad though he wasn't sure he would be "able" to do it again. "It doesn't matter," I replied, "I want to have you either as a friend or also for sex—either way."

"You are far different from the previous two. You see, I am fiercely attracted to you sexually." Yet I could tell, even on that golden and unforgettable afternoon, that his Cantonese Evangelical spirit felt in turmoil over gay sex—probably over any sex.

October 11, 1984, Melbourne

As we lunch at Monash University, Dick Bronowski, Australian Ambassador to Vietnam, recalls his days at Harvard when he took my course while a mid-career visitor to the university. "I still consult the notes from your lectures, especially when facing a visit from a journalist. Yet I must tell you that they make less and less sense to me in terms of today's realities."

It was a relief to hear it. I don't agree with all I said in those lectures on Chinese foreign relations in the early and mid-1970s. Nor does the topic grip me much anymore.

October 13, 1984, Melbourne

Henry meets me at the Melbourne University Union and we go to the meeting on "The Ugly Face of Racism" organized by the campus Fabian Society. Both of us were interested in Wellington Lee's talk on his experiences as an Australian-born in Australia a Chinese. I made contact with Clyde Holding; Henry did the same with Charles Khoo who heads the Federation of Chinese Organizations.

Afterwards, I suggested going back to my place, a short walk across the tree-filled campus. Henry agreed even as he murmured that he didn't know whether I had the right thing in mind. On the phone the other night, he had told me of his spectacular moral dilemma: "I will have to choose between you and the Lord."

As before, he didn't want to, but he did. Fortunately, I can read his mood well. Schoolboy-style we horsed around, until both of us had roaring hardons and physical contact made lust king. In bed, he said that today he wanted only to hug and not "have sex." That went by the board too. Few Chinese have turned me on more.

He simply could not resist me and I could not resist him. We drenched each other in cum and then sped in a cab to see *Silver City*, an Australian film about the experience of European migrants in post-World War Two Australia.

We dined at West Lake in Little Bourke Street on excellent garlic prawns and an indifferent dish made up of chicken and abalone—the two don't blend well together— with a Quelltaler Hock bought nearby at a bottle shop that reeked of Australian beer.

I was surprised that he drank a glass or two of the hock—was it to keep up with me, and prove that he is not irredeemably religious? He felt a bit tipsy afterwards. It turned out that he wanted to go to a gay bar. He'd apparently never been to one before; would I take him?

Henry volunteered his sexual background. "As a boy I had strong fantasies. And I explored every part of my body." Only in Melbourne did he have sex. There were just two guys, he said, before me. One he met at the Melbourne University swimming pool and didn't like. This tended to turn him off gay contacts. The other experience sounded successful, though both sides ended it out of guilt. Talking with the guy, from Singapore, whom he already knew quite well, he invited the guy to stay for the summer period when the colleges close down. One night in bed the Singapore guy embraced him.

"I was amazed when he told me this was his first time. I mean, to take the initiative like that when it's your first time!" For several weeks, they played around quite a bit, now in bed, now in the living-room, once in the kitchen. "But neither of us could handle it. The guy said it was better for him to move out. I still see him, but he doesn't like to talk about that subject."

He went on to say flattering things about me. "You know, Ross, your blue eyes made it impossible to resist. In your office the sunlight was streaming across the room and catching your eyes—that did it."

The perfect pattern for me is to make love in the afternoon, go to a movie, have a reasonably early dinner, then relax by walking the streets or sitting in a bar, knowing that the evening is winding down rather than building up toward love making.

October 14, 1984, Melbourne

Lunch with Mum at Chalkey's in Lygon Street. A good meal but my mother seems full of demons. She tries to conceal she dislikes many people—including ones long dead, like my father—but she does not succeed. No wonder she suffers from "tension." She creates much of it herself. I have never known her less happy. Her unhappiness becomes a burden on me, for much of what swirls beneath the surface of her conversation is from a past I do not care to recall.

Henry says on the phone that he has been haunted by the old issue of guilt. It's not quite as acute as last week ("I have to choose between you and the Lord") but it's still a problem. On the one hand, he thinks we shouldn't go to bed again. On the other, he feels on the brink of a dangerous emotional dependence upon me. Oh, to be young, Chinese, and tortured.

October 18, 1984, Melbourne

My talk on "Reassessing China: The Case of JQ" at the Institute of International Affairs seems to go well. A large crowd, some good questions, a genteel atmosphere of English sandwiches, tweeds, and three-piece suits. Dick Wolcott's father is there, apparently ga-ga, as is my former history teacher, Norman Harper, also ga-ga. God lost concentration when planning the twilight years of his creatures.

I drove back to Carlton in a taxi with Henry but dropped him at his place as I had an appointment with Steven. It took me a while to relax after the Institute event, but once I did the lovemaking was engulfing. In the middle of it, Geoffrey Blainey[184] phoned to ask if I could have lunch with him next week. I lost my hardon, but soon regained it

---

[184] Geoffrey Norman Blainey (1930-), Australian historian with over 40 books to his credit, described as "most prolific, wide-ranging, inventive, and...most controversial of Australia's living historians."

and turned my attention from Blainey to an Oriental who has been discomforted by Blainey's comments on immigration.

In the afternoon the Politics Department has its Third Term party. A good-looking waiter keeps every glass filled. In the middle of it, Arthur gives me a message to call Joan—I have to return two phone calls from Paris. Gough Whitlam wants to ask about a piece on UNESCO that has just appeared in *The Atlantic*; could I try to urge its reprinting in Australia. I mentioned to Gough that Santamaria told me he and Clyde Cameron (a former Minister in the Whitlam government) often get together and yarn. Said Gough: "I suppose that's because no one else wants to talk to him." But I wasn't clear if Gough meant no one wants to talk with Santamaria or with Cameron—or with either of them.

The other call was from Ramsay, my French publisher. Can I come to Paris for radio and TV in connection with the imminent publication in French translation of *White-Boned Demon*? A difficult decision. I am so immersed in Australian topics now that it would be quite an interruption. And would my French be adequate?

October 19, 1984, Melbourne

After I returned from interviewing Vernon Wilcox[185] downtown, Henry came in. He looked marvelous. We went to have lunch at Milliways and then drifted back to my office. As usual we could not keep our hands off each other. Cocks out, hair disheveled, bodies red-hot. For one in theory so timid, Henry is in practice quite bold. This cantor of passion was occurring in the office of his professor!

Eventually I said that we either should go back to my flat at Ormond and get into bed, or break off, put our dicks away, and go back to work. We decided to wait until tomorrow night. "Can I stay over with you tomorrow night?" I was surprised and pleased at the question. As he said goodbye at the door, his eyes looked right into mine. I think he is asking himself—and me—if I am capable of committing myself to him.

October 20, 1984, Melbourne

With boyfriends as with dentures, it is wise to have a spare. Something can always happen to Number One.

October 21, 1984, Melbourne

I went with Henry to the Market Hotel for dinner in new-cuisine style, with lilting white wine and country maiden-type waitresses. Henry sees a restaurant half with the eyes of a customer and half those of a waiter—he works part time at Empress of China in the city.

My surroundings—the Australian understated style, the gay scene, the dry Melbourne way—become normal after two to three months. I'm in universal mode; it's issues rather than "place" that I now think of.

---

[185] Vernon Wilcox (1919-2004), Australian politician.

After dinner we walk in the city and then go to the Laird. Later, Henry and I made love very happily. I did not sleep, however, because Henry was intermittently excited all night; even when he wasn't pawing me his way of sleeping in a close embrace made it impossible for me—though not for him—to sleep. By morning I was exhausted. But this did not stop me making love to him before he left for church.

In the middle of the night, he asked: "How committed are you and Edward to each other?" The question bothered me because for a week I have been unable to reach Edward on the phone. As soon as Henry went to church, I tried yet again to reach Edward on the phone—no answer. I called Glen; his number has been disconnected. Am I surrounded by men, or am I alone.

I read a biography of Bob Hawke during the morning. It set me wondering if Henry will throw off religion as Hawke did. Before lunch, we go to Carney Fisher's[186] for champagne and decadent conversation. In the dining hall, Henry keeps an eagle eye on the Hong Kong students down in the body of the room—and I dare say Raymond, Michael, and the others have a good look at him, too. They know and yet they don't know—it will go on being like that.

October 22, 1984, Melbourne

My mother comes into a dream which also features Edward. At one point she makes a snide remark to the effect that she doubts Edward can really be satisfying both a woman and me. How is it that even in my dim subconscious I permit her to have a say on this subject? In yet in another dream the tigress appears. I am standing before her, unable to agree to some request or other. Finally, I confess to her that my life is sagging, that I am not able anymore to competently fulfill my obligations.

October 24, 1984, Melbourne

With Steven at Ormond. He was cuddly and relaxing. I had a minor accident in the bedroom. I was switching positions in order to start screwing him sideways—which his chunkiness makes delightful—when I swung around quickly and hit my head against the edge of the bedside table. After a pause to put a band-aid on the cut, we resumed and I exhausted myself with a gigantic orgasm.

He has exams soon; he's going to stay here overnight before each one, so that he won't have to make the long trip from Footscray on the morning of the exam. I'm going to have to introduce Henry to him soon. How will Henry like that?

Steven gave me some tips on ensuring a good sleep: concentrate on your breathing, empty the mind and just think of sleep, focus on your body rather than your mind.

There are three things in his life: science studies, family, sex. The family is a constant—the balance between science and sex swings back and forth. "First term my grades were bad because I was obsessed with sex. Second term I did well and played around hardly at all." I fear I may have an influence on Steven's Third Term.

---

[186] Carney T. Fisher, China scholar; author of several books including The Chosen One: Succession and Adoption in the Court of Ming Shizong.

October 25, 1984, Melbourne

Two talks on the phone with Edward and thank God he sounds OK. Arlene's parents have been away in the Bahamas and he's staying at her place—hence not answering his phone.

"Anything wrong? What's wrong?" he begins the conversation. In fact, there was nothing wrong. It's his way of betraying that he's got something on his mind. I think it might be the old point: Arlene doesn't satisfy him but he's not sure he wants to do the gay flip—and my absence was supposed to give him the chance to try "going straight."

But is he missing something? "I can feel the tension built up in my stomach," he suddenly remarked. I have to put up with the attitudes that result from these repeated, futile experiments. Yet still I love him. He said Reagan "got many things wrong" in the foreign policy debate with Mondale last night but will win the election anyway.

October 26, 1984, Melbourne

Three more reviews of *White-Boned Demon* arrive from London. Two—from Ireland and Wales—are feeble and cool. The third is enthusiastic and, amazingly for UK, is written by someone qualified to comment, Collina McDougal, who used to write for various papers from Hong Kong. I was buoyed by her praise for a book that has brought me great joy and some pain. It helped withstand the disappointment of the royalty statement from Morrow in New York; book club payments are healthy but sales through the stores are weak.

October 27, 1984, Melbourne

I have become re-attuned to the Australian way. Sitting by my office window that overlooks the green beauty of the campus, I find many guys attractive. They are far away, yet even the walk conveys sexual attractiveness. This goes without saying in the USA, but for many weeks it wasn't like that for me in Melbourne. My eyes could see little. Now I have refocused, and the understated Australian traits no longer escape me. What will happen when I reach Boston in December?

October 28, 1984, Melbourne

Edward phoned, bubbling over with this and that. We talked for nearly an hour—so that's $60 spoken for. He talks about Arlene. The marriage question hovers, raised by family and friends. He says he doesn't want to marry Arlene—mainly because of the old Lion and Lamb issue. In bed she is a lamb; I (and I suppose other men) represent a lion. He likes to attack Arlene, but he also likes to be attacked. "If only there was something in between," he sighs. He is not sure Arlene has the wild streak that he requires; and not sure she could accept the wild streak in him that nature has made non-negotiable. "I am wild you know," he says. "Apart from you, I am the wildest person I know."

He said Arlene and I are "the two stars in my sky." For the first time, he asked me how old I am. I joked around and did not answer. I said he could do some research and find out if he really wanted to. "You shouldn't feel embarrassed," he said. "You should feel proud to have lasted as long as you have."

October 29, 1984, Melbourne

Juggling Henry and Steven is getting complex. I felt relieved when Steven today said he couldn't come in for our usual Wednesday afternoon "pash" and added: "You must see someone else; I don't want you to have to go without sex just because of my exams." So next week I'll tell him Henry filled in for him. This will be a way of breaking the ice.

October 30, 1984, Melbourne

This afternoon, I taught Henry a bit of squash, which was boring, then we made love at my place, which was not—anal stuff for the first time. He seems to be hooked on me sexually. I find him sensual and attractive. That he cannot compare with Edward does not mean he is not delightful.

October 31, 1984, Melbourne

While I'm at a dinner party, Simon Crean[187] and his wife came in with terrible news that Indira Gandhi is murdered by two of her security guards. Simon had been thinking about Hawke: "Sometimes I worry about his safety."

Every time such an assassination happens, anywhere in the world, it makes the next one that much more likely. The unthinkable takes place, and there will always be the odd tormented soul for whom that becomes a green light to another effort to avoid meaninglessness.

A little after midnight, the phone rang. I feared it may be Paris—I was not in a state to speak French, nor ready with a decision on whether or not to go to Paris to do promotion for *Demon*. But it was Henry. This evening he went to a Cantonese sex movie. It depicted nakedness and even an orgy. "I was shocked," he said. On Melbourne's behalf I was shocked, too, for he saw the movie in a mainstream cinema in Collins Street. This old dowager of a city goes from one extreme to another.

November 2, 1984, Melbourne

Lunch with Cheekun at "Trotters" in Lygon Street. Looking delicious on this golden day, he says he's decided to become famous. "I crave attention too much. The only solution to this is to be famous and then I'll have plenty of attention." I told him it's not easy, especially if you directly aim for fame, rather than pursuing creativity.

At night, Henry and I went to eat at the Shark's Fin, and he slept overnight. Even after coming twice, he did not lose his hardon. The years of deprivation have given way to a splendid harvest. In the middle of the night, he arrived—for the first time—at the point of begging me to fuck him. But it hurt him too much and I had to withdraw. "Enough! Enough!" he cried, like a Tang dynasty emperor ordering an end to a

---

[187] Simon Crean (1949-), a leading Australian politician and trade unionist.

ceremony. Later as we lay sated and relaxed in the moonlight, he asked: "Do Edward and you do that?"

November 3, 1984, Melbourne

My mother is on her high horse over Christmas arrangements. "There is a family tradition of getting together," she rasps. "Is it going to be broken!" She claims her rights and turns everyone off. If she made herself pleasant company for her family, which she is capable of doing, they would enjoy her company for Christmas. But who can save her from the consequences of her own positions? I can't, it seems. I have tried hard over many years and failed. For that matter, I am probably set on paths that are of my choosing, which one day will land me in unpleasant territory.

November 4, 1984, Melbourne

Henry and I went to two well-known Australian movies, *Phar Lap*[188] and *The Man from Snowy River*. How tough Australian history has been! As well as the convict origins, the battle against a difficult land made people wary and devious. The Great Depression of the 1890s did nothing to elevate the nation's moral standards. The young woman in *Snowy River* bursts out, "How changeable this place is. One moment it's a paradise, the next it's trying to kill you."

I had not realized that *Phar Lap* was born in New Zealand, or that his story was so intertwined with the US and Mexico. It seems that the world of racing is 90% money; even a horse as wonderful as Pharlap made no one close to him happy—except the boy who cared for him day by day. The Melbourne papers had a problem with deadlines when *Phar Lap* ran his first big race in North America. One cunning editor prepared two headlines. "AUSTRALIAN CHAMPION DEFEATS THE WORLD." And: "NEW ZEALAND HORSE LOSES IN MEXICO."

After eating a greasy chicken in Lygon Street, we went to the Hotel Laird, but like other Melbourne gay clubs it's terribly smoky. On the way home, I said sometime I'd like to meet Henry's brother and wondered if we might ask him over to my flat tonight. He looked at me for a moment, grinned, and replied: "Don't spoil the fun!"

November 5, 1984, Melbourne

Perhaps the French translation of *Demon* may not fall flat after all. A package arrives this morning from Paris with tear sheets of a serialization in Paris-Match and another excerpt in the women's' magazine Elle. A glass of Beaujolais to that.

A nice dinner at Hagger's in the city with Peter D. Likable behind a layer of South African reserve. Peter says being gay has made his whole life different. "Otherwise, I would still be in South Africa." He added that he would also have been an alcoholic. (The difference is not between Black and white on that point; during the evening we put down three bottles of wine between us and he added three brandies). It was partly

---

[188] Phar Lap (1926-1932), a Thoroughbred widely regarded as New Zealand's greatest racehorse.

the same with me. If I had been straight, I may well now be a minister in the Hawke cabinet. Yet I do not regret the course of events.

November 6, 1984, Melbourne

I'm juggling a lot of balls at the moment—and they're all nice. The problem is actually not balls but a dick—my dick. Steven can be rough. His teeth leave marks and Henry notices. I can't tell Henry again that I caught my dick in the zipper of my pants. He'll think I'm a spastic or a moron.

November 7, 1984, Melbourne

I'm coming back from a long Chinese emigration. Life flows back into my mind—it is a great satisfaction to wrap my mind around Australia.

November 8, 1984, Melbourne

A hot dry day on which I catch up with events. Steven stayed the night. Add to this the excitement of the Reagan election victory and the result was neglect of normal tasks. Lunch amidst the birds and bushes of Latrobe University to greet a bunch of China specialists. Then a dash into the city to interview the smooth vain Don Dunstan.[189]

Steven is staying the night, ready to get a flying start for his exam tomorrow morning. At my age I seldom wish—except on holiday at the beach—to make love with more than one person in a day. The wonderful thing at the moment is the Australian men. The legs; the eyes; the sunburnt hands—that quietly confident masculine walk.

November 9, 1984, Melbourne

Overnight Steven was with me. Two nice orgasms, night and morning. In between, I did not sleep well as he clawed and entangled me each time I dozed off. I think he has seen photos of Henry or else become disturbed at the tone of my phone conversations with Henry. A defensive, possessive streak has started to show up in him. He is all over me. It is too much. My feeling about him is changing.

November 10, 1984, Melbourne

I've been pushing my body too much. The squash games are strenuous with the English ball. Keeping two over-sexed Chinese happy takes its toll. Now I know how Edward feels as he keeps up with Arlene and me.

November 11, 1984, Melbourne

A call from Steven at breakfast time. The crisis is upon us. He says he's depressed because he has the feeling I don't care for him anymore. "Do you want me only for sex?"

---

[189] Donald Dunstan (1926-1999), Australian politician and labor party leader. At the time Terrill interviewed him, Dunstan was national president of the *Freedom from Hunger Campaign*.

I'm not going to tell him the truth until after his exams. Meanwhile, I admitted to Henry that the scratch on my dick—which won't heal properly—was caused not by a zipper but by Steven's teeth. Said Henry: "I certainly knew it wasn't done by a zipper." He told me that since he and I met he has not gone with anyone else and does not want to.

November 12, 1984, Melbourne

I took Mum to a grand dinner at the Hotel Windsor tonight. Have never spent that much on a meal for two—$145—anywhere in the world. But she loved it; the Victorian atmosphere was just her style. We put away two bottles of champagne in the course of a three-hour meal of many courses—a *menu gastronomique* concocted by a visiting French chef, an indication of the enterprising spirit that has come upon Melbourne hotels.

During the day, Henry came into the office and managed to divert me. I think he has had a hardon ever since I met him a month ago. We had lunch at El Gambero after putting our clothes back on. Like me, Henry prefers to let the cum dry on his body rather than wash it off.

In the evening, before I went off to meet my mother, Steven, who was staying at my flat ready for tomorrow's exam, fell upon me. Two sucking techniques, almost alongside each other. Steven wins. It is nice to come home "from a hard day in the office" and find there a cuddly companion. Maybe if I had this all the time, I would be less neurotic.

My French agent writes today from Paris to say that so far, the reception of *White-Boned Demon* in its French translation is "excellent." But no specifics yet. An old campaigner must meanwhile withhold any feelings of euphoria. In publishing, words and reality are sometimes far apart.

November 13, 1984, Melbourne

A squash match tonight: Pennant for Melbourne University against the Williamstown Club. We drive out as a team. All is highly organized. The rituals of politeness and procedure are firm. As Number One in the Melbourne University team, I played last. By 10 PM when my match began, I thought I would fall asleep. I lost the first two games but came back to win the next three. Just as well, for my win gave our side victory and a place in the finals, which begin at the end of the month.

My opponent, Tony, was a plumber, dark, blue-eyed, and good-looking. After the game, we showered together. His strong, sun-tanned body, "Australian dick," and blue eyes that bored through me made the shower memorable. Had I not been in a team situation, I would have propositioned him.

November 14, 1984, Melbourne

I sit at my desk, happy: my work on Australia begins to move; and the USA is there, just the same, waiting for me, and I can leave Australia and retreat to its charm any moment I wish.

John Young, an historian from Hong Kong with a degree from California, is to be the head of the new Chinese Museum in Melbourne. He's alright, but why not have an Australian? Guilt under pressure of "multiculturalism" is running riot in Australia—a strange thing for a country in the grip of nationalism.

November 15, 1984, Melbourne

A difficult evening with Steven last night, starting with dinner at Federici's and continuing with a night of maneuver. I slept little as I was warding him off. Finally, this morning we made love—perhaps for the last time. The magic simply has gone out of it now that his personality has become clearer.

I feel sad because he's appealing; also troubled and handicapped in some ways. He told me at dinner his mother died of overwork when he, Steven, was only 10; his father, a street hawker, has been an alcoholic and womanizer for years; he himself has had bizarre sex experiences with kids and brothers. "My father loved girls," he said as we walked down Royal Parade toward the restaurant, "and so I chose to turn to boys. My father drank wine and spirits, and so I don't touch them."

Like many Asian students in Melbourne, he goes to church and Bible class mainly for the companionship. "Religion is silly," he says. "I told God I was not going to change from being a gay. I didn't tell the people in Bible class; they would only argue with me. But I thought I would tell God—he is supposed to understand everything."

This morning Henry keeps coming into the office for reasons not clear. "Be patient, Mate!"

November 16, 1984, Melbourne

I took Henry to the party for the Australian-Chinese Museum inauguration at the snazzy new hotel Menzies-at-Rialto. Many Chinese were present, sipping orange juice and gobbling pastries. I knew few people there—how different from an equivalent gathering in Boston.

Don Dunstan, former premier of South Australia, happened to be at the door as we arrived, and I rather proudly introduced him to Henry. Don seemed effusively warm towards him. "It was nice being here with my boyfriend," I said to Henry. He flashed a lovely smile and gently touched my hand.

The speeches were good, including that of the Premier of Victoria. Arthur Huck[190] drank a lot as usual. Harry Simon[191] was so ignorant of the whole topic that he thought the museum itself was to be established at the Menzies-at-Rialto! So much for the China guru of Melbourne University.

Afterwards Henry and I decided to come home and have a pizza while watching the Liberal Party election "launch," rather than to dine in Chinatown as originally planned.

---

[190] Arthur Huck (1926-), professor of Political Sciene at University of Melbourne; author of *The Chinese in Australia* (1968) and *The Security of China* (1970).
[191] Harry Simon (1923-2019), a Sinologist at the University of Melbourne.

Peacock for the Liberals was impressive, developing at last a theme—standing up for the individual (at all levels) against Bob Hawke's corporate state.

Good that we came home for the evening, for we had a lovely time in each other's arms. He stayed overnight and woke me early to make love. He attacked with skill and vigor. Arranging everything, he did not neglect the setting; so that we could see the green leaves outside the window as we screwed. "I love you," he kept saying throughout. I am terribly fond of him.

"What am I going to do with you?" The words come at me from another time and place.

November 19, 1984, Melbourne

A long lunch with Tony Staley[192] at Federici's. He looks well and not very changed from our Melbourne University days. He said he wasn't that surprised when I told him I voted for Ronald Reagan. "You were never one to toe the line with the ideologues of your own camp." That perhaps understates my political transformation, but may be true, nonetheless.

Henry hands me a letter. It states his worry that he is becoming "a burden" to me. We talk about it as we sit outside the swimming pool overlooking the track. I tell him his fear is nonsense. One mistake I made yesterday was to muse on the question of costs if we go to Sydney. That made him embarrassed.

November 20, 1984, Melbourne

Barbara telegraphs to say that *The New York Times* magazine, "after much discussion," has decided not to commission a piece on Australia from me. So be it. It's better to get a negative reaction at this stage than after having written the piece. Perhaps I will approach *The Atlantic*.

November 21, 1984, Melbourne

I took Stuart Sayers, literary editor of *The Age*, to an expensive lunch at Copperwood, a nice Bistro in Lygon Street. He has the mouth of a Victorian Railways ticket inspector and the fussy manner of a master gardener. But he said interesting things about Melbourne and the fading of British influence in Australia.

I played squash with Peter Self.[193] My elbow hurt and I will have to rest it for a week. Henry and I then went swimming. At home we fell into bed and, considering that I still was not feeling one hundred percent fit—a touch of fever—had great fun. I wish he'd get his dick cut—if he did, I might really fall in love with him.

---

[192] Anthony Allan Staley (1939-), Australian politician.
[193] Peter Self (1919-1999), English academic and writer. At the time of their squash game, Self was Professor of Urban Research at Australia National University.

November 22, 1984, Melbourne

A letter comes from Curt Anderson saying I am pushing my body too hard. At my age, he gently says, what about a shade less sex? But I wish to cling to my youthful ways while I can.

I made a mistake today underestimating what a small world Melbourne can be. At the pool, I ran into Chris B and he happened to mention that he wanted to get interesting Chinese for his radio program on station 3CR. I thought of Wei, from Tianjin, and also of Henry and said that perhaps they could do a program together. Later Henry—when I explained this and described Chris—told me that Chris had often cruised him objectionably at the pool and elsewhere.

November 23, 1984, Melbourne

A night out last night with Raymond L, a gangling, sexy dental student who is my neighbor in Ormond. The night before, I had a dream about him. We were lying naked on a bed. I was on my back and he lay on top of me, also on his back. It was gorgeous—until small black ants appeared, the kind in my flat when rain comes. Then I woke up.

The movie we saw, *Strikebound*, was poor, full of leftwing propaganda. Only one memorable line was spoken. The wives of the "militants" went to a butcher shop to announce that, since the butcher had sniggered during the previous night's solemn meeting about their struggle, none of the Union families would henceforth buy meat at his shop. He was made to look a cowering man of privilege. But he shouted: "Silly Russian red bitches" as the angry women stood before his sides of lamb and trays of sausages.

Afterwards, Raymond and I dined at Café Sport on veal and white wine. I asked Raymond if he was surprised that there are a lot of Chinese gays in Melbourne—as in Hong Kong and China itself. "Not really, because the Chinese have a tendency to go to extremes. So, you get family conservatism on one hand; homosexuality on the other."

Back at my flat watching the tennis on TV and Henry phones. I think he really just wanted to find out if Raymond was there. Lo and behold, Steven phoned ten minutes later. These Chinese!

November 24, 1984, Melbourne

Outside my office window is Vincent Buckley.[194] The old poet and Catholic warhorse, dressed in a navy-blue pullover, trailing his wife and young kids, is walking across the Melbourne University lawn toward his office. I don't like him, but he represents quality. Do I lack quality? Or am I seen as a playboy, an impossibly romantic person, one whose life matters more to him than his art?

---

[194] Vincent Buckley (1925-1988), Australian poet and essayist.

November 25, 1984, Melbourne

Friday afternoon I got some letters off, which always makes me feel good, and Henry and I spent a leisurely evening. We bought pizza and a chicken and cakes in Lygon Street and ate in front of TV—a Diana Ross concert, discussion programs, wonderful tennis from Canberra of all places.

We made love, Henry stayed the night, and we did it again this morning, before going into the Ormond College dining room for eggs and sausages and the morning papers. Among other things, it is the innocence of Henry that delights me. Do I exploit it? I think I simply savor it.

Tonight, after he went to a church meeting and I pretended to do some work, we met again. In the city we saw the colorful, brash, but fascinating Australian movie *Coolangatta Gold* and then dined at West Lake. I thought Henry was subdued, beyond the fatigue which I also felt after much lovemaking and little sleep. There was a reason. It turned out that during the meeting, he was criticized for lack of attention to his religious duties. "I am not sure I can accept religion on the terms presented to us at this church." I was not surprised but I said nothing.

November 26, 1984, Melbourne

Henry brings in his young brother Kevin. We watch the Great Debate between Hawke and Peacock over pizza, chicken, and gorgeous desserts from Lygon Street. In the debate Peacock does well. Some of the journalists' questions are rude; others are trivial.

Brother Kevin is lackluster. Curiously, for one who is so religious, Henry pushed his naked feet at mine as he, his brother, and I watched TV together. I'm sure Kevin felt something was going on—when two people within inches of you get roaring hardons and lust for each other, it's unusual for companions not to know about it.

Kevin left. Henry and I watched satirical TV shows and then made furious love. It seems that for the time being we cannot resist each other's bodies. Up from bed, very late, we watched a summary of the second cricket Test Match before Henry went home.

As Henry and I were discussing the conflicting tug of work and personal affairs, I quoted Herbert Spencer's remark, as he played with one of his grandchildren on his lap: "This kid is worth more than all my books put together." Henry startled me by rejoining: "Just what was the grandchild doing to Spencer at that moment!"

November 27, 1984, Melbourne

Dinner with Patrick McCaughey[195] at Avanti's in Carlton—a sweet and sour evening. He's bright, but narrow. He touches a hundred topics with half-knowledge. Perhaps he has to be shallow in Australia where a gallery director is required to be a jack of all trades.

---

[195] Patrick McCaughey (1942-), Irish-born Australian art historian. At the time of writing, he was the director of the National Gallery of Victoria and had just published *The Pyramid in the Waste: The Search for Meaning in Australian Art* (1983).

November 28, 1984, Melbourne

The staff dinner to close out the year at Ormond turns out to be an enormous buffet; white table-cloths; gardeners in ties and cleaning ladies in 1950s frocks. The Master seeks me out to say the College would be pleased if it might be possible for me to come again next year.

As the white wine flows, I tell C of my suspicions that most of his job problems stem from his being gay. There is a long silence. "How different is it here," he eventually asks, "from in the USA?"

In brilliant sunshine, I took the bus to Footscray to see Steven and have him show me round "the Little Saigon of Melbourne" for my research. In a pinball parlor, where Asian and Italian kids concentrated fiercely on the machines, we fooled round almost to the point of coming. I am still attracted to Steven and if Henry did not fill my days, I would love to go to bed with him.

We had dinner at a poor restaurant. There are better ones, but I wanted to interview waiters and at Fairy Dragon Palace, Steven knew the guys and they spoke Mandarin.

November 29, 1984, Melbourne

I phoned Edward in Boston, who was in a good mood as he dressed for work. The short-term tenants for my apartment fell through, alas, which is a financial setback. The world of renting apartments seems to be as jelly-like as that of licensing foreign translations of literary works. Now you have it, now you don't.

The married woman he's been screwing each Monday is alone in the building because her husband is away from Boston for several months. "He's coming back in January," Edward says. "Do you want to take over Monday nights then?" I suppose I do. But a pang of doubt hit me; after being adored by Henry, who seems to live for me, will I take kindly to the spiritual lashings of the Wild One?

He begs me to warn him before I send any more "frank" photos of myself, Henry, or anyone else. Apparently, Arlene often gets to the mail before he does.

November 30, 1984, Melbourne

I am eager for my *Plu*Perfect* software—a clever hastening-up device to my Perfect Writer. This hunger may be a symbol of my need for the US in general and Boston in particular.

December 2, 1984, Melbourne

It is a relief that the election is over. Nearly all Australian politicians are determined never to have such a long campaign (seven weeks) again. Politics as a game (the Australian view of it) is not worth that many weeks on end. As I expected, the margin between the parties was much less than most people and all the media had expected.

I watched the polling with the Creans and other friends. I get the impression Simon wonders just why I am so interested in Australia when I'm supposed to be a world-famous writer on China, a grander subject. I can't explain why—I hardly know myself what odd mixture of nostalgia, materialism, and vanity drives me ahead with this project.

We dined at Asti's at a table that overlooked Swanston Street. Henry drank more than usual and as his face got pink he began to talk of death and of the cemetery in Carlton, which he says he often visits. "It's a museum of multiculturalism," he says by way of explanation. But I think there is also something very personal in his fixation on death.

Henry and I watched the election results on TV before going to bed at my place. There is no ebbing of our lust. He still gets a hardon whenever I look at him. (The previous night he also stayed over. We had finished making love and were drenched in cum, after lying together for some twenty minutes, when he got up to go to the bathroom; in the moonlight I saw that he was still rock-hard.)

Tomorrow, I lecture to my regular students on "Trends in China" and then begin my last two weeks of work on the Australian topic before leaving Sydney for Hawaii. I look forward to seeing Edward but not to the cold weather.

December 3, 1984, Melbourne

Trees alight with green. Beautiful guys on all sides. Hot dry days. A year winding down toward the summer holidays of Christmas and New Year. The lucky country?

December 4, 1984, Melbourne

A dreadful day. It begins well as I furiously write up notes from yesterday. Toward noon, disaster struck. I accidentally knocked the cord of the Kaypro out of its socket and lost my entire file of notes on Australia for the past week. Minutes later Kay phoned from Boston to say that part of the outside of the top floor of my house has blown off in a typhoon.

December 5, 1984, Melbourne

Henry and I talked things over during an excellent dinner at El Gusto in Carlton. He loves me too much, not too little. I think it helped him a bit to hear me say directly just how much I care for him.

At the start of the dinner, after I had reported on my difficult meeting with Steven, Henry said, "I fear that one day I may be in Steven's place." We came home and made love and again this morning. His ultimate cry is, "You're driving me crazy!"

December 6, 1984, Melbourne

A good meeting with Senator Button[196] this morning. And tonight, a fun party at a publisher's offices to launch Helen Garner's new novel.[197] Everyone drinks themselves

---

[196] John Button (1933-2008), Australian politician. At the time, he was Leader of the Opposition in the Australian Senate.
[197] Helen Garner (1942-), prolific Australian writer. The new novel Terrill refers to is *The Children's Bach*.

into a state of loudness and conviviality. Helen is sparrow-like and humble; it turns out she has read some of my books. Morris Lurie [198] announces he is writing his autobiography. Bill Garner, once Helen's husband (and my student) and now a screen writer at the ABC, asks out of the blue when I am going to switch from nonfiction to fiction.

Bruce Grant [199] is there making shrewd observations and asking thoughtful questions. His wife Joan makes the launching speech. Just as she gets to a passage in her speech about the "unforgettable children's characters" in Helen's novels, two kids who are playing with feather dusters on the balcony above where Joan is speaking burst into villainous laughter.

Afterwards, Rachel chooses a disastrous place for dinner—a London-derived, petty-bourgeois cabaret, accompanied by awful food. To make matters worse, she trots out trendy opinions. I feel she doesn't think for herself.

A wonderful session of lovemaking with Henry after we dine in Little Bourke Street. The best orgasm I have had with him. Afterwards I slept like a doll (though only for five hours). This morning when I woke, Henry was already up and reading in the living room.

December 8, 1984, Melbourne

A roast lamb dinner with Mum at her house. At first, she is in excellent humor, but when the subject turns to herself, she gets maudlin. Finally, I could hardly stand her. As I left, she said, "I'm sorry I was boring." I feel she is less ill than damagingly wrapped up in herself.

December 9, 1984, Melbourne

An idyllic day, green and golden with a suggestion of a breeze in the marvelous Melbourne trees. The city on a Sunday is full of people—mainly young—which is a far cry from the Melbourne Sunday of a decade or two ago. On all sides, attractive and even handsome men are to be seen.

Lunch in Hampton with cousins Len and Dorothy at their shady house near the sea. A relaxed, civilized meal. Len is in a convalescing mood after his recent heart attack. He seems for the moment to have turned into an old man. Dorothy is bright but a shade hectoring toward Len. She gives a hint she knows I'm gay by remarking (during a discussion of Vegemite!), "Make sure he has some waiting for you when you go home."

The nearby China Studies garden party is lackluster, and only Jack Gregory's remarks on how his career was shaped redeems it.[200] Jack is a real Aussie: talks like one, looks like one (in a floppy hat), and is at once self-deprecating and devious, as Aussies often are.

---

[198] Moses "Morris" Lurie (1938-2014), Australian writer. The autobiography, *Whole Life*, was published in 1987.
[199] Bruce Grant (1925-2022), Australian journalist, government advisor and novelist.
[200] John ("Jack") Gregory (1923- 2021), Australian professor of Chinese studies.

The king pin Harry Simon[201] is ignorant of everything that people at a China Studies gathering would naturally talk about. For example, it was news to him that John Fairbank has published his memoirs (though Harry chattered on about having once had dinner with John in Paris; of John having said Harry really ought to visit Harvard sometime; and Harry replying that Cambridge, Massachusetts "is not really on my train line.")

December 10, 1984, Melbourne

Terrible aches in the body and head. Have I got a repetitive strain injury? After a Serepax, I feel somewhat better. A pleasant drink with Mum at the Regent Hotel after her session with the psychiatrist (who said, when I went to pick Mum up there: "I'm pleased to meet you. Your mother has been talking a lot about you. When are you going back to America?").

Later I took Noel M for dinner at Il Vicolo, an excellent restaurant in Grattan Street, to thank him for loaning me his TV set during my Melbourne stay. He has become quite conservative politically. But, unlike me, he is also conservative socially—a closet gay who is still fiddling with cover-up girl friends in a way that deceives no-one.

December 13, 1984. Melbourne

I am getting excited at the thought of getting back to the US. No doubt when I reach Boston, I will pine for the Australian summer days—and realize how many things I should have got done here and failed to do. But on balance—however many more interviews remain ahead—it is time to step back, go over my notes, and see what stage I have reached with the book.

December 14, 1984, Melbourne

After we have dinner with Mum at Murrumbeena, Henry says to me: "Your mother envies you your independent life. She would have liked that for herself. But being brought up in another era, and being a woman in that era, made it impossible." Perhaps it is so. That may be the source of my mother's wistfulness, and of her fondness for me.

December 15, 1984, Melbourne

The amazing thing about Henry is that he blends three things seldom found in abundance within one person: intelligence; sexiness; a penchant for loyalty and domesticity.

Lunch with Dick McGarvie,[202] now a Supreme Court judge. Princely bearing, Scottish ways and values (self-reliance, participation, idealism but of an ordered kind), and a weak mouth like many Australians. Dick alludes to my role in the Labor Party

---

[201] Harry Simon (1923-2019), another Australian Sinologist.
[202] Richard McGarvie 1926-2003), a judge in the Supreme Court of Victoria, 1976-1992.

crisis of years ago. He was kind enough to remark I had played a "historic" role in getting together the group that lead to the reform of the Labor Party in Victoria.

As a judge, he's had cases where criminals decorated their rooms with clippings telling of their murders and of the trial. One time in testimony, it emerged that after an armed robbery the thieves went home and settled down to a night of thrillers on TV. Image and reality become blurred.

December 16, 1984, Melbourne

I feel experience is more important than knowledge as a springboard to art, happiness, and success.

My mother, it seems, came to dislike my father. And the reasons are perhaps the ones that led Pan to fall out of love with me. When Mum looks at me today, she may glimpse the man who disappointed her; for I am my father's son. A pity she and Pan (apparently) never got around to talking about this.

It seems strange to me now that during the Chum Creek sex episode in 1955, when G sucked off H during a high school country retreat, my main feeling was not eroticism. Perhaps I had a hard on? Yet I think curiosity, surprise, and perhaps awe at their boldness were my main feelings.

Now, years later, it seems incredible to me that I did not join in, or even try to join in. And I had to listen to the reaction of darling P, who, after G and H had finished, wrinkled up his broken nose and said, "Think of all the diseases you could get." My mind was not on diseases.

December 17, 1984, Melbourne

Australia is teaching me its abiding lesson: no human being is forever; only the land endures.

Henry Lawson,[203] the great if mysterious Australian writer, said drinking is a man's way of crying. Give up drinking? I talk about it with Henry and we agree that everything depends on what you have been doing the day of the evening you drink (or fail to drink). For my part, after a day on the beach, I have little desire to drink, but after a day of writing or other work I do. It boils down to an argument for rationality and moderation based on need—and a rejection of drinking as an obsession.

December 19, 1984, Melbourne

It is a wrench to leave Melbourne after happy months. The flat at Ormond College again resembles the bare spot at which I arrived in early August. Different and unforgettable are the friendships and good times and hard work that have filled the spring and summer days since then. It has all exceeded my expectations, even my hopes. How much of that is due to Henry? How much is due to a gut feeling of satisfaction at being "at home"? Henry has already left by train, and we will meet in Sydney tonight.

---

[203] Henry Lawson (1867-1922), Australian writer and "bush poet"; cited as Australia's "greatest short story writer.

December 20, 1984, Sydney

At the swank and marvelously located Sheraton-Wentworth Hotel, I feel like an American pretending to be an Australian. How to tip? I solve the dilemma by narrowing my eyes and tipping like a foreigner. The Australian bellboys despise this, as do I, but if they suspect the guest is a foreigner, there arises a weird duty for all parties to sink to an un-Australian level of condescension-and-superiority.

Henry is utterly rational—that is his greatest difference from Edward. Even in the midst of passion, he manages to be like an engineer over the practical arrangements and maneuvers.

In the morning, he loves to come over to my bed even before I'm awake. He says, "Hold me," and twines himself around me. Even when we don't make love again, strength to face the day flows into me from these morning moments.

December 21, 1984, Sydney

"I like your ears," I said to Henry as we ate lunch. "That's why they're just about hanging off," he rejoined with a lovely grin. He has a way of hesitating before making a remark, then when he has spoken, drawing in his lips, his eyes sparkling—a look which indicates satisfaction at what he has said.

Near our hotel, on a wall: WITH FRIENDS LIKE THE USA WHO NEEDS ENEMIES?

An Aussie remarks with typical disdain for the land to the south, "New Zealand has a population of 15 million sheep, 3 million of them humans."

I got stupidly tough with Henry when we were dining at the Albury Hotel. He kept glancing at a blond guy in a corner of the restaurant. Eventually I said, "If you like him so much, why not go over and join him?" Henry quite reasonably came back: "You don't even allow me the freedom to look around the room." Happily, he did not say it in an angry tone.

December 22, 1984, Sydney

On the way to Redfern, where Henry and I were on the prowl, our taxi driver got uptight at the mention of our destination. I was vague about where we were going, just saying we were looking for a hotel in the area. The guy said: "There is a hotel near Redfern station, but you wouldn't want to go there—it's where the Blacks drink."

"I'm history," says a guy who sways past me in the doorway of this Railway Parade Hotel. "Come home with me," says a woman as she grabs me to her flabby, smelly body; it is perhaps the most physically distasteful moment of my life.

Inside the toilet, a guy sits on the floor near the urinals with a liquor bottle in his trembling hand. A second man is curled up inside the one cubicle (you see the form beneath the door). At the urinals, piss pours out of Black cocks like water from firemen's hoses.

A guy called Steven is one of only two in the pub who looks sleepable. He seems like a pimp, the way he walks in briskly, dressed neater than the others. He spoke of his "missus." For a moment I thought he meant his mother, but he was referring to his British wife, who is now in hospital having their second kid.

"Not a real wife. You know, a de facto." Steven went to UK with her and loved it. "It's the best country in the world." Steven is just out of prison, for the second time. Did he regret committing the crime? "Not really, because I made $68,000 out of it—it was armed robbery, you see."

December 23, 1984, Sydney

At Lady Jane Beach,[204] we see a new Sydney. The atmosphere seems more medical than sexual, but we meet a gorgeous guy in blue trunks, dark complexion, well hung. He smiles at Henry and later at me. He is probably gay, but not "out"—getting away from the family, wanting solitude, but not knowing quite what he wants sexually.

From a ferry boat, women cry out in jest to the nude bathers in general: "You're all ugly. You score 1 in 10." Indeed, the naked people climbing on the rocks look more like insects than human beings—lacking their "human" colors, they lack much of their human character.

We see a scattering of Orientals—Henry is the only one of them who disrobes utterly—and as we leave a large number descend, including one old granny. This offers a vision of tomorrow when Orientals, swinging from one extreme to the other, will "discover" Lady Jane Beach and make it their own preserve of libertarianism, free from Asia's restraints. The old Australians will quietly move over.

Tonight, I visit Dick Hall[205] at home. He gets up every half hour for another bottle of beer. I begin to quiz him on Aussie politics. As he drinks beer, his face gets larger, redder, more animated. For him the Labor Party is still "we" and "us."

With FE, a fascinating session on the Australian fashion industry and Sydney life. Next time, I have in mind a more personal talk: the way we were at school and why and how we've changed; what does he recall of G; did his shift to Sydney have anything to do with his unconventional sexuality?

December 24, 1984, Sydney

My last day in Australia, after a wonderful week in Sydney. Henry and I play round early in the morning. Then breakfast with George Negus, the star of the Australian "60 Minutes," in the Pink Room of the hotel.

Back in the room, I furiously pack, and Henry and I plan our departure, before I go to interview Premier Wran.[206] As I was dressing for the interview, Henry saw a button missing on my shirt and quickly sewed it on. Then the question came up of what tie I would wear. He picked out a yellow and blue one—the very tie Edward bought me last time on the "Today Show" in New York. I looked at the pale blue shirt and, blow me

---

[204] Lady Jane Beach, popular nude beach in Sydney.
[205] Richard ("Dick") Hall (1937-2003), Australian writer and, at the time of Terrill's visit, president of the New South Wales State Library Council.
[206] Neville Wran (1926-2014), Premier of New South Wales from 1976 to 1986.

down, if it wasn't also the same shirt I wore that morning! Such eerie moments of connection make you feel like an ant on the surface of the universe.

Wran is a dream to interview; the session was excellent. The perfect prelude for one last hour of lovemaking. It was the best orgasm for weeks. As we writhed, I watched bits of the Test match against the West Indies out of the corner of my eye. We dressed and I said to Henry: "Well, that's enough sex for a while." He looked at me with wide eyes. All I meant was enough until I got back to Boston on Wednesday.

We staggered to the airport; would Henry like a drink? To my surprise he said, yes, he'd like a Tia Maria with milk. I had never heard of this drink, nor did it sound like one a born-again Christian would imbibe. We said unemotional goodbyes. I embarked for Auckland and Hawaii. Tomorrow, Henry goes to a Christian convention.

December 24, 1984, Aboard Pan Am

Many New Zealanders on this flight to Auckland: embarrassingly friendly, grinning with pleasure at making it home for Christmas (Air New Zealand is on strike). They are the country cousins whose rusticism you also find in Western Tasmania.

Auckland from its airport looks like a village in the north of England. But good to taste sweet NZ butter again. Nothing changes at this airport—even the sheepskin rugs are still for sale in the same spot; the only different thing is the plunge in the New Zealand dollar.

December 24, 1984, Honolulu

This spring and early summer in Australia have been important. The affair with Henry brought great joy. Putting my mind back on to the topic of Australia is satisfying. Now the US accent hits me. And I feel a twinge of the cultural aversion to the US that I felt years ago but thought had left me.

December 25, 1984, Honolulu

Back in the US, the dynamism amazes me. People get on busses faster, move faster, do more. Here on Christmas morning the *Today Show* and *Good Morning America* are on deck; and by "Boxing Day" tomorrow the stores will be open again to trumpet big sales. All this is unthinkable in Australia where holidays stretch out.

In the US, a dollar is a dollar; in Australia a single dollar is often treated with contempt. At the Ala Moana Hotel, I tip $1 for a $7 breakfast and the waiter is pleased. Americans have to strive more for their wages than Australians do, and are more on their toes and more appreciative of what they get.

December 26, 1984, Boston

I couldn't reach Edward on the phone from California, but by a wonderful chance he turns the key and walks into the apartment within 30 minutes of my arrival from Logan.

I am overcome. It has been so long. There is so much to say and do. He nearly had a heart attack to see the lights on in my apartment two days before I was supposed to arrive. "I expected to walk in and find the place stripped of everything, ripped off—why would the place be blazing with lights?"

December 27, 1984, Boston

As Edward and Glen are at my place, all thrilled at the reunion, Edward raises his eyebrows several times and looks at my trousers. Apparently, I was from time to time touching my dick. After Glen went, Edward asked where I had picked up this custom. I said perhaps Australians do it. "Well, I can tell you, Black guys do it. But this is the first time I've seen you do it."

Life is horrible—at the level of logic. Life is wonderful—at the level of imagination. I am in process, artistically and professionally, of moving from the basement of the first realm to the penthouse of the second.

I recall tonight that August morning I departed from Boston nearly five months ago: hot and hazy; my mind torn with sadness at leaving; a last rush to the YMCA. And now, this December day of return: Australia was good for me and changed me; at the same time, immense joy at seeing Edward again and picking up the threads of my life.

December 29, 1984, Boston

Quite a 24 hours. Last night, Edward called just when I was beginning to feel alone and flat. Soon he came around. We dined at Soom Thai—and came home and made love, first with the koala bear and kangaroo (it has a long hard tail) that I brought home as gifts, then long and gloriously with each other.

Soaked in baby oil, greased with Vaseline, we came like tornados. His asshole is my paradise. "Screw me," he shouted as I bore into him. For the first time, he rimmed me fully and lavishly—how I adored it. The orgasm left me trembling.

I thought he might want to go home, but he had no intention of doing so. This morning, we made love again. He began by saying, "Where are your magazines?" with an expression that suggested he did not mean *The Atlantic Monthly* or *National Geographic*. I was busy in my study when he called me into the bedroom.

I went on to Justin and Anne's for a small party. Mike Janeway was there, Penny looking dashing, and they had two pieces of news. While I was away, Mike was named Tom Winship's successor as editor-in-chief of the *Boston Globe*. And sad beyond belief, Bob Manning, Mike's chief editor at *The Atlantic*, has lost his wife Maggie, dead of cancer on Christmas Day.

Stratis said his new novel "came and went."[207] Anne said indeed in her view it isn't as good as his earlier work. Meanwhile, Justin told me that Jim Carroll's *Prince of Peace* is better than his previous work. I'll have to make another attempt to read it. Anne has changed publishers yet again. Her next book, a memoir, will be with Doubleday.

---

[207] Stratis Haviartis (1935-2020), writer in Greek and English. The novel referred to is *The Heroic Age* (Simon & Schuster 1984). A previous novel, *When the Tree Sings*, was shortlisted for the National Book Award.

1985

January 1, 1985, Boston

It is not easy this morning to get hold of 1985, as last night the new neighbors downstairs held a wild party with loud music until God knows when (I suppose the lesson is don't stay at home on New Year's Eve).

The major factor in my personal life is Edward; it comes as a shock that 1984 was our first year together. We are not quite together—even in the sense that Henry and I were together in Australia for three months—yet we are bound in an intense relationship. Sexually there has been no parallel in my life to a passion growing stronger after more than a year.

I know all the negatives. He is bisexual and has a girl friend who adores him, and is hooked on him as much as I am. He has not made enough progress professionally for his 25 years. He seems to have been brought up as a slightly spoilt child. He is not "in love" with me and I am not "in love" with him, or so we say. The bond with him has weakened my friendship with people whom I value deeply—Ray W, Michael Mao (neither of these have even met Edward). Despite all that, he is the great star in my life as 1985 begins.

The big event was publication of *The White-Boned Demon*. It did quite well. There was unevenness to its "performance." Being a featured alternate of the Book of the Month Club, also of the History Book Club, and a main selection of the Quality Paperback Book Club was a success. Bookstore sales, however, were modest. And the reception in general seems to be up-and-down. Great acclaim and sales in California, for instance, and an option for filming by the Shapiros of 20th Century Fox, while in Boston the *Globe* and the *Monitor* didn't like the book much.

Foreign editions have been quite good—about on a par with Mao. Striking differences so far in the pattern of sales. No German edition for *White-Boned Demon* so far yet a good French one—the opposite with Mao. The Sinological community has been so far sharply divided as to the book's merits. For everyone who is enthusiastic (Dick Solomon) there has been a silent one (Fairbank).

Wonderful to state, health during 1984 went from shaky to excellent. Toward the end of the year, I knocked off the anti-TB drugs. The right lung is presumed to be slightly damaged, but a recurrence of the TB is not expected.

The months of deliberation over my next book led to an unexpected decision to write about Australia. The stay in Australia confirmed the wisdom of the choice; I got into the material; it was good for me to distance myself from China. The *National Geographic* assignment on Sichuan will keep my hand in with the Middle Kingdom. The trip to gather material for it in mid-year went well.

The time in Australia was pleasant beyond work. I got back in close touch with favorite family members. It was fun to live in Ormond College for a while (I wouldn't like it year-round). The civility and convenience of Carlton life was great. Above all, the affair with Henry gave me one of the happiest few months of my life. He is a wonderful blend of passion and intelligence. But I think he feels my life in America—Edward in particular—is a shadow over his being with me.

Looking back on the drama of the trip to Australia in February to consider the job at the ANU, I can see that the problem (from my side) was the institution of academia, and to a degree Canberra, rather than Australia as such. The episode clarified things. I could live part of the year in Australia under the right circumstances. But I do not want a university post again anywhere.

January 1, 1985, evening, Boston

I asked Edward if Arlene would like to come out to dinner with us and he replied, "A marvelous idea." But he turned up alone. She had not felt like coming after all. "She slept all day," he said cryptically. It's new for Arlene to get miffed at Edward coming to see me; it always used to be me getting miffed at the time he spent at her place in Randolph. The Bandit—without making any pronouncements about it—may have upscaled me.

We had a talk over a glass of Italian white wine and then went to dinner at the Imperial Tea House in Chinatown. He repeatedly criticized Arlene: "I saw her lying on the bed today and I thought of the words of her mother, 'You look six months pregnant.'" She made a New Year's resolution to go to exercise classes, but Edward does not seem confident she'll keep to it.

It turns out she will take the bar exam again in July. "Maybe I'll break up with her before then and this will spur her to a big effort—just to get over me." It was a bombshell.

And yet it fits the pattern of his attitude toward her—and me—since I got back from Australia. He may go down to New York to comfort his about-to-be-divorced sister for a few months when Shawmut fires him, as he expects. No doubt this would help fix the moment of his break with Arlene.

After dinner we went to Washington Street and bought a video of seven Black guys "working out." For the next hour or so we were rivetted to the screen as these gorgeous Black guys did their tricks. We felt stunned when it was over. A good night kiss and he went home.

January 2, 1985, Boston

Dinner with Helen Rees at Copley's. She is pretty upset at finding out that her son is gay. I advised her to take the view that his studies and his health are more important than anything else; if she focusses on guiding him in these areas, that will avoid a counter-productive confrontation on the gay question.

I am not good at holidays and festivals. If I can calm down, do things step by step, think things through, listen to people, heed signals and realities around me, and not be too self-oriented, then my Golden Age is ahead.

January 6, 1985, Boston

I watch a movie with Edward, and we make love in front of it. He is in an imperious mood—do this, do that. At one point, I pushed my butt close to his face. (Last week he had stuck his tongue up my ass which nearly drove me crazy.) He growled: "You're blocking the movie. I can have your ass any time."

As we watched *Black Workout*, his cock became granite-like. Soon he pushed me into position, grabbed my cock, moved his thighs over, and impaled himself on my throbbing, yearning prick. As usual he was ready to spurt within one to two minutes of my going into him.

I showed him the pics of Australia that just came back from Fotomat and also Henry's letter. Of the pic of me nude on the beach at Sydney he declared: "the best photo of you naked so far."

In the letter, Henry spoke of meeting two guys at Lady Jane Beach, one a Rumanian, the other a Vietnamese who "was 25 but looked 16." Edward turned his huge sensual eyes on me and asked: "Do I look 16?" (he is also 25).

January 8, 1985, Boston

My appointment at the Fairbank Center of Harvard means less to me, and it seems only a matter of time before it comes to an end. Two years ago, I would have regretted this. Now I would not, except for a pang of injustice if they should summarily end it themselves.

January 11, 1985, Boston

Edward is unreasonably changeable. He seems to have forgotten about getting rid of Arlene. Of his gay side, which means his relationship with me, he says as we dine at St. Botolph: "Sometimes I don't think it's any problem, other times I think it is."

It's pretty clear that last week dear Arlene reacted. He told her he was probably coming with me to the Orient in March. She reacted badly and this set the pendulum of his ambivalence swinging again.

January 14, 1985, Boston

A difficult conversation with Edward late at night. We planned to meet tonight but he didn't call, nor was he at his number. He said he forgot; but later he said. "I'm not a good liar. I just did not trust myself."

So, I am the symbol of gayness in his mind. When he is in a 100% straight mood I am a threatening temptation. The one you care for, you threaten! At one point I said to him, with a touch of irony on my part, that evidently he was interested only in sex. "Yes, I am." This has long been a bone of contention between us—Edward saying that I am interested only in sex. You can't win.

January 15, 1985, Boston

Today in the mail, a wonderful review of *White-Boned Demon* in the *Glasgow Herald*. And a frightful and I think libelous one in the rag of the US-China Friendship Association. Will I sue? A negative review is one thing; a tissue of lies based upon political objections, is another.

January 17, 1985, Boston

I wonder why men like their girlfriends to have a lesbian interest, but women are terrified if their boyfriend has a gay interest.

January 18, 1985, Boston

With these appalling new neighbors beneath me, it's getting hard even to fuck in peace. Lunch at Ta Wei with Yang Bingzhang. He is in good spirits and we pick up just where we left off. Yang on American soil and Yang on Chinese soil are not identical. He even wants to do more work for me. Did he suffer any adverse effect in China last summer from having worked with me on *The White-Boned Demon*?

"No." After a pause he added: "But I did at Harvard. These professors are jealous of you, you see. Indirectly they discriminate against me as a way of expressing that."

January 19, 1985, Boston

The last few days have been like a dike long held back bursting forth. On Wednesday night, Edward was here playing music when David C phoned. After asking Edward, I rang David back and said come over. It had been many months since David and I saw each other.

Edward was his usual self as David and I carried on. For a while David and I played around upstairs until I said to David that I wanted to try to get Edward to join in.

David put his pants back on. I did not; I thought I would talk to Edward without them. Downstairs, Edward was still at his music, copying records on to cassettes. "Is David going to take a shower?" he asked with a little smile. He wanted to see David naked; but he was not going to take big initiatives, or even small ones.

David stayed over—Edward did not—and at 6 AM we made love again before he went off to his new job with the Federal Government. His huge dick was in great form. In the morning he began the lovemaking by first nestling close, then pushing his cock into my thighs, finally grabbing my cock and stroking the battered weapon as only he can do.

Later that morning, Wayne came. And during the afternoon, Reggie rang the doorbell! Reggie, a student, is perhaps the most irresistibly attractive guy whom I see, Black and lithe and dynamic. The day I met him at the YMCA, I was sure he was straight. A week later he begged me to fuck him, which I did, and I will never forget it.

Though I was, I thought, a spent force I got a hardon within 10 seconds of hearing Reggie's voice over the intercom. But I couldn't do anything with him at that moment as Ann Swift, my grim, hard, Buddhist cleaning lady, was in the apartment at work.

January 20, 1985, Boston

I phoned Luther in Louisiana. Luther had the yellow pages of the phone book open; he was about to call Delta Airlines to make a reservation for Boston. A few nights later, I was making love in the old furious way with Luther; he is staying for a while.

We went to Bangkok to dine in celebration of his readmission to law school. When we got home there was a message that Hank had called from Georgia! Hank of all people, the guy whose memory drove me crazy during the first month in Australia.

I phoned him. He gasped, he sighed, he couldn't bear to go any longer without me fucking him. I got uncontrollably horny. I told him he has the most beautiful dick in the USA, and I think he began to jerk off. He is going to visit soon. Meanwhile I went to bed and made love with Luther.

Luther was altogether superior to the first night. His dick nearly leapt through the ceiling—his worries about law school were behind him.

Perhaps all this is just my nature asserting itself as I prune my branches of lesser things, making my own world.

January 22, 1985, Boston

Dinner last night at Java with Luther. I fear I will quickly get bored with him. So few people are worth both sleeping with and talking with. Perhaps we will settle down. And if he keeps going to the gym his body will harden up again.

January 23, 1985, Boston

Dinner with Edward at St. Botolph . He is in a good mood. I had decided not to "pressure" him. "Sometimes," I remarked, "it seems to me that when you are in your present mood, even my existence is a threat to you." That was the only complaint I made.

When he first arrived (before we went to the St. Botolph) I introduced him to Luther, who was studying his law books in the green room. "Haven't we met somewhere?" Edward said. Luther didn't think they had but he politely said, "Perhaps at one of Ross's parties." But they hadn't.

Edward said both with his girlfriends and me personality counts more than physical attraction. "I'm not like you, you see," he explained. "You go and get handsome young studs. I don't do that. The proof is that I'm here with you tonight."

With Edward, the hurtful things are mixed with an enticing excitement that comes from homosexuality still being for him a novelty. I confessed that sometimes I am compulsive in wanting to have sex; as if I am trying to prove something. "You don't have to prove anything," he said. Did he understand me? Do I understand what I was saying?

January 24, 1985, Boston

Mum phones from Melbourne—she is "quite disturbed." Amongst the music tapes I left for her listening pleasure, there apparently were two sex diaries! "Anyone could have heard these," she pointed out, flustered. "Sex is a private matter, you know." I was amazed that such a mistake could have been made.

"Were they meant for me to hear?" she asked. When I said certainly not, she said: "Well, I am glad to hear that."

Later she said, "I suppose this is part of your memoirs—goodness me!" I did not ask why she listened to the tapes once she realized they were not music, not for her, and "not nice."

January 26, 1985, Boston

It seems that Luther is raising Edward's name again. Inevitably, I suppose there'll be some crunch. We make love almost every night now, and the good news is that Luther is getting better and better. I think that when he arrived from Louisiana, he was just out of practice.

January 28, 1985, New York

The lunch with Fred Hills at Sea Grill is pleasant. He seems happy with me. He wants a commercial book. He doesn't care if "everything" isn't in it. He warns me off "boring" topics that are merely informative.

He confides that he is not 100% happy with the Joan Kennedy biography that my friend Pam is helping with. The US fascination with the elite, he says, can bring its lesson for my book. Include stuff on the British imperial strutting in Australia—US readers will love that.

I made a lightning visit to 42nd Street. The strip was crisp and rugged-up, but exciting, nonetheless. I saw snippets of a few videos; I will buy (or rent) them when I get back. I met a charming Black musician named Tony. He said: "I have a big Black New York dick." Indeed, he did.

He was fascinated with Australia, and we talked almost as much as we screwed. He said an unexpected thing: "Have you got any weapons on you?" I, as the Australian visitor, might have been anxious about such a thing; but him too? He said he often saw Truman Capote at the place he and I met—until Capote's death.

A visit at Bantam Books leaves me grim about the paperback prospects for *White-Boned Demon*. Though the book is due out in April, they have just scrapped the planned cover and commissioned more proposals! Orders were disappointing based on the first cover (do covers matter that much?) They do not know how many they will print— "probably 25,000."

They do not favor a double page of review quotes at the front of the book. No reason other than they do it for rack-size books for not for trade. The reprint editor "thinks" the list of corrections that I submitted has been incorporated.

I report to my agent Barbara, later in the day, and she shrugs her shoulders. "Well, she is only a reprint editor."

January 29, 1985, Boston

A rushed day in New York, punctuated by a marvelous couple of hours watching the Australian movie, *Man of Flowers*. Then back to Boston to shop for the party I give tomorrow.

I did not want to make love with Luther, though it took persistence to get that clear. Just when I thought I could at last get to sleep, Edward phones, in a soft, probing mood. "You don't owe me a thing," he says. "I don't know how you put up with my incongruities."

The trouble is at present I don't even understand those "incongruities." Will he snap out of this straight mood? Or is it that I for a season bent him to a gay mood that is indeed beyond his nature?

"Have we anything more to offer to each other's lives?" I ask. There is a long silence. "As long as there is breath in our bodies, I think you and I will be offering things to each other."

He said he wasn't impressed with Luther. A little earlier in the evening, Luther told me he wasn't impressed with Edward (they had a talk while I was in New York). "He sounds like an imported Black American," says Luther of Edward. "At the age of 25, he should know what he wants to study and to do ... and it's immature to jump around as a bisexual that way." Edward thinks Luther is dumb.

I realized with a shock that sex with a guy does take it out of Edward; he remarked that after that evening when we made wild love in front of the TV set upstairs, he did not go to work next day.

Drawn on by his self-critical mood, I said it had been a shock to experience from him two totally dissimilar moods in the period since my return from Australia—one gay and the other straight. "Why bother with me?" Edward asks. It is a good question. But would he ask it if his interest had really gone?

January 30, 1985, Boston

I felt stronger today, in part because I had no sex yesterday (I sucked Tony in New York but did not come). With all the strain of last week, I promised myself that today nothing hectic or strenuous in order to be fresh for my buffet dinner party this evening. But life's timing can be amazing.

The doorbell rang and it was Julius. I hadn't seen him for months. He was always ferociously attractive and today more than ever, his eyes blazing, his cock perfect. I was going to keep my promise to myself, but I said I'd come downstairs and say hello. He had that look in the eyes that says, "My cock is hard and getting harder and will soon explode." We played with each other, stared at each other, moving from the lobby to the stairway near Kay's apartment, to the little corner where the electrical box is located.

My neighbor came bouncing down the stairs and we stopped momentarily. "I want it so bad," Julius kept saying. "Suck my cock just a bit." I did, as I knelt in the lobby of my own building. Then he grabbed me and said he wanted to get mine down his throat—a new theme for Julius. For some extraordinary reason, the neighbor then came bouncing back *into* the building! It seemed a tragedy to stop short of coming but we did. He will drop by again tomorrow afternoon.

The party went well, maybe one of the smoothest and calmest I have given: 21-22 people, rather diverse, but no one I think left out. Several people said I looked well and relaxed. David lingered and I started to fondle Luther in front of him as we watched TV. David began to touch Luther also.

I realized that Luther is not much into other Blacks, but when David told me he liked Luther ("Why do you think I stayed this late?"), I encouraged him. The three of us had wild sex. I loved ramming both their dicks down my throat at once. As David and I lay together, Luther did the same with our two pricks. Luther nearly went crazy when David and I sucked his tits at the same time. So did I when they did that to me.

We all came together., I brought Edward to my mind as I did this or that. The other two slept for a couple of hours, but I can never sleep after such excitement. At 6 AM the wake-up call came for David, but he decided not to stir. This made Luther irritated. "Move your butt and get to work."

"Yes, Mother," came a lightning, snarled response from David.

Was Luther just tired and hungover, or was he not pleased that David had joined us? I found myself hardly able to wait to hear the door click shut before touching legs with David and getting going. We got up, drank orange juice and coffee together, as he regaled me with stories about his grandfather, then he left and I sat down to work.

Later, Julius arrived, and we made love fairly quickly just before I flew off for a doctor's appointment. He had been been playing basketball at Charlestown and was sweaty but cuddly. Despite the earlier exertions, I shot about two meters. The old body is performing.

When Luther came home, he said he had been furious in bed that morning. "During the party, David had been complaining about the plight of Black people, and here he was being so weak-willed. That's what brings trouble to Black people." Luther felt David should have just got up and gone to work. "I was jealous of him; I mean he was going to stay there in bed with you while I had to get up and go to classes."

February 1, 1985, Boston

In bed, Luther wants to make love, but I only to sleep. That Southern pining tone enters his voice: "But I'm horny for you, Ross. We gotta get together today, OK?"

"We will tonight," I murmured. I try to get down to my book, but it is hard to get my private life locked back into a box.

I understand now why people mostly fuck at night: if you're to share a bed with that person you might as well have sex at the same time. I have been used to sex and sleeping being two separate activities, to be done at different times of the day or night. But maybe this is universal.

February 17, 1985, Boston

There's nothing to "get clear" with Edward. In the end, we need each other. We will go on—but we will go on being uncertain of each other, even as we fascinate and sometimes delight each other. What each of us ideally wants does not exist. But what each of us has with the other is real and probably more important than we now realize.

February 20, 1985, Boston

Reggie came in at last. The three of us were eating pizza upstairs when the phone rang. Luckily, it was for Luther; while he took it, Reggie and I slipped downstairs and did not emerge from the bedroom until next day. He came four times and me three. The bedroom was too cold for Reggie at first and he said, "The only thing warm about this room is your dick." Later, as he was rubbing our two cocks together, he said, "Your damn thing has grown two inches since we did this last."

February 22, 1985, Boston

Edward came around; we were to have dinner, work on his résumé, and spend the night together. But the Luther factor was a difficulty. When I went to make love to him, he said: "I've been attacked once, I don't want to be again." I took this as meaning last night, by Luther, at Edward's place. He jumped up. "You know I'm not into that kind of thing." Attacked? Not into that kind of thing?

The topic of Luther had been in the air, but I wasn't going to raise it. I didn't care about last night—if Edward and I had one of our sessions tonight. It accorded with what I told him the night after the dinner at Anthony's Pier Four: I don't care if he fools round as long as we continue to enjoy each other and be honest with each other.

I called him a fraud who didn't know what he wanted. He said I was addicted to "Black dicks" and didn't know what a love affair was. He said I had no idea of all the things I could give him. He said I had no idea how much he had confided in me—never had he told so much about his gay life and thoughts as to me; and never had he devoted himself to a man a tenth of the degree he had to me.

Eventually, I took his briefcase to the door once more, opened the door, and ushered him out. But he came back. He wanted a "tête-à-tête." We didn't get much further. I told him I didn't want him to set foot in my place ever again. We talked about giving back each other's things. He said that among those he wanted were pictures of himself. I said I couldn't find them at a moment's notice, and asked just which pictures did he have in mind?

Later he phoned, very sweet, wanting to exchange our things. This we did in the middle of that torrid night. But this time there was to be no weakness on my part. The guy who kidded himself I was easy game for a "Black dick" turned out to be wrong. My anger did not subside. At 1 AM, Reggie—pleasant as always—arrived with the car to help the move, so that was that.

So, he was jealous of my various Black friends. And I am accused of talking to Tony and other friends about him and me. Yet tonight, I was regaled with stories of Mrs. V saying this and that about Edward and me; and of Edward's mother having concluded that Edward and I are having an affair!

It's all to do with fucking. If I hadn't been fucking Edward—my dick up his ass—I doubt that his phobias would have been so strong. It's he, not me, that thinks of gay love as cocks and assholes and nothing more. His entire history is that.

Until he met me, sex with men for him meant the Combat Zone. The guy who always said he didn't want a relationship announces to me that I am incapable of a relationship. He also tosses in that he knows why Pan left me—because I can't resist any Black body that comes before me.

With a woman he can combine sex and friendship; with a man he cannot. Of his lovely qualities, I like best his smile—when it's real.

He thinks his Black dick can do all, but it cannot. To say it was "a mistake" to (as he put it) "have an affair" with Luther, and then to do it again, some days later, and the next day refuse sex with me—when I was leaving for China within 36 hours—that was not good.

February 23, 1985, Boston

I phoned Arlene this afternoon. I said I was sorry she was kept waiting last night (no doubt she rushed up the stairs because she feared the two of us might have had a reconciliation and be screwing). I told her I knew that my friendship with Edward may have been puzzlement—and a problem—for her but that from now on I would be out of the way. She said little, other than that the revelation of his bisexuality had "thrown" her and she would just take things step by step. I said I found Edward charming but also exasperating. She said she did too. I wished her well.

I also phoned Edward's mother. She clearly knew much about me. I began by saying I knew how close he felt to her. I stressed to her that I wouldn't be seeing Edward "for a while" as I was leaving the country. I said I hoped very much that he would have a chance to finish his degree. We talked about his character, agreeing on most points (how easy!). She hinted at flaws; I said each person must find his own way and standards.

Looking back, I feel the key is pedestrian. We both wanted two simple but enormous things: control and loyalty!

February 25, 1985, Peking

In this strange dinosaur of a Great Wall Hotel, every time I look at myself in the mirror, I think of myself as the one Edward rejected, or the one who could not put up with flaws of Edward's that seem, here in China, to be fairly minor. Now I've found a new way to be unhappy—dealing with China, instead of Edward.

February 26, 1985, Peking

Trying to solve problems that don't exist is my specialty—such as the imagined emotional bond between Edward and Luther. And here I am in Peking having a dream about issues that arise, months from now, on my arrival for my second research trip to

Australia! Some things I begin to see more clearly. I never got to make Edward see that I cared for him in a way totally above my lust for Reggie, Julius, or David. Why did I tell him about bouts with these and others, he may have wondered. Because I wanted to increase my attractiveness to him!

In a strange way, I caused him to play around with Luther, and yet I came to suffer from him doing it. Only because Luther was with me did Edward go for him (contrast while I was in Australia; he saw almost no men).

Perhaps he did want to love me. I recall that conversation in the St. Botolph restaurant when he wanted me to tell him how much I loved him. Yet he wasn't prepared to give more than about 20% of what would be required. People can be like that.

The lesson I can learn takes me back to the movie *Man of Flowers*, in which a man puts his passion into a strange vessel. Perhaps I can capture in fiction the love and excitement that I can't, it seems, sustain for a long time with Edward.

February 27, 1985, Peking

Shen is mystified as to what two guys can do together, or two girls, or various kinds of threesomes. Of course, the point is that he has had no such experience. Can there be any doubt that when the Chinese—yes, the Chinese—start to experience sucking dicks, orgies, licking asses, etc., that they will get addicted just the way anyone else who experiences these things does?

This aspect of modernization will come to appeal to them as all the other aspects. Someone who hasn't had his dick sucked while sucking another dick, and being rimmed at the same time, just can't imagine what a quantum leap ahead of normal Chinese sex practices it is. Give them time; people are basically equal.

February 28, 1985, Peking

This morning, I feel a little better. I didn't sleep much but I did sleep, and I didn't think of Edward and sex all night.

March 1, 1985, Out of Peking

I am on the train headed for Sichuan, slopping a bowl of noodles in a swaying dining car. I begin to feel I am in China. Like my father, I have been able to keep a young-looking body into my 40s. I hope that, unlike my father, I will not be overcome by illness in my 50s.

March 2, 1985, Shaanxi-Sichuan Border

Overnight I had a bitter-sweet dream. The doorbell rang and it was Reggie. He said: "Do you want to see me?" I said I did and pressed the buzzer to open the door. He didn't come in. I woke up—not in Boston, but on a Chinese train.

I feel my life is empty. A voice says that I have six books to my credit. That seems another realm. In one sense they exist, yet only the future counts. The train may be good for me because I have nowhere to go that would make me happy; to be in a place that is not one place may be the best.

Yes, I am insecure, as Edward said. But how to be otherwise? Someone of my sexual orientation, candor, and desire for intimate communication lives in a society where all three are rare, and dangerous to most people.

March 4, 1985, Chengdu

Having four or five regular sex partners, plus a certain amount of promiscuity, which I love, is a pattern with risks and stupendous rewards. Only at night do I constantly think of Edward. Twin emotions grab me in the gut: anger and regret.

March 6, 1985, Chengdu

Still weird dreams, tonight one about my mother. She had planned a party at a hotel. She didn't mention this to me. I had told her I was going to visit Rosemary and Barry, my likeable but slightly disreputable cousins. She happened to be getting the same train. She was all dressed up in a ballroom gown.

I drifted into the party, for some reason. My mother was elegant and an excellent hostess, but at one point she fell down, rather dramatically. It seemed she had invited all these people, though me had just casually invited at the last moment. I was very moved by her performance at the party. I left. Then, I thought, she was so magnificent for an elderly lady, I must go back and congratulate her. But at the hotel some people said she had hammed it, her fall was overly dramatic. This rang an unpleasant bell within me. So I didn't approach her. I just left.

The turning point toward a better morale is that I can do a fine article on Sichuan if I get to it.

Chengdu, Sichuan,1985

How best to please a foreign visitor? This lady's answer was to make extra-large dumplings filled with pork and winter bamboo, served with sugared lychees and sesame. Her father turns 60 today, so the lunch is especially festive. Girls at adjacent tables wear high heels even though the nearest street is full of mud.

March 8, 1985, Chengdu

China is changing. As we had sex in the park near the hotel, this young guy took my purse from the back of my pants. Just moved his hand from my ass to the pocket of my white pants. I said, "Don't be silly." He had little resolution or experience. I took my purse back. China is half-changing.

March 10, 1985, Chengdu

I got to fool about with Xu, though it took two issues of the *National Geographic* and a picture book on Sichuan to do it—sitting on a couch together leafing through the pages!

But I bungled a liaison with a guy in the fashion. Partly because my Chinese isn't good enough for his accent and partly because once more, I sniff a rejection when it isn't there; I gave up too early.

March 18, 1985, Chongqing

I think of times of sexual experience as among the very best times of my life. Some will say that is selfish, but nothing could be more wrong. My memories of sexual pleasure are as much of giving as receiving. I think I have given more joy to others through sex than through writing, teaching, friendship, or conversation.

March 27, 1985, Hong Kong

The time with Henry at the personal level has been fantastic, both the week in China and these few days in Hong Kong. In two weeks about 20 orgasms together—I doubt I have ever done that before with one person. I thought he was the sexy one, but at the end he turned me down once saying, "Ross, I'm too tired." I was amazed; I had found his limit.

Henry and I left many things unsaid. He hardly commented on the story of the quarrel between Edward and me. I did not broach the large issue of when Henry and I were to meet next. Nor did I reply to his declaration of love in Chongqing the day after our reunion.

March 30, 1985, Boston

Back again and so far, nothing seems real—jet lag is a disabling thing. But what a miracle that planes can whisk one around the world without mishap. The Sichuan trip was more successful than I dared hope. I found interesting material for my writing and at times even enjoyed myself.

If you really believe in yourself, do you need to project so much hope onto others—in years gone by onto teachers and heroes, in recent years onto lovers? Build them up too much?

George Johnston's wonderful book, *My Brother Jack*, convinces me that the 1930s were different from any period since WW2. Here are two friends sharing a cabin on the way to fight in the Spanish Civil War—on opposite sides! Yet they debate each night, without bitter quarreling, and remain fond friends. Until the one who enlists with Franco is killed in combat.

March 31, 1985, Boston

I had just gone to bed, wondering if tomorrow would really bring the start of spring, as supposed, when Edward rang. He hadn't taken long to find out I was back. He said he had got the torn-up photo of himself and my telegram from Kennedy Airport. I was flustered. I said I was sorry about the photo, "but that was how I felt at the time."

April 2, 1985, Boston

A long talk with Edward after he set up my stereo system in the bedroom. He said he felt we should go over our quarrel to see just why it occurred. I told him it had upset me greatly and I was reluctant to go over it. After long hesitation, I agreed to talk a bit.

For him, too, it turns out, it was a watershed. Several of his relatives and friends now "know" because the "break" with me made it inevitable; they already more or less knew that he and I were having an affair.

We each spelled out—very calmly this time—what had bothered us, though it was clear that he was basically puzzled as to why I had made the break so devastatingly. He did not like my phoning his mother: "it confirmed things for her." He hated me mentioning the money I had transferred to him. It hurt him that I had called him a liar, a manipulator, and a fraud.

When I raised the names he had called me—a pathetic human being, incapable of a relationship—he said this had only been a response to my tirade. I am convinced that it is he who cannot go into a gay relationship. For him, men mean Washington Street.[208]

He said he had not realized that I was so close to Luther that what he and Luther did could upset me so. It is true that I exaggerated the casualness of my affair with Luther when talking to Edward, so this misunderstanding was partly my own fault. He claimed that the second time he and Luther fooled about it was very much Luther's initiative (but then Edward asked Luther to his house).

He also said that he fully intended us to spend the whole night together that night (but why didn't he tell me, or even hint to me when I "attacked" him, by saying to wait a while or something like that?). I said if this was so, then I made a terrible mistake that night. Apparently, he had felt very bad about the whole thing, and especially that I said bad things about him; he wanted to know if I really felt like that. So it emerged that I took a certain amount of responsibility for the episode itself, while I also explained that the overall shape of the relationship had become unsatisfactory to me by that point.

But I told him I thought highly of him. I once more tried to convince him that I did not put him into the category of Reggie, Julius, Hank, David, or others. And this time I think I made some progress, by pointing out to him that the fact they are all Black, and he is Black, probably makes him tend to think that in my eyes all are just "tricks." Here there is some lack of self-esteem from his side. "You ought to see me with Chinese or with Australians," I said. "It's the same; the fact that you're Black is beside the point."

I said I had always considered him an exciting and stimulating person. "Just to have you walk into a room lifts me." I told him how watching him at the party made me proud of him, his style, his kindness to the guests, and that all this is not mere lust.

At the end, he said, gathering up his things, that there may be more things we will want to talk about. We gently kissed each other good night without setting any new time to meet. I said it's best to just see what happens. What I really mean is that the door is not completely closed but the next move is up to him.

---

[208] The main street through the "Combat Zone," one of Boston's gay cruising areas and a locale of prostitution. "A real and genuine place," Terrill would later write. "Its coin is sex and money."

April 7, 1985, Boston

A very miserable day, whether through a hangover from last night, my inability to start writing the Geographic piece (or even the book review for the Chicago Tribune), or the constant, nagging thinking about Edward.

I have questions for Edward. Yet the questions seem pointless. The only issue is whether or not we both want to resume the affair. Only within that context, at any rate, are the questions worth asking Edward. Still, I have to say that this Easter weekend, I have longed for Edward almost every minute—that is surely why I drank too much last night, and why I probably will go on doing that until we either get back together or I start living with someone else.

April 8, 1985, Boston

Hank has arrived. I did not look forward to him coming and yet, after one day, I feel a new peace. This has not come about mainly because of sex but mainly through his companionship (the physical side is there too). He seems calmer and more together than when we last met. Certainly, he is handsome and his cock is fantastic.

Today I got the *Chicago Tribune* review of John Hersey's novel done and feel better. Tonight, by an extraordinary coincidence, Hank, with his friends Tom and Toby, ran into Edward at the South Mall. Edward seemed stunned to see Hank and asked if Ross Terrill knew he was in town. "Yes," replied Hank. Hank then asked Edward something about his relation to me and at this point Arlene came up.

Tom later told Hank he was amazed to hear that Edward and I had been having an affair. "I thought," said Tom, "that he was the straightest of straights."

April 9, 1985, Boston

Why do publishing people think so well of me? Larry Hughes said letting me go to Simon & Schuster was the greatest mistake of his life. I get query letters regularly from senior editors here and there. My comments for a book jacket are evidently judged useful. Do they read what I write? Or is it just a legend that feeds on itself?

April 10, 1985, Boston

Tonight, I was starting to tire a bit of Hank, and when his friend Bill came, that somehow confirmed my feelings. After Bill went, Hank and I watched TV and cuddled up a bit. But his heart wasn't in it, and neither was mine. I said let's go downstairs but he seemed sleepy. He said he was hungry, and was going out to eat with Tom. He came in about 1 AM, hugged me and in the strange way these things happen, we began a bout of lovemaking. Before long, he was rimming me. I fucked him and as I came, he did too. "I've never shot that much in my life," he said.

April 11, 1985, Boston

Why does Glen keep calling me? I suppose to find out something from me for Edward, or convey something from Edward to me. Certainly, he has something tonight to convey to Edward. For Hank answered the phone—Edward will now know that Hank is staying here.

April 12, 1985, Boston

David came in, and Hank joined us for a drink downstairs. Then David and I ate at Thai Cuisine and came back and talked for hours. He said he wanted to stay overnight, but that we'd play around in the morning, not that night. However, once we were in bed, one thing led to another. I had a very long orgasm as he played with my tits while jerking me off.

After this I felt sleepy, but he started drinking beer again. I said, "Perhaps out of courtesy you ought to go upstairs and see if Hank would like to get fucked." I told him that last night I fucked Hank and he loved it.

No, David said, he wasn't going to go upstairs. But 10 minutes later, he changed his mind, put on his pants, and said he'd go out onto the terrace. I heard no noise and tried to go to sleep. However, I didn't succeed. Curiosity is a powerful thing. But after a while, David came back to bed, saying Hank had rebuffed him. This morning, though, Hank was in a good mood. Tonight, I want to screw him again.

April 13, 1985, Boston

Toward noon, Hank comes into the house and says, "Do you feel like fooling around?" I did. Later we lay on the couch upstairs in our underwear and talked for a long time, about our plans, our tie. Tonight, we joined up again and dined at Zachary's in the Colonnade Hotel. Excellent and expensive. Hank says I drink too much. He loves elegance, rises to it, makes me feel like a street boy.

April 14, 1985, Boston

A week ended leaving me feeling happy. Work done and wonderful moments with Hank. "You can do better" was his only comment on Edward.

This morning, in our last bout in bed, I loved it when, having felt he didn't want to fool around, he changed his mind during a session of photographing me (to send to Henry) and gasped: "You've got a nice body!"

"Pump it into to me"—that phrase was the magical balm, the magical link between Edward and this charming week with Hank. The last time Edward and I made love, he screamed out that sweet command. Suddenly I heard it from Hank!

Hank feels I am spoiled, that I need too much to get my way at any moment. This is a truer diagnosis of my weakness than Edward's wild incantation that I am a sex maniac.

At the last minute this morning, Hank said he wasn't sure he wanted to go back to Georgia. But I felt it was too late, so I urged him not to change his mind. He took the bus. I turned back to my *National Geographic* article, weary but relaxed.

April 15, 1985, Cambridge

BZY[209] says in my office today: "You should never go to China again." What did he mean? He says that when I got back from Sichuan a couple of weeks ago, I looked old and awful; now I look terrific!

April 20, 1985, Boston

I was in the Northeastern library going over a draft of part of the *National Geographic* piece, when I saw Alvin. Soon we were back here in bed. At first, we hardly talked, and hardly looked at each other. As the sexual enjoyment heightened—though there was neither fucking nor sucking—we both felt the need to gaze into each other's eyes. He's doing a master's in audio studies, dealing with people's hearing.

April 22, 1985, Boston

On the way to dinner with Ken Mayer[210] and Barney Frank the other night, I met this guy, Wyatt, at the corner; today he came by. Thin, pleasant. We made furious love—he seemed to love the head of my cock, and we both loved tit-play. I wanted it to go forever. Eventually he asked me to fuck him, but it hurt, so I came outside. Afterwards, he watched a favorite TV program, *All My Children*. I did not feel at all restless in going back to the *Geographic* piece while he stayed on in the front room. "Fierce," he called my apartment—which evidently means fantastic.

A second doctor says I should get a hernia repair. It will now be hard to resist. But these buggers can have a slip of the hand. That's all it would take for my sperm cord to be severed forever.

April 23, 1985, Boston

Talked to Ken on the phone—he's downbeat about AIDS. Evidently the proliferation of partners involved in the sheer process of living is just going to make things get worse.

I was impressed with Barney Frank. His mind is sharp as ever, but changed is his appearance. He must have discovered himself physically. Looks after himself, is aware of himself—and when you look at him, his eyes are beautiful.

---

[209] Benjamin Z. Yang (Yang Bingzhang, 1945-2020), a graduate student at Harvard at the time, and future author of *Deng: A Political Biography*.
[210] Kenneth H. Mayer, MD. At the time, he was on the staff of Fenway Community Health, Boston's LGBTQ health clinic, engaged in major HIV/AIDS clinical research.

April 24, 1985, Boston

Raymond, the banker, comes in after work and we fool about—he's a nice person. "A getting acquainted visit," he rightly calls it, as I apologize, and say I have to return to work. I tell him writing is a hair-raising job. He says banking is too. I want to see him again.

Tonight, I discover that a photo of Hank is missing from my bedroom! Hank is so sensitive about people seeing such things—though he's fully clothed in this one, a sudden snap of him in the little bedroom, trying on Pan's pink shirt-pullover. Horrible to plot out the possibilities, for it casts a shadow on those who shouldn't be questioned, but there are only two real possibilities—Wyatt or Raymond. Likely it was Wyatt—impossible to imagine Raymond taking it. Eventually, after denials, this charming, but terribly young guy says he wants to screw again, as do I. "I'll bring the photo with me when I come Sunday." Is this modern society crumbling about us, or do I just happen to deal with slippery people?

I phoned Edward and we had a better talk. I confessed I had cursed him to Glen. Today, I wrote to him in close terms. I took the letter around to Edward's and left it in his box; it reads:

Dear Edward,

I was going to write this shortish letter at the weekend but have been busy.

What do I want, you ask me, and that is a reasonable question. It is also forward-looking which I want to be.

First, I want us to bury the hurt and anger of the quarrel. From my side, that means for you to forgive me for what I did wrong.

Second, one time when we both feel like it, I want us to fool around, which will help us draw close and get into the present. It was over this that we had a misunderstanding, we both agree, that night of the quarrel, that can be repaired. And the memory of the misunderstanding, etc. can be supplanted by something new and nice.

Third, I want us to be friends again, learning from the mistakes, without illusions, but seizing the opportunity that we have in this strange but wonderful world. I will not project too much into this, or work myself up to some expectation that I know would be beyond what you want. I will be more sensitive to your identity, and your desire to preserve it intact.

I want a low-key but sincere thing between us, with all the different aspects there, but open-ended, and fairly spontaneous. I have some ideas about things to do together, for companionship, and am ready to help you in the realms you're interested.

Why should you trust me, you ask. Well, I suppose I couldn't blame you if you didn't. It's just that, with all the qualifications, I more or less love you—and a friend who feels like that is fundamentally very much on your side.

I said last week I didn't need you now, and I think that is true. I am not lonely. But my fondness for you remains. And whenever something happens,

I do keep thinking I'd like to tell Edward that; and I do keep wondering how things are going with you. I think my fondness is purer now that I have learned to be emotionally a bit more independent of you.

We can be original and find our own path. I expect for years to know you, and when you are married to see you, and your family. That itself may seem complex—but is it necessary to let complexity worry us? I suppose your life is going to have, as it already does, original patterns—maybe the time to pioneer them and get experience of them is now.

I feel that, having looked into the abyss, we can be kinder to each other now, and we can have a more mature, steady relationship. I just can't bear the thought that we let what happened destroy our friendship, much less let it make us negative about each other.

It sounds as if I do need you!—but's it's not quite that, just that I think there is something nice for us to grasp; we always need anything really nice.

These words seem inadequate—they do not match my feelings at all.

Ross

April 26, 1985, Boston

The draft of the *National Geographic* piece is done, and I think it's probably the best article I've ever written. Far too long, however—what will Mac[211] think of that, and what will he think of the irony in it? Before I cut it yesterday and today, it was nearly 30,000 words. I began it the day after Hank arrived the second time, Tuesday, April 9th, so that was two-and-a-half weeks work—not a bad pace.

These two weeks, I have been neglecting Henry in my thoughts. Will his family agree to him coming over? Do I want him to come over? I will phone him at the weekend.

April 27, 1985, Boston

Hank arrives from Georgia, looking wonderful, and we pick up from where we left off. As usual, he apologizes in advance. As usual, within 20 minutes he is reaching for the Vaseline to spread over my dick, and begging me to drive it deep inside him. Later we dine at Huskie's, quite a good meal, and Hank proposes that we write an article together about gay life in the South.

A letter came for him which I opened by mistake. As I told him tonight, I read it. "If you [were] to die tonight," begins this letter from the mother of one of his close friends, "are you SURE you'd go to live with God?" This lady, who, I was shocked to find out, is not Black, but white, feels "it won't be long till Jesus comes again." She says: "Beware of transcendental meditation, Hare Krishna, Jehovah's Witnesses, Mormons, and Moonies. And, Hank, be CAREFUL about the music you listen to. Much is definitely associated with Satan worship and sex perversion."

---

[211] Charles McCarry, editor-at-large at *National Geographic*.

April 29, 1985, Boston

Is it some silly wish to prove something that makes me want to fuck every day? No, it's just the pleasure of it.

April 30, 1985, Boston

My talk on Sichuan at Harvard seems to go well. Kuhn is effusive. Even Ben Schwartz comes up to shake my hand afterwards and say it was "informative." Afterwards at home, Hank is here, and we make love. He asks if I take "fertility pills." No, I say. "Then why do you want sex all the time?"

May 1, 1985, Boston

Yesterday the realization hit me that the Sichuan stuff is a book. I start to think of my editor at Morrow who wanted my next book to be on China—not on Australia, as Simon & Schuster wanted (and got). I write to Barbara with the extended Sichuan manuscript and a letter explaining my idea for the book.

Cary and the *National Geographic* legend writer come in to work on our piece. Over lunch at the St. Botolph, Cary says he wants to ask me if there may be a book in the Sichuan stuff, and could we do it together.

The phone rings and it's Pat. "I was thinking about you on the train this morning," she says, "I don't know why. Then I got to the office and there on my desk was a clipping from the *New York Post*, the Liz Smith column, with a big thing about Faye Dunaway being in the middle of reading your book, Esther Shapiro having asked her to play the lead in a miniseries based on *The White-Boned Demon*."

May 2, 1985, Boston

I am in the Northeastern library going over the *National Geographic* piece when this gorgeous Arab and I pass each other. His eyes rivet me. Almost hypnotized, I follow him into a men's room in the science building. We are in adjacent cubicles. Immediately his head appears beneath the partition. His lips open, he beckons me. It was a magnificent blow-job. As he sucked, I tried to grab him, his shoulders, his tits, anything. It's hard in that position. I said to him, let's go to my place. But he just furiously, lovingly sucked. He didn't even want me to reciprocate. In a flash he was gone—leaving me peaceful in the gut, staggered at his beauty, but also puzzled at the fleeting, one-sided nature of the encounter.

Hank and I went to the late show of *Amadeus* which is a rich and wonderful movie. He liked it as much as I did. We snuggled up a bit; no one seemed to notice or mind.

May 4, 1985, Boston

A dinner party here for which Hank cooks an excellent southern meal of stuffed pork chops, chicken, collards, black-eyed peas, and such. Hank's friend David P, who writes plays and is a leftwing activist, was here, but otherwise the people were all new to Hank.

Curt thinks Hank is spectacular. Curt lit upon a photo of me naked in Hawaii. "What a lovely cock," he begins. "That answers a lot of questions," he said with a grin.

I would like to have been with Hank afterwards, but he wanted to go out dancing with David. He says there's nothing between him and David, yet David looks at him with attraction, it seems to me—perhaps David is still waiting.

I phoned Wayne, and he came around looking great. Wayne and Hank met. As usual, I cannot handle these things. I get uptight, and others—in this case Hank—take it as guilt. Hank seemed to want to linger. I felt, OK, he's going out dancing and I'm with Wayne, let's get on with it that way

May 7, 1985, Boston

This morning, I asked Hank to leave a couple of days early, as I felt we were not close any more, and as his stay was getting longer, I began wondering about how to terminate it before Henry comes, as I so much hope he does. He threw a tantrum. As he packed, he denounced me and when Tom came to pick him up, he refused to leave. I said I'd have him removed. Tom pleaded with him to come. Hank shouted that I was "sick" and that I have "geisha boys" all the time.

Michael Mao is right when he says that in quarrels like this, everything that you say about the other person is true. Hank said I think too much of sex, I'm getting old, I'm changeable. I said his background makes it difficult for him to have a relationship, he lacks discipline, he's arrogant.

May 8, 1985, Boston

Henry calls from Hong Kong and says he desperately wants to come over. He's been thinking a lot, has talked his family into accepting the idea of the trip, and says he still loves me. He told me about two guys he sees and said that they mean nothing by comparison, and that I am the only one he has ever loved.

Alas, the US consulate turned down his visa application. So, I will scurry around today and write to Burton Levin, the Consul-General, and perhaps phone Washington, to try to reverse that.

Barbara phones and thinks the Sichuan [idea] is excellent but is against the book. After some going round and round, I realize why. The damned option clause in the Simon & Schuster contract. She insisted we agree to it. Now we can't talk about a Sichuan book until the Australia one is done, as it is first with Simon & Schuster that we will have to talk. I am slightly miffed. Yet it may be a good thing to set Sichuan aside for a while. And certainly, it's going to be a struggle to get the Australia book finished by the contractual deadline.

May 9, 1985, Boston

Mac phones to say he's been pruning my article once more. It's now down to 8500 words. I protest that we must have more space. "In the *National Geographic*," he explains patiently, "one page costs $50,000. What you ask would cost us an extra

$300,000." Anyway, I really don't think I want to see a yet further truncated version. I'll let him slaughter it, and wait until later in the year when I pick it up and turn it into a short book.

I play with fire and sometimes I get singed. Wyatt phones and asks what's the name of the guy whose photo he, Wyatt, stole from my bedroom. It turns out that last night, at some club, he saw Hank, went up to him (since he likes him—that's why he stole the pic) and, contrary to all his promises to me, told Hank he had a photo of him and that he got it "from" me.

It was good timing that, after going back to the compiling of my *National Geographic* expenses for a while, the buzzer rang and it was Jimmie, the guy who is painting the fence downstairs. He wanted to watch a video. "That must hurt," he said when a guy got fucked. We made love in my bed, more extensively and satisfyingly than I expected. He is not all that straight. On a shelf he saw my Mao in German and in Spanish. Thereafter, every time he looked along one of my shelves, he expected most of the books to be written by me. I explained that writing, like painting, is a slow job.

May 10, 1985, Boston

I've always wanted to cross barriers that are supposed not to be crossed.

May 12, 1985, Boston

In summer all things are possible. The three experiences which really engage me nowadays are: lovemaking; drinking; writing sentences. Most of the rest is so non-intensive by comparison that it can readily bore me.

A call from Hong Kong. My efforts with the Americans have borne fruit: Henry has his visa and will arrive on May 22 to stay for a couple of weeks. He sounded thrilled. I think I will be pleased, too, when I actually see him. Two weeks isn't too long to go without Black flesh, as I will probably have to do.

May 13, 1985, Boston

Alvin and I meet at Northeastern and later that day he comes in. We watch Ike's video—Alvin says he's never seen one before—and then make love in the usual way, with a big stress on tits and gazing into each other's eyes. We dine at Bangkok and talk at length. He is from a rather protected background, and perhaps spoilt.

"What do you do after fucking?" he muses.

"Wait for the next one," I reply.

May 14, 1985, Cambridge

One more sign of my low standing—or the envy of me—in Harvard circles: I got no invitation to the workshop on the social results of the economic reforms. Added to this, Phil's letter comes, saying I will have to share an office next year, and I begin to think I will myself pull the plug [with Harvard]. The Australian book, after all, will take me out of mental circulation for much of the rest of this year.

May 15, 1985, Cambridge

Deane Lord had a party to celebrate Alfred Alcorn's first novel,[212] and Joan Kennedy and I met there for our planned theater-and-dinner date afterwards. Joan brought Teddy, Jr., to meet me. God how he looks like his father. He seems pretty much decided to try for Tip O'Neill's seat next year, and Joan herself is very keen. "It will be much more fun being the candidate's mother than it was being the candidate's wife."

At the ART [American Repertory Theater]'s *Love's Labor Lost*, a charming effort to redeem a rather silly play—sorry, Shakespeare—Joan seems to know everyone. We chat with Eliot Norton, who has a dim view of both Rupert Murdoch and his old newspaper, *The Herald*. Joan is extremely charming. So youthful, so enthusiastic, such a fascinating blend of innocence and toughness. But I didn't really feel a strong passion for her.

During the play, Joan touches me, rubs against me, and turns to look me in the face. Afterwards, there is a cast party, and we meet the little boy who played a major role. Joan has an electrifying chat with him. He is 10, contracted kidney cancer at 3, and nearly died during chemotherapy. At that time a young man, also a victim of cancer, came by and told the kid that he, too, had lost his hair, but that it came back. The boy took heart. That young man was Joan's son, Teddy, Jr. When the little actor knew who she was, he cried. He said it was one of the greatest thrills of his life to meet her, the mother of the man who had given him hope.

Joan is still worried about the book by Marcia, her former staff member, but a bit less so than last year. The two women live in the same apartment building! "I do hate her sometimes," Joan suddenly said, disarmingly, with a smile, not a leer. "When I saw her with a mink coat. You know, she got the money for that from the book contract. And for years I wasn't able to wear a mink coat—Ted said it looked bad politically."

The *National Enquirer* is running excerpts, including the bit where Marcia quotes Joan, from when the two of them were in Alcoholics Anonymous, as saying that Ted in bed is "a five-minute man." Joan gets very worked up over this, but her objection is not that she didn't say this—perhaps she took it for granted that I wouldn't believe she said it—but that "Ted is still a public figure, and such things should not be published." She still sees quite a bit of Ted. The other weekend he called up; the Irish prime minister was going to be at Hyannis, would she like to come down? She did and enjoyed herself.

"I don't get through books anymore," she remarks. "They lie started but not finished all around my bed. It's the magazines and newspapers that I read through." When we reached her apartment, I felt it better just to kiss her rather than to go upstairs and get into things.

---

[212] Alfred Alcorn, Boston-based writer and friend of Terrill's. His first novel was *The Pull of the Earth* (Houghton Mifflin, 1985).

May 16, 1985, Boston

Exciting sex at Northeastern. An Oriental guy falls for my dick, does a lovely job, and in the middle of this a Black guy comes, watches, and eventually entices me to switch to him for a shattering orgasm.

May 18, 1985, Boston

A quiet day working over the first chapter of *The Australians*. I'm not sure it's that good; but pruning and polishing helps. At the Y, I meet an extraordinary guy, tall, rangy, with a huge dick, which he had flaunted to me in the sauna. He agreed to come home, but once here he got shy, or didn't like me much after all, and the sex was fleeting and disappointing. It is a relief to talk with Alvin, after that; something more settled (yet less settled than Henry) would be nice.

SBS Channel 0/28 phones from Sydney to ask if I'd go to China with them and make a TV program. I'll think about it, but I feel it would be a shoestring affair compared with the similar project I did with [Australian] Channel 9's *60 Minutes*. One good sign: the person who phoned was not ultra-romantic about China. She has read *The White-Boned Demon* and picked me precisely because they want to take a hard-eyed look at the China of Deng Xiaoping.

May 21, 1985, Columbus

After my lecture at Ohio State University, and a dinner with some professors, I went alone to east Columbus to check out some straight Black bars. Ended up going to bed with a guy called Dee at the Holiday Inn. At the Columbus airport, I phoned Henry who was packing for the trip. This made me realize with a shock how imminent is his arrival.

May 24, 1985, Boston

The days have been full and wonderful with Henry, who arrived two days ago. "I've come 10,000 miles for this," he said the first time he got my hard dick in his hands. He hardly seemed tired when he arrived. My guess is that he is still wildly attracted to me, but also a shade uncertain of me.

May 25, 1985, Boston

Dinner party here for 20-odd people to meet Henry. It goes well. At the end, we ask David to stay on, and the three of us go to bed, each coming twice. David and Henry get on well together, chatting and laughing.

May 26, 1985, New York

Henry and I flew down this afternoon and tonight dined in Chinatown with Richard and Shuchang. At one point, Henry makes a remark which I overhear and which puzzles me, to the effect that he's been "washing dishes and doing laundry."

At home, I tackled him on this. We both got upset. I said I was beginning to wonder what lies he told people about me. He said the big one is that he can't tell his family that I'm his lover. I saw once more the flash of anxiety in him at being gay.

I read the paper in my bed; he lay silently in his. Later when the lights were out, he came over to me. He never hides anything from me, he said. I guess I was not entirely mollified as I just said good-night. But later, I went over to his bed, said I loved him very much, and hugged him. Soon we made love. I fucked Henry for the first time, and afterwards he took both my hands and said: "I am so glad you did that."

May 27, 1985, New York

A wonderful boat trip about Manhattan, then to *A Chorus Line*, and dinner in Little Italy.

During dinner, I said to Henry to remember that I, too, have insecurities (he's had several dreams, the theme of which seems to be afraid of me abandoning him). About midnight, we left downtown and went to The Barracks, where there were few people, and Henry did not seem comfortable.

May 28, 1985, New York

Although we only got back from 42nd Street at 3 AM, and we made love. Then Henry jumped into my bed before 6. "Can I hold you?" he began, as usual. How wonderful he is!

During the morning, I went through the *National Geographic* article yet one more time with Mac, on the phone to Washington. It seemed strange to be back on this, after the magic of the weekend. Henry and I dined in the main dining room of the Club, then I flew back to Boston and he went out to Queens to Richard and Shuchang's place.

The Kirkland House Senior Dinner was one of most pleasant I remember. Derek Bok greeted me warmly. "I just read your *Mao*," he said, "while on a trip to Florida and enjoyed it very much."

I was intending to have an early night, but David joined me in bed. We talked for a long time, and I ended up fucking him for the first time ever. And perhaps it was his first fuck ever; the other night, during the threesome, I heard Henry ask David—as he put his finger on David's ass—"Do you like that?" and David said, "I've never tried it." I cannot recall any Black guy I've fucked who did not enjoy it greatly. It never seems to hurt them; many, bisexuals not least, crave it. This morning I woke up feeling sated, free, delicious. I moved my hand over and touched David. His dick was like a rock, as was mine.

Today I start to plan chapter three of *The Australians*, on history. It won't be easy, as I will have to be sketchy and opinionated.

Later:

Henry came in from the bus station and fell upon me. He couldn't wait to make love. We had some tender moments on the bed. He said how much he had missed me even for 24 hours. I said: "I now know I love you." Apart from the remark I had made in the middle of the night in New York, this was for the first time I had said I loved him. He cried.

May 29, 1985, Boston

Henry and David and I had a nice dinner at Huskie's. That David C is still staying here is a bit unexpected. It's my doing; I asked him to. In every practical way he is no trouble, but he is lonely, so he really wants to join us—and join in the sex—which goes against Henry's and my plan of being together for these weeks. I should not have fucked David Tuesday night; it has made me so conscious of his attractiveness.

I didn't really want another threesome late in the night. I was also conscious that I had perhaps broken my promise to Henry by sleeping separately with David. So, I suggested Henry might like to be with David for a bit. When they did that, in the small room, I got restless. A triangle of people in a house is never a completely easy thing.

May 30, 1985, Cambridge

Showing Henry around Harvard brings strange feelings. It all seems antiquity to me, now, and there is at times a surge of hatred. The symbolism of me being with Henry while everyone over there is busy with graduation week activities sums everything up: I have moved away from that world, so I should not complain that it seems odd to me.

I have not made plans to attend Commencement events—only Ken Galbraith's garden party—as Henry's visit has made them seem tame.

It's hard to accept that someone you are fond of does not love you, as I have had to do in the past. Curiously, it is also hard to accept that someone does love you. I now know that Henry loves me very much. My mind has been oriented to not believing this. I believe it now, but it slightly scares me.

May 31, 1985, Boston

David moved out today to the Beacon Inn, and both Henry and I felt more relaxed. Before he left, he and I had a very nice talk, and smooched around a bit upstairs while Henry was in the bathroom downstairs. David had been quiet for 24 hours and I asked him if he was depressed or if I had upset him. "How could you possibly upset me?" he asked. I told him to come back after Henry left. "If you really want me to," he said. I told him I did want him to. Sometimes I may be a bit soft when I fear hurting people.

A fun dinner at the Ritz Carlton Hotel with Deanne Lord, her mother, the Governor of Mississippi and his wife, one or two others—and darling Henry. Good meal, pleasant talk. "How did your friendship with Mr. W begin?" asked the wife of the Governor.

Afterwards, Henry and walked through the Boston Common to Sporters.[213] Later we went to Campus, and to Paradise,[214] before coming home and falling to sleep in each other's arms.

June 1, 1985, Boston

This morning Henry and I make love, long and delightfully. It is nearly 10 AM before I start work. The doorbell rings and it is Reggie. Soon it rings again and there are two of David's brothers. I ask them up. Both are nice. Where is David, they ask. A little later, yet another brother, Michael, phones with the same question. Meanwhile, I don't have David's phone number. But I think he's all right. Tonight, David phones to "apologize" for his brothers' contacting me. Of course, I don't mind in the least. A very polite family. At the same time a strange family.

Today the check for the *National Geographic* piece arrives. $9000 (Barbara gets her 10% of the agreed $10,000, which she negotiated). At the time I thought it a very large fee, but looking back on all the work—and the fact-checking is still to come—one cannot say it was a financially lucrative project. I put the $9000 in the bank on the way to dinner. It is good to have it under the belt. I will be alright now until I get to Australia, and there I can draw on my Australian account.

June 2, 1985, Boston

Last night we went to the Y, where someone cruised Henry in the sauna, shocking him greatly. Later we dined at the Copley Plaza Hotel. We were both too tired to go to a club. We watched videos for a while, went to bed, and this morning made love. He fucked me, I came a long and splendid orgasm in his hand.

Today was a beautiful day and we went for a walk down Commonwealth Avenue. We lunched in Newbury Street, at an outdoor cafe, then strolled on to the Common. There we lay and sunbaked, Henry listening to music on his Walkman (Walkperson?), me reading The New York Times.

At Sporters, we had a beer before coming home to change for an evening at the comedy Shear Madness. After that, we had a late dinner at the Imperial Tea House in Chinatown, and Henry talked for the first time in an extended way about JB. The conversation leaves me without any worries in this direction—beyond the universal one that none of us, in any relationship, can be certain that something will not happen tomorrow to change everything.

Edward used to think it was strange, and perhaps unpleasant, when my sweat would fall on him during sex, but Henry loves this. Few things thrill him more, he told me.

June 3, 1985, Boston

Shopping in Filene's Basement, where Henry cannot resist snapping up scarves, ties, ever more T-shirts. We see Ray W, and he is a bit cool. How to manage these things? If

---

[213] Gay bar on Beacon Hill.
[214] Two gay bars, both in Cambridge.

I'm with a Black, my Oriental friends can hardly hide their racism; if I go with another Oriental, the flames of jealousy soar.

David comes in—from the Y, where he is staying—to borrow my iron, and my heart jumps. Henry is out shopping. Scenarios rush through my mind. On the one hand, I desire David; on the other, I just want him out of the way until Thursday.

As it happened, the phone rang, I got into a long conversation with the *National Geographic*, and Henry arrived. David didn't stay long. When he went, Henry came into the study and both of us were for a moment a bit nervous. Then Henry noticed that my pants were unzipped. Naturally, he wondered if David and I had been playing. Actually, the reason was that when the *National Geographic* called, I was taking a piss and, in my haste to return to the study, I did not do myself up.

The *National Geographic* fact-checkers question whether Sichuan is really southwestern China as I say. The fact that the Chinese have characterized it as such for 2000 years does not satisfy the lady. I point out that although the Midwest of the USA is not an accurate description of where this region really is, non-Americans do not overturn the usage for that reason. She complains that if I send her down the Chinese-language materials for checking, she won't be able to read them. Can't the facts be checked through English sources, she wonders! By definition, then, work that goes to the source, and work that is original, is uncheckable to these *National Geographic* types.

Alvin phones and it's a voice from another world. I want him, and yet I don't. It is a delicious thought, anyway, that in a couple of weeks, when Henry is gone, Alvin will still be here.

(Now if Henry wrote that about JB, would I not feel a bit uneasy?)

Barbara is back from LA, where she lunched with Esther Shapiro[215.] Joel, her sub-agent for film rights, was there too. She says Esther is "absolutely determined" to make the Jiang Qiang miniseries, that Faye Dunaway is "sewn up" for the part, that an excellent script-writer is already working on the "book." However, ABC have not yet decided whether they want it. They probably will do so this week. Barbara says, "If anyone can make it, it's Esther." In other words, this is our last (as well as first) chance. Barbara seems to think it will come off. "Go out and buy a new house," she says in that nasal New York voice.

June 4, 1985, Boston

We go dancing at Chaps last night, together with David, and later by ourselves to Campus. At Chaps, Henry asks David to dance. Soon after Henry asks me and is surprised when I say yes. It is great fun. At Campus, the two of us dance a lot. As I dance so seldom, I wasn't sure how it would go. Late at night, Henry wrote some notes in his diary, which I could not help seeing at one point when he left it open to go to the bathroom. He didn't think I danced. He found I danced better than David. "No wonder Ross turned his face away when, not having asked him to dance, I went off dancing with David."

---

[215] Esther Shapiro (1928 -), American television screenwriter and producer.

A boat trip today on the *Spirit of Boston*. Pleasant enough but the company was not congenial: a Harvard reunion group, loud tourists, Europeans gobbling the buffet lunch. Boston Harbor itself is cozy, a harbor in decline, it would seem. The setting is certainly less striking than Sydney's or San Francisco's.

About six, we found ourselves in bed. The next thing I knew the phone rang, it was Dean, and he said it was 7:45. That was the end of our long, languorous lovemaking as we had tickets for a Boston Pops concert. It was fun; we sipped white wine and ate grapes as we listened to Offenbach and Mendelssohn. Later we dined at Zachary's in the Colonnade Hotel, an excellent meal. On the way into the Colonnade, we run into Glen, strolling with a friend. He says a warm hello. I do not stop, but he has time to add that I look "very sharp" (Henry and I are rather dressed up).

The champagne with dessert at dinner gave me a slight hangover, and when Henry began to kiss my tits at 6 AM, I just didn't feel up to it. However, he played with my balls and suddenly I wanted to fuck him. I did so. A bit later he said: "I really enjoyed what you did to me, Baby." After doing a bit of work, I went back into the bedroom, feeling very horny, and we galloped on; the orgasm, like last night's, was enormously long. "I love your cock, Baby," he cries out all the time.

June 5, 1985, Boston

After my squash match, we went to a party at Anne and Justin's. Mainly, Henry and I kept to ourselves, but Helen Rees was great company. Justin regaled me with the wonders of Jerusalem, to which he has just made his first visit. Anne seemed subdued; does she think I neglect her? I do a bit. John drove us home, bubbling about how he wants to bicycle through China. Henry packed for a while, then we seized the last chance for making love. I had one of the longest orgasms ever—I just did not want him to take his hand off my dick, even after I seemed (I could not see my dick at the time) to have finished shooting.

I no longer think of Edward as the orgasm approaches, which I was doing with people for a long while. Henry rather shames me by his remarks on this sort of thing. "In Hong Kong I generally thought of you when I was making love with someone. That's not fair to the other person, is it?" He says the only person he thinks of when with me is a film star called Rob Lowe.

Now I feel—as JQ did in Shanghai after sleeping with the soccer player—"half lost and half dead." I think I will be in a daze until Henry leaves tomorrow morning. Work is out of the question. I am just under the spell of him.

June 6, 1985, Boston

To the airport for Henry's flight to San Francisco. He tells me his weeks here have been "wonderful." He feels much better this time, he says, about our parting, than he did at Sydney or Hong Kong. I suggested the difference in feeling—in fact, I feel worse—is that this time he heads home, whereas the last two times it was I who was heading home. He replies that this is only part of it. "I am certain now of your love for me."

Back home, now, he says, he will have an anchor, a basis on which to limit this little affair with JB. The uncertainty he felt during the past two months in Hong Kong has gone. He knows without any doubt that we will be together again and again.

I cried—the first time I've done so in Henry's presence. We went into the men's room, where I cried some more, and we kissed a long goodbye.

Back to St. Botolph Street by the T, reading the newspaper on the way. Now I am free; but what sort of freedom is this? The freedom to merely screw around? The "bondage" of Henry raised me up, I think. But sex with the same person, day in and day out, is a strain too, as well as a wonderfully secure thing.

June 8, 1985, Boston

Before Henry left, I gave him, at his request, a copy of *The White-Boned Demon*. He was equivocal when I asked if the inscription could be frank, so I said I'd compromise, writing what I wished, but in very rapid handwriting which most Chinese could not read. "For Darling Henry, With All My Love." Henry looked at it; I asked him if he could read it. "Of course. As for others, they may think it's 'duckling.'" The rest of the inscription was pretty clear. No way he's going to hide this book. He wills himself out of the straight cage, I think.

Later:

Henry called twice from San Francisco before catching his plane this afternoon for Hong Kong. Meanwhile Cornell is here. I enjoy him; the sex yesterday was fantastic. Yet I feel uneasy at doing this so soon after Henry has left.

Cornell calls his father "old," but I find out today that the guy is 41. Cornell seriously doubts that this man is his real father. His uncle, whom everyone says he resembles, slept with all four of his mother's sisters, by his own admission, and some believe he slept also with Cornell's mother. The father drinks a lot, and this is why Cornell does not drink. Once the father pulled a shot-gun on Cornell, and a number of times he has ordered him to leave home. Regularly, when he gets angry, he says to Cornell: "You're not really my son."

June 9, 1985, Boston

Last night, Cornell and I together went to a party, Dean's housewarming at his new place on St. Germain St. A nice apartment, despite it being locked in Christian Science territory, but the people there, Cornell and I both felt, did not mesh.

We came home and realized we'd have to get up very early for Cornell to get his bus to the National Guard camp tomorrow. He suggested 4:30 AM. I thought that excessively early. "But we want time to fool around one more time." Most unusual for this silent guy to put such a thought into words.

Next morning, after Cornell took his bus, I luxuriated in my aloneness. To him that has shall be given, says the Bible, and to him that hath not, even what he has will be taken away. It's the same with sex. I seem to have become an addict. I think I should let the process of diminution take hold for a while.

Michael Mao takes me to Sunday lunch at Huskie's, but he has little to say—he's better on the phone than in person. He looks older, with much gray hair; this terrifies me, reminds me too much of what I cannot fend off much longer.

June 10, 1985, Boston

Reading Manning Clark's history of Australia, I notice that Aborigines and Chinese are repeatedly the marginals of society—not even counted, for instance, in the casualties at Darwin when the Japanese bombed in 1942. Yet it is Blacks and Orientals who have formed my sexual center of gravity ever since I left Australia. What demon am I pursuing?

This evening I feel restless, having been in the house all day, and go to Northeastern to read a few chapters of Churchward's *Australia and America*. Three guys suck my dick, though due to interruptions and my own hesitation about coming in a semi-public place, I had no orgasm.

Later, I phoned Will, who spent the day at Malden with his friend ("an older guy," Will says of him), and he came around. His friend had not taken all his energy. After we watched a video, and he sipped a vodka and orange juice, Will ate out my asshole, which I like immensely. He has a rock-hard dick and a passionate, determined manner.

He wanted to screw me, but this was out of the question with the memory of Henry so fresh, and my having told Henry that no one would screw me until he, Henry screwed me again. So he may have been a bit disappointed; and my own orgasm was slightly affected by this abortiveness too. But he stayed all night, snoring lightly.

June 11, 1985, Boston

At 7 AM Henry calls. I am hardly awake—Will had left at 4 AM and I dozed off after that—so I shower, make coffee and call him back. He has been thinking of me a lot. "People say love is very insecure," he says, "but I don't feel that. When I think of you, I feel so good." In San Francisco, he went with a guy called Bill, whom he met at dinner at Wyatt's. "I looked into his blue eyes, and thought they are not as blue as baby's. I touched his hair, but it was not as soft as baby's."

He said his weeks with me here were probably the happiest time of his life. In general, he did not enjoy San Francisco. Little chance to see the city. And thinking always of me. I didn't tell him how paralyzed I felt after he left. But I did tell him that my lovemaking with David was marred by my still feeling so close to "baby."

What especially touched Henry—he has dreamed about it every night since—was that moment at Boston airport when, under the cover of *The New York Times*, we held hands and looked into each other's eyes just before he boarded his plane.

Can I practice love across 10,000 miles? This was the question in my mind during 40 minutes on the phone with Henry. It is possible, but not certain. One way to do it is to write often and be totally frank—or nearly so.

Tonight, at Northeastern, I had my choice among several guys and chose boldly: a blond, nervous and inexperienced, far more sexy than he probably realizes. How delightful. Later, I decided to dress up and dine alone, which I have not done for weeks.

Strolling across to Zachary's, I met a nice guy by the Christian Science pond. But I did not want to invite him back straight away; gave him my phone number.

After dinner, who should call but David, just arrived in New York from London. Sounded older, said has hooked up with a Thai doctor, has been with him for two years, and has been "faithful to him." Can I believe him? It's now too late for David to come and stay. A pity in a way.

June 12, 1985, Boston

Barbara has not called. It seems that ABC must have turned Esther down for the *The White-Boned Demon* miniseries.

June 13, 1985, Boston

The week has flown away. Work-wise I am a bit frustrated still to be in the planning stage of the history chapter, and still reading; it's necessary but I will feel more fluent once I start writing those sentences.

Last night, while we were at 1270[216] Dean asked me what delights me most and upon reflection I answered three things: making love, writing good sentences, drinking in congenial company. It's true, Baby, and the work part of that is very important; when I am actually drafting something, a bit each day, I am happier than in the leading-up stage or afterwards.

As for the last point, we had a nice time. Dean just phoned me in the afternoon and said his friend Michael was singing that night at 1270 and would I go. The guy has a nice voice. There was not a huge crowd so we could sit and talk. Dean told me he is happy to keep our friendship Platonic; that is good for me also.

In my research, I came upon some regulations from the Gold Rush period which forbade Australians and Chinese to have sex together. A first offence meant imprisonment for the Australian; a second meant he was deported to China! Just imagine—here were we last year in Melbourne in that same society which once felt that way about "yellow and white."

It's interesting, as a play upon space and time, to notice that only this year South Africa de-criminalized sex between Black and White. Sometimes I reflect on the fact that the two groups which during my youth were outcasts to most Australians—Chinese and Blacks—are the two which in a personal sense have filled my life with happiness since I left Australia.

The question arises: can Henry's and my love for each other survive separation; will our love for each other make a difference to the lives we lead while we are one in Boston and one in Hong Kong? I am cautiously optimistic. I was slow to fall in love—it has been the same with me before—but once I do it means a lot.

I care very much about Henry's progress and happiness. Knowing he is "out there" will be an inspiration for me. And there is always our next time together to look forward to. While I feel these things, other sexual contacts will be casual, and will in no way be

---

[216] A gay bar and dance club located at 1270 Boylston Street, near Fenway Park.

the same as my tie with him. In some ways the separation is good; its stimulating, the painful aspects of it are a challenge; and when we are together nonstop there's a tendency to grow tired of each other sexually.

June 17, 1985, Boston

Monday night, when I like to dress up and dine alone. I was about to leave for Copley's when Dion rang. After dinner, he came over, we talked for a long time on the deck, and then made love. He is extremely nice, somewhat more stylish than Michael. I rather wish, now, for two reasons, that I had not done it with Michael. I don't know yet if each of them knows what the other did. Certainly, it is Dion, rather than Michael, who would interest me over any period of time.

I saw Will on the balcony outside his salon. I wanted to talk to him about the fucking issue, but there were kids there. He waved his hand and said never mind the kids. "They hear about it every day." I said I knew he wanted to fuck me, but that with the situation in regard to Henry I felt I couldn't. He said never mind; he loved my sucking. I said I loved his rimming. We shook hands on that, as the little boys looked up into our faces.

June 18, 1985, Boston

"I've retired from active sex," I said to Will, half-seriously, as I had to fend him off. "And what about passive?" he shot back. I just laughed. I love the guy's bull-like sexual strength. And I love the way he rams his tongue deep into my asshole.

Henry called and his sensual voice re-turned me on. He has told JB how much he loves me. He went to bed with JB on Saturday, "but, Ross, I did not enjoy it."

He has found exactly what I have found. "In the US with you, I was so interested in sex, but since I have come back, I'm not." I had thought my own similar experience was some kind of physical malaise, or an ending to my long obsession with Blacks. But the key may be that Henry and I are too close to each other to abandon ourselves sexually to someone else. At one point, I asked him if he was a strong Chinese gentleman. "Well, not always. For instance, when I'm in bed with you I feel very vulnerable." We decided we have to meet again fairly soon. Henry can take two weeks holiday before the end of the year. We will go to the Philippines or meet during my Australian trip.

June 19, 1985, Boston

Last night, the phone rang and it was Verny's cousin, a beautiful young Honduran whom I had met only fleetingly, one afternoon when Henry and I were strolling in the Boston Common. "I've been reading your *The White-Boned Demon*," this guy, whose name is Felipe, said over the phone. "Would I be able to meet you sometime?"

He arrived today at noon and looked even better than I remembered him when Verny introduced us. His English is quite good but far from fluent, so I was not sure he got one or two of the hints I dropped as to my admiration for his appearance. Curly hair, liquid eyes, smooth olive skin, and a most charming, gentle manner.

We sat upstairs and drank a glass of orange juice. I could see he had a hardon. But I was hesitating. Eventually the language of our eyes just took us over the threshold. It began with long kisses, and after that it was inevitable that we fall into bed.

All through a long session, he said nothing, only smiled. I thought he wanted me to fuck him, but since he wasn't talking, I didn't want to break the spell of quietude. I just played with his ass for a long time, until I was sure he was having a good time, and then banged my dick in. But it hurt him too much, so I stopped. The orgasm was fantastic. We showered together. Sitting in the living room, I took his hand and said, "What are we going to do?" I really feel I could go for him; he seems to feel the same about me. But, but, but ...

Afterwards, three to four hours on the phone with the *National Geographic* research department, going over my article for the 1000th time. It left me exhausted, and also quite unable anymore to see the article as other than facts and words.

I was so opened-up sexually by Felipe that after a squash match tonight with Ron— I won despite my fatigue—I wanted more sex. At Northeastern, I met this Black guy, and we sucked each other off. I treated it as a spin-off from Felipe, and I thought of Felipe as I came.

June 20, 1985, Boston

A talk on the phone tonight with Edward left me feeling good. I am going to take him out for dinner for his birthday. He didn't seem up-tight about Arlene anymore; "I don't see her as much as before." He says he is largely taken up with work at the bank, which is going well, and with family contacts.

He seemed very interested to know all about Henry's visit, and even about the new star, Felipe, who has swum with lights flashing into my firmament. He said nice things about people, including Cornell "I really like him; it's just that the night you introduced us, I was in a strange mood." At the minimum, it is so much nicer to be warm like this, than the way we were with our squabbling, for underneath, each knows that the other person is one he will, in some sense, always remain fond of.

After this phone conversation, I went with Dean to 1270. He is carrying on with a guy he met at 1270 last week, after I had gone home, and for once he's giving a relationship a sexual expression. Now between us, the shoe is on the other foot. That touching all the time, which I could not stand, especially in the presence of some of my friends, I was practicing a bit tonight—did I pick it up from him?—and it slightly irritated him. I suppose that this new friend of his—Platonic as my tie with Dean is and should remain—made me feel a shade insecure with him for the first time. How silly we humans can be!

I met a pleasant-looking Black guy called Cornell—yet one more Cornell, this one Cornell W—but being hooked up with Dean, I could do no more than exchange phone numbers with him.

June 23, 1985, Boston

A beautiful sunny day, quite a bit of work done, and then in the evening Felipe comes in. He looks fresh and adorable, in a red shirt, khaki pants, and good leather shoes. We decide to go to Chinatown for dinner. As we leave, I notice that he leaves his keys on my lobby table, with a quick glance at me, as if to give me a chance to say no. Of course, I merely grinned.

A nice dinner at Peking Cuisine, as we talk about Latin America and Felipe's family. His parents are divorced, and even the stepfather does not now live with Felipe's mother. He is pleased that he got a promotion yesterday at the drugstore in Allston where he is working for the summer. We stroll along Washington Street, peaking at a few places—but Felipe is too young to be admitted to a bar. We rent a video called *Sex Bazaar*, made by a Frenchman in Casablanca. Before the end of it we had to come downstairs and make love.

This morning we rose early as Felipe had to be at work at eight. He's the kind of guy—not like David, Reggie, or even Cornell—who when morning comes you ask courteously about his breakfast wishes. I got him a breakfast of orange juice, coffee, a banana, and toast and marmalade. "I had a wonderful time—thank you!" he said, and slipped away.

Some demon in me made me phone Cornell W, whom I had met and exchanged phone numbers with at 1270 last week. He came over this afternoon and talked so much that my sexual desire went away; I began to want to get back to work. He was once married, and had a confrontation with his father who intercepted a letter from a boyfriend of Cornell's. The father sent Cornell's brother to ask him about it. Cornell turned away from the brother, went into his father's room and said: "You should not open my letters. I could have you arrested for this." Later he told his father he would not have him arrested as long as his lifestyle was accepted by the father.

Eventually, as we sipped drinks in my bedroom, Cornell came on to me. He reached across to my chair, touched my gray gym shorts, and asked about the red inscription on them, his big Black fingers all the while going halfway up my thighs. Despite last night, I was quickly unhinged. He turned out a superb lover. He sucked my dick like an angel; we did all sorts of things.

As he was leaving, he started to talk of vegetarianism. You don't eat meat?" I enquired. "I certainly do eat meat—you just saw that." He grabbed me again in a lovely place, just below my waist; I felt like starting the lovemaking all over again.

When he was asking me about my writing he said, "Don't you sometimes take things from other writers?" This very point had been on my mind this week; in the chapter on Australian history, how to acknowledge my debt to Blainey, Clark, Collins, and others?

The doorbell rang; it was Julius. I could not resist him, and made a time to see him later. Yet all the time I was thinking of Cornell, of Felipe, above all of Henry—and wondering if I should be juggling so many balls in the midst of a beautiful Boston summer. I can understand why I promised myself, that burning morning in early August last year, that I would not again forsake Boston in mid-summer.

June 24, 1985, Boston

Inside all day today, the work mostly bits and pieces. I fall behind on my schedule; the history chapter won't be done by the end of June. Outside the window I saw a gorgeous Haitian. He strolled back twice, so I dropped everything, took the phone off the hook, and went down for a closer look. No sooner was he at my front steps than another guy cruised me. I quickly decided that a bird in the hand was better than a bird in the bush—and turned aside from the Haitian. Eric is an assistant theater manager, a nice Black guy.

June 27, 1985, Boston

During dinner at Soom Thai, Dean says if I was "ten years younger," he would fall helplessly in love with me. I feel depressed. However, he has a particular thing about age: his boyfriend David, in Melbourne, was older than he, and this one love affair of his life still haunts him. He cannot envisage getting hooked up with an older guy. It suits me, if not my vanity, because I am not fiercely attracted to Dean.

June 29, 1985, Boston

Cornell comes in, and we make love without the magic of the other day. Was the reason I loved him the other day because I hadn't fucked him for a few weeks? Is it surprise—that day I wasn't expecting him, while tonight was an arranged date? Perhaps Cornell was just tired or "oversexed," meaning to say "sated with sex," as Henry charmingly put it one night when he was surprised I didn't attack him. At any rate, it was perfunctory, and I was left amazed at how sex with the same guy a couple of days apart can be so different.

Almost every night, a banquet of hot male flesh! And yet tonight, in addition, I dreamed of my father sucking me off, he hot and sun-tanned in the kitchen of our house in Melbourne one night when the rest of the family were absent.

June 30, 1985, Boston

I love America; it has given me much. Working on my book about Australia, I feel a dual loyalty. I think Henry might understand because Hong Kong people are often "duals."

July 1, 1985, Boston

A chat with Henry on the phone—he recalls Felipe clearly. He saw at once that Felipe was attracted to me (perhaps my attention was on Verny, my friend, and I didn't look much at Felipe). Henry is a little upset—not much I hope—because he too finds Felipe very attractive!

Kam Sing and Henry's sister have been getting curious about Henry's contacts with foreign men. The sister even came to Henry and asked if it meant that Henry was gay. She said Kam Sing had told her he thinks Henry is gay. Kam Sing does not have regular work. "You see," Henry told me, "the fortune teller told him that anything he started before his 30th birthday would not go well. So he's waiting until then to start something."

The doorbell rang and it was Julius. I was cold but eventually went downstairs to talk with him. He said he was sorry for his behavior back in February; would I accept his apology? I was non-committal. He came on to me, and I could not resist. Before answering his question, I fell to his advances. I did not ask him up at that moment. We played about by the stairs, each sucking the other. I asked him to kiss me, which I don't think we have ever done before. He agreed. His lips are wonderful, and this made me feel better about seeing him again. Later that afternoon, he came back, I invited him in, and we made love. I enjoyed it immensely. That feeling I had, just after Henry left of not enjoying sex as much as before, has left me.

July 2, 1985, Boston

After a morning at Harvard, and a visit to my doctor to talk about the hernia operation, I went to see Felipe at the store where he works. I stole up to the counter where he was sorting films and surprised him. Smile the same; eyes as revolutionary as always. I gave him the maps and guidebooks for his mother and sister, who visit Boston next week.

I asked him a question that had been nagging. How did he originally get my phone number? "I asked Verny about you, and he said you were an author and that he had one of your books. I started reading this book, *The White-Boned Demon*. I got the spelling of your name from the cover of the book, went to the Boston phone directory and found your name."

A message from Barbara, and calling her back, I find she wants even more information about Australia—though she will be there only three days, on the way to search for the primitive in New Guinea. At the end of the conversation, I happen to ask about Esther and *The White-Boned Demon*. "Oh, ABC turned her down – she's going now to NBC." Is she offhand in order to try not to hurt me?

July 4, 1985, Boston

A delicious feeling of holiday; being a summer holiday, it reminds me of such Australian occasions. Yesterday, I finished the draft of the history chapter of my book on Australia; today, some housekeeping tasks and much taking it easy on the balcony.

I phone Mum and she's fine. When the money comes from the accident claim office, I think she will be even finer. There is in her an incurable streak of foreboding. I hate it because the same thing at times threatens me. On my back deck there is no rail. Standing there, I can get a feeling of panic. Alas, a similar feeling can invade my soul in the face of any task, anything new or unexpected. It is all irrational—one is not going to fall off the roof without getting to the edge.

Cornell comes in. I am not in the mood. But after a while I see his hardon—he never wears underwear—and suddenly I am in the mood. A long loving 69, and a good orgasm. He is as hot as Hades; have never known the head of his dick to swell up so big.

In the afternoon, I happen to look out the window and see Edward walking along Mass Ave with a guy, sandy haired, medium height. Each of them carried a gym bag. My heart leapt. Edward is seldom around at weekends; to see him with a guy was extraordinary—and it hit me full in the stomach. I could not even stay in the house, but went wandering around, and sat on a bench at Northeastern to pray for a calm spirit.

At night I watch America's celebration of its birthday on TV and feel very patriotic. Later, I start a letter to Henry.

The Blacks I go with are all such unsatisfactory substitutes for Edward. That is my emotional problem. While I am with Henry, I forget all about Edward, but when I am with Black flesh, I compare the nickel with the quarter.

July 7, 1985, Boston

In the morning I worked, then Yang came in; he is going to Peking tomorrow and we lunched at the St. Botolph .

I had not been back long when the buzzer went. It was Edward. Flustered, I said I would come down; there was silence; I amended this to an invitation to come up. He looked very good in white shorts, white tank top, white socks, white sneakers. In between all this white was the Black flesh I love.

We caught up on all the news. We talked of work. We talked of family. He confided that he had been "a couple of times" to the Combat Zone since our quarrel. Oddly, he added with ferocity in his voice: "If you ever go there, I'll crucify you!" We talked of mutual friends—obsessively he returned to Hank, and I realized that a deep jealousy exists there. When we got to the point of planning for dinner on his birthday, I said that Zachary's and Apley's were amongst the best I know. He replied that the former was out of the question, since I had told him that Hank developed a liking for it!

We went upstairs to the deck. I told him about the Moroccan video that Felipe and I got from Washington St., and he said he wanted to see it. We moved to the couch and the VCR. *Sex Bazaar* didn't seem to turn him on that much, though my dick jumped out of my shorts and he took a good look. We looked at photos, as the hours went by, and as we seemed to be drawing closer, and every topic we touched we seemed to be trying to conciliate each other, I began to feel that sex might rear its gorgeous head.

Something took us to the couch in the front room, and he wrapped my arms around his shoulders, as I sat behind him. In this position, he seemed rapidly to doze off. At the same time, he was cuddling very close to me. I reached for his tits. The same as always—he begins to unhinge! I could hardly believe that we were at it again after so many months. From his part, there was the same edging in sideways to the initial acts of passion; his cock pulsates when I touch it, but his eyes are still closed—as if he does not yet want to acknowledge what is happening.

Soon I have his tank top pulled back and am sucking at his tits, and he is clearly not dozing as he has my dick pulled out of its rather feeble protection, my gray gym shorts. He is groaning in his usual way. I fall upon him, and the two parts of the combo-couch move apart. We pick ourselves up and tear off each other's clothes. On an impulse, I pick him up. "You cannot possibly carry me," he gasps. Indeed, he is heavy, but I carry him across the room, dump him on the bed of our old acquaintance and begin to work seriously on his enchanting tits.

The madness had two startlingly new physical twists, and an aftermath of new communion. In my dreams for many weeks, I had got to the point where I wanted to rim Edward; this was it. I spun him round, parted his legs, drove my tongue deep into his asshole. He gurgled, he whimpered, he pulled back, he pushed closer. Meanwhile, I had my first real taste of going into someone like that.

He began to rim me also, which he has done many times before, and then to suck my dick. All hell broke loose, as I gave my lips, tongue, face, and head to his balls and his cock and his asshole. Suddenly I found myself on top of him, he face-downwards. This was not one of our usual positions. I was not sure that he liked to be fucked this way. I moved tentatively; the groans multiplied. I charged. He shouted, he cried, he begged me to pump harder. I thought for a moment that all I had ever hoped for in life had come together in this coupling.

My bed lies solidly on the floor. It does not creak. But on this occasion, it did creak; it first hissed, then squeaked, then began to sound like the mattress on a wire bed in an Australian village. Meanwhile, I was sweating like a pig. This bothered me; unlike Henry, Edward does not like this. I looked up at the broad Black neck. He groaned. I thought I must be hurting him, yet all the signs were that he was in heaven. I increased the depth and speed. The combination of baby oil and sweat made a river of the glistening space, the intermittent space, between our bodies. He arched up his back and I grabbed his rod, thicker at the base than I ever remember it being. I could not stop myself—I came, shooting into him. He felt it and cried out like a man dying.

"Do you always fuck your boys like that?" he asked me as we lay together. For a long time, I did not answer, because the question feeling of friendship bothered me. Eventually, I said he was not a boy, no-one was a boy, and that with him there was a element that sex entirely different from Reggie or Hank.

"I have never had such satisfaction," he said. "No one has ever fucked me like that before." He said he felt like the French guy in the video *Sex Bazaar*. We lay side by side gazing into other's eyes for a long time. I told him I had been obsessed with him for several weeks. He said I am "amazing." I said that to me he is unique in all the world. I ventured our old phrase, "What am going to do with you?" and he grinned beautifully.

"You look happy," he said. I was indeed. "And so you should be after what you gave me then." I said, "I don't know why: I'm not sure we should do this too often; just from time to time."

We made a bubble bath and luxuriated. He spoke of his Irish ancestor who, he thinks, is responsible for his dick not being as huge as he would like. I asked him why this issue is so important to him—after he had again made a sideswipe remark about Hank. "Because I'm a Black man, that's why."

Later, we dined at Thai Cuisine and then went for a walk about the Christian Science pond. He said what he'd love to find is a "female Edward." That means a girl who is bisexual, promiscuous "up to a point," a bit wild, but also serious. He told me about his plans. To finish his degree, get a car, pass the real estate course. I may help him with the car and see if I can get some tax advantage from doing so.

Why did I change my mind about you, he mused—but did not give an answer. I have some possible answers. One, I did not pressure him. Two, he is in a "gay phase."

July 10, 1985, Boston

Edward and I dressed up—me in the suit Henry's brother made for me—and dine at Bay Tower Room for Edward's 26th birthday. A nice setting, a reasonable meal, not worth the price. The wines were especially expensive. Our two bottles of Asti Spumante cost $40 between them—plus Edward's two exotic champagne cocktails. We shared a rack of lamb; to precede it, he had clams broiled with bacon and I had a seafood casserole, which would have been good had it been hot.

He talked incessantly about his family and relatives, and I tried not to let it bore me. I love being with him—even in the bourgeois stuffiness of the Bay Tower Room. Will I recommend this restaurant to my friends, he asks, as we take a cab home. Well, no. When the check came Edward became a bit gloomy. Did he doubt the dinner was worth the money? Does he find it difficult to accept things given him?

July 11, 1985, Boston

Back home after squash, I had a glass of wine and then phoned Will. He came around on the way home from his salon and after he told me all about his vacation in Kansas City, we went to bed. This only whetted my appetite, so I called Eric, and within 15 minutes, our long delayed first meeting began. I had invited him for a drink, but those eyes at the door bowled me over, so we made love first and had the drink afterwards.

I began to "talk dirty," as Michael Mao would say. Eric became crazed. I gradually realized that my dick was the focus of his attention. He wanted me to fuck him, but we encountered a cultural problem. "I want you to fuck me, but do you have a condom?" I did not. "Next time," I murmured, thrusting my bursting dick into his huge soft balls.

He is keen to meet again, and I am agreeable. He works at the Wang Center for the Arts, having graduated from Emerson just two years ago. He is lean and Black and well-hung. Does he like himself? This is my only doubt.

After I had gone to bed, DG comes in. He wants to go upstairs for a while; I go to sleep. About 5 AM, he comes down, having, it seems, watched videos and read all night. We make love. It is excellent, but I kick myself that I don't like getting fucked, and with a dick the size of his, I sometimes dislike getting fucked. I envy people like Edward who really get off on it. At the same time, I worry for their health, and I half believe that if over the years I had been constantly fucked, I would be in a bad way today.

The bursitis has gone. I don't think the squash brought it on; more likely the weight lifting, using a faulty arm position. But then RT was never one to study the rule book before plunging in to try any new toy.

July 12, 1985, Boston

Tired today but managed to write a page or two to start the new chapter. DG was around most of the day, for the first half of it in bed, looking beautiful wrapped tightly in a blue sheet.

Tonight, I became extremely depressed on realizing that my camera has gone, and in it the film Edward took last Sunday, including nude ones of me. There must be something wrong with me. Do I attract theft? Only three people were here during the period the camera went: Will, Eric, and DG—all of them last night. I just hate to think of the possibilities; one is dealing with friends, after all, and people that one goes to bed with in high passion.

July 13, 1985, Boston

Mum phones this morning to say that her compensation has come through. A check is in the mail to her. She asks about Edward; it is her peculiar genius to ask nothing about him while Edward and I are together, then once she is told of the breakup, to ask. Meanwhile, no questions about Henry—no doubt because she suspects Henry is "in." With a mother like that, who needs enemies?

I get going on the "British or American" chapter and sense it could be good. Felipe's mother, after all, is not leaving today, but tomorrow, so we will not meet tonight. So be it; I need time to myself.

July 14, 1985, Boston

I am getting nervous about the coming hernia operation, and perhaps for this reason played today a "you come to me" game with Felipe. I phoned Eric, got his answering machine and told him I was upset about my camera disappearing. Had he, by any chance, seen it? Did he, by any chance, borrow it? I said all this in a calm and non-accusatory way.

July 15, 1985, Boston

After squash with Ron at the Y, I play around with a couple of guys at Northeastern. No sooner am I home than Felipe calls. He wants to "wish me a good trip away." I am silent, hardly knowing whether to curse myself for having spent myself at Northeastern, or suspect him of waiting until the last moment so that it would be difficult for us to meet. He said, yes, he did want to see me again. The damn trouble is that I simply do not know when my body will be able to perform again after the surgery.

A letter comes from Eric. He is a little bothered by my message, but offers to replace the camera if I really think he took it. He wants the "issue" resolved as soon as possible. A reasonable response, if he's the nice guy that I think he is.

July 16, 1985, Boston

This morning, I phone Henry, make love with P, then go into hospital—that place of bad memory on Parker Hill. At the admissions office, I find I have to share a room. Can I share with a Black, I ask. The girl, a Filipino, look startled. She searches but the last room, with a 24-year-old Black engineer, has just been assigned. I kick myself. She says brightly, "We are putting you with a Chinese. We thought you, as a famous author on Chinese affairs, would like to be with a Chinese." I try to smile.

July 18, 1985, Boston

The hernia operation is over and apparently successful. Waiting for it, and going back and forth over what kind of anesthetic, were worse than the thing itself. I had decided to treat the whole stay in the hospital like a hotel stay, a break between chapters of my book, and this worked as an approach. In fact, in a good hospital you are waited on hand and foot more than in a good hotel.

The night before and the morning before the noon operation, they dosed me up with Dalmane, so by the time they put the needles into my thighs I really was quite mellow. It took about an hour, and only two or three times did I have to request an extra shot of Novocaine.

Just before I went into the operating theater there was a lovely moment. On first entering the hospital, I had noticed a handsome Black guy with curly hair; he was dressed in a surgical-type gown. This same guy came up to me and said, "Pull down your pants!" In his hand was a shaver. His job was to shave off the hair near my cock on the left side so that the surgeon could do his incision! I loved it so much. I said, why not do the other side as well? He just grinned a beautiful grin, and I was wheeled in, like the Sunday turkey, to face the knife.

Back in my large, airy room, which I shared in essential silence with the Chinese, shots of Demerol kept me comfortable. The only difficulty was turning in bed; once in a given position, I was OK. I took music in with me and this proved a great idea. When the Chinese guy had visitors, I simply began a Mahler symphony or some Saint-Saëns and went into another world.

The Americans certainly believe in asking questions and documenting everything at exhaustive length. I tried to be patient—in fact, I was patient—and giving all the answers enabled me to make the point (precautionary for my surgeons, I trusted) that last time I was in this hospital sloppiness cost me dearly. But it must have been at least six times that I told someone I drank about a bottle of white wine a day. Are you addicted, one asked. Look, I said, I'm addicted to several things, including wine, sex, and work. This amiable person decided to go on to the next question—any allergies?

Leaving hospital, I got a form which said what I could and could not do. "Driving: not for two weeks. Housekeeping: unlimited, but no heavy lifting for six weeks. Sexual activity: unlimited."

Tonight, I was scarcely home when the phone rang and it was darling Henry. The sound of his voice made me feel a new person. He cares so much. He said he cried when he read the end of my last letter, which spoke of my feeling that we really must live together, spending a few weeks here and a few weeks there is not enough. "Ross, I have been thinking exactly the same thing."

July 20, 1985, Boston

A glorious Boston summer day; the sun fills every niche. Alas, my wound is sore. Yesterday I spent mostly in bed; Tony came in with food and conversation and the hours passed pleasantly. This morning, I rose at five, tackled my "British or American?" chapter and after a couple of hours felt bad. After phone consultations with the clinic, they told me to come in. As I was waiting, an attendant come up to me and asked if I was a historian. Sort of, I replied. "I thought so," he said, "I read your biography Mao in a course last year and it just made the course." I felt slightly less pain.

Tonight, I feel lonely. The terrible thing is not the absence of people here, but the realization that I am not fit enough to fuck with a friend, or find a new one. I went to the gym, met a nice guy, but did not want him to see my wound; a nice fish swam back into the sea.

I will leave Boston about September 15. That way, I can attend the opening festivities of the Harvard season—then disappear. If necessary, I can spend a few days in New York, see Fred Hills and Barbara, and take off for Brisbane from there. Great if before departing, I could get the "Race" chapter done, and maybe the "Two Cities" chapter.

July 26, 1985, Boston

Wyatt, evidently having overlooked the fact that I am an "asshole," phones up; can he go to bed with me. The answer, at the moment he phones, is yes. He looks good and feels good, though he still has a fussy streak, his drink, this way, temperature of the room, that way.

July 28, 1985, Boston

Reading a new book, *Confessions of a Concierge*, a social history of 20th-century France, I find a couplet which brings to mind "that Sunday" when Edward and I re-met in heaven: "Said the mattress to the sheets, I have never seen such feats. Said the pillow to the case, "We've been shaken to the base."

July 29, 1985, Boston

At night, dinner with Curt Anderson at Genji's. While we are having a pre-dinner drink, a fluttering bird called Kevin comes by, and Curt asks him to join us for a moment. Beacon Hill type: longish shorts, blond hair, a novel in his long white hand; mannerism always to pretend not the hear or understand what is said.

Walking back along Mass Ave, we ran into Edward—done up in red. From the moment we looked at each other, it seemed inevitable that we would spend time together. When we reached Curt's bike, Edward sort of joined me and we farewelled Curt. In such a situation, Curt is very cautious.

"Let me fix my bag on right," Curt said, bending over his bike. I looked at Curt's ass, Edward was looking at me. "His bag has an excellent book in it," I said to Edward. It was my *Mao*, which Curt recently bought and brought along for me to sign. When Curt mentioned that it was softcover, I said "soft" seemed to be all I could manage these days, "hard" being beyond me. Both roared. Curt said: "Not from what I've heard."

Upstairs Edward was imperious. After pouring himself a Dubonnet, he phoned to get a ticket for a music show late tonight. A button was off his shirt; I scurried to sew it back on. He softened, and we sewed it on together, the new button coming from my collection in the green box. "Any new videos?" he cried. "I thought you were going to a show?" "Not yet."

Upstairs, we watched one full of aggressive fucking. Edward loved it. At one point, as he oohed and aahed, I said he had an engineering view of sex between men. He asked to see my scar, which I last week playfully told him was due to Felipe biting me. After a brief inspection, he resumed watching the video, and resumed criticisms of many things around him—including the lack of blinds.

"We can watch the rest another time," he suddenly says. As we approach the bed, he announces that this is going to be a quickie, as he still wants to make the music show, so what would I like. I said nothing; I was unhinged by the sight of him naked (still, after all these times!), and by his—on this occasion—taking charge of the situation.

I fell back on the bed, my cock pushing out from my underpants. He looked down at me, pulling his shirt off, his dick wildly on the right in his white briefs. I merely murmured, as he pulled off my underpants, that I hadn't thought I'd want it again after sex with the Texan student, Richard S.

"That will be the day, when Ross Terrill does not want more," he says, hurling his red shorts toward one of my plants, in that flat voice that people in heat use on every topic, except a sexual instruction or a moan of response.

He sucked me for an age, hoisting my legs over his shoulders, and put a finger into my asshole. He towered over me and rammed his dick down my jaw. It seemed hotter and bigger than I'd known it. He does not concern himself with the angle. For Edward, style eclipses convenience, and the style of the moment was the Big Warrior act, grinning down at me from a great height. My mouth had to struggle to cope.

In what ensued, there were many positions, many twists. He rammed his tongue deep into my asshole. He lay back and I sucked him. Then he drew me up. The whites of his eyes rivetted me. He was beseeching me to do something, but I did not know what. I had to ask. "Sit on it," he gasped. In that position, he began to fuck me.

Some time later, he pulled me off him, drew me higher, and croaked: "Shoot on my face." As he worked my cock, a great pain gripped it and soon I did indeed shoot into his mouth, nose, and forehead. He wiped my dick all over his face, as if pushing a vacuum cleaner into every corner, then thrust it into his mouth to lick off the remaining cum. Meanwhile, he was shooting into my back his own load of thick, sweet cum. I could never forget the excitement. I will never possess this man. He could never be mine, nor me his—as with Pan, and may be starting to occur with Henry.

July 30, 1985, Boston

A long letter from Henry, together with photos and extracts from his recent diary. The letter is beautiful and devoted to me. The diary is vivid. He is complex, intelligent, sensitive.

Lunch at the Harvest in Cambridge with Tony Lewis of the *The New York Times*, who is going to China tomorrow, and Nieman boss Jim Thomson. Tony's leftism is sufficiently under control that we get on well. I give Tony a few tips on Sichuan, on which my *National Geographic* piece should appear in a couple of weeks, and suggestions on themes for him to take up.

July 31, 1985, Boston

Have been reading Henry's diary and letter again. He seems to think my idea of being together more may just be casual words. Actually, if I get this Australian book done by February 1986, I can be quite flexible as to where I am and what I write about. It would be interesting to tackle the novel set in Hong Kong; then I could divide my time between Boston and Hong Kong, and see a lot of Henry. When in Boston, he made a lot of remarks against USA, and he thought I was too pro-US. Now in his diary I find that he likes the US and even compares it favorably to Australia—which I did when we talked, and he generally did not agree with.

Edward comes around. He's lost his keys; could I help him with a loan to get a locksmith? In the end, John, the elderly gay guy from down the street, does it for $40. Edward has band-aids on his right leg. He sucked a taxi driver off, and bending over to his left, scraped himself against the front of the dashboard.

I think he's getting closer to going back and finishing his degree, which is good news. But will he sit for the real estate exam? I told him that if he does, and if he passes it, I will give him 395 to sell as a first task. He was pleased.

August 3, 1985, Boston

Henry's dreams are remarkable. And his capacity to reproduce the dream on paper! Everything is there—Hong Kong society, family life of the Chinese, situation of a student returned from the West, gay life, problems in dealing with me.

It is natural that he should go on with JB. I think he is the kind of person who needs to have a concrete, local person. He seems to be comparing, looking out for a possible replacement for me. I am not doing this, but perhaps he thinks I am. Maybe, in the end I am not as attached to him as he is to me.

Separation is separation. I'm sure there are things I do that bother Henry to some degree, too, including one I haven't told him about yet. I know there is one for him; he told me he found it difficult to think of me with Felipe. He is young and relatively inexperienced, and so is likely to change as he gets around. I am older and experienced and, as he mentioned after he had talked to his friends in Sydney, less reliable because of that.

Henry could distrust his emotions; he could distrust mine—but really, it's just the problem of being far apart. And there is too much joy to be had by thinking of the positive and remembering that friendship requires overlooking flaws. It also involves giving the other person the space to be himself.

August 6, 1985, Boston

I should not have seen Wyatt last night, after seeing Reggie in the morning (and the previous night). And then I drank again. There's something in me that just does not know when to stop, especially on gorgeous warm days and evenings.

The talk on the phone with Edward last night hangs in the mind with a gentle melancholy. I felt sorry for him. I felt sorry for myself. I felt the weirdness, the cruelty of life; so many brick walls are thrown up against the human spirit. Yet we have to live with compromise; that is what society is about and it is amazing that the whole thing can hold together at all, given the passions of the human heart.

I thank my mother for my blue eyes, I thank my father for my body—both have made my life.

At 6 AM, Reggie and I woke up. It was the end—for the moment. We bustled. We fumbled. We embraced. At 9 AM, his plane for Dallas took off.

Aaron came in at lunchtime, after I had spent the morning in the BPL[217] trying to plan my chapter on race in Australia. He is even more attractive than I feared to hope when we met yesterday. He made love like a house on fire. And he's an interesting character.

John A phoned. "I'm lonely in Boston," he said. He is pretty, he sucked like an angel, and in the end the sex was fantastic. He is a dancer in New York.

I retreat to my study to write letters. Chris rings the bell, but I need to write letters and be with my books.

August 11, 1985, Boston

A strange phone call to Texas. I got Richard S's mother. "Where are you?" Then: "Who are you?" So blunt, so rude. By the time Richard came on the phone, I was cowed, and he was a mouse. I hope—in a way—it's just a case of a tyrannical mother. Or is it that for him a dream has come to an end? Probably the former. I think of Felipe, terrified of his family's reaction; said he would call but has not. But who am I to talk, for in Australia as a youth I did not face this issue in the way these kids do—not to speak of the awful health complications that are making today seem worse.

August 16, 1985, Boston

The Spanish translation of *White-Boned Demon* arrives from my agent, looking good—but they left out the documentation. It is an Argentine edition, distributed from Buenos Aires to the Spanish-speaking world. I wonder if it was the parallel with Eva Peron which made the Argentine company leap ahead of Mexicans and Spaniards to buy the rights?

---

[217] The Boston Public Library in Copley Square.

August 17, 1985, Boston

Jimmie comes in, and for once I'm free to see him. He's extremely attractive; he becomes less and less straight. Tonight, he sucked me and rimmed me. Straight afterwards he said he must go; he was only on an errand to the corner store. But it was 1 AM before he left.

August 18, 1985, Boston

Edward says he is "stalled" at the moment on all fronts. I am not sure I can help. Is he an evil genius? Or is he an innocent, bound to be broken on the rocks of the near future? We may together enroll in a health research study at the Fenway Clinic.[218] After declining ever to discuss the topic, he now talks much of AIDS.

August 19, 1985, Boston

Phone call to Henry this morning, and progress on the chapter helps me ditch the migraine. Henry sounded great. Says that as long as we really love each other, other things don't matter. I said when we meet, we will pick up exactly where we left off, and that any playing around in between won't affect anything.

August 20, 1985, Boston

Wyatt brings his friend Tyrone and we have a drink and watch a video. The guy is extremely attractive, if not handsome, and I felt horny. On the couch, we all played around a bit, but both were shy with each other. One would suck me; a few minutes later the other would—but they didn't want all three of us in action together.

Wyatt asked if I had any "bad books." I said I wouldn't answer until he called sex books by another name. He called them beautiful books; so, I went downstairs and got some.

Tyrone goes right off the radar screen when you suck his tits. On the couch, I also went out of control—while Wyatt was downstairs—when Tyrone went into full throttle sucking my swollen cock. "Not tonight," Tyrone kept saying, his big eyes sending a message opposite to the one coming off his lips.

Eventually, Tyrone, after carefully watching Wyatt, said: "I'll come downstairs, but I can't take my underpants off." Fifteen minutes later, as we rolled around in bed, he was pulling off his underpants and begging me to fuck him. He is a superb lover.

Wyatt is a flirtatious, gossipy, indecisive character who makes a loyal friend, but is hopeless in this situation. What did he want—just to watch? Twice he came in while I was screwing Tyrone, who was begging me to "pump that white dick into me, pump it harder." Tyrone would become embarrassed when Wyatt came in. We would stop. Then we would resume.

---

[218] An LGBTQ health clinic in Boston.

Tyrone kept saying "You're teasing me." What did he mean? I don't know, but he said he loved what we were doing. I gave him my number, on a tissue when Wyatt was not looking.

Wyatt ended up jerking off in the bathroom with one of the "beautiful books," but he didn't seem to mind—he must have realized when he brought Tyrone in that this would happen.

August 22, 1985, Boston

By chance, on my 47th birthday, Luther calls after a long silence, and Felipe calls, also after a small silence. Luther is coming up to Boston and wonders if he can "leave some stuff" here. I suggest he stay for a couple of days; he will arrive tomorrow. Felipe has been busy and is tired. He sounds wonderful. We are to have dinner next Monday at 10 PM when he gets off work.

Writing about Australian aborigines and seeing US Blacks daily makes for an eerie contrast. The Australians have none of the grace, dash, and dynamism of the US Blacks. But they have an almost painful sincerity.

August 27, 1985, Boston

I leave the house with the package of my manuscript to send to Corgi [Press] in the UK, planning to go to the post office on the way to meet Tony for lunch in Boylston Street. Just outside the door, I see a slim guy walk towards his car. I smile. He smiles. I linger, and I see him leaning down to look out the car window at me. After a few moments, I stroll to the side of his car and murmur a silly remark about the hot day.

"Where do you live?" I pointed upstairs. Silence. I asked if he could come back tonight. "No, I can't." Another silence, then he adds in a kind of severe whisper: "How about now?" He is a Tanzanian Moslem, very charming, with a lovely dick, a student at a Boston community college. It was the quickest of quickies. He drove me to my rendezvous with Tony. When I took my leave, he leaned toward me and kissed me on the forehead, Islamic-style.

August 28, 1985, Boston

After dining at Pizzeria Uno, one of Edward's favorite places, we went for a drink to the Top of the Prudential. At one point, we both went to the john. "This is what they do at Northeastern," I said, kneeling down in my cubicle and sliding my knees under the partition, and my throbbing dick up into Edward's cubicle. He grabbed my dick. I nearly went through the ceiling of the Prudential Tower with ecstasy. Later, I stood on my toilet seat, peered down at him, and said, "I want that Black dick." Just as I said this, the door to the john swung open, someone came in. I jumped down from standing on my toilet seat and resumed a normal position. None of this fazed Edward; sometimes so cautious, sometimes so wild.

When we walked back to 200 [St. Botolph Street], he made to go in, but I said brightly, how about going to your place. He looked startled, then grabbed my arm, and off we went. I said the bed is comfortable. "Arlene gave it to me," he said quietly. After a night with Edward, you feel you've been communing with both heaven and hell.

The difference between the writer on the one hand, and the drunk and prostitute on the other, is only that the latter two never record their experience.

August 29, 1985, Boston

Henry phones early this morning. "Why so much sex, Baby?" After a long talk, what he said made a link with doubts in my mind. But action on these doubts? We confirmed our plans for Christmas and January. He has found, at last, a Chinese guy he likes—Albert, a student in UK who is back in Hong Kong for vacation.

Took the bus to see my surgeon. Dr. Shuyler said my post-hernia operation guts look fine and the only thing I can't do for a few more weeks is ride a bike. Later I played squash with Ron. I lost, but it felt great to be back on the court. In fact, I just fooled around, so happy to be there, with a racquet in my hand and my bare legs scampering across the court.

August 30, 1985, Boston

McCarry calls from the *National Geographic*: will I come down and lunch with the chief editor next week and talk about doing a special article on Australia for the Australian Bicentennial.

September 6, 1985, Boston

I was feeling funny from the anti-VD injection, but that did not reduce the magnificent sex with Tyrone. Afterwards, I was tired, but no rest. Cornell phones, agitated, his tone quite different from this afternoon. "Cheap trash" he called me, for picking up VD. I was soft for a while, but after a while I got sick of his narrowness and his moralizing.

September 8, 1985, Boston

I was preoccupied with the US Open, while pretending to work, when in the evening Ted came in. I wasn't sure about making love. It was just over two days since the penicillin; enough according to the doctors, but I didn't want to take a risk. Happily, Ted had in mind prudence; for once I was of the same view. We did not "exchange bodily fluids."

September 12, 1985, Boston

Cleared the decks for writing politics and economics, a chapter I may call "Public Ways." I itch to be at it; writing gives a daily satisfaction that planning can never give. I might have started this afternoon, but Tyrone came in. I could tell by the look in his eyes what he "wanted." He said he wouldn't interrupt me—he had an hour to kill—but I was happy to be interrupted.

He is uncontrollable when I eat his tits. He started biting my arm—a new trick. He didn't want to be fucked. As we jerked each other off to the climax, he talked as if I was fucking him; a good turn-on, and my orgasm was so roaring that I felt tired for hours. Have I seen Wyatt, he asks. I haven't seen much of Wyatt, but the sad thing is since Wyatt introduced me to Tyrone, the two of them are slightly estranged.

A long talk with Joan Kennedy about the book on her by Marcia,[219] now out. Joan wants to ignore it, and so far, the plan is working. She has been in Hyannis to get away from the insistent TV and radio invitations. Ethel and Eunice "have been wonderful." She feels the *National Enquirer* excerpts are a worse ordeal than the book can be. I told her Tony Lewis is interested in a column on the privacy theme, and that Bob Manning has suggested Mike Barnicle[220] write on the same point.

Joan wants to see if Marcia's publicity tour makes a splash before making her next move. I am going to find out next week what the printing was and how the orders are coming in. I suggested if the book is going to be big, she should hit back, if it's going to sink—keep silent. I am on Joan's side, right or wrong.

September 15, 1985, Boston

A third day on the chapter on Politics—a long gestation may be frustrating, but it bears fruit when you start writing.

Tonight, Edward calls, back from Connecticut, and says can he come round and we watch a video. He is horny; he tears my clothes off. On the couch, I find myself up-ended, sucking his toes, while he sucks my dick. When he gets his tongue near my asshole, I say I'll take a shower first. We take a shower together, and soon are rimming each other. I love to hear his whimpering when I get my tongue inside.

He had decided he was going to fuck me tonight. In all sorts of positions, some of which hurt a lot, but he liked it. Actually, it hurt so much that I lost interest after a while and did not come. He stayed all night, leaving early for the bank.

September 16, 1985, Boston

Tyrone calls and comes in. Nice sex. Afterwards, I have to get busy, and he stays upstairs watching TV. I am already in bed when he tip-toes in to say goodbye. "Sometimes I think I'm going crazy," he said mysteriously.

September 17, 1985, Boston

Edward and I work on the ad about selling my condo in Cambridge. He is in a good mood and looks gorgeous in a purple shirt (he prefers to call it mauve) and faded blue jeans.

Later, I meet a Puerto Rican guy Rafael at the laundry. At first, he says he doesn't have time to come to my place. I say, well come up on your way home and we'll write

---

[219] Living with the Kennedys: The Joan Kennedy Story, by Marcia Chellis.
[220] Michael Barnicle (1943 -), American political and social commentator. At the time, Barnicle was a columnist (1973-1998) for the Boston Globe.

down each other's phone numbers. He agrees. Walking along St. Botolph Street, he sees a pigeon in distress in the middle of the road, and gently lifts it and puts in a more comfortable position on grass. A nice person. We go into my place. I fuck him, as I expected he wanted me to do.

September 18, 1985, Washington

Breakfast with the *National Geographic* brass; little discussion of substance, much stroking of feathers and registering of consensus. They love to pepper the talk with remarks like, "One issue of the *National Geographic* takes 1200 acres of trees to have printed," and, "stack one issue of *National Geographic* up and the pile is six times as high as Mount Everest."

Later, a session with the Australians about my forthcoming trip. On the way out, I run into diplomat Murray McLean[221] and we lunch at the Grammercy Hotel and talk China. Beautiful sights all over the streets of Washington.

I take Amtrak to New York, and get a message that Mark Barty King from Corgi is in town from London and wants to talk with me.

September 19, 1985, New York

Ran into Henry Rosovsky at breakfast at the Harvard Club; he is down for the day for an Asia Society meeting. Full of sighs about academic life.

Mark Barty-King[222] thinks my first three chapters are "absolutely superb." No worries about different versions for US and Britain. "The high opinion is not just mine; others in the house have read it and think the same." "Utterly fascinating" he found the three chapters. All well written. "A Memory" he found "beautiful." Likes the "I" weaving in and out of the story. Says this could have been the most difficult chapter, but it's moving, and the themes are there. Sometimes metaphor overused. If the book comes in at about 100,000 [words], this chapter at present is too long. We'll see.

After lunch, I went down to Eighth Ave to buy the video, *Black Sex Therapy*, and in the downstairs store I could not resist a young Black guy. He was up from Virginia, he said. He sucked me off in one of the booths, while a film ran without us watching a thing.

New York sparkled on this warm September day. The variety of people in the streets stimulates; you never know who or what you're going to see next.

September 23, 1985, Cambridge

To our "open day" at 395 [Broadway]. Eight or nine people came to enquire. Probably we should advertise again next weekend. But I am leaving for Australia in a week. Edward was excellent with the visitors. A woman entered and announced herself as

---

[221] Alistair Murray McLean (1947-), at the time Political Counsellor in the Australian Embassy in Washington D.C. Later, Australia's ambassador to Japan.
[222] Mark Baxter Barty-King (1938-2006), known as "the Captain" of British publishing,

Beverley. "A lovely name," says Edward, "my sister's called Beverley." We brought white wine and orange juice but only Edward and I drank any of it.

Later, I went to a PEN party at the Harvard Bookstore Store cafe. Steve Goldberg annoyed me by asking yet again about my health; half my straight friends seem to think that any man who has loved other men is going to drop dead of AIDS.

September 24, 1985, Boston

A wonderful evening with Edward. We ate upstairs, Chinese food by candlelight, and talked about Black life in Boston and marketing my Cambridge condo. Afterwards, downstairs, he was in one those I-want-to-be-attacked moods. I attacked. Every time he said, "Don't" or "Stop," I redoubled my attentions.

He drew me close to lie quietly. This I liked enormously; but after a while I wanted some action. The compromise was that as we lay together, him kissing me with deep tongue, I wangled a finger up his ass. Since it was his night to be "controlled," I also had the delight of tearing off his pants, his socks, his shirt, and more or less "raping" him. There comes a point where the gasps if protest become gasps of encouragement. This time I ended up fucking him in what Tony calls the doggy position; it seemed more comfortable for him than my preferred flat-on-top way.

How am I going to present all this to Henry?

September 25, 1985, Boston

During the day, I was wondering what to do with Rafael, with whom I had a 3 PM appointment when, at 2:30 PM, the doorbell rang and who should it be but Reggie. "You're a sex maniac," he said when we finished. "Never tell anyone we fool around," he demanded as we showered. "If my girlfriend knew, she'd kill me."

"Why are you hot for me today?" I asked him.

"Because it's something different." He added: "You're like a Black guy; are all Australians like Black guys?"

Tonight, Tyrone came in and we made slow love. "You're teasing me," he kept saying. He had to work a bit harder than usual, but both had good orgasms.

September 26, 1985, Boston

I have arranged to give Edward the power of attorney, concerning my Cambridge condo, for while I'm away. Edward is dressed in a nice blue suit, and he's excellent in these situations. The lawyer we consulted was no doubt intrigued at what kind of relationship exists between Edward and me. We had lunch together at Skerington's—cave-like—and talked about Edward 's future study plans. He's taking French, like many other Black guys; a reaction against Anglo-Saxon culture.

September 27, 1985, Boston

Panic as Hurricane Gloria hits; the shops close, and on my last full business day before the trip, I find I have no empty discs or extra printer ribbons. Nor have I picked up my ticket from the travel agent—whose computers are today all shut up. Pray to God, Gloria will pass today and the shops will open tomorrow.

September 28, 1985, Boston

Edward has just gone, and I have the day to pack. He came in last night depressed; today he is not. We watched videos last night, then went to bed and I fucked him strongly. This morning we did it again, but he came before I had shot into him, so I pulled out. Then I brought him a glass of orange juice in bed, and we chatted. I said goodbye to his dick.

We do not sleep well together. Or perhaps it's just that neither of us sleeps well. I hear him tossing and turning, and murmuring all night; he says he hears and feels me do the same.

The Diary manuscript is missing entries from late September until early March 1986. Presumably, Terrill was back in China during some of that time.

Photographs

Ross at the summer place, Beijing 1964. Author's collection.

Ross Terrill with Rupert Murdoch and Murdoch's second wife, Anna Murdoch Mann, at Murdoch's farm. (Right to Left: Ross Terrill, Rupert Murdock, Anna) Author's collection.

Ross with famed Chinese scholar and poet Guo Moruo at the Great Hall of the People, Beijing. Author's collection.

Ross Terrill and the Prince Sihanouk, Cambodian King and Prime Minister. Author's collection.

Ross Terrill and Australian Prime Minister Robert Hawke, 1983 - 1991.
Author's Collection.

Ross and Zhou Nan at the Ming Dynasty tombs. At the time of this photograph, Zhou Nan
was about to be named Chinese Foreign Minister. Author's collection.

Ross Terrill and Rachel, who at one time had been his girlfriend. They remained lifelong friends. Author's collection.

Ross and his mother. Author's collection.

Ross and Pan. Pan was a Thai grad student with whom Ross had a deep relationship. Pan succumbed to AIDS. Author's collection.

Edward, a young bisexual man with whom Ross conducted a long and sometimes unsettled affair. Author's collection.

Ross in his study. Author's collection.

Ross Terrill. Author's collection.

1986

March 7, 1986, New York

A leisurely morning at the Harvard Club then strolling down 5th Avenue, prior to seeing BL and then Fred about my manuscript.

Edward arrives and it is nice to see him. We go to Better Days,[223] which boggles his mind. "How did you find this place?" he keeps asking, his eyes swiveling around the room. My friend Mathew is there, but for a long time I don't go over to him. Eventually I do, and later, predictably, Edward says Mathew is "too effeminate."

We decide to go to The Garage[224] but Edward screws things up totally—getting the wrong address, then losing his temper with the cabbie just as we could have tried to sort our location—so we went back to the hotel about 2 AM. I suppose the meetings with BL and Fred had left me a little down. And I began to feel Edward is not at his best. All night he was restless, jiggling his feet, hurling himself from side to side. I don't think I slept ten minutes.

March 8, 1986, New York

Cold again, but we enjoy a brisk walk down Madison toward a cinema. On the way, we lunch at Fino, a high-class, totally empty Italian restaurant. Edward asks for a glass of water to take his Alka Seltzer with. Six waiters scurry to get it. Tired and a bit troubled, I drown myself in white wine. We have a great time chatting away. At $70 for lunch for two, one can understand why Fino's patrons apparently go there only for dinner.

After the movie, I went back to the Hyatt to rest, while Edward wandered off to the Village. When he came back, I saw that the zip of his trousers was undone. I pointed it out, and lightly said I hoped he'd enjoyed it. He said it was nothing, the zip just keeps sagging down.

March 9, 1986, New York

Edward goes back to Yonkers late in the evening, and oddly I felt a desire to go out on the town. First to the "bookshop" that I found yesterday and this time, when I find Anthony, I feel relaxed about letting things go where they will. Though he has a cold, he sucks masterfully as yesterday. We go on for so long that the cubicle becomes stuffy, and keeping up the supply of tokens is a major undertaking (no token, and the light outside the cubicle goes off, which brings the staff by, knocking on the door, saying either leave or pay up). Anthony puts on his clothes and goes out for more tokens.

Each time we think what he gets will be enough, but each time we run out and he has to go out again. I came with a wonderful rush and exhilaration. "You're an animal," this charming hustler says.

---

[223] Better Days was an East Side dance club that operated from 1972 until 1990.
[224] Paradise Garage, also known as the Garage or the Gay-rage, was a New York disco (1977-1987).

Heading for Better Days, I call in at the Adonis Theater on 8th Avenue, a huge place in which few watch the screen and many walk around looking for a partner. The types do not turn me on; too much moustache and whiff-of-leather style. In the freezing streets, as I head for 42nd, I feel the need to break my walk, and pop into a Spanish bar. As I sip a glass of wine, a guitar plays, Spaniards in three-piece suits and ties sit drinking, and a Mexican who lives in New Jersey tells me the joys and sorrows of his life.

Next stop is a straight porn cinema where for $1.99 you may see reasonable pics and a surprisingly bi-sexual crowd of patrons especially in the balcony. I sat in the second-to-last row of the balcony, cock out, and watched a handsome Black guy in the back row get sucked off first by a white guy and then by a Black.

Further up 8th Avenue, I find a nice quiet bar where I sit sipping white wine, vaguely watching a TV above the bar, and feeling that tired tingling in the body that comes after each phase of a canter of lust. It is very late when I reach the corner bookshop near the Port Authority where in the past, I have bought videos and found guys. A short, dark, chunky guy sucks me off. He complains that it takes a long time! I never get to Better Days. At the Hyatt, I shower, fall into bed, and sleep a hundred times better than last night.

March 10, 1986, Boston

Lassitude as I pay for overdoing it in New York. I start this, start that, but have insufficient energy to complete anything. Mike phones and comes over. His body is beautiful, but still, he is uptight, and insists on leaving his boots on as we make out. "Can anybody see us?" he keeps asking weakly. I don't think he's all that straight, and he makes a dive straight for my dick as soon as he gets heated up. He wants me to fuck him but thinks it will hurt too much.

March 11, 1986, Boston

I take Joan Colebrook[225] to lunch at Huskie's and we talk about our forthcoming books. How strange that after 20 years friendship we are suddenly "competitors" (as she can't help thinking). As always, she likes to know about my love life. It's impossible for anyone to properly love both men and women, she says; against the logic of our genes. Alas, she's also racist. "Can you really trust a Black man?" She insists that I ask myself if "intellectually" I believe Edward and I can last together; of course, that is never the point with passion.

Reggie comes in and we make love. I have never said no to him, and though tonight I should have, I was not strong enough to make a departure. He smoked some reefer, began a large bottle of Budweiser, and together we watched the video Jailbait. Soon he was begging me to fuck him. His very dark, smooth body grabs me even in my saturated state. As we slide and grind around, he cries, "Boy, man; God, man, that's good."

---

[225] Joan Colebrook (1910-1991), Australian writer, among whose books was *A House of Trees: Memoirs of an Australian Girlhood* (1987)

Inspecting my asshole, hoping I might let him fuck me, he says it looks different. "It's been opened up. Has that Chinese guy been fucking you, Ross? Ro-uss ?"

He is so sexy I forgive him for asking me, constantly, whether I like eating out girls, and for remarking that I'm getting fat. On one matter, Reggie and I vary: unless he drinks, he can't get fucked; unless I drink, I can't sleep.

March 12, 1986

The special luncheon at Kirkland House is nice. I sit next to the Master and feel relieved that he talked about Cambridge real estate

Sitting at lunch in the Junior Common Room, which is directly below A Entry, where I lived, ghosts of the past rose up. The past with Pan, much of it spent in the apartment just above the ceiling over this spring luncheon. My Harvard past:; it is really a past, though I cling to it sometimes, and in my public image I am still Harvard-linked. I think this is a great difference between me and Edward (and other friends): experience just slides off them, whereas for me, it's mulling everything over, with regrets poking up.

March 13, 1986, Cambridge/Boston

Vinny was to come in today at 1 PM. By chance I was in the Boston Public Library during the morning and ran into him. Deep in a paper, he asked if we could postpone our meeting till Monday. Sure, I said. A day's rest from sex would for me be all to the good, I thought.

Moments later I ran into a guy dressed in red from head to toe. We came home through torrential rain, wiped ourselves dry with towels, and went to bed. After careful and repeated checking with him, I fucked him uproariously. In the shower, he said; "Almost never did it feel that good." His name is Cornell—yet one more—and he works at a local college.

March 14, 1986, Boston

Am I running out of steam and discipline? In the past, I have always told people who asked that, no, I will never go back to Australia to live. But God, now with the dwindling Australian dollar, and the future prospect that my riotous sex life will die down, can I really rule out the possibility?

March 15, 1986, Boston

It is easy to blame Edward for something, or the state of the relationship between him and me for something, when the source of the problem is really within myself. This summer I want to understand myself better, to become more stable and realistic.

I went alone to see *Kiss of the Spider Woman*. After a slow start, it is a fine movie. As always, it is the hopeless that moves us. As always, it is the perilous effort to build bridges—in this case between love for a person and belief in a cause—that moves us.

A long, pretty good talk with Edward on the phone. He didn't feel disappointed at the New York stay as I did. I spill out everything, including all doubts; he doesn't.

Which is the best way? He's working for UPS. I simply feel that a person of Edward's talent and personality at age 27 should be doing something better.

March 18, 1986, Boston

Henry phones from Hong Kong. His voice is rich and sensual even on the phone. And I had just last night been thinking about him because of his letter and the photos which came back in the afternoon.

Planned out an article for *New York Times* on recent American writing about China. Funny, after all this Australian stuff, it was nice to think about China again for an afternoon. But another book on China?

I was just going to have a rest—for Tyrone is coming in for dalliance and dinner tonight—when the doorbell rings and it's Cornell. Few people ring my doorbell unannounced. Even fewer are so arrogant as to say—when you ask who is there—"it's me." But then quiet Cornell has his arrogant side. Anyway, he was thrilled to get the postcard from Henry and me and came by to say thanks. His night job ends at 3:30 AM; his day job starts at 9 AM. Between 5 PM and 6 PM he has one hour off between jobs! No time even to shower. Alas, Cornell, who was always so clean, smelled dirty. And looks so tired.

March 19, 1986, Boston

I feel I am making some progress in clearing my desk of accumulated tasks, and my sleep is getting toward normal. How much more time there is in the day when one is not writing those slow sentences!

March 21, 1986, Boston

With Tony O to see two Victor Bumbalo[226] plays at the Triangle Theater Company, and we laugh our heads off. A sell-out house in the tiny upstairs theater on Berkeley Street, to watch a gay farce with moments of pathos, on the theme of gay relationships in the pre-AIDS era.

Afterwards, we dined at an Irish pub, Claddagh, where I had an excellent steak, and Tony drank Manhattans and ate raw vegetables. I still find Tony attractive after all this time, especially, as tonight, when I haven't made love for 4-5 days. We go back to his place, and I meet Jim, his nephew, a charming and handsome youth of 17.

One hears birds in the morning, a magnificent sound after the long privation of winter. Sex really does drain energy.

March 30, 1986, Boston

It was nice to be with Edward yesterday. When he came in. he looked magnificent in a purple shirt ("lavender," he corrected me, his ass tight in mid-blue jeans). But at the end, there was a silly little quarrel. I foolishly referred to the piece of paper he left in our

---

[226] Victor Bumbalo (1948-), gay American playwright.

room at the Hyatt in New York a couple of weeks ago. To me at that moment, it was merely a pleasant topic of conversation. But when I handed the piece of paper to him—something on it made him feel embarrassed that he had revealed too much.

I had introduced the whole damned matter by saying, "Isn't 40 old to start having a family?" This is what his map of his future life on the paper called for, along with things like visiting Cairo and studying law at Howard University.

After taking the rented videos back to Liberty shop in Washington Street—it satisfied me that they gave me back my money in twenties rather than trying to fob me off with two hundred-dollar bills—something made me pop into the Pilgrim Theater.[227] Soon a very attractive guy appeared. I smiled, and he did. He beckoned me down the stairs to a lower level. Soon my pants were off, and he was grabbing my balls, murmuring "beautiful balls" (that should have made me suspicious; few say that to me) and began to suck my cock. By now my pants were around my ankles. Suddenly the guy stopped and was gone. Putting back my pants, I found my wallet gone.

Having just got the deposit back on the three videos ($210), I had not only a wallet heavy with cash but my Mastercard, bank card, YMCA card, Harvard card, and much else. In my dusty pants, I found 80 cents, just enough for the subway ride back home.

Standing on the platform of the Orange Line,[228] I felt stupid and mad. How could it happen! Of course, one reason was that the guy's attractiveness bowled me over and distracted me. Another was that I'd been drinking. I realized. as I thought back, that a third was that the guy had an accomplice; he didn't bend down to get into the pocket of my pants, his mate did—that's why the choice of location had been made.

On the bus home from Copley, I saw this nice Black guy. By now, I was still a bit tipsy, feeling very sorry for myself, but also starting to feel a kind of satisfaction that I had my life and limbs, and my keys to get back to my nest. I was not so disgusted with myself and the world that desire could not again shoot up.

Keith—as he was called—got off at Symphony as I did. He looked at me and then walked down into the subway station. I said, with a smile, "It's closed." He said, "I know," and grinned broadly. I followed him down the grimy steps into the gloom. He grabbed me, but I said I didn't like it down there, and how about coming to my place, which is "one minute away." He agreed.

"I don't kiss," he said with a nervous, lustful smile. Indeed, he was largely straight, but hot as a furnace, so who cared. (I must do something about the top of the curved window in my bedroom; the nervous ones glance up there, imagining an audience of millions is watching).

This morning, as expected, I awoke depressed about the theft, as well as hungry and hungover. There was a lunch date with Luther. How was I to get money? I didn't want to have to tell Luther about last night; nor is he a person to have much cash on him. I rang Dean, but he said he was broke. I was beginning to feel forlorn and abandoned. And the more I thought of the origin of the whole disaster—in a quarrel with Edward—the more forlorn did I feel.

---

[227] Porno movie house in downtown Boston.
[228] One of the then four subway lines in Boston.

But lust is a great consolation. I was so lusting for Luther that I let the morning go by thinking only about his body, and taking, as preparation for lunch, only the step of unfreezing a Cornish hen. He looked good and we were soon in bed. He sucked me like an angel, played with my asshole, and generally put me on fire. All those rough phrases we used to utter in the heat of things came back. As a sentimentalist and as a writer, I find great pleasure in recapturing an affair from the past that has flickered out. It was wonderful. Only after we had finished did I casually mention that, having no cash on hand, I was going to cook. We ate the hen, done in tarragon, and shrimp with eggs, accompanied by an Italian white wine.

Luther is thrilled that he's got a clerkship with a leading LA judge. We made plans to spend a weekend in New York on his way there. We talked much of gay issues, about which he is not so self-conscious these days.

After Luther went home, I had no dilemmas about what to do. After buying milk and orange juice for tomorrow morning, I had about 15 cents left in the house. I stayed in. Talked to Tony B on the phone but we decided to wait until tomorrow. That was my Easter Sunday.

At midnight, the doorbell rang, and it was Chris. I was weak; I said yes, and we fooled around for a while. Halfway through, he said, "Ross, what do you do when your cock starts hurting as you take a piss?" For two days he's been this way. Chris, dear Chris, might have raised the matter before we got into bed. I told him where to go at City Hospital.

March 31, 1986, Boston

I felt better about the theft after I started to get replacements for things. It's good for the soul to feel the insecurity of no money and no means of getting any for a couple of days—but a couple of days is enough!

Pleasant surprise to find $600 in my account at the Harvard Credit Union. This will help me bridge the period until Simon & Schuster, or Corgi in London, accepts my manuscript and pay me the rest of the book advance.

Well, Tony B from Barbados is hot. Despite my fatigue we had a nice time. He said he enjoyed it, too, and we're going to meet again. He's socially fairly conservative, it seems, and this suits me.

April 2, 1986, Boston

A guy comes in to measure for the closet fittings. He spots the *National Geographic* with my article on Sichuan in it and asks for a copy. As often in such a situation, I am unable to say what I wish to say—I don't give away my services any more than you do—and tamely hand over a copy. I suppose it's vanity that weakens me.

Now Cornell's phone is disconnected. Yesterday it was Will's. Sometimes my gay friends seem nomadic.

April 3, 1986, Boston

I went to Washington Street[229] and ended up spending many hours there. First in a "bookshop" with a nice TWA flight attendant who is originally from Tennessee. Later to the Pilgrim Theater, where all sorts of safe-sex things went on. One beautiful guy of about 45, a very straight and uptight type, just wanted to sit together, he stroking his dick and me mine, without us touching each other!

Near the front was a guy, virtually naked, who had covered himself with baby oil from a bag of tricks at his side, and was playing with himself to the accompaniment of loud groans of joy. The front of a large cinema is very bright (from the screen) yet also isolated (few want to sit that close). The combination was good; I sat beside this guy with my pants pulled down, and every time he said, "I want that cock-head up my ass," I all but came.

Eventually, as neither of us could stand the solo suspense any longer, he leant across the vacant seat between us and with his oily hand jerked me off magnificently. I was a mess of cum. I put my pants and shirt back on and took a cab to the St. Botolph restaurant. Sitting in a window, my clothes sticking to me with dried cum, I ate wild mushrooms grilled in garlic, chili with cornbread, and prosciutto with buffalo mozzarella, washed down with white wine. Then I fell into the shower and soon a deep sleep.

April 4, 1986, Boston

At the post office in the Financial District, I see this young half-Black guy delivering packages. Instead of going into the area for sending parcels—I had my memo on publicity to send to my London publishers—I followed this guy into the elevator and upstairs where he was to deliver a package. I got out when he got out. He didn't know where he was any more than I did. I looked at him. Quickly he got the message; one of his big, brown chunky hands went to his dick. We found ourselves in a stairwell, groped and writhed around. "Do you like to get it?" he enquired, breathing heavily, his cock out like a dark pile-driver.

I explained that I came in to post a package, and when I saw him getting into the elevator, I followed him. "Am I that attractive?" he asked with only half a smile. Unfortunately, I not only was dressed up in a jacket and tie, on my way to a Harvard seminar, but I had a squash racket, a bag of blank videos I had just bought at the Ritz Camera shop, and another large bag of stuff from Chinatown. He kept asking if I liked to "get it." We couldn't do more than a certain amount there, so I gave him my number. He is called James and lives near City Hospital.

April 5, 1986, Boston

I meet Menelik, an Ethiopian, in the Roberts Club and he comes home. He is straight and up-tight. The window in the bedroom, like much else, terrifies him, so we do it in

---

[229] The main street through the "Combat Zone," at the time, an area full of strip clubs, porno movie theaters, prostitution.

the small room. "America is too permissive," he says, his cock in my mouth. I had never had an Ethiopian and wanted to try one.

April 6, 1986, Boston

No squash today and perhaps my body needs a rest. A terrible fatigue and numbness once more. It is a gray day and I sort through Sichuan stuff, with a view to doing more articles. After a while it begins to come alive. It's as if I'm married to China; hard to cut loose, comfortable to sink back in.

At the Y, I noticed this slim, young Black guy going up and down between the general locker room and the downstairs exercise room. When he showered, I showered too. In the dry sauna, which was crowded, it was easy for me to press my leg against his. At one point, I grabbed the head of his dick—all I could reach as I leaned forward with my newspaper spread out—just to put matters beyond doubt.

Would you like to come back to my place, I asked when we were together by the lockers. He cocked his head, and after a moment said he would. Dressed in a bright red track suit, Chad has a tiny moustache and lovely smile. He is not that young, 33, and married with one kid and another on the way.

Nice to be with someone mature, who knows himself. "My wife knows I'm gay, but she doesn't know I sometimes do it with another man." He had a lover for some years before getting married three years ago. I think he wanted me to fuck him but when I started, it hurt him so I stopped. He's never done it, he said.

Late at night, he phones from work—a second job at Charlestown Navy Yard, to pay for his wife's college—to tell me he smiled all the way home from my place to his. Still obsessed by his wife, I felt like asking if she noticed the smile, and the smell of cum all over him—he didn't shower afterwards—but I held my curiosity in check. "I like older men," he said, when he asked me how old I was, I said guess, he guessed 34, then, bowled over and pleased, I cribbed a bit on the real answer I gave him.

April 8, 1986, Boston

I dined alone at Copley's and thought about the Sichuan material. I am drawn to the idea of a short book. If BL could get $40,000, I think I'd do it. $20,000, no. Perhaps something in between. The beauty of it for a publisher would be that I could deliver in December.

Reggie says, no, he doesn't carry round a photo of his girlfriend. "I see her every day, what would be the point?" We talked about Hong Kong and I remarked, when he asked if I might go and live with Henry, that I couldn't because there are no Black people in Hong Kong. "Ross, you're kidding. No Black people live in Hong Kong?"

Even Reggie the natural man feels guilt—that he cheats his girlfriend by seeing me. The world is getting nibbled to death by guilt. If we were all more candid, 90% of the guilt would be unnecessary.

April 9, 1986, Boston

Decided to get decks cleared today. Off to City Hospital for the periodic VD check-up. As always, a long wait and by the end of it I felt I might as well give the day away as far as work goes. But it's fascinating to read the faces in the waiting room. Each time, there are ravishingly good-looking people. Today, a girl who could hardly be more than 13. I try to read the story of precocious lust from an impassive school girl's face.

There were pimps and prostitutes, gays and straights, Whites and Blacks and Hispanics. One of the best-looking, whom I chatted with as his girl-friend went in, was Portuguese. Something would have come of it but for her.

I had to smile at the nurse who administered the tests to me. She pulled out a calendar of months, weeks, and days for the whole year and put it in front of me. "Can you work out when you last had sex?" I felt a bit silly in saying yesterday. "And the last time before that?" I told her the day before. She took back her calendar and closed her notebook.

On my way to Kirkland House, I ran into Y.T. Feng[230] in Harvard Square, and she was caustic about her China trip. "After democracy," she says, "the next most important values, I now see, are central air-conditioning and plumbing."

More seriously, she feels the spirit is less hopeful than when she was there two to three years ago. In particular, she points to the ambivalent, unstable attitude to the West. They double-charged her and husband Philip (chief of Boston Public Library) on the ground they were foreigners. Yet there is aping of Western things out of sheer trendiness. Whether it's ignorance, or latent resentment, either way it's awful. She says she spoke out and condemned the practice, and at the end, she was mildly encouraged when at a banquet to farewell her it was said, "Miss Feng speaks from the heart."

Tonight, Chad calls. "Can I come by?" He still amazes and delights me. This time I was very horny and he sucked me—expertly. Laying there afterwards, he said he'd love to stay all night, but he had to go home to his wife. What does he say to her when he arrives home at 1AM after having finished work at 10 PM?

April 10, 1986, Boston

An hour on the phone with Henry this morning—one step further toward bankruptcy when the phone bill comes in—and I find him worried. He's not sure I love him as I used to. In a way that is silly. We have just been together and picked up from where we had left off. In another way, he uncannily puts his finger on the heart of a problem. Somehow, he hopes my anguished talk with him may help me toward greater realism over the impossible Edward.

Henry says he just feels overwhelmingly jealous when he reads the Diary notes I send him. It would not be so bad, he says, if he'd met Edward when he was in Boston— but at that stage, last summer, Edward and I were not in touch. He feels uncertain about

---

[230] Yen-Tsai Feng (1923-2019), at the time of writing the Roy E. Larsen Librarian of Harvard College.

the future of my commitment. I explained some realities. That we are distant. That my feeling about all things Chinese is a bit different from two years ago when we met in Melbourne. That Hong Kong and the USA are different worlds. That the surface feeling of romance does change over time. I also said I still love him, and that I am not in love with Edward. I think what he really wants is for me not to drift away from him anymore.

I asked him to send me his diary; sharing his anguish and criticisms of me will help the atmosphere. If he does that, I'll send him more of mine. If he doesn't, I won't. He leaves the Aberdeen branch today and returns to the central office of the bank. He has joined a health club. I say laughingly he should have an affair with a Chinese but preferably not with a Briton.

Vinny comes in and we have a great time. Hadn't seen him since his accident. I really felt in the mood to be rimmed and that's what cuddly Vinny did, long and lovingly. I sucked him a lot and he said, "You like my dick?" I was glad to be able to say I did—especially since his eyes and his dick are the things about his body that one can most like. He saw my organizing of my new closets and was amazed at some of the clothes. "So, you're trendy!" he kept saying. I don't think he realized they are not all mine.

April 11, 1986, Boston

Got VD results this afternoon, all negative. The old body is holding up quite well through storms.

At last, I have replaced all my cards following the theft at Pilgrim Theater. The new wallet I bought has a smooth skin but the slip of paper inside it says: "This NATURAL leather is beautifully enhanced with natural scars, barbed wire scratches, wrinkles and creases that affect the animal in its natural environment."

Two long talks with Edward, and I feel better. He regrets his "overreaction" to my seeing and mentioning his life-plan document. He's working two jobs now, so he can't make it to Manhattan during my visit next week. I mention Chad, and Edward's capacity for hypocrisy soars. "That marriage won't last," he pontificates. "Playing around is playing around—even if it is with one person, and that a man."

Oh, and what about Edward and Miss M? Having fucked the ass off that married woman week after adulterous week, he is not in a good position to lecture Chad on the morality of his marriage.

Another card from Chad today, saying "It only takes a moment to start missing you." If he gets to the gym on Saturday morning, he'll come over afterwards. That would be nice—love in the morning beats love at midnight with someone like Chad.

April 12, 1986, Boston

The article on the criminal trial in China is printed out in first draft this morning. It's been fun to write. Now who will publish it?

Sorting old letters in that file labeled "CV" (Clairvoyant, a code word I years ago adopted for gay stuff) brings to mind some wonderful friends from the past. Try to contact them? Perhaps not. They will have changed, as I have changed, and the world has changed.

I find to my astonishment that, as early as 1976, I had the idea of a novel about Hong Kong's future under Communist rule. To think I've been dithering about it for ten years!

April 13, 1986, Boston

The Eastern shuttle is chaos. I arrive for the 7 PM and a roomful of angry people—the 6 PM people—have been put off their plane because of a mechanical problem. No one leaves till 8 PM and by then the 6 PM people are furious beasts. Women with shoulder bags swing them like cudgels. There's nothing like the affluent bourgeoisie to show upset human nature.

Then at the Milford Plaza, it takes 45 minutes to check in! Oh, for the Harvard Club! But this time the dress code would make it unworkable. Meanwhile, at the Milford Plaza, you get an ordinary room, not terribly clean for $95 plus tax, and you must leave a key deposit and $25 deposit to be able to use the phone!

I went to Better Days, but there was hardly anybody there, so in the street, I met an extremely attractive guy from Queens. We went to a place near the corner of 8th Avenue and 42nd Street and inside a booth he sucked me magnificently. I shot in his mouth. "A lot," he said as he spat it out. "Gee, you're hot." Why is there such an embarrassment of riches around these days? Has AIDS scared many of the middle-class away that the few who continue can take their pick of the bi working-class guys?

April 14, 1986, New York

I retreated to the Harvard Club in the morning, had a long, leisurely breakfast, and then worked on my Sichuan travel article in the library.

Afternoon tea with Michael Mao, who smokes furiously and tells me AIDS patients in New York go to traditional Chinese doctors. "The Chinese think this disease has been around for thousands of years, and that herbs can build up the immune system." He lives in a tiny studio apartment, virtually without furniture. It gives me a shiver of gratitude down the spine for Boston.

In the late afternoon, I was in a "bookstore" when I saw Yves. The moment I saw him, I lost interest in all else except getting into bed with him. He is tall, big-boned, taciturn. At first, I thought he might be a Haitian. He has the cheek-bones, the elegant gestures, and the cock of a Haitian.

Yves works for a post office in Brooklyn, delivering letters in a Jewish neighborhood, and does hustling on the side. I said this was fine with me when he suggested $15. We went back to the Milford Plaza. As soon as we were in the room, he began to peel off his clothes.

It was one of the loveliest bouts for a long time. Straight as he says he is, he did not hesitate to suck, and he was willing for me to fuck him, but it hurt so I came between his gorgeous legs. We showered together and then I rushed off to dine with Mike Bessie at the Harvard Club.

Mike is older and slower but otherwise the same effervescent, eclectic publisher of *Mao* and *The China Difference*. A note of pessimism has entered his overall view of the world. He thinks it quite likely that something scientific will go wrong, with genes or bombs or both.

April 15, 1986, New York

Again, breakfast at the Harvard Club. Somehow, I need respectability in the morning to steady me. In the dining room, I meet Friedel Ungeheuer, the journalist who wrote the profile of me in *Time* 15 years ago! He's still with *Time*. As he pointed out, his hair has gone gray, but mine has not.

A visit with BL, who tells me the bad news that Esther Shapiro has not renewed her option to film *White-Boned Demon*. Very sad. That virtually eliminates the possibility that she will do it. Someone else? BL is vague. She feels we can't do anything about a Sichuan book possibility until Simon & Schuster react more fully to the draft of *The Australians*. "Get on with the novel," she cries, but I can't in an atmosphere of such uncertainty. She doesn't bite much on *China on My Mind* but then she isn't the biting type—perhaps agents shouldn't be.

Just back to the Milford Plaza in time for a return date with the fantastic Yves. He comes in with his mail bag and dressed in his post office uniform, which soon however is off. Beneath the windows, the sounds of a demonstration against US bombing of Libya rise up, faint, irrelevant to the business at hand.

Even better than yesterday, and it went on and on. Happily, I had just found out that Yvonne's dinner party was changed from 7 PM to 8 PM; all the newly available time was spent with this hot hunky stud. This time I sucked him too, though I found that when I had his dick in my mouth his concentration on sucking me sagged, so it was better to do it *ad seriatim*. He wants to go to Washington next weekend with friends, so instead of $15 I happily gave him $25.

Yvonne's dinner party was as expected. Elegant, exquisitely polite, gastronomically superb. But socially pompous and intellectually trivial. Too many Council on Foreign Relations types for comfort. Libya was the only topic of conversation.

After I got home from the dinner party, I should have read and gone to sleep. But I felt restless. The wonderful time with Yves before dinner had somehow triggered me; the more you get the more you want. And the essential dullness of the dinner party required an antidote.

I dropped into the nearby Spanish bar for a glass of wine. It was now very late and some of the cinemas on 8th Ave were closed. I went into one on 42nd Street. The balcony was a nice scene. A scattering of guys, some straight, some less so. I was sitting there with my dick out eyeing a couple of good prospects when a very attractive guy walked in, hesitated, then sat down quite near me, just to the rear.

I got even harder, and this new guy was unable to take his eyes off it. In a moment, after smiling, I got up, half did up my pants, walked over to his seat and asked if I could sit beside him. Sure. He had a huge and extremely hot dick. It was almost impossible to get it out of his pants, since it reached in its massive stiffness up beyond his stomach, so

I suggested that Dave, as he was called, just take off his pants as I had done. I said he was big, and he said, "You looked big too; that's why I was staring." Dave works out in a far suburb, and tonight is a rare foray for him. He just felt he had to get into the city.

We were writhing around, but Dave felt there wasn't enough privacy. We went back to the Milford Plaza, and the bastards there said no visitors could enter the rooms after 2 AM. The "bookshops" were also not so good at this hour, so we went back to the same cinema and jerked each other off there. You never can tell with orgasms. Despite the magic of Yves, earlier the same evening, I felt unsurpassable pleasure in Dave's hands in a grimy movie house when we couldn't even be naked.

April 17, 1986, Boston

The New England China seminar at Harvard yesterday jogs my thinking back onto the China path, but I learn little new.

Today Mac calls from *National Geographic*; they are commissioning the piece on Australian aboriginals. Very good; now I can plan my summer. They will pay $10,000 for the article. and it is to be "not one word longer than 6000 words" and delivered on August 15.

BL is thrilled. "They're a classy operation," she says when she calls me. Perhaps she forgets that *National Geographic* came to me; at that stage Barbara had never dealt with them. Perhaps they thought I was a classy operation. BL now feels we could approach Simon & Schuster with the Sichuan book outline if I wish to.

I will spend another week carving out articles from the Sichuan notebooks. Then I will tackle the revisions to the Australia book. In June, I go to Australia for the *National Geographic* piece, and do checking and updating for the book, too. Money-wise I think I am out of the crisis. The *National Geographic* cash in August. And the clear signal now from both New York and London that the Australia draft is going to be acceptable means the second half of the money should hit me during the summer.

April 18, 1986, Boston

I phone Chad, and his wife answers. "Oh, Chad told me all about you." We talk for twenty minutes. In the evening, the man himself reaches me just before I go to sleep. I said, "I spoke to a lovely girl on the phone today." The two photos of myself that I gave him are prominent in the living room, he says.

May 1, 1986, Boston

I celebrate May Day in the arms of a white guy, Rick. Well, not quite in his arms. "Just safe sex," he says. "You see I work in a hospital, and it makes you stick with safe sex." Very attractive and I have not enjoyed mutual jerking off as much for ages. He was brought up in Roxbury—the white part—and he does not do it with Blacks. "I've got nothing against them," he says in a tone of voice that makes it clear that he doesn't like them.

May 2, 1986

At 1 AM last night, the doorbell rings and the voice says, "Reggie." This was the moment I had been somewhat fearing for many weeks. Apart from "my" Reggie, whom I adore, there's another Reggie, friend of a friend, who has taken to ringing my doorbell. He is dirty and arrogant. The catch is, on the intercom his voice sounds just like my Reggie's. Normally the real Reggie phones first, on the 661 number, which the other guy does not have, and so until tonight there was no confusion.

"What do you want?" I said a bit coldly after the caller announced himself. I thought the answer would tell me who it was. In fact, it took several more sentences before I knew who it was—and poor Reggie (whom I have never once, as far as I can recall, been unable to see when he asked to see me) was staggered at my attitude. He looked like a sad spaniel when he came in. "I failed the real estate exam," he said as he sat on the side of my bed.

Anyway, we had a wonderful time. "I've been fucking so much, and tonight I want to get fucked," he cried. He has his Beck's beer as usual. We went up to watch movies, and he could not wait to come downstairs, or even for the end of the movie. So we unfolded the sofa-bed and began operations. God, he wanted it. This time we got the right position and it didn't hurt him. Far from hurting him, it drove him into the Seventh Paradise. "More grease, Ross," he said at intervals. He has decided now that it's better for me not to come inside him, which I agree with; I had to keep coming out to avoid coming, and he would then turn back to the movie, get worked up, and scream for me to start fucking him again.

You have to wait on Reggie hand and foot. I understand why his girlfriend, her mother, and especially the mother's brother, find him a demanding person in the house. The childlikeness of it appeals to me though.

This afternoon I made a curious visit to someone I had never met. Two days ago, the phone rang, and this guy said I did not know him, but he was calling because he had found my wallet on his deck—would I like to come and pick it up. "By the way," he said, "about that Club Baths card inside the wallet—it's no good anymore because that baths burned down."

He is quite a pleasant man who lives with many dogs in a mansion of a place just up Mass Ave. His back deck abuts a side street. After pouring me a glass of rosé wine, and trying to keep three or four of his dogs from raping me, he hands me the wallet. I hardly glance at it and put it in my pocket.

As he tells me about his chocolate importing business, and I tell him about Australia, which interests him, he chips in to ask when I lost the wallet. Thinking back to that crazy night in the Combat Zone, I said about three weeks ago. As he went on about Swiss chocolate, my mind's eye went back to the wallet I had put in my hip pocket: this was not the wallet stolen that night! This battered old crocodile skin was the one pickpocketed on the Dudley bus much earlier, by the guy who pretended to collapse in front of me as we were both getting off at Huntington Ave.

"I gave you the wrong answer when you asked how long ago I lost the wallet," I said. When I explained that there have been two recent losses, he laughed, asked how long

I've been living in the USA and said I should be more careful. "Never carry money in your wallet—and never carry much money."

May 3, 1986

At last today, I really got into the revisions on *The Australians*. The book came alive again, and I began to see some of what Fred Hills means in his memo of suggestions. The break away from it has been good for my perspective. And I think getting back to it clears away an anxiety that has been building up in me—the anxiety of leaving a task half-finished.

At night, I went to the Pilgrim in the Combat Zone for an hour and then to Haymarket (totally devoid of interest). In the Pilgrim some great fun, all safe sex, with a Latino type and a Black guy who jerked my cock off as well as anything I remember for months. Two incidents cooled my ardor. While the Latino was jerking me off and sucking my tits, another guy touched me from behind. Seeing this, the Latino said to this guy: "You take your hands off him or I'll stab you!" Later, I sat down quite near a handsome guy, also Latino, who already had his dick out as his eyes stayed glued to the screen. I began looking at him as my own cock soared. There was a clink, and I saw that he had pulled out a knife to "deter" me.

May 4, 1986

A strange, desiccated day. Work on *The Australians*, but also a terrible headache—I suppose a result of last night, the mental aspects perhaps of last night. Chad is going to come and then he says he cannot—his son is sick. I go off to Somerville to see the art exhibition that Ann Swift is part of, and buy her painting called "Faces." Later, I learn that minutes after I left, DH comes by, hot as hell, and that Chad calls to change his mind again and say he's coming round on the way to work.

In the evening, Tyrone comes in and we make fantastic love. I felt guilty about Chad—in the sense that he is on my emotions—but after a while, I just enjoy Tyrone's passion. "You're teasing me!" "Ooh give me that white Australian cock!" I went over to Betty's and when I came back, I sprang into the shower. The phone rang and it was Chad—contrite, charming. Leaving the shower on, I talked to him for nearly an hour. Later there's a knock on the door: Eileen from downstairs says water has been coming through their ceiling ...

I am still haunted by the TV movie *An Early Frost*.[231] Overdrawn and yet powerful. Such movies must have an enormous impact on the vast majority of viewers who know little about gay life. One thing in American dialogue which drives me up the wall. "I'm sorry, OK?" Jesus, if you apologize, you wait at last five seconds before demanding that the other person let you off the hook! Yet this is common. It's almost a case of turning aggressive at the moment of apology. Is it then an apology?

---

[231] A made-for-TV movie by John Erman. Starring Aidan Quinn as a young lawyer stricken with AIDS, it was, according to IMBD, "many people's first look at an AIDS victim as a human being instead of a statistic."

May 6, 1986

A long day's work on *The Australians*, and perhaps I am at last making progress.

Menelik calls and waits to come again. It reminds me of the bank waiting ten days for a check to clear; Menelik, the prudent, middle-class Ethiopian businessman, waits ten days to see if he gets VD from me and when he doesn't, he roars back for more sex. What class!

I watched this young Black guy as he walked across the open area on the second floor of Boston Public Library, but it seemed he wasn't interested in me. He had on a baseball cap, gray pants, and a blue jacket, and his body was first-rate. He looked about 19. He sat at a corner table, a sort of booth, with a book and I went over to the shelves nearby. By now, I realized that I was fiercely attracted to him. I felt myself and through the shelves he looked. I went further—and soon I sat down at the table beside him. His smile was great and when I experienced it, I pulled my dick clean out of my pants. He leant over and started jerking me off.

I grabbed him and he soon pulled his dick out of his gray jeans. I suggested we go to my place, and soon we were on the 39 bus. "I'll meet you out on the street," he had said. He is called Kip, from South Carolina.

For three hours and 15 minutes we made love, and it was the best, at least since the second last time with Edward—which is a little time ago. It ranks high. I would have to compare it with that first night at Luther's place, with Hank in Detroit, and with Edward, not at the start, but when I started fucking him. Kip is built but he is not that beautiful. I am not that beautiful. But somehow the sensual chemistry just did it. We could not get enough of each other.

He is slim, a bit hairier than my taste, with a cut cock that has a splendid head but is not overall large. The kissing knocked me out. That gooey Southern kiss, tongues sucking, fucking tongues. Each time we got into it, he stopped, laughed, and said he was going to come but didn't want to yet. In the end, I shot meters past his shoulder into the brick wall. "Do all Australian men make love like you?" he asked.

"Take one in front of the flower," he said as we fooled around with the camera afterwards. (The "flower" is my huge tree.)

May 10, 1986

Menelik comes to work on his résumé. He really is charming. He is also inquisitive. Each time I was keying a passage in at some length, he was looking round the study. One minute he came up with some sex magazines. The next with pics of the criminal trial in Sichuan. Then with an issue of *BW*. He wanted to have sex, but I had decided against it; with so much available, I do not need one who, attractive as he is, is elitist and not sufficiently reciprocating.

"Just kiss him," he begged pulling out his handsome dick. "Look, I bought new underpants specially to come and see you." But I didn't. "Now I'm aroused, I'll have to masturbate—can I go into the bathroom?" I said I had to get ready to go out to dinner. "Just turn your thoughts to your résumé," I urged, "and to the brilliant career ahead of you."

John Roderick[232] took me to dinner at Club Café. He is vigorous and charming as ever. Still has that slightly sinister way of the man from Maine—as if somehow in secret Maine people commune with rocks or fuck pigs and feel uneasy that the world may guess. On this occasion, an excellent meal, chicken for him and prime rib for me—with an appetizer of beef in herbs and cheese. He liked my *National Geographic* piece very much. Talks always of sex; perhaps the older you get the more that happens. Is writing his memoirs but has left the personal stuff out. "You see my generation just can't get over its reticence on such matters." Tomorrow he's off to Madeira where he gets boys of 17 to fuck him or ram their dicks (70% cut he says) down his loquacious throat.

His long-time Japanese companion has now married. I told him briefly about Edward. "With a bisexual person," he said, based on his Japanese experience, "the friendship is more likely, than with a gay person, to last in some form or other for a lifetime."

May 11, 1986

Kip comes in and after a while I am not sorry that I got diverted from going to the Signet Society's Strawberry Night. He loves the pics, so I give them to him. He is hard from the moment he comes in the door and we are soon in bed. We didn't have that much time, but allowing for that, the sex was just about as good as the fantastic first time.

It was a bit embarrassing when Kip arrived. He hadn't called during the afternoon as he was going to. Around six, Robert called and wanted to drop by. I said OK, and ten minutes later Kip called to say he was on his way. When Robert arrived, I went downstairs and lied that people connected with a dinner I was going to later had already arrived to pick me up. While the two of us were in the lobby Kip rolls up! I introduce them, walk Robert out into the street, come back and take Kip upstairs.

May 13, 1986

Took a Mogadon[233] last night and slept without interruption for the first time in a long while. Despite too much sex, I feel better today.

The article on the criminal trial goes off to Andé Zellman at *The Boston Globe*. I improved it by adding local color on the village where the crimes were committed and the city where I attended the trial.

The editor of *Signature* magazine phones from New York to chat about the possible tourism article on Sichuan. He sounds OK, but it is a bit of a long shot when I haven't seen the magazine and he knows little of me. Still if BL can get a fee of $2000, plus a kill fee of at least 25% of that, I think I will go ahead and give *Signature*'s readers an armchair trip through my dear old Sichuan.

In the evening, Robert came, and it was nice to spend time with him, chatting and watching TV. As always, he was horny as hell, but I didn't go crazy about the sex with

---

[232] John Roderick (1914-2008), American journalist and correspondent, considered a major "China watcher."

[233] Brand name of Nitrazepam, used for short-term relief from insomnia.

him. He's not masculine and enthusiastic enough for me. In the middle of it, Chad called and how I wished I was free!

So my friend Shengde wants to leave China! I vowed not to help anyone again after the case of Mark Sun, but Shengde is so vulnerable. I think I will write to the US Consulate on his behalf, even though I don't hold out much hope of him getting a visa. As it happens, Maynard Chen is going to Shanghai soon, so I can introduce him to Shengde and also have Maynard explain a few things.

May 16, 1986

Luther came in at 11 AM on his way to New York. He looked great and we sort of fell on each other. That long Louisiana dick became longer; my fantasy about his father whom I've never met become more intense. "There's no time," he gasped when I proposed moving from the lobby into bed. But soon we were on the bedroom floor—a good substitute for the bed as it turned out.

Teddy White is dead. His was a great career, and it will not be matched in kind again—his time was special, and his blend of the scholarship boy rising from disadvantage into a stream of opportunity is less likely to be found at the end of the 20th century than it was in mid-century.

I remember him taking me to lunch in an Irish pub not far from his house on New York's East Side. I remember the TV program we did organized by the Asia Society, when he arrived in a temper and by the end of the program was at his most charming. He said a pretty nice thing about my *Mao* (not on the jacket—he did not believe in that—for in ads and the release): "A Major and enduring contribution to the classic literature on the Chinese Revolution."

May 17, 1986

Brian didn't call, so I put on a pair of shorts and went for a walk. At Northampton station, a guy turned me on. At first when I looked at him, he gave me that "mind your own business" look. But then I felt my dick and in a minute he did too.

Unfortunately, even when we moved down the platform, we were still visible, thanks to the elevated nature of Northampton station, to pedestrians on both Mass Ave and the cross street. We just flirted like that until his train came—going in the opposite direction to mine. I continued on to Essex station and was not disappointed by the Combat Zone.

May 19, 1986

The patient approach with Menelik worked. Twice he has come in to use the computer. Today he was extremely hot. After finishing the work, it was all kisses and hugs. He was hardly recognizable as the guy of several weeks ago who hardly deigned to even touch a man's dick. He told me that he "started with boys" when he studying in Italy. "The young men of Venice and Rome are almost without comparison," he says.

Once we were interrupted by *The New Republic* calling to say they wanted my piece on "Politics and Economics in China." Then I was hardly back in bed—the small room, as he hates the window in my own bedroom—when *The New York Times* rang about me doing a couple of travel pieces on Sichuan. Back to bed where Menelik tried very hard to persuade me to let him fuck me. Judging by today's progress, I may well be fucking him this time next week.

May 25, 1986

I bought the Sunday *Globe* and came home. The Focus section has my article about going to the dance with Henry in Chongqing. Next week's *New Republic* will have another piece on the Chinese economic reforms. The *Chicago Tribune* published my two shorter pieces last week, on birth control and student protests. It's kind of fun, if much work, to be doing magazine pieces again. The money is not as good as the boost to the ego. There's something much more immediate about the whole process than the long haul of a book.

Before going to Australia, I have two pieces to do for *The New York Times*: one on the ancient wonders of Leshan, and one on the Yi people in the southwest of Sichuan. Also, a long piece for *Signature*, the magazine of the Diner's Club, for which dear BL has secured a contract for $2000, or $500 if they don't use what I write.

May 25, 1986

Today is Luther's graduation from law school. Once again, as last Sunday, I put on a suit and tie. It's quite a nice occasion, in the open air on the beautiful campus. I meet Luther's mother, sister, and grandfather. The mother seems so young! Both she and her father ask me how long Luther and I have known each other. The old guy turns out to be a Jehovah's Witness preacher (and part-time insurance worker). He bashes my ear on how he transferred from Baptist to Jehovah's Witnesses, and how the latter is genuine "because based on the Bible" and the former is "just opinions."

Later we say goodbye. The orgasm is the clearest, the most honest farewell. I wonder how much of him I will see in the future?

The Orange Line is really a boon. On it tonight, I meet Bernard, a very nice guy from St. Kitts. He is handsome, on the short side, with a chucky, gymnasts-type body, and a very sensual voice. He does not suck that well, but to my great delight he wanted me to fuck him. This I did very slowly and with enormous pleasure.

May 26, 1986

Today in the morning, Bernard phones and we arrange to meet tonight. It is a day of calm and brightness, with that feeling of irresponsibility that Memorial Day brings. I work on my "In Search of Frontiers" chapter, which I think I will break up into segments on the North, the West, and the Center.

I print out the chapter, feeling very good, and Bernard comes in. He drinks a few Foster's and looks around the horizon through the binoculars, while I watch the video

Black Taboo. He gets interested, quickly becomes hot, and we go downstairs. It was similar to last night, except a bit briefer. We showered, then I went out to eat at Soom Thai while he went back to his girlfriend's

Now Bernard gets interested in the girls downstairs. Bernard wants to fuck them, and I want to kill them.

May 31, 1986

Quite a good trip to Washington and New York ending with a happy rendezvous with Edward. *The National Geographic* performed their ritual blessing of my aboriginals project. Garrett[234] said he'd never seen a better outline. Mac just said to do for the aboriginals what I did for Sichuan and all will be fine.

In New York, I did a Radio Free Europe interview. A waste of time in a business sense (I did it at the urging of BL who has a friend there), but it turned out to be interesting—a table-full of people firing questions of some subtlety at me.

A wonderful night on 8th Ave., which perhaps didn't make much sense in light of the fact that I was going to Yonkers to be with Edward the next day. Again, the straight movie houses seemed the most exciting. On the way home, a young guy who needed five bucks to get back to Brooklyn offered to suck me off in a parking lot. He was so lovely and so good I gave him ten. The first place we chose did not work. It was in an alley just near Sardi's restaurant. As he sucked my willing cock, a pile of timber leaning more or less horizontally in a corner started to come down upon us. We moved to another lane. I kept trying to take my shorts off completely, fired by the risk and excitement of the situation. He kept saying, "Leave them on!" and looking up to see if anyone was coming down the alley.

In Yonkers and White Plains, Edward was in wonderful form. We went shopping, and then back to La Reserve in White Plains where I had reserved a room. I love driving around with Edward and seeing him in a buoyant mood. We had a rather luxurious dinner in this rather luxurious hotel and then went to bed.

I can't deny that these six months have been difficult for me—as it has been for Edward—but I just feel I want to stick with him despite all the limitations. We must find more and more ways of sharing things that both of us want to share. That's what living's all about.

June 5, 1986

Ken Galbraith's garden party has to go indoors this year and we stifle in the humid rooms. But as always, everyone is there. These days, it is the only event on Harvard's Commencement Day that I bother going to, and the academic types whom I talk to seem like people from a previous incarnation. Martin Peretz[235] comes by and says, "Very good piece" (referring to my recent *New Republic* article, which broke a very long period

---

[234] Wilbur Eugene Garrett (1930-2016), editor of *National Geographic* during the 1980s.
[235] Martin Peretz (1938 -), a former assistant professor at Harvard, he was, at the time, owner and editor of *The New Republic.*

of non-contact between me and that persistent magazine). As I leave, I ask Galbraith about the comment on Robert Menzies he is supposed to have made—"like someone imitating King Edward VII"—and he says it is indeed his.

David stayed with me all night, and the latter part of it, he spent upstairs in his usual insomniac way. Apparently, he browsed very carefully in the foreign editions of my books. "You're a year older than my mother," he declares at breakfast. "I didn't know you were that old."

An interesting reflection on sex and the ego in a *New York Times* review. Why do eyes matter so much (and other parts of the face) in sexual attraction? Because in the face you read the interest in you. When those eyes express interest, the person looked at is transported by a feeling that he is wanted, that he's of much worth. When there is reciprocated feeling, the pair are wrenched from their actual surrounding into an intense universe of their own.

June 8, 1986

I begin to think that Edward is not below what I think he is, but above. I miscalculate him only because he and I are so different—in age, race, culture, experience.

June 10, 1986

Mike Leahy from *The New York Times* travel section phones to say my article on Leshan is "lovely." They will publish it July 20.[236] The second one on the Yi people I will do on my return from Australia.

A long talk with Judy Rascoe,[237] screen writer for Ray Stark productions in Hollywood. They want to do a love story set in China and wonder if I could be a consultant. Well, I have been through this before. The amazing thing is how intelligence can be wedded to such total vagueness as they approach a new (to them) topic.

One gets anxious about something, it passes, and all one is left with is a couple of years off one's life because of the strain. It isn't worth it. Sometimes I think that nothing matters enough to let it worry you. Perhaps Helen Rees was right when she told me you just have to enjoy the process of things—that's all there is.

June 14, 1986

Another marathon talk with Judith Rascoe. She's bright; she's tenacious; but I wonder if I'm being led up the garden path?

June 17, 1986

I was at the gym just going upstairs to play squash when I saw this attractive pale-Black guy in the foyer. He was looking for a safe-box. I said I would loan him a padlock and

---

[236] "New Slogans, Old Shrines in Sichuan" by Ross Terrill was published on September 14, 1986.
[237] Judith Rascoe (1941 -), American screenwriter.

he accepted. He has big lips, a sensual face, and a chunky body. From Mattapan, he is in the military and going to a college in Arkansas under military aegis. I gave him the padlock with the numbers in Chinese on the back. All through the game with Ron—which I lost—I thought of Paul exercising and swimming downstairs. Sure enough, he was in the locker room at the time I said I'd be there. I said he could keep the lock. Then he said he needed a towel to wrap his swimming trunks in. I couldn't sneak one from the Roberts Club at that moment, so I suggested we get one at my place on his way home. He agreed and by this time I think the die was cast.

As I turned the key in the lock, I heard voices. Bob Lee[238] was there with his project manager and a designer! That did not stop us. Thank God for a large apartment. Although he kept saying he hadn't done this before and hadn't done that before, he was an excellent lover. He sucked beautifully. He loved getting his asshole tickled and the next time I'll probably fuck him—but alas, that will be quite a while away as the deserts of Australia beckon.

Paul's lovely visit put me behind schedule for the day's work, and I was just getting going again on the manuscript when the doorbell rang and it was Jerry, the guy I'd met earlier today. At that time, I was on my way to play squash with Ron, and he said he couldn't meet later. Anyway, we exchanged addresses and tonight he just came in. Like one or two others of my friends, he works at a bank. Is it the security-minded types who now and then like a bit of excitement?

June 18, 1986

I sent off the revised manuscript to London, New York, and to BL. I really think it is a good book. But then, each time I hone a book, I think it's very good, and that is no guarantee of its success.

There is a nice symbolism in going off tomorrow to talk with Ray Stark at Universal Studios having finished a big nonfiction book, I turn my mind to my "Hong Kong novel," and at the same time go to see a movie man and his script writer.

June 19, 1986

At the last minute, I manage to get off two articles to Nick King at the Focus section of *The Boston Globe*. One is on the religious revival in Sichuan, and the other is the story of how the West China Coffee-house came into being. Hope he likes them.

June 25, 1986, Sydney

I went nowhere at night, but one lovely thing happened. A slim, young concierge called Greg—looking not unlike my nephew Greg—smiled at me a couple of times in the Regent's lobby. This morning I asked him if he would like to come up to my room. When he came in, he asked what job I had for him to do. This threw me momentarily. No job, I said, but I thought he might like a little break. I took his hand. But he said, "Auh, nooo." He sat on the couch and mentioned his ex-girl friend. When he asked

---

[238] Contractor for the condo renovation.

again if there was anything he could do, I said I found him attractive and would like to suck his cock.

"Oh, I haven't done that," he said as insouciantly as saying he was unfamiliar with a new variety of ice cream. He said his ex-girlfriend "sucked only for the sake of it" and wasn't that good. I pointed out a man sucks better because he knows how it feels. Greg said that was interesting.

"I'm too thin," he observed. I said I didn't think so, and I went to the couch and sat down beside him. Moving my hand up and down his leg, I said he wasn't too thin at all. His cock was big and quickly-stiffening. In bed, he loved everything, including getting his asshole tickled. Soon he gasped, "I'm gunna blow." As he got dressed, he kept saying, "What an experience!"

Can we do it again when I get back to Sydney? "Yeah, yeah."

June 26, 1986, Sydney

I phone Gary Foley, head of the Aboriginal Arts Board at the Community Council, and told him of my project. "No way, it would be a waste of my breath after all the shit *National Geographic* published about the Black people." He's a Black Panther type from the 1960s. "All over Australia the Black people wouldn't want to have anything to do with anyone from *National Geographic*." Well, we'll see.

In Sydney, the Aboriginal Development Corporation sponsors the Aboriginal artists gallery at which there are bark paintings—not so much the sand paintings. You see the expression of a cosmology in which mythical beings created the environment. The prices are steep. A Greek-born lady runs the shop. The government wants them to be self-sufficient, but the rent is high and Aboriginals insisted on a fancy location. "We could break even if we had a smaller, simpler shop—but the Aboriginal people say why can't we have a fancy shop like the whites."

June 28, 1986, Canberra

In Canberra, it's cold and all three of the Federal ministers I contact are off in Cairns. None of the secretaries are able to tell me what meeting is going on up there. "It's so cold in Canberra, wouldn't you want to be going to Cairns?"

July 5, 1986, Melbourne

Nice to do it again with Steven, though it lowers the standards a bit as he's overweight these days. Recently he went to a party in Toorak of some Australians who are into Asians. A guy cruised him all evening and he ended up going home with him—it was Don Dunstan. He said he fucked DD for such a long time that the ex-premier of South Australia had to take a rest between bursts.

"Your cock's gotten bigger," Steven said as we undressed at the Regent; I just smiled, mystified. "You love fucking, don't you?" I just nodded and looked into those deep, passionate eyes. He insists on a condom and I preferred not. He'd brought a tube of KY as well as a box of condoms.

He's thinking of immigrating to Australia and has contacted a gay group that specializes in getting permission for this based on gay ties.

After two weeks, I miss writing, music, squash, and Black flesh. But the trip is going well. Quite a bit done on the book: checking facts, seeing Transamerica, the Bruthen visit, getting Grant, McGregor, Wombwell and others to read bits.

July 7, 1986, Melbourne to Bairnsdale

As you move from Dandenong toward Warrigal, green hills and gum trees, and a tea tree-like scrubby tree. Cattle grazing. More suburban-type residential housing on the outskirts of places like Bunyip, some with white-painted railing fences, well kept up. This is called a "country train." The huge fat belching chimneys of Yallourn. A pipeline, no doubt bringing gas back to Melbourne.

On this July morning, the train is some 60% full for the four-hour trip. It's now called "Intercity Train to Bairnsdale" (not "Gippsland Train," as it used to be). At Morwell, the one town with much new development, drive-in bottleshop [liquor store]; 24-hour hotspot (snacks, etc.) This valley is a sad reminder of how Australia has put itself into the hands of energy and resources at a bad time—I mean when the prices for these things have slumped.

A bank of steely, battleship gray clouds, and then below and above a silver-aluminum-colored bank, with an on-line decoration of ice-cream type twists. Chinese restaurants, caravan parks, everywhere the supermarket, the Japanese car, internationalized youth culture. The familiar red and yellow arches of McDonald's. Houses set absolutely flat on the ground.

Toward Sale, sheep, and tree trunks in grotesque shapes without leaves or small branches, some at amazing angles. Dairy cattle drinking at water holes. Mountains to the left, a brilliant mid-blue despite the wintry weather. Greeny-beige grass, barbed wire fences along the railway, broad spreading gums with broken dry branches underneath them, dams here and there, and the red gravel of the siding.

To one side of the Princes Highway, the side roads in orange gravel lined with trees in that Gippsland way—like the French countryside except that they are gums not poplars. Under the trees, bracken fern, though the leaves are not soft like ordinary ferns—they get very dry and become a menace to farmers as they feed off the soil. Can be burnt off. Bottlebrush trees, and twisted branches that in the winter light look like so many animals frozen in angular postures.

Galvanized iron tanks by the houses, at the railway stations the tiny wooden dunnies [239] with a metal entrance-way, most painted in railway orange. Stumps everywhere, stumps on which we used to sit, or at a picnic rest a cup, or put out the ingredients for a barbecue, or use as a table. An occasional huge cypress in whose multitude of boughs a kookaburra sits.

On the outskirts of Bairnsdale, a timber yard. As the town comes into view, each house has a rotary clothes line and paling back and side fence just as in Melbourne.

---

[239] Toilets.

Here in the Lake Tyers cooperative room, a picture of a gumleaf band, and of a dog, the three colors of the Aboriginal flag, a stove in the middle of the room, three typewriters deployed, a photo of Charlie Carter with the Victoria Governor taken around 1970. Dennis was taught by my father in Bruthen and stayed in the Church of England hostel. Alan says the sleeper cutting is now often done by machine, and not in Bruthen.

The guy (Ron Edwards) who kicked 43 goals in one match confirms that he kicked one while standing on his head. "I just put it through, that's all. Anyone could do it— if he's good enough. You've got to be fit for these things, then you do anything. In those days, I didn't drink, just a few beers after game and that was all."

"White and Black get on well when its people you know," Edwards remarks. "This land, what are the Blacks gunna do with it. I mean, we're all Australians, Black, white or anything—we gotta share this land."

July 12, 1986, Adelaide

The three-week mark. With this schedule, it's necessary to turn off at the weekend, and I'm not good at that. Going to the gallery and the library and walking around helped ease the strains of the week in Melbourne and here.

Talked with both Edward and Henry, who seems to think I've let him down. But I feel just as frustrated as he that I probably can't come to Hong Kong. I am constrained by many forces, including finances, and would prefer not to be.

The Pulteney Sauna wasn't exciting, but that's because I don't like such places much anymore. Actually, it was big and crowded, and quite good as such places go. I should have been strong, and when nothing appealed to me there, come home and read a book. But I jerked off, and did so again this morning—weak behavior.

July 17, 1986, Alice Springs

At the Sheraton, "Barbecued Kangaroo Meat with Witchetty Grub Sauce" is on the menu; also a clear kangaroo soup with rabbit dumplings. Is the barramundi fresh, I ask the maitre d'. "No Sir, we are in the middle of the desert," replies the brusque German.

July 16, 1986

In Papunya,[240] houses with curved galvanized iron roofs, iron verandah posts, brick walls. Houses started—large brown bricks—but thick tufts of coarse grass grow up beside the pillars of unfinished walls. Some finished homes unoccupied, and some people live in tiny lean-tos beside a finished house. Streets but no street names, houses but no gardens.

I see no shops. I tread on some glass and the label on the flagon says Orlando Moselle. Peter Garrett alleviates the dry problem by smoking grass. After our fire is lit, Aboriginal kids join us, dripping noses, the stuff dripping into their mouths. Two girls

---

[240] Location of an Indigenous people's art cooperative.

of 13, asked about what they will do on leaving school: a holiday; then go to college in Alice Springs.

A Northern Territories cop, one of several in Papunya, is tomorrow moving elsewhere and is relieved. Says there's no way of stopping the import of drink because there's 20 roads into here. Used to have a brickmaking outfit but it got wrecked—kids with nothing to do wrecked it. Authority of the cops here same as everywhere in Australia. Petrol sniffing is not against the law; it goes on, but it's not matter for the cops. Courthouse is held here—bush court. Cooperation with Community Council is very good.

Midnight Oil[241] thump and dance away, the glitter of their drums and mikes and console under a spotlight. Immediately in front of them, a row of tiny kids who spring to life as each song starts and jive and rock. Then a large empty space and under gum trees a row of spectators, some on bonnets [car hoods], in back of trucks, or leaning against cars. Album and song titles: *Big Name, No Blankets*, "Out Of Jail Back To Wurumpi," "Why Don't You Give Up Drinking," "Bread Line."

At the end, a tired-looking Peter Garrett announces: "We've got some Black fella/white fella shirts over there, so if you've got some money why don't you buy one?"

Wurumpi[242] very good—essentially because they're deep. I have different criteria for rating bands from most people, but by all my criteria, Wurumpi is good. They've got a great rhythm section and the guts of any rock-and-roll band is the rhythm section. And their drummer is one of the great drummers. The blending, the voice, the language—all tremendous. Fairly good song-writers, certainly not bad song-writers. A bloody good band; we're encouraging them to keep at it, with all their internal difficulties—you know whites and Blacks together. Easier for us as we all come from similar background. And they come under much more peer and family pressure than we ever do.

Get up on beautiful morning with the crows singing, go to look at Dinny's painting done in waterproof acrylic. At 9:30 AM, no activity in the town; and no farming around this area. Some 70 earn a living in the Papunya area from sand-painting (not the other kind). Colors are subdued, like the environment here. Most artists are old. As Dinny says, it's because the youth don't know the stories.

Everywhere in Papunya dogs, almost like wild ones, you never know to whom they belong. Seized cars lie everywhere; they're sold at government auction if liquor has been found in them. Papunya has the image of being a bit conservative. Clinic is under-utilized but the most elaborate building in the township. At a playground most equipment is not functioning. No activity in mid-morning at the workshop. Outside the clinic, mothers, kids, and dogs sit on the dirt. Brightly-colored clothes. As we make noodles for dinner, Aboriginal kids gather round. Wendy, who is visiting from another township, says the kids laughter is at the noodles, which they think look like snakes.

---

[241] An Australian rock band.
[242] Wurumpi was a country and Indigenous Australian rock group.

Geoff Barden, who was in adult education, introduced idea of canvas painting. Out in the bush, they paint on bodies, but viewing of them has to be sexually segregated. Midnight Oil was shown artifacts in segregated fashion this morning.

After visiting Papunya, one must say it is not working; yet that it's probably better that the government did what it did, than that it failed to try this. Not one Aboriginal flag do I see at Papunya or Hermannsburg.

July 14, 1986, Alice Springs

"Journalists shall respect personal privacy. Journalists shall not place undue emphasis on race"—notice at front desk of Central Land Control offices. In Pat Dodson's office, a TV and a VCR, and that stick-like thing in the corner is not a spear but a film screen. Rosie, the secretary, comes out to fetch me and lead me in, gets excellent coffee. Pat wears jeans, his long beard comes down over blue check flannel shirt. He smokes as we sit on armchairs at one end of his tidy office. On the walls, photos of last year's pilgrimage to Canberra, and one of Lester. He's an impressive mind; too much, though, of the ex-priest and the administrator. He actually said quite a bit to buttress lines of thought I already have. The government-mindedness of Australia is carried to a climax in the realm of Aboriginal affairs. They have been influenced by it and in turn they perpetuate it.

CAMA[243] says its potential audience is 46,000, and it broadcasts in five Aboriginal tongues. On the wall, THE GROG IS KILLING US, with a bottle that has a black cross through it. A casual rhythm of activity in the office. Another poster: SAD BOYS ARE SNIFFING. They broadcast the Coloured Stones quite a bit.

July 17, 1986, Darwin

The plane from Alice Springs to Darwin has a fold-up table in the toilet, labeled, "Baby Changing Table." Somehow in the north, Aboriginals always seem to be in back of the planes.

Compared with Darwin's lively cosmopolitanism, Alice Springs seems sullen. "Are you a detective?" asks the young hunk whom I cruise. Then a bit later, "Maybe me and my friend could help you out?"

July 20, 1986, Darwin

At the Casuarina Free Beach, a vast wide desert of a place, one feels little eroticism. But there's an extra dimension of freedom in walking around nude. I see this Black—can I sit down beside you? He says yes. With sand all over my hand, I was loathe to do much, but he was hot, so I asked him if he'd come back to the hotel with me. He was very hesitant, but eventually agreed (I had to be very patient and very persuasive)—as long as we walked separately from where we were to the spot where the taxi was due to come for me.

---

[243] The Centre for Applied Macroeconomic Analysis.

Arriving at the Sheraton in Darwin, I gave him my Air France bag to carry, and passed my sandals to him. In this part of Australia, it's better for the white guy to go in bare-foot than the Black guy. Compared with US Blacks, there is a dullness to Aboriginal lovemaking, but Guy is a quantum leap ahead of the guy in Cairns last year who was my first Aboriginal sex partner. A lovely dick, lovely lips, lovely smile.

July 21, 1986, Over the Gulf of Carpentaria

When the plane for Groote Eylandt is announced, a girl in the bar beside me rolls her eyes to the ceiling, puts her empty glass down, and says to her boyfriend, "Back to Alcatraz."

Over Gove, the soil is not so much pink as red. Like Cairns, it has mangoes. There is a customs plane and a Skywest charter. Some Aboriginals are loading onto a charter what looks like the instruments of the Midnight Oil and Wurumpi bands. Gove has 4000 people and 250 million tons of bauxite reserves being mined by the Nabalco Company.

Several people are away today at smokingout[244] operations here and there, following a death in the community; wherever the person has been has to be smoked out. For this purpose, a little plane hops here and there. Last night's absence of Aboriginals from the Club was due to a ban imposed by the chairman after an incident when people drank on till 10 when the chairman had said stop at eight.

Smokingout also occurs if someone has put a curse on, say, a shop, in anger at something. Shop closes; to get things back to normal again, there has to be smoking-out and a ceremony. In recent times, the Community Council has laid down that a person doing such a cursing pays a fine of $500 to the Community Council.

July 30, 1986, Perth

Talking to the kids from the RC Chinese school, I ask what are you going to learn at the school? "Try to learn things that'll help me get into white society." "Try to be sort of like them, but not exactly like them." Laboring job (George, 18.) Only mother alive. "She hasn't exactly got a job, she just does home and does the house job."

In the school's "personal development" course, something of Aboriginal tradition gets taught. Is there any criticism directed against the kids for going to a white man's school? "It'd be the same anywhere in Australia—such as when you go to college. Sometimes the whites can't understand our talk, we use some of our Aboriginal words, you know." George used to drink Scotch and Coke; the other guy never, but his girlfriend got him to give it up.

I'd been looking at Craig all day without receiving a flicker of encouragement. Next day, I said I'd like to interview him. He came to my room in the Sheraton in his gray sharkskin pants and gray Indonesian-type shirt. He's applied for a hotel job as he thinks that during the America's Cup, they'll want some Aboriginals "up front" for the tourists to meet.

[244] Indigenous Australian spiritual cleansing ritual.

I arranged to be in the shower when he arrived and dried myself in the room as he looked around and admired the view of Perth from the window. The big window came to my aid. As we looked out on the sunset, I leaned against his shoulder. Then as he read the Room Service menu—to see if he could get cigarettes sent up—I massaged the back of his neck. Would you like an entire body massage? Yes. He lay down and his beautiful ass, brown back, and superlative neck just drove me on like wild horses. I turned him over, squatted on him, and discovered a huge hardon at my crotch. It all became pretty clear. Soon he grabbed my cock. We took off our pants. "I've never done this before," he said. But from his sucking, and the way he took my dick in his two hands and rubbed it like a fire-stick, I wonder if that's true.

As we were getting dressed, a maid came in to make up the room for the evening. I took the chance to ask about the America's Cup and generally draw her into a three-way conversation with Craig.

July 31, 1986, Melbourne

Australian Labour Party state conference is like old times—here is the Liquor Trades Union getting total support for its position against allowing alcohol being sold at more outlets and for longer hours, on the ground that jobs would be lost in the hotel industry. A letter-writer in the *Australian* countered that in the *Weekend Australian* one time in June there were 460 public service jobs advertised at a total salary bill of $16 million per year.

August 1, 1986, Sydney to Hong Kong

The steward in Qantas first class wakes me up and says with a cheery smile: "We're going to feed you again." On the one hand, this airline can play the haute cuisine and high formality game; yet if they have a passenger who is dressed informally and addresses the steward as mate, a Qantas steward can slip into egalitarian mode.

August 5, 1986, Boston

A pleasant flight from Paris, and there is Edward in shorts and a purple shirt. It is wonderful to see him. He has become very used to the apartment and has looked after everything pretty well. He massages me long and lovingly. I say extravagant things to him, and they do not seem to bother him. He still drives me as crazy as ever.

Edward said that while I was away, he browsed through the books I've written and he's come to the conclusion "you've done all you can on China—I mean you've brought the story right up to the present and until something else big happens to China, maybe there's not much more for you to write." Indeed.

August 7, 1986

To Cambridge with Edward and after dining, we went to my office to clear things out. Once inside, he came on to me. After a while, he had to go to the bathroom. I said there was a ladies' room down the corridor. He went there and eventually emerged without his trousers and wandered back into room 303. I was kind of amazed at this boldness. We got onto the desk, which, being steel, was rather hard but cooler than the carpet and away we went.

August 9, 1986, Boston

First talk with Kip since getting back and he says his "heart and soul" is no longer into sex with men—he thinks—and he's going to "look for a female." I said take it step by step: get the female first and see if that takes care of his desire for men.

I'm having trouble re-entering even though I was only away just less than seven weeks. I must have got into the swing of Australian life; back here I seem off-balance. Only Edward gives me a sense of where I am spiritually. As usual, it will take plunging into the next writing burst to overcome the alienated feeling.

So often Edward is wise about others but less so about himself. He understands me pretty well; does he understand himself as well?

I must review my relation to drinking and the way to do it is probably to think in terms of what I advised Michael Mao on smoking—think of what you can do if you don't smoke (drink).

August 11, 1986, Boston

A lovely morning with Edward, who is fresh and bright after a weekend with the family in Connecticut. He is somewhat recovered from the shock about the apartment. I think there is a law at work between Edward and me: the more I show dependence on him the less he desires me, and vice versa. Several times in the past week Edward has asked me about sexual encounters—I mean about whether they occurred—and he didn't used to do this. I suppose it's a good sign.

Tomorrow to Washington to see the all-devouring *National Geographic* editors— and perhaps pop into the Martin Luther King Library, where I do the concrete grass- roots research that is a rough equivalent to that which I do in order to write a story for *National Geographic* on Australia.

A welcome talk with Fred Hills. He says I have done "a wonderful job" in meeting the points he made about the first draft. He is sending me a memo tomorrow and wants to go hell for leather now to get *The Australians* into production.

August 13, 1986, Washington

The Washington trip was necessary but hardly exhilarating. Mac was very pleased with the stuff I've gathered and congratulated me. Cary, however, after hemming and hawing until the last moment, pulled out as photographer. (He has a good reason: the Russians have been holding him up on his Kremlin story.) It is irritating that I will have to start from scratch with a new photographer.

The city looked beautiful in its green summer dress and for once was not humid. I strolled down from the Governor's House to the Combat Zone and met a very handsome straight guy who was in the mood for a bit of fun and the meal which we had afterwards ("I'll be candid with you," he said, "I'm hungry.")

When I arrived home, Edward was in the middle of setting up the new stereo. He is still in a charming and affectionate mood, and this is the best thing about my life just now.

August 14, 1986, Boston

I called to see what's up with Chad and I reached Linda. "Chad's at the doctor's." Linda says she's worried that he's too thin. "I keep telling him he's young, and he should enjoy life and have some fun," she says. I wonder if she realizes how much I agree with her.

August 22, 1986, Boston

Unfortunately, moving the stuff was a bigger job than Edward realized—I tried to tell him about it as we were shopping—and we both got pretty tired moving everything into the truck. He busted a bookcase. This didn't matter much but, on the way, home he grazed a car—a bit of damage to the fender of each vehicle. After this began the huge task of getting everything three floors into my house.

We dine late and well, then come home to bed. Most of the lovemaking waited till next morning when we were fresher. We had breakfast together—a rare thing.

In the afternoon, I met Mark, a carpenter from Chicago, and fooled around with him in the Roberts Club. At night, I stayed in, phoned Edward, and ate his leftover shrimp and pork from last night—which of course "outraged" him; anything he orders in a restaurant is indisputably his—like a piece of land he holds.

These days, Edward and I see each other every day. We are very close. I am relying on him. I have doubts about the apartment he has taken; it's a large monthly expense for one without a job. But I have learned not to try to advise Edward when he has made up his mind.

My segment on Mao for *All Things Considered* seems to go quite well, though I expected [Bob] Edwards to ask more about the years since Mao's death and less about Mao's career. A lot of people listen to this show. Alex calls to praise it. The article I wrote has also been widely bought—even in Japan and Korea. I should make $2000 from it if everyone coughs up.

One lesson is to write pieces when they're linked with an anniversary that lazy editors feel constrained to take notice of. Meanwhile Australian Broadcasting Corporation canceled the broadcast on Mao I was to do for them from WGBH studios. "We cannot afford your services," they said primly when I merely enquired what the fee would be.

These days with Edward are sweet. A "gay period" does not normally last this long; what's going on? He hasn't even asked me to take down the (half-nude) photo of him that I currently have in the study.

August 28, 1986, Boston

The transcription of these Australian tapes is a scarifyingly costly business. Slow too. And the resulting typescript is mostly not good. What is the solution to this problem—perhaps I shall have to go back to recording everything by hand in a notebook? Then at least the moment I get home from a trip, I have the material in front of me, ready to use.

September 2, 1986, Boston

To the Fenway Clinic for the second round of test results in the "AIDS study" and once more I am negative to the virus. One cannot say it isn't a relief. I told Edward about it—again he says he is not surprised. I would not be surprised, though, if the third round produces a different result, and this for a particular reason. Some weeks ago, after Reggie fucked me, there was blood in the rectal area. It was soon after that that Edward fucked me (without coming inside me) and if there's anything to the theory that pre-cum carries the virus, this I suppose could have been a moment of transmission.

September 3, 1986, Boston

I went to the Harvard University 350th bash on the banks of the Charles. Not bad, especially after I saw a guy who later turned out to be named Harry. He had been in Mather House about the time I was in Kirkland, and I think it lingered as a possibility in the back of both of our minds that we once had a quickie in Lamont Library. Anyway, all we could do under the circumstances—he was with a family from California, a guy who has been his mentor—was to exchange phone numbers.

September 5, 1986, Cambridge

Another Harvard University 350th event, this one at the Kennedy School on the theme of de Tocqueville Revisited. The general idea was to bash Reagan. But Shirley Williams[245] is always interesting. At the party afterwards, Dan Bell comes up and says how do I like being featured in *Time* as an elitist. I didn't know what he was talking about, but I soon did, as several others had noticed the mention of me in the magazine's covering of the Harvard birthday. It is said that—preoccupied with my own research—I turned away the request of a brilliant student for a consultation.

Jonathan Moore[246] is once again extremely nice. "Any time you're in Washington, I'd like to have lunch with you." As the head of the refugee program, you wouldn't think he'd have many lunches free, but maybe I'll take him up on it. I suppose that now he's left th#e Institute of Politics my line to that place—and its kindness to me—will come to an end. It's nice to keep in touch with Harvard University, and it's also nice to get on the MBTA and come back to Boston.

---

[245] Shirley Vivian Teresa Brittain Williams, Baroness Williams of Crosby (1930-2021) a British politician and academic.
[246] An academic and public servant who served six presidents. Moore was the first full-time director of the Institute of Politics at the Harvard Kennedy School of Government.

September 11, 1986, Boston

This morning, Edward had his last college exam. He came in afterwards and got a long and loving massage. We both felt terrific and relaxed after the lovemaking. He took a bus home to Connecticut, and I zoomed back into the bottomless pit of my manuscript. He will bring back the car at the weekend, and we may make a few excursions in it.

I felt peace this evening. Not that I wanted to be alone. But being alone after being with Edward this morning complemented the togetherness. How difficult it must be in a marriage to keep a balance between the pleasure of being together and the pleasure of being alone.

September 12, 1986, Boston

Annual check-up and all looks fine. On the way, taking the Orange Line to Forest Hills, I twice had encounters that would have led to something if I wasn't on the way to a medical appointment. Someday, I ought to just ride the Orange Line around and prove how few straight guys there really are.

September 18, 1986, Boston

For the last time for some weeks—I hope—I rose to face the pressures of *The Australians* manuscript. There was the ending to play round with. By eleven, I had it more or less as I wanted. By two, I was at the Federal Express with the whole manuscript to send to Simon & Schuster. I wrote Fred a long letter about what I have done to each chapter. I did not mention my anxieties over the timetable for the book; in about a week or so, when the ball is back in his court.

In the evening, the annual Nieman Foundation party and a chance to see a few Harvard types. Adam Ulam[247] is getting sick of working on Russia and for a reason parallel to my lack of appetite for working on China: the stuff you have to read is tediously propagandistic. Dan Bell regales me with an attack on Weber's views on China: instead of Confucianism being an enemy of capitalist development, Dan says, it's a spur to it. I tried to explain—in vain I think—that this oversimplifies the issue.

Chatted with Dan Wakefield[248] about his new book, which grew out of a *New York Times* magazine piece. It turns out he had experiences with the *Times* that were very similar to those of Ward, Danny Yergin, and me: rejection of pieces or the throwing up of a blank wall at any proposal. Dan says that in his case a philosophic barrier is that the *Times* just does not like personal stuff—or any article that's written heavily in the first person. Interesting in the light of the fiasco over my "Mr. Li" article.

September 19, 1986, Boston

Long talk on the phone with Henry from Hong Kong. He's doing well at the bank. We are trying to meet at Christmas; I will need to be in Australia soon after then, but don't

---

[247] Adam Ulam (1922-2000), Gurney Professor of History and Political Science at Harvard.
[248] Dan Wakefield (1932-), American novelist, journalist, screenwriter.

particularly want to join in a family gathering—picking Henry up in Hong Kong and going, say, to the Philippines or Malaysia west coast for a week might be nice. He is keen, so we will each think about it.

Spent the morning with Cary Wolinsky,[249] who is going to Australia to shoot pics for my *National Geographic* Aboriginals story. He really is a thorough and impressive photographer, and I think I'm lucky he's working on the project. He's going to be there nearly three months, so the article isn't exactly going to jump into print even if I write by the end of October.

A drink at Harvard Square with Joan Colebrook and she tells me Farrar are "rushing out her book, *A House of Trees*. Roger Strauss got her manuscript on a Friday and read it over the weekend. Compare with Fred Hills's leisurely pace. And Chatto in the UK are sending Joan on a trip to Australia at their expense to do publicity, even though she's terrible at radio and TV. She warns me against intertwining my life with that of a Black American. "There'll be so much pain," she says.

It never crossed my mind that Joan and I might be thrown into competition next spring, but it did today when she said: "I wonder if *The New York Times* might ask you to review my book? The friend I'm staying with says he read your article in last Sunday's *Times* and it reminded him that you're very well connected there." I said I suppose I would have to decline any invitation to review her book—unless we reviewed each other's, in tandem, in the same issue of the Book Review! I wonder if that's ever been done. If it were done "blind," I don't think it would be unethical.

September 20, 1986, Boston

Edward drove us out to a pancake shop in Brookline where we ate a huge breakfast—he had just knocked off work—and then to Cambridge for the annual East Asia center conference. Quite good this year. At night, David C and I went to *The Fringe Dwellers*, a Beresford movie about Australian Aborigines. To my surprise, David found it very interesting. "Live how we wanna live," says one guy as he urges a girl to marry him and get away from the community. "Ain't nobody then gunna tell us how to live." I would judge that's a pretty important concern with many Aboriginals caught between white and Black pressures.

September 22, 1986, Boston

Finally, the Harvard guy, Harry, and I got together last night, and the sex turned out fantastic. I felt comfortable with him from the moment he walked in. On setting eyes on him again, I wasn't crazily attracted to him. However, I was horny enough to pursue the matter. He wanted to get fucked, and fuck him I did.

As we looked back on that night on the river bank, during the Harvard University 350th party, Harry said as he put his clothes back on: "I really admire the way you go for what you want and get it."

---

[249] Cary Wolinsky (1947-), American photographer.

"Didn't you have some part in that?" I enquired, and he conceded that he did. He said he was astounded at my energy. But he didn't know that I'd been deprived by King Edward for several days and was as hot as hell. He is unlikely to get as much cum next time as he got last night—the orgasm just went on and on.

Have been thinking over the legal case involving Jiang Qing and Radic's play in Australia.[250] At a gut level, I think I want to pull out of it—either that or hit them now with what we have and see what happens. I don't think I want a protracted bout unless the outcome is all but certain.

Talked with the lawyer on the phone and we are going ahead with a list of alleged infringements. This seems best. The response to it will then determine whether I actually take legal action. Until then, it's only guessing, speculating—and fearing, as Radic murmurs about defamation action against me.

Edward in the middle of the night, with one hand, stops my snoring mouth as he goes on sleeping. Earlier in the evening he read *A Boy's Own Story*[251] and this probably made him restless.

September 22, 1986, Boston

In the USA, I make no assumption that problems can be solved and chaos reduced to order, whereas in Australia I do. Am I, in America, irresponsible, or am I a realist?

Got the article on the Yi people off to *The New York Times* and this just about completes the cycle of China articles, mostly based on my Sichuan material. Now it's head down to the *National Geographic* piece on Aboriginals and after that another go at *The Australians* for UK-Australia, and after that, I hope, a start on the novel.

September 24, 1986, Boston

First meeting of the Kirkland House Senior Common Room for the year. It's a pleasant association with Harvard—more so than is the Fairbank Center in a way—and I'd like to continue it.

Reggie came in and we made fantastic love—except that he came before I'd finished fucking him—and also talked a bit much and certainly more than usual. In his life he's done with it six men, he said, but in recent times I'm the only one. When he and Caroline were talking about their pasts, she told him one of her boyfriends had a cock 10" long and 2" across and after fucking she could hardly walk. "Why did she tell me that?" says Reggie, whose own dick is lovely but not out-sized.

Just after we got out of the shower and dressed, Edward came in. Reggie got a shock as the key turned in the door. So, at last the two met. Reggie had to go very soon after, but later Edward told me he seemed the nicest and the most "average" of all the guys I've ever introduced him to.

---

[250] Thérèse Radic (1935-), Australian musicologist and playwright. Terrill alleged that her play with music, *Madame Mao*, first produced in Melbourne in June 1986, borrowed extensively from his book without his permission.
[251] Novel (1982) by the gay writer Edmund White.

September 25, 1986, Boston

Cornell phones and apologizes for hanging up on me the other night. "I was in the middle of an argument with someone." I feel better. He wanted to come around, but I was busy. We plan to meet on Saturday night. It is so much nicer to be in harmony than in disharmony.

September 26, 1986, Boston

Sure enough, Tsai turns up. I half hoped he wouldn't. I felt it was worth a try if I felt extremely hot and deprived. But having had Edward yesterday and Reggie the day before, I was not in that state. Also, Edward had just come in, bubbling, after a very good interview. So, I made love crisply with Tsai, while Edward remained upstairs, and Edward and I went off to Top of the Hub for a nice lunch.

Bantam writes at last with suggestions for the UK-Australia edition of *The Australians*. Happily, their proposals are few. A reader they employed in UK said he "enjoyed the book enormously." This round gives me the chance to put back material that was squeezed out as Fred's trowel moved over the manuscript. I wonder whether the Bantam edition should start with the Pacific flight to Australia as the Simon & Schuster one does?

Can I persuade Edward that if he holidays away with me, his parents will not be terrified he'll return to Boston only in a plastic bag—as they feared when we went to Mexico?

I have had the bright idea of doing a short book on Aboriginals with all this material I am so painstakingly assembling in order to write the *National Geographic* article. Perhaps BL will bite at this idea more than she did at the Sichuan book idea—she is into primitive chic.

Supposed to phone Cornell tonight, but I haven't done so. On the one hand, he's attractive and has great qualities. On the other, his temper has shown itself now three or four times.

September 27, 1986, Boston

The decks are gradually clearing and, in a few days, I'll be able to start writing the *National Geographic* piece; some of the material is wonderful.

October 5, 1986, Boston

After my unforgettable trip to the feuding undersea world of the Great Barrier Reef last year—the way fish carry on makes human society seem a Sunday school by comparison—it is interesting to see this new book from Harvard on sex and fighting amongst animals. According to *Females of the Species* by Bettyann Kevles, lesbianism, incest, and promiscuity are common in the animal kingdom. Prostitution too: pygmy chimps in Zaire barter sex for food.

October 18, 1986, Boston

The Emerson College writing conference goes off all right, with my own session fairly lively. It is nice to have BL up for the occasion. I don't think BL is crazy about me doing a book on the Aborigines.

Before she went back to NY, I took her to Helen Rees' 50th birthday party. Helen's son was there, and he tells me he is writing a novel. Gee, I hope there's still some readers around as well as would-be writers. It was pleasant enough until late in the evening when the World Series sort of took over, and not being a follower of baseball, I came home.

I'm really into nibbling carrots at my desk these days. Edward irreverently suggests I could use them to practice getting fucked. A nice end for a story or a chapter of a novel: "He fucked himself with a carrot and went to bed."

October 21, 1986, Boston

Reggie came in the morning which is very unusual. After watching *All of Me* upstairs, we went to bed. I really get spoiled by the fact that every time Reggie comes by, he's horny as hell. I just couldn't imagine him not so.

Rachel is in the USA, and she comes by for an afternoon, having spent a day inspecting the Children's Museum in Boston. She seems a little more peaceful in her soul now she has a job. We are learning not to flaunt our political prejudices in front of each other. I still get the impression there's a chip on her shoulder. Is it only with me— does she still hold it against me that I did not marry her—or is it a general left-wing thing?

Paul Nagano's[252] opening at Pucker Safrai Gallery, but I find his Bali far too light-hearted and colorful to seem real. Nevertheless, there were some nice canvases, and I regretted that his prices have soared through my range.

October 22, 1986, Boston

I talk—dragged by Jim Thomson—at a Boston University seminar. The topic is American writing about China. One guy asks me about homosexuality in China and later comes up to chat. I give him my home phone. I got the impression Jim wasn't comfortable to have this guy and me huddle.

October 23, 1986, Boston

Early in the morning the phone rings, and I think it must be Edward about to leave work, suggesting breakfast. But it is Will. He's been up most of the night, I would judge, and wants to come round and have a shower, before starting the working day at his salon. Sure, I say. "Just a shower," he keeps saying. In a way, he meant it, yet he did suck my cock for a while, and then he said "one day next week" he'd like me "to screw" him.

---

[252] Paul Nagano (1938-), Hawaiian-born Boston watercolor artist.

Fascinating guy, Will. He brought me a new calendar which the salon and other nearby businesses sponsored. I'm really glad his place is doing well.

October 29, 1986, Boston

Pleasant Kirkland House autumn lunch at which the charming Y.T. says she liked my piece on religion in China in Sunday's *Globe*. She is skeptical how deep religion runs with any Chinese. This accords with my view that the appeal of Christianity in China is mainly the world of Western individualism it presents.

In the afternoon, I got a revised version of *The Australians* off by express mail to London. What a relief; I have been chained to it for so long. I told Kate Parkin in the covering note that I felt she has a big success on her hands. Will London—and Sydney—think likewise?

Edward is in a strange mood. I went around to his place tonight. Once more, he is lying fully clothed on the bed, this time clutching a bible. Opposite the bed, is a painting of hands praying. He is physically fine, he says, but not in his spirit. Yet I cannot communicate very well with him at these times. I just lay on the bed beside him for two hours.

Among the few things I said was that I have come to the conclusion there are two dangers in being gay: one is to worry about it all the time; a second is to allow sex to play too large a role in one's overall life. At the end, he felt slightly better. His pillow—a polyester one—is giving him problems and I will buy him a feather or down one tomorrow.

October 30, 1986, Boston

Ellen Goodman writes in her *Boston Globe* column about AIDS education of the young being likely to "once again make the young afraid of sex." Yes, they used to be afraid for moral reasons, now for health reasons. Yet the truth of the matter is that sex is a terrifyingly powerful thing. It is a metaphor for death as well as life.

October 31, 1986, Boston

A transformation—almost—in Edward yesterday and today. He came in last afternoon saying he would like to have dinner together. After squash at the Y, I came back, watched *Cosby* and another program with him, and then we went off to Allegro for an excellent, if overpriced late dinner. He stayed overnight, using the new duck feather pillow, and brought me orange juice this morning. After classes today—when I had finished a morning's work and played squash with Joe—Edward back and watered the plants. But he didn't really want to make love; I guess I have to give this fit of depression a bit more time.

In the circumstances, I was not ready to resist Will when he came round for a break about six. As he had requested last time, I fucked him, and we showered together like two birds in the rain. He went off to a Halloween party, I read for a while, and then Robert arrived. At last, we could get down to serious one-on-one. As I expected, it was great. Strip him of the effeminate touches of his circle and he is very attractive. Wyatt phoned and Robert and the pair went off to some club.

I went to Deanne Lord's party at the Cambridge Tennis Club for Dorothy Austin's birthday. Erik Eriksson[253] was there, dressed in a black suit and one of those Sunbelt-style string ties. He still is as interested in India as when he wrote *Ghandi*. Deanne starts dancing with everyone, and there's no chance to say goodbye and thank her for a pleasant party. Fox Butterfield is there, now split up from Barbara, and he tells me *The New York Times* is "in chaos" as Max Frankel moves into Abe Rosenthal's old job and looks around for people to replace and people to promote.

Today Edward and I talked during the morning—about his study habits, his (lack of) health coverage, my clothing, the state of his apartment, the need for further blinds in my place for privacy. We sort of asked each other what things we wanted each other to get done.

November 7, 1986, Boston

Over lunch at the Back Bay Bistro, Jim Carroll[254] expresses a certain amount of disappointment with the reception and sales of his new novel *Supply of Heroes*. God knows a sale of 30,000 in hardback seems OK by my standards; and anyway, the book has only been out three months. But as Jim said, "Dutton paid best seller price for the book and it's not going to be a best seller." Jim's thinking of tackling a "Washington novel" next.

November 16, 1986, Cambridge

Cambridge seems almost alien to me now. The other day, a talk on Hong Kong at Harvard that seemed absurdly optimistic from all I know of the situation—yet the academics just sit there and write it all down, the big picture and common sense absent from their minds.

November 22, 1986, Boston

In the lobby of the Y, something made me sit down—on an opposite bench—beside a chunky stud who looked tired but marvelous. I had no real hope of him. I just thought I'd read the *Globe* and observe him. Soon Miles and I got talking and he seemed fascinated that I am a writer. He is from Baltimore and works at City Hospital. I had to go off to continue working in the Northeastern library, but I left him my number and said I'd be home at ten.

A bit to my surprise, soon after ten, Miles phoned and drove round in his car. We had a drink and watched the video *Black Taboo*. I got horny, and as we sat on the old couch, I began feeling myself through my pants. I stretched out a bit so that my head was almost on his knee. He didn't pull back. I took my cock out of my pants and stroked

---

[253] Erik Erikson (1902-1994), eminent developmental psychologist ranked as "the 12th most eminent psychologist of the 20th century" the *Review of General Psychology*.

[254] James Carroll (1943 -), American author.

it. He moved his hand closer to me and then put it on my chest. Soon after this—as the gorgeous Blacks fucked and sucked away on the screen—I gently moved his hand from my chest to my dick. He was fantastic and soon we were downstairs in bed (it was he who said, "Let's go downstairs"). I suppose it was a classic seduction; no explicit words were said—only comments on the movie. He's straight, he said. For safe sex, it is safe to say it was a near-record enjoyment.

November 24, 1986, Boston

Edward comes in the front door, smiles, throws off his coat, comes over and grabs me. He starts undoing my belt in the front room. Virtually an attack, a sweet one. I vaguely protest that I must first go to the bathroom, but little room for maneuver is left to me. Soon, he has my cock out, and he falls to his knees in the hallway by the bathroom door and starts sucking. I weakly protest, saying I feel flat (Reggie was here last night), but there's no stopping this guy. I'm allowed a little break at one point to get into the bathroom and wash myself—just as well because when I return to the bedroom, I get rimmed. I did the same to him and eventually he sits on me, and I screw the blazes out of him and come in a lovely orgasm just at the same time as he comes.

November 26, 1986, Boston

Reggie and I are in bed when in the front door comes Edward. I jump out of bed and reach the bedroom door just as he reaches it from the lobby. "I'll be out in a few minutes," I gasped lamely. When I went back to bed, Reggie was almost trembling. At first, he just wanted to go home. I persuaded him to calm down. Eventually, when I asked him—as I felt bound to do—if Edward could join us, his eyes showed a weighing up of the issue. "Could I fuck him?" I said probably he could. I went into the lobby and Edward was sitting primly on the white couch with a silly look on his face.

Edward accepted the invitation to come in. How do you feel? he asked Reggie "Very nervous," replied Reggie. I said I also felt a bit nervous. Reggie asked Edward how he felt, and he smiled and said, "I feel very excited." Reggie and I tried to resume, but it was difficult while Edward was sitting fully clothed in an armchair. Soon he got into bed and took over by announcing he was going to give Reggie a massage. And a very thorough massage he gave. (Reggie later said it was excellent.) After a while, I thought it was getting too scientific and I got on top of Reggie—thus interrupting Edward, who takes pride in his full non-erotic massages. "Leave him alone," says Edward, getting into his high-horse mode. This turned me off for a while. But soon I was kneeling at Reggie's neck, and he started sucking me and I got into the swing of things.

All sorts of things happened, including Reggie fucking Edward and Edward sucking me after Reggie finished, and me sucking both Reggie and Edward. Reggie wouldn't let me fuck him, which Edward noted and raised afterwards. After Reggie came, he kind of backed out and Edward and I—we hadn't come—sort of stopped and chatted until Reggie left. A tension hung in the air. I just wanted to resume the lovemaking. Edward wanted to talk. I guess I prevailed for once and fucked him deliciously. It was exciting to get into him an hour after Reggie had been in him. Afterwards, though, it was

Edward's turn to fall silent. Exciting as these encounters are, they are not easy to manage flawlessly.

December 1, 1986, Boston

An intestinal specialist, German-born and fresh as a milk maiden, examines me—mostly my record, with my brother and sister's problems, and some recent bleeding—and suggests a colonoscopy. It's something of a relief to hear that this is the "gold medallion" of the field because I really couldn't face another sigmoidoscopy or even another barium enema.

This one, she says, after pulling her rubber-gloved fingers out of my asshole, will really tell her how things are. And if the recent bleeding means—which I doubt—that there's a polyp, the thing can be removed there and then. The plan is to do it in Beth Israel just as 1986 gives way to what one hopes will be a banner year of 1987.

December 3, 1986, Boston

Yesterday Reggie comes by—first visit since the threesome with Edward—and for whatever combination of reasons the sex is fantastic. We drove our tongues into each other's asshole—the first time I've done it with him—and then he led me to fuck him. He goes on—exaggerating I think—at how he regretted what we did, how Edward is not his type ("too skinny") and so on. I said he had appeared to enjoy it, and he said, "Edward just kept putting my cock inside him."

Reggie is depressed about his exterior situation. Caroline is keeping him now and he feels bad about it. He wants a job. Of course, being of his type and generation, he wants a job immediately and he wants a job with high pay, great satisfaction, and few burdens. He took another plant home with him, though he says the first one staggers.

December 6, 1986, Boston

A letter from Mac at the *National Geographic* with a mixed response to my draft on the Australian Aborigines. He has a theory that I'm writing too much for my sources, not enough for my readers, but he doesn't illustrate where this is evident. It's as if there's a hidden agenda to his reservations. Carey's absence as the photographer?

Dinner with Robert at Soom Thai—after reasonable sex, though he didn't suck me which I would have liked. As we nibbled Thai dumplings, he told me his father is serving a long prison sentence for murder. Apparently, Robert's parents split up a decade or so ago, his father married again, and it was the new wife—or girlfriend—that he killed.

December 9, 1986, Boston

I think I see now Mac's hidden agenda. A long talk on the phone with Wolinsky, the *National Geographic* photographer, who says his just-completed trip to Australia was a major disappointment. Couldn't go here, thrown out of there. Perhaps Mac is embarrassed now that my piece won't see the light of day for some time, and finds it easier to quibble with it than to tell me of the visual problems facing the project?

Who should ring the doorbell but Julius. I went downstairs and soon he was sucking me off on the stairway down to Kay's apartment. He's just as electrically sexual as ever though getting a bit overweight. He came as he sucked—then complained that I had not brought down tissue for him to wipe up his cum! He's been in California, and he'd brought me a front cover of *Playmate* of which he is the feature.

Next day he comes back. Here a problem arose because I don't really want him in the apartment. I said Edward was upstairs, brought out Vaseline, and we did it on the staircase two floors up, near the front door of the unit that is empty.

December 10, 1986, Boston

United magazine arrives with my Sichuan piece in it. It looks nice, but above all it brought in $1000, less $100 to Barbara. Writing is like prostitution, as Molière said long ago. First you do it for the love of it, later you do it for a few friends, and in the end, you're doing it for money.

Edward and I are having once more that conversation about flesh and spirit, and once more I try to convince him that it's not mainly his body that draws me. "I don't want Black flesh for its own sake," I insist. He grins and rejoins, "No, you want it for your sake." He thinks he's hit the nail on the head.

December 11, 1986, Boston

Off *The Australians* goes to NY once more and with what a sigh of relief. I was working on a new ending up to midday—probably a bad sign—but at least it's now over to Fred. The copy editing wasn't all that good, which made my task harder. At the same time, I decided to put in some of the passages I had prepared for the British edition and this all took time.

December 12, 1986, Boston

Weary, yet a lovely day because the pressure of *The Australians* has gone and because it was a day spent with Edward. As he worked on his paper about Africa, I caught up with letters, tidied the study, made phone calls. Later in the day, I polished some of his paper.

Reggie came in and the two of us made love. During this Edward interrupted his paper to go upstairs and check out the video—*Water Colors*—that Reggie and I had watched before jumping into bed. Afterwards, the three of us chatted in the study. Edward hardly feels any jealousy in such situations, and the three of us rapping together afterwards removed any tension that might have existed. We continued work on the African paper and then went out for a late dinner to St. Cloud. It was a superb meal, ambience, and service. Edward had rack of lamb, I had goose, and we drank a French red. Later, though I wanted only to go to sleep, he initiated love making. This was fun for a while, but I got tired. He also tried to fuck me about 3 AM. In the end, neither of us came and I think he got disgruntled.

We spent a pleasant morning doing this and that. We decided to go to Thornton's. He took a shower, and then I made a Big Mistake. I took a photo of him before he was dressed. This threw him into intense fury. The brunch was off. So, too, he said was the trip away next week. He gathered up his study books and swept out of the house like a hurricane.

I felt wretched during the afternoon and tonight decided to go to the dinner party at Kirkland House. Cambridge takes my mind off the way of life I lead in Boston. The academics drank and ate away and talked about trivial things. How astonished the world would be to know what Harvard gatherings mostly talk about. Yet for me it was pleasant. I wandered around Harvard Square, bought books at Wordsworth, took the bus home and went to bed.

December 17, 1986, Boston

I phone Kate in London to check on the schedule for *The Australians* and get a bombshell. No, the copy-edited manuscript will not be sent to me. Neither will the galleys. "We are going straight to pages." I scurry round to prepare a memo of points to be slotted in, hopefully, before the printer does his work and comes up with pages in early January. Kate is so nice on the phone that I didn't manage to complain about these arrangements.

December 18, 1986, Boston

To Washington today and the usual winter air travel hassles. An hour's delay at Boston, circling Washington for 40 minutes, two delays due to fog in leaving wretched National Airport to come home. In between, a genteel *National Geographic* lunch where few seem to say what they think.

Mac approved the idea of two trips to Australia to get the Bicentennial material. The idea is that the first should be soon—maybe late January if I can get both Simon & Schuster and Corgi galleys out of the way by then—and the second in June just prior to writing and delivering the piece.

December 19, 1986, Boston

A tense week goes on. Edward is as busy as I and we try to share time at the computer. He has two papers due this week and a final exam today as well. We are both over-strained. I work all day on the memo for London. In the evening, Bob Lee comes in and at last his figures are final. I have a flickering doubt about the greenhouse parts—there are too many partitions—but I think we've probably got about what my budget can permit. Demolition of my old deck will begin next week.

At night, Edward and I dined at St. Botolph Restaurant and went to see a silly movie called *Crimes of the Heart*. He didn't want to make love, having a splitting headache, but we made up for that this morning.

December 22, 1986, Boston

Judy Kerr rings from Sydney to pin down dates for my radio and TV tour in Australia. We fix on the second week of June. She says the book is their Number One nonfiction title for the six-month period, and that they're printing 10,000 copies. She could tell I thought that was a bit modest, but she insists it's "big for us" in Australia. The Murdoch people are still interested in first serial, though they don't pay much.

December 23, 1986, Boston

Various work and business pressures and frustrations. I have been impatient with others as well. We are different races. It is a challenge to be close across this barrier, but one I find worth it. I hate a boring life. On the other hand, intensity is awful when it boils into a quarrel. Is there no happy medium—excitement, risk, but in the context of respect and affection—that is unshakeable?

December 24, 1986, Boston

Edward awoke early to go to NY. I gave him his Christmas present and the money to pick up the car, and he left with a tiny smile but no hug or kiss. Perhaps one should accept, as Michael Mao always tells me, that everything one says about the other in a quarrel is true, and go on from there if you can.

Late in the morning, I went spinning to the Boston Public Library in a daze. I played around with a Black guy in a cubicle, the door locked, and a bit later I saw a gorgeous sandy-haired white guy sitting on one of the johns that has no door. Eventually, he made a gesture with his mouth indicating that he wanted to suck me. He has lovely eyes, nice skin, and a large cut dick. He just gobbled me up, and it was so good I didn't care who was watching from behind.

Many times, I stopped him because I got to the point of coming, and again I didn't want to come, for the same reason as with the Black guy: I needed the excitement but if I came that would have made painful the gap between my affection for Edward and the necessity I'm faced with of seeking sex elsewhere. He wanted to come home with me, and perhaps I should have done that.

The Combat Zone in the early evening had a half-closed up yet exciting feeling. Half-closed up in a salute to Christmas, exciting because there was a fellow feeling of being orphans from Christmas. In the bookshop near the Chinese movie house, a nice white guy came up to me. Knowing he was a hustler, I said no, but he said he was so horny he'd suck me for nothing. In one of the booths, he indeed sucked beautifully. However, after a moment, I felt a movement near my left ankle—the guy was trying to get at the pocket of my pants which were around my sneakers. I moved on.

The Pilgrim Theater was quite crowded, I think, because they seem to have closed off the top floors. I hadn't been there for months. First, I had a pleasant time looking around—despite the smell—watching these husbands out for a quick look. Other husbands for a little flexing of their bi muscles. Orientals escaping the suffocations of family life in Chinatown, Black hustlers in leather jackets, and people who have come in mainly to keep warm and have a little sleep.

I became aware of two Black guys getting more and more smoochy with each other. One tall guy was in a cap. A shorter guy, sniffing something that seemed like cocaine, was in a blue sweater and soon had his pants down, bent over in front of the stud in the cap. Things advanced. I kept saying. "Fuck him! Fuck him!" It spurred them on.

During this, several men came by to grope me, but I swished them away with the same gesture used by the Black guy in the cap who was fucking the cocaine guy to swish me away. Then a slim Black guy appeared at my side. This was a different cup of tea from the others. He looked enticing, and when he reached down to my cock, he stroked it nicely. In a moment, he was on his knees, sucking me. The proximity to the other couple was fun. I pushed against the thighs of the guy fucking the other guy, and, as well as pulling down my pants. I took off my shirt. Elliot—as he is called—alternated sucking my cock with sucking my tits. Suddenly, I felt a sharp pain. I had leaned against a heater and burned my ass. I screamed and explained to Elliot what had happened. He continued.

Eventually, with me pouring sweat because of the hot confined space and him, having worked like a soldier on the battlefront, he said, "I think I'll take a little rest." I said I'd give him my phone number. Neither of us had a pen, so I said I'd go to the cashier and meet him there. It was dark in the lobby. I put out my hand with the piece of paper and—it wasn't Elliot! The guy looked amazed: why was I smiling and putting a piece of paper into his hands? I hastily turned and there was Elliot.

When I got home and showered, I phoned Li-li and we talked for a long time. About China and her bad back; about Christmas in America when you're not American-born. Then I began the various calls to Australia, and this went well—everyone was waiting to hear from me, and they sounded well and cheerful. The burn was quite spectacular, and I wonder what Harry will think of it tomorrow night.

December 25, 1986, Boston

Well, I needn't have worried about the burnt back-side when Harry came, for he phoned this morning and said, a girl he knows is having a baby today, so he's not coming over after all. (Actually, it's the girl with whom and with her husband he had a simultaneous affair when he was in Mather House.)

Edward phoned. It was a phone call with long silences; these, though, can be eloquent. Is he happy with the family? "No, not at all. Everyone here pisses me off except my nephew." I am very glad he called.

Mass Ave is warm and quiet and clean-swept as I go to Oceanic. In the window of the Mother Church's office, a book is opened at an underlined passage from Mary Baker Eddy: "In the late 19th century, I discovered the divine rules of Christian Science." Some century, some lady, some rules.

After I got home, Robert came round and we just of drifted into bed. The sex was OK but not inspired. When I told Robert that I was resolved to go ahead with the renovations, he said, "You're right. In life, you get a ticket, and it's only one time around."

December 26, 1986, Boston

Quite by chance, after a nice lunch at Hillary's, I met Skip, a medical student. I wasn't looking for such a thing, being on my way to Jordan's to check out mini-blinds. Anyway, we went into the Boston Public Library, sat side by side at a big table on the lower level and talked and played with each other. He is handsome and polite, with a very small cock. We decided to come home. He carefully showered—me with him—and then sucked and rimmed me in silence and with great care and concentration. I had a sort of double orgasm which surprised him. Afterwards, when he saw the upstairs, he commented on the lack of blinds. "It figures," he said. "No one would have done what you did in the library if he wasn't the type who doesn't care about blinds."

Skip was in the kitchen and looking down at a carrot. I glanced over and nearly died. I swooped across, took it away, and said, it's an old one. The carrot was the Vaseline-smeared one I had experimented with fucking myself a couple of nights ago.

December 28, 1986, Boston

I try to focus on getting bits and pieces done, but few get done. Elliot phones, and in the course of a long talk, he mentions he's just out of Plymouth. A 10-month sentence for assault. This depresses me all afternoon. I didn't ask him over—I had to meet Dave for squash.

In the evening, letters to be posted to Japan and elsewhere that are urgent, so I go to South Station.[255] Afterwards, I drop by Washington Street. In the video shop, a lovely guy with frizzy hair and light skin wants to suck me though he is not himself aroused. This puzzles me—he is in no way a hustler—but I enjoyed him. Then a drink of wine—no food allowed—at Playland,[256] where I hadn't been for years. Enormous fun, especially with Dean, a tall, built auto worker. Not the type I'd invite home, but extremely attractive and a great drinking companion. He asks me if Australia is inside or outside the USA.

I think he sometimes hustles, but he didn't ask for anything—I bought him a White Russian and a beer, which he drank simultaneously—after we fooled around a bit in a musty back room. He has one of those huge snaky, droopy uncut dicks, like a tiny baby's arm.

Going home, the white cabbie was very inquisitive. Did you have a good time? Are you sure you want to go home now? He was nice, but I felt he was on drugs, and I was terrified of his driving. I was so relieved that he made it to Mass Ave and Columbus that I got off there, bidding him warm farewells. He was too far gone to count money or get correct change.

December 29, 1986, Boston

I finish up the article on Chinese student demonstrations for the *Globe*. Starting to feel weak from no food—only liquids until tomorrow noon—I feel up to little, so I decide to take the article out on the Red Line to Columbia Point.[257] Then squash with Jim.

---

[255] Location of an all-night post office.
[256] The Playland Café, a Combat Zone bar, was known for its "sketchy clientele, banged-up piano, and year-round Christmas lights." (Robert D. Sullivan, "Last Call," *The Boston Globe*, December 2, 2007).
[257] Location of the Boston *Globe* offices.

Ansaphone tells me Edward called twice but did not want to leave the number. Well, I know it, but he does not want me to call at work, so I won't.

I turn things with Edward over in my mind. My emotional impulse is to say I'll do anything to adjust to him. But my mind won't let me say that. However much we dislike it, or don't face it, there is something transactional about relationships.

I call Dr. Taitlebaum, who will do the procedure tomorrow, to ask her the difference between "clear citrus fruit juices" and other sorts, as stipulated on the instruction sheet for my dietary preparation. She laughs and says she does not know. I ask if I can have tomato juice. Again, she does not know! Such specialization. Are colons all she knows about?

Kip comes in and we talk a lot. He's still on with the girlfriend who is his classmate at Bunker Hill Community College. But he wants it with me so much. We just hold hands and I say, "Well, don't come and let's just pet around." But he says he wants to do it till he comes. I let the contradiction lie in the air.

He still remembers the photos I took the week before I left for Australia in June. Where is the one of him in the green shorts, he demands. He says he loves to cruise, even though he nearly always doesn't do anything with someone he sees or meets. This is hard for me to understand.

Kip said he wouldn't suck today as it's not possible for him to suck a man and kiss a girl on the same day. He also didn't want to kiss, which he is great at doing. His devotion to my dick, fortunately, hadn't abated. I had a very nice time, but I decided not to come and, in a general way, explained to Kip the reason. He's a delightful guy. As for his agonizing, I don't think I can advise him.

The *Globe* calls to say they like the piece and will run it.

December 31, 1986, Boston

A lovely end to the year. Edward comes around and we chat intimately. He says he's sorry for implying that I manipulate him and acknowledges that it's difficult for him to receive things. Beyond that, neither of us say much about last week.

We dined at Oceanic with Ray and the two of them got on well. At the end, Edward said we ought to go out drinking. When Ray suggested Paradise[258] and Edward agreed, I almost fell off my chair. At the bar, we had a great time, Edward drinking Slippery Nipples, Ray, beer, and myself, white wine. I could hardly believe my eyes to see Edward in a Boston gay bar.

At home, he fucked me and he jerked me off as his cock was inside me; then he pulled out and came all over me. We slept like kittens. Early next morning, I fucked him.

---

[258] A gay bar in Cambridge.

1987

January 1, 1987, Boston

A lovely peacefulness. I slowly arose and did clearing up; later sent off a China article to the *Baltimore Sun*. Edward stayed in bed under the blue sheets and telephoned as he loves to do.

Later, lunch with Edward at St. Cloud. As so often, a lovely meal, though Edward orders me around about the size of the tip and does not like it when I ask whom he spoke to on the phone this morning. "Have some respect," says the man who comes into the house when I'm in bed with someone and opens the bedroom door.

January 3, 1987, Boston

Last night, I had a lottery ticket in my hand for the first time in my life and looking back, I think it might be the last. For my flutter—not on the lottery itself but on the lottery of befriending a stranger—turned into a nightmare. Unfortunately, it doesn't always do to do a good turn for a stranger—you realize that when you feel the click of handcuffs on your wrists.

Toward 6 PM on January 2, I was walking along Huntington Ave after going to the gym and making purchases of coffee and wine, when near the Bay State House of Pizza, a cheerful young man in a hat said hello. He was holding something in his hand the way people proffer a handout. I returned his greeting with a remark about Happy New Year and kept walking toward Mass Ave. Noticing my foreign accent, this thin Black guy asked me where I was from. When I said Australia, he said that was nice, and I remarked—at the liquor store, the person in front of me at the cash register had bought Foster's beer—that Australia had a line of beer that was becoming quite popular in the USA.

By this stage, we were at the Mass Ave lights. The man asked me if I would cash in a ticket for him at Christy's. I was intending to pop into Christy's, where I often shop, to buy New England magazine, which has an article about Hartford—Edward's hometown. "Why not do it yourself?" I asked. "Because I once got into a fight in there, and they don't like me." I thought the request was a bit of a nuisance, but I was going in anywhere, and it was the New Year, so I said I would. "Just give it to them and they give you the ten dollars," the guy said. He then took up a position by the entrance to Symphony Station to wait for me.

The cashier said yes, they cash these tickets, but he added that the manager has to do it, so he called this man from the back. I went over to the magazine section to get *New England*. When the manager came out, tension rose. He seemed agitated, and soon he was at the door of the shop with a key in his hand. When I went over to him, he said he'd lost $40 recently through having forged lottery tickets tended to him. It was only at this stage that I even knew the thing was a lottery ticket. I said the person who asked to me to redeem it was just outside, and if I went out with the $10, I could lead the manager to him. "You just explain all that to the police" he said. I thought this was stupid, but I was not unduly alarmed and browsed in the magazines.

Police arrived with a big flurry. I told them briefly—for they weren't interested in listening to my story. They, too, were uninterested in getting the forger (assuming the ticket was a forgery) and clapped handcuffs on me. A number of people in the store watched this unpleasant moment. I felt the eyes of accusation and then of relief as I was hustled out the door into the snowy night.

I felt a certain futility that all the hullaballoo with several police cars and noise would certainly have led a forger waiting at Symphony Station to flee. But as I was hustled out of the store, the cops would not even make the attempt to look for the young man who gave me the ticket. "Tell that to the judge,'" grunted the senior of the two cops, dressed in blue, who drove the car as I repeated my story.

The second cop, dressed in an orange jacket, was so much less zealous that I wondered if he thought the arrest was the sensible thing to do. As we reached the curbside, I asked if I could leave my shopping bag—wine, coffee, disks from my locker at the YMCA, a clipping from that day's *Globe* of my op-ed article on China—at my home, which was a stone's throw away. No.

If I was a suspected forger, wouldn't it have been worthwhile having a look around my house for the instruments of forgery? If I was trying to defraud the state of $10, would it not have been relevant to check out my house, which a bank valued at $250,000 this year?

At the Boston Number Two District police station, glaring lights, and much paperwork. The numerous porky, all-white cops are quite curious, as they lounge around, to look over the new criminal. "It's a quiet night," I hear someone say in a neighboring room. "All the college kids are away."

But at least they'd found one victim, and they made the most of it. It took three of them to count out my money—just over $150. They wanted me to watch. I tell them I trust their arithmetic. Their spelling is another question. My birthplace of Melbourne gives a scribe endless trouble, and he cannot spell at all. Three times I spell it out letter by letter, but the catch is he hasn't heard of this country, and so he still gets it wrong. But why point to details, for mindlessness rules in this place: why else would someone not wonder why a man with $150 in cash in his wallet plus various credit cards would be hurling himself into danger for the sake of $10?

I was shown a notice on the wall that listed my rights. Two points from it stuck in my mind: that I had the right to remain silent and that I was allowed to make one phone call. Call a lawyer? But the case seemed so trivial. Call the *Globe* and dispose of it by having a reporter put the glare of publicity on the absurdity of arresting a fairly well-known citizen for forging a lottery ticket? I had a residual fear of antagonizing these cops; if things could just proceed rationally without doing so, that might be better, I felt. And I had some anxiety that in my shopping bag were disks that contained much of my personal Diary for the past two years—backup copies that I was bringing home from my locker at the YMCA to update. Big fuss, angering the cops, press story—might I end up having my Diary being read?

I asked the cop in the orange jacket just where I stood. "Look, you'll be out of here on bail in an hour," he said. How much would I need? He laughed. "You've got plenty in your wallet. It couldn't be more than $50." Armed with this knowledge, I decided to phone a personal friend, Tony O, and in a low-key way, ask him to stay in touch. While on the phone with him, I repeated the question to the officer about bail and the adequacy of the money I had; he gave the same answers.

Naively I asked Tony if he'd be home later in case I needed to call. Also, in retrospect, I probably sounded too relaxed and casual to Tony. Had I realized that the cops tell lies to prisoners as casually as many Boston people throw litter onto the pavement, I would have asked Tony to arrange for bail there and then by an independent bondsman.

The remark about an hour proved a bitter illusion. More than 16 hours later, I was still in my cell. Had I been told I could call a bondsman of my own, I probably would have been able—it was not yet 7 PM to get out quickly. Instead, I was told a Massachusetts bondsman would come, and I believed what I was told.

Millions of people have been in cells before me and, alas, millions of people will be after me. It is little different from expected, but after a few hours, it is absolutely awful. Cell Four is metal except for a concrete floor. There is a freezingly-cold metal bench and a toilet which is unflushed as I arrive (and cannot be flushed from inside the cell). On the walls and the ceiling are names and dates and scrawled messages of anger and defiance.

For a while, it is not much more irritating than an airport delay. You just don't know when you can leave. But you assume the wheels are turning, and you just make the best of it. That feeling did not last beyond a couple of hours. It was not only that there was nothing to do. Looking up and seeing the cell bars gave the awful, amazing realization that I was a prisoner of the law.

Through the night, this point got rammed home progressively. "I have a problem," I said to a lady cop, hoping to broach a request for a blanket or some heating in the nicest possible way. "Yeah, your problem is that that you're in there," she said in a tone that was half chuckle and half rasp as she disappeared down the corridor.

In my cell, I didn't worry about my galleys or my mortgage or unpaid bills. AIDS and the travails of the Middle East didn't enter my mind. For most of the time, I didn't even worry about how I could get off the charges laid against me. Only one thing concerned me: getting out of that cell.

Being a slow night, the cells were mostly empty. On one side in Cell Five was Al, a Black guy, perhaps in his late 20s, who was brought in about an hour after me. He was in possession of heroin, and he had been nabbed also because there was a warrant to get him for falling behind on child support. On my other side in Cell Three was 18-year-old Jerome, also Black, a talkative "card" who was in on a charge to do with cocaine. He had been in since 2 PM that afternoon. For neither guy was it the first time in a cell.

When he first came in, Al cried quietly. Later, bemoaned his separation from his girlfriend. He didn't talk much, but the silences from his cell were punctuated with the passionate cry "Damn!" Jerome said there was no way he would have sex with his girlfriend even if, by some miracle, she appeared in the cell. "Man, a damn cockroach might come at your dick just as you've got your pants down."

Jerome, even colder than me because his jacket, having a string on it, had been taken away from him, tried all night to pull his jacket into his cell from out in the corridor. With exquisite sadism, the cops put it in view but just out of reach. Jerome used his paper coffee cup, pieced together with coffee cups passed in by Al and me, to make a clumsy pole, to try to hook the edge of his jacket. Repeatedly he did this. After breakfast, with more coffee cups, he tried again. But never did he get hold of the jacket. Sometimes after he failed, he quietly cried.

Many times, I called for an officer to ask if the toilets could be flushed, but I could never get it done. Ninety percent of the time, there was no answer, just as when Jerome and Al called out to ask about a match or a phone call. Sometimes a cop would respond and then, as you spoke to him, just murmur, "Yeah" and walk away without listening to the question. In the same way, I called out to various cops that the cells were too cold, and the answer, if any, was always a variation on "M'm"—except once, when a young cop said he'd look into it. Perhaps he did just that; the temperature did not change.

Various of us would shout "Officer" to get attention, but it was like the cry of a baby for an absent or unconcerned mother. In general, I learned that those [cops] without influence were more likely, at least, to respond than those who could do anything. Many times, Jerome tried to get permission to call his father, and several underling types said they'd see about it. More senior cops didn't answer his beggings. He never called his father.

An opening door always seemed a welcome sign, and when a cop came by and opened all three of our cells, this was positively exciting. "You and you can get bailed," he said as he pointed to Jerome and me. "You can't because you're in default on a previous charge," he said to Al, no doubt referring to his failure to keep up with child support payments. The three of us were manacled together and, in a bizarre stumbling line, were led to another building for fingerprinting and photographing. At least, that was the idea. When we got down there, only I was declared a "nay." Jerome and Al had records and didn't have to be processed again.

In this department, there occurred the only normal human conversation of the evening, one between prisoners and officers. The photographers, and fingerprinters, and our escorts, none of whom were directly responsible for any decisions about our cases or treatment, asked questions and made comments. This was also the only occasion during which Jerome, Al, and I could actually see each other. Jerome was a genial, slightly overweight guy with a friendly grin, wearing jeans and a ski cap. He would chat about his case and his previous arrests with anyone who wished to talk with him, gesticulating extravagantly and evincing no bitterness. Al, good-looking, rather taciturn, and glum, was in a US Army jacket and kept his hands in his pockets whenever possible.

A Puerto Rican was brought in, struggling, kicking, and screaming in his rich tenor voice. "I've done nothing," he kept roaring. Apparently, he was in under the four-hour rule for drunks: he wasn't arrested or charged—and couldn't be bailed out—but he could be held for up to four hours for being drunk. One wonders why he was picked up, but that I will never know.

The Puerto Rican hurled himself against his cell wall and door, and Jerome and I felt sure he was hurting himself badly. As he cursed and argued with the cops, they, instead of going away and letting him cool down a bit, in effect goaded him on. He would scream that he shouldn't be locked up. A cop, outside his cell, would retort that he should. Each would repeat this basic sentiment a dozen times. Meanwhile, the cops who hung around, adding to the Puerto Rican's fury, could not be got to light a cigarette for Jerome or Al.

When the sparring between the Puerto Rican and the cop died down, Jerome and the Puerto Rican began an argument over the noise Puerto Rican was making. The argument itself mightily added to the noise banging into the ears of Al and me. "Shut the fuck up" was Jerome's basic line. "You shut up the fuck up" was the Puerto Rican's standard rejoinder. All this was not spoken but shouted across the considerable distance that separated the Puerto Rican's cell from those of Jerome, Al, and myself.

One phase of the spat was cast in sexual terms. "You suck my dick." "No, you suck *my* dick." As Al got annoyed with the noise, he joined in. "Hey, bitch, bend over and I'll fuck your ass." Raising his voice from a shout to a scream, the Puerto Rican said, "You bend over, queer, and I'll fuck your ass."

"Let me out. I'll do anything to get out," roared the Puerto Rican again, and this time Jerome decided to imitate a cop and lead him up the garden path. Putting on an entirely different voice—indeed sounding like an Irish-American cop—Jerome shouted: "If you suck my dick, I'll let you out." Silence. Then in a calm voice that tried to hide the Puerto Rican's excitement, the corridors echoed with the shout: "Yes, come over now and I'll suck it." Jerome said he was on his way, and the Puerto Rican elaborated on what a fantastic job he would do.

Here one learns that sex is an appetite, like food, and affections and situations are another realm. In terms of straight and gay, the distinction is never so blurred as in prison, because expectations and options are so tiny that a chance to satisfy any of life's appetites is like winning a lottery (no joke intended). I don't think this is a moral question. The brotherly gesture or the shared risk involved in furtive sex between cells can be moral behavior. But two dicks poking out from the bars of adjacent cells, with the hand of each man straining through the bars to jerk off the other, brings the gay/straight gap to the vanishing point. The straight's dick looks pretty much like the gay's. The two hands are, well, human hands.

I thought of all this when, after the argument between Jerome and the Puerto Rican had died down, through the silence came the question from Jerome's cell: "Number Four, would you like me to suck your dick?" Minutes after a big shouting match about who was the most macho, the macho-in-chief quietly asks to suck the cock of probably the only one among the four prisoners who is gay.

When so many moments of hope slip away, a fear grows that hope itself is futile. Scores of times, the opening of a door or the sound of a fresh voice made me think the bondsman had arrived and I would soon be free. An equal number of times, nothing happened. By this morning, I felt that hoping all the time would, before too long, damage my mind if not my body. The only thing to do—for as long as is possible—is to turn off from the march of events, or non-events, and open up the inner world.

In the real world, there were big decisions to make—I don't mean which adverb to use or which restaurant to dine at. I mean whether to put my head at the corridor end of the metal bench and fail to doze because blinded by light, or whether to put it at the other end a couple of inches from the unflushed toilet. I mean whether to lie clothed on the bench and after ten minutes feel too cold to stay that way, or whether to take off outer clothing and make a base out of this, and then after ten minutes feel too cold on top to stay *that* way.

Always I preferred to put my head at the lighted end, though at home, I cannot sleep without a face mask, and as a boon, there were fewer cockroaches that end. The choice over clothing was impossible. There was no right choice; one just oscillated like a child who cannot make up its mind between vanilla ice cream and chocolate ice cream.

By the time, which I later found out was about 9:30 AM, I was feeling very down, and I devised two arguments to get some action. The first was that, when I'd been told 14 hours before that I'd be out on bail in about an hour, I didn't worry that household appliances had been left on in my home, but now I did. The oven was on; the situation may be dangerous. The second argument was to be that I needed a doctor, having had the removal of polyps from my intestine in a colonoscopy procedure three days before (true) and now finding myself in acute internal pain (untrue). The first worked, and I called Tony.

He had realized—last night—that we had to get our own bondsman and had been working on it. But he later said my tone of voice made him realize how awful things were and that had galvanized him to speed things up. A principal purpose of the call was to mention conditional future steps to Tony in order that the cops, who all listen to a prisoner's phone call, would hear them. I told him if I wasn't out by noon to call Professor Chen, Dr. Thomson, and Robert Manning, who would contact the *Globe* about the story of my incarceration, as well as my lawyer.

I paced my cell, talking with Jerome and Al. Each gave me a phone number to call, which I memorized. Each wanted cigarettes, Al from his girlfriend, Jerome from his father. Neither had any chance of getting out before Monday when they go to court. I told them both that if I couldn't arrange for their people to bring the Newports, I'd bring some myself.

"Peril, come here," said a cop as he unlocked my cell and grabbed my arm. A bondsman called Mr. Christmas had arrived. He wanted $15. I would have given him $1500. I said I had the money. My hand was shaking as I reached for my bag of things, which was now pushed across a desk to me. My wallet wasn't there. Mr. Christmas looked as if he thought I didn't have any money after all.

With the stupidity that had marked the cops' behavior from the start, a cop said what was in the bag was all the possessions I had. My keys? I enquired. "There's no keys!" Of course, enough cops knew that I'd brought in $150 in cash that, eventually, the matter was rectified. "Be in Boston Court Thursday morning," said Christmas as he handed me a receipt.

The Boston tax-payers weren't any nearer to getting the problem of forged lottery tickets solved, but some Boston police had given themselves work on a slow night, put another name in the books, and flexed the muscles of their important but dangerous authority. As so many of them put it to me during those 16 hours, they had "done their job."

January 4, 1987, Boston

I woke up feeling sore in my hip bones, the fruit of the night-long effort in the cell to make a cold metal bench into a place of rest. But, oh, how lovely a bed is! The pleasure of being able to walk from one room to another. Something to read! The unheard-of luxury of being able to ask a question and get an answer. The magic link between me and the rest of society and the world of the phone. I never knew it could all be so sweet.

Edward and I were sitting with arms wrapped around each other in the big black study chair when the phone rang. He happened to pick it up, and it was his mother, calling to see if I was OK—he had called her to tell her the story of my arrest. He never mentioned to her that I was in the chair with him.

Dinner at Commonwealth Grille, a rather fun atmosphere on a Sunday night. I am staggered and delighted when Edward says to me, "You're the best-dressed person in the room"—it was he who has chosen what I have on. Back home, Edward chats for a while as we lie on the bed. He's come to appreciate me more lately, he said, and it's partly having Todd around—some sort of comparison there that got a bit misty in the telling. I've come to like kissing, hugging, and stroking with him even when it's not going to lead on to the fire and brimstone of an orgasm.

January 6, 1987, Boston

I plead not guilty and ask the judge for a trial date. Politely, he gives me January 27, after checking that the date will suit my attorney, Lopata.

The Diary is missing an entry that records the outcome of the court appearance. At the proceeding, Terrill was acquitted of all charges.

January 22, 1987, Boston

A flurry of newspaper writing on the events in China stimulated by a phone call from *Yomiuri* in Tokyo asking for a piece. Some papers that haven't taken anything from me for a while have come in this time—*Miami Herald* and *Philadelphia Inquirer* among them. *Globe* ran the piece nicely at the top of the page with an illustration. I hope the Koreans take it—they pay better than anyone else except the Japanese when in a good mood.

Norma Nathan has twice written about me in "The Eye" column in the *Herald*. Though a possible film of *White-Boned Demon* was the topic once, I think the trigger both times is an underswell of interest in Australia. She'd seen the Simon & Schuster ad for *The Australians* in *Publisher's Weekly*. On the phone, I was able to give her the news that Book of the Month Club has taken the book as an alternate.

I notice at the gym intense Black nervousness about homosexuality. Upstairs by the basketball court, these lovely studs haul on their street clothes over their gym gear. Few go down to shower and take a sauna, for fear they'll be thought interested in looking at other men or having other men look at them. They doth protest too much.

January 24, 1987, Boston

Winter is hitting home with icy winds and snow everywhere. The strain of the start of the renovations adds to my burden. Leaks from the roof; plumbing problems; ensuing diplomatic problems with my fellow condo owners; escalating costs. I have let the plan to get away to the sunshine slip and slip, but I needed the money for the renovation.

March 3, 1987, Boston

A rather sad farewell to Edward. We embrace but do not make it to bed. I leave notes on various practical matters, for he will look after the place.

Later, the doorbell rings. "It's Elliot, Baby." He brings Coke, vodka, and a little jar of poppers. He also brings his magnificent lips and an asshole that wants—but in the end, cannot take—my cock. "That's a nice bit of meat," he kept saying, "I want it inside me." But apparently, the head was a shade too fat for his comfort.

His thighs drove me to distraction. His cock is the size of a salami, slightly marred (for me) only by his wearing a cock ring. All this just a couple of hours after Edward said goodbye before my trip around the world. Before 2 AM, I had to say it was time for me to resume packing and for Elliot to go home. I walked out into the night with him; he took a cab to Dorchester, and I posted letters. A cold, clear night.

March 4, 1987, Los Angeles

Luther picks me up in a smart new car, and we go to his pad in San Pedro. He is pleased to play the host; I am pleased to be his guest—though as his eagerness for sex becomes plain, I half wish I had not received Elliot last night. Right at LAX, he asked about Edward but thereafter not.

"I feel OK about AIDS," he says as we whiz along an LA freeway, "because I haven't had anal sex since I was a child." I guess he has forgotten at least one golden evening with me when he was a law student.

Before dinner, we shower and then make love. "That's the best blow job I ever had," he says as he pulls on a pair of underpants. Next morning, we did it again. I was amused that the first time he said, "Gee, we both had a lot saved up." Tell that to Elliot.

I should not have drunk so much wine on the Boston-LA flight; the hazards of First Class.

The next morning, we ate breakfast at one of those wonderful Californian coffee shops where the booths are grand, the waitresses are great fun, and the coffee flows without request.

"Have you had any more parties?" he asks with a lovely smile. Alas, I have had few. I suppose it is Edward plus AIDS.

March 6, 1987, Honolulu

As I look around the Hyatt-Regency Hotel, I feel an aching loneliness. Edward would love this, I think, as I look over the lovely rooms and view of the ocean. Or I imagine being here with Henry and feel a surge of pleasure. I'm just unhappy at being here by myself.

I have a yearning for perfect unity and harmony, and not being able to thrill at getting fucked is a detraction from this. Yet if it had been otherwise, I might have been dead by now. Oh, the anguish of beautiful things being flecked with ugly flaws; and of life itself being a losing game with death!

I need to think things over one at a time, come to a resolution, and then think of something else. While I'm away, there is very little I can resolve over Edward and me. Of course, I can gauge how much I miss him. I can see how much I enjoy the reunion with Henry. I can test the possibility that I'm becoming sexually addicted. I can try to face my overall insecurity. But except for Edward's handling of renovations to my condo and the mail and messages, I should not think about Edward in the coming weeks.

Two issues nag: growing older and the feeling that nothing has quite replaced religion and socialism as a raison d'être for my life. Mistaken the pair may have been—but is writing itself, with its egotism and necessary self-preoccupation, a sufficient moral purpose?

Is loving another person that purpose—but then you're wanting things from him all the time, and he from you. Perhaps my fiction can stand upon a moral concern? I must reread George Orwell's "Why I Write."

March 7, 1987, Honolulu

Being a fairly candid person, I see that I just don't know the answers to many political and philosophic dilemmas, or I'm agnostic about the answers. It's a small step from that to say you can't write because you're not convinced you have anything to say. Maybe exploring some of these things could help me meet Jim Thomson's question of why I have become more conservative and with a half-belief in Buddhism. (Yet the moment Buddhism became a philosophy in my mind, I'd reject it as a system too).

AIDS reduces the worthwhileness of mounting a long-term quest for meaning or achievement. AIDS is a metaphor for the basic helplessness of the human condition. Never admitted, there are gaps between what the newspapers say and what doctors say to patients, and, thirdly, life as its actually lived; what people do with each other in bed defies prudence, reason, and certainly science.

Somehow the past is never enough. Even if I were to publish my huge Diary, and some may marvel at the fun I've had, it wouldn't help my future—I'd still have to strive, still have to be good, and still feel the ebbing away of youthfulness.

So much of what we call love seems to be sex, and so much of what we call friendship is a contract of people wanting things from each other—if they don't get them, the friendship sags. When I have a lot of sex, I get tired. But when I don't have it for a couple of days, I think of nothing but sex.

The lesson Henry and I have learned over two to three years is that absence doesn't always make the heart grow fonder; it can lead to detachment.

The magnificent thing about youth is that it's the unexamined phase of life. In middle age, everything gets appraised, one sees the flaw, and feels the doubt. To me now, looking closely, everything is unsatisfactory, including myself. Youth doesn't know what it wants, a state of grace. Youth doesn't think twice; how splendid.

So far, this trip is proving that I want Edward, not because I can't do without him but because I love him.

March 18, 1987, Melbourne

Dinner at Ormond College, which has a strange power to delight me. The first and second crews have won the competition today, and so there's a celebration. Master David Parker, whom I sit beside, says morale in higher education is low. "We have a government," he says with his little half smile, "that pays people more to be on the dole than to study."

Carney Fisher is in good form, stressing his Catholicism. Like me, he doesn't any more enjoy the company of his mother. In our culture, he argues, the lack of big households and compounds and extended families makes it all the harder when an old person loses accustomed independence. Others are not there. Others are not used to caring for such a person.

"I'm too old now to fall in love again," he says as we drink at the Exchange Hotel on Commercial Road amidst the cigarette smoke and timid cruising of Melbourne youth. "If I lived with someone again, it would be separate bedrooms, and a separate way of life."

A scattering of men attracted me, including two Timorese. After I dropped Carney at OC, I went to the Steamworks. Pleasant to relax, take a sauna, and shower. I don't think anyone was interested in me, though you never know with Australians. So soft and coy, you have to approach them three times, whereas, in the USA, one glance is enough. In Australia, a tiny look out of the corner of the eye is the equivalent in America of lunging at your dick.

March 24, 1987, Melbourne

Multicultural Australia, for all its improvements over the old Australia, will be less engagingly modest than that old Australia.

Martin, of Maltese origin, sitting with two girls in a bar of the Regent Hotel. Glances are exchanged. He goes to the bathroom; I go to the bathroom. Nothing as crude as showing a hardon. Just, "G'day, how are you?" I said we ought to get together sometime. "I could be free now," he responds.

Brazenly, he leaves his female companions and comes to bed with me. He sucked and rimmed well. He had trouble not coming the moment we got into bed. Probably he was puzzled by me. I loved talking with him. The way we could look into each other's eyes and understand each other—it's not that often with an Australian this way.

March 31, 1987, Sydney

At the post office in Darlinghurst Road, is that an Aborigine making a phone call? I touch my dick and lean over the balustrade opposite the phone booth. Soon he looks. When he gets off the phone, he sits down on the step. It only takes a couple of remarks, and I ask him back to my room at the Gazebo. He is not Aboriginal but Maori. "I love shaved balls," he says as he sucks them. We each want to fuck, but the compromise works fine. I love his tongue and his thick lips, and his thick brown hand, which gets eight-days' worth of my cum.

At night, Sut, an MA student in Bangkok, comes over and creeps into my bed. The only preliminary was a glance in the street and my mention of my hotel and room number. He's engaged to a Singapore girl. "I'm going to get married eventually," he says before he leaves.

April 2, 1987, Sydney

With Mark, the American basketball player, it was a case of seduce-me-while-I-don't-look. We sat there watching TV—talking and watching *à la fois*—not my style. "Do you mind if I get comfortable?" he asked, and I made as if to go and let him go to bed.

But no, he didn't have that in mind. In his red robe, he lay down to watch TV and, bit by bit, I moved from a sitting position to a reclining position at right angles to him. Somehow the robe moved up his leg a bit, and soon I saw this lovely Black dick stretching along one leg. I could also see the balls and most of the crotch. The more I looked, the harder the dick got.

As we chatted on and he drank beer, I grabbed his leg in a friendly locker-room way. When he didn't move away, I just leaned across and started licking his cock. From my angle, it was hard to get under the thing enough to start licking up the shaft; but eventually I got the telegraph pole to stick up. Throughout, he kept watching TV. His only word was a halfway suggestion that I get Vaseline from the bathroom.

April 4, 1987, Hong Kong

At Kai Tak,[259] Henry meets me and Alan is with him. I wasn't really upset about this—I half expected it—but Alan's proprietorial way with Henry did surprise me. We talked in my room at the Shangri-La Hotel for an age. I was on Sydney time, three hours ahead of Hong Kong time, so I was tired. At one point, I asked if they'd care to stay the night rather than go all the way back to Shatin. "There wouldn't be anywhere to sleep," says Henry. This made things clearer. At another point, Alan, assuming the role of planner-in-chief, said, "Tomorrow night, will we eat at our place, or would you rather go out?"

When Henry came in by himself to see me next morning, I knew what I wanted and, in the end, I got it. I wanted to tell him it was fine with me about Alan, but I also wanted to establish that we were still close and could still enjoy our occasional get-

---

[259] Kai Tak Airport was the international airport in Hong Kong from 1925 until 1998.

togethers, free of what he was doing with Alan or me with Edward or whoever. Later we had an excellent lunch in the Chinese restaurant of the hotel.

During it, he was not the Henry of old, and I think we both realized we had an agenda before us. Yes, he had a grievance against me. He felt I wasn't frank about the resumption of my tie with Edward. He didn't like my Diary. He felt my visit last year was terribly short. He was upset at the delay and further delay over my coming to see him this year.

Wanting to change our relationship to a lower gear, I basically welcomed all this—though emotionally, there was a pang from last night—and I did not greatly resist his points. Their implication—that I was no longer head over heels for him—was correct. In his own mind, he has been torn and may still be so; but I did not try to grab him back from the brink of his growing obsession with Alan.

We went back to my room. I think Henry didn't intend for us to make love, but I just tempted him beyond the point of him being able to say no. "You're so hard to resist," he murmured as I pulled his shirt up and started licking his tummy and chest. It was enormously satisfying.

So, I felt in the end that despite the emotional pangs, we had enjoyed seeing each other again. It was a safe landing in what could have been a wrenching situation. "Do you respect my new choice?" he asked me, and I said I did, and that I wanted to go on seeing him from time to time, as we had just done at the Shangri-la.

April 7, 1987, Bangkok

A ravishing pleasure simply to be in Thailand. Handsome, polite people on all sides. Warmth. Amiable hubbub. Sense of an ancient and proud culture. Near the Montien Hotel, a guy on the street urges me to come to a festival to watch "fighting fish." Another offers "lady doing it with snake."

At a bar on Suriwong Road, an *embarras de richesses*. I end up fucking a handsome guy of my own height and weight, called Nai. Square-faced, he is from Pattaya. Just as we emerge from our cubicle to shower, from next door, the guy whom I had admired second best to Nai emerged; he smiled and grabbed my sticky cock as he walked by. Exhausted from the passion with Nai, I lamely murmured, "Next time." Meanwhile, I had left Lung at the Lonely Boy; he expected me to return by eleven. Affectionate, but hardly a match for Nai's sensuality and athleticism.

Thailand: the shaft of light in a temple foyer; orchids; purple silk; patience and grace.

April 8, 1987, London

Not traveling often from the Far East direct to Europe—though I did go from Hong Kong to Paris last year—I'd forgotten how long the trip is, and today I felt a wreck. Apart from phoning a few people, I did little.

One has to come to Britain to be addressed as "Governor" by a cabbie. But in many ways, the country is doing better than in the recent past. I love the big solid, comfortable dining rooms and the recent innovation of a phone card that allows you to make all calls without coins.

Although the Park Lane Hotel is quite stylish, British men in cardigans troop in at breakfast time and sit down grim-faced to bowls of porridge.

At the hotel, I meet a nice Portuguese-British "hall boy" with blonde hair and wearing a maroon uniform. We talk a bit. I ask him up. "Sir, there's something I must tell you, Sir. I'm straight, Sir," he adds as apologetic as a spaniel. "You're a nice man, Sir, but I've tried it, Sir, and it's not my style."

All this didn't stop him showing extraordinary curiosity when, later on, Russell came upstairs to my room. He waylaid us both near the lift. "When am I going to see you?" I do not have the patience for these British games.

Calls back and forth to New York after I discover that the fax of corrections to the Simon & Schuster pages that I sent from Sydney never reached Fred Hills. Can Corgi have been so careless, or did the thing reach the vast empire of Simon & Schuster and get lost on its way to Fred's office?

Anyway, Leslie Ellen is efficient and charming on the phone. The indexer loves my book, she says, "and this is rare because indexers get so jaded." She tosses out the shaky opinion that the book is going to make me "rich and famous."

April 10, 1987, London

Kate Parkin comes in for breakfast—which I pay for—and I am left with the impression that with Judy Curr taking over the running on my book, London folds its hands and merely hopes. "Word of mouth will make this book," she purrs, in the classic cop-out. Her enthusiasm at the moment is for the Sinatra book, *The Rotation Diet*, and a novel, *Destiny*.

Leisure Club has turned mine down. The second book club, BCA, is taking a "second look"—and, according to Kate, is in its Australian version just now considering the book. The National Maritime Museum is gorgeous as a French palace—I can see why it loses money—and the Australia 200 exhibit, which I get a preview of, is good. A wonderful old Dutch globe, the first one ever to show Australia. A newly-found portrait of James Cook. The staff betray touches of fuddy-duddyism and elitism. Mr. Christopher Terrell, whom I talk with, loves and knows the seas more than he does Australia. One cannot blame him; Australia is very remote for most Britons.

A drink with Abner Stein at the Park Lane Hotel, and I am pleased to find he's a nice guy after all. Abner thinks I should be more demanding with Radic over *White-Boned Demon*! He wants me to send him the gist so that he can approach Heinemann's lawyers about it; a letter from them could help the bargaining if, indeed, bargaining is going to occur.

April 13, 1987, Boston

The BA flight at Heathrow is delayed, but happily, the First Class lounge (still thanks to *National Geographic*) is a beauty. I drank champagne and read the Sunday papers.

It was quite a good trip though many achievements were indirect. I corrected the Bantam pages. I laid plans for Australian publication with the excellent Judy Curr. Got some feel for the atmosphere in which the book will come out there. Corrected the

Simon & Schuster pages and their funny map. It all took a lot of time. It was a rich trip in terms of keeping up with friends and family.

April 16, 1987, Boston

Felipe comes in for dinner and we look at each other. It is nearly two years since we made love. We embrace, we kiss, and for a long time, we stand in the hallway holding each other, then we get too hot for equanimity and go into the bedroom, take off our clothes, and make love. Still the quiet, passive, lovely Felipe.

April 17, 1987, Boston

I feel stronger today, and a glimmer of hope appears to clear the mountain of paperbacks that sit on me. Julius phones from prison. Will I visit him; will I send him some money?

At night, after Edward has gone to Connecticut, I watch Bernstein conduct the Vienna in Brahms Second Symphony and peacefulness comes over me, as if Good Friday still has some hold even over an infidel. As last night watching the *Cosby Show* with Edward, I find TV in the evening—a bit of it—good for me, cancels my various compulsions. I suppose, in the end, it could become another compulsion.

April 21, 1987, Boston

Good to catch up with the gang at Helen's party for the Boston Marathon. A Japanese guy won the race, though few at this ritual party pay much attention as the sweating entrants grind past the windows.

The old problem of Edward's ghost arose. Not only in Lee's questions, but in bed. Knowing Edward was coming over tonight, I didn't want to come, hot as I was. Lee begged me to fuck him, but I resisted. Then, with my cock between his massive smooth legs, I got to the point of no return and pulled my dick above his body and jerked off onto his neck and chest. A good orgasm, but spiritually a silly compromise that got the worst of two worlds. In the end, Edward and I slept together in the big bed after dining pleasantly at Bangkok, but he, too, was not in the mood to do much.

April 22, 1987, Boston

A difficult conference call with Fred and the chief copy editor at Simon & Schuster over the index for *The Australians*. Fred reads me extracts from the *Chicago Manual of Style*, which says you don't index all references to a name or place—only "significant" ones. Trouble is the omissions I noted in my letter the other day are significant ones, even by the Chicago definition.

I felt an engulfing sadness all day, and it only intensified when Edward came in at midday. The reason was that last night I gained pleasure but not happiness from the sex with Lee; in the thought and company of Edward, I find happiness but no sexual pleasure. I didn't tell Edward about Lee's visit; it seemed too sad to speak of the anguish I feel.

Reggie comes by for our first meeting since my return. "You look different!" he keeps saying. At times it is thinner; at other times, a new look in my eye. The same routine. That always pleasant reacquaintance and almost re-sizing-up. Happily, it each time issues into lust. But in between is the stage of Reggie expressing anxiety. Often it is about AIDS. Tonight, it was about Caroline "finding out." The setting of a wedding date—thank God, not until June 4, 1988—has focused his mind. Soon we go upstairs, which is the beginning of the physical stage.

Watching a film called *Getting It* was the occasion for our entry into the kingdom of the flesh. I had shaved my balls, using a fancy French shaving cream, hoping for his tongue—not his cock—up my asshole. In the end, I got only his finger because we got so hot on the couch that we both came there, never making it downstairs, full nakedness, baby oil, massage, and the rest. How do you say: "If anything should happen between you and Caroline, I would be here to welcome you."

He likes the feel of my skin and attributes it to using Vaseline lotion that he suggested. I smile and agree, though Edward thinks that it was he who introduced me to this product. Having told me as he arrived that he's given up drinking, he put away four Heinekens.

April 23, 1987, Boston

Well, John from Roxbury is nice. How I love that color skin—a sort of cinnamon. A cut dick, an insatiable love of sex, and is a capable guy who studies hard at community college. I hope we can meet again. Halfway through, as we stared into each other's eyes, I said, "Oh, we can have good times together!" and he rejoined: "Yes, we certainly can!"

April 25, 1987, Boston

I tell Edward I am under too much strain with the loss of confiding in each other, and his physical withdrawal. I cried when I sensed a lack of warmth from him. I told him that three and a half years of knowing him had taught me, for the first time in my life, the meaning of loneliness. In the end, he held me in his arms and said, "I think we can work this out." Yet I am beginning to wonder. If I hear one more word about "pressure," I will suggest that, at some point, pressure turns into masochism.

Later:

I found out tonight it's very hard to cry and maintain a raging hardon at the same time. In some ways, the Combat Zone is a real and genuine place. Its coin is sex and money. Out in the suburbs, these two also fuel nearly all, but few admit it.

April 29, 1987

Reggie came in and we had a great time. I'm going to rent a beeper for him, and he's to do some shopping for me. This will be explained to Caroline, who will then find my contact with Reggie entirely reasonable. That is the theory.

Edward came in to look at the front deck problem. I thought he was quite nice to Reggie, but a little incident happened at the end. Saying goodbye, he said "Jimmy."

Reggie corrected him, apparently (I didn't hear this) in a tone of voice that Edward thought smart-assed. As he swept down the spiral stairs, Edward said, "Reggie, Arthur, Jimmy, whatever ..." Reggie felt this was insulting, and I did too. Later Reggie asked me how I let Edward behave so arrogantly.

April 30, 1987, Boston

I asked Edward if anyone had fucked him while I was away. "If the answer's no, you won't believe me, and if it's yes, you'll be upset." He did tell me about a guy he met at the Y, who fucked him; they just met the once. He tried to think I was upset, but I wasn't, and I didn't let any flicker of sadness show.

Junior comes in and insists he's a straight guy. From Jamaica, he's lived in the States for quite a while. He's had sex just about only with girls, but "I like being with men, I know that." We sat and talked for a long time, and I didn't know whether he'd accept an advance. I had my hand on his knee. He didn't move away.

Then he just put his arms around me and embraced me and kissed me. He didn't want to get fucked or to suck, but we had a great time. I began to suck him, thinking he would then do the same to me. He came almost immediately in my mouth. I soon had a fantastic orgasm in his hand, shooting across his chest.

Afterwards, I felt disturbed about the danger of having had his cum in my mouth. I just didn't expect it; he said he didn't either. But when he said he's only done it with girls for a long time, and that rarely, I forgot about it. Since January, he said, he's been very lonely, and meeting me was a great thing for him. I noticed he liked us to lie, holding each other tightly, as we did this and that. He is studying for a management exam next month. He is working hard and I do hope he passes.

May 1, 1987, Boston

BL calls to say *Omni* magazine wonders if I'd do a piece on the I Ching and the concept of *qi* in China. I say I'll think about it. Later in the day, I call BL back with the suggestion that I do two pieces, the China one and one on crocodiles in Australia. She is dubious.

I write to Fred Hills about the welcome, but in its detail amazingly gauche, notice in *Publishers Weekly* last week about *The Australians*. "Hot Hardcovers for Summer" was the heading, and under "Etcetera" was a paragraph about my book as one which traces Australian history from its origins to today! The cheapest possible effort—by Simon & Schuster, I assume—to piggyback on *The Fatal Shore*. And the crazy thing is that the strengths of *The Australians* are totally different from those of Hughes's book[260]—contemporary, warm, personal, and somewhat upbeat.

I was not looking for anything today, but Davey's body and especially his shapely, cut dick caught my eye in the gym. I got a hardon in the sauna. He saw it, and I saw him seeing it. Later, I took the chance to brush against him. Drying ourselves by the lockers, there was a chance to talk. I simply asked him: "Would you like me to suck your dick?" And this rather conservative half-Hawaiian replied, "Yes, I would. Where do you live?"

---

[260] Robert Hughes, The Far Shore: The Epic of Australia's Founding (1986)

Davey is handsome, smooth-skinned, and possibly a little vain. As a graduate student, he was fascinated that I am a writer. But after the excellent sex, he remarked that he was still stunned at how quick it all was: "I mean for someone to play with his cock like you did in the sauna, and then for me to find an hour later that I've been to bed with this man ..."

May 2, 1987, Boston

I awake with thoughts of two things racing through my mind—the renovations and Edward—and by the time I've finished my first cup of coffee, I'm convinced that during this weekend, I must keep every thought about those two matters out of my mind.

Spring seems here, in time for the opening today of the new Orange Line.[261] The nearest station, just outside my study window, is smart in brick and silver, with its glass windows a match for my new greenhouses.

Reggie calls at noon and comes puffing and panting with fatigue and "the heat." He watched a video while I finished up a paragraph I'm working on. I persuade him to take a shower. He feels fresher, and I then show him how I feel about him by rimming him. He nearly dies, gasping that this is the best thing that's ever happened to him.

He wasn't in all that passionate a mood, but I was quite content to caress, ride, and pump him. His body turns me on every bit as much as that first afternoon I met him at the swimming pool several years ago. Later he reckoned it was more than five years ago.

At one point, I mentioned that I'd been to *Room with a View* with Nancy last night. He asked me questions about her. Then he said with a smile, "You know, I love to hear you talk about a girl."

Just after the orgasms, a key turns in the door. It's Edward, and Reggie is furious. "I'm getting out of here," he rasps. I calm him down, and turn on the shower for him when I find that Edward is safely ensconced in the other bathroom. Reggie subsides and, in the end, the three of us chat very pleasantly. Later, after Reggie leaves, Edward says with pleasure that Reggie noticed how nice his arms look. Edward volunteers that Reggie is extremely good-looking.

Ken Mayer is overworked and wanting to dissect the whole world as usual, would not go to any of the restaurants I suggested. We ended up in a poor Vietnamese-Chinese place. My only meal out in two days is a fizz. Still, it's always a stimulus to talk with Ken. No good news on AIDS. In fact, a little bit of evidence has emerged from the Boston Study that receptive oral sex can turn someone who has repeatedly tested negative seropositive. Compared with three to four years ago, I have become reckless in regard to this issue.

May 5, 1987, Boston

Reggie comes in as planned, and it happens that Edward is upstairs, watching TV and eating two hot dogs. Edward has a meeting within 40 minutes, but that does not stop

---

[261] It replaced the old Washington Street elevated line. The station Terrill refers to is the Massachusetts Avenue station, around the corner from his condo on St. Botolph Street.

him throwing Reggie and me into a funny frame of mind. "Take your coat off," he says to Reggie as the three of us sit before the evening news. "Take all your clothes off!" This pissed Reggie off.

Later, Edward said to Reggie, "Do me a favor—take some of the Star Market shopping bags upstairs." Reggie, moving to do so, says, Sure, anything you wish. Edward. eyes gleaming, says, "Anything I wish?" This sort of thing turns Reggie off.

May 7, 1987, Boston

Hank called. He's in Boston. Two nights ago, driving down from Montreal, he was approaching my house when he saw two things that decided him against ringing my doorbell. Edward walked into my house. And a little while later, Edward and I came out of the house and walked down Mass Ave. Hank drove away to David P's place. Beauty makes prima donnas.

An evening with Edward which brought us closer than we had been in weeks. When I got back from playing squash with Ron, he was sprawled on my bed. I massaged him, taking his clothes off one by one, and an hour or so later experienced a massive, sustained orgasm. Afterwards, he looked at me like a child examining an animal in the zoo. Troubled as I think he is—by something—as long as we can have times in bed like that, all is fine.

May 8, 1987, Boston

Bill Garrett, boss at *National Geographic*, summons me to his presence. I accompany him from Boston University to the airport. Bill doesn't seem to care a hoot about the Aboriginals story, he just likes me, but I am sending it to Mac anyway in a couple of days, and I will get Barbara to exact payment; enough is enough in delays over pictures.

May 9, 1987, Boston

Tonight at Harvard, a grand retirement dinner for Ben Schwartz, who turns out to be quite dignified in retirement. Everyone is there with all their small talk. As Hart dominates the informal conversation, Henry Rosovsky recalls for me that he once met Mandy Rice-Davies—she was running a Chinese restaurant in Israel.

I should learn a lesson: stress the positive; nearly everyone has given you something; of course, it could have been more—as with Ben not backing me for tenure—but precious in a flawed world.

There was much reference to how Ben surmounted Harvard's non-welcome to Jews. If so, that's well in the past.

May 10, 1987, Boston

Lee says he's having "hallucinations" about me. Can he come over; can he sleep the night? He'll do everything in the book all night long, he says, except clean out the kitchen ... I said I'd think about it.

I am reading the Sarah Davidson biography of Rock Hudson. She has done a good job. Hudson—a bit to my surprise—comes over as immensely talented but shallow, a real American hero, but not the kind I like much.

Hart[262], again, all day. He could have had a great campaign theme: Make Love Not War. And Mrs. Hart could have saved the situation by announcing from Denver: "I too spent last weekend with someone. I forgive Gary, I hope he'll forgive me. In this era of a new understanding of human ties, I hope America will forgive us both."

On a golden early evening, I took the Orange line to Washington Street, and there was Elliot. He'd called once while I was out of the country, and Edward had told him to wait until I returned. Back home, he sucked me as gorgeously as usual. As I began to come, I cried out loudly and Elliot said to shush, "The Manager'll hear you!"

I asked him about the coke he did while at my house. He said it was given by a friend and normally he doesn't shoot coke. I hope that's true.

At Chinatown station, I was propositioned by several girls; all seemed surprised when I wasn't interested. "I didn't know you were gay," one eventually said. The ultimate weapon.

May 11, 1987, Boston

Cheekun descends from Melbourne. He is sad in the eyes, no doubt because he's recently found out he's positive to AIDS. He says, after hearing my summary of the situation with Edward, that I shouldn't end it, if I don't want another stable tie. Just withdraw the house keys. The type of tie Edward and I have, he says, normally doesn't last long.

May 12, 1987, Boston

Unexpectedly, Edward and I talk to a Gay Collective Line, and after it, talk until 2 AM. It may be beyond my capacity to satisfy him, he says. Last time we made love, he said, it was better for me than it was for him. It's hard to satisfy the other if he doesn't let you touch his cock, his asshole, or his tits. "It's not that I don't want to go to bed with you." Now what does this mean?

Has Edward willed that I dissatisfy him; not accepting the gay aspect of himself, he must oppose me as a gay and his link with me. I said he seems to dehumanize everything to do with Gay-ness.

May 14, 1987, Boston

In Mass Ave, as I wait for the bus to a party for Fudan University, a woman with a leaflet in her hand says, "Would you like to live forever in paradise?" "Why not?" I ask and smile.

---

[262] Gary Hart, frontrunner for the 1988 Democratic presidential nomination until he withdrew in May 1987 amid allegations that he had had an extramarital affair.

May 15, 1987, Boston

Cheekun and I went to a concert at Emmanuel Church to benefit the Aids Action Committee, then we slept together. At lunch at Huskie's today, he talks about his recent feeling that "nothing matters" and that "people seek unhappiness." His mother does the latter, he says. The former seems to be his way of coping with family strains. He meditates now—I wonder if it is since he found out he was positive to the AIDS virus.

Why does Edward see gays—with the spectacular exception of myself—only once? How come he can say of the guy at Lawrence, if his dick was 8 rather than 6, he would have put down the phone and gone out to see him? It must be taken into account that I am much older than Edward. Also, that I do focus more on sex.

May 16, 1987, Boston

Edward and I are lying—chastely—on the little bed when Reggie rings and is on his way round. I tried to delay Reggie, but they overlapped. Reggie came straight into my study and, when Edward had finished his exercises and shower, he knocked on the door and then came to chat. I was so hot for Reggie that I could hardly keep from coming as soon as we got into the bed. Eventually, I came a huge, long orgasm as he squatted behind me and finished me the way I like. Afterwards, instead of jumping into the shower, we stayed lying together and talked. He's worried about Caroline's questions, though he acknowledges it could be more his imagination than her suspicions. One trouble, he goes home high on Heineken and perhaps smelling of cum—at least of a shower.

May 17, 1987, Boston

At the Y, the new guy, Sam, responds to my overtures. "Where do you live?" he asks. On leaving, I gave him a slip of paper with the address. Soon after 5 PM, the doorbell rang and it was Sam. He came up, left a bag of stuff on the couch.

We watched videos upstairs, on the couch in the far side of the room. Moving to the floor, we made love watching *Forbidden Black Fantasies*. We overturned a bottle of baby oil on the rug and Sam's underpants. He went home without any.

In the evening, Ken Mayer calls, and the hidden agenda in his recent chats with me came out. "I think you should exchange your bisexual boyfriends for a gay boyfriend." I doubt it.

May 18, 1987, Boston

Mac from *National Geographic* calls to say the Aboriginals piece is "quite brilliant." It has "everything in it that anyone could possibly want, with wonderful quotes, and a superb laying out of the issues." The second $5000 will be on its way. I phone BL to tell her to send in the invoice for the extra monies due for extended fieldwork, now that the piece is accepted.

She says so far, no foreign rights sale has been made for *The Australians*. "It will be more difficult than with *White-Boned Demon*," she said ominously.

When Reggie comes in, I talk of dildos, and he doesn't like it. "Remember, I'm in love with Caroline." I said I was sorry. It transpired that he doesn't like people saying sorry. I live and learn. He has on new brown shoes—Caroline bought them for him, just a week after I bought him a new black pair.

Later, Edward calls. Reggie answers the phone and, later, I take it downstairs. Edward wants to come round to work on a paper. I replied that it probably wasn't a good thing for our friendship for him to come round now. Pause. "I'll go now," said the spoiled kid.

Reggie feels caught in the middle. It's nothing to do with you, I say, the tension between Edward and me.

Often, I have proffered facilities to Edward. But since he flirts with people who are in my house—given the unsettled nature of our own tie—I felt I should sound a note of caution about him coming round.

Reggie hands me back my keys, his eyes clouded with sadness. How important keys can be! Upstairs, after the call from Edward, Reggie's chief complaint was that despite all, Edward still had the keys. Tonight, it may be that I lost both Reggie and Edward. If so, Ken's remark last night becomes prophetic. Will Edward and Reggie together destroy my tie with both? The bisexual impossibility!

May 19, 1987, Boston

Some more first serial submissions sent off; at times, I have a sinking feeling that the book will be taken as a travel book—and reviewed as such.

At Harvard, BZY gives a good, if slightly over-academic, talk on the prospects for the forthcoming 13th Congress of the Chinese Communist Party. I drop the bound galleys of *The Australians* off to Deanne Lord and then come home, filled with a desire to talk both to Reggie and Edward.

Edward wasn't at work, but I left a message. Reggie phones and, at the end of it, we both felt better—he's taking back his keys tonight or tomorrow. He said his main worry—it really tossed him—was that he was getting into the middle between Edward and me; and that possibly Edward would get mad and "do something" to expose Reggie's tie with me to Caroline.

May 19, 1987, Boston

As the weather improves, the Korean guy opposite on Mass Ave starts to be visible again. How I like it when he has engine trouble and he pushes his head down inside the front of his sports car. From my study window, I watch him bend and twist, those perfect limbs making a ballet.

May 20, 1987, Boston

I'm expecting Reggie when a key turns in the door and Edward appears. He puts my iron on the desk. He goes to the pile of gay magazines and takes away two or three that are his. He fetches his blue jacket from the front room. He hands me back my keys. He says he owes me "an infinite amount" and "wishes me well." He is so hurt that it kills me to look at him. And the guy who somehow has got tangled up in things is due to walk in the door at any moment. Edward leaves—that talk he and Reggie were going to have is not appropriate for now.

Reggie got intrigued by the ginseng and tried some. He said he'd take some home, but I pointed out that Caroline might ask too many questions. Why would he be needing ginseng if the sex with her was all the sex he was having? Within two hours, Reggie and I had made tender love, and I was in a suit sipping white wine with Caroline. (In between, I played squash with Dave, trying to hide my red eyes).

May 23, 1987, Boston

A talk with Edward goes quite well, and we end up more realistic but with a tender embrace. We are going to take a step back from each other—but, once more, it's probably not over. I just wasn't ready to call it quits, and in his own way, I guess he wasn't either.

"Study hard," I say as he leaves. I know it's for the best that he no longer has the keys.

I'm still the little boy who used to feel abandoned when his mother went into town for a day's shopping. And I'm still the romantic who loves the impossible chase. Anything I really have—

at present, Reggie—threatens to disappoint. What really entices me is what is almost out of reach.

Not long after Edward left, I took my *COMM*[263] outline to the Northeastern University library to review it, but hardly had I begun when, in the music section, my eye fell on a handsome guy with a bag of books. "Why don't we drop by your place, then?" he said when I told him where I lived. He's a musician and a waiter.

Jayden has a lovely body and great charm. I wanted very much to fuck him, and he enjoyed my finger up his ass, but he demurred. Soon after we finished, he was talking about renting my small room. His only fault was talking during the sex.

May 24, 1987, Boston

After the afternoon seminar on Chinese historiography, Mike Bessie asks me what I'm going to write after *The Australians* (which he kindly dispatched to Colleen McCullough in the hope of a comment from her) as we drink a glass at 33 Dunster. I tell him about my quandary over the moral purpose behind writing. "You write because its 'you' to write," he says.

During the drinks at elegant 17 Quincy, preceding JKF's 80th birthday party, John Rawlinson and his wife come up, introduce themselves and say that for years—God, it's more than a decade—they have wanted to tell me of their delight at my "annihilation" of Bill Buckley on a *Firing Line* program. I thanked them. Then I asked, "But was the point of view I expressed right?"

---

[263] China on my Mind, eventually published as China in Our Time: The Epic Saga of the People's Republic from the Communist Victory to Tiananmen Square and Beyond (1992).

"Oh, don't ask such a thing," says this quiet scholar.

I did not speak during the dinner session—what more is there to say about John?—though I was tempted to mention his global reputation, which had not come up, and also to muse aloud as to whether Wilma and John might not go one more time to China, she to look for walls that no longer exist, he to point out that there's been a revolution.

May 25, 1987, Boston

Memorial Day, and as so often in America, there is death to mourn—the 37 soldiers killed last week in the Persian Gulf.

Ideal for my next literary steps would be a two-book contract, the novel and *COMM*. To get that, I'll have to write a couple of chapters of the novel. Later, contracts in hand, I could perhaps work on the two books together, alternate days or weeks.

A melancholy sets in and it seems more than the hangover from last night's festivities. Perhaps it stems from a stark fact: in the past couple of months, I have lost intimate touch with three people of enormous importance to me. Henry as he accepted my withdrawal and turned to Alan. Edward as he pulled back for his own mysterious reasons. My mother as her mind fades within her body.

A talk on the phone with Joan Kennedy, who is correcting her proofs. Hopelessly unworldly, as usual, she won't discuss concrete action to help each other's books. She seems to think that books can make their own way. She'd even overlooked that, these days, booksellers send the things back to publishers in 60 days if they are not sold!

May 28, 1987, Boston

A lovely evening, whose genius began when I phoned Dion at work and asked if he'd like to drop in for a while before dinner—which I had planned with Ken Mayer, just before he goes off to a big Washington AIDS conference.

It was hot. We sipped soft drinks and caught up on all that's gone on since we last talked privately. But not of intimate things. I wasn't sure whether this sleek Black banker would be likely to take off his smart three-piece suit until nearly two hours after he arrived. Then came a moment in the front room when it seemed natural to touch each other. I found myself standing behind him with my hands pushing deep into his trousers' pockets, moving against those hard, smooth thighs.

His body is as lovely as ever. I gently went to fuck him. "I still don't do that." One can forget, or one wants not to remember. After that, I got nervous for a while and lost my hardon. We talked for a long time before Ken arrived. I told Dion I had felt intimidated by him. He looked at me quite sharply and asked how I could possibly feel that way. I didn't say anything; what I felt was that I don't often go to bed with a handsome Black guy who is also a masterful banker.

Ken and Dion get on well, so we linger over a drink before Dion goes home and Ken and I dine at Capriccio Più. Ken can't get over how different Dion is from Edward. "Dion seems so responsible."

May 29, 1987, Boston

Brunch with Curt at Thornton's and a great reunion. He is still involved with Claude, the French-Canadian, and still slowly evolving away from Bob. A bit like me with Edward, there is a feeling of deep regret and a desire—is it age creeping up?—to keep the door open.

He's going to employ Claude this summer, in the decoration of his Montreal home; we'll compare notes later as I have experience of giving Reggie odd jobs (mainly to dispel Caroline's suspicions as to why he comes to my house).

"Sex is a bugger," as the husband says to the wife in the film *My First Wife*, Paul Cox's saga of love and separation in Melbourne. Put money into the scales and one has an even more volatile mix.

Paranoid about Chinese, Curt tells the sad story of a former intimate of his who died of the disease last year. A macrobiotic diet prolonged his life for a time, but eventually, the guy grew tired of it and tired of life as it had become.

Full of questions about *The Australians*, he remembers a day in my study when he saw on my computer screen a draft of a passage about a visit to the nude beach in Sydney. "I think it will be the best-written book you've ever done," he says, and I cling to the remark like a drowning man to a piece of driftwood.

Li-li calls. "You should be in a posture of celebration, now that *The Australians* is done." I suppose she is right. But why didn't it occur to me? I fear everything, and I lack the will to live, that's why.

Jayden and I dine at Thai Cuisine, then talk long and seriously, moving from room to room in the house, about the plan of him moving in. We learn much about each other. He's a serious professional—30 years old on June 22—and rather attractive. We lay on the bed in the small room, smooching in front of the mirror, neither wanting to do too much, lest that uncertain territory between roommate and intimate friend become too quickly defined.

May 30, 1987, Boston

"After you're saved, we won't be able to do this anymore." This sentence of Reggie's blows my mind. Of all the wobbliness of bisexuality, this threw me as much as any ever has. Before we relaxed, Reggie did some shopping and other chores most efficiently. We'd agreed that he wouldn't get high anymore while he was working. As he did get high, he made another startling remark. "You're a pervert, you know that. You're teaching me bad things. The other night I was saying to Caroline things I got from you, 'Take that dick; eat that Black dick!'"

I think there's something in Cheekun's theory that, in a close tie, we unconsciously seek unhappiness at times. So perhaps, beckoning unhappiness, I put Lee into Edward's path!

Reggie and Edward are so different. Reggie is cautious yet wills his own destruction as an ordinary straight. Edward has a reckless streak and yet is fundamentally conventional. Of course, Edward does not drink as Reggie does—this, at crucial moments, makes a big difference.

June 1, 1987, Boston

The weekend discussion with Jayden about his coming here has been illuminating to me. I had to face much in looking at why I wanted it to proceed and why I didn't. My privacy I take for granted. Yet my rigidity requires a breaking down of that privacy—this was the charm of the request from Jayden. We got very close this afternoon; he said he couldn't come (at the $300 a month) if he wasn't guaranteed beyond June 21; I said that looking after everything when I was around the world was such a big thing that I needed a trial period first. Later we watched *Salt and Pepper Boys* and smooched around pleasantly.

I dined late and alone at Oceanic. Afterwards, I took a bus back. The bus was interesting, so I continued on to Dudley. Outside Roscoe's, guys hung around. Three gay types pretended to hustle.

On the bus coming home—the last bus, I think—a guy at the back looked good, and after looking at me a bit, he got off at St. Botolph Street as I did. He walked into the alley and took a piss. I did the same. Within a minute, we were in my bed. There were few words. I assumed he was pretty straight. But things just went sensually. We each fucked the other, but without coming inside. In the end, we came in each other's hands while spreadeagled against the brick wall. Soon after, we fell asleep. Intermittently through the night, he would push a leg against me, or I would lean over and stroke his dick.

I awoke and found no one beside me. A noise in the lobby had perhaps woken me. John was there, with his bag preparing to leave. We embraced. Only later did I notice my video camera was missing. And my Olympus autofocus. In the lobby, the Mitsubishi VCR was sitting; it would have gone with John had I not come out of the bedroom when I did. I rang the number he gave me and got a disconnected recording. Later I reported the theft to the Boston police and called my insurance agent with a preliminary report.

June 2, 1987, Boston

A good talk on the phone with Reyna Mathes in Sydney about Simon & Schuster's publicity plans for *The Australians*. She sounds good. A pusher but not a mindless one. Things begin with a party at Kinsella's on June 24. It should be fun—that's the way I will approach it.

June 3, 1987, Boston

Numbness is bad in legs and fingers. I suppose it has a spiritual cause: I seem to have lost almost everything that was dear to me. Reggie sets a wedding date. Signs abound that *The Australians* will gain little First Serial sales ... At the gym, Ray W tells me the

Mitchell twins, old friends of Pan, are feverishly treating themselves with experimental drugs against HIV.

Americans never ask about the basic nature of man; they ask what can a man do.

Wyatt comes in after work. and we make love for the first time in months, he first looking at his pictures of "men with the ladies." We have a great time. I love the way he cries out about my "big white dick" as I do this and that. Moreover, he sucks well, which in this day and age, one comes to appreciate. He's settled down at work, which also makes him unusual around here.

June 4, 1987, Boston

A fantastic morning with Reggie, joined at the end by Mikey. Reggie was in wonderful form, doing jobs and then getting uncontrollably horny (though when he arrived, he said his cock was worn out by too much sex). This time he made amends for his "disgusting" outburst by talking lovely dirty-talk stuff as I shot all over the bedroom.

Jayden called. Since he'd wanted to contact Reggie's sister, who works as a DJ at a radio station, I suggested he come round right away while Reggie was still here. Reggie and I were busy elsewhere, and Jayden, to my slight surprise, went straight into the bedroom. There, as he must have seen, was a trail of glistening cum across the cranberry sheets, with a baby oil bottle and Vaseline jar sitting nearby.

June 5, 1987, Boston

A Chinese boyfriend, I can hardly believe it. One from Hong Kong, moreover. I suppose I viewed Wilson through a midday session as a surrogate for Henry. We had noticed each other in the neighborhood. In fact, had he not been a Chinese—when I saw him in Mass Ave, I thought a Mainland Chinese—the hookup would have come sooner.

He is slim, handsome, slightly effeminate, a third-year engineering student at Northeastern. A bit frail, he sucked excellently. Yet the main glory of the was the kissing with which everything began and ended. His father is in construction in the New Territories area of Hong Kong. All next week, he'll be busy with exams—after that, to see him again.

June 6, 1987, Boston

Spent the afternoon with Edward, who looked refreshed and beautiful. We caught up on each other's activities for a hectic week. He has finished all his courses. Only two weeks now till graduation. His company hasn't given him a commitment for the future; nor has Barry. This bothers me.

On the couch, we lay looking into each other's eyes. When, at excruciating length, I asked what was on his mind, he said, "I am thinking about what to do with you."

I gave him the beeper as a gift for finishing his courses. I think he was pleased. Typically, he asked me when I got it and whether anyone else had the beeper number!

Later in the study, we talked about the need to realize that, though you cannot control the behavior of another, you can control your own. One gets power from this realization. You can say no to another, and at the same time, you can face the fact that only you yourself are responsible for your own affairs. You can be in charge *chez soi*; you need not worry that you are not—never can be—in charge *chez l'autre*. This point gives relief to many and offers vision to others. One is not often the source of others' problems.

He lingered on and on, and eventually the doorbell rang. It was as I knew—and by now Edward knew as well—Jayden come to fetch me for dinner. At this point, Edward, who had not wanted a drink when previously invited, said we all should have a drink. He fetched them all himself, becoming, to my dismay—yet fascination—the householder. The effect on Jayden, as later conveyed to me, was powerful.

Edward gave Jayden a detailed critique of his album, which we'd listened to during the afternoon. This was great; that was passé—as always, Edward knew so much better what others should do than what he himself should do.

Edward left, and Jayden and I dined well at Thai Cuisine. Back home, he suddenly said, as we leant over the desk together, "I know who you look like—Rock Hudson!"

June 7, 1987, Boston

My crocodiles piece is in the *Globe* today, nicely displayed. Upstairs, I do bits and pieces on the sun-dappled dining room table. My travel plan for Australia. The revision of my will. Checking over transcripts from interviews at Broken Hill, the Australian mining town.

Yet one more *National Geographic* photographer, calls with the news she's on the assignment and could I tell her something about Australia. I mention one or two Australian organizations, and each time she asks if they have a branch in NY. After that, I take it gently. I give her only bland names and addresses. God knows what she will shoot—yet in some ways, a blank slate is not a bad idea in approaching Australia.

Down in Washington Street, I met a nice young guy from Plymouth, who sucked me off. Then I dined at the new Thai restaurant and read the *Sunday Globe*.

June 8, 1987, Boston

Howard Goldberg of *The New York Times* Op-Ed page impatiently says the piece I sent him on Australia is "too background—we don't do those sorts of pieces anymore." If I do something on the Australian election, it will have to be a wholly separate piece.

I sent my article on the prospects for democracy in China to my little group of newspapers. I wonder how it will go? *Newsday* asked for it—I am a darling of theirs at present.

June 10, 1987, Boston

Sex is still a potent force in the air between Edward and me, even though we have little of it together these days. Today he calls and we arrange for him to come by. Later,

Jayden calls and says he's coming over. The timing gets out of kilter—Edward is delayed—and when Edward calls a second time, I say: "Jayden is coming over too, but that's OK with me if it is with you." His divided mind got to him. By the time he arrived, Jayden and I were in bed. Edward looked around upstairs, but he was clearly in a bad mood. He said he'd come back later, and I agreed to that.

Later, Edward and I had dinner at Commonwealth Grille and spent a lovely evening. He understood, when I explained, that my handling of the afternoon arrangements had been designed to leave the door open to a threesome. "Jayden likes you," I explained.

It's all settled about the graduation. I said I was prepared to come "anonymously" if that was best for him. He said he appreciated very much that I understand his dilemma.

June 11, 1987, Boston

Harvard commencement and in the afternoon, Ken Galbraith's garden party. He apologizes for not yet having got to the proofs of *The Australians*. Oh dear, will we have no quotes for the publicity? Frank Friedel[264] talks about FDR, on whom he is doing yet another volume. No, he wasn't like Gary Hart, he says when I ask. "The most he would do is put an arm around a woman he was drawn to, as they drove through the countryside. It was a romantic era." Some AIDS advertising stresses this, rather than condoms and so-called safe sex.

Robie Macauley is retiring from Houghton Mifflin next year. I think he feels sad about it. We talked about the double moralism and libertarianism of America, which seems this season to be especially on display with the TV evangelists, AIDS, and the Hart affair. Like me, Robie gets discouraged at times about the way images dominate public affairs.

I chat with Arthur Rosenthal[265] and Margaret for the first time in a long while. He is extremely affable. He had no idea in advance, he said, that the Welty book[266] would be a best seller. Robert Maxwell once offered him a job, but he does not like him. Margaret, now editor of *Boston Review*, rails against minimalist short stories.

Toward the end of the party, David Greenway[267] grabs me, and soon he and JB, Frankie Fitzgerald,[268] and I are eating dinner in the fish restaurant of the Charles Hotel. A time of catching up, and of savoring the process of growing older.

David and Frankie get off on the Middle East with great passion. We all feel mad at the free ride Israel gets in Washington.

June 12, 1987

Mike Lally sadly hands me back the keys to 395 after more than three months of futile efforts to sell it. Just afterwards, I met a lady from Fred Meyer's and another from

---

[264] Frank Burt Freidel, Jr. (1916-1993) American historian.

[265] Director of Harvard University Press, 1972-1990.

[266] *One Writer's Beginnings* (HU Press, 1984).

[267] Hugh David Scott Greenway, American journalist; chief of the Boston *Globe* editorial page.

[268] Frances FitzGerald, American journalist and writer. Her *Fire in the Lake: the Vietnamese and the Americans in Vietnam* won a Pulitzer Prize in 1973.

Levaux to show them round. Monday, I will select between them once I have their report, proposed price, and marketing plan.

In the evening, Tony O comes around in some distress over his tie with his boyfriend. The boyfriend is taking him for granted, playing around all the time, and it's difficult to talk to him. For the first time ever, Tony broached to me money matters over his boyfriend. "He pays me no rent, and I have no idea how much money he makes."

June 13, 1987, Boston

What a way to spend a Saturday afternoon! There should be more of them. I did letters during the morning, rewrote the will after the talk with Edward about arrangements, and then Reggie came in to do jobs. I went to the gym, and when I came back, he'd finished work and was getting mellow.

Reggie put on a gay movie called *A Matter of Size* and got horny over it. I, in turn, was horny over him, almost naked on the big old couch. Soon I was on the floor in front of him—stark naked—and he had his underpants off.

After sucking Reggie while I was on the floor, lying on my back, I got his asshole fired up with my finger and then knelt up, flipped his legs over his head, and while he continued to watch a video of a guy begging to get fucked, I got my prick inside him. I've never seen him come so much. "You finally got what you wanted, didn't you?" he said, typically, as he limped downstairs. Later, I massaged him as we lay and listened to his favorite music station. He then massaged my asshole with the vibrating machine, and I came in his hand with the machine strapped to the back of it.

"What do you use those for?" he asked, picking up a condom from the bedside table. He went on to say, "they're supposed to take away the feeling." Probably Reggie, like me, has never used them seriously.

June 14, 1987, Boston

These summer days, I think of rural Australia, playing marbles in the dust under the flowering shrubs in the churchyard. And I think of erotic summer days around the world, when everyone seems a bit more human and vulnerable than when heavily clad and when the rays of the sun lift the looks of everyone.

I turn back to my draft chapters on "The Legitimation of Chinese Socialism." Bearing in mind the style is overwrought, it isn't bad. But rather than return to it as a research project, much could be got into the novel. A character who is a professor has been working for a decade on the May Fourth Movement and the evolution of Chinese socialism...

Horrors: Tony calls late at night. He confronted his boyfriend over Reggie, despite my asking that no mention of it be made, and Richard said he does not know Reggie. God knows what this will do to my relation with Richard—in the middle of his rebuilding the second floor of my house.

June 15, 1987, Boston

Edward came in to have a look at upstairs. The weekend party for his mother went wonderfully, he said, and his parents are well. We talked about the extraordinary events of my weekend—and found ourselves in the front room. At one point, after we'd been talking about my need for some new clothes, he went over to the phone, lay on the bed, and dialed a number. It was Arlene!

He invited her to shop with us tomorrow afternoon. As they spoke, I lay on the bed, silent. After he rang off, we lay touching and talking. I began to rub the top of his head. Suddenly he leant down and grabbed my dick from out of the leg of my little blue shorts. As I massaged his head, he stroked me. Soon I took his cock—he was still dressed, tie, shoes, and all—in my left hand as I rubbed his head with my right.

"You have no finesse!" he cried when I pushed my throbbing cock at his lips. Like a stately galleon, he rose to undress. He lay on his tummy as I took the massage machine and, helped by a little oil, rubbed his back, his neck, his ass. When I also lent underneath and got at his tits, a gentle groaning began.

I licked his balls and rimmed him. Did he want his front massaged? No. At this stage, I judged he wanted something else, and I proceeded, step by step, to give it to him. First, I used my cock to play with his buttocks, slapping it against them. As a change, I rimmed him again, my thighs around his neck, and took his balls and his cock into my mouth as well. Then I got into him, first guided by his hand. I watched his expression, as his head was tilted to the right, and all his gorgeous features were on display. I pumped away. Halfway through, he rose a bit on his knees. That way, he could grab his cock. I finished off in a crouching position, a sort of double orgasm, the first flowing on into a second. He shot a big load onto the green sheets. We lay panting and then quiet like kittens.

"What's that rash on my neck?" he asked as we showered. He worries about every little spot on his skin. "I'm just not pure anymore." He told me his grades—an A and three Bs, including a B+ for French. He seems to do better when he is not with me too much. We chatted on about everything under the sun until it was time for him to go and change for tonight's harbor cruise with his graduating class.

The night of the graduation cruise, he came home in the middle of the night, having slept for a few hours in the park. Next morning, he kept asking, Why did they leave me? Friends left a bar without him, evidently because he poured beer over the head of one guy named Mark. But it seems Mark had forgiven him because when I met Mark on graduation day, he was very nice toward Edward.

We go shopping, and Arlene overwhelms. Capable and resourceful, but not as pretty as Reggie's Caroline. Wednesday, while I'm in New York, he has the class's Cape Cod picnic.

As he got dressed, I said perhaps we could ask Arlene to come to dinner with us tomorrow night. He winked and then grinned. "It's fascinating what a little sex does for you—or not such a little."

June 16, 1987, Boston

About 4 AM, Edward comes in, drunk, after some class event. He's in an adorable mood, and later in the morning, I fucked him. Later still, he stirred, I started biting his tits, and as I put my finger in his asshole, he jerked off.

June 17, 1987, Boston

Last night was a milestone. Arlene, Edward, and I went shopping, then had dinner at Atlantic Fish. Edward remarked during the steamed mussels, "Finally, after three years, the three of us are sitting down to dinner." We met at Longfellow Park, where I was at a PEN picnic. At SYMS,[269] we whizzed around, picking up this and that. Reggie has fairly good taste and is practical and seems to have my (sartorial) interests at heart.

One image I loved: as we sped toward town, the sunroof panel of Arlene's car drawn back, a song called "Lean on Me" blaring from the cassette deck, Edward was waving his arms, beating to the music, his left hand thrust high through the roof, his right out the window, the long brown fingers just in front of my gaze. It's great to see him so happy.

Behind Edward's spontaneity, I think, is a love principle. Behind my calculation is a tit-for-tat principle—debts to pay and to receive. "That'll be all. I'll have the check." It's that same "close up the hatches" spirit I have just after finishing sex, as if to say, let's tie up the transaction and steer away to something else?

NY today was brief indeed. The session at Simon & Schuster was well worthwhile. Barbara was subdued, and I think there's something on her mind, either about me or in general. Julia, the publicity director, and her off-sider Lisa struck me favorably. But the "word of mouth" phrase, which they uttered often, is a synonym for, "It's not worth us doing much publicity."

On 42nd Street, I met Eric, who came with me to a nearby cinema. I liked him, handsome and straightforward. As we watched the movie, I jerked him off. He did it to me but not to the point of coming.

After that, I went to a 25¢ video place, where—for $10—a sad, beautiful Black sucked me long and lovingly. Then I went to the hangout on 8th Avenue just off 42nd. This construction worker type from the West Indies was hanging around the sidewalk. I loved the sight of the rim of his cut dick through his pants. He wanted to fuck me. I intended only to jerk him off—an exceptionally well-turned rod. In the end, he also jerked me off.

June 18, 1987, Boston

"Letting the situation evolve" is probably good for Edward and me. It gives him space. It gives life itself its proper chance. As the poet Rilke said, "Be patient toward all that is unsolved in your heart. Try to love the questions themselves."

I was terribly depressed when, once more, no renovation work was done upstairs. I wandered the streets, went to the Y, and there met Michael, a gentle, lovely guy, a lithe

---

[269] Clothing store chain, closed 2011.

brown body and nice cut cock. We spent a pleasant time in bed, which I had to cut short to see Kay for dinner. Edward comes in looking strained. His rash has spread and is now very visible.

June 19, 1987, Boston

Richard comes in and Edward is naked in my study. Richard strides toward the study to talk to me. Edward hides near the washer and dryer. When Richard actually gets to the door, he sees Edward through the crack by the door. Edward grabs a pair of my pants.

June 28, 1987, Sydney

A difficult few days, but perhaps I will be revived a bit by tomorrow morning. In the rush of interviews, I was looking forward to contacting Johnny and Mort. When Johnny didn't call back by Saturday afternoon, I called Mort; no sooner had I invited Mort for the evening than Johnny came! I'd never had sex with Johnny and was intrigued. So, I did it with both—I couldn't get Mort to re-schedule what he had canceled for my sake.

Johnny is sensual, as I expected. Mort and I dined at the Kwangtung Palace, a Chinese restaurant in mid-city, then made love through the night. He's a nice person. Both of them I fucked.

This morning, I caught up with notes, thinking about my schedule, reading papers and magazines. I walked across the domain. The sight of the harbor in the winter sunshine, with hills in the background, and people in relaxed enjoyment of the city, all improved me.

A good ABC program on the playwright Dorothy Hewett. An ex-Communist, she now likes only people who believe in nothing. Another on Diane Cilento, on art as a way of avoiding causality. And the electrifying Greek youth prodigy pianist Sgouros[270]—despite this morning's horrible review of *The Australians* in the *Sun-Herald*, this kid's piano playing has given me inspiration to go on.

The topic of a novel: nothing matters, yet because nothing matters, every concrete little thing and act matters.

June 30, 1987, Sydney

The different interviewers teach me about the book I have written. Ray Martin, who stayed up until 1:30 AM the previous night reading the book and marking it up agitatedly, said he felt I started out a bit negative about Australia and then, when I got to the frontier states, the book warms up. Some truth in that. A Tasmanian guy, Rick Patterson, focuses on my childhood, which makes an interesting change, and I am relieved when he says Neil Brown's remarks on Tasmania are a "wonderful quote."

Roy on *Good Morning Melbourne*, asks whether I really like Melbourne, having said waspish things about it. Don Willessee on *New World* ends up by asking if I wish to

---

[270] Dimitris Sgouros (1969-), Greek classical pianist. He was not yet 18 when Ross heard him.

return to live in Australia. Derryn Hinch gently criticizes the idea that the Windsor Hotel stands for values which remain central Melbourne values.

July 3, 1987, Melbourne

Almost for the first day of the trip, I wake up and don't feel under pressure, though there's lunch with Jean Chesneaux[271] and an SBS interview on China tonight.

Judith Barr of an Adelaide radio station says of my first chapter, "It's the most evocative thing on an Australian childhood that I've read for a long time."

At the Melbourne City Baths, more cruising than in the past. A nice guy, body like mine, gets a roaring hardon. I want him. But he's terrified; he only wants to watch. He follows me wherever I go, and eventually gets me to jerk off, naked, in a cubicle while he watches from over the partition in the next cubicle. Such is Australian sex.

Another time, a Chinese, to whom I gave my phone number. Next morning, he called me at the Windsor. He's from Shanghai and is studying English. Kept saying: "You want sex, I want to talk." Eventually, we had sex—with a certain amount of talk. One flash of Chinese hypocrisy came out. "There's so many gay people in the City Baths—it's awful."

July 5, 1987, Brisbane

At a TV studio in Brisbane, the producer settles me into the guestroom upstairs with coffee and sandwiches. In bounces an effervescent blonde who says, "Well, what'a we going to talk about?" I said, groping, "Well, what's going on in Queensland?" She was a nice person, and it happened I had just seen her photo in that morning's *Courier-Mail*. She was pleased that I recognized her.

I start to think that maybe she—and not the person, a male, I thought, who the producer told me would be doing so—was going to interview me. So I started talking about my book. Then she interrupted and asked, "Well, what do you think we should put in the big rooms?"

"Do you know who I am?"

"I'm beginning to think that I don't." She was expecting the PR director for David Jones Stores; she interviews people in interior decorating for "Good Morning Brisbane." I was hustled to an adjacent studio.

July 9, 1987, Gold Coast, Queensland

Phoned Edward for his birthday. Arlene had just taken him out for a dinner of veal and bomb Alaska at an Italian place in Brookline. He had drunk wine and Spanish coffee and was bamboozled. What to make of this Arlene thing? I don't really know, and I'd rather be genuinely uncertain as to how much physical stuff there is. God knows, she's aware of the virus status, so she's making her own decisions.

---

[271] French historian (1922-2007), specializing in East Asia.

Interview at the *Townsville Bulletin*, and I'm hoping he hasn't read the bits about his city in *The Australians*. He hasn't; only got a book and the assignment yesterday. Scottish-born, he came here ten years ago and turns out to be a leftist. But what he's read of the book, he says is "extremely well written."

A radio program with Dave Perkins is excellent, with much praise from him for the book. I even managed to say which bookshop had copies—I saw them in the mall on my way to the studio.

July 12, 1987, Townsville

The general election campaign has exhausted me almost as much as the poor wretches who are in it. So hard to find mental room for talk of *The Australians*.

I look better when sun-tanned. Two half-days here are my first in the sun for a long time, and already I feel better. Not one cloud in four days. At the airport, a cabbie, who says many people in Townsville still don't lock their homes when going out for the day, gets out of the cab and takes my luggage to the curb. He finds a trolley and loads things for me—all this with too much pride to accept a tip.

July 12, 1987, Darwin

The journalist from the *Northern Territorian*, Chris Anderson, arrives in the lobby of the Sheraton to interview me and says: "I believe you've written a book; what's it about?" I remained civil.

July 17, 1987, Perth

A message awaits me at the Merlin Hotel; they want me for *Good Morning Perth*.

So sad that Craig fails to turn up. Was it AIDS fear; or Aboriginal unreliability, the kind Cary Wolinsky met in dealing with Craig last year? I lay on the bed waiting for him for so long.

On lampposts near the hotel, leaflets show a Black guy in shorts reclining beside a blonde girl in a one-piece bathing costume—the two photos have been spliced together. The heading: "Is This Your Daughter's Future?" It's from the Australian Nationalist Party, based in Victoria. Not nice.

July 24, 1987, Murdoch's Farm, near Canberra

Just after we viewed kangaroos, I asked Ian (Rupert's UK publisher) and Rupert [Murdock] both about the film *Crocodile Dundee*. Ian said it's a real reflection of Australia. Rupert's comment was on Paul Hogan. "We distributed him in Europe. Hogan's a regular Australian guy. They got to Paris and Mrs. Hogan was taken around all the great couturiers, and she came back with the sort of thing you'd buy at Woolworths in Sydney. It was hard to drag Hogan to Europe. "Aw, it's cold over there; I love Sydney, mate; do I have to go?"

When Rupert, at the end, said to me, "Are you seeing Hawke tomorrow?" it was almost like the PM saying, "Are you seeing businessman X tomorrow?" Roles reversed; Rupert, rather than the PM, seems the man of real power in this country.

July 28, 1987, Sydney

At the elegant fifth-floor bar of the Sheraton, businessmen come in for a drink after the end of a conference. "Pull up a pew." The half-sincere modesty of it. The harking back to an era of the hegemony of working-class culture, especially in Sydney.

Anzac Day[272]: The veterans remember, and then they drink until they forget for one more year.

July 29, 1987, Sydney

In the streets of Sydney, you hear quite a bit of Japanese. I think back to the 50s when if you spoke a language other than English, you'd be rebuked. I can see Sydney, which doesn't have much in the way of roots, getting almost overwhelmed by the Japanese.

Fraser McEwing[273] called from downstairs to see if I was "in the middle of something." I said I was in the middle of something. I was fucking Reggie, who said, as the phone rang, "Stay inside me as you answer it." But the cord wasn't long enough, so I had to come out, and Fraser kindly gave me ten minutes to finish up.

July 30, 1987, Sydney

A talk on the phone with Fay just before leaving for the airport. She is very taken with the USA at the moment. "We're so out of history here. In Washington, I loved the monuments and the self-confidence behind them. The Lincoln Memorial is fine because they had a Lincoln"—she cannot enthuse over Australia's new Parliament House.

Another point in America's favor is that it has, far more than Australia, blended the ethnic groups. In Australia, they come, but they don't really move into the center of things." Of course, Fay does live in Perth.

July 31, 1987, Washington

A classic *National Geographic* ritual session—projection of the Australian photos. Bill pronounces them very good, so everyone else says the same. Later in Mac's study, I point out some gaps—few prominent Australians are included, and little on city life—and Mac calmly says, "they'll find that out later on." Bill's view is that "we have covered Australia without using a single cliché" (this before I've written a word!). He's thinking of devoting a whole issue to the story, and it's to be February, rather than January.

---

[272] Anzac Day, a national day of remembrance in Australia and New Zealand commemorating all Australians and New Zealanders "who served and died in all wars, conflicts, and peacekeeping operations."
[273] Fraser Beath McEwing, Australian writer and magazine publisher.

I ask veteran Joe Judge[274] if he has any do's and don'ts for me. He doesn't. "Just take the money and run," he says mysteriously.

Afterwards, we all lunch at Joe and Mo's, and over celebratory drinks, Mac regales us with stories of Reagan, whose memoirs he is ghosting. I tell tales of Hawke and Murdoch. At National Airport, par for the course, my Eastern flight to Boston is canceled. Tired, I get onto a USAir flight and leave my baggage behind to the tender mercies of Eastern.

August 1, 1987, Boston

Boston is beautiful in the sunshine. Still, jet lag is jet lag; it gets no less as one ages. And having to go to Washington on the way home added to the complexity of the trip.

What did I accomplish in Australia? Some good new material for the *National Geographic* piece. With regard to *The Australians*, my impression is that a lot of effort has borne modest fruit—there's just too much resistance among the intellectuals to an expatriate writing about Australia. So at this stage, I expect sales to be fairly slow. It may go on selling quite well through the bicentennial year of 1988.

I'm not sure that a separate Commonwealth edition was worth all the effort and expense. One edition—published first in NY—might have done; a good reaction in the USA first might have led to a better Australian reaction.

My house is a mess. The task, I suppose, is to learn to live with grace among the fragments (sorry, Tillich). Edward comes in looking marvelous. I feel happy for him.

A first copy of the Simon & Schuster edition of *The Australians* arrives via Federal Express. Fred Hills says in a cover letter that he thinks it looks wonderful and, at first sight, I agree. Maybe the US edition will lift both the Australian and UK efforts. Australia is not yet free from the desire to have a foreign imprimatur put upon a product before it enthuses about it.

August 2, 1987, Boston

Last night turns into a reunion with Edward and a sort of review and celebration of the arrival of the book. He breezed in during the afternoon looking very good, having slept 12 hours after a birthday party last night for his former roommate. Is it nice to have no more courses to do? "Yes, but in a way there's a gap." It seems his employer doesn't have much in mind in training him for extra things. Must get him to do that résumé over. We dined at Zachary's. Later, I fucked him, but as he noticed after a while, my cock stopped being properly hard. Then he fucked me—with a condom. I asked him if it broke. He said it didn't.

Later as we prepared to sleep, he asked me why I lost my hardon. "Mind you, I'm not complaining," he said, with that grandfatherly look of strain and great responsibility on his face. He asked if it's because I'm more interested in the conquest than the act itself. A good question, but that is only a small part of the reason.

---

[274] Joseph Judge (1928- 1996), writer and editor for *National Geographic* magazine.

August 4, 1987, Boston

I must get the *National Geographic* article out of the way quickly so, that by late August, I can brace and organize myself for Simon & Schuster's publication of *The Australians*. Thereafter, I expect a tranquil period, which will give way to indecision about what book to write next—then some mad gallop will again begin, I'll be on a treadmill once more, and the idea of "getting control of my days" will become a mirage.

August 6, 1987, Boston

A bit of smooching with Jordan at the library. He was on duty in the audio section. When our eyes began to get a message, one sent from the other, Jordan told me to go into a side room. Soon he joined me. From time to time, he would say, "I must go and check," and disappear to make sure no customer was waiting. I took off my pants, but he couldn't. In the dark, we knocked over chairs, and fumbled except for an unerring grip on each other's body.

August 9, 1987, Boston

What a land! What a people! Willis sucked my cock as I hardly recall it being sucked. It was in the Pilgrim Theater. I caught his eye as we sat fairly near each other in the stalls. I took out my prick, but there were others watching. I signaled with a toss of the head for Willis to follow me down the front. He leaned over and, for the next 40 minutes, at least, devoured, adored, possessed, and all but ate my cock.

I tried to get at his, but he was so single-minded on mine that it was difficult. I was able to squeeze his tits. Then I got a finger down against his smooth Black ass. At length, I managed to reach his cock, all this while being inside his lean, handsome head. Nothing I tried to do for him distracted him from his holy task. I shot into his mouth. As he spat it out, I looked at him and just said lamely, "That was fantastic!" "Sure was!" he said. "Would you like a cigarette?"

August 10, 1987, Boston

This afternoon, Round Four at the Fenway Clinic. This time, some new questions: do the pair of you know the other one's antibody status, and a series of sex questions specifically on the activities of the pair of us together. Walking home, I felt a heavy consciousness of my sexual restlessness. Part of it was a sense of wonder that I had been with so many people. But, as well, I could not help asking myself, whether all that sex in the past six months was really necessary. Well, I suppose it wasn't; but nearly all of it was immensely pleasurable.

August 11, 1987, Boston

A whirlwind hot morning with Reggie. He falls asleep, stark naked, face down on the sofa upstairs. Later, he didn't even know that I had gone upstairs, caressed him, anointed him with baby oil, and briefly stuck my throbbing cock on his silky ass. What a few beers can do! We went downstairs and had a great time, though without orgasm. I didn't really want one, in my new mood of conservation. Orgasm is a kind of death.

In outback Australia, much anal intercourse and some bestiality. We don't have AIDS, it was reported to me. Is this because there is very little or no AIDS there? If so, why?

August 14, 1987, Boston

At night, something propels me to Washington Street. I went into the place with the little booths, talked, and played around with a Black guy from New Jersey. Very sensual, with a lovely complexion. I went over to the Pilgrim. In the stalls, I see this shining Black face with classic features. I move closer. Not close enough. Then he moves several seats closer. In a moment, we are eating each other's tits.

This gorgeous guy is Laurent, from Guadeloupe. We went at it for a long time. Afterwards, I dropped into Playland for a drink. Nice—until the smoke drove me away. At the Chinatown station, I was sitting waiting for the train when a half-Black guy dressed in a white shirt and shorts walked by. I thought he cast a quick glance at me. I moved along the platform to where he had taken a seat—toward the end, where they were no people. He sat with one leg lifted high and idly caressed his thigh. He was stunning-looking with a lovely complexion. I sat beside him. I had on shorts and soon got a hardon. With a glance around to make sure no one was near, I pulled out my hard cock for him to see. He stared at it and started to play with his asshole.

The train came. We sat together. As we looked at each other and he gave me his phone number to memorize, and kid opposite said to no one in particular, "No drawers." I looked down. Part of my hard dick was poking out beyond the leg of my shorts.

August 15, 1987, Boston

The distortions you find in Black America! At the gym, this quite attractive guy asks, when I get a half-hardon near him, "Are you a homosexual?" I replied, "Sometimes." He then said, still quite loudly, "I am too. But I do it for money."

He was hilariously inexperienced at such things. I scoffed at the money idea, especially when he said what he charges. Later, he followed me to the back of the locker room. "Come downstairs." I didn't know there was a downstairs. But this guy knew. It was a weight room beyond all the weight rooms. "You can suck me off for free," he said, now very hot. He was rather arrogant, perhaps a result of nervousness. Anyway, I did that, in front of a huge mirror, as he alternated between looking down at my eyes and looking across into the mirror. I asked him to tell me before he came, but he didn't and shot into my mouth.

August 18, 1987, Boston

Susy Gordon says I look fine. God, is this how doctors calculate things? While I was waiting to see her, I read a piece in *The New York Times* about the fallibility of condoms.

But how do they know—it is assumed people tell the truth in the surveys. Even in private, people do not tell the whole truth about sex.

August 19, 1987, Boston

A day of lassitude and vague thinking about plans. Perhaps to Australia for Christmas. Some work on the novel in Hong Kong? Nothing can be decided until the renovation of my house is finished. There is still much more to do on the *National Geographic* piece, though the creative agonies are over.

Later at night, I took a snack at Thornton's and chatted with waiter Dan. He bangs away at two jobs because of his vision of the need to get a degree. Tell that to Australian kids!

August 20, 1987, Boston

My birthday dinner, and Edward and I go to L'Espalier, a new place for us, and a splendid one. We both loved it. We talked a lot about American history. Edward more or less gave me a lesson in the Revolution and the Constitution. Interesting to hear it from his lips.

It seems to take me a couple of days to recover from the intensity of being with Edward. Or is it the combination of him and the other guys, who don't blend in with my relationship with him—an apples and bananas situation. He seems more resilient. In he comes with Arlene the other night. She seems to have put on a few pounds. I have a terrible headache from long hours in front of the word processor. Arlene—ever the resourceful "mother"—pulls out two Paladin from her ample purse.

As she sat there in my lobby, I developed an overwhelming desire to fuck Edward there and then in her presence. She has the face of one who suffers. Will she and I both, in the end, be victims? Why doesn't she pick someone else? Why don't I pick someone else?

August 23, 1987, Boston

Mum phones for my birthday. Unfortunately, she had a fall last week, tripping over her walking stick. Just as well she has the two Chinese guys renting a room, living under the same roof. I wonder how long she can go on living in the house. Aged parents. You feel you disappoint them; you can never spend as much time with them as they would like. And they disappoint you. Memory fades; they are not quite the friends they were before.

Alas, the *Boston Globe* review today did not please me. As soon as I saw it done by an Australian journalist, my heart sank. Justifiably. For although he could not manage to obscure the book's quality—his quotes from it were the highlight of the review—he went sour at the end. Maybe he would like to have written such a book himself. I wandered around the Christian Science pool[275] in a stunned daze. I called no one, and no one called me. At night I got drunk.

---

[275] The reflecting pool outside the Christian Science complex in Boston's Back Bay.

August 24, 1987, Boston

Laurent ticked me off in a friendly fashion for getting depressed over the *Globe* review. You will naturally have some bad ones, he insists. We make love, but I am not quite in the mood. He was, and I think I am, the only sex partner in his life just now. Later, to St. Botolph restaurant.

He is a serious person. Probably he is strong-willed. Maybe as a child he was difficult and grew up early. He is half Syrian and half French-Caribbean. And maybe he has a streak of vanity (pretty justified). But he has a good mind and a wonderful personality.

In the middle of dinner, he asked if he could put a personal question to me. Yes, I said without hesitation but with much inner trepidation. "How come a person of your standing and achievements was in that place where we met?" I said there was an excitement about the Pilgrim Theater. The unexpected, the forbidden, the dangerous—step in there and it's another world. He said he felt a bit the same way.

He only went there twice. Once a straight friend took him. He was intrigued by people who went into the dark corner. Being with his friend, he couldn't investigate. The second time, the night he met me, he was there to investigate, but after meeting me, he never made it to the dark corner.

August 27, 1987, Boston

A whirl of work on the article plus pleasant time in Edward's company. We really seem to enjoy each other these days. In between times, I allow myself the space to get nervous about the coming reception of *The Australians*. So far, some very nice short reviews. As well as *Kirkus, Harvard Magazine, Atlantic, Vis-à-Vis,* and *Library Journal* have all given it raves.

A time to be sober, and a time to drink some wine—I think this is my reaction to the experiment, prompted by Edward of these past days to drink little or no alcohol. The good part of it is testing one's own ability to control things. Edward noticed I worked at night, which is rare for me; I suppose one is a bit more efficient when abstaining. On the other hand, I am not going to make a fetish of abstinence. That would bring its own demons.

August 30, 1987, Boston

Quite a night last night. Michael came around as planned. He brought me a beautiful gray-and-red sweater for my birthday. We dined at Thai Cuisine. Edward was in but declined the invitation to join us. It was a very spicy meal. Michael got red in the face and drank much water. Afterwards, Michael and I went to bed. Just as we both came together, I heard Edward come in the front door with his slice of pizza.

Much later, I took Michael upstairs to say goodbye to Edward before we called his cab. I was a bit tired, Edward and I having made love this morning, and I wanted to go to sleep. As I expected, and half-hoped, Edward got into him, rapping (as I learned this morning) for several hours and then going to bed. Michael fucked Edward—coming almost immediately, which "pissed me off," said Edward.

I later phoned Michael to thank him for the sweater and to assure him that I didn't mind Edward and him getting together. He said a striking thing. "I hadn't been to bed with a Black man for four years. This broke the mold—and now I've thrown the mold away." He's going to Chicago this week as his godfather is ill.

The mad stampede to get this draft of the *National Geographic* piece continues. Just as well I didn't go to Wellfleet. As it happened, I had time only for a half an hour break with Stewart, the guy with some American Indian blood whom I met last week. Very affectionate, if not terribly good-looking, and a sincere, straightforward person.

September 1, 1987, Boston

Fred Hills calls. I'm on the phone to Seattle about an invitation to speak at Evergreen College and have to call him back. I had just dictated a note to him with yesterday's good news from Australia. He, in turn, had good news; they decided today to do a second printing of 10,000 copies. "[Robert] Hughes has hurt us, but we haven't bombed," was the chaste way he summed up the situation. There was a certain excitement in his voice. "For a good book like *The Australians,* it's worth striving. I have an emotional commitment to this book." When he said I had worked very hard on it and "put a lot of yourself" into it, I said that he, too, had contributed much.

Laurent came in after I'd played squash. I was happy and relaxed, and we had a great time. We talked for a long time. Then we went to bed. Then to dinner at St Cloud. He asked me another "personal question," and again, it took him about five minutes back and forth to decide whether he'd ask it. Once more, I thought it might be how old am I. "How many lovers do you have?"

It took care to answer. In terms of specifics—no names—I only got as far as Edward, Reggie, and Henry. He said he's been involved with three men—I am the third—in his whole life. The other two, one a pastor and one a fellow student at Howard, were both in DC. The pastor didn't last long as he had strange habits like wanting to dress up as a girl. The student turned out to be "childish." He liked to go in "in a group." For Laurent, a night out with someone should just be with that someone.

September 3, 1987, Boston

Two radio programs this morning to promote *The Australians* go well. The Charlie Brennan show in Newton—I arrived with 30 seconds to spare—and the Christian Science program, which they say now goes to more than 1200 stations. The interviewer, Steve Webber, was good and well-prepared, as was Charlie.

I had hardly gotten into the house when Edward called. Back from the funeral in Connecticut late last night. Today his boss said he's going to make him an offer of a job in Chicago. Would he relocate? He called me straight after the interview with the boss. He may accept such an offer, he said. A pang of sadness went through me. A little later, I wondered if it might not be such a bad thing if he goes to Chicago for a while.

September 4, 1987, Boston

Edward and I both must share. We both must be thoughtful of how the other feels. And in terms of the health angle, I want to narrow my circle of sex partners, and would not feel comfortable with the idea of Edward going into a wild, promiscuous phase with men, in Chicago or anywhere.

September 5, 1987, Boston

Reggie is in a great mood despite a hangover from going with Edward to Paradise last night. Before he goes to Star Market, he suggests "a bit of head." Later, after we moved the TV downstairs, we watched a pic. "Your cock's turned green," he said. Today he paid that "green dick" extra attention, sucking it with an expertise that belies him saying he "never does that."

Talkative about everything, he said both Brenda, a former classmate, and I suck his cock better than Caroline, whom he continues to deeply love. "I want a nude picture of myself," he announces. I take several, all marred by the fact that he's prancing around with a joint of grass in his mouth. Then, as he said at the start he would do, after enjoying enormously the pics, and discussing the details of them, he starts talking about Caroline and goes to the bathroom and gets scissors and slices the pics into pieces. The pieces he puts in a paper bag in the depths of the green bag to go out Monday morning.

"You work so hard," he said as he inspected a list of my books that appears in the front of *The Australians*, "how come you've only turned out seven books in your whole lifetime?"

He asks me to inspect his asshole. "Caroline says I've got moles." I didn't find much; maybe warts, or hemorrhoids. This didn't stop me poking my cock in, but it hurt him. I suggested he go to the doctor, but he said he was embarrassed to go into such details with the doctor.

Later, Caroline comes to pick him up, and I see the famous ring. The three of us eat a pizza before Caroline and Reggie go off to investigate leasing a car. Caroline brings me some booklets about her crystal business to be distributed by me to God knows whom. An afternoon of peace and calm, in which I get back some control of myself and my days.

September 6, 1987, Boston

Perhaps at the back of my mind is a lack of full acceptance of sex. Because it was at first presented to me as forbidden fruit, I feel an overly strong push to win that fruit. Some thoughts about sex, which are normal to other people, are not so to me. For instance, a man takes a second wife. His pumping his cock into her—when juxtaposed with the memory of the first wife—to me has an offensive strain. Some half-conscious childhood memory? I invest sex with much significance. Edward is free to treat it, on the one hand, like food, and on the other, a branch of engineering. To me it is life at its most intense.

"What would be fascinating is if you wrote about your homosexuality." Li-li's words of a week or two ago hang in my mind. Diary bits maybe, efforts to answer certain questions, some utopian dreaming, confession, portraits of certain people. The sensibility behind such a book would be my moon-struck awe at the experience of being a homosexual. The saturating impact of it on one's life. The continual excitement of it. There would be no need to drink while writing this book. It would be Ross facing up to Ross. But people would object to the sex.

This evening, as arranged, Laurent comes in. We talk for a long time. He probes, almost to the point of discomfort. He reckons I should "talk to" Edward. Ah, how little does he understand that demonic charmer! He says he's never known anyone to be involved, as I am, with two guys, both of whom have steady girlfriends. We made love as Charles Aznavour's songs played, then dined very late at Oceanic on huge salty shrimp balls and scallops in garlic sauce.

September 7, 1987, Boston

I was heading for the Orange Line stop to go to Commonwealth Grille, when this attractive young Black guy looked back and smiled. My plans changed. Alan G, slim, with a nice smile and a nice ass, is from NY. He is not as young as he looked—35—but very sexy. I fucked him as he cried out for more and harder. Then we ate late at the Bangkok and drank a lot of white wine.

His father, who was Irish, he never knew. His mother, a French-speaking Black, has had two other husbands since, neither of whom has behaved well. Alan recalls following the present stepfather to a bar, where he was drinking with his girlfriend. Alan was 12 at the time. The guy punished Alan for this act of loyalty to his mother by throwing him down a staircase. He still has the scars on his legs.

September 8, 1987, Boston

Lunch with Li-li and her back is much better. As we walked by the Christian Science pool, she urged me very strongly to make my next book autobiographical. She feels my writing on such material—as in the first chapter of *The Australians*—is the best writing I do. I pointed out the Diary is there. "But it's the way you would put it all that would make it a masterpiece." She feels the novel can wait. The stuff about my own life is more unique.

When I got back from squash, Edward, whom I thought would be home cleaning his apartment, was here watching TV. I was getting packages off to *National Geographic* and Simon & Schuster with Federal.

We had a fairly nice dinner at Hammersley's. When I told him about Li-li and marriage, he said why not marry her. In talking about that, I said one reason is that I don't have a desire to fuck her. "Lovemaking and fucking aren't the same," he said. Perhaps in Edward, I have neither lover nor "fuck-mate."

We talked of ethics, and I remarked that some guilt is necessary to the living of a moral life. Otherwise, we would be beasts in an immoral jungle. "How wonderful that would be," Edward said with a grin. When I looked perplexed, he said he was only joking.

A welcome reunion with Curt, who has come back a little chastened to Boston from Canada. It's home after all, he's learned, and you must have one home. "What you want is always clear," Curt said to me as we dined at Thornton's. "Your motivations are not—they seem incredibly complicated." After I left Curt, "my" Sam came in. We watched a video and made hot love. He's mellowing, no longer grunting instructions as we go along, even expressing his pleasure. Is he still straight?

September 9, 1987, Boston

"Why Edward?" people ask, and I ask, and now he asks me. Because he has style!

September 10, 1987, Boston

A TV show to promote *The Australians* at Channel 38. The hostess liked the book and praised it for her audience. It was the same studio where I met Helen Caldicott while promoting *The White-Boned-Demon*, and a fellow guest on today's show knows Helen well. "She burnt out in the USA and went back to a cottage on the Australian east coast."

At noon, a white guy almost bites my tits off in the john at Northeastern. Two others watch, jerking themselves off, as the preppie guy swoops up and down my prick with a saliva-greased hand.

September 11, 1987, Boston

At noon, a phone call from one Bruce Chapman in Oregon. "I just had to find your number and call you—your *The Australians* is wonderful. So much information. So entertaining!" I told him this is what makes writing books worthwhile.

All day, Laurent is without a phone. He experiences what I did when I moved in here six years ago—the maddening inconvenience of being cut off. Yet Edward prefers to have no phone. What a difference of temperament!

Keiji Samejima from Japan invites me to tea at the Hilton. He says I haven't changed in four years. Nor has he—the optimistic, busy China-watcher as in the 1970s when we both were busy in the Pacific China-shuttling community. I told him I do a piece for *Yomiuri Shimbun* about twice a year. "Only twice a year?" he said.

Late at night, I ponder my tie with Edward. Reason says I ought to let his thing with Sam run its course. If Edward gets something, that doesn't take anything away from me—from what I have and from what I enjoy with him.

September 12, 1987, Boston

Long hours on the *National Geographic* piece, interspersed with hopping into bed to cuddle Alan, who came after work at 7 AM to rest in peace. I'm pretty pleased with the article. Mac is such a skillful editor; that helps.

A nice review of *The Australians* from the *Hobart Mercury*, and a reasonable one by Hawke's girlfriend Blanche d'Apulget, in typescript form from Fred, that will appear in the *Los Angeles Times*.

Today, illness looms from two directions, one a hint, one a body blow. The hint came when I woke Alan in the mid-afternoon. He was utterly bathed in sweat. Some things seemed to fall into place. Bartender at Buddies for some years. Went to NY. Came back to Boston to live just last month. Loves to get fucked. With him dripping with sweat, I can see in his eyes something has cropped up between us.

Tonight, Wyatt phones with the astounding news that Tyrone is dead. At 22, he died yesterday of AIDS in Brigham Hospital. One of the most mature 22-year-olds ever. A kind, handsome, uncomplaining person. For months, I asked Robert to have Tyrone call me. Why wasn't he calling? I didn't know. Now I do. Wyatt says Tyrone's friend Frank, a Black guy of 29, died of AIDS last year. Said Wyatt: "And Tyrone's family didn't even know he was gay." Life goes on, Wyatt said. And sex will go on. If I were to be far-sighted, I should prepare myself for what might happen to other people—such as Edward and myself. But seldom are we far-sighted.

September 13, 1987, Boston

A disturbed night. Too much red wine at Thai Cuisine. And thoughts of Alan, who'd been in my bed all day, and of dear Tyrone. I woke with a stiff neck, headache, and an utter unreadiness to work. I drank coffee and reflected.

With this terrible plague, you can't even talk candidly about it. For instance, poor Tyrone's death—can I tell Edward, who knew him. Probably, but it will be difficult. Certainly, I cannot tell Reggie. And I doubt I will tell Laurent. We dissemble in the face of monstrous things. We are gamblers who know little and lack courage to explore what we know.

On the way back from the Y—its first Sunday open since the spring—a bout with a white guy named Rick. The head on his brown cock drove me out of my mind.

Tonight, Laurent was just getting out of the shower when the key turned in the lock and Edward came in. So they meet. They talk about their respective college experiences. Later as Laurent and I dine at St. Botolph Café, he says he was embarrassed when Edward walked in. He thinks "Edward has something missing." He was astonished that Edward had instructed me about how to use the washer and dryer in a dictatorial manner in my own house. Laurent does not yet quite understand.

In the Marian Christy interview out today in the *Globe*, the thing that intrigued her was that I have become a US citizen. She could hardly believe it.

September 15, 1987, Boston

To the Fenway for the report on my fourth round of tests in the AIDS study. Once more, I am negative to the virus. One feels thankful. Clay, the nurse, says pre-cum does contain the virus. "People get pregnant from it," she points out, "so we treat it as one of the fluids which can transmit the AIDS virus." I will try once again to convince Edward that this may indeed be true.

Li-li calls to say she loves the article about me in the *Globe*. She was anxious to hear today's medical news. She is insistent that, from now on, I take extra care.

September 16, 1987, Cambridge

The Nieman party is fun though not well attended. Mark Feeney[276] introduces himself but prudently waltzes off before I have a chance to tell him what I think of the *Boston Globe* review of *The Australians*. I ask Ken Galbraith how Europe was. "Normal," he replies. Paul Soliman has a view on whether I could use the Rupert Murdoch chat at his farm in an article. "Treat the microcassette recording as a jog to memory; check with RM before making any use of it." That leaves the passage on birds, which I have used in the *Geographic* draft. I am near-certain Rupert would not object to that.

The annual Louis Lyons[277] award is presented to a South African. Sometimes in leftwing Cambridge, you get the impression that South Africa is the locus of world oppression.

Susan Bray phoned from Sydney to say *The Australians* did not remain on the Australian version of *Publishers Weekly*'s bestseller list during August. "But it's still selling, and the reps are really behind it." Last week's *Bulletin* has a nice mention, she says.

September 17, 1987, Boston

We had a talk about the incident with Edward the other night. I told him, What the two of you may do is your affair—but please not at my place under my nose. Reggie said that was reasonable.

Cornell looks fine, with a haircut that, typically, he finds not what he wanted. He has had quite a time since we last got together. The affair with Tony, which has left him bitter about relationships. Feuds at home. The death of his grandmother. A new job with the immigration department.

Wyatt called to say he cannot face tomorrow's service for Tyrone. Lee called to tell me there was no service. Robert called to say he's going to wear a black turtleneck and a black blazer to the service.

Cornell told me his brothers came into his bedroom at home when he was in bed with Tony. The fight led him to leave home—once more. "I wanted them to say, 'You're a faggot,' but they never got to the point of saying it. The break-up with Tony was with fist fights, as is usual with Cornell. His tie with his father reached another horrible low.

As we dined at Thai Cuisine, Cornell remarked, "I see now that nothing's perfect," as he gobbled up chicken and scallops. He looked at my stomach and said I was getting fat. Combative, single-minded, yet exceedingly gentle in my presence—he is still the same Cornell I have known for three to four years.

---

[276] Mark Feeney (1957-), author and arts writer for *The Boston Globe*.
[277] Established in 1964 by that year's Nieman Fellows, the Louis M. Lyons Award is given for "conscience and integrity in journalism."

September 18, 1987, Boston

I took a cab to Johnson's funeral home in Roxbury. About 25 people gathered as music played. Almost all were middle-aged or above and dressed up. At the door, I signed the open book which was headed "Relatives and Friends." Wyatt, Robert, Lee, Joe—none of them were there. Nor any others who looked remotely like Tyrone's gay friends.

His elder brother was seated at the front with Tyrone's mother. I was the only white person in the room, but I was welcomed like everyone else. There were prayers and a bible reading. A man sang "Abide with Me" very beautifully. The pastor spoke briefly and well. One has to ask why, he said, when seeing an obituary with the birth year as 1965 and the death year as 1987. But he was honest enough not to give an answer. "Think of the people you know who are inconsiderate, who snarl, who are arrogant. You think the world would be better without them. Tyrone was a person of the opposite kind. More people like Tyrone and the world would be a better place."

A former teacher of Tyrone's spoke movingly of his politeness, cooperative spirit, caring attitude, willingness to listen, and uncomplaining nature. "He always had a smile for me." Throughout the ceremony, no mention of Tyrone's life as I knew it. Deluding oneself with a religious smokescreen. Yet who am I to say they should integrate sex with family life and work life? I find it impossible to do it myself.

I came out of the funeral home, my mind full of memories. The pastor was outside smoking a cigar. In light rain, I walked down the hill to get a bus at Dudley.

I changed my clothes and went to the Sheraton for an appearance on behalf of *The Australians*. I sat signing books at the New England Booksellers meeting and thoroughly enjoyed myself. Simon & Schuster had provided a hundred or so books, at their expense, to entice the booksellers. I was to chat, smile, and present a signed copy to each one who lined up for the privilege.

One of the reps, Harvey Berliner, wants me to go to the Dartmouth shop—"a natural for *The Australians,*" he says. In his region, which seems to include NH, VT, Maine, and a bit of Mass, there are about 3000 copies of *The Australians* in the stores. Some reordering has begun. Saul Gillman, the boss who is cocky for Simon & Schuster sales here, says the book is doing "quite well."

Steve Morgan introduces himself. He reviewed *White-Boned-Demon* in the *Herald* four years ago and now edits the book page for the paper. Is he going to review *The Australians*? "We reviewed it two weeks ago," he said to my embarrassment.

Francine du Plessix Gray[278] comes by—she is next to autograph books after me—dry and snooty as I expected. "This is my husband. He has to go and have a sandwich while I sign," she squeaked to Saul. "Please tell me exactly where he can find me after he's finished eating."

At Northeastern, I meet the amazing Rick with the riveting eyes and soft black hair. I saw him in the quadrangle; he followed me upstairs. We tore into each other. At one point, I thought the wall of the john might give way. This time his previous rule of no sucking proved not to be a rule after all. He almost ate my cock. And I thrived on the

---

[278] Francine du Plessix Gray (1930-2019), writer and literary critic, nominated for a Pulitzer Prize.

beautiful head of his. Meanwhile, we fantasized about fucking each other. This led to such heat that we almost did fuck each other—but for interruptions, probably would have. Again, I loved his locks, eyes, and swarthy dick; again, he went for my tits. The new thing, apart from sucking, was that he stuck his tongue in my ears and his fingers up my asshole. Once more, no phone numbers. It can only work so magnificently in that strange insecure situation.

In the evening, I went back to the Booksellers' meeting for the champagne party. Frank Kramer of Harvard Bookstores said the book business is doing "wonderfully, especially in New England." His theory—beyond the buoyant Massachusetts economy—is that American book prices are really very reasonable. He's right, as I told him by way of illustration of the relative price of *The Australians* in the US and the British Commonwealth.

As champagne was poured into the glasses of myself and a charming bookseller from Vermont, I overheard a woman seller say to her companion of some book: "Look, I might be able to sell it at $8.95, but there's no way I could sell it at $10.95."

September 19, 1987, Boston

Laurent looks wonderful tonight. We make love as rain pelts against the windows, and dine late on noodles at Oceanic.

When he was 12, a priest at his school in Guadeloupe, while tutoring him, had sex with him. Laurent could not tell his parents, but he did tell his 17-year-old brother. Laurent refused to go anymore to tutorial. The mother complained that Laurent was neglecting his studies. The brother went to the priest and told him if he touched Laurent again, he'd report him to the police. The priest stopped, then began with another boy, a good friend of Laurent who now lives in Chicago.

As we lay in bed, Laurent asked me another "personal question": how many times a week do I have sex? He said I'm sometimes "on the moon." He says I worry too much about other people's problems and don't look out enough for myself.

September 20, 1987, Boston

Laurent and I slept very peacefully together, and the next morning he went off to Hyde Park. A great disappointment today. A very grudging review of *The Australians* in the all-important *NY Times Book Review*. Oddly, like the *Globe* review, which also failed to lavish praise on my book, the review, despite itself, managed to make the book sound rich and interesting.

Tonight, at the PEN party, some condolences on the review. Justin informs me that the reviewer is Australian-born. It fits the pattern. I enjoy meeting Mark Kramer, author of several nonfiction books, and Chris Leland, a gay guy who has written a novel for Houghton Mifflin.[279] Frank Kramer puts on magnificent food—the company is hardly worth it, except for a few, including darling Pam [Painter], who is teaching like crazy to pay the bills for her kids' education. She feels disappointed with Fred Hills over

---

[279] Christopher Leland (1951-). The novel was *Mrs. Randall*.

the book she ghost-wrote for the Wall Street guy. But then, aren't we all always disappointed?

Afterwards, I walked down wonderful Newbury Street, starting to feel and look a little like autumn, and bought Marian Christy's *Invasions of Privacy* at the Ritz kiosk.

September 21, 1987, Boston

Everything is made more difficult by yesterday's review. How can I push the Simon & Schuster publicity department now? How can I reproach BL for not yet getting any foreign translation rights? There has been a cost to me of the two years spent on writing on Australia, putting me out of touch with China. I must focus on my next book. There comes a point when you have to let go of the old plant and cultivate a new seedling.

During dinner at St Cloud, Joan Colebrook quotes lovely lines from Emily Dickenson. She urges me to "draw back from that life, and write about it." But which makes for more happiness, living that life or analyzing it? "That life" is my bond with youthfulness.

She also urged me in my next book to "be less journalistic and more literary." I can be, she says, referring to passages I've written that she's read. It's a choice I can make, she insists. If she's right, what I should do is disengage emotionally from Edward—not take it all as seriously as I have. Then I would be less obsessed, I would have more energy for other things, and I would feel less often hurt.

September 22, 1987, Boston

Julia Knickerbocker from Simon & Schuster rails against "the bloody *New York Times*" for Sunday's Jane Perlez review. She reveals that we lost the Today Show because of this same Australia-born reviewer. Emily Boxer of NBC, wanting to do the book in a Jane Pauley segment, sent it for evaluation to none other than Perlez! After her report, the idea was dropped.

At dinner with Don Butterfield—he persuaded me to try the Promenade Café, and it was excellent. He heard one man's testimony about the stages of life. "My 40s were hell. 30s were better, and now my 50s are also better." You go through the midlife crisis, Don reckons, and you come out happier. His crisis, he says, lasted much of his 40s

Edward got take-out lasagna at Thornton's and came back to my place. He told me about the wedding of the guy at work—Greek music and much food and drink, but in-laws who didn't like each other. We went to bed. Next morning, he woke me early to make love. He decided not to go to work. Later Don said to me, "Don't let this beautiful man go to Chicago!"

September 23, 1987, Boston

Barbara is in town and takes me to lunch at Copley's. I decline to go into future book arrangements. I think she got the message—I await action on foreign rights for *The Australians*. She urges me to consider writing something for *Traveler*, the new Condé Nast magazine, which Harold Evans edits. After lunch, I read the *Boston Herald* review of *The Australians*, which is good. Also, the *Washington Post* one arrived—I heard this is an attack, so I didn't read it. At night, Edward read it. "This lady doesn't like you," he said. He thinks I shouldn't read it for a month.

September 25, 1987, Boston

Reggie comes in so hung over he can hardly stand up. Last night was the celebration party for his victorious team. As he gets into bed, he says how much he dislikes the Aboriginal painting on the brick wall. "That serpent. It's like a devil. Are you my devil, Ross?" I take the picture down. He grins.

While I had Reggie in bed and Edward on the phone, David Scott from the *Christian Science Monitor* arrived to interview me. He is pleasant, intelligent, and well-prepared. He leaves for a posting in Sydney next week.

I went to a seminar on China at Harvard—excellent by the German scholar Rudolf Wagner on the Tang Dynasty—and then came back to see young John. Charming as ever, with just enough naivety to add to his appeal. Tomorrow, he goes to New York with a group to be photographed—building a portfolio for a possible modeling career. But tonight, his mind seemed to be less on his career than on things of the flesh. I love the color of his skin, neither Black nor White, but caramel.

September 26, 1987, Boston

I am in a great rush to get the *National Geographic* manuscript into Federal Express when Edward comes in. He drinks a beer or two as I finish up. He's never been in love with anyone, he says. Is it a double standard that I see all these men and he very few? I replied that, well, there's never been much symmetry to our relationship—it's a maze of double lines. He has access to my place, but not me to his. He keeps family in a box sealed away from his tie with me. He generally has a girlfriend going, which I don't.

I had not realized how sharp Edward's break with Arlene had been. "I won't restart with her unless she calls first. Her birthday will be the big test." But her birthday is not till January. I asked him if he could imagine settling down with a man. "Only if they don't find a cure for AIDS." He says what he needs is a girl who, like him, is positive to the virus and who therefore understands that the marriage cannot produce kids. I wondered if he might advertise in the *Phoenix* for such a girl. He said I should avoid treating sex with him as a repeated re-capture of him.

We went to the late session of *Fatal Attraction* at the Cheri. Some gory, violent scenes, during which Edward laughed. A couple of people nearby glanced at him in surprise or discomfort. Beforehand, Edward bought popcorn while I tried to save two seats against a rising tide of young patrons. Why do youth like to see a movie about the horrors of family life?

Long after Edward had gone home and I'd gone to sleep—perhaps about 3 AM—the phone rang. It was Cornell. He was bored. Could he come round? So we did it again after quite a long break. Slow, gentle love. That lovely body. At one point, I got at his asshole, but he just said quietly, "Uh, uh." We slept in each other's arms

September 27, 1987, Boston

It's not that I lack belief in myself—it's that I lack conviction that I'm typical and that what I want is what others want, and that what I produce or do, others will like or understand.

In the evening, Chris came in and told me his woes. His fiancée has now gone to a psychiatrist—to help handle the abortion trauma. We went to bed. He asked me to fuck him—but I wasn't desirous of that. We had great fun with other methods.

September 28, 1987, Boston

At Northeastern, I sucked a white guy as a timid Black guy watched. I was aware that it was Edward's night with Melvin, so I wanted to do something. Later a great peace. I made some clam chowder, listened to music, and went to bed. Before sleeping, I phoned Skip in Pittsburgh. A roommate answered, so I was circumspect. Tomorrow Skip has his Boards exam in the medical program. I merely wished him well.

September 29, 1987, Boston

As Edward said the other day after reading the *Washington Post* review of *The Australians*, it hasn't been a good year for me. It began with my arrest at Christy's. The problems with the condo renovation have clouded every month. *The Australians* doesn't look as if it's going to be a roaring success. Henry and I parted. My mother declines by the month. Perhaps Don B is right about one's forties.

Later a dinner party at Don and Cathy Pfister's in Cambridge. My book is a centerpiece of the pre-dinner drinks session. I autograph the one they've got in the room. "I bought it at the Coop," Don says, "and the salesman asked if I'd like an autographed copy. I said I'll get the autograph personally; thanks very much."

I am lauded for my success by many at the party. Yet I don't seem convinced of it. At dinner, I am seated next to a science academic. Sophie Ducker is an Australian of German birth who taught at my old university for many years. She told tales of Madagascar. In search of seaweed and other plants, she found many prize specimens in that exotic isle. But regulations about what to take out hit her. In the end, she smuggled key fungi out in her brassiere. For two days, they were against her breasts. She reached Mauritius and took them out—and had a bath.

When I come home, Edward is here. We have a nice time exchanging news. I told him of my doings. He warns me of the Northeastern place. "I know firsthand. I was in a stall when a cop came in and demanded to see my ID. He said, "This is a problem place, with many homosexuals," and he wanted to see my ID. Fortunately, I had it."

"Were you alone?"

"No one else in the whole john—though minutes before there were three of us in my stall."

September 30, 1987, Cambridge

A hot day. I went to Kirkland House Senior Common Room. Introductions, as it's the start of the academic year. Larry Wylie tells a true story about a guy who goes into a drugstore on Linnaean Street. "One packet of Trojans," he asks briskly. Then he lowers his voice and puts his hand to his mouth: "And a packet of Marlboros."

The taping of the radio show for Sunday week with Matt Schaffer goes well. He is always prepared, and he told his listeners *The Australians* is "a delightful book." It was a beautiful day and I walked home from WBCN across the Fenway.

A candid talk with Fred Hills as I listen through the phone to the sounds of him munching his lunch. He lost out on getting more publicity for my book. "Dollar for dollar, they don't think it's worthwhile." He won on an ad. They will follow my suggestion and put the warm review quotes into a *New York Times* Sunday ad. "I'll send it all over to the agency." It makes me shudder to hear of all these intermediaries. New York is like that, and it's a big reason why so much goes wrong down there. "I said to them, we've got a second printing; do we want to move it or just have it lie in the warehouse?" He believes *The Australians* can be a Christmas book. So it still has some time yet.

I planted a few seeds for *The Australians*. A copy to the Activities Committee of the Harvard Club of New York City. One to Lehmann-Haupt at the *Times*. A release to the San Diego Chamber of Commerce, where Hawke will appear in a couple of weeks.

October 1, 1987, Boston

A white guy comes up to me at Northeastern and turns me crazy. Olive skin, honey-colored hair, medium-sized rubbery cock. We spent almost an hour with many interruptions. He wouldn't come home. Many things he also wouldn't do, but he was so attractive that anything we did delighted me.

I worked on the article for *The New Republic* about British and American influences in Australia. In the evening, Edward came in, fresh and buoyant from a safe-sex encounter with a guy called Steve, whom he met at the Y a few days ago. He ate fried chicken, watched *Knot's Landing*, and went home.

A phone call to my mother, who seems in fairly good spirits. Health is the main factor in life, she pronounces. But I wonder if love is not more all-consuming even than health.

October 2, 1987, Boston

Fred calls to say that *The Australians* is indeed doing better in the Boston area than anywhere else in the country. He also says I should call Julia directly and talk with her about some West Coast publicity. "A publishing house is a collection of human beings," he says, "and you are not only a good writer but you have a good way with people."

After squash with Joe, a good seminar at Harvard given by Chinese artists who've left China. A big futile discussion over whether their work is "Chinese" or "Western." Actually, the issue is a different one. These young men have rejected the political meaning of life. They reach for self-expression of the individual in a society that prefers conformity. That doesn't make them any less "Chinese" than your average Chinese official.

As it happened, on the way to the seminar, I took my water-damaged Chinese scrolls to the Fogg[280] for an opinion on how to repair them. Traditional paintings! I have been collecting the landscapes in old style while, in my heart, what I really admire about Chinese art is the anti-traditional and anti-social realism work of these young dissenters!

In the evening, Paul X and I dined at Newbury's. He regaled me with stories from his summer on the island of Madeira. He is strictly no-risk—mutual jerking off is as far as he goes. Well, it takes all sorts to make up a world.

I must try to depend more on my inner resources and less on what comes upon me from outside myself.

October 4, 1987, Boston

Laurent comes in and we make love. At lunch afterwards at Harvard Bookstore Café, he tries to convince me that Edward probably is affected—deeply—by my having other friends, often very desirable friends.

On the way to Copley, I noticed—as we left the train—that Edward was in the same car. Cap, leather jacket, that set expression; I don't think he saw Laurent and me. We returned the videos on which Edward gorged Saturday night. As we came out of the shop, the wind whipped at our faces and legs. Fall is coming. We went back to 200, and Laurent fell asleep on the bed as I read the Sunday papers.

October 5, 1987, Boston

A golden autumn morning, though I find it hard to face the day. I have been thinking over what to say to Edward when we next talk. Perhaps there is nothing new to say. I don't want him to call. But I do want him to love me. I suppose I expect too much.

October 6, 1987, Boston

Laurent is here much of the day. He doesn't think I should write a letter to Edward as I had been planning to do. At the library, I revised the article for *The New Republic,* and now I think it is in fairly good shape.

October 7, 1987, Boston

I write letters—endless task. Li-li says I ought to be more self-reliant. She says because I felt abandonment as a kid, I have this too-great desire to please. She reckons writing is my best available therapy at the moment. On the whole, she says (having heard only my side of the story), I have handled this latest Edward crisis in a balanced way.

---

[280] Fogg Art Museum at Harvard.

October 8, 1987, Boston

I decide to send the letter I have written to Edward despite Laurent's advice. I take it round to Worthington Street and put it under his door. In comes Robert with his friend Mikey. The moment Mikey and I set eyes on each other, I think the die was cast.

As I worked in the study, the two of them watched videos. I put on Stallion one from yesterday, but Robert had put on *Black Workout II*. Perhaps Mikey wasn't as fixated on Black as Robert because he eyed me as much as the movie. I lay on my tummy on my bed wearing my brief blue shorts—in the line of view between Mikey's gleaming eyes and the TV screen he was supposed to be watching.

Later I took him upstairs to show him the view. We tore into each other. "Does Robert mind?" "No." So we proceeded. He is tall and lean and sexy. In the middle of it, Jim Bradley phoned about a game of squash. Mikey didn't even let my prick slip out of his mouth during the call.

October 10, 1987, Boston

Sam is good in bed yet again. Two things he likes above all: for me to suck his balls; and for me to drive my prick between his legs under those huge smooth balls, as his gaze rivets on my shaft.

I make a rare foray to TV and am amazed at the pussyfooting on matters where I, now, just speak my mind. Donahue[281] talks to people about marriage and relationships generally. Much talk about why people do this or don't do that, especially get together or stay together. Two things were glaringly missing: does the woman like the guy's cock; is the guy hesitating about a marriage commitment because he's got men on the side (at least one guest clearly did).

October 11, 1987, Boston

At last, Loring catches up with me and we lunch at Huskie's. He talks of his sex (non)life. It all takes me back many years. It recalls Pan and me 10 years ago. "It's so easy for a gay couple to quarrel and break up," Loring says as his big pretty eyes bore into me. Indeed. He wanted to go to a movie and make a day of it, but I gently disengaged myself after the pleasant lunch. In the pouring rain, he insisted on walking with me to the Dodge Library, where I was headed to consult periodicals.

October 12, 1987, Boston

I talked on the phone with Nancy Sayles in California, who is setting up media appointments for me in Seattle. She seems capable, though it is all rather too much by remote control; New York asks LA to make plans for Seattle!

I wrote to *The New York Times* suggesting the news on Tibet makes it a good time to run my article—already paid for by them—on the Yi ethnic minority in

---

[281] Phil Donahue, "King of daytime talk," whose TV show ran for 29 years, from 1969-1996.

southwestern China. The $500 isn't everything; one still wants the thing to see the light of day.

October 13, 1987, Boston

At the NE seminar at Harvard, Lucian Pye grabs me by the arm and says he and wife Mary are reading *The Australians* out aloud to each other. "It's a wonderful book," he says. The pair of them were in Australia last year and found it disappointing—"blah." At the seminar, Tu Weiming[282] speaks on the "Confucian revival" in China, but it sounds to me much less than that. Returning to a day-by-day study of China materials helps structure and stabilize me.

Carl buzzes and comes in. His smile and shoulders dazzle me as always. But the purported reason for our chat is religion, so we plough through various New Testament texts. Do you have a bible?" I think he is amazed when I produce many editions from various dusty corners of my shelves. We discuss a variety of passages as we sit together on the lobby sofa. Looking at his legs and his neck, I thought of what Henry said to me at the start of our relationship: "I will have to choose between you and the Lord."

October 14, 1987, Boston

I suppose for Edward, since the affair didn't ever begin at an exact moment, in the same way it cannot have a moment of ending. Yet, as in the case of Pan, I was slower to fall in love with him than he to fall in love with me. Edward said those golden words, "I love you," quite early on. Glen recently told me that for about nine months, I was Edward's "perfect flower—you could do no wrong in his eyes." I suppose the affair did have a beginning. But it's sometimes oddly difficult to notice a beginning at the time.

The Condé Nast magazine, *Traveler*, is indeed very good. Barbara sent me a piece from it by A. Alvarez on a visit to the Daintree Forest in far north Australia. It is eloquent, travel writing with flair. So I'll do something for them.

At the appointed hour of seven, Edward came to get some more of his things.

October 15, 1987, Boston

Laurent, then Reggie—on a day like this, I can easily think I can get over Edward. Did I perhaps—in line with my gushing personality—put too many eggs in one bastard?

In the afternoon, a conference call with the people in Seattle over my forthcoming visit there to speak. The seminar is jointly sponsored by Evergreen College and AT&T. As we discuss the theme of my speech, the AT&T guy, urging more stress on doing business with China, says crisply, "Recall who's paying for this seminar" (i.e., AT&T, not Evergreen College).

---

[282] Tu Weiming (1940-), Professor of Chinese History and Philosophy and of Confucian Studies at Harvard (1981-2010).

At the Fairbank Center, a seminar on Mao during which Ben, Rod, Merle, and others attacked Mao so strongly that I felt like saying a few words in his defense. But what's the point. Academic seminars are, well, pretty academic.

I gave Bing Yang a draft of my article on China for his suggestions. I want to get it out this week, and perhaps to the *Globe* tomorrow.

October 17, 1987, Boston

Just as I am getting a package together for the Federal Express relating to my trip to Seattle in a couple of weeks, Cornell comes in. He has with him two friends, John, his classmate, and a bank clerk visiting from NY for the weekend. They watch TV while I go to the Federal Express amidst the warehouses and fly-overs of Albany Street; then we all chat pleasantly. They smoke a joint. John is quite attractive, but I have learned to do nothing in Cornell's presence. He doesn't like spontaneous things. And now that I know as much as I do of Cornell's hot temper …

Later, Junior phones and we end up sleeping together. He really is a quiet, conscientious guy, doing well, it seems, at his job with the Harvard Coop. It turns out he's a member of the same church as Carl downstairs. I must read some of the studies of Black religion; no doubt there would be links or parallels with experiences I have of Black passions.

October 18, 1987, Boston

A white guy called Todd, a librarian, wants to suck me. "I love your shaved balls," he says when we meet in Mugar. "Let's get together at my place and shave each other's balls."

October 19, 1987, Boston

At Northeastern, I fucked a nice Black guy. "Come out before you come," he cried. I got home in time for our condo meeting. David came in first, and he looked as if he'd just woken from a nightmare. He brought news that the Dow Jones average dropped more than 500 points. At first, I simply could not believe it. Oh, this will have repercussions!

October 20, 1987, Boston

Called cousin Ivy in Melbourne. Mum's operation went smoothly. But much else looks grim. She may not be able to live alone soon. Her mind is not very clear. Ivy seems to have had enough for the moment of worrying about her two ailing aunts.

Reggie and Laurent meet. Later as he smokes a joint, Laurent looks straight at me and says, "You're strange. And naïve." There are probably many layers to that statement, but one of them is that dear Laurent absolutely cannot understand why I get so involved with men who also have a woman.

To Kirkland House for the Sophomore Dinner, which turns out quiet and sober. These new kids are all into the stock exchange and small business enterprises. They dress neatly and even elaborately, guys in ties and polished shoes, girls in frilly dresses.

October 21, 1987, Boston

Recipe for a sad period: you miss someone very close to you, but at the same time, intellectually, you doubt you could be happy with him back.

Wyatt and Robert and the amazing Mikey come in unexpectedly. Laurent is in bed. Reggie is due any moment with some pot. The three of them sit with me upstairs at the dining table and have a drink. They're all cool. Soon Mikey is grabbing me under the table. I eventually conclude that Wyatt and Robert know about this, so I give in. Mikey and I go down and do it fairly quickly in the small room. Meanwhile, Laurent does not stir. Reggie comes in and is terrified that "someone will see me."

Later, Laurent awakes and, at my suggestion, comes upstairs to meet the terrible triplets. Mikey blatantly attempts to seduce him. With great dignity, Laurent declines. I think Wyatt and Robert are a bit embarrassed. I cannot help contrasting Laurent's response to Edward's response in similar situations. Laurent's hair just about stands on end when Wyatt and Robert refer to each other as "Miss" and "she"—as does mine.

Downstairs, Mikey told me that he and his brother (who is now in the military) used to fuck each other when quite young. "Down south no men are straight. You see, in the little towns, guys go through all the girls, then they have to start on the boys."

October 22, 1987, New York

After last night, I hardly needed NY, but I warmed to it. The Harvard Club is its same welcoming self. The meeting with Selma Shapiro was, I think, worthwhile. She would like me to hire her for PR when the paperback edition of *The Australians* comes out next year.

The Simon & Schuster party at Dick Snyder's was something else again. Dick says he liked *The Australians* very much. He hopes to go to Australia soon, he says, and if he does, he'll call me for suggestions.

Apparently, the party is not "for the Fall list" at all, as someone told me over the phone it would be, but to smooth the feathers of the literary agents after all the negative vibes from Simon & Schuster recently, in particular in the wake of Joni Evans leaving for Random House.

Most of the room is talking about money in general and the fall in the stock market in particular. Barbara, gaily drinking white wine, says I shouldn't "waste the China articles collection on a university publisher," but sell it together with my next book to a commercial house.

Some of the young editors, like Bob Landow, whom I vaguely remember from Harvard, were impressive and even tentatively friendly. Julia and her chicks from the Publicity Department take on a lesbian tone when seen all together.

Helen and Marlin are there and, for a moment, Barbara and I join them. A foursome with some memories, but little is said. Later I joined Michael Bessie and his colleague Clayton from the San Francisco office of H & R for dinner at the Harvard

Club. Mike is full of his Gorbachev book.[283] When he and Cornelia were given the manuscript to read in a Leningrad hotel and told they must say yes or no before leaving the city, "I wondered if we might end up in Siberia should we have said no." But he said yes.

Clayton wants me to write a book for him on how religion comes back as Marxism declines in China. We all talk for a while—with examples from our various recent experiences—of people's amazing capacity to compartmentalize. Intellectual consistency is seldom present in the average person. Later, I went to a straight-sex movie house on 42nd Street and to another on 8th Avenue where a very nice mulatto guy sucked me off.

October 23, 1987, New York

At breakfast in the Harvard Club, the chairs smell the same, the marmalade is there, the coffee has the same bitter taste, the waiters are familiar. At the long table, few look up from their newspapers.

On the shuttle from NY home to Boston, I see Lew Jones, looking just the same blend of businessman and street kid. After listening to Larry Sullivan talk interestingly about fascism in China—a new thought, at least since the Blue Shirts of the 1930s—I joined Lew for a drink at 33 Dunster Street.[284] The Dunster Street/Kirkland House tradition draws us in. We're still all students at heart.

In the evening, I sit alone and think. I realize I am in the midst of a life crisis of the kind I've had only once before—at the time of the "Strasbourg decision." I know in the best part of my mind: Edward can't help me more in this crisis—he's too scared of getting close for good reasons of his own.

October 24, 1987, Boston

Reggie never fails to turn me on in a big way. Of all the people I've made it with, say, 30 times or more, he is the definite winner in this respect. He gets high, and in hooking up my VCRs for copying—I find much later—he gets one of the audio-video plug sets around the wrong way. Damn the stud!

Later, Laurent and I dine well at the Café Promenade. Discreet to a fault, Laurent doesn't ask about Reggie, though he probably smelled him on me and in the bedroom. He has plans to go to Washington next weekend for a Homecoming at Howard University.

October 26, 1987, Boston

The Chinese Party meeting has begun. How many newspapers will run my preview piece that I sent out last week?

Fred Hills' comment that *The Fatal Shore* "hurt us" takes on a particular meaning as I hear more and more reactions to both books. People bought, but often didn't enjoy,

---

[283] Perestroika: New Thinking for Our Country and the World (Harper & Row, 1987)
[284] A pub in Harvard Square.

Hughes—or even get more than part-way through. This hurt me. These people's Australian purchase for 1987 turned out a (quiet) disappointment for them: they were not inclined to risk a second book on Australia.

Li-li calls. She feels strongly that I should start on the autobiographical stuff, that this will absorb me as well as produce fine writing.

I spend part of the day at a seminar on joint ventures in the Communist world at Harvard. Of very modest quality. How does Harvard get away with these seminars to businessmen, when many of the businessmen know more of the topic than the professors?

I must develop the habit of simply rejecting unpleasant thoughts when they appear at the doorstep of my mind. Negative example here: my mother. She flings open the door to bleak thoughts. At my peril, will I go on doing the same?

October 28, 1987, Boston

A mad rush through traffic to catch the plane to Seattle with a connection through Chicago. The Checker driver bungles as we head for Inman Square. I become furious. He, in turn, is fed up with my fury and refuses to take me further. At Inman Square, I am forced to try to find another cab. I do—and catch the plane—but the lesson is that I am brittle at present (or that America is coming apart at the seams. Or both).

In Chicago, there is an airport "Red Alert." A captain hisses this to a hostess, and I overhear it from my front seat. Another United plane is approaching O'Hare with a crippled hydraulic system; fire trucks and ambulances swarm across the tarmac. Meanwhile, we sit in our seatbelts and wait.

At a lavish dinner offered by AT&T at a Seattle waterfront restaurant, a company executive says to Joe Olander, the likable science-fiction writer president of Evergreen College: "I hate my job at AT&T; I live for my hobbies."

David Aikman is one of my fellow speakers. The *Time* magazine correspondent is in white collar with colored shirt and a well-scrubbed face. About the only thing a *Time* writer doesn't do is write. He hasn't heard of *The Australians*. Depressing. Unless, of course, he has heard of it but prefers to pretend otherwise—depressing in a different way.

Seattle has a wonderful market, more a working market than Boston's or Baltimore's, yet with tourist and handicraft elements as well. All in bracing clear air. Beside the market lies a tame night district. The peep booths delicately have the bottoms of the doors cut off so the attendant (and others) can get the gist of anything going on inside. I manage to get together in a booth with a clean, healthy, polite, handsome Oriental.

In the street, I met a well-built ex-marine named Curtis. He came back to the Sheraton and we made love. He said, "Be sensual, not sexual." I think he felt I overwhelmed him a bit, and perhaps came on too fast. The sex went ahead of the feelings, he later said, smiling, in explaining why he did not come. "Have you ever been to bed with a Black man before?" he asked me.

October 30, 1987, Seattle

Seattle is clean, buoyant, hospitable, with the buzz and sparkle of a port, and a people who love the outdoors life. A journalist at the *Seattle Post-Intelligencer*, Wanda Anderson, interviews me about *The Australians* over a British-style afternoon tea at the Sheraton. "It's a hard book to talk about," she says. Is this because it doesn't have a "line"?

Two radio interviews bring wonderfully warm praise for the book from both hosts. "There's such a lot of affection in this book, Jim Altoff says at NBC Radio. "Such a lot of affection."

Compliments come in about my talk yesterday. How weird that I got so scared about it. Yet if I hadn't gotten scared, maybe I wouldn't have prepared thoroughly; if the speech was good, it was because of the preparation.

October 31, 1987, Boston

That tired but exhilarated feeling that comes from a night in the plane on the way back from a trip. I took the bus to go get back my computer. Sitting a few rows away from me was a very handsome and charming-looking stud. When I looked, he looked back. When I put my hand inside my thighs with fingers on my cock, his eyes were riveted to that spot.

At Beacon Street, he got off. I decided to get off too. He had a hardon, pushing high to the left in his pale blue jeans. I walked along with him toward Kenmore Square, where he was headed to go bowling. Chiseled lips, lanky body, flashing white eyes, dick soaring up. Yes, he'd done it before. "With a coupla guys." Does he like getting sucked? "Yeah." Did you suck them too? "Of course."

We installed ourselves in a bathroom within Boston University Bookstore. He turned out to be a magnificent kisser and cocksucker. He wanted me to come in his mouth. I didn't, but after I shot huge loads over his hand, he bent down and lapped cum up from my swollen dick-head.

Off he went to his bowling. I walked in Kenmore Square trembling with happiness. "You're old," he had said to me as we walked along Beacon Street. "Gee, are you 28 or something?"

November 5, 1987, Boston

I got an article on China done for *Yomiuri*. From the Colonnade Hotel, I faxed it to Tokyo. In the early evening, I got a message from Mr. Hori that it had arrived but was too small to read! Would I send it again? I dispatched it to FE, recklessly spending money on a piece that may, in the end, yield me nothing. I sent the article also to the Korean paper *Dong Il Ribao*, with which I have a tie as Guest Columnist.

A lunch at the Harvard Club with the Sobins. Well-connected at Boston University, Julian[285] urges me to consider "doing some things" for them. Lee and Julian have made a lot of money dealing with China, but they have not ended up with a rosy picture of China and the Chinese.

November 6, 1987, Boston

I dreamed about Edward erotically during the night. In the morning, I lay there, unable to rise and face the day. The phone rang. It was Edward; he said he had to speak to me right away. In he came looking tense and clutching a copy of this morning's *USA Today*. Its front page had a story saying warts and other skin problems may be a result of the AIDS virus. He told me he has had a rash for some weeks and that he's developed a rectal wart as well as the flaring up of the wart on his toe. "The whole pattern is one of deterioration," he said tightly.

I went over to the Harvard Coop to see bookseller George Stephens. He was very affable and asked me to sign 20-odd copies of *The Australians*. "It's a welcome book," he said, without saying it was selling like hot cakes. He was very interested to hear that Simon & Schuster is putting an ad for the book in the Christmas issue of *The New York Times Book Review*.

At the Fairbank Center, Marianne Bastid was good, as always, in her talk about education policy in 20th-century China. Bird-like and precise, she has taken on the slower aura of middle age as well.

November 7, 1987, Boston

At length, I drag myself out of bed. I must face Edward though it is without enthusiasm. I remarked to him (Li-li's prognosis) that I am insecure because, as a child, I sensed— with a working mother—abandonment always just around the corner. Edward said that was perhaps the truest thing I have ever said. I went on to say rather sadly that I have been finding that the world is not as I had thought it, that I myself am not the person I imagined myself to be, and that in this life, what I want I often cannot have.

"Write that down," he said. "That's good."

While I was at Kenmore Square, Kay's apartment was broken into. Consternation at my condo building. All eyes seem to be looking at me and asking how many young Black men have keys to this building.

From prison, Julius phones. When he asked what I was going to be doing in NH, I told him promoting *The Australians*. "You wrote a book? I didn't know you had the potential!"

Emotions all at 6s and 7s, I go to the Combat Zone. Furious sex on all fronts. Then I descend from the mountain to eat a wonderful *moo shi rou* at Peking Cuisine.

---

[285] Julian Melvin Sobin (1920-2001), a chemical manufacturer who became part of a small group of Americans invited to attend the 1972 Canton Trade Fair. At the time of this entry, Sobin was a fellow at Harvard's Center for International Affairs.

November 10, 1987, Boston

The people at Concord Library in NH have prepared for my visit very well, but there is a snowstorm, and few come to my lecture. The sad-faced man from the local bookstore has brought 50 books; he sells six. Afterwards, Mrs. Gross, together with her grumpy son and his wife, take me to dinner at the Ramada Inn. They are well-informed about NH politics, which is almost as local and convoluted as Chinese politics.

November 11, 1987, Boston

Changing trains from the Red Line to the Green on my way back from NH, I see this guy almost alone on the platform at Washington Street, seemingly in difficulty. Amazingly it is Edward. His back is giving him agony; he had just stepped off a train in order to get away from crowds of people. He is on his way back from Randolph. So sore is the lower back that he cannot even lift his briefcase or the canvas bag he also has with him.

I took him home. He couldn't crouch to get into a cab, so we took the T. Halfway there, he said perhaps he should come to my place. I didn't say no. He took a hot bath, phoned work to cancel, and slept under sedation until Reggie came in to fetch him in the late afternoon.

While he slept in my bed, I glanced into his appointments book that was on the bed in the small room, learning that he visited Chicago, had pizza and rum and coke with Sam, and, two days after that, helped Sam move house. The entry for October 5 read: "Choked by Roscoe. The End." I am sure Cheekun, were he to know, would say that I willed my own unhappiness by looking at that appointment book.

November 12, 1987, Boston

Reading *House of Trees*, with its Australian language, I find the phrase for my character weakness. I "drop my bundle" rather readily. Down the decades, my grandmother's voice echoes, "Ross, please don't drop your bundle."

November 13, 1987, Boston

Who should call but Randy B It is seven years since we met in Indiana in a hotel swimming pool. The night together at that time was memorable; I had all but forgotten about him. Now working in LA, living with a Finn, he was on his first visit to Boston. Today he came over and we fell upon each other with passion. "You have such energy," he said in his slow sincere way, "whether in bed or at the word processor."

He likes my "hairline." I think he wanted me to fuck him—the quite amazing size of his dick precluded any urging of him to fuck me—but he's pretty wary of AIDS, so we stopped short of that.

November 14, 1987, Boston

I am in the middle of writing a review for the *Chicago Tribune* of Joan Colebrook's memoir when Reggie breathlessly arrives. He's going to shop. Afterwards, we try to make love. But first, Caroline phones. Then a buddy of Reggie phones. Then the groceries arrive as neither of us has clothes on. He says Caroline is complaining about the time he spends here. I said doesn't she need her space. "I'm her spice," he rejoins quickly, falling prey to my Australian accent.

Caroline calls yet again—where is Reggie? She decides to come and pick him up. Reggie straightens himself up. I said surely, it'll take 30 minutes for her to get here. No, five, he says. Twenty minutes later, as we are still watching a video, he pulls off his pants. "Let me fuck you now, Ross." The horn soon toots below.

November 16, 1987, Boston

A letter from Shengde with the bombshell that he is going to Australia to study! God, will there be any talented young Chinese intellectuals left in China within a decade?

A mad night ride to Hanover, NH, after a lovely dinner at Copley's. What am I doing in one more chase to urge two men and a dog to buy and read *The Australians*?

November 17, 1987, New Hampshire

The lady who runs the radio program is ill. A substitute has not read my book. She also lacks umph. At the book signing in Dartmouth Bookstore, there are but three people to sign books for. But how pretty Hanover is. This is America as few people around the world know America.

Forlornly, I board my bus back to Boston. I turn my attentions to a lovely blond jock across the aisle in our big speeding bus. He wants. The tragedy of my spiritual condition is that I didn't want him enough to risk reactions in the daylight bus. A couple of years ago in Texas, I was so much bolder!

November 18, 1987, Boston

A nice evening with Ken at the new restaurant Columns. He reckons Edward must have felt overwhelmed by me, that maybe I don't realize the impact I have on people, and that my accomplishments, which I take for granted, can be a problem for a younger friend. With some younger people, yes, but I'm not so sure about Edward's case. He is a very bright and tough guy.

November 19, 1987, Boston

I speak at a luncheon of the Institute of Politics at the Kennedy School at Harvard. A pleasant occasion. They quiz me alike about Australia and China. One of the fellows, a former premier of a Canadian province, tries to revive the social democratic vision, but I think I convinced the audience it wilts. Only sherry is offered—Oh, Harvard—so I drink water and enjoy it.

After playing squash, I receive a visit from Wyatt, Robert, and the mercurial Mikey. We sat upstairs, as they like to do, enjoying the view. Mikey and I fooled around once they all got into some grass. We don't seem to be able to keep our hands off each other.

Later downstairs, I had Robert's and Mikey's dicks in my mouth together, but Wyatt was left out—my mouth isn't that big—so we eased off. Just as the four of us were setting off to eat at Huskie's, David C phoned. After consulting the others, I asked David to meet us there. We had a great time. David, of all people, had no ID, so could not order a drink. Instead, he shared my white wine and the waiter didn't mind. Like most waiters I have met at Huskie's, he was on his first night's work.

When we went back, there was some fooling around, but as it settled down, it was David who stayed. We made love very happily indeed, and he slept with me all night. Maybe Mikey was surprised by David's fairly masterful personality. I hope to God he wasn't upset, for Mikey is sensational. Early in the morning, while David and I were still in bed, the electrician came to put in the new lobby lights downstairs.

November 20, 1987, Boston

I told Edward, we are not in a dress rehearsal, this is life. We don't have endless chances to choose what we are going to enjoy and to do. Both of us have to be honest. I have prayed about this; perhaps he has, too. If we value each other deeply, either we look ahead, repair the damage, work on the relationship—or we cut the thing off.

"You don't understand friendship," he said. I replied that I had fine friends.

I said he had damaged me. He said I'd damaged him. Then I said, let's not exaggerate, we are both adults, and we'll be OK; let's even be a bit light-hearted about it, have a drink together and a laugh, and then shake hands on it. But for God's sake, let us get out of each other's lives.

He became silent and gloomy. But I did not want to prolong the occasion. At the door, I gripped his hand and begged him, "Let's not exaggerate this. And let's part on good terms." He said this was going to hurt him far more than I realized. As he left, he said, "I hope you find someone who will make you happy."

Straight away, I phoned Li-li. In the middle of our conversation, Edward called to say he'd forgotten his umbrella; could he come back for it? Somehow, I wasn't as shocked as I should have been. I said OK. I also mentioned that, at last, I'd found the comic books that he'd been looking for. He said he was on his way to get both.

He came upstairs and quite unexpectedly started a new tack. It must have been no coincidence, he said, that he forgot the umbrella. It followed on from the other two recent circumstances that had thrown us together again. Wasn't there a meaning to this? He said he had decided there were two choices. A cutoff. In his opinion, that was impossible. A new beginning—accepting each other just as we are. I was too far gone emotionally to re-open everything. I said let's talk about that sometime during the weekend. I wanted to go to sleep. He said he was hungry—wouldn't I share a pizza? We went to Huskie's to dine with the understanding that we would just chat about this and that.

November 22, 1987, Boston

Continued goings-on with the research department of the *Geographic*. I am sick of my article now. I care little what changes they make because it hardly seems my piece anymore.

November 24, 1987, Boston

Wyatt and Mikey arrived. Mikey was determined to fuck me, and this he did. He had my legs high up against the bookcase, and long unread tomes on socialism and Russian history came tumbling down as he rammed his huge prick into my rather unpracticed white asshole.

November 25, 1987, Boston

Kay drove me to Copley Square, where I picked up a film. Lovely one of Reggie in the bedroom; weak one of him in a suit. Some nice ones of F. Some of Edward that would seem to justify Laurent's remark the night he met him: "There's something wrong with that guy."

At home, I found Laurent asleep in bed. I joined him, browsing in a copy of *Publishers Weekly* until he awoke and we made nice love. Later a pleasant dinner at Columns. Tonight, his brother and detested wife arrive from Washington. Laurent has to ferry them about. The obligations within these sprawling families!

November 26, 1987, Thanksgiving Day, Boston

With Laurent down at Providence, I collect myself this afternoon. Some re-ordering of papers and furniture gives me slivers of satisfaction. Much indeed to be grateful for— even the house is lovely when I tidy and clean and then sit on a sofa and drink in the vistas. Even growing older isn't bad if you think of the alternative.

November 27, 1987, Boston

Just as I was thinking about Reggie, he arrives. Spent yesterday *en famille,* and his brother got leave from prison for the day. We were both really in the mood. I think he has something on his mind about Caroline, but I didn't push him to talk about it.

In the evening, I took Laurent to a dinner party that Van Long gave at the Boylston Street restaurant of his brother. Nearly all Chinese. Van looks well. Chuan is there and masterful as always. Her daughter Felicity is now a graduate student at Columbia; tomorrow, she wants to come and see me about her thesis. I gave Van, who is a nephew of Chuan, a copy of *The Australians.* He said a biography of his father, the former warlord of the southwest, has just been published in Hong Kong, and the same edition also within China. This pleases him immensely.

November 30, 1987, Boston

Ann Swift comes in to clean bearing a nice clipping about *The Australians* from yesterday's *Boston Globe*. The travel editor has a round-up of books about far-flung spots which he recommends for Holiday Reading—my tome *The Australians* is there. It will help the book in shops like Banana Republic.

Late at night, the phone rings and it's William. I had almost forgotten him. "Is your cock hard for me?" he asked on the phone. Eventually, I invited him around, not one hundred percent sure who he was. It turned out to be the Latino guy I met on Huntington Ave. Each time we met—only three or four times—we just about devoured each other, and tonight was the same. "I need it now" were his first words. There was no need for me even to get out of bed. William is tied up with a guy who has three kids. The guy's out of town this weekend, hence his "need" for me.

December 2, 1987, Boston

Feeling that I had not expressed much gratitude to Edward last night for his role over the renovations, I phoned him at work. I said he had been right to push me to hire Stuart. Was there something I could buy him, or something we could do, to say thank you. He said he was "flabbergasted." He would think about it.

I told him I was probably going to Santo Domingo tomorrow. He said he'd phone tonight to check—if I didn't get away, we could meet in a day or two. At last, in the early evening, Laurent leaves—I like his company, but I have so much to do. Mikey and Wyatt come in, and although I am packing for my trip tomorrow, I can hardly resist some dallying. Mikey looks great in a green jacket. He and I alternately suck each other; Wyatt jerks off as he watches from my bed.

As the two of them watch TV, I go to Newbury's to dine. While I am out of the house, Edward calls from Randolph—twice—to see if I am leaving as planned and to wish me a good trip to the Dominican Republic. The first time he speaks to Wyatt and the second to Mikey. The pair of them, cum wiped away, go off to a club and I go to bed.

December 3, 1987, Santo Domingo

A delicious feeling of freedom as I board the plane for San Juan. No overcoat, little luggage, heading for a country I haven't been to for twenty years. By 4:30 PM, after a second flight from PR to Santo Domingo, I am by the pool under a blazing sun at the Sheraton Hotel. Drinking in the sun, dreaming.

Jealousy's root, it seems, is a kid treated as the center of the world. Perhaps I was a modified case of this—the third and last child spoiled by a mother who wanted to hang on too much.

A guy hangs around the pool garden. We smile. Hector is a security guard at the hotel. But this afternoon he's off duty. The beauty of the situation is that he has access to a very restricted hotel. I accept his offer of a massage in my room for 40 pesos. Hector is married with two kids. He is thin and brown and cheerful. He sucks me nicely. I like his ass and suggest fucking him. "Have you got a condom?" I didn't have one on hand as it happened. His lovely asshole could hardly take all the cum I finally shot hotly into him. I speak no Spanish, and he has ten words of English, but it mattered little.

December 4, 1987, Santo Domingo

Overland magazine from Australia has a piece by the lively Richard Falk on the world scene. He urges that something in between capitalism and socialism would be best. I think individual self-fulfillment should be the centerpiece of any social philosophy. Kindness as a virtue should have a place, too—even a smile counts. Sexual joy—though there are two sides to that one, for it can accentuate conflict as well.

By the parapet overlooking the sea, I meet Carlo. A sunny personality, brightly dressed, straight with a twist. I liked his eyes and his smile and his chunky ass. He told me it was impossible for him to go into the Sheraton. I said let's try, but Carlo was right. We were firmly turned away even from going together to the second-floor coffee shop. We will meet tomorrow.

December 14, 1987, Santo Domingo

On a golden morning, Carlo takes me for a walk to a bank of rocks where people fish. He thought no one would be fishing so early. But every time we positioned ourselves for sex, we caught sight of a guy with rod and line. Walking back, Carlo said the nearby Napolitano Hotel posed none of the problems of the Sheraton. I decide to move there in the early afternoon and asked Carlo to come by at 4 PM.

Before I moved, I met an airline steward at the Sheraton. Born in the Dominican Republic, he now lives in New York. We looked across the pool at each other and "wanted," as Roger Casement says in his diaries. He was a bit uptight, but he followed me into the shower room, and I jerked off his meaty, big-headed prick as he panted out his pleasure. Greasy with sun-tan oil, I wanted to get my dick into him as I did so, but he was not so bold.

The shift to the Napolitano worked beautifully. The hotel staff is like a big Spanish family. Carlo was a delight. We began in the bar downstairs with a beer or two. It seemed easier to move upstairs from there than from the lobby. I asked him to massage me, but he had no idea how to do it. This was charming—I taught him by doing it to him. When he took over, he focused on my asshole and nearly drove me crazy. Soon he was rimming me as I looked down on his handsome brown face and flashing eyes, facing down the length of his lithe, smooth body.

After a while, I lay across him and sucked his silky balls as he went on driving his hot tongue into my bum. I shot a huge double orgasm load in his hand as we stood together, he just behind me, in front of a large mirror, six floors above the shimmering sea.

I dined alone on magnificent seafood in the restaurant of the Napolitano. After that, a stroll along the waterfront was enough; I didn't feel like going to a club, though Carlo urged it and the guidebooks list several.

December 5, 1987, Santo Domingo

In Santo Domingo, it is a huge decision whether to keep an appointment with Carlo to drive to Boca Chica, whether to go alone, or perhaps just explore the Spanish city where I am on foot. I must have left Boston behind me to be so preoccupied with indulgence.

The city reminds me of a Catholic school: conservative yet coquettishness on all sides. It has some grand places from the Columbus era. But it is not clean and resembles a provincial city, not a great capital.

In the end, I go to Boca Chica alone in a huge broken-down taxi. It is a gaudy place. I expected waves, but the protected water is quite flat. A stroll along the beach under a sizzling sun. I stop for a beer at a little kiosk under a palm tree. I share my large local beer with a beautiful guy named Julio. Wearing only swimming trunks, he was curled up on a cane chair, eyes flashing, smooth skin gleaming in the sun's rays. But he did not "want." The one that did at this kiosk was a half-crazy guy who talked wildly as the others laughed. Embarrassed, I walked on.

Coming back in the wonderful jeepney, a tiny boy of perhaps 9 looks at me with the eyes of a 40-year-old. With astonishment, I realize that he is flirting with me. As we are crammed in the bus with legs tightly pressed together, he tells me the fare is only one peso. I can hardly believe this. Later the conductor comes by, and I give him $5. No change is immediately forthcoming. The tiny boy, now sitting behind me in a minibus that grew more crowded with each stop, hisses that I should get change. Sure enough, the conductor, with whatever feelings toward the urchin, then hands me four pesos. Back in Santo Domingo, the tiny boy wanted to escort me back to the Sheraton. I was terrified of the possibilities and had to shake him off.

I walk in the evening gloom by the monuments of Avenida Washington—what power Spain showed in perpetuating its influence!—and then dine at a sidewalk cafe on the usual seafood delights.

Carlo arrives to take me to the Penthouse Club. It's quite elegant, but there are few people. I suggest we go to another one. "No problem," Carlo says each time a problem arises.

On the way out, we saw a group of guys hanging around in front of Penthouse. One of them, a dark guy called Luis, I invited into our taxi. Luis knew the scene and suggested Anna Maria, a bar that Carlo had never heard of. It was a nice place, with white-washed walls, fancy prints, a clientele of ordinary Santo Domingo guys. I had both Carlo and Luis in tow, which was not an ideal situation. In the end, perversely, I had to take my leave from both of them in order to avoid choosing between them and hurting the other. But I arranged to meet Luis tomorrow.

December 6, 1987, Santo Domingo

I tire of Luis after a while. The sex with him was ordinary—less than ordinary after Carlo. He says he doesn't have a girlfriend, "because they talk too much"—he meant in the sense of gossiping. Speaking English to a degree, he told me a leading gay bar mysteriously burnt down recently.

I probably should have stayed with Carlo and not gotten entangled with Luis. That lure of the new can be addictive and dehumanizing. In fact, Carlo—under tutelage—was a magnificent lover.

As the afternoon wears on, I pack my bags. A short stay, but it is time to leave. I like short vacations. Nice to get away and nice to get back. I feel better in spirit than when I left Boston. At Santo Domingo airport, the immigration people idly chat with each other as passengers wait to have their documents examined. My Eastern flight to San Juan is late, and as I would have missed the connection to Boston, they put me on a flight to Miami instead.

December 7, 1987, Boston

It is Laurent's birthday, and though I'm exhausted and wish to postpone the celebratory dinner, I think he wanted not to. So we went to Capriccio Più and had a lovely meal and a nice chat about his courses, the Dominican Republic, and life in general. I doubt he will go to Haiti for Christmas. Maybe we can go away together briefly somewhere else—if I don't decide to go to Australia, and if my condo gets renovated on time.

December 8, 1987, Boston

Quite an evening which turns into quite a night—but I think I earned a little fling, as things begin to fall into place for me. I returned from the Northeastern seminar, and a stop at the gym, and was going to have some soup, read, and go to bed early. But Jonathan came in and we got to know each other better. He didn't drink to excess as before. His body is smooth and sexy. His dick, once aroused, is big and sensual. Eventually, I think he will let me fuck him.

"You're very aggressive," he kept saying. Then he would complain that I was hard, but he wasn't properly so—this was my fault, he felt. But he is very handsome and has a sparkle to his personality.

I went downstairs with him a bit after midnight, intending to dine at Oceanic. Waiting for the bus, I saw this attractive man in shark-skin pants walk toward my building and then go in. I moved closer—it was Miles.

He was like a furnace. It was all I could do to delay his orgasm long enough for me to enjoy that tight, hard body. We sucked each other, which I don't remember us doing before. He decided to stay the night. I was just dozing off at about 1:30 AM when the doorbell rang. It was Reggie on the way home from an office party.

He was quite high. I handed him back the negative of the photo of him nude on my bed that I got developed (for discretion's sake) in Seattle. He hardly glanced at it. Two months ago, it seemed a matter of life and death to him to deliver that picture into his hands.

"Who's in your bed?" he asked. I said a friend from Baltimore. He said he would like to come to bed with Miles and me. He was in a great mood, and I was very turned on by being in the middle of these two Black hunks.

But Miles wasn't keen—he played with me but not with Reggie, and he seemed to be keeping his face out of the way. I mainly sucked Reggie, though at one point, Miles suddenly drove his prick straight up my asshole. Sometime after two o'clock, I gently asked Reggie about letting Caroline know where he was. "Let me go," he said, "I want to rest." A few hours later, he awoke cursing and raving. The whole household had to mobilize to get him back to Brighton.

"Call me tomorrow," I said to Reggie as he rushed downstairs to his cab. "If I'm alive," he replied—it was a reference to Caroline's likely reaction to him getting home at 5:30 AM.

Later Reggie insists that Miles isn't from Baltimore but from Mattapan and that he knows him. We'll see—Reggie can get these things wrong on occasion and feels he knows nearly everyone in Boston. He's brilliant in assessing character, fallible on facts.

December 9, 1987, Boston

A long evening with Edward, which ends up with a late dinner at Oceanic. On the way home in the cab, he astounded me by saying he wasn't sure whether he'd come to my party on Sunday or not. I hadn't asked him. It never occurred to me to ask him. As a courtesy—especially since I have asked Glen to the party—I told Edward about the event, mentioning that, of course, it wasn't his cup of tea.

December 10, 1987, Boston

It is the Christmas season with a vengeance. Parties roll by like tramcars in the streets of Melbourne. A nice office party at Stu's in Newbury Street, mainly real estate, legal, and business types.

Then to Harvard for a lavish do at Dan Yergin's consulting firm's new offices by the Charles Hotel. Nadav Safran[286] and I discuss the parallels (and non-parallels) between what has happened to Beirut and what might happen to Hong Kong. Dan thanks me for sending him *The Australians*, but seems too busy to read it. A lawyer who is occasionally retained by Dan's firm says, "I know who you are: you were recently written up by Marian Christy in the *Boston Globe*." Then he is gone. Harvard Square has become glitzy and costly; few of my old grad student days' haunts remain.

December 11, 1987, Boston

I told Laurent that Edward may worm his way into Sunday's party. Laurent is easygoing about such things, happily. Laurent is in bed when Reggie comes by to go liquor shopping. Reggie astounds me by saying Caroline has come with him; she's in the car downstairs. "I'll take her with me, and we'll see about her coming up when I'm finished." Meanwhile, Reggie pops into the bedroom to chat with Laurent as if it were the kitchen, and Laurent were clothed rather than naked.

When Reggie comes back from the store, he announces that Caroline would like to come up. Meanwhile, Laurent had agreed to the idea of him meeting Caroline. We all gathered upstairs—Laurent clothed—and Caroline and I drank Folonari Soave as

---

[286] Nadav Safran (1925-2003) was professor of government and director of Harvard's Center for Middle Eastern Studies.

Reggie and Laurent drank Heineken. We had a great time. Laurent and Caroline hit it off well, and Reggie was proud as a peacock at bringing everyone together.

December 12, 1987, Boston

Last night, Caroline said to Reggie, "Is Ross's friend Laurent gay?" Reggie said he nearly fell over. But he recovered and said he had no idea. "You know, Ross, Caroline doesn't suspect anything," Reggie went on. And if she did, she'd come right out and say, 'Reggie, are you gay?'" Maybe he's right.

At six or so, Edward comes to decorate the Christmas tree. He does a wonderful job. At one point, I said: "Edward, I didn't invite you for tomorrow. But now I'm inviting you. It's Christmas, and now I know you'd be interested in coming, I'd like you to come—and it's you who's made the tree so nice."

I then said if he came, I would ask him to bear in mind the rather delicate situation. First, Laurent is going to be a kind of co-host; that is already set. Second, there are people coming who don't know that Edward and I have quarreled, and tomorrow's party isn't the time for shocking them or explaining things—so if he comes, please just slide over that and not present a new atmosphere.

He said it wouldn't be a "condition" of his coming for him to behave this way or not, but to be assured that he would be considerate of these points. I said that was fair enough. We ordered a pizza from Domino's. Edward laughed his head off when the guy came to the door with it, and I asked cheerily, "Are you Mr. Domino?"

As we decorated the tree, he told me how dumb I was, tying things the wrong way, putting the right balls in the wrong place and the wrong balls in the right place ... but it was a lovely evening and very late when he said goodbye.

December 13, 1987, Boston

The party is great fun. Some twenty people. Laurent gets the food from Chinatown without a hitch, and the dishes are delicious. Before the meal, there is a gathering by the fire in the front room. Loring is in great form. Don B tells stories. Laurent mixes affably (he told me later this was his first-ever gay party). Dion and Peter, his friend from Connecticut, both look gorgeous.

Just as the meal starts, Edward comes in and I introduce him to those he has not met. When he sees David Parker, I think for a moment he forgets they had once been together. Don soon reminds him. In fact, as the meal proceeds, they eat lunch together and gaze at each other from the couch and loveseat, respectively. Later, Laurent told me Edward was very cordial to him. During much of the party, I was far away from him. I did try to introduce him to Peter at one point. "I'm in the middle of a conversation," he rejoined.

Many guests had left when Mikey arrived. At once, he and Edward hit it off. Edward engaged him in a tête-à-tête. It became a rampant flirtation. Eventually, I had a chance to talk alone with Mikey—Edward said perhaps he should help me clear up; I said, sure, you stack up dishes and I'll do the trash. Mikey said Edward is "really hot." I said we must have a threesome, but tonight wasn't the occasion. Mikey said he understood.

Soon after Mikey left, Miles came by unexpectedly. I tried to draw Edward into a conversation *à trois* at the table as Miles and I ate dessert. But Edward wouldn't. At times, it seems he doesn't know what a shared, multi-sided conversation is. I did not want to be in a long tête-à-tête with Miles, so I drew back and helped Edward with cleaning up.

Edward and I gravitated downstairs to sit together and talk. Miles had a long phone call to make, and shut himself in the small room to do so. At first, we had a great time chatting and reminiscing. Edward grabbed the vodka bottle. "Since everyone is an alcoholic, I might as well be so, too." I went in to tell Miles that he should take his time, as Edward and I needed to continue our talk.

December 14, 1987, Boston

Laurent came in and we made love. Halfway through, Miles arrived; I had an appointment to come with him and see his apartment. When I returned, Laurent and I resumed, pleasantly enough, though, as usual, he enjoys it more than I. Then we dined long and garrulously at Huskie's. The waitress, for once, was very experienced.

December 15, 1987, Boston

I felt better this morning and I read and wrote some letters. Then I fetched Joan Colebrook from Jamaica Plain and took her to the airport on her way to Florida. She said I look very Australian today. Once more, she warned me, as we ate clam chowder in the Eastern terminal, that I am taking silly risks with my body by my sexual behavior. The mind depends on the body, she insists, but she knows little of gay sex. On the other hand, she speaks from experience in that eye and heart problems shadow her; I guess she knows more than I that if you lack good health, you lack almost everything.

McCarry phones me about my Hong Kong outline. He likes it, but he drops a bombshell. Joe Judge wrote an article on Hong Kong 15 years ago for the magazine, and ever since then, he considers Hong Kong "his topic." Mac doubts that Joe would accept me writing about it. A pity. From an economic point of view, I don't think I can embark on the book about Hong Kong unless I have a *National Geographic* commission.

Kirkland House Christmas Dinner, but I did not stay long. The turn-out by the Senior Common Room was thin and, by the end of cocktails, those who had come may have begun to wonder why they did so. Paul Freund shocked me by saying it is a decade since he retired. He was very interested when I mentioned *Madame Mao*. But in these situations, my reaction is first to be amazed that a well-informed friend had not heard of the book!

December 16, 1987, Boston

Lisa from Simon & Schuster calls all very businesslike to say she's working on media appointments for my trip to Los Angeles. Good. Nothing like a publisher paying for the air ticket to make them focus on good use of time in a city. We may even include Chicago in the mini-tour since Selma Shapiro has an invitation for me to visit libraries in Chicago in connection with a "Bridging the Distance" program that links Illinois and New South Wales. Also, the Harvard Club of New York call to invite me to speak about the book in the early spring.

December 17, 1987, Boston

Christmas party at Kirkland House. After dinner, Arthur Smithies and I together sang the folksong "Waltzing Matilda" before the assembled, wine-sunk, sex-starved multitude. I introduced the song as one "impregnated with the Australian spirit," and then ask darkly if they knew who had impregnated Waltzing Matilda—adding only that both she and Arthur Smithies came from Tasmania. This is the way you do things at KH when Christmas comes.

December 18, 1987, Boston

To my amazement, anger toward Edward rose in me yet again. This passion is a fire that seems impossible to extinguish. I thought the emotional switch was off, but it isn't. I tried to calm myself and say something as candidly as I could. "I love you, Edward. Because I love you, and because, since I 'tried to strangle you,' the physical tie between us has ended, there is too much tension involved in us meeting. I find I cannot cope with you. There is no pleasure or sharing or joy left.

Luther calls and we have a nice chat. I think he's lonely. There was no chance for me to tell him that from my side, too. It was a welcome time for us to be back in touch.

Laurent comes in after his last exam. He smokes a joint, we watch a video with half attention, and then the evening news. He has canceled his ticket to Haiti at his father's insistence. Port-au-Prince just is not very safe. We dine at Thai Cuisine—an excellent duck and a poor curry—and then Laurent went to work at the nursing home.

December 19, 1987, Boston

The money position after the sale of 395 Broadway looks OK. My home will probably look nice not too long from now. *The Australians* may still have some life left in it. But I think Edward really is over. And I see my mother's health in decline. I will be more alone. I do not see Laurent as a replacement for Edward—even for Henry. Can I use the bleak circumstance of my aloneness to face myself more fully?

December 20, 1987, Boston

A lazy weekend. Copying some movies for Luther in Los Angeles—he has just bought a VCR and has nothing to play on it—turns into one of the day's major activities. Laurent comes in from work at breakfast time and we spend the day together. We read the papers in the morning. Then I played squash with Dave. I won by a hair's breadth in the fifth game. When I had Edward in mind, I lost points; when I got him off the screen of my mind, I won points. Later over dinner at the Commonwealth Grille, I told Laurent about this and he seemed amazed. He predicted that the relationship will come back together again one day.

Today, *The New York Times* publishes my article on the Yi people of southwest China. They do it handsomely with nice photos. The mention of my books is good and will probably sell some copies of *The Australians* in the Christmas rush.

December 21, 1987, Boston

I wake up feeling desolate, morning after morning. No doubt I should follow that old boy scout maxim of leaping out of bed the moment I awake to avoid morbid thoughts. Reggie comes in and we have a lovely time, erasing any clouds that still existed from the day before the party. He is an open book—I hope I am to him as well.

December 23, 1987, Boston

Edward rings and asks if he could come by to wish me Merry Christmas. I broke the rule I'd made about phone contact only—Li-li will criticize me!—and said yes. He was charming. He'd brought a gift to put under the tree. Eventually, I cried. We ended up embracing before he left for Connecticut. I cry for a while. Later Bryan S comes by. That lovely smile. That darting, nervous conservatism. "Show me that dick again." Then he is off to the airport to fly to Memphis for a familial visit.

December 24, 1987, Boston

I feel happy bringing my Kaypro back from Inman Square, apparently in good condition again. Later I shopped for computers at the Boston University bookstore. IBM looks like the choice for my next one—after I eventually say goodbye to the faithful Kaypro.

In the sauna at the Y, an electrifying question. A tall, handsome Black guy sitting in the sauna reading the *Boston Globe* says a moment after I enter the room: "We've met before—do you remember where?" It was not the place where I welcomed that question asked out so loud. Never could I have expected who it was.

"It was in the lobby of the Gazebo Hotel in Sydney, Australia," the guy said as everyone in the room swiveled to listen. This handsome stud was Mark, the basketball player who was training a team in Sydney. After that meeting in the lobby, one thing led to another. I ended up sucking him off in his room at the top of the Gazebo—the night before I left Australia to go to see Hong Kong.

I phone Mum at home and later Poppy at her old folks home—both seem in fairly good spirits. The expected warm day Down Under did not materialize. How lackluster Melbourne is at Christmas when the weather is gray and drizzly.

With Laurent I dine at the Café Promenade in the Colonnade. My mind is on Mikey. Should I tell Edward I don't want him to fool around with Mikey? Should I tell Mikey I would prefer that he didn't see Edward?

December 25, 1987, Boston

A relaxing Christmas Day. Laurent comes in from work and we loll around and make love. It was painful dealing with his huge prick and massaging him with the gash in my right hand.

He goes home to sleep for a while. To clear my head, I go for a walk. At the Y on the 3rd floor, a nice old Black guy rims me and sucks me off like an angel. In the afternoon, Laurent and Ray S and I hookup, dine in Chinatown, and then drop into Tony's apartment.

Tony is an excellent host as always, though his guests are lackluster. I was pleasant to his boyfriend but did not talk to him for long. As they prepared to eat turkey, Laurent, Ray, and I went to see Bertolucci's movie *The Last Emperor*. Visually stunning but wooden in its storytelling. For a nightcap, the three of us popped into Sporters. There I found Arthur Maass, who told me how much he liked my article in last Sunday's *New York Times*. Laurent was tickled when I told him this guy was chairman of the Government Department at Harvard.

December 26, 1987, Boston

A peaceful but melancholy mood. Laurent goes home, it seems, with a certain reluctance, yet I needed to be alone, even if I am not completely happy when alone. Last night, he snored without ceasing.

Met a white guy at Boston Public Library and sucked him off in the small bathroom. Later another old sensuous Black guy sucked me in his room at the Y. I drop by Playland and meet two pleasant guys, Glen and Connor. Connor is a cook. I gave him my number and took his.

Later I went to the Pilgrim and had a rather wild time. My firmer chest is bearing rich fruits in terms of men who get worked up sucking my tits. One embarrassing thing: walking along Washington Street, I ran into Laurent. Can our ties survive this mishap? I think so; he's a very mature person and I think he understands me pretty well.

December 27, 1987, Boston

I like these words Gore Vidal wrote some time ago: "In their youth most people worry whether or not other people will like them. I survived by understanding that it is I who am keeping the score. What matters is what I think, not what others think of me; and I am willing to say what I think."

Julius calls to say he is moving to another prison in Bridgewater. The Puerto Rican friend is back behind bars and Julius is angling to become his roommate. One ludicrous barrier to their reunion is a prison policy that roommates must be of the same race! The other day, a Portuguese guy sucked Julius off in the shower. From time to time, this guy watches Julius jerk off. "I come a lot because we don't have as much sex in here as on the outside."

1988

January 5, 1988, Boston

For the first time in a while, I had a white guy. Chris is a young singer from the Conservatory, blond and cheerful with a large cut dick. We made love for a very long time, interrupted once by the arrival of a man to fix a roofing leak. While I was on the phone, he browsed in my front room bookshelves and discovered two of my books. "I'm impressed," he said with a touch of a smile.

A good PEN meeting on the topic of "independent scholarship." Panelists are an impressive tribute to the combining of academic training with the pull of the writing marketplace. But how cold the weather is. Even a little outing becomes an ordeal.

January 6, 1988, Boston

I must be tired from yesterday with Chris. For whatever reason, I feel on the moon this morning. Then unexpectedly Reggie comes in. To set eyes on him is always a tonic for me. Nah, he can't stay. But after he copies some document and then goes to the store for me, he gets mellow and we end up making love while watching *Ebony Humpers*. He asks, "What's the time?" This is his way of asking whether I think we have time for a bit of fun.

January 8, 1988, Boston

On the bus from Harvard, a crazy man is shouting. Then at Central Square, another crazy man gets on and starts his imprecations. The pressure goes off us passengers; the two crazies are in competition. They assume an audience for their ravings. When, instead, they face a rival's ravings, they are thrown back to silence.

Will I go to Puerto Rico tomorrow? Half of me sees the need to get to the sun. The other half wonders if the effort of getting ready is worth it. A big snowstorm has begun—it may make the decision for me.

January 9, 1988, San Juan

A flight to San Juan takes me back in time; it's a decade since I last went to Puerto Rico. That was the Harvard period. Pan's love. Quick getaways at times when my students were preparing for exams. I even took undergraduate blue books to San Juan and graded them on the beach. A shadow hangs over the tourist industry here from the terrible fire a year or so ago at the Dupont Plaza Hotel—98 dead. I stayed at it when it was called the Sheraton. This time, I find the Dutch Inn satisfactory—and safe.

January 11, 1988, San Juan

Golden sun, the smell of sun oil, renting a beach couch, riding the high blue waves. Wandering back from the beach after the sun goes down for a drink at a bar, Italian food, evening prowls.

I see José sitting on the steps of a shop in a side street off Avenida Ashford. He sucked well, though his anxiety about avoiding getting pre-cum in his mouth was a little off-putting.

Finished *Iron and Silk*, a memoir of living in China by Mark Salzman. Touching, biting, refreshingly economical—one of the better books on China of its type.

January 12, 1988, San Juan

I met Willie on the beach by the Atlantic Beach Hotel. He smiled nervously as he told me he had just had a scare with a dog that rushed at him. It seemed to mark him as a soft person. We had a drink at Atlantic Beach, sizing each other up.

The curvaceous type, Willie was sensational in bed. He had told me beforehand that he was a good lover. At that stage, I just looked at him and said fine. But it was true. By the time he began to rim me, I was quite out of control. The only thing I wanted that I couldn't do was fuck him. But the pleasure was so intense that even this did not matter a great deal.

"You're nice," he said with his broad smile. "Not young, not old, but a middle man."

January 13, 1988, San Juan

The clubs don't appeal. Vibrations was full of New Yorkers gazing at a porn movie screen. The only attractive local was the doorman. In old San Juan, the bars I'm familiar with are no more. Lion's Den is shuttered up. La Vista seems to have turned straight, as has Small World.

However, the bathhouse on Calle Luna—now called Steamworks—was a pleasant surprise. At the desk, a condom is given with the towel. I played around mildly with several young guys whose Hispanic curves turned me on. Then three guys who seemed to know each other drew me into a room with them. Only one of them wildly turned me on. Still it was fun, exciting in the novelty of the form. Two of them sucked me. I sucked one. One wanted me to fuck him as he rimmed another and this inflamed me well and truly. With four, though, it's likely—as in this case—that the lines of attraction are uneven.

January 15, 1988, San Juan

The party to honor Jim Williams on his appointment as director of Boston Human Rights Commission is stilted. I felt the speeches were clichés. "Discrimination," everyone cries as if the meaning of the term was quite clear. In fact, it is murky. Every day our lives are one long chain of discrimination. How much of it should be resisted by darling Jim's office?

Don Butterfield is there, worried about his high blood pressure, still trying to hang on to E. Jealousy is more complicated among gays than among straights. Consider this scene: a man's wife is being cruised by another man at a party. The husband comes across, beams, puts his arm around his wife and says, "Isn't she gorgeous?" That defuses all. But if the "wife"—as well as the third person—was a man it would not be so simple. For it would not only be the "wife" choosing between her husband and the new guy; in a gay situation, the new guy and the husband could like each other and leave the "wife" out. This is actually close to what I feared when Mikey met Edward that fateful night of my party in December.

Sexually I'm full of curiosity. But I'm not desirous of really giving myself to anyone. There's no equivalent urge, as I had with Edward (and Pan before him), to merge myself with the other person, share everything with him.

January 17, 1988, Boston

Pretty nice time with Connor. A double orgasm inside him. But I felt it was hurting him a bit. I am still eaten with jealousy as I speculate about Edward and Mikey. How feeble is the human spirit, or at least mine, requiring an anxiety to fill any vacuum.

The February *National Geographic* arrived. The cover is ordinary—two Australians looking glum—but the issue itself is great. I am pleased at the treatment of my own piece and delighted at the warmth about me in "On Assignment."

January 18, 1988, Boston

I could do a nonfiction book on China that would be more "literary"—as Joan would put it—than I have been planning. Another *COMM*, but less structured, more discursive, more whimsical.

January 19, 1988, Boston

At the gym, a smiling, handsome guy called Joseph. He talked about a thesis he's writing on the various categories of friendships and social ties—drew a diagram in the shape of a pyramid to express it all. In his blue tracksuit, he was good to look at. We exchanged phone numbers.

A nice, if restrained talk with Edward in the late afternoon. He is feeling good. There is the job with Wang. He's going to church. And he's been watching TV shows that have given him the idea that mind is stronger than matter, and that if he has a positive attitude toward tomorrow, he won't get sick.

What ties bind him still to Boston, I asked. He said they are the same as for some time, with people who range in length of closeness to him from 18 years to four years. We embraced and held each for a moment, without kissing, and then he was gone. The end of an era.

I think I can stand back and learn something: to respect people as people; to accept my own irrevocable separateness and thus avoid super-romantic notions of oneness with another; to avoid falling into the trap recalled by Kierkegaard's remark that comparison is the source of all unhappiness; to be less thin-skinned about rejections and set-backs.

With a new friend, I should go step by step. Only as far as I feel comfortable. Sex only as it is matched by a context of feelings and respect. Is that possible?

January 21, 1988, Boston

Joseph, whom I met at the Y, came in late in the afternoon. We drank wine and talked. He was handsomely dressed in jacket and tie. As we sat on the green couch and got closer, he suddenly got up and said he had to take something off. In the lobby, he put something in his bag. Returning to the couch, he explained that he had had his pistol on and felt he should take it off before we got closer.

Was I upset, he asked, that he had a gun with him? Well, for a moment or two I was. We embraced and played around mildly. There wasn't time for more than that—he is not the type for a quickie—as I had squash with Jim at seven.

My article on the Australian bicentenary is out now to a number of papers. So far acceptances from *Chicago Tribune*, *Los Angeles Times*, and the *Sacramento Bee*, a decent start.

Newsday passed—not a sharp enough viewpoint in the piece. Likewise, the Japanese didn't bite as they felt their own man in Sydney could cover the topic. Koreans are too taken up with their own domestic politics—but they will pay for last year's article at long last!

January 22, 1988, Boston

Swarms of carpenters and electricians. I love the sound of the drilling and banging. I go on errands downtown and to Arlington station to get my air ticket for Los Angeles and Chicago. On the train, I suddenly saw Edward. I am sure he didn't see me. He was deep in thought, dressed smartly in beige overcoat and French cap. I started forward to go down the carriage and speak; something stopped me.

I stayed where I was and juggled my emotions. I felt his attractiveness. I felt an understanding for the rumination he may have been engaging in on the eve of his departure from Boston. I felt a surge of conviction that homosexuality is a volatile, perilous condition.

Above all, I felt love for him that contained acceptance of a certain distance. For those few moments at least, as I held back from walking over to him, I believed that I could pull back from him while still loving him and hoping for the best for him.

January 23, 1988, Boston

In the evening, Chris comes in. He has a new girlfriend and this is helping him get over Angela. "This one's 20 years old. I tell ya, after Angela, I'm not having any more young ones."

January 24, 1988, Boston

Laurent snored a lot last night and early in the morning I moved to the small room. I don't like to raise it with him again—he won't be here much longer.

A really great game of squash with David, which I won by a shred at the last moment. Striving for a positive mental attitude at key moments—this won me the match—I kept thinking of Edward. A delicious physical tiredness afterwards, good for mental exertion.

A packet of reviews of *The Australians* from London. A very nice one in the *Daily Telegraph*, two good ones from the provinces, and a blistering, bitter attack in the *TLS* from confirmed enemy Sylvia Lawson. I think I'll reply to her for the many factual mistakes in her venomous piece.

This afternoon in the BPL on the second floor, my eye catches a handsome young guy who looks vaguely Mediterranean. The great squash game this morning made me feel good in my skin; I just bored in on this prince. At one point, something made me take my dick out of my pants; he stared at it, and I could see his cock rising in his sharkskin pants. When the library was about to close, he put together his papers and went out the front door. But he lingered. I spoke to him—no it "isn't safe" to do anything. "Do you have movies?"

"Are you sure you don't want to do anything?"

"I'd just like to watch you jerk off."

I decided to give him my phone number and not meet now. A few minutes later at the bus stop, he came up to me. I was quite surprised. He wondered if I knew a place where he could spend a couple of hours until going to the airport to meet his girlfriend.

"Come back to my place." We jumped into a cab. I was immensely excited at this guy, Giuliano, who has an Italian father and a mother, part-Seychelles and part-Chinese.

"What's the biggest cock you've seen?"

I tell him about the guy in Puerto Rico whom Pan and I jointly sucked off years ago. Then I asked him what's the biggest cock he's ever seen. "Yours, I guess." So, he isn't all that experienced. In the end, movies did not constitute the full agenda. I shot a great load across his magnificent chest.

January 27, 1988, Boston

My Australia article is having a mixed career. *Boston Globe* thinks it's not opinionated enough. Even the *Boston Herald* did not bite.

Mikey looked so mature tonight. Rich eyes, experienced eyes. Evidently, he felt uncomfortable over what was going on between Edward and me. He said he and Edward didn't do anything. Why had Mikey and I become estranged for those weeks? Mikey was reticent. Perhaps he had indeed felt I saw "many people." Later he said this did hurt him, and also was a mirror to his own behavior, with which he's not completely happy, for health and other reasons.

We made wonderful love. His sensuality is almost without equal. He can suck a white boy's cut cock as few others can, playing on the head, applying just the right degree of tongue pressure. This weekend he's going to New York. He hinted that he and Joe, his older boyfriend, have had frictions.

January 28, 1988, Boston

A nice time with Reggie. This despite the fact that there wasn't much sex and neither of us came. Probably if Laurent had not been in the house, we would have gone further. But what fun you can have even if a blinding orgasm doesn't bring it to an end. I'd felt a bit bad about postponing him last night because of Mikey. It was good to draw close again.

Thinking of his approaching married status, he asked if I'd mind much if we had to give up sex afterwards. I didn't actually say I wouldn't mind. "You're not in love with me or anything, are you?" I assured him I wasn't! Perhaps he felt better.

Julius calls and Reggie talks to him for a while. Afterwards, Reggie has that serious expression that never quite looks serious. He says, "Be careful of him." I don't know whether it was because Julius is behind bars or whether because at one point, Julius said to Reggie, "When I get out, you and Ross and I can have a threesome!"

I suck Reggie in the study, sitting on the floor and looking up at him. His eyes are riveted on his cock and my tongue. "Why do I like this so much?" he gasps.

Reggie's brother gets out of prison this week—maybe the apartment in Connor's building, cheap at $190 a month, might suit him. Reggie hasn't decided whether or not to introduce me to his brother.

A message from Norman Lear, the producer, in Los Angeles thanking me for the copy of *The White-Boned Demon*. It turns out he is an admirer of mine through years ago reading *800,000,000: The Real China*. But, oh, that was such a leftish book. What will the famous producer make of the anti-communism of *Demon*?

January 30, 1988, Boston

Many compliments on the *National Geographic* piece. Lee Sobin[287] said she and Julian had never been interested in Australia—until reading the article, and now they want to go. Of all people, the playwright Bill Alfred, whom I bump into after lunching with the Melbourne poet Chris Wallace-Crabbe, has just read it and thinks it "marvelous."

Laurent tells me he actually married one of his many girls—Jackie!—before he turned to boys. Reading further in Nancy Friday's book[288] about jealousy, I feel that in my case jealousy is often self-centeredness: if I want something and can't have it, I react badly. That seems to be the core of what could look like envy (the success of another when I don't succeed) or jealousy (another actually taking what I am reaching for).

---

[287] Leila F. Feinburg Sobin (1920-2011), first American woman to do business in China.
[288] Nancy Friday (1933-2017), author of *My Secret Garden: Women's Sexual Fantasies* and other books on female sexuality. The book Terrill refers to here is *Jealousy* (1985).

January 31, 1988, Boston

I sent the employment section of today's *Boston Globe* to Hank in rural Georgia as requested. Will he really return to Boston? His sister lives in Augusta, so perhaps he could come to see me when I speak to a college there on April 5.

At the BPL this afternoon, I half-expected to run into Giuliano. But I don't think he was there. Last Sunday, a win over David at squash and the lovely time with Jayden went together. Today, a loss to David and no Jayden. Lovely things seldom repeat themselves.

A strange night of mixed excitement and qualms—both teaching me once more the colossal power of sex. Connor came by with his friend Luther, an appealing rough diamond who had already drunk quite a bit. Then Laurent arrived with study books in hand. Connor wanted Laurent, and I had no objection. He'd been waiting for such an opportunity. As Luther and I watched a video—he having showered and made himself comfortable on my bed before I knew what was happening—Connor popped in on Laurent, who was studying in the small room.

As Laurent and Connor got it off, Luther and I did the same in my room. In the end, I fucked Luther, which I had not expected. He came as his body was crushed against the bed by the weight of mine.

Laurent resumed studying. I had to go out and was anxious to wrap up the Connor-Luther visit before Luther got any drunker on the rum and beer which he sipped alternately. When he showered for the second time, various items could be heard clattering to the floor, including, I later discovered, my electric razor, its tiny parts spread to all corners of the room. The noise was so loud that Laurent and I wondered if another golf ball had not arrived through a window.

Connor asked if the two of them could stay the night. I said really that wasn't possible. He said at his place, the landlady didn't like him to have overnight guests.

All this time, Laurent had seemed very quiet; he had gone back to his study books. I got ready to go out—Laurent and I were going to eat—and after a while, when there was silence from the front room, I went in. Luther was fucking Connor. Ten minutes later, I went back and the pace had not let up. Insatiables. Connor's knees were high in the air, Luther was grunting.

In my heart, a jumble of reactions to two handsome Black bodies fluently fusing. Envy, fear, contempt for the animal side of our natures. Also, I was getting hungry and wanted to go eat. Eventually we all left. Laurent and I dined at Huskie's and had a nice talk. "So how was Connor?" I asked Laurent cheerfully. He frowned. "That was a mistake." I was surprised, but left the topic there.

February 1, 1988, Boston

A malaise, I go out. At Northeastern, I suck two white boys. I fantasize that these dicks I am licking are plunging inside Edward—the way I watched Luther go into Connor last night.

Back home, my CD player decides to work and I listen to *Cats*. When the song "Memory" is played, I think, again, inevitably, of Edward. In the night, I dreamed once more of Edward; we were under a sheet together in some sunny clime. I ducked my head down right underneath the sheet and leaned against his thigh, kissing his upper legs and his smooth brown tummy.

Today I was supposed to be preparing my lunch talk at the *National Geographic*, but I made little progress; dramas of personal life intrude.

February 3, 1988, DC

I awake in a Washington hotel room. The same numbness and pessimism that greet me daily are here—leaving town solves nothing. I am weak with nervousness about the speech I am to give today. The Australian press gathers. Each person grunts greetings in the usual Aussie way.

A beautiful meal full of calories. Then an elaborate parade of brief remarks by distinguished people. Eventually, the editor himself rises to make remarks and then introduces me with high praise for writing on China and the ability to blend academic and journalistic approaches to my material. I spoke.

Bill Garrett and Joe Judge were both ecstatic about the speech I made. "Eloquent," said Bill as he pumped my hand. "Put him on the road," he said of me to Joe. "I knew you were a brilliant writer, but I didn't know until today that you were also a brilliant speaker!" Joe was even more extravagant in his praise. I had to cut him off out of embarrassment.

But Bill was not encouraging on my prospects for doing a Hong Kong article. "They'd kill me here if I gave you that story," he said. At the evening party in honor of the movie *Dreamtime*, I tried to convince Tom about my idea for the Hong Kong story.

At night, a lovely encounter with a Black guy called Tim. I ended up fucking him— at his suggestion—though the whole idea was supposed to be that he was straight and that I'd buy him dinner in return for him doing "an unusual thing." You just never know. Well, he did one more unusual thing than he expected. As I shot loads into him, he said, "Don't come inside me." I think he knew I had.

Downstairs for a late-night drink, I ran into Steve Cuddy from Kirkland House days. He's working for AFL-CIO in Seattle. We reminisced, and dissected the labor scene in the USA, West Europe, and Australia. Everywhere labor is on the defensive, it seems to him.

February 4, 1988, Boston

A gathering snowstorm and I land at Logan just in time to avoid problems in the air. Having risen at 5 AM, I am not as able to socialize with Laurent as perhaps he expected.

The phone rang and it was Keith from the Y. Though I was tired, and I knew Reggie might still come in, I trembled with excitement. Since the first time I set eyes on him, this Keith had my heart in my throat. He has the impish manner and the liquid eyes of Edward. That's the key to my infatuation. Once or twice our eyes met at the Y, but he would always be in a hurry. Then a couple of weeks ago, we came together briefly but explosively in the shower. He grabbed my dick and I got a finger up his wonderful asshole.

Tonight, I was certainly not inclined to delay his coming to my home. It happened, though, that Reggie had already arrived when Keith got here. Reggie was terribly late. I explained that when Keith phoned, I assumed that Reggie wasn't coming over. He is good about accepting such a situation. But Reggie wanted to linger and have a bit of a look at Keith. As the three of us are chatting and drinking, the key turns in the door and Laurent enters. Now we are four! *Quoi faire?*

But I was quite determined that this would be Keith's and my moment. I think Laurent got the message about this. I sat beside Keith on the green couch and looked at him quite a lot. Eventually, Laurent went into the little room to study. Reggie breezed out to go and dine with Caroline.

Showing Keith around the house, we got to my study and somehow found ourselves embracing. Heading hotly for the bedroom, we walked along the corridor half-naked. The door of the little room was half open, so Laurent could see what was starting. An hour or so later, he called out "Bye," and the front door closed—a little firmly, I thought.

"Can I fuck you?" I asked Keith.

"With a condom—sure, I want you to so much." He is cuddly and dynamic and charming and intelligent. A civil engineer. Afterwards, he dashed off—a bit like he always dashes off from the Y. "I get up at 5:30 AM," he said as he left. "Engineers have to arrive early in the morning at construction sites. You're a nice man." Then he was gone.

February 5, 1988, Boston

I should have stuck to my desk—plus supervising the Never-Ending Task of the condo renovation—but Connor came in. Soft and unassuming, just having a shower and watching TV, he calmed me down, won me over, and soon had us wildly thrashing about in bed. I wouldn't have thought it likely, given last night with Keith and the night before that with Tim in Washington.

Later in the day, on coming back from errands, I found Connor on my doorstep with two suitcases. He can't stand his room at Brigham Circle. He's going to stay with David tonight; could he leave his stuff with me?

February 7, 1988, Boston

Laurent comes in early as I sit at my desk in my robe. "So you're up already." No comment on Thursday night. Maybe he wasn't upset at all. At any rate, with Laurent, being upset doesn't (as with Edward) equate with making a huge issue of it.

Connor calls. After chatting with him, I pass the phone to Laurent, and they talk for a few minutes. It seems Laurent isn't that keen to see him again. But what was the nature of Laurent's "mistake" last time?

A long talk with Ken Mayer on the phone. He is a kind and caring guy. He gets the impression I am stabilizing myself. "But I am not very happy," I say to him, as if still wanting to be the patient and he the doctor.

The 267 line rings. "Collect call from Edward X, will you ..." A click. The operator says Edward hung up, must have been a wrong number. If this is not a sincere call by him, does he realize the impact of his psychological terrorism!

So "Jern" turns out to be Cleveland, who used to work at the Roberts Club. Sam had told me about this friend of his whom he wanted me to meet. I wonder if Cleveland got as big a surprise as I did when the two of them arrived at my front door tonight. We watched *Black Workout II* and then had a pleasant threesome.

February 10, 1988, Los Angeles

Who should be the steward in the first class cabin of the American Airlines flight to Los Angeles tonight but Douglas, the Black guy I met at the Boston Public Library and see now and then at the Y. He looked really smart in his uniform. He had never told me he worked for an airline; it explains his coming and going. During the flight, he looked after me very well and smiled his head off. On board, I continued Nancy Friday's book. In LA, a warm and balmy day. Early to bed, ready for a hectic round of media tomorrow.

February 12, 1988, Los Angeles

A good two days, capped off with a fancy party at which Chris Carmody introduces me to Norman Lear. After the first show, a TV taping with Michael Cart done in a public library, I ran into Anna Murdoch. She came in to talk of her new novel as I left after talking about *The Australians*. "Have you seen Rupert lately?" Not a usual question for a woman to ask in reference to her husband. Her novel *Family Business* is evidently doing well. It's a better topic than the bleak domestic drama of her first one set in the Australian outback.

Two ladies who escort me around are heavily into animals. One, it seems, thinks better of animals than of humans. We discuss—to get my mind off Australia between studios—whether it's better "to know" or not to know about something terrible: an infidelity, an impending disaster about which nothing can be done, such things.

"I'm the kind that doesn't want to know," says Sherry. "For instance, if my dog had a brain tumor, I'd just rather not know that." During the earthquake last year, she and her husband and three of their dogs got into a closet until the movement subsided.

Steve Futterman of NBC radio turns out to be a friend of Ray Martin in Sydney, and a cousin by marriage of Rick Baum at UCLA. He is overburdened with doing a story about this morning's earthquake—it hit as I breakfasted at the Century Wilshire hotel—and he also has the flu. After he has made me feel thoroughly sorry for him, he begins the interview. Turns out well, and he says it will go to many radio stations across the country.

I proceeded through Jim Simon's live *Midday Magazine*—he didn't pretend to have read the book—and then the important *Connie Martinson Talks Books*. Connie is a character indeed. Reminded me of Marian Christy of the *Boston Globe* in her probing personal questions, and of a Spanish medium in her appearance: 1950s clothes and hair-style and slow, penetrating expression.

We were running late for the next show and Karen was pissing herself. Nervous, I devoured the greasy doughnuts that lay in a cardboard box in the green room. After a radio interview on a campus in Pasadena—which I was 30 minutes late for—a chance to talk on the phone with Laurent. So, Sam came around to move his things from the landing to my study. The workmen let him in. My place has become a bus station.

I would like Edward to have observed me today. On the road, with a job to do, I had no desire to drink, and was perfectly content without any drinks. The second day, I needed a valium to deal with a sharp headache. It was made worse by the fact that, after a good interview on the phone to San Diego with the Copley Radio Network, the woman from the *Los Angeles Herald-Examiner* canceled her meeting with me. "Another story has come up." This plunged me into depression and the ache over the right eye became acute.

An ABC radio interview was slight. Then a pale young intellectual from *Los Angeles Daily News*, who could not resist asking a couple of questions off the topic: Did Simon & Schuster pay for all that travel in Australia? What material is your black jacket made of? *The Paul Wallach Show* at KIEV was one of the highlights. Paul loves the book and told his audience so at frequent intervals. Vera Gold of *Vera's Voice* was likewise enthusiastic, though I think her audience on KMNY is much smaller. She invited me to return to the program and talk with her about China next month.

I rushed back to Westwood to meet Chris at the party given by Norman Lear. Sixty-five years old and expecting a baby in July, Lear was quiet and affable. We talked mainly of China. Chris says Lear's been so successful that now he's reluctant to sign off on a new film for fear it will be less well-received than so much else he's done.

On the second night, almost as an afterthought, I went to the opening of the UCLA conference—which brought me to Los Angeles in the first place. A Black journalist from the audience came up and introduced himself. He recognized me from the photo on the back of *The Australians*. He loved the book. I let him drive me back to my hotel.

There I discovered Chuck Bahmueller, the organizer, wanted to confer with Tom Keneally and me about the morrow's sequence of talks. I rather boldly asked Cary, the Black guy, to join us. Over drinks at a nearby Holiday Inn, Cary and I sat side by side on a couch—the others to either side—and our hands and legs brushed now and then.

"Would you like to come up to my room?" I asked Cary as the quartet broke up. Straight away, he said yes. The sap rose inside me. But as we entered the lobby of the Century Wilshire, who should be sitting there but boring Randy B. He'd been waiting there two hours for me! Cary's eyes were nearly popping out of his head. He is a gentleman and he said he quite understood. We'd reschedule. I still felt bad—the more so as Randy turned out to be in one of his tortured moods.

February 13, 1988, Los Angeles

The city is dazzling in its color and greenery (at least the UCLA area) and bright light. Happily, this week it has not been smoggy; nearly 80 degrees each day. Take away the autos and it would be a paradise—but it could not do without its autos, physically or spiritually. "I had to choose between a decent apartment and a good car," Chuck told me. "I chose the car."

Karen mentions that her husband is 50, and the remark hits me. First, surprise; Karen looks an ageless type, maybe somewhere in her late 30s. Second, one realizes that, after all, 50 does come down the pike and take people by surprise, even spouses.

My speech at the conference on "Australia: The Last Frontier" was evidently a success. Tom Keneally and Geoff Blainey both complimented me warmly, which I did not expect. I went up to Cary and apologized for the night before. He said it was quite OK. But when I asked about getting together, it proved hard to find a time—I guess he was a bit hurt or put off. I don't blame him.

On a sparkling warm evening, the hosts of the conference take the speakers for an Italian dinner at Mario's in the heart of Westwood. Afterwards, I finally get hold of Luther—he'll come by at 7 AM tomorrow, on the way to one of the endless series of study sessions that precede his bar exam.

Tom Keneally, after five years of socialist government in Australia, extolls the atmosphere for writers in America as compared with in Australia—the way they can get support. So maybe the USA isn't, after all, a bleak capitalist jungle? When I told Tom what I thought of the Sylvia Lawson review of my book in the *Times Literary Supplement*, and why I thought she was so bitter, he told me such types criticize him even for visiting the USA. He also gets basic, sustained criticism for not setting all his novels in Australia. He notes that feminists in Sydney object to "Anglo-Celtic sexual imperialism." Evidently, then, "Australia has been able to do what Ulster has not: unite Anglo and Celt in some wider cause."

The Australian dream, he remarks, "is a barbie on the back lawn, a fridge full of beer, the kids all around you, the sun shining on the second car in the carport." Responding to my remarks about Australia's suspicions of declarations of liberty—and a formal bill of rights—Tom said Australians think only the baddies would get into pleading the Fifth Amendment (as in the movie *The Untouchables*). He says Australians think you only hear eloquence from people who are trying to sell you something.

Tom has a serious bitch with Simon & Schuster and, for the moment, is withholding a decision on whether or not they'll get his African novel. It seems it had to do with the Dick-Joni break-up. Tom's editor, Patricia Soliman (who once approached me for a book!) was close to Joni. Dick, in his wisdom—or under the weight of his emotions—ordered withheld various payments Joni and her mates had decided upon. The result was that only six months after delivering *The Playmaker* did Tom get the delivery payment. He was furious. He says, unappealingly: "I'll just tell them: Look, I don't have to publish in America anymore. I can afford to ski four months of the year!"

Blainey begins his speech with a potentially good joke that falls flat. "I thought my marriage was going well until I moved from Los Angeles to San Diego and found I had the same milkman." For Americans, he should have said "the same plumber" or "the same newspaper boy." Milkmen went out here decades ago.

Before going to sleep, I phoned Cary. He was very nice on the phone, but he couldn't come around. We'll see. Next morning, I was lying in bed, at once horny and depressed, wondering if Luther would come, when the phone rang—he was downstairs.

I jumped out of bed, opened the door a couple of inches, took off my T-shirt, and sprang back into bed. He's less in shape than he used to be, but still has raw sexuality.

We made love pretty much like old times. At one point, he said perhaps we should use a condom. I said I didn't really think so. He seemed to have got it into his head that Edward might have caused me health problems—no doubt he deduced this from his own experiences with Edward and what Edward likes to do. But I have a certain influence on Luther; I was able to allay his fears. Luther said that his mother was looking at the photos from his graduation one day and noticed me in one of them. "Oh, that's the guy that likes you," she remarked.

February 15, 1988, Chicago

In Michigan Avenue, a woman says to her companion, "What a gorgeous day!" It's 22 degrees. However, a ray or two of sun comes out—and Chicago is pathetically grateful. Never mind that the Chicago River is topped with huge sheets of broken ice. Never mind that an expedition without earmuffs is pure masochism.

I gather from various sources that the liberal academics are ferociously jealous of Allan Bloom.[289] Such principled people! I speak to a large conference about Australia—they clap. I leave. Then to a women's club, where there were few questions along feminist lines.

I sign dozens of copies of *The Australians* at the flagship store of the Kroch and Brentano company. Now will there be people to buy them?

February 16, 1988, Chicago

I awoke feeling happy that I was near the end of my tour, and also buoyed by what has been a good trip. One more day! First, to the Chicago Public Library for an address to a gathering—in my honor—of heads of all the public libraries in the city of Chicago. About 50 people and quite delightful. The Black guy who was chairman had his fly unbuttoned. I didn't tell him; he was sitting beside me at the top table—there was always the possibility that I might get a glimpse inside his blue trousers.

I was answering a question after my address when someone came into the room and said there was an urgent message for me. I ended up leaving instantaneously. Mary had mistaken the time for the Roy Leonard show. The studio was waiting for me! They had told her I was due "ten to eleven." She took that in the British sense of 10:50 AM, whereas what they really meant was that I was to arrive at 10 AM and depart at 11 AM.

Panic. I was embarrassed to rush out on the librarians and unsettled to begin a radio show in such circumstances. But the show went stunningly well, like the library meeting. Leonard became enthusiastic about the topic of my book, and I think that was conveyed to his huge audience. He kept praising the book as "a marvelous read" and "the best book in existence on Australia."

---

[289] Allan Bloom (1930-1992), American philosopher and professor, best known for *The Closing of the American Mind,* a critique of contemporary higher education

As normal in Chicago, lunch was opulent. The Illinois Center for the Book is no threadbare operation. At least its ruling board believes in a nice lunch—with a magnificent view of the city from an extraordinary height. I sit next to Carl Kroch,[290] who reminisces about publishing paperbacks before World War Two.

Mary toasts me and I make a few remarks. I tell the story of being mistaken in a Brisbane TV studio for a furnishing man; "What mattress do you recommend?" I comment on China. I explain the genesis of *The Australians*. Then I ask the gathering to tell me how it is that Chicago is such an internationally-minded city. This question pleases them. Trade is the gist of the answer.

Peggy has no idea of how to get to the studio for the NPR segment with Jeremy Komanic and his program *Book Gallery*. We get lost. We are late. JK is understanding. And in the end, this show too goes very well.

At O'Hare, I am too tired to phone people, or to cruise. I check my messages. Tricia of the *Los Angeles Herald-Examiner* earnestly asks my forgiveness for the cancellation and proposes to do the interview by phone from Boston. Hank called from Georgia to say he has found a job and can I help him get to Boston.

February 18, 1988, Boston

Felt very good last night; nice to be home and to know the trip went well. In my absence, some progress was made on the renovations upstairs. The bathroom is mirrored, the kitchen takes shape, the living room has been painted blue.

This morning, Connor came in on his way to the dentist. As always with Connor, the purpose of the visit is not precise; he's the kind of friend that just likes to pop in. He began sucking me beautifully, expertly in my study. I wonder if the dentist will notice the flavor of my dick in his mouth.

This afternoon when Laurent came in, I felt strongly attracted to him. This hadn't been the case for a while. We soon fell into bed for a lovely session—he rimmed me and then playfully (I hope) tried to fuck me—and later we dined at Saint Cloud. He went home to study for Friday's exam. I was still exhilarated and watched a video and came again—thinking this time of Edward. My binoculars have disappeared from the study. Connor, I suppose.

A really nice time with Reggie. He is riveted by *Powertool* and hardly seems to notice I am getting into a position to fuck him. Eventually, after he has murmured "No" many times, I suggested a condom. No answer but a few minutes later, "How about getting a condom?" It didn't hurt him at all, and I nearly went crazy inside him.

February 20, 1988, Boston

Laurent seems icy toward Connor—perhaps something went wrong, or maybe Laurent is just a class above the seductive chef? At Northeastern, a Black guy and I get it off as

---

[290] Carl A. Kroch (1915-1999), pioneering Chicago bookseller who transformed the family business, Kroch's & Brentano's, into the largest privately owned bookstore chain in the United States. Named a "hero of American culture" by the Library of Congress in 1986.

others watch—a stern, masculine, taciturn character; he bit my tits just as I like them bitten.

Tonight, at last, a one-on-one with Cleveland. Turns out fantastic. I shot and shot and shot all over his head, neck, and chest—as, indeed, he shot over me. "How did you do that!" he gasped.

As I was waiting for him to arrive—he wanted to make a copy of the video cassette *Black Workout Two*—I discovered, to my annoyance, that this exact cassette was missing. Connor!

I told Cleveland it was missing. He immediately said Connor probably took it in order to prevent him, Cleveland, watching it! He said Connor had asked several times if he was coming over to my place.

February 22, 1988, Boston

Reggie, Laurent, and I had a nice time together, smoking grass and dining at Huskies. Back here, Reggie wanted to get into something—very much—but he also wanted me to start it. I wasn't that keen, in part because I couldn't quite read Laurent's mind on the issue.

Eventually, Laurent—pretty drunk—went to work, and then Reggie and I went to bed. After massaging his back for an eternity, I poked my dick at his ass. He kept saying no. I rimmed him. Before I knew what was happening, he came—in a very happy mood. (Laurent later told me that the fact that he didn't leave—when Reggie was getting very horny—showed that he was willing to join in if something started. But he said he and Reggie would never have started it—it had to be me).

February 23, 1988, Boston

A very British phone call—from the secretary of Ian Chapman, chairman of Collins Publishers. A check has come from *National Geographic* for the snapshot Ian took of Rupert Murdoch and me on Rupert's farm in Australia, which was published on the "On Assignment" page in the February issue. What should Mr. Chapman do with it?

I wasn't quite sure what the lady meant. I mean, most people put checks into their bank account. She explained that he couldn't possibly accept it. Wasn't it my camera? Would I like the $100? Should Mr. Chapman perhaps give it to charity?

February 25, 1988, Boston

I drag my feet on writing the reply to Sylvia Lawson's attack on *The Australians* in the *TLS*. Such an unpleasant task. As with many other undesirable things, I just wish they would go away. I don't want to face unpleasant realities—never have.

Reggie and I have one of our impromptu crazy canters after dining late at Oceanic (Caroline had to take a girlfriend—soon her bridesmaid—to the bus station). I knew Reggie should already be home, but he wanted to come back to my place. He didn't leave till 1:30. He's tough, resourceful, but also a romantic. It was Laurent the other day who mused on how extraordinary it is that Reggie and I have been close for six years.

February 26, 1988, Boston

How could Laurent reckon me patient! Yes, he said that—he said I'm a patient person.

February 27, 1988, Boston

This guy is sitting at a desk in the Boston Public Library, reading a book, yet also with a handsome brown hand thrust down the pants of his tracksuit. I sit next to him. I play with myself, first down the front of my jeans, then by pulling my hard cock right out of my pants. He watches. I lean over and play with him through his pale blue pants.

At my place, Nick turns out affectionate and experienced. He rims me. I fuck him, withdrawing just as I come. A quiet type, he smokes a cigarette and then takes the Riverside car to his home.

February 28, 1988, Boston

Lunch with David C and then, a little bit to my surprise, we make love again—after many months. God, what a wonderful cock. Briefly, he put it in me. "I like your body," he gasped as he sucked my tits, and the remark made my day. He told me that he wants to have children of his own. We talked of Steve, whom neither of us has heard from for years. I think David's scared to phone the family in New York for fear all is not well heath-wise with Steve.

February 29, 1988, Boston

On the phone, I told my mother I can't come to Australia just now. She was understanding. I suggested she consider coming here. She had the sad news that our local clergyman killed himself, jumping from a high tower on the campus of Monash University. Murrumbeena is not used to that sort of thing. Tongues wag. How could a "man of God" take his own life. Can they not allow him the dignity of his final act of courage!

March 1, 1988, New York

The Asia Society affair on the topic of *The Australians* is a great success by all measures. Big crowd. I spoke well it seems. Bob Oxnam, the president, said it was "a fantastically good speech." Sold and signed about 40 books. One woman born in Orange, NSW, bought three copies.

During the wine and cheese reception afterwards, I notice a face that seems familiar. The guy comes up smiling and introduces himself—it's Eddie H, the Chinese-Australian guy I had a fling with in Canberra years ago.

March 2, 1988, New York

Lunch with Barbara at Sam's, a pleasant restaurant on 52nd Street owned by the daughter of Ernest Hemingway.[291] By strange coincidence, who should we literally bang into by the front door but Fred Hills. He hugs me. He fails to recognize Barbara.

Over pasta, for me, and an omelet, for her, we make progress about future plans. Norman will tackle my last burst of Australia articles. Then I'll decide whether I want to tarry with the Sichuan and Aborigines material. Or straight to the novel. In the latter case, once some of it is written, a two-book contract linking the novel with *COMM* might be good.

Barbara thinks Pat could be the editor for the novel. She grumbles about Fred and his slowness with manuscripts. She doubts Simon & Schuster has a line into which the Sichuan and Aborigines books would fit. She worries that I must get the right tone for the travel books. She doesn't want the give editors the 90 pages of the original Aborigines piece. "They have better things to do than read that sort of thing," she adds mysteriously.

I hoped to go to a Broadway matinee but felt too tired. These lectures exhaust me, especially the strain beforehand. I felt I should try to nap and then start to prepare my thoughts for the speech at about 4:30 PM.

The Harvard Club occasion is less well organized than the Asia Society one—the man who introduced me told the audience he'd been asked ten minutes ago to do the job—but in substance, it was good. Speaking in that brown cavernous Harvard Hall is nice. Quite a few questions on Australia's international position, unlike Tuesday night at the Asia Society.

Michael Mao is there. He said the parts about my upbringing told the audience an awful lot about Australia. "Write a novel," he burst out.

March 3, 1988, New York

Walking in Manhattan is nice, even in this chilly weather. I am so taken with looking at buildings, people, incidents, that I nearly bump into striding, grim-faced New Yorkers.

Sushi is now a big item at the Harvard Club. The head waiter rushes into the grill room and hisses to the other waiters: "A wait of 20 minutes on sushi!" The poor Japanese guy who cuts up the fish is overwhelmed.

Fred Hills phones before I have a chance to phone him. *The Australians* is trickling along at about 100 a week. Fred said he is disappointed at the sales, and re-iterates that the Hughes book hurt us. If we'd come out before Hughes, sales would have been double what they are, he said. But the sales do not shake his admiration for the book, he added. I made three points in looking back. I regret the delay that led to us coming out after the Hughes. I admired and appreciated Fred's editing. And I felt the publicity effort was minimal.

---

[291] Terrill means Hemingway's *grand*daughter, Mariel. The restaurant was Sam's Café.

"I agree with you on the publicity. There should have been an author tour." So what is the bottom line? We agree to a dangerous degree. But does he have power within Simon & Schuster or not? (At the conference in his office before publication with Julia, Lisa, and Barbara, he said, "This is not a book that wants a national tour.")

I plunged out into 8th Avenue, changed clothes at the Port Authority, and left a bag with my "Harvard Club clothes" at the parcel counter there. Then to straight sex cinemas. The Cameo Theatre seemed a purely drug scene. Everyone—including transvestites—too concerned with shooting coke to crave sex. Another one around the corner was better. All sorts of scenes, seductions, glances, maneuvers. Then, as time began to run out, a guy from Brooklyn sucked me off expertly.

Barbara's party is interesting. She lives on the West Side in a rather ordinary building. The apartment is one bedroom, rather garishly furnished, except for some primitive-chic carvings and paintings. The other guest of honor is a guy who's just written the Columbia University guide to coping with life after 50.

On the Eastern Shuttle coming up to Boston, I run into Ken Mayer, who tonight was inducted into the College of Physicians at a dinner in Manhattan. As usual, he asks me about Edward. As usual, we are soon gently arguing about politics.

March 4, 1988, Boston

In the afternoon, the report at the Fenway Clinic is a great relief, together with a warning sign. Once more, I am negative to the AIDS virus. Wonderful. But my T-cell ratio has declined in six months from 1.5 to 0.5. A serious weakening of my resistance.

Possibly the strain of Edward and the contractor, and the extra drinking entailed, has caused this weakening of my immunity. Troubling. Should I go away and ask Laurent to handle things so that I can recover?

March 5, 1988, Boston

I finally tell Connor—who calls this morning—that I feel he should give me back the things he's "borrowed." This put me in the posture of accusing him, or at least casting my suspicion upon him. I said when he comes to collect his suitcases, he could take the opportunity to bring me back any things he's borrowed.

March 6, 1988, Boston

Reggie bursts in, looking flushed. He's had a quarrel with Caroline and has run all the way from his place to mine. "I'll kill her," he gasps. It began over who should clean up and do the laundry. Reggie was tired. He's working extra hours. And because he's working those hours to pay for the wedding, a tiny issue became explosively large.

"Well, fuck your wedding," he said at one point. As he talks to me, he is holding his hand in pain. In his fury with Caroline, he banged his fist against the apartment wall, and two fingers and thumb are hugely swollen. Sounds awful, but I think they'll patch it up within 24 hours. They have before.

On the other hand, the flare-up was preceded by a curious, pregnant incident. Caroline came in from the laundry crying. Meanwhile, Reggie had been on the phone with me. He was telling me about his visit to J and how J came on to him. "But I'm getting married, you know, so ..." he said at one point. Caroline may have heard this from the laundry. A deeper issue than who is lazy.

Edward phones from Lowell, where he is doing a training course for his new job. He is a shade prim but not unfriendly. I get slightly miffed when he asks about my plans to celebrate my 50th birthday.

I wonder—especially when I compare Edward with Reggie—if I sometimes failed to respect his "bi" status. For instance, I would never take the liberties with Reggie that I did with Edward—touching, saying certain things. But then Edward did not behave towards me on these matters as Reggie did. Edward would often initiate kissing. Reggie and I have never kissed in our life, and if I tried to do this, Reggie would kill me. (Well, first, he would laugh.) I virtually never ask Reggie about his (fairly few) sexual contacts with men—as I sometimes did with Edward.

March 7, 1988, Boston

I told Reggie I got my test results from the Fenway Clinic, including the AIDS virus test. Once again, it was negative. He looked pensive. "I guess I should get tested," he said quietly. "My God, the baby!"

March 8, 1988, Boston

Reggie reads me well as always. The last two times we met, I felt a touch unsatisfied, and I think it registered with him. This morning he came in and, within a few minutes, his shirt was off. "It's hot in here." After a bit of prowling around, exchanging news, and criticizing me for this and that: "What happened to my massage?"

It falls to Reggie to take the first-ever piss in the upstairs bathroom. With a quick jerk, that handsome dark prick comes out; then, with a quick jerk, it snaps back inside the blue tracksuit. In the afternoon, Robert is here; he needed money to go to a club, so I said if he helped me in the house for a couple of hours, I'd pay him for that. He vacuumed and arranged things well. Afterwards, we ate at Atlantic Fish. "We all thought Wyatt would be first," he said when the conversation turned to Tyrone's death from AIDS, "because he is the most promiscuous of our group—no one thought Tyrone would go!"

Robert's easier to work with than Reggie. On the other hand, he cannot hold a candle to Reggie when it comes to personality. His dick is good—Reggie's is great. His body is pretty good—Reggie's is fantastic. Reggie takes no bullshit—Robert would say pink was blue if I asked him to.

March 11, 1988, Boston

Few people were in the YMCA's Roberts Club, but among them was Eddie, the handsome Black tennis player. I entered the steam room and sat opposite him. Soon I became aware that a very ordinary-looking white guy in the corner and Eddie were eyeing each other. Eddie had in his hand a bottle of baby oil.

Suddenly the white guy reached across and grabbed my dick. This didn't thrill me much, but I was angling to get close enough to Eddie to do the same to him. Then to my amazement, Eddie put some oil on his dick and moved in position to sit on the mingy little prick of the white dude (who still had hold of me).

Happily, this un-promising scenario was interrupted when the door opened and an old coot entered, talking his head off. A little later, after Eddie and I had looked each other up and down in the shower, things changed. Eddie signaled me into the steam room. The white guy was not in evidence. This gorgeous, sensual Black guy, about 40 and probably married, closed the door very tight. Then he leant against it with his back to me and grabbed my throbbing prick. He put baby oil on it and thrust me inside him. Like that, I fucked him this way and that, twisting, pumping, zigging and zagging, going in deep thrusts and then for a change in quick, shallow jabs—until I shot a huge load into him. All this time, he was leaning against the steam room door to make sure no one opened it.

Exhausted, I sat down. Soon I began to suck his very big, uncut cock. But we were interrupted before he came. Later, I spoke to him privately. I explained I had to go to an appointment. And I said there was something I wanted to mention that there'd been no opportunity to mention earlier: I have been tested for the AIDS virus with a negative result. Eddie smiled, thanked me for telling him that, and said he was also negative.

Then I went to see my doctor, Suzy Gordon. She wasn't helpful. Doesn't know what T-cell ratio means. Hadn't received the detailed documents I sent her anyway (had she phoned and told me this, I wouldn't have gone out to West Roxbury to see her). A negative test, she intoned, doesn't necessarily mean you are not carrying the virus, so for the blood test today, we'll go on full precaution as a courtesy to the staff. Somehow this pissed me off.

March 15, 1988, Boston

Laurent stays over. During the night, I feel him fondling me. I have a hardon but prefer to wait until the morning. The morning, however, is a circus. Morgan phones. Soon Charlie arrives. What we started got aborted.

This evening, Laurent and I began again. He was hot. Alas, I was tired and distracted. I didn't come. But he did in his usual torrent. Then we dined at Turner's Fisheries. The food was nice, but Laurent detected Irishness in the place. Funny, it had not impinged on me the way it did on Laurent, who is Black. Now I understand why the napkins and everything else are green.

March 17, 1988, Boston

Hank is coming for a few days en route to Provincetown. I sent him bus fare. In return, he will work with me here in the house, and perhaps do some keyboarding stuff into the Kaypro.

Edward phones and, a few minutes later, comes by. He's just had a consultation with a neurologist. Lately, he's had problems of numbness just as I have had. Also, "psychological problems." Medical issues are much on his mind; he has talked to Ken Mayer several times since getting the phone number from me last month. He looks around the house, loves the blue, loves the new bathroom—and the island. The aqua in the small room made him squeal with delight. So, too, the relocation of the study to the front of the house.

All this went along with a warm attitude from each of us to the other. Does he think, at last, that I respect him as a person?

March 18, 1988, Boston

A morning phone call from one more Australian expatriate who loves *The Australians*. He finished it last night and "could not resist" phoning me. "It's a fair book, and it brought Australia back to me completely." He is a veterinary surgeon in Colorado. Still an Australian citizen and married to an American.

Nice, gentle, silent time with John G. He is living at present with his parents—spends the weekdays up here. Lovely body; elusive soul. I come as much as Laurent does—which is to say, I drench John and the bed alike. We are just finished when Laurent calls. His best friend in Haiti has died at the age of 24. Moreover, the guy's father and uncle died last year. Laurent's mother said on the phone today from Port-au-Prince: "People are dying all over the place round here."

March 20, 1988, Boston

I wake up in the middle of the night with a horrible feeling that I'm "leaving the field" of academic China studies. Yet rebirth always involves dying to a previous life. I think I should just set aside these pangs, plunge into the novel, and see if it works. I can always go back to the Sichuan book and the *COMM* book.

I feel almost guilty at how nice this apartment is going to be. The way to assuage that guilt will be to work hard on a new book.

California seems to be picking up clues from *The Australians* faster than the East Coast. Edward said that, in September, the West Coast is less hide-bound in its reception of the work of someone like me. The trees are tired, but the wind will not subside.

March 26, 1988, Boston

A stunning experience down the street this afternoon. Restless for some reason—despite Hank's presence in the house—I went to the Y and, after desultory exercises, went into the general locker room to shower. This guy was just coming out of the pool. Dark, slim, with a wide smile. I asked him if he was he going to take a sauna. He didn't know about it; I explained it was good for the skin.

He came into the sauna a moment or two after I did and sat down beside me. He was in the corner, and me next to him. As I read my newspaper, I got a hardon, which he saw. I pressed my leg against his. His brown dick was held between his smooth legs; otherwise, it would have popped up like a tulip in spring.

When I went to the shower, he came to the shower next to mine. In a quiet moment, I offered to soap his back. I included in this definition his lovely buns and soon had a finger in his asshole. His cut cock stuck out in front like a coat hook.

We went to the fourth floor of Mugar. What do you like best, I asked him. He smiled and shrugged. We did just about everything, standing up or kneeling. When I started to fuck him, he said, "It's easier to do this lying down." He got his dick inside me but came outside. Huge load. His family is Moslem, living in Dorchester. I hope he comes back to the Y next Saturday.

Though the February *National Geographic* has been out for a while here, it is just available in Australia. I sent copies with a cover letter to PM Hawke, several ministers, and most of the other Australians I quoted in my article. I would rather they all read *The Australians*, but people read articles yet hardly ever books.

March 28, 1988, Boston

On the doorstep when I returned to the house, I found Connor. With him was an attractive Puerto Rican called Tony. I was cool toward Connor and said I was busy. Could he collect his luggage? I said OK.

Upstairs the liquid eyes and curved body of the guy from San Juan got to me. In the red bathroom, we started a three-some. Downstairs we came to continue. As the Puerto Rican fucked Connor, I fucked the Puerto Rican. He is very sexy indeed and his dick is huge.

"He's got to have a blood test today," Connor said of Tony. "He's getting married next week." After they left, I discovered that my Ricoh camera was missing. I am such a fool. Connor took only half his luggage. Shall I throw the rest out or keep it as a bargaining chip to get back my camera—or at least the half-exposed film in it?

March 29, 1988, Boston

The mirror has gone up over the fireplace. And the first closet in the new bedroom is finished, complete with mirrored folding doors. I think I will order a second to match.

Reggie suggests a condom. Halfway through, it came off. I went back in without one—though I did not come inside him. Afterwards, he looks at me with that cheerful suspicious look of his. "Did you have a condom on?" I point to it lying on the sheet beside us. He looks. Then he picks it up and smells it.

April 3, 1988, Boston

Delightful Hank materializes from the Cape. He has a job, though not the one he went there for. He will stay overnight as he has shopping to do and must go to the Fenway Clinic. We realized we had missed each other since that pleasant week together. I said he might as well sleep in my bed for the night. "Yeah, I thought that'd be a good idea, too." Even the Georgia accent is enough to drive me crazy. "Nice yams," he says when I take off my pants. Next morning, he asked me if he had been "too wild" the night before. I didn't think so at all.

As usual, I find it difficult to have someone in the house the morning I am going off on a trip. Hank thought I wasn't paying attention to him as I packed and prepared my speech notes for two lectures at Augusta College.

April 5, 1988, Atlanta

A night on the town in Atlanta at a place called Loretta's on Spring Street, which Hank recommended. Mostly Black gay disco. Big, friendly, extremely loud music. "I don't think of Australians as being gay," said a charming Black guy at the bar. At one point, he said something about white men, and I said, Well, I'm a white man. "You know," he said with his head tilted to one side. "I don't think of you—an Australian—as a white man!"

April 5, 1988, Augusta

I am whisked directly from the bus station to my first lecture at a class. The town is ablaze with azalea and dogwood. My visit is well prepared. The place drips with history. Everyone is normal and pleasant. I enjoy myself. My evening lecture seems to go well. Beforehand, there was a dinner and afterwards a reception, so it was a five-hour performance that left me drooping. I went back to my inn—charming with paneled walls and a fireplace in my bedroom—and changed for the streets.

As people drove me around during the day, I had noticed a bar called Twilight in the Black district, and that is where I headed. Run down, lively, all generations, all sexual preferences—a perfect place for me to change gears from being the dressed-up VIP discoursing with authority on all topics.

I sat down with a nice guy who was, however, pretty drunk. He pointed to a couple of boys at the jukebox. "They suck dick. I want my dick sucked. It doesn't matter who does it, don't you think, as long as it gets sucked. Why don't you get yours sucked, too? Which boy do you want—you can go first."

This was not exactly what you expect in straight bars in the great cities of our nation, but it was exactly what I like. Later, I talked with the boys by the jukebox. They seemed gay. Talking with them were women who were very much available. At the back of the bar, in comfortable booths, were older men. Everyone was friendly. Once people got over their amazement at the sight of me in the bar, I could more or less have anything I wanted.

I arranged to go home to the hotel with Dwayne, one of the kids, and we called a cab. Had the cab come quickly, all would have been fine. But it didn't and in the interim, as it sank in that Dwayne was my choice, complications arose. Women leaned against me. A very handsome, tough-looking guy smiled. In the john, he said, "Don't go with him [Dwayne], he's a faggot, you could get AIDS. Go with me, I'm straight." I felt his cock, and it was the lovely big cut rural Georgian variety that I love. It was Hank all over again, before my eyes, on the home turf of Georgia.

Back at the bar, Dwayne says, "There's three outside scheming up something." I felt uneasy. When the cab still didn't come, I told Charles—the straight guy I'd talked to in the john—that I was leaving on foot and he could follow me at a distance.

About six blocks into the night, I looked around for Charles, but it was Dwayne and one of his friends who first caught my eye. They were following me. I explained I couldn't take him home after all. I felt bad. I gave Dwayne my number at the inn and said let's meet tomorrow morning. "I'm going to call you tonight," this slim charming guy said, "to make sure you've got home alright."

Charles followed on as I walked through the lovely soft night. The last few blocks, we walked together. He took a shower and then we went to bed. He was too straight to suck, he said. But it turned out he wasn't too straight to get fucked. I ground against his perfect ass and shot a big ease-the-tension load into his Black gut. "Kiss my cum," he hissed—a new phrase to me—as he shot his load at me.

It was 3 AM when I went onto the veranda of my suite to sit in the cane armchair and drink in the smell of the flowers and the tranquility of the night.

April 6, 1988, Augusta

I sit on my veranda after a hearty breakfast served by waiters in black tie. Golfers fill the inn; it is Masters' time in Augusta. But in the streets, I observe a hometown atmosphere. Much sensuality. Guys politely but nakedly look. These Southerners with their lilting voices are slightly embarrassed to receive a tip.

Augusta is full of history. Down the road from my inn is the house where Woodrow Wilson was born and spent his first 12 years. Mansions on all sides. Sites from Civil War battles. Grand hotels where presidents stayed to get spring air and watch golf. And the locals are so proud of it all. To them, Atlanta is an upstart.

The flight back to Boston was smooth. At about 10 PM, I was on the phone with Laurent when William called. After last night with Charles and the trip back from Georgia today, I wasn't that keen. But William is persistent. He came around and, as usual, I received him in bed. "That's sexy," he said when on the phone I told him to come upstairs and into the bedroom and the bed. After we finished and he was showering, he said, "So you shaved your balls?"

"Yeah. You like it?"

"Well, it's different, it's interesting," says William. Still, he can't give me his phone number. "My lover is so jealous! You are just my secret." Off he runs down the stairs into the spring night.

April 7, 1988, Boston

A flutter of activity over Shen in California. He is worried that his college may not get him a good internship for the summer. As a trustee of the college, can I help? I make phone calls. I say Shen is good stuff. The academics prick up their ears and say they will report back to me.

Lunch at Joe's with Laurent. Laurent, who had read part of my diary, was appalled that professors could complain so about their students' demands and the burden of having to plough through student essays! His eyes nearly popped out of his head. "I mean professors are not supposed to think that way about students!" (Really—whoever said so?)

Another theme from the book—reassuring to many people, Laurent thinks—is that nobody is perfect. Here is even this Harvard professor unable to resist being sucked off in public in a Bangkok street, as passersby nod and smile in greeting. So other people must be forgiven other things.

In the Diary, Jayden reminded Laurent of his brother Jean. Is Jean that sort of academic, Laurent asked himself. Why do people become academics? I explained to him how I stumbled into it purely by dint of doing well scholastically.

As we walk away from the restaurant, Laurent says of himself, *tout m'amuse, rien m'attache* [everything amuses me, nothing ties me down]. Striking, revealing, impressive. Before lunch, I wanted to grab at the big dog in his pants. Afterwards, I wanted to be with him as my best friend. The French saying comes from his father, who also taught him one about starting slowly but getting there surely in the end.

I went to Harvard for the film *Girl in Red*, and then Fred Wakeman's[292] excellent talk on the Chinese secret service. At midnight, the bell rings and Sam comes in. He's nervous about something. It turns out, as we lie on the bed, that his mother is having an operation at 2 AM tonight. For the first time ever, he sucked me—but I was tired, not in the mood, and I didn't come.

April 8, 1988, Boston

A fairly good visit with Joan Goldberg, a physician at the Kenmore Center of the HCHP, whom Suzy had suggested I see. Like Suzy, she seems to like me—a touch here, an intimate question there ("Exactly when do you use a condom?"). Her specialties are cancer and blood; she is HCHP's overall AIDS coordinator.

The gist of her preliminary impressions: My helper cell figure isn't too bad—no call for preventive drugs, I'm not especially vulnerable to things at present levels. Stress could certainly have lowered the number of helper cells. The other Fenway test results are all fine. Skin looks fine. She thinks that maybe I ought to see a neurologist, but her own tests do not suggest alarm. Alcohol could add to the numbness problem, she said when asked. Coffee? No problem.

When I said I was having trouble reading the phone book and the stock tables, she merely smiled. My feet look "very good for feet," she pronounced.

April 12, 1988, Boston

A good PEN panel on ghostwriting. Everyone is very nervous with the concept, yet it's a growing one and people like Bill Novak, Fran Schumer, and Larry Rothstein—all on the panel—are extremely capable. Bill said he loved working with Lee Iacocca. Fran fought with Mary Cunningham all the time. Bill Phillips, a senior editor at Little,

---

[292] Frederic Wakeman, Jr. (1937-2006), American expert on East Asian history.

Brown, is urbane, charming, reasonable. He sits on the mountain and watches the tigers fight below.

April 14, 1988, Boston

At lunch with Reggie at Huskie's, I realized his absence lately is because he's nervous about the wedding (and busy over preparations). As we ate, he outrageously flirted with two white waitresses. Never seen him do this before. I playfully pointed out that he is "a married man" (a phrase he sometimes applies to himself). "Not for six weeks," he said with a grin. "I've got six more weeks!" Both girls were attractive. When Reggie said let's ask them home, I agreed. Then he backed off. "Well, I'm nearly married."

In the YMCA before lunch, he had been similarly dualistic: lingering long in the showers and flirting; but when it came to the point, drawing back. Right there in the locker room, one guy said to him, "Fuck me." Reggie had cruised the guy. But when he told me the story, he spoke as if it were outrageous of the guy to ask that. We greatly enjoyed the lunch of chili, spare ribs, chicken, and baked potato skins.

Charlie was painting the new bedroom cranberry and white, but Reggie nevertheless insisted on seeing a movie. We took the TV inside my study door from the lobby and lay on the black rug. Naked, he looked great against the black rug. In the middle of things, Caroline phoned. Reggie mouthed at me to say he wasn't here yet. He had told her he was coming around to my place to help. She asked me to have him call her as soon as he arrived.

When we'd finished—at least after he'd come—he phoned her and she was mad. Were you there or not, when I phoned, she demanded to know. If not, where were you? When he said he'd arrived but gone out again for a while, she said, "You two had better get your stories straight."

He charmed the pussy off her and she calmed down. Later, when we resumed our fooling around, I came and he came again. Of such are pre-marriage nerves made up.

April 15, 1988, Boston

It never rains but it pours—Mikey comes in. After many weeks without Mikey, and several without Reggie, they materialize within 24 hours. Mikey is thrilled with the renovations. "I can't believe this house," he kept saying. Of the red bathroom, he said, "I've never seen a bathroom like that, even in books."

Mikey became the first to make love with me in the new cranberry-and-white bedroom with its mirrored walls. To my surprise, the mirrors made him shy for a while. He licked me all over and sucked me. Then he oiled me and asked to fuck me ("Let's do the real stuff"). I let him do so for a while and up to a point. "That was great fun," he said at the end, and indeed it was for me too.

He is tiring of the closeness with Joseph. For some months, they have been living together, alternating in cooking breakfast. And he lost his job at the shoe shop; without his paycheck, he has no independence. I sense I may be seeing more of Mikey in the coming months. Yet I, too, would fear too much closeness. And at close range, I would no doubt see a more humdrum side to the magnificent Mikey than I see now.

April 16, 1988, Boston

Lunch with Yang Bingzhang at Huskie's. He's worried about his future career. The Harvard research project won't go on much longer. Always that question for short-term academic workers—what comes next? He talks vaguely of going back to China, but I think he will join the vast army who, without making a clear decision, drift into staying in the USA.

April 17, 1988, Cambridge

A talk with Joan Colebrook over coffee and a snack at Harvard Square. She's launched on the second volume of her memoir. This one takes her to the UK and her love affair with the scientist. J.D. Bernal. I envy her the obsession of being into a new book.

We seem at cross purposes when we talk of AIDS. She is horrified at the risks she thinks I run. I am surprised that—her concern for me apart—straights like her get so worked up about a limited danger to those who aren't gay or heavy drug users.

David calls, but, alas, I don't have the energy for the lovely activity he has in mind.

April 18, 1988, Boston

Cleveland calls again. As with David, we just don't seem to be able to hookup at the moment, much as we wish.

On the phone, Mum seems fine, which takes pressure off me to visit Australia. She has two students boarding, one from Bangladesh and one from the Victorian bush. She loves the company. It seems to help her health as well as her morale.

At a Harvard dinner, Bob McNamara[293] speaks of China's future. He's pretty rosy. The elegant dinner is a fund-raising technique, with fat cats from business in attendance from all over the USA. It wouldn't do to present China in dismal terms on such an occasion. Before dinner, I recalled to Bob that when, as Secretary of Defense, he came to speak at Harvard during the Vietnam War, students jumped on his car. "We all learned something from it," he said uneasily.

Fat cats come up to say they've read various of my books; wealthy New York women, who, as they visit Cambridge, try to look bookish and not wealthy. I suppose Harvard invited me because I am more of a draw card to affluent outsiders than most of the current East Asian faculty.

In his speech, McNamara praises China's self-reliant way. Yet I wonder: can a quarter of mankind hold back from interdependence; and can the world's problems be alleviated if it does? Surely the future of China should include the important dimension of how much internationalism tomorrow's China will display. McNamara condescends to China, as many do. He praises the Chinese for material progress. Yet the Chinese, like ourselves, have values, and love freedom. Cassette recorders and fridges do not sum up their life any more than ours.

---

[293] Robert McNamara (1916-2009), Secretary of Defense from 1961-1968.

No Marathon Day party at Helen and Marlin's this year. End of an era. After all, it hasn't proved easy for Helen to resist New York. Or to run a literary agency from Boston.

April 19, 1988, Boston

Joan Colebrook comes, and we have great fun going through my books on Britain in the 1930s. I have many that she does not know of. She borrows some to help for her memoir. When she comes in, I happen to be wearing Laurent's tee shirt that says BLACK BY POPULAR DEMAND. It seems to irritate her. Before leaving, she yet again alludes to the "risks" that I take. After she left for her appointment with the eye doctor, I thought mischievously that I should have lent her Coleman Dowell's wonderful *White on Black on White*.

Mikey came in again. While I went down to Kay's to a trustees' meeting, he watched *Black Attack*—loved it. Later we made brief love before he went back to Joseph. "You know, I hate going back there," he said with a furrowed brow. Until they go to California, he's going to help me with shopping and rearranging.

April 21, 1988, Boston

Some exciting hours as a new book project on China takes shape. Called *The Failure of Marxism in China*, it will be a collection of my best articles since about 1980, together with a new lead essay on the main theme. Probably the book will begin with a report of a trip to China later this year. It will be published in 1989 to mark the 40th anniversary of the Communist Revolution. Reading over some of the pieces, I must say—once I get beyond the leftism of the 1970s—my stuff stands up.

Dinner with Laurent at Icarus. As we come out, I see Keith walking with some older white guy. Laurent is starting to get into a cab. Not noticing what he is doing, I hold my hand up to hail another cab. Laurent does not realize my distracted eyes are following Keith, watching his gesticulating hand and the beautiful undulations of his ass.

April 24, 1988, Boston

On a quiet Sunday afternoon, a Marine phones. He worked at the US Consulate in Melbourne some years ago. Now he lives in Western Massachusetts. Has just read *The Australians* and could not resist finding my number and calling me to say how much he liked it. Says the Australia I described is the Australia he knew. It happens that while in Melbourne, he lived in Murrumbeena, where my family lives.

April 26, 1988, New York

I fly down to visit Chris Hurford, the new Australian Consul-General, before going to a lunch with former PM Gough Whitlam. Our first spring day in the Northeast, and how grand to feel that sparkle in the air. Hurford knows of me. "The first time I walked across that bridge at Lo Wu, I thought of your book *800,000,000*," he said.

Whitlam, chief guest at the Asia Society lunch, talks well, if egocentrically, about the state of the world. He is in town to drum up American support for the Australian National Gallery, of which he is chairman. I am given the honor of being seated next to him. But the man is not in a mood to talk. I know him in this respect. Sometimes he is very warm; sometimes close to chilly. Today was the latter; something had got under his skin.

Did he expect me to send him personally a copy of *The Australians*? Were there passages in it he didn't like? Has he not read it yet and feels embarrassed? Does he feel I've become too conservative? At any rate, at the end, he addressed me as "Comrade" in our old style.

My lunch talk about Australia took me back in time in a double way. To my experiences in the Labor Party in Gough's time. And to experiences in writing *The Australians*. I did not feel entirely comfortable in this time warp. I'm anxious to move on from the "Australian phase" that *The Australians* lead me into. Which is not to regret that phase.

At William Morrow, Pat Golbitz throws her arms around me. She is so proud of *The White-Boned-Demon*, she says. She has always wanted to work with me on another book. *China on My Mind*, she thinks, will be an important book. "Commerce isn't everything; I like to publish important books like yours as well as the very popular books."

"Novels are harder to sell than nonfiction," she said after I described my Hong Kong novel plan. "But, of course, a China novel by you would be different because you know the subject so well." I said I'd discuss my plans with Barbara and see where we stood with the Simon & Schuster option.

I mentioned to Pat that, while sales of *The Australians* have been OK, *The New York Times* review was disappointing. She threw up her hands. "All they like is books from university presses. Anything people really enjoy they attack. And look at the advertising dollars we pour into that *Book Review*!"

I went to Barbara's new offices in a seedy, ethnic part of downtown and handed over two draft book proposals, *China on My Mind* and *The Failure of Marxism in China*. The latter was quite new to her. She looked as pleased as an Avon lady who finds her customer of the day is Tammy Bakker.

She was surprised, I think, that I'd done some work on something at last, after all my agonies over Edward, the house, and the fairly disappointing sales of *The Australians*. She will study the proposals next week.

After leaving my stuff at the Harvard Club, I went to 42nd Street and got sucked off by one Black and one Hispanic. Then a cab to La Guardia. The driver was talkative. I was not in the mood for his chatter. But when he spoke about cricket, my interest perked up. He was a Pakistani. "I am very lonely in New York," he said.

I mentioned, almost as something to say, that in Australia, we always sit in the front seat of a cab; if we don't, the driver feels it is unfriendly. "You can sit in front," he said in that chirpy Pakistani tone, smiling. It was raining as I hopped out of the cab to change seats.

Approaching La Guardia, I could see the mood was OK. Just before we reached the Eastern Shuttle building, he stopped the cab. I sucked his hot, cut cock. He came almost as soon as I began. He asked me to stay with him next time in New York.

I had a glass of white wine while I sank into my seat for the flight to Boston. It was a night as clear as crystal. The privilege of living in Boston while being so close to New York hit me anew.

April 28, 1988, Boston

A nice lunch with Pam [Painter] at the Harvard Club on Commonwealth Avenue. Again, she urges me to start a novel. "Don't over-plan it or you will lose the vigor of the narrative. You shouldn't now know exactly how it will end," she says when I complain about just that. She has a story of Mary McCarthy telling someone—apropos a lost manuscript—that she could never sit down and write the novel over again, "Because I now know how it ended." She and Jim Carroll are teaching writing at Emerson College and love it. Pam says I ought to join them. But all what I want to say on the subject, for nonfiction, could be said in two lectures.

April 29, 1988, Boston

At Harvard, the year winds down. Scholars look tired. Summer travel beckons. People begin to dress informally. The program of seminars comes to an end. Yet, for me, this cycle has reduced meaning.

In the shower at the Y, I saw Dion. Something hung in the air between us on this late Friday evening. I saw he had a half-hardon. When others left the shower room, I looked across, and he saw me do so. He was soaping himself. I moved to him and began to soap him. He grabbed my dick. I got a finger into his ass. His cock was hot and long and hard. Through the soap, we blindly, madly sucked each other's tits. Amazing—and lovely—that two friends who've been to bed quite a few times should come on to each other in a public place.

I knew I had people at home. Leaving the general locker room, I said goodbye to Dion, mentioning this to him. With regret, I departed. By eleven, however, Mikey had left. I phoned Dion and asked him if he had gottten home safely. This amused him. Within half an hour, he was at my place. Upstairs we began to make love. Sucking each other, me rimming him. I had forgotten how ticklish he is. He came soon. "I didn't mean to come that quick. But just give me ten minutes." I wiped him clean with a cloth from the nearby kitchen. "Haven't you got any hot water," he cried as I mopped his lovely dick with a cloth that was only warm.

Later we went downstairs and, after I came, he came again. He stayed all night, sleeping like a baby. During the night, while still asleep, he reached across and gently, silently felt my hair, mouth, and eye mask.

April 30, 1988, Boston

After Dion last night, I wasn't sure whether I'd be ready for Caleb. But I was. I was delighted to see him and he stayed all night. The sex began naturally after the lights were turned out. For some reason, it excites me that his father is in prison. After the rendezvous with Dion and Caleb, two events I had lined up for the weekend—Chinese Cultural Institute party and Signet Dinner—got sacrificed. I suppose my priorities get spelled out by my actions.

May 2, 1988, Boston

I went to Joan Goldberg's office to have a Western Blot test as a double check on my HIV status. Suzy had thought this a good idea. It seems it seems that there is new evidence that a few people are getting AIDS even though they have tested negative to the virus.

May 3, 1988, Boston

Not for the first time, Reggie seeks to fuck me in order to bring about my fucking him. I like the procedure, actually. This time there was a difference. He really did fuck me. He just wooed me very charmingly. We rolled around in that "two animals" posture which I remember so vividly seeing Connor do with one of his mates in my bed. But he didn't come inside me.

Later, as we sat in the study, he talked of his brother and remarked, "He'd love to fuck you." But Reggie hesitates to bring Robert round. "You see, my brother might be real nice to you and then suddenly turn on you, denounce you as a white man, and rip you off."

I sent Caroline and Reggie their wedding gift in advance. They are short of cash to pay the wedding bills, so I gave them a check for $200.

May 5, 1988, Boston

I was sitting at a large table on the second floor of the BPL when I glanced up and saw a young Black guy in jeans and a baseball cap. He had thick lips, huge eyes, a slightly gangling walk. He looked at me more than passingly. When he moved to some shelves, I got up and strolled over there. The die was cast. He signaled me to follow him, but it turned out, rather charmingly, that he didn't have a clear idea of where to go. We took elevators, grabbing each other madly, fleetingly, between stops at floors. Despite the tiny patches of time at our disposal, he managed to suck my tits, and I got his cock out of his pants. We tried the corner of various floors, but there always seemed to be some old creep within view. At length, I realized that he wasn't that experienced. He agreed to meet me later near my place. It was complex, as I was on my way to City Inspectional Services. I said goodbye to Mike, not at all sure I would ever see him again.

After my meeting at the city offices, I rush back to Saint Botolph Street and change into shorts. I find Mike, as planned, sitting on the concrete parapet near Christy's. How we made love that warm afternoon! I got inside him, but it hurt, so I didn't stay long.

On the big bed, as things went on and on, I began to feel a trifle exposed. The extreme pleasure of it, and the desire to string it out, made me attentive to perfect it. Visions of someone with binoculars in the white building calling the police did not help my concentration.

We moved to the small room. With one or two sweeps of my arm, I got rid of the manuscripts—my articles from the 1970s—that I had been painstakingly sorting on the bed. With the mirror alongside us on the little bed and the green walls nicely matching Mike's brown skin, this setting was even better. He got inside me and I loved it as much as he did. He sucked my cock and my tits. His big lips drove me to distraction.

An afternoon party for Al Alcorn's new novel,[294] but I knew few people there. A nice chat with Stratis Haviartis. But nice to be—after all these years—again in the Poetry Room of Lamont Library; for me in the 1960s a place of intellectual and sexual discovery. Afterwards, our first squash League match of the season, and our YMCA team won handily.

May 8, 1988, Boston

At last, a chance for Caleb and me to spend time. We dined at Thai Cuisine, catching up with each other's tribulations. He was very interested in Edward. It was good to talk about it with him because he had a lingering doubt that he shouldn't have gone to bed with Edward that night at my place. I reassured him on that. After all, I facilitated it.

His own saga with David is not really over. Caleb seems to have a need to be dependent. It leads him—such a pleasant, sunny person—to suffer. After dinner, we came back and, with that slow step-by-step approach I had almost forgotten, we made the decision to spend the night together. I came a lovely orgasm in his sensual brown hand. He makes me feel peaceful.

After phoning Australia for Mother's Day late at night, I went to sleep and had a weird dream. A floor sander is working in my back room. I come by to check progress. He is holding a photo of me naked with a couple of other guys, also naked, fooling around. Perhaps he found it somewhere in the room. This floor sander has no nose; he has eyes and mouth but simply no nose. He holds the photos toward me, drawing my attention to them. I ignore them and talk to him about arrangements to get a glass table and a new rug...

There was a second dream. I am sitting at a bar in a tourist-type setting. With others I am talking about the price of airfares to Europe—evidently, from Australia to Europe. We are all naked, perched on our bar stools. One of the people—my parent? my rival? my lover?—flirts heavily before my eyes with a third person. The gender of most of these people is indeterminate. As does the relation of the flirter to me. At any rate, this person starts to get a hardon. I feel upset. I wake up.

---

[294] Murder in the Museum of Man (Houghton Mifflin, 1988).

May 10, 1988, Boston

It felt weird to dress up in suit and tie first thing in the morning. Down to the Courthouse. My first experience of jury duty is anticlimactic. After being lectured by a judge and others on how to do it, there was nothing to do. The lawyers made deals with each other, and we jurors were sent home. "See you in three years," we were told in farewell. They said they would send a document to verify that I had served. This way, my employer can pay me for the day. But as a self-employed writer, who will pay me?

Everyone asks me lately how did I become so successful as a writer. Problem is I don't feel successful.

Ron Sidman is back from China and, after our game, he came back for a drink and a chat. He visited factories near Canton that are making toys. He was impressed—largely for reasons due to the factories being Hong Kong managed. The wages the workers are getting are pegged to Hong Kong wage rates. Women making the toys are paid half the Colony rate. Of this half, they get half—Beijing gobbles up the rest.

May 11, 1988, Boston

Tony Staley phones from DC. He's on a visit from Melbourne on behalf of the Australian company Geostar. One of their projects is to make a film based on Barbara Tuchman's *March of Folly*. Tony wanted my advice as to whether Kissinger would be a suitable narrator. I said he has a dignified voice. On the other hand, I pointed out that the book is anti the Vietnam War; Henry was pro. Maybe such details don't matter to filmmakers.

The doorbell rings early and it's Mike. A plumber was in and out, but Mike is prudent and rational. He stayed upstairs while the plumber ripped installations from one of the downstairs bathrooms. In the end, Mike stayed all morning. We had sex in the green room. Later on, I sucked him off again in the lobby, where he'd been watching movies as I worked.

Later a magnificent time with Mikey. As we writhed in the green room, he gasped, "Oh, you turn me on!" Later, he begged me to come so he could watch the spurts. I had a great time, but I had a reason not to come just then—so he shot alone. Mikey then went out to shop for orange juice and wine. Laurent came in—we had a date—and I forgot all about Mikey. Laurent and I were sitting on the green couch holding hands when the lock turned in the door and Mikey walked in with his parcels.

Laurent and I—never mentioning Mikey—dined at Columns and then came home and made love. He stayed all night. This morning, he went off to DC for a week. I noticed on the new mirror by the bed that his cum had gushed against it and left a large stain, tall and white like Guilin's mountains.

May 12, 1988, Boston

My VD checkup at City Hospital produced negative results in the cultures for gonorrhea and the blood test for syphilis. During the tests, Lorraine, a veteran of the clinic, complained that people who need to be tested (for everything) don't want to get tested.

Work on *China on My Mind* and *The Failure of Marxism in China* for Barbara's digestion. They are coming along. I use my polish-and-print-out technique. I don't know any alternative to this process of putting writings through draft after draft.

I got a second batch of letters off to Australian notables whom I had cited in the *Geographic* article. Meanwhile, a letter comes from Prime Minister Hawke congratulating me on my article. It is quite intriguing that Hawke likes me. I mean, I have never shown excessive enthusiasm for him. I have done much for Whitlam, and he is hot and cold with me. Same to a degree with Fraser. With Hawke, the warmth is probably due to my China reputation plus a good personal chemistry.

May 13, 1988, Boston

Mikey again. The eyes, the long, hot, cut Black cock, the imperious bearing. Amazing that we have become close again. He does the teak tables upstairs with oil from Scandinavian Design, and the result is excellent.

May 15, 1988, Boston

The American press and smart opinion in Cambridge assail Reagan for having a mild interest in astrology. They never assail the Chinese elite for having had, for thousands of years, a strong interest in astrology. Another one blind spot on Reagan glares out from *The New York Times* every day: editorially, they portray him as dumb; in the news pages, they report him as popular with the American people! One is not left with the conclusion that *The New York Times* has a great respect for the opinions of the majority of Americans. Two days later, they declare him a danger to the US.

May 16, 1988, Boston

At the BPL, I finished some work on *China on My Mind* and was debating whether to go to the gym and play squash with Serge or go home and put the revisions onto my computer. Then in a yellow jacket appeared a guy I had seen around and admired. Cinnamon color, smoldering eyes, ardent nature, solid build. Our eyes met and that was that. His name is Mark; he works somewhere on Huntington Avenue. I think he may once have worked in the library. Perhaps because he knows people there, he didn't want to talk or linger on the spot. After the eye contact, he just walked slowly out into the street. I followed him. There we arranged to meet on Huntington Ave after I went back upstairs to gather my things.

Walking along Saint Botolph Street, Mark asked me if I was hard. Without waiting for an answer, he poked the tip of his beautiful cut dick above his waistband. "I am." It looked at the bursting point. He asked me when I last jerked off. With a start, I realized this is the usual mode of sex for him.

Inside the house, he was the sergeant-major type of straight Black. Going up the stairs, he announced, "You've gotta to be hard and long. Otherwise, it's all off." He began to tear off his clothes. "I've got to be quick. I'll just lie down on the bed and you can do what you want." I was crazy with lust for him, but at the same time, I prefer an evolution.

"Is it hard—ah, yes, it is." We ground away at each other. First, I took the initiative. Then he said he'd show me the "Boston way of doing it." He lay on top of me with our two cocks pressed together. His body is cuddly and sexy, and his cock was hot as a fire. It was a struggle to keep from coming as we writhed there on the bed in the green room. I sucked that lovely tool. I licked the yellow-brown body all over. Have seldom seen anyone cum as much, lashings all over me. He yelled out that his cock was stinging. What did he mean by that? Then he said he was late for work and must dash off. A passionate, excitable young man worth his weight in gold.

With relief, I got the package for Barbara into FedEx. I have spent much time on these two book outlines. *The Failure of Marxism in China* may not make it, as it is mostly stuff already published. But *China on My Mind* could be a big book.

May 18, 1988, Boston

A fantastic time with Reggie this morning. From the moment he walked in—very late—there was electricity. After a couple of beers, he asked about videos. In bed, he asked for a massage. One thing led to another. "Don't do that, Ross." A few minutes of my writhing and pumping later, "Don't do that without a condom, Ross." I leaped to the closet and got a Trojan. It didn't hurt him today, once he arched up his bum, head toward the big mirror to see everything. As I rode him, he jerked himself off. I came a huge load. After coming out of him, I realized the condom had broken. There was just no room inside the thing for all the cum. Reggie didn't notice.

May 19, 1988, Boston

Dreadful rainy weather. Everyone complains of lethargy. I caught up with reading and correspondence. Then a Summer League squash match at the Newton Y. I lost, but overall, our team won.

A chaste evening with Nori, the Nigerian I met last week. He is an interesting person, without most of the arrogance that Nigerians at Harvard had. We went to Thai Cuisine and then talked back here. I think he was expecting me to make a move. But I wasn't that keen. I like to have a friend who knows and loves books, and Nori does. He borrowed *A Boy's Own Story* by Edmund White.

May 20, 1988, Boston

Laurent was trying to call me, just as I was to call him. The second chandelier is in and looks good, he said. So, too, the "Theatrical Light Strips" in the second downstairs bathroom. Bit by bit, we get there. Down at Canal Street, where I went to look for navy blue material for the redone sofa bed, a wall shouts out a sign: "Follow Jesus." But where is Jesus going?

On the way to Washington Street, I sucked a Black guy in the Ell Center.[295] Who should I find at Playland but Cornell W. He had a book of poems with him. As before, I had the impression of a stunning body and a wayward mind. "I want to spend the night with you," he said at the Orange Line station, where, on the way home, I found him and Sam B talking together.

May 22, 1988, Boston

With David C, talk, sex, lunch at Huskie's. David has gone back to his old job. Couldn't stand the pressures of the financial world. His new female boss looks at his cock all day. A junior male worker said to David, "You only got this job because she likes your cock." David looked at this young man. Didn't he know him? Otherwise, how come he was talking in a familiar way about David's cock. The young guy smiled but said nothing. David remembered. "Of course, you know me," he said to the young Black guy. "I once fucked you." They had met in a park in the Fenway.

May 24, 1988, Boston

A talk over lunch at Our Town East with BZY about *China on My Mind* and *The Failure of Marxism in China*. He likes the tone of the memoir. Urges me to reach for a higher plane in it. "Most scholars in China studies start out excited by ideas, then view everything in career terms," he says. "Only a few go on to a third stage of getting wisdom from the study of China."

BZY has a contract for his own book from Westview Press.[296] It gave me some satisfaction to help him fill out the promotion questionnaire. Here is a guy who began as a querulous PRC student, arriving at my house on Broadway Street to seek a research assistant job, now equipped with his PhD and his first book contract. All in seven years. He deserves his success.

May 26, 1988, Boston

When Reggie asked if he could come over, I had not expected that the contractors would be here working on the green bathroom. Undaunted, Reggie did a few things upstairs then called me up to have a drink. He looked fabulous in blue jeans and a shirt of blue and green.

When I began to suck that elegant Black powerhouse, Reggie looked at me and said, "Won't that guy come upstairs?" His look suggested I shouldn't stop, and I didn't. But sure enough, Bob, my contractor, came up swiftly and silently. When he reached the top of the stairs, I had got up from kneeling between Reggie's legs but was still naked to the waist. It was warm up there, so perhaps this didn't look odd. Reggie managed to get his pants zipped up before Bob's little cap appeared at the top of the staircase.

Reggie's back in Lowell for the week. Got his results from the Fenway today and is in the city. The results are "good." I guess this means there is no deterioration in his

---

[295] Classroom and community building at Northeastern University.
[296] Bingzhang Yang, Revolution to Politics: Chinese Communists on The Long March (1990).

various ratios. I told him Reggie was here, and he comments on the impending marriage. I think he can't quite believe the setup with Reggie and Caroline and me.

Reggie had another beer and rolled a joint. With sixth sense, he had guessed it was Edward on the phone. To my surprise, he praised me for how well I recovered from the whole affair. We were sitting on one of the beige couches when he stuck out a hand to my white "cook's" pants. He cupped my cock and balls inside the cloth. His eyes riveted me. So, the scare with Bob had not exactly deterred him. I fumbled with the belt and pulled down the pants. He put his beautiful head near me and took my cock in his mouth, licking and sucking, as the noise of the hammers and drills wafted upstairs from my half-finished bathroom.

"Do you want to fuck me here on the floor?" he said, as if asking me if I wanted a cup of coffee. I just grinned. He got down on the Indian rug beside the kitchen island between the two beige couches. "Get some grease." As fate would have it, there was no Vaseline upstairs, and I wasn't about to go downstairs. Baby oil was on hand. Reggie was already on all fours, so I banged my prick in. He had made no mention of a rubber. But that didn't matter as he came quite soon after I went in—so I did not come inside him.

Then Laurent came in and we all had a drink. At length, Reggie went home to Caroline, who had phoned to see "where he was."

May 29, 1988, Boston

Memorial Day weekend is upon us. Wonderful sunny days. I shop at Workbench for a desk chair and small table for beside the desk. Walking back from the Leather Center on Boylston Street, I come through the Fens and lie down on a rug with Randy, a thin, attractive Black guy who seems to live there. He bites my tits. He puts a cool Black hand up my scanty shorts. We lie embraced, the green leaves above us. Here and there, people are cultivating their "victory gardens." They glance over now and then, but tomatoes and cucumbers pull their attention back.

I must avoid being reductionist. Pushing everything to its "logical conclusion," scrummaging deep until I come upon the bare bones. For things are not always logical; especially people are not always logical. And the last layer of reality is not a pleasant place to be. True of people's lives. True of our world. True of the physical universe?

May 31, 1988, Boston

The sunny weather is gone. We have clouds, rain, and humidity. Deng Yiming phones from Chengdu to eagerly enquire when I will be "returning to Sichuan." They have a list of requests from writers and journalists, she says, but they want to give me the priority as to timing and places to visit because I have been "so helpful to Sichuan tourism" with my writings. My letter of intention and requests is on the way to Chengdu.

Very late, Van Long phones from Washington. "There's someone I would like you to meet." I agree to have Hassan, visiting from Singapore, stay on his first trip to America.

June 1, 1988, Boston

Mikey called and asked if he could come around. While we were together, the doorbell rang; it was Sam B. It turns out Sam was Joe's lover prior to Mikey taking over! All this time, Van's friend Hassan was resting in the green room.

One thing led to another, and I suggested we go into the bedroom. There we had a threesome. I shot a huge load on Mikey's chest. "Wasn't that fun?" Mikey kept saying as Sam and I went upstairs to shower. Mikey had never done it with two others before. And he and Sam had never done it with each other before. Hassan, I think, would like to have joined in. But he had kept saying he was going out, and by the time he knocked on the bedroom door, the pattern seemed too set to accommodate a fourth. Mikey and I walked to the Orange Line. He headed home to Joe, and I to Commonwealth Grille.

Hassan came in from Haymarket about 2 AM. Since he hadn't been able to join in the threesome earlier, I sat on his bed in the green room. He talked of his cooking work in Europe. I stroked his chest and later we got into my bed and made love. He went back to the small room to sleep and I, spent, slept well until eight.

June 2, 1988, Boston

If I could see we are part of nature, I would handle sexual jealousy better. Sex is natural. We are here because of sex. We are made to want it regularly. One should put a lover's indiscretions in this context.

Anthony Grey's novel *Peking* turns out quite good. I do not—as *Publishers Weekly* did—find the span of time too great. And the characters are memorable. Grey demarcates the novel into sections, with a historical note preceding each, and makes his chapters within these sections short. Jumpy? A little. But each one keeps you wondering what will happen next.

June 3, 1988, Boston

In the afternoon, I got the outlines for *China on My Mind* and *The Failure of Marxism in China* off to Barbara in New York. Of course, an outline is never final, but these are in sufficiently good shape to get publishers' reactions. Barbara will aim for $100,000 for the pair. First, we go to Fred, as I have an option agreement with him.

In the evening, Hassan cooked for a table of six, and it went well. Tony O brought his sister; Laurent came and also Cornell. Afterwards, Cornell and Hassan went off to a club, Laurent went to work, and I went to bed.

This morning, before Hassan got his bus to New York, he watched a video. I came out of my study at a good time, found him horny, and lifted the towel he was clad in. I was curious to really see his body carefully, as when we had made love the other night, there was little light—we had been like a Chinese married couple, making out but never seeing each other. Hassan has a nice Moslem cock, and a nut-brown body. His weakness, if any, is passivity of spirit.

Laurent doesn't arrive for our trip to pick up my chair, shelves, camcorder, and table. I fume. As I fume, Edward calls from Hartford. He's having a day in bed. Work continues to go well. Also hectic. I ask about Arlene, and he says, "Who?" When I tell him about my recent purchases, he, like one or two others, wonders where I am "getting the money." The answer is selling 395 and the rise of the Australian dollar. Also, the clock ticks by; one's resources are not to be hoarded.

Edward and I talked on the phone again. He seems ensconced in family and work. Tomorrow, he goes to church; he urged me to go, too. I quoted to him Camus' words: "Don't walk in front of me, I may not follow. Don't walk behind me, I may not lead. Walk beside me and just be my friend." He liked this.

June 5, 1988, Boston

A perfect, non-humid summer day. I stay home, reading, tidying, and arranging upstairs. I begin to sort through Pan's huge trunk. His letters in Thai. His term papers. His class records from Deerfield Academy. A notebook from the Chicago period. Pamphlets about the cultural glories of Thailand.

I run into a "Californian" in the Ell Center at Northeastern. A blond is sucking him off. He looks into my eyes and then, in his authoritarian way, he commands the blond to switch from his dick to mine. The blond complies. As I get sucked, the Californian smacks the blond on the back and shoulders and rasps for me to "fuck his mouth, fuck his mouth." Then he sucks my tits as the blond gets our two cocks in his mouth together.

June 7, 1988, Boston

I woke up this morning and remembered I had not bought orange juice last night on the way home from dinner. A storm of passion had diverted me. I was coming home from the Park Plaza Hotel when a voice called out my name on Huntington Ave. It was Greg N. Eyes still gorgeous, though he looked thinner. He came upstairs and sucked me with a passion and skill as constant as a perfect blue sky. I don't think he is in good health. He begged me to fuck him, then changed his mind. No, you wouldn't want that at the moment. He said the same in reference to his cock going into me. A clouded, sad look came over his face.

BZY phones to say that last week at Harvard a group from the Nationalist Party in Taiwan had a day's talk with Mainland China students and scholars. They amicably discussed visits by the PRC people to Taiwan and the long-term issue of reunification. As with Reagan's trip to Moscow, it seems a sign of a fluid world.

I am sitting on the back deck reading when I notice a Hispanic guy in his 30s snooping around the grassy area on the near side of the vacant lot. Is he going to have a piss? Is he looking for Coke cans to redeem for 5 cents each? No, he beckons to someone. Soon a Black kid comes down the alley. He finds his way through the gap in the fence and goes toward the Hispanic. The Black guy is slim, attractive, and young. The two sit down together, glancing left and right. Alas, they see something, possibly me. I curse myself.

June 9, 1988, Boston

Reggie comes by full of wedding problems. X isn't attending rehearsal. Y has the wrong-sized tuxedo. The minister warns him not to come smelling of liquor. He kindly drives me over to Francis Avenue for Ken Galbraith's garden party on Harvard's Commencement, making himself late for an appointment with Caroline and others.

Fewer people at Ken's bash under the trees this year. Yet one catches up with friends; it is a measuring rod for the march of time. As I greet Ken at the gate and congratulate him on his Honorary Doctorate this afternoon, he tells a story of JFK. "I was in the Oval Office the day after the Inauguration. Kennedy said to me, 'Well, what did you think of Cardinal [Spellman]'s talk to God yesterday.'" It had been a long and evidently boring speech.

In the midst of a talk with John Bethel about the span of time at Harvard over which his magazine *Harvard*, in various forms, has appeared, he invites me to join the Advisory Board. I accept. No duties, no pay—just like my present appointment at Harvard itself.

I chat with Jim Carroll about how Little, Brown mishandled his novel *Prince of Peace* (leading him to shift to New American Library). Ken comes over and slaps each of us on the back. "Time for a drink," he announces in a British locker-room tone, having gone through the enormous chore of welcoming every single guest at the gate. "Is there any sherry?" But there wasn't any.

Amazingly, Jim Carroll had not seen the recent *Publishers Weekly* mention of his new novel. It was a tremendous plug in the Leonore Fleischer column. How come, he wondered, and so did I, that his editor did not send the piece to him? Maybe my publisher isn't so bad after all.

After leaving Cambridge, I dined well at Saint Botolph restaurant. It is going through a good phase—at least in the café—with an enticing new menu and attentive service. Ramone comes over after his rehearsal. We talk, then go to bed. I fucked him again, but again he twisted me to withdraw just as I began shooting. Afterwards, we go upstairs to shower and talk for hours over a glass of wine, then downstairs to sleep.

June 10, 1988, Boston

Ramone stayed around as I tried to work. I gave him a couple of guidebooks for the choir's tour next week. "It's like taking a shower out of doors," he remarked of the red bathroom. That made my day because my aim was to remove barriers between indoors and outdoors.

Much coming and going over Reggie's wedding tomorrow. My new video camera is being used to film it. I hope I get it back in one piece. No work done.

June 11, 1988, Boston

A magnificent warm day. Chris Lydon[297] of Channel 2 phones to ask about terrorism in China; his concern is the music group about to leave for Peking. Chris is overanxious for whatever reason. There is no danger of terrorism in Peking, I assure him.

Even on the morning of his wedding, Reggie is at my place, fussing over a light for the camera, phoning this one, cursing that one, grabbing a beer between calls. So the man who, of all my fairly regular sex partners, I have enjoyed most with over an extended period of years leading right up to this week—leaving aside one—has got married.

In one way, it was an anti-climax, even boring; we sat for an hour in the overly-warm church waiting for the ceremony to start. But there was fascination to the social mix. The appearance of the two handsome brothers electrified me. When Caroline came down the aisle, I cried.

At the Christian Science compound, there was a lovely time of fellowship with Caroline and Reggie and some photos. By the end of the day, I was extremely moved.

Everyone was in blue and gray—very smart—though Reggie's gorgeous elder brother, Robert, was an exception in deep pink. Lovely little children marched in with the ring on a satin cushion. Standing at the altar, brother Robert bantered with Reggie; a knowing older brother's smile at some words of the pastor, a dig in Reggie's ribs with some private joke. At one point, the minister, with a smile, leaned over to adjust Reggie's bow tie.

After the wedding vows had been sternly stressed by the preacher, a solo was sung on the theme "Just Give Me One Night." The preacher had a folksy way to his prayers. "Lord Jesus, help us to understand that shacking up is not the way, but Holy Matrimony is the way." Almost everyone in Reggie's family—and many other families—has broken that particular rule.

To the vows, Reggie replied, "I will" instead of "I do." Cleverly, the minister phrased his questions to Caroline so she could answer, "I will" to match Reggie's answer. I asked Robert, the older brother not long out of jail—who looked terribly pleased with life out of jail—what he thought of the church ceremony. "Great wedding." He looked around at the bridesmaids. "And I just might find my own bride amongst all these."

I talked with Reggie's father about Boston and his life out West; he does not live with Reggie's mother. How many sons and daughters do you have? "Three sons, four daughters—Oh, let me think, no three daughters, it's hard to keep track." A fourth daughter is the baby he recently had by a girl in Las Vegas.

Juliano has been calling. *Quoi faire?* He's at a pay phone. At the Y, I meet Kevin, a new member of the Roberts Club. From Los Angeles, he has lived in Atlanta recently and arrived in Boston on an internship with John Hancock. Egotistical, charming, conservative, an only child.

---

[297] Christopher Lydon (1940 -), a former journalist with *The New York Times*, anchored "The Ten-O'clock News" on Boston's public television station WGBH, from 1977-1991.

At midnight Reggie phones to say he's coming around with the camera. An hour later, he arrived with Caroline and also Mike and Edgy. We partied upstairs. Reggie made phone calls now and then. He showed Mike and Edgy around the apartment. In a few hours, the entire hurricane will depart for Jamaica. Nearby shrubs like me will get some peace. He's one of a kind, Reggie, a dynamo of charm and emotion in the wake of which the world adjusts as it can.

June 14, 1988, Boston

I ate at home, then walked in the Ruggles-Columbus area. On the way home about midnight, I met Grady, a lean young guy, on Mass Ave. After exchanging glances, he said, "You want to take a little walk?" He attracted my attention because, by the bus stop, a taxi stopped and the woman sitting beside the driver harried him [Grady]. Didn't he want a lift!

Inside, Grady carrying a huge red stereo radio, looked around as if to say which room are we going to do it in. How we sucked each other! I loved his cut dick with its big head. He wanted to fuck me and indeed started. I wanted to fuck him but was so absorbed in getting sucked and jerked that I came before the opportunity came around. He said he would ring my door buzzer sometime.

I went upstairs to drink a glass of wine, take the warm night air, and read magazines. It was well after two when I went to bed. I was woken by the phone. It wasn't morning, and it didn't seem like evening. Indeed, it was the virtually unknown hour of 4 AM. The caller was Edward—he couldn't sleep, had things on his mind. Is he an aggressive person? Is he, after all, rather difficult to get on with? I answered no to the questions which I have on other occasions answered yes to.

I went back to sleep. About 8 AM, I was woken by the door buzzer. It was Mike. We made love in the cranberry room (the previous time, we'd moved to the green room since the shades hadn't yet gone up). Then he watched videos till noon. I went in from time to time to chat and caress. Of the videos, he liked *Salt and Pepper Boys* the best. A peaceful, self-contented guy.

June 15, 1988, Boston

A rap at the apartment door. A voice: "It's Peter Pan." Hank was in wonderful form. At the start, he announced, "I'm horny," and I had to fall in with that mood. Various things jostled inside his lovely head on this summer morning. "Have you been behaving?" he asks. I don't have time to answer.

"Have you had a shower?" he asks as we get into bed. I obviously had; I had still been dripping when he arrived. What he wanted to say was that he'd like to have a shower. Soon he was back in bed, and I deliciously sent my tongue curling around his balls and asshole. When I shot a big series of spurts, he said, "So you have been behaving!" Hank does not realize his capacity to make my body lie.

Recently at the Inn in Provincetown, where he was working, there was a transvestites' convention.[298] These guys came with their wives. They dressed up in women's clothes. It didn't seem to involve sex; after the parties, they went back to their hotel rooms and waiting wives!

At night Hank and I were ready to go out to dinner when Mikey, Wyatt, and another guy arrived. Mikey had a good look at Hank and then took me into the study: "He's beautiful!" Upstairs, it was too hot to sit on the sofas, so we gathered at the table where the air-conditioner gave direct benefit. Mikey and Joe have parted. He complained that Joe seemed to find him "too old" and promptly took up with "this child of 16." Wyatt asked if Mikey had always been faithful to Joe. "Yes, I have," lied Mikey. I looked at him, but he was looking away.

All this time, Hank, to my surprise, resisted totally the incredible importunities of Mikey. His eyes screamed, "Come to bed with me now." And indeed, he cornered Hank in the bedroom. But Hank was playing it cool. At length, Hank and I went out to Saint Botolph Café and dined well. "You know, Mikey wanted to spend the night with me!" Of course, I knew. What I also remembered was that Hank, that night when David tried to get onto him, more or less said he prefers white guys. Come to think of it, I don't know of any time he's done it with a Black guy.

June 18, 1988, Boston

I took Somchat to the Gay Asian party so he could meet locals. He enjoyed it. Loring, who had invited me to come, kept a hawk-like eye on Somchat. Though I mentioned casually that I had just met Somchat, who is from Thailand, as we came in, I think Loring, who perhaps fancies me, suspected a longer attachment. In fact, Somchat and I met a week or so ago at the BPL. He slept one night at my place. Even that degree of intimacy shows when the beholder is keen-eyed like Loring.

At the party, I chatted with a Harvard graduate student who is trying to write a history of homosexuality in China. Loring, when I said I had recently been in Georgia, announced that the South is very oppressive toward gays. He has been reading some stuck-up treatise by an ill-informed Northern academic.

June 20, 1988, Boston

Hot again. I finalize all three *National Geographic* outlines. Out of the blue, Fred Hills phones to discuss *China on my Mind* and *The Future of Marxism in China*. Is *The Future of Marxism in China* any more than a collection? Can it be made otherwise? And is *China on my Mind* about China, or is it about Ross Terrill? Good, probing questions.

---

[298] Fantasia Fair, held every year in Provincetown since 1975.

June 21, 1988, New York

At the Hyatt Hotel, Australians are to the fore at the Asia Society's annual dinner. Alan Bond[299] chats about his university on the Gold Coast—"We just have to come to terms with our region"—when a guy comes up to us. "I'm Mike from Pittsburgh," he says to Bond. "Iron Bridge. You bought us. How ya doing?" Bond is short, bouncy, with an open, kind face. Someone asked Bondie about his beer companies. He held up a glass that appeared to contain a highball. "I'm keeping off two topics today—beer and gold mines."

Jim Wolfensohn[300] is pleasant. Both he and his wife compliment me on *800,000,000*. He is a refined, predictable man. Jim makes an eloquent speech in response to receiving an Asia Society award, referring to Australia and America as "my two parents, both of whom I love." He seemed to think I'd come with Prime Minister Hawke's party and was surprised when I told him I lived in Boston. The only other time we met was at a party for PM Malcolm Fraser at Rupert Murdoch's.

During a lull in the dinner, I went up to Hawke at the head table. He greeted me very warmly. He said some of the themes we talked about in Canberra last year he incorporated into his Chicago speech earlier today.

I was seated next to a Mrs. Kunstadter, a pleasant and polite China-lover and devourer, she says, of my books on China. At our table, also the Bhutan ambassador and a silly dentist from Sydney who deals in real estate. The PM spoke well about Australia and Asia. A little rosy, perhaps, about China and its "reforms" (such a safe, irreproachable word!).

I left carrying a huge and beautiful book on Australia given to all guests and a large soft bear which I won in a raffle. Walking back to the Harvard Club, stares from the crowded Manhattan streets, and some cheery smiles at the sight of my white koala bear.

June 22, 1988, New York

I woke up weak and numb in the limbs. An hour of sex fantasizing before I developed the will to get out of bed. Manhattan melted under a fierce sun. I checked my book review for the *Los Angeles Times* one last time and posted it to the excellent Jack Miles.[301]

At Simon & Schuster, James Nicholls, editor at Touchstone, seems upbeat about the upcoming paperback of *The Australians*. He did not dismiss out of hand my suggestions for publicity. I don't know if this was mere politeness or an indication of serious intent. I gave him review excerpts. "This book really has been well-reviewed," he murmured. In the second Touchstone edition, they will put in a page or two of quotes.

[299] Alan Bond (1938-2015), high-profile Australian businessman noted for his corrupt business dealings.
[300] Sir James David Wolfensohn (1933-2020), Australian-American lawyer, investment banker, and economist, known as "banker to the world's poor."
[301] John R. "Jack" Miles (1942 -), American author, winner of the Pulitzer Prize (for *God: A Biography*), a Guggenheim Fellowship, and a MacArthur Fellowship. At the time Terrill was writing, Miles was the literary editor at the *Los Angeles Times*.

Barbara took me to the play *M Butterfly*. Worthwhile, but not dramatic enough until the wonderful last act. Throughout, it stimulates thought. "No Oriental is completely a man," says the character René Gallimard to his lover at one point. When they quarrel, there is a strong scene which has René calling Butterfly "my little one," and he throwing it back in René's face—"Come here, my little one!" How well I know that particular conflict.

The play is about fantasy. Do we want the truth? We so often hide from it. And about the pride of East and West. Perhaps the playwright is gay. The wife is absurd. There is silly talk of penis size. Not enough romantic dramatic excitement as M "turns" into a man, and the lovers deal with each other as males.

You can go in and out of the Harvard Club now, through a back door, in shorts and sneakers and tank top. I just said to the man at the door that I was going jogging. On 8th Avenue, I got sucked off by a muscular Hispanic guy—who rushed me, but otherwise was great. In the steamy heat, I walked back along 44th Street as the delivery trucks for *New York Times* geared up to take away their cargo. It seems a primitive mode of getting news to people—in today's world—to print it on paper every day and deliver the physical product across a logistically clogged metropolis.

June 23, 1988, New York

I catch Mike Bessie on the phone before leaving for Washington. With his Gorbachev manuscript coup, he is still full of Russia. Tonight, he has a party for the Maly Theater troupe from Leningrad. He believes the changes in the USSR are "extremely important. I know a bit of what John Reed felt," he gushed. Can Gorbachev be that important?

Later in DC

A nice time amidst suffocating heat last night. It is more convenient to be staying in a hotel, rather than in the Harvard Club, as in New York, with its dress code. In shorts and sandals, I walk to Malcolm X Park. A few types but not many—too hot for outdoor promenading.

The movie places around the MLK Library prove interesting. I see a fantastic stud in a blue track suit. He bought $5 worth of tokens. By himself, he went into a booth to watch a movie. Then he changed booths. As he walked, his huge prick was bulging to the left within the blue pants. He went to get more tokens and again I could not take my eyes off his lovely ass, the smooth round line of his neck, and that waving prick. Unhinged, I went into the booth next to his and lay down flat on the grimy floor. This way, I could see up toward his body sitting on the seat as he faced the screen. This big, cut Black dick was in his hands. His pants were not down, just opened at the fly. It seemed too sad to see him solo like that, so I uncoiled myself from the floor and left.

This morning, another guy, Phillip, came to the Holiday Inn, and we made nice love. He has smooth baby's skin and is good with mouth and lips. I could hardly keep myself from coming. He wanted me to fuck him but asked that I use a condom. By the time I had fiddled around with the thing, I went half soft. In the end, I came in his hand—wonderful orgasm. He gave me his address, his sister's place in Virginia, to which he is moving in a couple of days.

The meetings at *National Geographic* go well. Mac is buoyant over Don Regan's memoir's success, the good prospects for his new novel, and, I think, over the excellent publicity he himself has finally been receiving as a master ghost-writer and spy novelist.[302]

I gave Susan an idea for pieces on the Chinese army and Chinese youth. She thought the latter was great, wondered if the first was really good pictorially. She's in the middle of a story about cocaine. She could hardly believe her ears when I told her I had been offered coke the night before a mile from the White House. "Who would buy coke in the street?" she kept saying. One wonders how trenchant her story will turn out.

At the *Geographic*, there is always a great calm. I don't know if this is because of super-efficiency or over-staffing. Mac is in a great mood as he sweeps me off to the Madison for an over-priced lunch. I can't write about the Aborigines in another publication until my story is killed. As he considers the prospects of it being published almost zero, he will seek to have the story killed—then I would be free to write on the subject elsewhere.

We talk of American politics. He thinks Bush will win. He likes Don Regan and thinks he got bad press—thanks to Nancy—toward the end of his White House years under Reagan. He has read the Reagan-Gorbachev transcripts and says RR is a terrific negotiator. In his view, people expect too much of a president. "By the time a problem gets up that high, it generally means it's unsolvable. But American people don't want to know that problems are unsolvable."

He hopes *Bride of the Wilderness*[303] will get a better go in *The New York Times* than he has been used to. He tells a story that may explain his bad run with the *Times*. He was living in Geneva, working as a spy. He gave a dinner for Abe Rosenthal, then covering the UN, to meet some Genovese. Mac's wife prepared an elegant meal. At the table, Rosenthal took no food; instead, put his notebook on the table and questioned the guests. At the end, when guests rather prematurely departed, Abe turned to Nancy and said, "Now you can get me some food, Nancy." Mac reached for Abe's notebook and threw it on the crackling fire.

Mac says a good *National Geographic* piece is like a screenplay. He asks what my colleagues at Harvard think of my writing for *National Geographic*. It wasn't an easy question to answer. Yet again, he praises the Sichuan piece. "Neither you nor the magazine got the credit deserved for that breakthrough piece," he observed. Of the three ideas I submitted, it is "Youth in China" that interests him.

Mac today resembled some of his characters in *Bride*: tough, intelligent, bon vivant, believing in nothing, stoical, given to humor as a remedy.

---

[302] Donald T. Regan (1918-2003) was Secretary of the Treasury from 1981 to 1985 and the White House Chief of Staff from 1985 to 1987 under Ronald Reagan. His memoir, ghostwritten by McCarry, *For the Record: From Wall Street to Washington*, was published in 1988.

[303] Charles McCarry's sixth novel in the Paul Christopher spy-thriller series.

June 24, 1988, Boston

Dr. Joan Goldberg gets back to me at last with news that I am negative to the HIV virus by the Western Blot as well as the more primitive Elisa test. Short of a very experimental test splitting the DNA not yet available, that establishes that the virus is not within me. Thank God.

I go out to West Roxbury for my annual physical with my physician, Suzie. She says I look fine when I walk in. If doctors can say that when you open the door, why do they bother with tests; are the tests but a ritual, like saying mass or the Queen's speech from the throne? I should have a colonoscopy, she says, and get my eyes tested. I will see a second neurologist over the growing numbness.

BL calls with the good news that Simon & Schuster wants to hang on to me—the president, Charles Hayward, in particular, does—and that they can come to three-quarters of the price she is asking. I want to hold out for the 100 grand. They want to talk to me next week, after I'm finished with the Australian film people on Monday.

June 25, 1988, Boston

I am woken by the silky voice of Somchat. While I was out of town, he busied himself at the BPL to find out more about me. Got a print-out of reviews of all my books. He has read a number of reviews and now started to read *White-Boned Demon*. He wants to come around and "go for a walk together."

My guilt is no good; I must slay it. First, understand it. Guilt that my Chinese language and Chinese expertise have sagged in the past three years. And guilt over being gay. There's a third: so many gays have died or are dying that one feels guilty about still being alive!

Sam came in for a quickie before going to dance at Haymarket. I drove my dick endlessly against those great balls and beige thighs. But I didn't want to come as it was not the moment, he said, for me to fuck him. Perhaps something to do with the exigencies of dancing before an audience.

Reggie comes by briefly. Once again, Caroline and others are waiting in the car downstairs. He has a dramatic story. The start of the video cassette they used to record the wedding rehearsal "had some man on it jerking off. There was you in your house, and there was this man." Reggie's eyes were popping out of his head. "Caroline saw it and she said, 'Is Ross gay?'" The incident shows Reggie's post-wedding state of mind.

June 26, 1988, Boston

Perhaps in the next couple of years, China can be for me what religion has been for Dan Wakefield. Beyond despair, is there something?—that is the question. If there is not, one just obliterates the pain with booze or drugs. But Dan found that if he prayed, the anxiety went away. I suppose it's a case of transcending self.

Lately, I have been too subjective with my writings and brittle publicity. Indulging myself, getting the conditions right for me to feel how I want to feel, and mostly being able to do so. In Chinese language and the study of China, there is an objective discipline. To get back to it will steady me beyond anything I can contribute in writing about China.

Li-li calls to comment on my outlines. She says my detractors will say *China on my Mind* is egotistical. But she thinks the "people" angle of it will be fascinating. She is persuaded I should do this book before the one about my sex life.

Greg N rings the doorbell, and we go to bed—literally—almost for the first time. First time was in a library. Second time was in the Zone. Third time was in my lobby. He doesn't seem a bed person. Once more, I find his cuddly sexuality irresistible. Is he ill? He may be—so I did not suck him. He seems conscious of some barrier and withdraws. Meanwhile, he sucked me beautifully. I had to come before I liked because of my trip to New York tonight.

I am trying to prepare for the New York meetings tomorrow when Sam comes in. He wants to lift a few weights. He wants to watch a video. My old classmate Tony Staley calls to say the producers of the Australia film project are late and we won't convene until tomorrow morning. I'll take the 7 AM down to NY.

June 27, 1988, New York

A lovely morning to fly down on the shuttle. Tom and Tim, the Australian producers, are intelligent and well-prepared guys. Tony Staley, dear friend from Melbourne who brought me together with them, is the enthusiastic host. Their scheme of putting Barbara Tuchman's *March of Folly* together with Henry Kissinger as host of a TV miniseries seems bizarre. But who knows, on TV, apparent opposites may blend together by the trickery of the producer. I advised them on the shape of the project and how to approach Kissinger (they didn't know basic things, such as that Kissinger has a contract with NBC).

My session at Simon & Schuster was tough. Fred said his colleagues did not like the outline. To reinforce this, he had brought along Alice Mayhew as hit person. This charming lady urged me to rip up the outline and start again. I could not help thinking that everything BL had urged me to put in the outline, Alice found "off-putting," such as protracted personal experiences, mention of prizes won for my writing on China.

He still wants *China on my Mind*, Fred says, but he wants more of the drama of China in it and less of the memoirs of RT. He linked his point with the money angle: his idea would be a "bigger book in every way" than the one I was proposing. In other words, what the outline proposed (plus the essay collection) was not worth the phrase he Delphic-ly chose to use. I got antsy at this and said archly that I had not come to talk about money.

Whom should I meet on 42nd Street but the postman Yves. After so long! "I got your postcard," he said with a big smile. "But you never replied to me," I rejoined. Anyway, he is still very sexy, though thinner and strained. We didn't have a proper place to go as I had just left my bag at the Port Authority prior to catching the 12:30 AM bus to Boston. In a peep show place, he sucked me off with his old skill, passion, and good timing.

June 28, 1988, Boston

The bus trip back to Boston was neither restful nor exciting—bus trips should be one or the other. Dawn was beautiful, though, as we approached Boston about 4:30 AM. I was tired but didn't sleep for long.

Over lunch at Saint Botolph restaurant, Jim Thomson argued strongly that my *China on my Mind* outline is good and that I should go ahead. Biography, he says, is the nicest way to read history and contemporary affairs. He made a few suggestions about toning down the ego of the outline (was this what Alice didn't like about "tone"?). He thinks the sex stuff ought to be in if it is done delicately. I told him the story of Lan Hua at Vassar and New York, and he said this indeed sheds light on Chinese culture.[304]

The answer has come on how Reggie feels now he's married. We spent several hours together tonight with our usual goings-on. He was here when I got back from squash, looking stunning in a white shirt and faded gray jeans. We did a long post-mortem on the wedding, and he told me of the honeymoon in Jamaica. He loved the photos I took on my Nikon at the church and by the Christian Science pool.

June 29, 1988, Boston

Li-li feels I may well be able to put in more of the sweep of Chinese history to satisfy Simon & Schuster. But she still feels the "RT perspective on China" is a "valid and exciting lens" for the book.

I see three alternatives. Try to see the thing Fred's way. Go to Pat at William Morrow. Forget the memoir idea for a few years and start on the Hong Kong novel.

Greg N comes in for his jacket. He wanted more than his jacket, but I couldn't turn my mind to sex—Reggie last night and Dion the night before had spent me. Greg is amazingly attractive.

July 2, 1988, Boston

Harrison Salisbury is back from China and can hardly stop talking about it. Great diversity across the land, he says. Canton booming but not the north. Hong Kong people have too much influence—"Is it really PRC that will take over Hong Kong, or Hong Kong that will take over the PRC?"

I raise whether the absence of a believed public philosophy is not a problem for China today. "You and I know that 'preliminary stage of socialism' is a ridiculous formulation, but it's the only fig leaf they have." A fair comment. He didn't like the Paul Theroux book *Riding the Iron Rooster* as much as I am liking it—and reviewing in the *Boston Globe*.

Edward phones to say he laughed a lot at the birthday invitation with its little jokes and ambiguities. In principle, he accepts a birthday dinner; he will propose a time later. He could not resist asking if Reggie and I had had "post-nuptials."

---

[304] In 1980, Lan Hua, a 35-year-old graduate student at China's Dong Normal University, came to Vassar as the first foreign language intern from the PRC.

I want him to see I am not interested in a "recapture." Our meeting—or not—is a matter of friends enjoying each other's company; our going to bed again—or not—is a matter of whether pleasure awaits.

In the evening, Reggie comes in and does shopping at the liquor store. I thought Reggie would like *Beyond Hawaii*—white guys on the beach—but no. "I don't like watching them do it outdoors—only indoors." Afterwards, he and Caroline went to a late movie.

In the wedding post mortems, only one false note was detected by Reggie, Caroline, and their friends: the minister shouldn't have mentioned "shacking up" being the wrong way and marriage better. "Too crude."

July 3, 1988, Boston

A leisurely time with Li-li, including lunch at Atlantic Fish. She says there are few people of quality, and those that exist should be cherished. She feels I lower my standards at times and juxtapose fine and mediocre in a puzzling way.

July 5, 1988, Boston

Has the resumption between Reggie and me turned Laurent off? He was eager to know, "Has Reggie changed since the wedding?" When I said he hadn't, Laurent said nothing, but since then we haven't met and haven't talked that much. Is it really a case of *rien m'attache*?

July 6, 1988, Boston

It is wonderful on my new decks, the back one especially. I almost feel guilty at the comfort and beauty! As I predicted to Laurent, plunging into the next book will assuage the guilt over my wonderful house. "Peter Pan" calls out of the blue. My heart leapt at the sound of his voice. Yes, of course he can stay here.

Another hot day. I plunge ahead, catching up with the China academic journals. Good to read *China Quarterly*, *AJCS*, and *JAS* in a bunched way; one learns more as themes emerge than by reading the issues as they hit the desk. In between times, I inch ahead with understanding how the *China on my Mind* book could be done à la Simon & Schuster.

I got my Australia article off to *World Monitor* at its plush paneled offices on Columbus Avenue. Next week, I should tackle the Melbourne Cup piece for *New York Times*. I am getting to the end of these spin-off pieces from work on *The Australians*. Then will come the change of gears into China material—a year from now, I'll be producing China articles the way I've been doing Australia articles this past year. In some ways, 1988 will resemble 1971: in that memorable spring, I finished the Tawney manuscript, then headed for Peking. This year, I tidy up the Australia project and head, yes, once more to Peking. It's like a disease, this Sinological grip.

July 9, 1988, Boston

Reading Theroux's *Riding the Iron Rooster*, I think back to my *Flowers on an Iron Tree*. I even dip into this book of 13 years ago. It is quite good, but some things lack by comparison with Paul's: humor; digression in pursuit of the bizarre or literary effect. I was too hung up on facts and figures. And I lacked irony in *Flowers*.

A nice time with Ramone after we dine at Legal Seafood. He devours oysters, announcing they are an aphrodisiac, "but only if you take no alcohol with them." He stays all night. He is a quiet sleeper and a nice presence in the house. I only wish he didn't come from a preacher's family; he has an impulse to showmanship and opportunism.

July 10, 1988, Boston

Sam saw me on the back deck, called out, came up. He wanted photos for the owner of "The Gallery" in the hope of landing a new dancing job. We shot some upstairs and then in the bedroom. He looks very nice indeed at the right angles. I love his legs and his balls.

We turned from art to pursue lust. Soon I had my cock deep inside him. "What are you doing?" he said with a grin, as if he didn't know. But I knew what he meant, so I pulled out before I came.

July 11, 1988, Boston

The "Evoked Potentials" neurological test at Kenmore Health Center causes no pain at all despite warnings. This test will probe the "low grade neuritis" that Dr. Teres found. I chatted my head off with the girl as she fed me valium. The last I remember before going into a drowsy state was telling her about how Australian kangaroos bite.

Reggie says, "I'm going to stop drinking. I'm going to stop everything." I say nothing. I don't want to discourage him. I have heard it before.

July 14, 1988, Boston

At the squash club, I was going upstairs to play Serge when I caught sight of this well-built Black guy. Solid, tall, lovely eyes. His name is Kyle. Within two minutes, we had hooked up. I explained I was in a rush and gave him my phone number. He said he'd call that afternoon. He did, and we had a marvelous time. Few have sucked me more lovingly. He wanted me to fuck him so badly. I did, though the usual caution in this era aborted the exhilaration of pumping my rod deep up into his stomach. He has a sunny, relaxed way.

July 20, 1988, Boston

Glued to the TV screen—my wonderful new one in the bedroom—watching the Democratic Convention from Atlanta. Jesse Jackson was magnificent. I think the party made a mistake—or Duke[305] did—in not putting him on the ticket. Mayor Flynn said after Jesse's speech: "I have never been so proud to be an American." I felt the same way.

Is there a self-indulgent streak in all gays? Barney Frank on TV discusses the character issue of the presidential candidates with himself as the pivot. I suppose, as a group, we are subjective. I will never forget Prof. Mac Ball saying to a colleague, with much exaggeration, during the month I left my tutorship at the University of Melbourne to take up my Knox Fellowship at Harvard: "While not marking our exams, as he was supposed to, Ross wrote a hundred personal farewell letters."

July 21, 1988, Boston

Delivered the revised article on Australian character to *World Monitor*—driven to Earl's snazzy office by the excellent Marilyn.

Relentless cruising. The words from the Chinese novel *Golden Lotus* spring to mind: "There is a limit to our energy, but none to our desires. A man who sets no bounds to his passion cannot live more than a short time."

The political TV from Atlanta draws me, but Reggie draws me more. Going up the staircase to fetch a beer, he looked back at me with those huge eyes and rasped, "Where's that cock?" I turn down the volume as we make love. Then, when we are done, Reggie wants to discuss politics. As tricks left and right turn out fickle, the married guy is the steady one!

July 22, 1988, Boston

The TV show at Cape Cod Television on Marion's *Books and the World* program goes OK, but she does not inspire or provoke. And she threw me at the start by inviting me to quote a ditty from *The Australians*, which I could not remember.

I was hardly back when Mike came around. A workman was upstairs, but that didn't stop us. He is going to Connecticut with his family for a short holiday next week. He's still abstaining from sucking and fucking.

Sam has landed the dancing job. The boss loved the photos I took—wants more. What with hangover, lack of sleep, orgasm, and hazy heat—I felt tired. But revived after a message from the *World Monitor*: "Mr. Foell[306] said to tell you that the Australia article is absolutely splendid."

July 24, 1988, Boston

Chris has written a poem, "Walking and Thinking." He has things on his mind. He realizes, I think, that being handicapped is going to make it hard for him to marry. He wanted me to fuck him, and I did. I like it with him in the green room, watching in the mirror at close range as we writhe.

---

[305] Michael Dukakis (1933 -), Governor of Massachusetts (1975-1979 and 1983-1991) and Democratic candidate for the presidency in 1988. His running mate was Lloyd Bentsen.
[306] Earl Foell (1929-1999), senior editor of *The Christian Science Monitor*.

At times, my numbness is not there on first awakening, but comes later, after I have dozed off to sleep for an hour or two and then re-awakened. If so, is it a consequence of thoughts which fill my subconscious in the last phase of the night's rest?

July 26, 1988, Boston

My South African-born neurologist, Dr. Teres, has found nothing in the blood tests to explain the abnormal performance of my peripheral nervous system. No auto-immune problem. No thrombosis. He is virtually certain the central nervous system is not damaged. Anything in my diet to watch—coffee, alcohol? "No, no, not at the level you drink." I say nothing. Then I ask, "Have you read the file?"

"Well, I think so. Let me see." I mention that I drink half a bottle of wine a day or a bit more.

"Oh, I didn't realize that." In other words, the genius hadn't read the file. I had put the thought into the mind of this empty-headed peanut. That doesn't mean it wasn't a good idea to do so. The possibility of wine as a culprit had been hanging in my mind. Dr. Teres announced with great authority that for 60 days I should take no alcohol at all.

"Now there's no point in not doing this properly," he said. "Don't compromise. It will be harder than you think."

I walked out feeling like when I was going into National Service—nine months in the army—in Australia in 1957. But I had a feeling of satisfaction after National Service. Dr. Teres said that, if drinking is hurting the nervous system, "at your age," the decline should be reversible after I stop drinking wine.

July 28, 1988, Boston

At Tremont Street, I notice this glorious stud in jeans and white satin tank top. He is at the traffic light. The stud has just reached Columbus. Dressed in my gym clothes, carrying a squash racquet, I stare. I walk a little behind him as he goes along Mass Ave. I considered him the perfect Roxbury stud—unavailable—and looking was all I hoped for.

At the bus stop by the Orange Line, he stops and sits down. I do too. Some looking occurs. I began to think it was possible after all. I let my half-hardon show in my long white pants, rocking forward and back against the parapet of the station. I said hello and asked where he lived. He asked where I lived, and I pointed up at my greenhouses.

"Would you like some company?"

Paul W is of medium height and curvaceous and a lovely cinnamon color. He kissed me fiercely after I knelt on the floor and came up his body inch by inch while he sat on the white sofa. In bed, I began to fuck him as he lay on his tummy. "Just a minute. I'll switch." He lay on his back. It was simply paradise as I rammed him that way, squeezing his tits and looking into his eyes in lust's conspiracy.

July 29, 1988, Boston

Three days without drinking any wine is tough but interesting. At best, I may reclaim the pleasure of really using my mind to the extent possible. I will test whether the tools at my disposal are in good order.

July 30, 1988, Boston

I reach Luther at last. He has changed his phone number because of legal action against his former employer. He sounds fine, almost childlike. But he doesn't have a new job.

I am puzzled by Laurent. We ran into each other after his exam. He was rushing off to Malden to study in a group for the next exam. Said he'd be home at nine. I phoned many times after nine but no answer.

Li-li often phones these days. Tonight, she is worked up that professors seem to be slipping behind economically in American society. Were they once over-valued, I suggest gently?

Withdrawal symptoms as a newly-minted teetotaler are rather bad tonight. I trust they will get less.

August 2, 1988, Boston

Prayer would be important as meditation if for no other reason. I also find a step-by-step approach to getting things done essential. You can only do one thing at a time; while doing it, don't worry about the next thing. I have developed a post-Teres passion for sweet things. I eat ice cream every day. I stop at little shops for banana splits. A wine substitute?

I got my test results from the Fenway. For the sixth time, I am negative to the HIV virus. All other tests are normal—except the T-cell test, which was not done. How grateful I am to American medicine!

Magnificent time with Reggie tonight. From my side, and I think from his, the desire has not dimmed in the five or six years we have known each other. I fucked him hard and deep without a condom as he gazed deep into my eyes and held my body with unusual tenderness. It helped—though I didn't shoot inside him—that I got the test result this afternoon. Reggie's declaration of some time ago—"I can't get fucked any more"—has gone the way of a politician's words in an election year, or a single man's on the eve of marriage.

August 5, 1988, Boston

At the BPL, a nice Black guy. Overweight but with a huge, handsome weapon. I follow him into the music section. He utterly ignores me, goes on doing a crossword puzzle. Later, I am in the men's room, in a stall reading the *Boston Globe*. This same guy comes near, kneels down, and sucks my throbbing cock.

Dinner with Caleb at Thai Cuisine. He is in a rigid mood. He wants another lover. This person must give "150% of himself" to Caleb. I get restless with such standards.

Caleb senses this. After dinner, he goes to meet relatives who have just arrived from the Midwest. For the first time in a long while, we meet without making love.

August 6, 1988, Boston

Breakfast with the AP journalist John Roderick at his favorite haunt, the Parker House. He still fiddles with an autobiography. Also with a book about the history and renovation of his old farmhouse at Kamakura, out of Tokyo.[307] He does not favor putting sex into a memoir. Says to keep it out of *China on my Mind*—do it in a separate book. "How I envy your ability to write books!" he exclaimed, unsettling me.

John has some bitterness about AP and himself in 1971-72. After his great reporting from China in 1971—he had a background on the subject, having met Mao in Yan'an in the 1940s—he was not included in the team that went to Peking for AP to cover the Nixon trip in 1972! John nearly resigned from AP over this. How curious are the workings of large organizations and how happy I am not part of one.

He told me BW—I had not known he was gay—said that in Peking you can do well with boys if you observe one rule: they don't like being groped in front, but you can do anything you like with their ass. Thus did Bob pass his time, it seems, at Peking University during the Cultural Revolution.

August 7, 1988, Boston

Am I turning into a chaste old scholar? I felt that way as I dressed up in a Somerset Maugham-like outfit and dined alone at the lovely restaurant in the Colonnade Hotel.

August 9, 1988, Boston

My evenings have changed. I drink coffee. I eat ice cream. I go for late-night walks, I read until 1 AM.

Li-li is urging *qi gong* on me—a second way, in addition to diet changes from Dr. Teres and others, to regain control of my physical future. It chilled my spine when she remarked that her libido has almost disappeared. "Fifty's the watershed," she said without grief. If this ever happens to me, I will prefer to lie down and die.

August 10, 1988, Boston

Dr. Troy at the HCHP says my knobby knuckles are nothing to worry about. It is an arthritic condition, but not a bad one. Surprising to see it in "one so young." But unless it becomes dysfunctional, there is no point in surgery. He mentioned diabetes and too much alcohol as factors in some arthritic or loss-of-feeling conditions. But how physicians vary! The moment he mentioned drinking, he added: "But that can't be basic; otherwise, the Italians and French wouldn't be able to walk."

Hank arrived from Provincetown. He is tired but looks great. We made love at noon. Then I played squash and later joined him for a late lunch at Legal Sea Foods.

---

[307] Minka: My Farmhouse in Japan (2007).

But Hank has a distracted air. Is there something on his mind? Or does he have—he would not be the only one!—a generalized sense of malaise, anxiety in this AIDS era?

He is working in the Boatslip's[308] kitchen—$8 an hour—as well as being a waiter—$2 plus tips. "The worst tippers in Provincetown are the French Canadians," he says. In October, when the season on the Cape ends, he and his sister Sandy plan to take an apartment in Boston. Should I let them stay here while I'm away? Once more, the slight change in the Laurent/Ross tie becomes a variable—and imponderable.

Edward phones and we talk for two hours. He received the *National Geographic* on Australia and has been devouring it—also the clipping of funny fashions from the *Village Voice* that I enclosed. He is coming up on the evening of August 22. We plan a joint birthday dinner.

August 11, 1988, Boston

A prowling foray into Roxbury. How much more exciting, generous, and open are the young, especially the young straight ones! Dudley Square, Washington Park, Martin Luther King Blvd, the Roxbury YMCA—all physically battered but socially intriguing.

At the bus stop near the Washington Shopping Mall, I see a slim young guy of dark complexion. We looked, we jiggled our legs. "Walk up this way," he said, jerking his head toward the hill. We sat on the steps of a high school. I played with him through his pants. "Would you like to see it?" he said charmingly. Indeed, I would. Jean-Maurice is Haitian. His cock was a beauty—long, thick, cut. I sucked it. He came very quickly. I had my towel with me from swimming, which was convenient for mopping up delicious Port-au-Prince cum.

August 12, 1988, Cambridge

A long talk with Michael Bessie at the Harvard Faculty Club before his talk in Coolidge Hall on the experience with Gorbachev and his book, which Mike is editing and publishing. He is slightly uneasy being beneath the shadow of Murdoch's colossal power.

More friends of his and Cornelia's—and two colleagues at Harper—have succumbed to AIDS in the last year. He quizzes me again on my health, as if he never really believed I recovered from that years-ago bout with TB.

A seminar at the Russian Research Center is similar to comparable ones at our East Asian Center: bereft of theory; blinkered in focusing on "our country" as if it were the universe; hungry for scraps of information in the face of Communist secrecy.

Later in a sweltering afternoon, Lu Chunyi comes in to read to me the memo his mother wrote on his father's troubles at the hands of the Communist Party. Such pain and passion of a family! Yet what would be the point of a newspaper story by me about his family? That the new society is the same as the old one? Or that the new was better than the old, but something bad happened along the way?

---

[308] A resort in Provincetown popular with gay men.

Lu is avowedly a *chong yang*.[309] I was even constrained to say: "Look there is but one moon. There is nothing wrong with the moon in China—it is only that clouds cover the beauty and roundness of the moon." This is actually the planned theme of my novel.[310]

August 13, 1988, Boston

My brother Peter is coming to the USA next week. Alas, his days in Boston coincide with my days in Jamaica. Shall I respect the older brother's shadow and cancel Montego Bay?

Lunch and a long talk with Somchat. He makes me feel peaceful, but I am not attracted enough for total sex. We were turned away from Atlantic Fish because I was wearing a tank top. We took the line of least resistance in terrible heat and went to Pizzeria Uno. Somchat will leave the US soon. He is going to explore Japan on the way back to Thailand. He is self-contented and enjoys traveling alone.

August 14, 1988, Boston

As I reflect on my feelings about China, I remember Joan Kennedy saying when explaining her unhappiness with Ted in Washington. "It wasn't that I didn't like politics, just that I didn't like the Kennedys." A good part of my aversion to "things Chinese" is really to communism and all its ways. I pick up an issue of *China Spring*, the dissident journal from New York, and the Chinese world seems as lively as my own.

Waiting for word from the *Times* over the Melbourne Cup piece. Also, from the Big Enchilada, Fred Hills, over my *China on My Mind* project. Must get both fixed up—in the latter case, a two-book contract if possible—before China draws near.

Chen Mingming calls. He is in Washington as aide to Ambassador Han Xu. He wants to be back in contact. In 1986, he went to Australia, a "marvelous country." On Chinese developments, he is fairly optimistic. "In the Boston area at present are concentrated some of the best minds of a new Chinese generation. They cannot fail to have a big impact on our nation's future." He says the biggest problem is "bureaucracy." Haven't we heard that before?

August 15, 1988, Boston

Who should phone at 6 AM but handsome Chris O from Melbourne. He is coming to New York—and wants some tips for his first visit to the Big Apple. Paul Theroux was very grateful for my letter to *The New York Times* over their mean review of *Riding the Iron Rooster*. "Your letter was the act of a true friend," he wrote to me.

I sent the Aborigines manuscript to Barbara. I need her to read it carefully and advise me whether to stay with a magazine piece or think in terms of a short book.

---

[309] *Chong yang* (重洋), i.e., someone who looks up to the foreign, in this case, the French.
[310] The novel, entitled *Only One Moon*, remains, to date, unpublished.

Nice sex with Reggie, who showered first and enticed me to rim him till he screamed. He sucked me—in fact, he was great, but I was a little lacking in inspiration. "You didn't come like you usually do," he said with those huge white eyes boring into me. Was I thinking of Paul?

August 17, 1988, Boston

I try to "clear the desk" but fail. The pile of letters and papers has been a little reduced. I even wrote to Henry—that took a nine-months wait. There are no articles I can think of waiting to be written. Why not, then, dear Ross, do some real work and start a book? Then no one would care, least of all me, if my desk were clear or unclear.

I meet a lovely guy called Danny on my way out of Legal Seafoods. He is carrying a radio that almost seems part of him. Back home, he is charming. Lovely lips, nice eyes, an impish manner.

He has "sore nuts," he says, through coming too much. I don't know about that, but there was nothing wrong with his asshole. I fucked him long and hard on the bed in the green room, our panting bodies inches from the mirror, our mouths half open as we writhed and watched.

August 18, 1988, Boston

I am trying to plan for the China trip. Would like to catch the opening of the academic season at Harvard before leaving. Who to look after my house and mail and phone? Laurent and I don't seem to have the same rapport as before. Somchat would be good in many ways. Kay could do it in her fashion.

August 20, 1988, Boston

Chris O, visiting New York, says on the phone in his thin, dry voice that he has "settled down." This means he hasn't moved house for a year and intends to stay in his present one—just built—for at least two years.

When I told him of my various writing plans, he said, "Do the novel." Thinking about that, I feel that, in my fictional world, things will look bleak—yet certain individuals will rise above the mire and shine.

I don't know why Chris asked when I am coming to Melbourne. When I do call him there, I do not feel an overwhelming welcome. But he has "fallen in love with America." Perhaps that will thaw his British-Malaysian reserve a bit.

It has always been an offense on my part in the eyes of Australian intellectuals that I took up residence in America. England would have been fine in their eyes, but not the citadel (supposed) of capitalism.

August 21, 1988, Boston

I called Laurent and we spoke as if there's been no gap in time. Has he just been busy? Has he not, after all, interpreted me as losing interest in him? The full sex act at last with Somchat. It was a going away present (Japan, Korea, Thailand) for him. A bit of an effort for me—but he's a nice person.

August 22, 1988, Boston

Well, the day has come, 50. More than double Pan's 24, when he cried all day that he was "over the hill." The best thing is that virtually no one knew of it. I told Li-li only. She insisted that each stage of life has its special joys. "Think of yourself as a bottle of Chateau Lafite," she said. "With each year you get better." I bought myself a birthday present at an antique shop on Columbus Avenue: a mahogany triangular table for the corner of the green bathroom.

Reading the last part of the Capote biography does nothing to lift the spirits of an aging gay. When gloom and doom replace an objective view of things, I should:

- do some tasks one by one, a step at a time
- open the current writing project and do a few sentences.

August 24, 1988, Boston

The Truman Capote biography by Gerald Clarke[311] shows that talent has little to do with morality or happiness. Also, why are some women incredibly patient with impossible gays?

The surprise in this "60-day experiment" is that I have reclaimed my evenings. But the mornings are not improved, I mean the early mornings. Still hard to rise, still slow to start. Yet late at night, I am more alert; I read, I phone, I don't merely fall into bed clutching a book or magazine that I scarcely read before going to sleep—as Bob Manning says he does.

Edward arrives and we go off as planned for our mutual birthday celebration. He is very interested in whose photo is where. A group on the bedroom dresser included Hank, Laurent, Reggie, and Pan. Where is Edward? To tell the truth—which I didn't— Edward had been there until a few hours before.

Tonight, he looked wonderful with a new haircut and immaculate in a blue suit. We dined sumptuously at Aujourd'hui, each saying nothing to displease the other. He drove back to Hartford late the same night. I felt happy, righteous, and anguished. I packed for Jamaica and went to bed.

August 29, 1988, Montego Bay

Jamaica is a lovely island. Too much togetherness on this press tour, but an experience. A lady from the *Toronto Sun* fell in love with me. When I didn't whisk her off to bed, she asked me: "Tell me, what sort of women do you like best?" I replied, "Actually, I prefer men." Our relationship got even better. She then threw herself into the arms of a man she didn't like, had the first orgasm of her life, and attributed it to a fantasy about me. Next day, she told me she had fallen in love with my mind.

---

[311] *Capote* (1988).

I fucked two Jamaicans. Both handsome, with big uncut cocks, chirping accents like Britons. Both showed a Boy Scout coyness which had to be brushed aside in favor of real action.

"Put it in now," said Peter, who until that moment had given no indication that he wanted to get fucked. "Ooh, I like that," he gasped as he held his balls with his fingers.

With Canute, alarming Briticisms came out at wrong moments. I was pumping him when he enquired, like a restaurant lady asking if I would take my tea black or with milk, "How long do you take to discharge?" "Oh, a real man," he cried as we writhed. "What a man!"

August 30, 1988, Boston

Sheer joy at returning to a house I now love. Dr. Terespolsky has the good news that "no cell was found" in my spinal fluid. That means no infection—HIV or anything else—in the central nervous system.

Reggie comes by and we watch a movie I got today—*Backstrokes*—and have fantastic sex afterwards. When we are done, Laurent arrives, and it is nice for the three of us to rap. Laurent is terribly depressed. School is not going well. When Reggie goes home, Laurent and I dine at Thai Cuisine. He is going to phone his father to "be comforted." I advised him to drop the second job and sell the car he needs mainly to drive to that job. Otherwise, I don't see how I can help him much. Nor, I suppose, can he help me with my problems.

Barbara talked with Fred, and Simon & Schuster have made up their minds. They feel I have achieved the "meeting of minds" needed on the concept of the book. They want it. But they don't want the collection of essays, *The Failure of Marxism in China*. The deal is $100,000 for *China on my Mind*. The requirements are that foreign rights be included, and that I promise not to publish *The Failure of Marxism in China* anywhere else before *China on my Mind*. Barbara says a good point is that she got half on signing rather than one-third as we got with *The Australians*.

September 1, 1988, Boston

I walked out into a warm late-summer sun, and the first sight was a swarthy, black-haired guy on the steps of Symphony Hall. We looked at each other. I stopped walking, touched my hand to my dick. He touched his. I went over to him. "Sit down," he ordered. It was the first of several commands.

He arrived from San Diego this morning. A dancer, he is here to study. These are his first few hours ever in Boston. He was waiting for his brother, who lives here, to pick him up. "Do you have underwear on?" he asked. I did not. "Do you have a big cock?" I said it was medium, big head.

"I want to suck it."

Then began various commands. To stand in front of him facing Huntington Ave. As I did that, he felt up my bare leg and into my shorts from behind. Then he asked me to stand facing him. "I can suck it here." This I was not willing to do. He may have been from San Diego, but I live two minutes away, and I was once arrested at this very corner—not for sex, but for doing a good turn over a lottery ticket.

I said I would give him my phone number and we could meet sometime soon. I explained that I had people in my place at that moment. He insisted he needed it straight away. "Isn't there a restroom somewhere?" I was terribly attracted to this wild Californian. I compromised. I suggested we go to the Northeastern library for a few minutes.

Amidst the bookshelves on a third floor that was pretty quiet, the commands began again. "Choke me!" He wanted me to stand behind him, digging my prick into his bum and locking my arms tightly around his neck. This I did—a first. "Tighter," he gasped in a strangled voice. Meanwhile, he grabbed my cock and pulled it out of my pants. He wanted me to use my hands, rather than my arms, in order to choke him tighter. Anyway, this turned him on. He said, "Push my head onto your cock!" Obediently I did. All this went on amidst the shelves of the Dodge Library. As it happened, no one came by.

I gave him my phone number. Also, at his request for information on nearby gay bars, I gave him the name and address of Chaps and 1270. Panting, I fled to the gym for my squash match.

Hank doesn't seem himself. Tired, leaves things around, has little to say. I took him to a party in Cambridge; Hank perked up a bit. At home, I massaged him and we made love. I had to do most of the work—he was on the verge of sleep—but in the end, I enjoyed myself greatly. I shot off in his hand and sprayed his handsome neck.

While at the party, I phoned Li-li. Her house was just around the corner. I was going to pop in, introduce her to Hank, and pick up the garden chair she is giving me. Alas, she is down with two pieces of bad news. Her favorite sister is dying of cancer. And— worse for me—Richard Hsiao[312] is in his last weeks with AIDS in Sloan-Kettering in New York.

We all die—but so soon! It's like a wonderful party from which favorite guests depart one-quarter way through the evening.

September 2, 1988, Boston

Hank again raises the question of my "settling down with someone." Perhaps he guesses I am not thinking of that, or that he would not be my choice of "running mate." At any rate, a few minutes later, he says he thinks I am too set in my ways to live with another. That point is correct. Also, if from now on, at fifty, I am going to want sex two times a week, rather than five, why live with someone?

I got a rough draft of my Jamaica piece done for the *Boston Herald*. Then I began to look into the documents on Lin Xiling, the Chinese dissident. She is not worth a book. But her story could come into my *China on my Mind*.

---

[312] Richard Hsiao, art history professor at Mt. Holyoke College.

Danny arrives unexpectedly after playing basketball in Washington Park. We make delicious love. I could not fuck him, though, as he was sore. "I haven't done it for a while," he said. For how long? "Since the last time with you."

September 3, 1988, Boston

It seems strange that after stopping all alcohol, I should find it not easier but harder to get up and get going in the mornings. I am so tired today. Five sessions of sex to orgasm in the last seven days—Peter and Canute in Jamaica, Reggie and Hank, and Danny here. There was a time when I would take five in seven days as a minimum. Now it seems to be a maximum.

Michael Mao has the sad news that Richard Hsiao is dead. There will be a private funeral this weekend. Some memorial is planned at Mount Holyoke College later.

September 4, 1988, Boston

Some work on *China on my Mind*. The writing of this book will be taxing, but the research is comparatively light. A couple of hours on the phone with Edward last night. He is pleased that everyone likes the clothes he gave me for my birthday.

He is concerned about my contact with Barry! "We have to be careful," Edward said. "I am just warning you that certain people can make trouble." He recalls that Barry may have seen "the two us walking down the street on the way to dinner." Edward despises Barry.

Tomorrow, he goes to Yonkers to see his sister and his beloved nephew. On romance, there is a big difference between us. To me, sex is a part of friendship; not always, but a natural extension of friendship in those cases where attraction arises. To him, sex is akin to magic. It's another world into which you make periodic plunges (at least, for him, this is the case on sex with men).

Despite his present wonderful mood, I can't help feeling Edward tries to live as if he is not in the universe with everyone else. But the clock does not stop ticking for him. He cannot be a mere spectator of others' lives forever. The rules he throws out for others apply to him, too.

Mark Sun phones from Paris. Wants to talk. Yet I hang up, not knowing what he wanted to talk about. In a Chinese bookshop, he recently found a book, *Meiguo ren kan Zhongguo*,[313] which contains a chapter by me. He bought it and read it. It is a collection of analyses by American writers of current life in China. My essay is lifted—without permission—from *Foreign Affairs*.

September 6, 1988, Boston

This seems to clinch matters. Reggie says that after stopping the Folonari white wine, I look healthier. At least his remark clinches my resolve to stay off it for the full 60 days, and then to be very sparing with it, at most, after that.

---

[313] 美国人看中国, Americans See China.

September 8, 1988, Boston

I sent photos to my two friends in Jamaica—Peter and Canute—saying they made Jamaica lovely for me. My sore throat has not gone away. Mysterious—I don't normally get these! It tears through my mind that if it did happen to be gonorrhea, a terrible crisis would ensue with Reggie. If he then got it, and also Caroline, I suppose it would be the end for him and me, even for him and Caroline. Laurent is busy with exams, but we keep in touch on the phone.

September 9, 1988, Cambridge

"What's the point in being straight-out anti-communist?" Miss Lin kept asking me. Indeed, it is worth thinking about. What can be the *end hope* for policies that the China Spring leftist people push?

I'm glad I went to the Chinese "political scientists delegation" lunch. It annoyed me, though, when Benjamin Schwartz introduced me as a newspaperman. He was speaking in his limited Chinese, so maybe he was groping for the right word when he said *xinwen*.[314] But it's the sort of moment that makes me want to never set a foot inside Harvard again. Except the libraries.

I asked the Peking scholar Li, "By whose authority was the Politburo 'enlarged' on the occasion of the decision to sack Hu Yaobang; who selected the participants?"

"Deng Xiaoping!" he replied without hesitation. "I'm of the old school," he said when asked if separation of party and government will mean Li Peng will grow more powerful and Zhao Ziyang less. "As long as Zhao is party secretary, he is number two man—to Deng—and so he is more powerful than the premier." Amazing that American political scientists—in this case, even the most perspicacious, Lucian Pye, (who asked the question)—can be so naive as to trust structures in a Leninist system.

September 10, 1988, Boston

Edward and Arlene visit. Ghosts of the past dance. Yet it is a pleasant visit. Arlene looks huge; Edward wonderful in a tank top. On a lovely day, we all sit on the front deck. Edward tried to assert his ancient control over both of us—Arlene especially. He treated me nicely and by no means "protected" Arlene against any shafts of light from another world. Only on politics was there any disagreement.

As they looked here and there and saw photos, including some of Jamaica, I tried to bring in Sandy Naiman as "my girlfriend in Toronto that I went to Jamaica with." But Edward looked curiously at when I said that, as if to say, "You are mine, not Sandy's."

At other points, I essayed discretion (in front of Arlene), only to find him going in the opposite direction. When he put the shirt and braces on me, he grabbed my arms, felt my arms, in full gaze of the seated, matronly Miss Vaughan. At another point, he asked me to put on the handsome new trousers he had bought for me. I went to do so

---

[314] *Xinwén* (新闻), news.

there and then. Edward said nothing, but Arlene threw up her hands: "Now don't you two start anything!"

When they left, I tickled Edward's asshole from behind on the landing outside my apartment door. He did not resist, much less rebuke me. In fact, he was smiling his lovely impish smile. He and I are meant to be in each other's life. At present, the damn fool is fighting against that in a very weird manner. I had my head so full of Edward that after they left, I forgot all about Cary Wolinksy's photographic opening at the Pucker Safrai Gallery.

In the evening, before dinner, Shen Chunyi and I phone his brother in Shanghai. How much easier to phone there than to hinterland Chengdu! The brother seems nice, but, as I expected, his English is very limited. I told him I would hookup with him next spring when I expect to be in China again for *National Geographic* on the topic of Chinese youth.

Chunyi and I dine at Thornton's and talk of China and America. "I had been trying for so long to get to USA—four years—that the actual departure from Shanghai airport left me feeling nothing. In Boston the sky seemed so beautifully blue! In China I had never seen a sky like that! I prefer American people to Chinese people. They are open, they say what they feel." When he extended this admiration to American women, I asked why he wants to bring his wife and baby daughter here.

"It is my duty."

"But wouldn't your wife find out that you now prefer American women to Chinese?"

"I would tell her! I mean, this is freedom. This is not China. You can speak your mind here."

So much, it would seem, for his marriage. But later, he gave another reason for wanting to bring them here: "I just don't want my daughter to be shaped by the narrow Chinese cultural world."

His viewpoint makes me think of May Fourth era Westernizers like Chen Duxiu. A few years ago, *chong yang* was a pejorative term. But now most of these Mainland Chinese students "worship the foreign."

September 11, 1988, Boston

The Chinese trip dates are pinned down at last. Deng phones from Chengdu tonight to say I should arrive on October 20. She says that, because of the weather, I cannot go to the west of the province. Still, it will get me back onto the China track; that is a big aim of the journey. Then a delicious time with Danny, and a quiet dinner alone at Saint Botolph.

September 12, 1988, Boston

Hank unexpectedly comes to town. He will stay with me. On arrival, he had that look in his eye, and I knew there would be some moments of diversion before evening. It happened about 5 PM when I got back from the library.

A lovely evening with Reggie. He and Hank meet and like each other. Then Hank goes to see his friend in Somerville. Reggie and I talk for a long time. I even told him the story of Miles—he thinks Miles might be on cocaine, desperate for money for that reason. We meandered in and out of conversation, then odd jobs, and dinner at Saint Botolph. At first, Reggie was busy glancing this way and that. I knew what was on his mind—will someone see me. But I said nothing. In the end, he enjoyed the dinner hugely. As did I. The beef satay with peanut sauce remains excellent.

Afterwards, he came on to me in a winning way. He curled himself on the bed, began to suck my cock, then my balls, then my asshole. Then he begged to fuck me, and indeed he did fuck me—coming out just before he came. I loved the position: he held me in his arms like a baby. As soon as he had come, he phoned his wife Caroline.

September 13, 1988, Boston

The election now finds me partisan. I see little to commend Dukakis; I hope for a Bush victory and will cast my vote for him in Chengdu.

Hank remarks that Reggie loves me. Absurd. How could Hank know such a thing! Yet on reflection, if Reggie did love me, I would probably be blind to it. I have him in a certain category, and I keep him there. Does Hank have insight on this tie—some six years old—seen from outside?

While I am at the gym, Edward phones. Hank answered and spoke. I wonder if Edward realized who it was? Later, I went out to dinner with Laszlo at Club Café. While I was gone, Edward came round. Hank buzzed him in, and he stayed for five to ten minutes. At first, Edward called Hank "Luther." He said Hank had changed. Hank told me Edward had changed—"improved." When I went to my desk, I found a note: "I was here, you weren't—Edward."

Sex with Hank before we go to sleep. I sleep well in a bed with him. Should I be doing these things, night after night; will my energy hold out?

September 14, 1988, Boston

Rereading reviews of my *Mao* nearly eight years ago is both instructive and—in a way—good for the ego. I can see much more clearly now what I achieved, and didn't achieve, than I could see at the time. But the number of U.S. reviews, more than seventy, may turn out my highest ever.

Far from expected, sex with Laurent tonight. The presence of Sandy tended to reduce the time I spent with Hank—and my desire for this. Tonight, I thought Connor would have left, but she had not. So I told Hank our plan of dining at Hammersley's could wait till next week.

I phoned Laurent. He had just come back from work and was ravenous. We dined at Club Café. An excellent meal, and who should be sitting next to us but luscious Dion. With him, once more, was the cheery Gary, plus two other guys.

When we got home, we watched an outstanding documentary on Thurgood Marshall. One thing led to another—though I felt a bit uneasy at the thought that Hank and Sandy might walk in at any moment. Laurent shot as if he hadn't shot for weeks. Whether that is true or not, I do not know; he and I never discuss sex—probably a good thing; we just do it. No post-mortem that we did it again after many weeks. It was as if there had been no interregnum. Just lovely.

September 15, 1988, Boston

Joan, as we breakfast at Thornton's, is quite keen about *China on my Mind*. She urges me to be candid. And to plunge in with a long article that sums up the book—and publish it. She thinks I should also start a book on myself and what makes me tick. When I object that I have lost my idealism and American readers don't like such a lack of zing, she says such an evolution can still be interesting. She doesn't think I should leave out the Australian background. And she reckons that what was happening in China while I was growing up in Australia should be part of my story.

At the Nieman kick-off reception, Liu Binyan[315] is almost stately, with an owl-like face, holding his cigarette like a Hong Kong businessman. He tells me nearly everyone in China is pessimistic, but he himself is optimistic. There are two advantages in China as compared with Russia, he says: the Cultural Revolution scared everyone off the leftist path; the reforms have been going a decade and much experience has been gained.

I pointed out that, on the other hand, economic levels in China are far below those in Russia; to the degree that economic attainment precedes political change in an authoritarian system, China must be behind Russia. I mentioned my concern about a lack of believed public philosophy, and he said he had been thinking deeply about just that. Altogether, it's no wonder he's looked up to by millions.

A Chilean journalist is awarded the annual prize. In her graceful speech, she says: "In a dictatorship, you either go along with it or you fight against the oppression." As she says these words, I look across the lawn into the sculptured face of Liu Binyan. "In my writing," the Chilean said, "I tried to ensure that no one could any more say, 'I didn't know.'" Surely in the Cultural Revolution, people did know—there was hardly any need to "report" it—yet almost no one resisted. But Liu Binyan did.

September 16, 1988, Boston

Lunch at Locke-Ober's with John Roderick, who is en route from Europe to Los Angeles and on to Tokyo. He stays with gay friends all over Europe, going to concerts and museums. He had asked me to show him photos of "people." I complied. In the formal atmosphere of Locke-Ober's, I passed him shot after shot of half-dressed and even naked men. He nearly died with delight. Walking out to get a cab to take him to the airport, I happened to mention how important the eyes are in sexual excitement. As he climbed into the vehicle, he said, "By the way, your eyes are lovely."

Hank got an SOS from his boss in Provincetown, asking him to work tomorrow night. He will go and come back Sunday afternoon. I surprise myself that I'm pleased to be a night alone.

---

[315] Liu Binyan (1925-2005), Chinese writer and dissident. In 1990, his memoir, *A Higher Kind of Loyalty*, was published.

September 17, 1988, Cambridge

The Harvard conference on India and China was quite good. I felt back into the swing of the field. I met a Shanghai scholar, Wang, on a Luce fellowship to study the life of an American missionary in China. We got talking of publishing, and I told him of my *800,000,000*: how it came out, *nei bu*,[316] censored, with an unflattering preface, and only years later did I see a copy.

"Oh, that was in the Cultural Revolution," said Wang, looking embarrassed. "That was a special period." Was it?

September 18, 1988, Boston

I wake up filled with fantasies of Kemal. Soaping his back in the shower that afternoon. A finger at his asshole. The mad cantor in the fourth-floor men's room of Mugar. Then I fantasized about what we haven't done yet: he brings his two friends with him to the house. In every conceivable combination, we twist and writhe until all are sated and at peace. The boys go off to eat at Burger King.

Reading the German reviews of my *Mao*, I see they are better than the American and English reviews. A study of the man with psychological overtones. Little extended inquiry into the social causes of things. One sharp criticism in a Zurich review sticks in my mind: "I miss the fight with the facts that forces one to take a firm standpoint. What is lacking is engagement and depth of perspective."

On a calm Indian summer evening, I give a little party. A moment to pause and be thankful for blessings. Health good. A real delight in my renovated house. Nearly all the spin-off articles following the Australia book have been written and published—and earned a respectable sum. Looking forward to the China trip as a point of re-entry to the China topic. An agreement in principle with Simon & Schuster on a contract for the next book, giving me income for the next two to three years. A certain (sad) stability to the ongoing tie with Edward. Plan in place to spend Christmas in Australia and see to family and other matters there.

September 19, 1988, Boston

As I shower, I find "Apricot Face Scrub" on the shelf before me. It is a sign, one of many, that various people are still in the house from last night. It was a fine party. By very late, there was Laurent, Ramone, and Nori all in a position where the possibility of doing something with me was in the air—plus Hank, who was at a club with Craig but due back around 2 AM. In the end, Laurent and I went to bed. We made love—he came twice despite being drunk—and then he started to snore so loudly I had to retreat to my study. There I read Ackerley's exquisite memoir *My Father and Myself*.

The waiting and maneuvering that precede sex in a party situation turns some people on. For me, it is just tiring, especially late at night, and a strain, if diplomacy has to be practiced before lust can sprout.

---

[316] Nèibù (內部), inside, internal.

Loring and I discussed the "bisexuality in the South" issue that we touched on glancingly previously. Still, he doesn't understand how freedom comes from ambiguity. Don B told everyone about plans for the next dinner of the Human Rights Campaign. Ray brought his friend Enrique, the Cuban-born filmmaker, a pleasant small mouse of a man with large spectacles.

Advanced a Melbourne Cup piece for *The New York Times.* Widener Library at Harvard has much more on Australia than it used to—thanks to the Australian Fund, which I was instrumental in getting here.

September 20, 1988, Boston

Dr. Terespolsky has found that all the tests on the spinal fluid are negative. "My work can end here," he says. He says it would be a good thing if I kept off alcohol indefinitely. "One bottle of wine a day is certainly too much. I think one a week is too much."

"Don't do any more damage," he sums up when I ask why, after the 60-day test, the numbness has not gone away if wine was the culprit. That is to say, he argues that stopping may not restore the peripheral nervous system to normal, but going on drinking might resume the damage. Of course, he doesn't really know. In the first place, it was I, not he, that brought up the wine issue. It turns out that he himself drinks "fine" wine and malt whiskey.

Edward calls. "Do you miss me?" I said I did at times. Later I asked if he missed me. "Yes, I do." His mother called him in for dinner. After dinner, he is going back to work. Sunday, he spent ferrying his grandmother around and then picking up his parents, who were back from Maine. A new life indeed for Edward, sex left behind.

September 22, 1988, Boston

A VD check-up at City Hospital. Probably nothing doing, but my sore throat has persisted for a week.

I finally did the phone interview with Les Carlyon in Melbourne on horse racing; so the material for the revision of *The New York Times* piece on The Cup is now all in.

Liu Binyan's lecture at the New England China seminar lived up to expectations. He is part David Halberstam, part Studs Terkel, part Roy Medvedev—yet very Chinese.

I really felt like seeing Reggie but we kept missing each other. It was his day off. Eventually, tonight, on my return from Harvard, Caroline called to ask if Reggie was still here. I said righteously that he was never here today. Wyatt comes by with John S. After drinks upstairs, we watch a video downstairs. Wyatt gets frisky and, while John is in the bathroom, begins to suck my cock. I think John saw him move away from me as he returned to the room.

Later, when Wyatt went to the bathroom—both were drinking steadily—John and I locked eyes in a new way. "Wyatt and I are friends, you know, not like that," he said with a smile. "I couldn't do anything with him here." Oh. Eventually, I said Wyatt could suck my dick and I'd suck John's at the same time. They both laughed. Wyatt went upstairs for something; John came onto the bed and began to fiercely suck my tits—by now, after Wyatt's ministrations, I had almost nothing on. Then he played with my ass and plunged a finger in. "I want to fuck you so much!"

Wyatt breezed in again with a drink for himself and one for John. When John and I could talk, he said, "I'll dump Wyatt and come back later." I said maybe Hank would be here then, and it might not be possible.

"Cornell said you were hot, but I didn't think you'd be that hot." This pleased me, coming from such a stud. At the times he was in the bed with me, he did not take his pants off, even his hat, as Wyatt was never far away.

As it happened, he did phone me much later. It was 3 AM. I explained that this wasn't a good time. Call again at the weekend, I said. If he does, I will also have to explain that I didn't mean to encourage him to just come right in and fuck me. Why, I might prefer to fuck him!

September 23, 1988, Boston

Hank is still here, but we are both so busy we hardly see each other. The China plans take shape. All the air bookings are done. I agree with Miss Deng on this occasion that no changes should be made; I have learned my lesson that altering flights within China is a losing game. I now await only my passport back from the Chinese Consulate and the AA award for my ticket from Boston to Los Angeles and back.

Maybe Hank's remark about Reggie "loving me" has a kernel of truth. While I was not watching, something happened to our tie. We are in very frequent contact. There are many secrets between us now which require big trust. I think he does depend on my friendship. And I realize that I would be upset if he should go with another guy. Yes, I would be jealous—that was unthinkable two to three years ago.

September 25, 1988, Boston

A nice portrait of Horowitz at 85 in *The New York Times*. Of course, he has retired again, as he has done many times before. "You cannot live a second time," he remarked. "It's much better to live nicely the first time." He says he drinks only water these days.

Few Americans appreciate the freedom they enjoy. In particular, the privacy they enjoy. Looking back, a big reason why I came to the US is freedom and privacy. My experience of China has reinforced my regard for both. The reasons behind the contrasting American and Chinese situations are instructive: two different social-political systems. A media that is part of the state is no good. I am beginning to see, however, that private media ought not be so powerful as to dwarf the state.

September 26, 1988, Boston

Four talks on the phone with Edward tonight in between watching Louganis dive and Johnson be stripped of his gold medal. His life seems to be largely work, family, and church. He hasn't seen Arlene since that Saturday he brought her here—to impress both Reggie and me, in different ways.

"I've got 40 inches here," I said in reference to the new TV in the bedroom. "Don't you wish you did," he rejoined with a giggle. His mother knew I was on the phone. "Isn't it time Ross went to bed?" she inquired with delightful irrelevance.

September 27, 1988, Boston

Golden days. Boston in the early Fall can be perfect. The weather induces me to look back on the entire summer. Months like this are precious, and, like the golden days, will not go on forever.

Reggie comes by. Though he is in a "safe sex" mood, we have a great time.

September 30, 1988, Boston

A lovely Friday afternoon winding down at the hands of Danny. He sucked my tits to get me going. He came down my body and began to suck me slowly, concentrating on the head of my dick, using his tongue on its underside as his lovely lips encompassed the top side. Then I fucked him slowly, watching him in the mirror as he himself looked into his own face.

He says he is going to be spending more time with Frank, this 40-year-old with the 12-inch cock that he occasionally mentions. "But Frank doesn't fuck me."

Dining at Copley's, I looked ahead to my plans for Australia. Maybe the solution to the problem of how to take my computer, or hire one in Australia, taking all the research notes for *China on my Mind*, is to work only on the novel for that period?

October 1, 1988, Boston

I love Saturdays, especially when the weather is lovely as this morning. I always have loved Saturdays in America. Calm, with a touch of the festival, yet everything is open—such a contrast with Australia. One could spend a whole day—a week—in magazine reading. There are so many in America. Yesterday Ric the barber showed me some issues of *Illustrated London News*, which I hadn't seen for years. There's another world in these British magazines.

October 2, 1988, Boston

A good day's work on a lovely day. Drafting the outline for the grant application. Yet one more round on the Melbourne Cup for the ravenous *New York Times*. The editors there remind me of a child that bothers you with a question every five minutes for days on end.

Dinner alone at Commonwealth Grille, dressed up, taking the splendid Orange Line there and back. I can do nearly everything—except one crucial thing—very happily alone. Actually, the best reason for living alone is that sex with others is better, and probably more than when not living alone.

October 4, 1988, Boston

The *Geographic* has not yet decided to go ahead with my China Youth story. Worse, Garrett hasn't yet read my proposal. "I'd rather have a Yes in February than a No next week," says Mac. He points out there have recently been two China pieces: Theroux on the railways, and one on China photographed from a balloon.

A damned disappointment all round. I really will have to apply for that grant to make sure I don't go broke next year. But the bottom line is that I'd rather wait for the *National Geographic*, than go now to *World Monitor* with the Chinese Youth idea. I wish Barbara could run into Garrett at a dinner party. It is hard to imagine Mac playing a big role in the magazine when he has just been away, again, on a six-week leave writing his fiction.

A good lunch with Yang at Thai Cuisine. He urges me not to compete with what my critics hold up as a measuring stick against me. They say RT doesn't have the detailed knowledge of the situation in China. Forget the details, he says. Write something that will satisfy yourself and that, in 50 years, will still be read and admired. All this is out of the blue from dear BZY.

Only two things count in China today, he says: agriculture and foreign money. These are the only two success realms. I suppose all that Vogel is reporting about south China really falls into the second category—Hong Kong's proximity explains all. The pathos of it! In the case of Russia, he says, it is always possible to step back from the reforms—not in the case of China.

October 6, 1988, Boston

Wasted today after staying up late to telephone Melbourne for "betting details" on behalf of *The New York Times*. I was short with everyone. That included Edward when he interrupted our phone conversation to speak with Glen. And when I dined at Oceanic about 12:40, I quarreled with the waiter when the dishes I wanted were "not available."

Hank comes by and looks awful. He has pneumonia. His fever has been going for days. He is on antibiotics which are supposed to work within a few days.

October 8, 1988, Boston

In the evening, Chris comes by. Long and lovely. He came a second time as he watched a movie of a Black guy fucking a white chick in her kitchen. Well, in China there will be a season of abstinence, so I might as well give myself a decent send-off. So much to do before I leave for Chengdu, and three days to do it in!

October 10, 1988, Columbus Day, Boston

The opening PEN meeting of the season. A modest crowd. Some are on the verge of being ratbags. And yet, today's ratbag might be tomorrow's successful novelist. When it was time for a photo to honor those authors who have had a new book out during

1988, Dan Wakefield and I crouched conveniently near the camera in the front row, holding copies of our books—in my case, the Touchstone edition of *The Australians.*

A lovely autumnal peace. Letters of preparation for Peking. Ramone calls. I would love to see him before I go. But dinner with Laurent tonight and a visit from Danny tomorrow, and probably Hank, how can I give him what he wants?

Li-li hopes I won't be "too disappointed on this trip to China." Now just what does she mean by that? She urges me to see relics unearthed at Guanghan in Sichuan. She brought me an Italian garden chair as a birthday gift.

To China tomorrow—via Alabama and Hawaii—and how much I will miss things here for six weeks. Forays to Roxbury. Sex with various friends. Seminars at Harvard. Calls from Barbara, Fred, and Mac that plug me into writing and publishing. Squash with Mike, Serge, and David. Talking on the phone with Edward. My lovely redone house. Above all, the endless stimulus and treasure that is America.

November 3, 1988, Chongqing

Sexual expression is delightful; yet withholding it can also be pleasant—that sense of pent-up power, readiness, the excitement of the spirit leading the body.

November 5, 1988, Boston

A nice time with Chris. He has found a new girlfriend. I was happy about that; the happier some guys are with a girl, the more they want a cock up their ass.

"Ross, how do you get that big?" he asked as he grabbed my cock. I was embarrassed and dealt with this by saying I was cut and he wasn't, and that makes a difference to the size of the head.

"In the Bible," he said, "it states that you get circumcised at the time you become saved."

Often, I have to excuse myself with Chris as I have something else to do. Tonight, it was me who wanted to go on and he who had to break. Because his girlfriend is out of Boston, he has to feed her cat.

I finished transcribing many of the dictated notes—sign of the times that I did it myself—and printed it out. For these China articles, I am making elaborate preparations; but when will I get to the writing stage?

November 8, 1988, Chengdu

Young Wang has rushed into my world these final days in the Southwest. I met him in the bar at Renmin Hotel in Chongqing. A waitress frowned upon my buying him a drink. "Why are you buying him a drink?" Incredible rudeness—from hotel staff no less—but I ignored it to concentrate on Wang.

He is extremely handsome, hyper-active, chain-smoking. He came to my room and, despite the risks, we made quick, fiery love. I would love to have lingered—and got totally naked—but it didn't seem wise. He is a real sex bomb. The next day, we did the same thing, while Zhang Bingzhang hovered in the neighborhood of my room, checking to see that my luggage was ready for our night train.

November 13, 1988, Hong Kong

A smoother transfer to city and hotel than at Tokyo recently. Kai Tak Airport is so handy to everything. The harbor still has magic, despite coolish weather, high prices, and the dark shadow of 1997.[317] A lot of fractiousness in Hong Kong as they talk of how the chief executive will be chosen after the takeover. I suppose after years of pent-up political passion, they could go for a blend of enthusiasm and disunity, thus giving Peking a perfect excuse to be strong in the name of avoiding *da luan* (disorder).

Now that I have spoken with the Governor, my friend David Wilson, I see that what I suspected in Peking the other day is true: the CCP is starting to treat Hong Kong as just one more Chinese city, and its government as a mayoralty. Amazingly enough, many people accept that! Actually, Hong Kong is the equivalent of a nation, and should be treated as such.

To get into the spirit of Hong Kong, I went to the President Sauna. Hot pool, sexual goings-on under the water. A finger in an asshole here, my cock in a golden hand there. I have the impression that these Hong Kong bodies are getting more robust. Also in the sauna, the self-image of effeminacy weakens—Chinese gays can be real men nowadays.

November 18, 1988, Boston

Lovely to be back in my beautiful place, with fresh China material securely under my belt. I go to Harvard to see Joan and get mail. She had sad news that the Korea scholar Gregory Henderson died after a fall from a fruit tree. Edward phones to welcome me back and to say he's coming to Boston tomorrow for his report at the Fenway Clinic. A friend is coming with him; would I like to meet this Steven? I said I would, and perhaps we could meet alone for a while as well?

November 19, 1988, Boston

Canceled the Signet Society dinner tonight. Just too much to do, unpacking and getting to work on my notes and cassettes.

Edward came in mid-morning and we talked upstairs. His work is not going well. He wonders how much longer he'll be there. He is under therapy; the medical guy constantly interrupts Edward, who rebukes him for this.

Due to his late arrival in Boston, he had to re-schedule his Fenway time. This meant friend Steven would come to my place just at the time Edward would be at his appointment. I said that would be no problem; Steven could wait here, and then the three of us could have lunch when Edward got back.

Steven came on time. He is a short, compact, good-looking Black guy. His manner is cheerful and talkative, and he was wearing gaudy satin pants and an army jacket with

---

[317] 1997: the year Hong Kong, a British crown colony, was to be handed over to China.

badges and ribbons. We sat on a sofa upstairs and talked. A hand on a leg and something had begun. Do you think we'd be better off downstairs, I said.

"Yeah, a bedroom's always better."

I sucked him like I was going out of business. Partway through, I asked him what he thought we should do if Edward came back when we were still in bed. "Get dressed quick." I had considered staying there and asking Edward to join in, but Steven felt it was too risky. He lay on top of me with my cock throbbing and pushing between his legs. Two sexy bodies going crazy. I gurgled: Ooh, I'd like to fuck you! "Go for it!" As I started, he said, "Gee, I haven't done this for a while." (Later, he told me Edward fucked him once.) I came inside him as he knelt, looked into the mirror, and shot a big load onto the green sheets. We had each showered, me in the red bathroom, he downstairs when Edward arrived back—delayed by running into lovely Hazel at the 200 front door.

Lunch at Thornton's was pleasant. Edward was in a flirtatious mood—with the world in general—saying things that he would have killed me for saying in a restaurant. "Now, I think there's two homosexuals here," Steven said at one point.

"Gee, I'd better go home," I quipped. This cracked Edward up. So far as Steven and I knew, he didn't guess Steven and I had gone to bed.

November 20, 1988, Boston

Fairly sober Sunday lunch with David C at the Club Café. He's been leading a quiet life. Afterwards, we came back and he found a couple of new letters from my mad admirer in Hawaii. They were written in three colors. He just couldn't believe the stuff. Nor could he readily believe that I no longer even open her letters—yet still keep them. I went into the bedroom and found he had taken off his clothes. After we finished, he said he hadn't had sex with anyone since July!

Much later, I was asleep when the doorbell rang. In came Reggie. I looked at my little red watch; it was 1:30 AM. He'd been to a club with some mates. He wanted beer; he wanted food.

"I missed you." How I loved those words from Reggie's magnificent lips.

The other day he had trouble with his German-born athletic director. "Every single thing that crops up this guy sees in terms of black and white."

"I'll have to get out of here soon." It was the sign that he wanted sex. Getting home could wait.

November 22, 1988, Boston

I had been wondering about Edward—and Steven, who drove back to Connecticut with Edward on Saturday night—when he phoned. He said Steven liked me. "He wouldn't want to go to bed with you or anything, but he thought you were a nice person." That removed the issue. The topic of conversation was his health. On Saturday during lunch, unbeknown to Steven and me, he had heavy news on his mind: his helper cell count has gone down to 413.

November 24, 1988, Boston

I try to lie low with my mountain of work. But when Ramone asked keenly, I went to a little party. As it happened, I made a mistake by going late. As I arrived, five attractive Black guys were leaving. Remaining were a dull white couple, a fat woman, and a plastered Ramone.

A Thanksgiving call from Edward. He is now just waiting to be fired from his job. I told him why I had resumed moderate wine drinking. One reason, I said, was that there isn't a strong positive inspiration to keep on abstaining.

November 26, 1988, Boston

Another talk with Edward. His therapist says he has a fear of success. I told him that years ago. He also now says that he's a sex addict. Last night, he went cruising very late—after a quarrel with Steven—and met a fat Black guy called Iran. Iran had that all-important (to E) "abundant dick."

I am reading an interesting book, *Seeds of Fire*,[318] about Chinese dissidents, to review for the *Washington Post*. I will certainly praise it.

November 27, 1988, Boston

The lovely quiet of a Sunday morning and some work done upstairs on the dining room table. The China notes are starting to form patterns.

December 2, 1988, Boston

Busy cooking a roast lamb dinner for Edward's arrival. He arrives very late from Hartford. We dine about midnight on the lamb and a banana split. No wine.

The bed in the little room is covered with my papers; whether for this reason or others, Edward joins me in the cranberry bedroom. I show him the black-white video segment from prison, which I had mentioned to him. This excited me, and I played with myself a bit, but he didn't seem to look at me. Eventually, I turned over and put out the light on my side. He patted my shoulder: "Are you going to sleep already?"

I could hardly believe we were having sex again. It had been more than a year. Those tits, those balls, that long thin hand gripping my dick. Had he planned this? Next morning, I massaged him and started banging my cock up against his balls. The damn phone rang, and we didn't continue.

December 3, 1988, Boston

Last night the Writers' Union party in red-hot-left Cambridge. Nice woman called Debra, who writes on dance for *The Boston Globe*, came up to me. She's a "tremendous admirer" of my writing, she says. Maybe of me, rather than my writing.

---

[318] *Seeds of Fire: Chinese Voices of Conscience* (Hill and Wang, 1988).

Edward was still there when I got back. He decided against going dancing to the Haymarket—with his female cousin—after all and just rested. He went to sleep while still wearing his shorts and tank top.

December 4, 1988, Boston

I worked for a while. Edward seemed subdued, but he popped his head in the door after a while and looked brighter. He'd arranged to see cousin Lenore for lunch. Meanwhile, we went to Trinity church—where we'd last been together on his birthday years ago—a dignified service. But Edward was moody. I realized he wouldn't be likely to come with me tonight to Ken Ishiwata's housewarming party.

December 5, 1988, Boston

I rose early to talk with McCarry, who is in Guatemala. We went through the detail of my commission to write on Chinese youth for *National Geographic*. I will make two trips to China to gather material during 1989.

Edward seemed to want to talk, so I went back to the bedroom. I said I knew it was a difficult time for him. It turned out he didn't have his firing from his company on the front of his mind, but rather the relationship between us.

"I don't require you sexually," he said, elaborating his theme that my need for love and affection from him was greater than his need for these from me. I don't think he requires anyone sexually, only a video and his own right hand. He loves cocks, rather than people. It's the "require" or "don't require" approach to friendship, even more than the fact that I'm declared "not required," which is depressing. Like the pandas of Chengdu, he has the desire to conquer rather than to care.

The phone rang while Edward was still undecided as to whether he'd stay over tonight or not. It was Steven, ready to come over! Holding my hand over the receiver, I asked Edward for his decision. Yes, he'd stay. So I told Steven that he could not come tonight but that we'd hookup tomorrow night, and he could stay at my place. Within half an hour, Edward had arranged to have dinner with Ruth.

Steven arrived. Long sex. I fucked him in the doggy position again. He stayed upstairs until the early hours as I went to sleep. I heard him come down toward dawn and liked his presence beside me in bed.

December 6, 1988, Boston

Steven told me fantastic stories of his life. He's been a "faggot" from early years. He went to a private school—must have been unusual for a kid from Roxbury.

December 7, 1988, Boston

Rushing off to Harvard, I looked back, and there was Steven waving from the front deck. A remark of his spun through my head. We were talking about job satisfaction; I said that in the end, we must satisfy ourselves. He rejoined with a smile: "That's what jerking off is all about."

As I walked down the stairs, I realized that he was probably referring to last night. I felt bad—I wanted to explain that I was just too tired so late at night. As it happened, I got my chance. When I got back from Kirkland House, he was still there—unexpectedly—as his father had called off some job of work. He was on the bed. I took off my clothes slowly and lay down.

"This is only the second time I've made love in the afternoon, and the first time was also with you," he said as I held his silky, sexy body in a hard embrace. I fucked him riotously for the third time. "I feel guilty about someone." I knew who he meant, but I pretended to be unsure. I said secrecy was the problem—why not find a suitable moment to casually mention it to Edward?

I asked would he still have gone for me that Saturday noon even if he and Edward had not had a difficult evening the night before. "Yes, it had nothing to do with that." So far, so wonderfully good.

December 8, 1988, Boston

It is Wyatt's birthday, and he is "feeling his years" at 24. "I wish I was 18," he says when he phones for a philosophic birthday chat.

"Would you do anything different if you went back today to being 18?"

"Yes, I'd go straight. I'd play sports."

The two of us feel closer since I fucked him. It happened that John S came in one night soon after Wyatt and I had fused. He hung around. I wasn't sure why. Later, I realized he wanted to get into bed with me. I mentioned that "Wyatt and I did something we'd never done before." So John related some version of this to Wyatt. He was at once proud and embarrassed.

Pleasant to attend the NE China Seminar, though Tony Saich[319] is pedestrian on the 13th CCP Congress. He takes the formal-legal level—as political science calls it—too seriously. I dined with Ezra, who was affable, and the lawyer Bill Alford from Stanford, who has "read all your books" and has an involvement with Sichuan.

Afterwards, Reggie comes in. He looks older, wiser, more tired. Part of it is winter, part is two jobs, plus the strain of the house issue and married life in general. His cock looks ever nobler and granite-like. He had brought jewelry, so while we were in bed, I phoned Laurent to tell him it was here at last. We had hardly shot off when Laurent arrived at the apartment door. He didn't buzz. This I didn't mind at all, but in fact, he generally does buzz. I quickly put on a towel.

Laurent and Reggie really like each other. Quickly they get into a mutual groove. I mentioned Edward was staying. "And you love him!" Laurent burst out. Laurent smiled broadly. Reggie looked at Laurent and then looked at me. His head went up and down. "Yes, he does love him!"

December 9, 1988, Boston

Ric, my barber, gives me a short haircut; I am ready for the hot weather in Australia.

---

[319] Anthony Saich, at the time he was Associate Professor, Sinologisch Instituut, University of Leiden.

I finished a draft of my article on food for *World Monitor*. Then I took the Aborigines piece around to their offices. I hope Earl takes it; it is time I wrapped up the Australia topic.

I told Edward on the phone about the affair between Steven and me. He was not annoyed. It seems he had no idea this was going on. If I astonished him, he then astonished me: he has asked Steven to join the Turner family for Thanksgiving. I felt stabbed by a knife: I have never been asked to Hartford for Thanksgiving.

He ended up slightly annoying me by not acknowledging that I had shared friends sexually with him. After we finished our phone conversation, a list popped into my mind: Tony, Richard, Calvin, Lee, Reggie, Caleb, Hank, Julius ...

In the early evening, John G came in, and we made long love before the mirrors in the Cranberry Room. Few words. Afterwards, he lingered to look around the study, talking of books. A nice guy. His family is Cape Verdean. Hence the quietness, grace, *politesse*.

December 10, 1988, Boston

Darling Greg N administered the finest sucking I can remember for goodness knows how long. He is muscular yet curvaceous. Masculine, yet affectionate. Wild, yet a gentleman. I sucked him too. He pushed the great black dog down my throat to the point of choking.

"Oh, fuck me, Ross. Split me apart!" We began in the stare-at-each-other position. With Greg, that's important because his eyes are wonderful, and he likes to get that soul-communication in place. Then I sought a flat-on-the-tummy phase. This really gets me beyond all reason. The third position was modified doggy. After three positions, I ended up pouring myself into him as he half slipped off the bed.

"Where did you learn to fuck like that?" I did not say. I do not know.

December 11, 1988, Boston

Drama builds over Steven. He left a message saying he'd be late as he had a car accident. Since Edward told me various things, I tend to question the veracity of every detail Steven give me. A pity, yet if Edward is right, I do have to be wary.

When we did get together, Edward was very down. After all, he has neither a job nor a place of his own to live. He used the phone and announced with a curse that he'd missed the last train to Hartford. Wasn't there a bus?

Overall, Edward's response to the saga of Steven and me is very fair. He might have flown into a rage or gone into a depression. I told him I think his "fear of success" is linked with the tie between him and me. He didn't reject this idea; we'll talk about it when I get back from Australia.

A fantastic time with Reggie, as we both feel festive. Unusually, we talked sex— "dirty," as Michael Mao would say—and this fired us up. I got my tongue further up his asshole than ever before. First, I had washed him with a cloth, he having been too lazy to take a shower. He giggled with embarrassment at this, but it was a good idea. He ate a jar of macadamia nuts. I shot hugely all over his right shoulder.

Tired but very happy, I dined alone at Copley's on pasta and an end cut of prime rib. Back home, I fell into bed with a vow to rise early and pack. I think I am in a well-prepared condition for this trip. Gradually over weeks, I sorted the papers required.

I don't think Reggie and Caroline will buy a house. It seems that Caroline will really make the decision, and she doesn't seem ready for the psychological leap of home ownership.

December 12, 1988, Boston

Ferociously cold, the streets white, people bundled up. I took the article to *World Monitor,* stopped by the Y on the way back.

I couldn't reach Wyatt—so be it; there was hardly time left to do much with him anyway, though I dearly wanted to fuck him before I left.

How nice to get on the plane and let irresponsibility seep over me. In Denver, I reached BL to talk about the Aborigines story and *World Monitor.* I told her it was 59 degrees—she's going there next week for skiing. She sighed.

December 14, 1988, Sydney

Yesterday, December 13, went down history's hole. I did not see it, or feel it, or do anything with it. So much for crossing the dateline.

The Australian cabbie who drove me to the Hyatt Kingsgate grumbled about Asian immigrants. "Who built this place up?" he said with a wave of his hand toward Sydney's landmarks. I was about to say, the British. "Greeks and Italians, that's who!" he cried.

He said when he came from Greece in the 1950s, he had to undergo five medical examinations. He had to sign a paper giving the Australian government the right to send him to work in any part of the nation it desired for two years. "The Vietnamese never go to the bush. They have everything, We're the second-class citizens now."

I was hardly checked into the Hyatt when a Black American took my fancy in the lobby. Short, curvaceous, sparkling eyes. Turned out to be from LA, and he looked like it. I felt myself postponing my spiritual entry into Australia, bringing what I loved most in the USA into my first days in Sydney.

"Yeah, I'll take a massage." After a while, I'm rubbing oil between his legs and very near his asshole. I got to the point of stroking his oil-glistening cock, a large uncut piece of work. He smiles. "OK, let's cool it."

I dined at Fountain Bistro, a lovely Australian meal served by a willowy girl. Octopus and then steak. No frills. I watched the life of King's Cross go by as I ate.

December 15, 1988, Sydney

Most of the day, I feel like a physical and mental zombie. But I've secured the hire of a Kaypro from the sister of the head of the Kaypro User's Group here, who works at a Bible college. (I mustn't print out personal things at her place!)

A superb dinner at Encore, the restaurant of Sebel House. The Albury Hotel restaurant has gone Thai. Back at the Hyatt, I was too tired to seek sex with Dan from LA or anyone else.

December 16, 1988, Sydney

Spoke to Susan at Bantam. Judith and Reyna are both traveling in the USA. Susan sounded cheerful and was very friendly. Didn't phone others as I was so happy to have my computer. It's almost like having a friend with me on the trip.

Returned a call from the ATC office in New York. Perth is too far away, the lady reasoned; how about Darwin instead? An American, has she glanced at a map of Australia? But "California"—the place of decision-making in these things—is "favorable" to my request.

The smell of Woolworths: plastic, candy, paper. Will they develop my film without questions being raised? Greg N naked, Steven in the same state (with cum on), myself in various positions.

December 17, 1988, Sydney

Rain here, and Melbourne, amazingly enough, is hot and sunny. Phoned Mum early and found Peter had jumped the gun in calling her to tell her I had reached Sydney— whence this new filiality on Peter's part?

Johnny called last night, but I was out at the bank. Hope he calls again today. Wonderful couple of hours at Bondi Beach, blazing sun, perfect blue sky, some lovely bodies (many Italian). Talked to a Singapore banker named Jimmy. I told him he had beautiful eyes, then gave him my phone number.

In the early evening, after finishing a draft of a book review for *The Washington Post*, coffee and a stroll to Rushcutter's Park with Cheekun. He looks well, but his spirit is flaccid. He has been seeing a therapist for a year, ever since he found he was positive to the AIDS virus. He wants to get out of architecture and into fashion. He has finally decided that his family is not good for him. His experience with them has made it difficult for him to relate to other people. Cheekun goes swimming a lot and says the pools—in the Botanic Gardens, Milson's Point, University of NSW at weekends—are cruisy.

Jimmy from Singapore comes by in the evening. He is very nice but utterly straight. We have a drink in the bar downstairs. He is one of those intelligent Chinese straights who have enormous curiosity about gay life. If it is totally outside his interests, why is he obsessed with AIDS?

Continued the China reforms article for *World Monitor*. My usual little trip down the street for a cappuccino and errands. Sunbathing in the back garden. Then Sivi comes in to discuss her housekeeping role for Mum, starting soon after I return to Boston.

I shower and get ready for Shengde to come and pick me up in his car. Hard to believe the transformation. The construction worker from Shanghai whom I urged to learn English as a necessary first step to getting out of China—right here with me, where I grew up in Murrumbeena.

I feel as I used to while getting ready for a Saturday night date in this very house decades ago. Then it was a girl to dance with. We would dress up. Standing under that same shower, I would wonder what my chances were that night of a kiss. And getting a finger in her...

December 18, 1988, Sydney

I fucked a dark guy from Madras in his room in Surry Hills—intermittently pleasurable—then finished a draft on Chinese economic reforms for *World Monitor*.

The Qantas flight was delayed, but the hotel kindly let me stay for a few hours. In the Captain's Club at the airport, Bob Carr and his wife were waiting for their holiday flight to Munich. Tom Hayden recently phoned Carr, now Leader of the Opposition in NSW. Having found my portrayal of him interesting in *The Australians*, Hayden would like to meet Carr. And how did Bob find Hayden? "Very hung over from the Dukakis loss. He told me he doesn't expect in his lifetime to live again under a Democratic president."

December 20, 1988, Melbourne

The nice thing about our family house in Murrumbeena is the garden. It's what I don't have in Boston. You smell and see greenery and flowers from every room. Peter, the boarder from the country, seems a nice guy. I can understand why Mum likes to have "someone under the roof."

Lunch at Hagger's given me by the City of Melbourne. Hugh Rogers, full of energy and still in his 60s, tells me of plans in the Boston-Melbourne sister city tie. Two colleagues are there. They all feel sad that Melbourne has to take the initiative on most of the programs.

The diners at Hagger's just about fell off their chairs when I tell the story of Ms. Jordan at the Australian office in New York, thinking the Melbourne Cup was a "car race" and that Cooktown was the Cook Islands. At Flinders Street station, I meet a cute Vietnamese guy. Later he phones me from Dandenong and we talk. He knows little English.

December 21, 1988, Melbourne

The party last night went quite well. My brother Peter had catered it meagerly, with mushy things like ladies' tea-party sandwiches, but people ate the stuff. Happily, I had bought some extra wine on the side, which was needed.

December 22, 1988, Melbourne

Coming to Murrumbeena is like coming to China: the cycles of life loom larger; one makes time for people; elaborate rituals; a sense of the past.

Shengde is remarkable—and different. He looks fuller in the face, he is a little heavier, he is far more confident. He has fallen in love with Australia after just one year. He wrote to Singer Australia, pointing out that his grandfather had been manager for Singer Shanghai before the revolution and asking for a job. He got one. In East Malvern, he was staying—free—with a German woman whom he'd met when she was at the German consulate in Shanghai and who is now at the German consulate here. At Singer, the manager turned out to be a Hong Kong Chinese—he helped Shengde in many ways. Last week Shengde bought the guy's wife's car.

"I want to be a crane operator. I'd get $5000 a month instead of $1000 which I get now." Indeed, in China he did such work.

As we begin to make love in the apartment he's just moved into, the pragmatism of the Chinese enters and gets in the way. He mentions that Carney Fisher asked him to come to his mother's funeral, which he agreed to do. He said my cock had got smaller since we did it last in Shanghai. And as I began to suck him, he said, "Tell me, why do you like men?" I felt like replying that, actually, I think I might like women better. None of his remarks helped the occassion. He drove me home—a long way from Thornbury—with great pleasure; he is so proud of his car.

December 23, 1988, Melbourne

A good morning's work on the reforms for *World Monitor*. A piece like this hinges on the quality of the material gathered in China, good judgments, and felicitous imagining of the right words.

Noel M came in with a gift of bush leaves and nuts set in glass. Very pretty indeed. We took lunch at Chadstone and then saw Meryl Streep in *Evil Angels* (as they call it here), about the woman whose baby disappeared in the Outback. A first-class movie, one of the best Australian films I've seen.

Memories. A distant past floods back. The sound of the birds brings back my childhood. The sight of Armadale station puts my Wesley College years in front of my eyes. I think of the classmates from those days, realize they are now middle-aged; despite all we have shared, I don't know if I want to see them again.

December 24, 1988, Melbourne

A searing day of 100 degrees, and I love it. I am still Australian since hot weather feels more like Christmas than frigid.

After a little work in the morning, and lunch at home with Mum, I set off in burning heat for the train station. First to the cricket test match between Australia and West Indies. Jamaicans in Jamaica and Jamaicans playing cricket in Australia are very different. The Black man remains an exotic person under these southern skies. The crowd is crude and very nationalistic. "You Black bastard," someone yells when a West Indian is not given out as the crowd wished.

Then I walked into town past the magnificent Olympic facilities and took a tram to St. Kilda beach. Asians everywhere, including in the men's shower room. Round brown asses to raise my spirits.

In Prahran, I had a glass of wine at the Exchange pub—until they asked me to leave: "After eight, you must have covered shoes," the guy said to me pleasantly, as he stared at my sandals and looked at the clock which showed 8:15.

Nearby, is the new 55 Porter Street.[320] Nice place. A Thai guy and I fooled around a bit. Then a Greek-Australian took me in hand. "I'll give you a super head job," he said, and he did. I did the same for him. Then we sprawled in the jacuzzi.

I took a cab home, and the driver asked me: "Do you think Australia was right to recognize Red China in 1972; do you think we should have done it sooner?" I said I thought whoever did it arranged it all pretty well.

December 26, 1988, Melbourne

Christmas Day, we went to Cousin Ivy's and had a sumptuous feast of turkey, ham, and rich plum pudding with custard and whipped cream. Kevin was there and plied us with wines. Before we left for Ivy's and after we got back, people kept popping in. I felt again the warmth and affection of an Australian Christmas.

I did work on my carvings-at-Dazu article for *The New York Times*; the back of it is broken. In a few days, I should print out the draft pieces I've done in the past 8-9 days— in case there may be complications in formatting on a machine which my disks are not used to.

Appalling zig-zag weather. Roasting one minute, freezing the next.

December 27, 1988, Melbourne

Good morning's work on "Reforms" article for *World Monitor*. Then a few hours in the wonderful reading room of the State Library. So quiet. When eventually there was chatter, I said to a child, "Shhh," and it shut up immediately. Its mother apologized.

Met Shengde at the Southern Cross hotel and, from there, we went to dine at West Lake. Reasonable meal. Then a great movie, *Baghdad Café*, an off-beat German-American production of great humanity. Shengde drove me home. I slept in Peter Brisbane's room, where the bed is more comfortable than in my little room. Pity PB isn't still here.

December 28, 1988, Melbourne

A quick stop at the cricket, long enough to see Richards hit a magnificent six off a short fast ball. At the home of a Kaypro user in Kew, I was able to print out the stuff I'd been writing in Melbourne. Great relief; this really can be a successful working trip.

---

[320] A Melbourne gay bathhouse.

1989

January 1, 1989, Melbourne

Shengde introduces me to Eve. We go to her place and await her return from Castlemaine, where she went for New Year's Eve. Soon after she came in, we drove in Shengde's car to Elwood beach—I hadn't been there for 20-odd years. Eve and I got on well. I didn't really know—at that stage—what she knew about me. Only that she'd read *The Australians*, about which she made appreciative remarks. We dined *à trois* at a Chinese place in Acland Street near St Kilda beach. Eve is not the masterful German lady I imagined but rather a fairly feminine, youngish secretary at the West German consulate in Melbourne.

Who would Shengde drop off first? He went to Eve's place, then later brought me over to Murrumbeena. We talked really for the first time about sex. He likes girls mostly, but with a handsome man he jumps, though not fully reciprocating—that's the gist.

January 2, 1989, Melbourne

Spontaneously, a meeting with someone who once bulked very large. Chris O phoned—he'd left a message some days before, asking me down to Airey's Inlet, but Mum had forgotten to tell me. I went to his new house in King William Street. It is superb. It has the grace, eclecticism, and love of the old that one would expect from him. We dined at a Malaysian restaurant in Lygon Street.

We behaved with a mild flirtatiousness toward each other yet did not go to bed. I was in his house, so I didn't press the issue. He generally knows his mind. We will meet again later in the week. "I'm going to bed. Shall I call you a cab?" I gave his attractive bare brown feet a squeeze and rose from the couch.

He fell in love with the USA. Typically, it impressed him when a Wall Street type built a house in New York in which guest rooms have the smell of freshly baked bread piped into their rooms in the morning. He's restless in his job. Stock brokers are not the most interesting people in the world, he has discovered. He has bought an antique shop in Armadale.

I left my glasses at his house, and also the lovely gardenia he picked for me from his garden. The glasses can be replaced; the gardenia is only for an evening...

January 5, 1989, Melbourne

Carney joins me at the "Pub"—as we used to call the state public library—and we went to the Exchange Hotel and drank and dined. His mother died a few months ago; for him, it's a major watershed. "The grief is great—people should be given six months off from work for bereavement."

"This will be a good book," he said when I outlined *China on my Mind*. No comment on *The Australians*. For friends, one's next book is always more enticing, more remarkable than one's present book.

January 6, 1989, Melbourne

At the City Baths, I feel my body again. In the locker room, a lovely guy looks at me. I look back. He comes over. Within a moment, he grabs my dick, expertly starts to jerk me off. A Thai queen, who had cruised me earlier, chose this moment to arrive. My friend with the golden hand—Malaysian—got rid of him and we continued.

Really good progress on what may turn out to be a prologue to *China on my Mind*.

January 8, 1989, Melbourne

Lovely day at the beach. Shengde and I drove down to Rachel's, and from there Rachel drove us to Lorne. That little town! Just the same as when our family went there for summer holidays, renting a house (hardly a holiday for Mum, as she took with her half the contents of our kitchen!). Yet, in spirit, it is totally new, almost Californian in a low-keyed manner.

Shengde talked his head off, even as I dozed off while lying on the beach beside him. About all his conquests in Shanghai. How he loves sex more than money ("as long as I'm not poor"). His desire to bring Miss Wu here ("I must have a wife; it takes two hours to get myself dinner at night.")

While we were in the house of Rachel and Wade, Shengde noticed that an inscription in Chinese characters of gleaming brass was upside down—at least one of the characters, *fu*, was upside down. He went across to the wall and put it right side up. Rachel looked embarrassed.

Last year Carney Fisher behaved rather oddly toward Shengde, questioning (stupidly, since it was Shengde himself who was testifying to it) whether I could have conducted my tie with Shengde in Shanghai in Chinese. And kissing Shengde on the mouth outside the church at his mother's funeral! The guy is either unhinged by grief or else he was trying to pry Shengde away from me. In the latter case, he failed; Shengde told me all.

Should I recommend Carney to Don Price for that job at UC Davis? Some say friends are there to betray one. But friends surely are there to be turned to no matter what.

January 9, 1989, Melbourne

How timid these Australian men are. They look at you, then they scamper away like frightened rabbits. What exactly is the message of this behavior? I got emboldened to talk of neighbor Mick as Mum's "girlfriend," which did not seem to throw Mum. Shengde was charming and, at the same time, masterful all through a splendid meal.

Next morning, as Shengde drove me into the Qantas check-in at the Hyatt Hotel, he said he'd been disappointed that I didn't come on to him after "lights out" last night. "I know you were tired," he said, not getting the whole point.

Mum is very proud. There was no pathos as I left this time. She had held on to her independence, stood up to me at times. No groveling. Is this better? Or is it merely a result of her mind ebbing?

I worked out at the City Baths, then went to Tullamarine and relaxed in the Qantas Captain's Club, eating delicate Melbourne sandwiches and drinking chardonnay. Emotions to calm down, sort out. I think it's draining to be with Mum because she is a mirror to myself. Also, she makes me feel old.

January 14, 1989, Sydney

Night of horror at Bondi. I brought a handsome young Australian guy up to my room. At least, we got halfway up. At the parking level, this dark, young Australian guy got into the elevator. I nodded, but he was bent on offense. He knocked me down. The elevator stopped somewhere and a colossal attack began. Punches and kicks to the head. This guy had two accomplices waiting. I was hauled down the concrete stairwell as they punched and kicked. They said little, mainly just "Kill him, kill him!"

I managed to say I didn't have money with me. It had no effect. I really came to believe I would be terribly damaged and probably die. For I was trapped in this stairwell. Doors out of it all seemed to be closed. Each time I tried to open a door, I only exposed myself to more punches and kicks by losing my focus on the attackers. What went through my head was: and this is Australia! This is where my life ends, and just look where it is—a motel stairwell, in Australia!

By 4 AM, I was at the casualty ward of Prince Wales Hospital in Randwick, exhausted, depressed, aching like a dog. Yet I was lucky. My eyes were not damaged. Nor, I think, the top of my head. Nor, according to preliminary X-rays, was my jaw or nose broken.

This morning I felt dreadful in body and spirit. I dragged myself off to the beach. I went to put on my sandals—then realized that they'd got lost in the fight. I'd returned to my room, not only with my trousers in tatters but barefoot.

January 15, 1989, Sydney

Thinking back on the reunion with Shengde, it seems that cultural context is terribly important to sexual excitement. When we talked of his coming to Boston, I tried to allay his expressed fear that my Black friends would be jealous. But I think he may have a point; a problem might be *my own* feelings about the Black-Chinese gulf. If Shengde were staying in my house in Boston, I would find it hard to get it out of my head that the two sides didn't like each other. Given my feelings for Reggie, Greg N, etc., I think the result would be lack of desire for Shengde.

In Australia, Shengde has become too normal! The Shanghai element recedes; the fact that he likes girls comes to the forefront. So I am left with the conclusion that only in China would I eagerly want to make love with Shengde.

A nice lift out of a dark mood by getting together with Kazu last night. Son of a wood-cutter and kindergarten teacher, he is a homespun Japanese. I saw his ad in *Campaign* and replied with my photo. He is chunky, direct for a Japanese, and affectionate.

It was pretty clear as soon as he walked in that we'd do something. We sucked each other. For a long time, I had my cock around his asshole; only health prudence prevented him putting it in. And I have seldom seen such a big cock on an Asian, long and fat and hard.

We dined at A Fishy Place, an overpriced but quite good restaurant just near the Cosmopolitan Motel. I had oysters, easy to eat with my swollen mouth, and a seafood omelet—most of the dishes were 30% higher in price than in Boston, and inferior in quality. Many diners were painted Sydney bourgeoisie of the seaside variety. I fell into bed exhausted, still very sore about the head. Hope there will be sun tomorrow.

January 16, 1989, Sydney

I phoned Mum to thank her for my stay. I told her how pleasant it had been, that she has a lovely house, that the stay proved it can work for me to bring writing there and do it, and that I'll come again.

On the beach at Bondi during a glorious afternoon, I am reclining on the sand when I notice a kid looking at me. He is a sharp-featured Mediterranean type of guy. "Gd'day," he said. I beckoned him over. He was a Greek. "Looks good," he said as he stood over me—my cock was peeping out of one side of my trunks. He urged me to follow him to the toilet. But when we got there, he said he saw a friend of his in there, so that was no good.

I took him to my motel room which was very close. He had only a very few minutes. He had a lovely brown body with a leaping cut cock. I got inside him but it hurt, so I didn't finish. Then he fucked me, panting and groaning.

January 17, 1989, Cairns

It is good to get out of Sydney, though it is pouring with rain here. All the airlines, even Qantas, have gone downhill when it comes to staff courtesy and initiative—the stewards gather chatting in groups about low wages while passengers wait for anything, a fault I associate with US airlines, but until today not with Qantas.

Gorgeous new hotel with marble lobby and tropical cane furniture. A lovely boy at the pool—from the Islands north of Australia—but shy. "Sheilas" [321] everywhere. Phoned Boston at great cost—the hotel puts a surcharge on phone calls equal to the greatest luxury hotels in the world.

January 22, 1989, Cooktown

Everyone asks what happened to my finger, but it's my head that hurts. The hand has benefitted from the northern air. So my brother Peter's friend, Don Fry, built the Quicksilver boat I traveled to Cooktown on. He did a good job.

One feels a class gulf when the Bushies are around. I want to be on a level with them, but they seem to think a guy from the Big Smoke is a "gentleman" who will do things

---

[321] Australian slang for girls and women.

differently.[322] And it is true I stay at The Sovereign, a lovely hotel, while Strikie and his friends stay at the backpacker's hostel.

Searing sun at last. Local identity Hans Looser, cheery and overweight, received a copy of the *National Geographic* with my Australia Bicentennial article not only from me but also from a friend in Germany.

January 23, 1989, Cairns

The Cairns Colonial Club is garish, costly. From the start, I noticed two bad signs: low ceilings and many children. In far-north Queensland, announcements start, "Ladies and gentlemen, boys and girls." Not much graciousness in Australian life.

"Are you the gentleman who has been exposing himself under the water?" So began an incident—or ended one—with unpleasant race overtones. In the city pool, I was talking to two young Black guys. Sex was in the air as we splashed around. No one really touched anyone else, but we all had hardons. I was wearing underpants, not swimming trunks (since I had none), and my dick popped out.

Evidently, some people didn't like the fraternizing of the Black kids and me. They told the pool supervisor, who decided that I should be asked to leave for exposing myself underwater! Exposing myself to whom—the fish?

My behavior and personality, it seems, are more striking in Australia than in the USA. Perhaps I stand out both as a gay and as a Yank.

January 25, 1989, Honolulu

My jet lag is dissipated by a romp with Peter V in the ocean. We play around in the waves, and soon I have my cock inside him. Fucking under water is not only possible but exhilarating. A wonderful guy called Curt in the shower room, but he turns out to be all enthusiasm and no follow-up. I think he didn't know his own mind.

The Outrigger is a good hotel for a short stop-over, with a convenient location. In the shower room, an older Japanese guy got nearer and nearer to me. He began to soap me down, smoothly, expertly, erotically.

Downtown in Hotel Street, in the movie house, a Chinese jerked me off, but the clown stopped the rhythm just as I started to shoot. Chinese often do that. Instead of rejoicing in the stream of cum, like Blacks, they get scared of it; it says reproduction to them maybe.

Talk on the phone to the Committee on Foreign Relations in Boston. At last, *The Australians* has made an impact on an institution in my home state: they love the book and want me to speak on Australia at a dinner meeting next month. I was happy to agree. It made me feel plugged back into Boston after too long away in Australia.

---

[322] Bushies, less sophisticated people from the Australian Bush; Big Smoke, the city.

January 27, 1989, Boston

Trying to get out from under a mountain of mail. Surprising how many Christmas and New Year's cards there have been; a large number from China!

Financially things look OK. I have brought back about US $10,000 from Australia to take advantage of the high Australian dollar. This, plus the first half of the advance from Simon & Schuster for *China on my Mind*, gives me a healthy balance in DLA. Meanwhile, *National Geographic, World Monitor*, and other articles will bring in a bit during 1989. As a bonus, my monthly payment to the bank for my house loan has fallen below $800.

Steven rings the doorbell and once more, I really go for him. Afterwards, it dawned on me that just as he was the first person I went to bed with on my return from China in November, so he was the first on my coming back from Australia.

Amazingly—he and I have some incredible telepathy—Edward phoned in the middle of it. Later, I called him back and Steven came on the line—it cleared the air of any feeling that Steven and I were doing something behind Edward's back, for the three of us to chat for a moment together.

January 28, 1989, Boston

Boston is crisp and beautiful. At the YMCA, I saw Troy and my heart leapt. I could not speak to him; we only stole glances as before. He focused exclusively on my asshole as I bent over to dry myself.

From the postal service, letters arrive that are three to four years late. There is a covering letter of explanation: "Enclosed is mail addressed to you which was recovered incident to the arrest of a postal employee for the delay and obstruction of mail." Sincere apologies are offered. Meanwhile, the ten letters are a recap of my existence four years ago, but all can be thrown away.

A wonderful reunion with Reggie, who looks magnificent. He's been working out as coach of a junior basketball team in addition to his regular job. "I needed that massage" was the nearest to a sexual comment; no matter, we each know after six-plus years pretty much what is liked.

I read in the Dodge Library, and this steadies me. Dinner at Thai Cuisine, where the same lovely waiter as last night expresses the same Thai charm. At three, the phone rings. It is Wyatt. He's been at the 1270 bar and is lonely—could he come round? I told him yes, but only to sleep. In the event, I fucked him before we went to sleep.

If you drink a glass of beer, a glass of fine champagne will immediately arrive! Greg N, whom I have been adoring from afar, phoned while Wyatt was still in my bed and asked to come round!

January 29, 1989, Boston

A pleasant day of reading. As Kay told me on the phone from Australia, it really is the mildest of winters. I phoned Auntie Pop for her 90th birthday, and she was thrilled. One can only wonder which of us in the present generation—if any—will live to 90!

Dined at Copley's with today's *New York Times Book Review*. Then Chris came in; despite my vow of restraint (I want to see Greg N tomorrow), we had a passionate time while watching "Heat Waves."

All the magazines to catch up on. From some of them, like *Publishers Weekly* and *Free China Review*, one learns quite a bit. But the opinion magazines are starting to seem dispensable.

February 1, 1989, Boston

D came in. Shapely, soft-skinned, silky asshole—my sixth welcoming man in five days back. I finished the revision of the review of *Seeds of Fire* for the *Washington Post* and chose pictures with Jean at *World Monitor* for my China article.

February 2, 1989, Boston

Reggie came in. I wasn't sure he wanted to do anything. He just sat on the chair against the wall on the Orange Line side. Then his tone changed. After a lapse in the conversation, or even a dead-end, he said softly, "How ya doin' buddy?" Then, "Go down on it." Before he was through, he had fucked me twice. Just as well we know the signals.

February 5, 1989, Boston

An amazing weekend with Edward. He had decided while I was in Australia that he was going to come and make love with me again. In he came from Hartford, and I soon fell absolutely under his spell. He arrived late, as usual, and I got out of bed to welcome him. I was wearing just the gray-white-black underpants by Calvin Klein that he gave me for my birthday. A few minutes later, he was lying on top of those underpants—and me. The warmth, the vitality, the rising lust!

I fucked him in the facing position, coming out of him just before I shot. He spurted much at the same time. We slept.

On Saturday, we dined at Thornton's on his favorite dishes. He told me he's decided that "it's easier with men than with women." He will "come out" in Hartford sometime this summer. The physical relation with Arlene is "all over." We'll see.

That night I had an engagement: he went out with Glen and, I think, his cousin Lenore. When he came in, he lay down, tired, beside me and we watched a video. "I shouldn't have had those two drinks," he said.

I massaged him. This led on to playing with his asshole. Soon I had my prick in him. Then began one of the loveliest experiences of any kind anywhere that I have ever had. I twisted, I pumped, I curled, I jabbed, I went in short and then suddenly in long. He groaned, begged for more. After a long, long time, during which I felt him responding to me by his muscle twitching, I shot into him. After he showered, he said, with I do not know how much seriousness, that I should not have shot inside him.

It was clear Edward was bent on seducing Greg N, so I went into my study. Sure enough, he did. The door remained open, so I kept in touch. Greg screwed Edward in the two-insects position. It was a magnificent sight, the two athletic Black bodies writhing against each other.

Later, Edward phoned Cavalieri—I think—and reminisced with him about the past. "Was it twice we did it with a third person?" I do feel envious of Edward for the way he feels ebullient after sex—I become subdued. Edward and I dined at St. Botolph restaurant before he drove back to Hartford.

February 6, 1989, Boston

I felt depressed, then Brian came in. It was our first time, and it was fantastic, despite his hang-ups about extreme safety. From Georgia, he is a medical student. "I've never done it with a writer," he said as he caressed me all over and gave my cock the biggest comprehensive working over it has had for a long while. "I hope when I'm your age, I have a body like yours," he said.

Later, John S came by and toyed around with his dick in my asshole. He was so drunk that I am not sure he will remember this evening. I like his personality very much and think he is attractive.

February 7, 1989, Boston

Mac at the *National Geographic* says I should go ahead with the China Youth coverage. My first trip can be by myself, he says, without waiting for a photographer to be named. He would like to see Cary named to do the pictures.

Mac complains that his new novel has hardly been reviewed in the UK. Because he has previously written spy novels, everyone wanted a spy novel, and *Bride of the Wilderness* is an historical novel with much American reference.

A Nieman evening seminar on American Indians. Issues are very similar to those of Black people in Australia. Same talk of federal money, of tension between fitting in and being "sovereign." Same stories of accusations of mishandling of government funds. Nothing new.

Liu Binyan was there. When I told him the story of the bribe (not by me) being necessary to get permission for my *Mao* to be published in Chinese in Shijiazhuang, he said: "In that case, a bribe is a good thing. It increases freedom of expression."

As for 1989 in China, he said he expects a crisis "bigger than any since 1949." A Malaysian journalist came over, and Liu added to us, "There are now opposition groups in China."

February 8, 1989, Boston

Still very cold. I feel my suntan ebb away. Can't settle to the Cooktown article. Perhaps I should just start to write it without more attempt at planning. Not having my printer working does not help.

A memorable line from Updike's new book, a sort of spiritual memoir: "To be in print was to be saved. And to this moment a day when I have produced nothing printable ... is a day lost and damned."[323]

Danny brings in his cousin Neal. Neal is nice, and he "wants." But I am not sure about doing it with the two of them together till I know them better—influence of the Sydney mugging? Neal had on pink pants. His lovely eyes bored through me. The two of them reminisced fondly about their days together in the Job Corps and about going to Kung Fu movies together.

Françoise Lepage[324] phones from California to ask me to speak at Dominican College on my way to board the *Pearl* cruise liner in April. I said yes.

In the evening, John S phones and I ask him around. Three hours later (and, on his part, many drinks later), we have sex. I am attracted to him, but you have to get through a maddening shield of "Nos" and passivity to get what you want. "How was I?" he asked afterwards.

A Bill Terrill from NJ writes to say he is thrilled with *The Australians*. He praises Australia extravagantly. "They have what we lost—a thousand miles of nobody." This from a man who lives in the central NJ megapolis.

February 9, 1989, Boston

Lunch with *World Monitor* editors at Claddagh. They seem pleased with my reforms article. Also, nice remarks about the already put-to-bed Sichuan Food piece.

After lunch, Reggie and I went to bed for the afternoon. It was rimming day. I dearly wanted to get my dick inside him, but he stood out for our rules. I shot a huge load all over him. Later, he came a second time—he had come the first time when I went to the phone to take a call about my printer—and then, late in the afternoon, he fucked me and came (outside me) for a third time. Now he really may be tired! We finished just before my fellow trustees arrived for a condo meeting.

February 10, 1989, Boston

Some good work on the Dazu article for *New York Times*. Sex with Danny, as usual, is very good. A lunch meeting at Harvard at which Andrew Walder talks about new patterns in Chinese industry.

February 12, 1989, Boston

A welcome call from Edward and a long talk. He had been at Beverley's, plus a side trip to Manhattan. He had sex with four men in 42nd Street. So much for Arlene. I told him of my increasing interest in being fucked. "So now you know how I feel!" he said. He gave me suggestions for exercises I can do even with a sore left wrist. We will meet in Hartford or New York in a couple of weeks—he can't get away before that. A DC trip, staying with Van, is another possibility.

---

[323] *Self-Consciousness: Memoirs* (Knopf, 1989)
[324] Françoise Lepage (1945-2010), Canadian educator and writer.

I went to Legal Seafoods with David. On the way on the Green Line, in a crowded train, I got horny for him, brushed against him. He got a hardon. He said I was a *cochon* (French for hog) to come on to him in a train. But he was smiling.

February 13, 1989, Boston

A party for Liz Shannon's book on Irish women[325] at Helen Rees's. Very charming, but I cannot enthuse over Irish topics. Each time I looked at Liz, I felt so sorry for her loss in Bill's death.

Tomorrow my Fenway appointment. Mental preparations. The neurologist, Dr. Troy, is going to sign off on me; the problem still exists in my peripheral nervous system, but it can be lived with. At any rate, he can't think what to do about it.

Gentle sex with Michael in the morning before his classes. He is getting more quiet and passive. But we enjoy each other's company, I guess, silent as it is mostly is. He seems to have ruled out fucking nowadays, and I do not feel I should persuade him otherwise.

February 14, 1989, Boston

Fantastic time with David in the afternoon. "He rims me for the first time, and I just about go through the ceiling. Kneeling, I came in his hand. "Gee, I could never cum that much!" he said as, my ass aching with pleasure, I shot across the bed.

"Don't trust Neal too much," he said mysteriously of his cousin.

Off to the Fenway Clinic for my round of tests and interviews. It turned out that I had, in the past 6 months, 56 incidents of sex with men more than 3 times in that period. Not an exact science, of course, as the woman stares at you, pencil at the ready, as you recall and add things up and sort out categories.

Mark comes in, but I do not have much time for him. I love his big brown hands and the way he plays with my cock.

February 15, 1989, Boston

Got some important discs off to the bank vault. The box is filling up, and soon I will need a bigger one. Though my nose was broken in the Sydney attack, my head, the X-rays now reveal, was not damaged.

February 16, 1989, Boston

Cornell phones and is very nice. What I feared some time ago—that John would tell Cornell various things I said to Jayden about Cornell and me making love—apparently had no basis. Good, for Cornell can be sensitive, very private about such things. Anyway, it was Cornell, according to John, who told John that "Ross is really hot."

Dr. Troy looks gravely at my wrist, then says I will have pain for one year. The only test of what to do, or not do, is pain. How brilliant are these doctors.

---

[325] Elizabeth Shannon (1937 -), *I Am of Ireland: Women of the North Speak Out.*

Reggie comes in. He has a sore throat, but this does not stop us. How I wanted to fuck him! If I was very cynical, I would just get him a bit higher than usual—even higher—and then just do it.

Elegant party at the Giffords for Henry Brandon, whose memoirs[326] have just come out. Joan Kennedy is there and greets me warmly and with the reproach that I have been out of touch. As she and I stand together, someone comes up and snaps a photo—perhaps at Joan's prior request.

As he signs my copy of his book, Henry makes generous reference to my work on China. Everyone says I look fine. Various folk say they are pleased to see me—why, then, do they never phone me? Dick Neustadt[327] and his new wife Shirley Williams chat about social democracy. "It will have to change," says Shirley. The talk turns to Kissinger. I say I do not recall having been lied to by him, but Dick insists he knows of times when Henry lied.

Tired from the big orgasm, drunk from the party, I ended up with a hangover.

February 17, 1989, Boston

I meet a guy called Mark C. He sucks well, a shade too vigorously. Sex like that doesn't make me feel happy afterwards. A long talk with Li-li about Edward. "Isn't there another young man you could better put all that hope in?" she says delicately.

André told me today that his friend Gary died last year. And now this new friend, the gorgeous Tim, has been diagnosed with HIV, too.

February 18, 1989, Boston

Talk with Edward for an hour on the phone. He's had the flu. He said he has a fantasy of being in the middle of Reggie and me: he fucking me as Reggie fucks him. I told him Reggie is a most improbable candidate for this. But we both think Greg N is an excellent candidate for a fucking sandwich. Edward would prefer to be in the middle, but he would also like to do it with Greg in the middle. Come to think of it—though we didn't discuss this on the phone—I'd be happy to be in the middle, too, if Edward did the fucking of me.

He's had to lie pretty low this week. No therapist, no aerobics class, no gym workout, no work at the church. He sounded very passive, coming to life only when we talked of sex in raw terms. He couldn't believe his ears as I spoke of buying a Black dildo. As I explained to him, I am only interested in being fucked by either young guys or people I feel close to—really Edward himself and Reggie.

I printed out a draft of the introduction to *COMM*. It is taking shape.

---

[326] *Special Relationships: A Foreign Correspondent's Memoirs from Roosevelt to Reagan.*
[327] Richard Elliott Neustadt (1919-2003), political scientist and author.

February 19, 1989, Boston

Hank asked me to tell him all about my recent sex life. I said I would as long as he didn't judge me, and as long as he realized that he wasn't some outside observer but a person I was very attracted to and fond of. Sure, he said. But soon, he became highly agitated that I was seeing "many men."

We dined at Legal Sea Foods and talked of his work—we never talk of mine—and a little more of the Big Topic. But as soon as I get close to the idea of living with him, I pull back. He said he thought he'd go home and "cool out." I thanked him sincerely for his advice to "settle down."

February 20, 1989, Boston

Following a quiet night—after Hank went home, I read in bed—fireworks this morning. Greg N phoned and soon came by with a new recording of wonderful Spanish music. We kissed at the start, and before long, he was sucking my dick as only he can.

We tore off each other's clothes and sprang onto the bed. He begged me to fuck him. Suddenly, as we writhed, I started to come; he made me spray on it on his chest, then he came too. All this within three minutes of us getting into bed and five minutes of his arrival. A mistake, but a beautiful mistake.

I got a joint Reggie had rolled, and we lay down and talked. To my surprise, he said he found Edward "ugly" and "too big for me." And that "there is something I don't like about his personality—over-eager." Greg N said Edward forced him to fuck him. "I did it to get it over with." I began to massage him, and we got hot again. But having just come, I wasn't hard enough to fuck him the way he prefers. I sucked him long and lovingly as we talked in nameless superlatives.

Eventually, we got our two cocks together and came together in four hands on his smooth brown tummy. "God, that was good," Greg said.

We went upstairs to the red bathroom, showering while listening to Spanish songs. I said I regretted that I was not strong enough to fuck him after coming the first time. He just laughed. I said I was getting old. "You're not!" Of course, I felt better.

As I went to the library, I pondered the fact that, as he said, he jerked off four times last night while lying alone in bed. "I didn't think I'd be aroused this morning," he said after he came the first time. All the nicer to know I turn him on. Should we go to San Juan together?

In the evening, after doing some work on my speech for tomorrow and playing squash with Alan, I phoned Edward to see if he's got over the flu. He has. I said of Stanley: "I'm too old to waste time on people who don't know what they want." He loved this—"You should write that down."

February 21, 1989, Boston

Much of the day spent preparing for tonight's speech to the Boston Committee on Foreign Relations, held over dinner at the Saint Botolph Club. All very successful. One of the co-chairs is Dick Nenneman, the new editor of the CSM.[328] He thinks well of *World Monitor*, thinking it should be bigger with six or seven—not just three—major pieces in each issue. He particularly liked my Australia piece in the first issue.

Richard Epstein, the other chairman, said he'd never met an Australian he didn't like. He asked me which Down Under poets I liked best. Some guests were curious to know why I should "leave" the topic of China to write a book about Australia.

During the afternoon—rain-drenched—a Black guy stared at my dick in the Robert's locker room. When it got hard, he whispered: "Come to the TV room." There in the gloom, he sucked me, sitting in an armchair in the corner as I stood over him. This made me a few minutes late for my squash match.

After the game, I was planning to just take a quick steam—to aid my sore wrist—within the Roberts, and then get back to work on my speech. But something made me go to the general shower room. As I went in, a Mediterranean-type was finishing his shower. Modestly, he wrapped a towel around himself. I smiled and said hello. Before he put the towel on, I saw the muscled, shapely thighs, meaty cut cock, smooth skin.

When I'd showered, I went to where he was drying himself. He didn't hurry. I dried myself and got excited. Meanwhile, there was a third person in the section, a very handsome, straight Black bodybuilder. Before anything could be tested, he had to be gone. Soon this magnificent Mediterranean guy—probably in his early 30s—was sucking me. I watched out for any passersby as he did so. We switched. Soon he said, "I'm nervous." I was, too. I said how about giving him my phone number and meeting later. He agreed and I went to the Roberts desk for pen and paper. He gave me his work number. No one was there, he was still naked above the waist, so I began to suck his nipple. He moaned gently. "Do you like that?" "Yeah."

I rushed back, by now very late, to complete my preparations for the talk on Australia. It was pouring with rain and very windy.

At night Chris came in and wanted me to fuck him. We did a lot, but I had decided in advance to save myself and not come. It was very difficult, watching my rock-hard dick against his lovely ass in the mirror. He twisted around, toying with it, wanting it inside him.

February 22, 1989, Boston

Tired after the dinner lecture last night, but still my mind turned to Stu, the Mediterranean guy. I phoned him at work—state offices. He said he didn't know his schedule yet. This puzzled me and, combined with him not giving me his home phone number, made me feel he was gently backing out. Anyway, I suggested he come around that lunchtime. I had the Kirkland House Senior Common Room, but I was prepared to miss that for this guy. He said that sounded alright. I said phone me toward noon when you are ready to leave.

I wasn't sure he would, but he did and shortly arrived on the Orange Line. We had a superb time. He sucked me wonderfully, and rubbed my cock all over his body, saying,

---

[328] *Christian Science Monitor.*

"Ooh, I'm so excited!" Then he rimmed me, and I stuck my cock inside him. At one point, he said, "Lie on your back!" He sat on me, and I shot into him.

"I haven't done this for a while," he said when I first went inside him.

Since it went so well, I asked him why he hadn't given me his home phone number. "I'm married, you see."

February 23, 1989, Boston

Still under the shadow of the passion with Stu. His licking of my asshole seems to have "licked" that hemorrhoid; it has gone down. I am tired, erotic, restless, work-oriented—all at once.

I got the article "Australia Revisited" off to Melbourne, and the one on race and immigration to David Chen at SCMP[329] in Hong Kong. Agonizing over the *Los Angeles Times* request to do an article on the Asia Pacific region for their "Calendar." If only Simon & Schuster—typical stupidity of publishers—had not got the message wrong! The Touchstone editor rang to say the *Los Angeles Times* wanted to interview me about *The Australians*. Alas, when I spoke with them, they wanted an article. Meanwhile, I worked like a slave on a long piece for *World Monitor* on the Aborigines of Australia.

February 24, 1989, Boston

At the YMCA, a young Black guy cruised me. But he looked exhausted; perhaps he was sick. I stroked him, but he was passive. He just gazed with lust at my dick but didn't seem to have the strength to grab or suck it.

Cornell phoned and said he'd like to come round. We drank tea upstairs as he told me about his life. He's still going strong—since September—on his no-sex vow. Despite this, we fondled and hugged a bit. His cock was hot and hard in his pants; as ever, he wore no underwear. Later he went off to meet a friend at Luxor's, a video bar that is evidently the rage.

February 25, 1989, Boston

I think I'm projecting onto Edward some of my own addiction, my own lack of a center.

February 27, 1989, Boston

Work on the Cooktown piece for *New York Times* in the morning, and then lunch with Liu Binyan at the Harvard faculty club. He will not return to China when his Nieman year is up in June but will go to Trinity College for a year. "All my friends in Peking say, don't come back now." He doesn't think the military will dispute power in the old way when Deng goes but sees regionalism—Guizhou as leading case—and the prospect of military in one province being at loggerheads with military in another one. The false (NPC) can turn into the true (Democracy)—he still believes it, "but it takes time." Did

---

[329] *South China Morning Post.*

he ever believe firmly in the Party? "Oh yes, Liberation was a wonderful thing. I didn't even think the 1954 constitution was necessary. Let the CP handle these matters, I felt; we trust the Party." I gave him a copy of my book *Madame Mao* and a newspaper piece I wrote after the 13th congress of the CCP.

I read papers and magazines in the club lounge for a while and then came back to try and finish up the Cooktown piece before Nuke was due at 5 PM. But Michael arrived, on the way to see his aunt in hospital, and with Mike one thing always leads to another. The sight of his legs, cock, and balls sends me off. "Safe sex," I realize when I have to stick within its limits, is something I'm not used to. It's hard to pull back from the sublime.

February 28, 1989, Boston

I started the article on Pacific Rim for the *Los Angeles Times* and revised the first part of the book Intro—it could itself be a whole chapter.

Went to a concert with Greg N, and there we ran into a clergyman who apparently used to suck Greg off in Roxbury. His specialty was to take out his false teeth first. "It's different," Greg said. We dined at Atlantic Fish. Greg remarked that I am "a gentleman," and this he likes about me.

March 3, 1989, Boston

An interesting talk at Harvard on nomadic poets in China and their quiet dissent from orthodoxy. I polished the reforms article, the op-ed, and the Pacific Rim piece for the *Los Angeles Times*.

Shengde writes from Melbourne that he wants to become an Australian citizen. It is amazing to align the Shengde of today with the Shengde of not so long ago in Shanghai. I booked the dates for San Francisco for my lecture at Dominican College on the way to China and probably sojourn with Greg N on the way back.

March 4, 1989, Boston

At Roxbury YMCA, a couple of nice young guys in the locker room, for once. One of them takes furtive glances at me whenever he thinks his mate is not watching— especially at my cock. If only they did not go around in pairs or groups.

A nice concert of the Boston Symphony this evening, Brahms the best. I took Harold A, and afterwards we dined at Thai Cuisine. Harold wants to truly fall in love, and live with that one person for the rest of his life. "I know I would have to make compromises, but I'm prepared to do it." He makes me feel flighty by comparison, yet I am not sure he's very happy. "I feel very lonely," he said twice. Strangely, the more he talked this way, the less I wanted to be intimate with him.

March 5, 1989, Boston

A fine performance of *Aida* at the Opera House. I was in standing room far up—the only space available. During the final act, two Black guys came up. It turned out they were part of the cast; their roles were finished, and they came up to watch the last act. "It's the best place to see it from," one said to me.

One of them stood very near me. We played with each other as the arias soared. It was the second one, however, who turned me on. But when the second one and I drew closer, maneuvering in the dark like ships entering a harbor, it turned out the guy was Brian, the singer from the Signet Society at Harvard. We said hearty hellos and left it at that.

March 7, 1989, Boston

What is odd about the Rushdie fuss[330] is that it isn't really the book that comes under attack, but the publicity pushing the book. If we writers just want our books read, as we should, the whole business of death threats by people who never see the book has nothing to do with books.

Got the article off to *Los Angeles Times* on the Pacific Rim. Greg N phones, wants sex, so I turn Chris away—then Greg phones an hour later to say he's come down with a fever. Chris has gone.

It's bitterly cold. I would like to go to San Juan. Will I ask Reggie to come—or Greg? Or will I go alone?

March 8, 1989, Boston

I got my report at the Fenway clinic. Once more, I am negative to the HIV virus. With gratitude, I walked slowly back along Mass Avenue to my home.

March 9, 1989, Boston

I must say no sometimes. It would have been better, for instance, to have said no to the *Los Angeles Times* request to write the overview for their Arts feature on the Pacific Rim. Too much work for too little reward; a diversion from larger tasks.

I was still in bed, dozing, when the doorbell rang at 7:45 AM and in came Michael. He had decided to take the day off. He watched videos, and at intervals, I popped in to chat, cuddle, or suck his lovely weapon.

Edward phoned halfway through the morning—wanted the new phone number of the Fenway health clinic. I told him of being depressed because I had not been invited to the "literary lions" dinner and because of the refusal of the grant from Washington to do research in China. He reassured me; he is marvelous in that.

Stu came in as we planned last week. I have learned that this terrific guy can be relied on and doesn't feel he has to say things twice. We made love long and deliciously. "I'm going to stay for hours," he said, "I'm going to take a long lunch break." It hurt him today when I went inside, both on his front and on his back. This took away some of my desire for a while. Then as he slid all over me, he came before he expected.

---

[330] Salman Rushdie's novel *The Satanic Verses* (1988) was accused of blasphemy by certain segments of the Muslim world. Death threats were issued against him, and Ayatollah Khomeini, the Supreme Leader of Iran, proclaimed a *fatwā* on 14 February 1989, that sanctioned Rushdie's assassination.

Upstairs we showered together, talked about his family, and got to know each other better. "What are you doing Tuesday night?" Evidently, his wife has something on. So we will meet after work then.

Just as Stu and I were getting into bed, Greg N phoned. I said I'd call him back, but it took a while. Anyway, he came around to show me his College of Art application and borrow $10 for the filing fee. He said he was horny, but he knew I'd been with Stu. So, I suppose there was no expectation. I also had to leave for Harvard by 4:15 at the latest. And there was the *Los Angeles Times* material to be sent.

I went to the FAX office while Greg tried to hook up the new VCR. When I came back, I looked at him, and the vitality of the guy turned me on. One shouldn't compare people, but it's the sensual that distinguishes Greg from Stu (and lots of people). I said I'd suck him off quickly since he was horny. One thing lead to another. We tore each other's clothes off. I'd shaved my balls and got my asshole snippety clean, so I was ready to go. He sucked me like an angel, and that was it. We swung into the "son" and "Daddy" routine. This was the answer to the vague anxiety I had felt last week at the syndrome: embrace the depression, use it as a sexual framework. "Fuck me. Fuck me, Daddy !" So I did.

I suggested he roll on his side. We were very close to the large mirror. He faced it, my white hand gripping his huge, rippling Black prick. Going on with the father-son stuff, I rammed it into him, exploded like an atom bomb inside that kitten of love.

March 10, 1989, Boston

Tired but happy. I got the package off to the Chinese Ambassador, requesting cooperation on the "China Youth" project for *National Geographic*, and the manuscript to Edward for his opinion, then took a quiet lunch of sea trout and mackerel at Legal Seafood.

Greg came by, and Reggie called. I said Greg N was here but to come by. He sounded dubious. But he came. The two of them got on well at a polite, general level. I think it was striking for Reggie to see someone else so much at home in my place—Greg was working on the hook up of the VCRs.

Reggie and I talked upstairs about his job situation, which is calming down. As Reggie had a few beers, he became more relaxed. Greg showed us his stunning paintings of prostitutes, tornadoes, and peepshow life.

"Is he reliable?" Reggie whispered when we were upstairs alone, while Greg was in my bedroom getting the video camera ready to film his paintings. "Completely." At another point, Greg put on *Gypsy Kings* rather loud, and Reggie went up and changed the record to another one without comment. But I think Reggie found Greg's paintings talented, if way-out.

I must get back to that bum-enhancing exercise using the spiral staircase that Reggie taught me. And the guy at the YMCA today told me that the leg exercises he does—sitting on a machine—is good for the bum as well as the thighs. If so, I will try it. My wrist is markedly stronger than a week ago, which is an immense pleasure. I am able to do some arm and chest routines at last.

March 11, 1989, Boston

The decks are getting cleared, at last, for work on *China on my Mind*. The arrival the other day of the Simon & Schuster royalty statement for *The Australians* has concentrated my mind. I do have an advance from them for *China on my Mind*, and there is a deadline laid down in the contract.

Something made me think back to Wilson and the Brazilian guy I was with in Geneva years ago. One night in the bunks, Wilson said to me that I was all words. At that moment, I should have got into his bed, just upstairs from mine, and started kissing him. I missed so many opportunities in those years—including one day when the Brazilian, sitting on his bed at the Foyer John Knox,[331] had a lovely hardon and smiled at me as I looked at it.

In those days, I was one to study all the time. And I was one to agonize over moral questions. I suppose the only good thing about my abstinence during the 1960s was that, had I plunged in then, I might have gone to the extreme—as I have been known to do—and undermined health and career alike.

March 12, 1989, Boston

Edward suggests I add the term "boy" to the vocabulary that Greg N and I have been using in our dad/son games. For whom?

Met a handsome guy in the sauna who works for Northeastern University and lives in the YMCA. "I have never met anyone that way before," he said, of my having stroked his ass as we sat in the sauna. "You're bold," he said. I pointed out that he didn't move away when I touched him. "I didn't want to move away," he said with a nice smile. "But I thought, Gee, will we get thrown out of the YMCA for this." As we made love, he kept saying, "Are you having a good time?" I was, so I didn't mind him talking too much.

My aim now is to get chapter two of the book pretty much in shape before leaving for the Orient in mid-April.

March 17, 1989, Boston

Fucked Chris in the legs-up position last night, and it was tremendous fun; he said he loved every thrust. Got a batch of letters off. My wrist is at last showing improvement; I mustn't do anything that will set it back. Reggie is brooding, demanding today – what's on his mind?

Sergei is again suggestive. He knew I was late to meet someone back at home. "I hope he's not angry with you," Sergei remarked. Then he pressed me to name a time when he and the magnificent Mike could come round "for dinner." I hadn't realized that I'd invited them.

The magnificent Greg N is down, very introspective. It was our first-ever talk about homosexuality and its problems. He confessed he's frightened about the upcoming HIV test result.

---

[331] A student hostel in Geneva, where Terrill stayed in 1964.

Meanwhile, his fever goes on. In the hospital, they could not work out why, but before they'd finished their tests, he walked out—he hates the regimentation of a hospital. He said it's me alone that he has sex with nowadays.

We made love—safe sex—before dining at Thai Cuisine. But he was too weak and exhausted to eat much. He stayed overnight. Next morning, I came again soon after he started working on me.

March 22, 1989, Boston

I guess three orgasms in a bit over 24 hours is just very tiring for me now. But the session with Hank on Monday night was worth every cost. Whichever way you look at him, Hank must be the most attractive man I have ever been involved with over any length of time.

I wanted to fuck Jodi last night, but finally he made it clear he doesn't really like it. I came on my own, watching the new stud in *Black Rage*. I hadn't done that for ages.

Wyatt did shopping for me and happened to impart shocking news. Of course, his statement that Greg N has AIDS should be treated with caution. Still, it threw me. He said Greg had a bout in hospital some months ago. The second piece of news is more factual, one would think but hope not: Sam Brown is in prison, ten years for drug trading.

I phoned Greg to see how he is getting on. Not very well. His eyes are red and he's depressed. Everything seems different now that Wyatt has told me what he did. I checked on whether Greg feels he may recently have picked up the HIV virus. No, he doesn't think so. With Edward, he happened to remark, he received no cum (and pulled out of Edward, also, before shooting). He remarked in what may be his declining years that he dislikes threesomes. "It's not real ."

March 19, 1989, Boston

Airways magazine in Australia has accepted my "Expatriate's Reflections" article. Good—$1100 credit on Qantas, and some nice exposure to Australian elites. Work on China back in 1964. It will be the easiest chapter of the book to write, but maybe the thinnest in content on the story of 25 years with China.

March 23, 1989, Boston

Will I go to Charleston or Savannah next weekend? But perhaps by then—I must book a week ahead—the weather here will have improved.

I told Chris Carmody that his coming with me on the *Ocean Pearl* did not work. "They say a spouse is a spouse," I told him, a shade misleadingly, after talking with Pearl Cruises. He said he could dress up in drag.

I think about Greg N taking poison when he was 12. If things don't turn out well health-wise, will he get that depressed again? Our indiscretions! I remember that Tyrone readied himself to make love with me minutes after I told him I was sick with gonorrhea. Everyone and everything is flawed; that's what is so sad. So much is beautiful and exciting, yet the flaws appear.

Squash with Sergei, last time with the hard ball. He is so warm these days that I said with a glint in my eye: "Next week, with the soft ball, you'll be able to do anything you like with me!" He grinned. But Mike de Forrest is even more enticing. How to conjoin squash and sex.

March 25, 1989, Boston

The 19th century was an age of economics. The 20th century, has been an age of politics. It looks as if by the end of it and the coming of the 21st century we will once again be into an age of economics.

Edward is coming to Boston for his Fenway tests on Monday, but he "absolutely" will not stay overnight. Then he asks me a question I am not comfortable with: having nice ties with Greg N and Reggie and Hank, why do I want him, Edward? I didn't really answer. Probably because of this phone conversation, I have a terrible headache this morning.

March 28, 1989, Boston

I thought about the question Edward asked and called him to answer it better. He is intelligent, I said. He knows me better than others. He had a conservative, good upbringing which I like. He's more of a real man than Hank, more sophisticated than Reggie, at least as sexy as Greg N. He loved all that.

Above all, I said—and this is the only point that really counts—I just think he and I are destined to intertwine our lives. I think he also feels this but resists it. The maddening thing about him posing the question to me is that it implies that he is somehow outside the issue. But what he thinks and wants is really at the heart of the matter. I linked the postponement of our New York trip with his "fear of success." He was very reasonable and reflective. I said I loved him, and this was probably a mistake.

Neal was here. He said of my massage and other things that even though he's been married, he's never felt pleasure like that. When he could not wait anymore to come, he said, "Beat me, beat me!" I hadn't heard the term for a long while, since my Melbourne days. I was very happy to beat him—jerk him off.

March 29, 1989, Boston

Got a Chinese-reforms op-ed off to several newspapers, spurred by a call from a Korean newspaper, saying Seoul wanted one. Now I will do a longer version for *Newsday*, work on the latter part of the Intro to *China on my Mind*, and after that take a break in Charleston. After a long seduction, in this room and that, I fucked Wyatt.

April 3, 1989, Boston

Have been on a trip to Charleston, semi-successful. Next time, I will call ahead for a weather forecast and book a hotel in advance. The cool air that came to Boston also came to the Southeast, so the beaches weren't appealing. And the place was chock-a-block with people visiting for the spring tour of the Great Mansions.

Charleston is charming. And I made good use of the time by revising the Introductory chapter of *China on My Mind*. I had taken it only as a security measure—not wanting to leave the only copy in existence in my study—but, as it turned out, I went to the public library each morning and polished it.

At Folly Beach, I went over to these two brothers in their 20s, each with a couple of kids. They were surprised I spoke to them. Local whites would not have approached them, they said. One of them I quite liked. We talked—their rural South Carolina accent and vocabulary wasn't easy to follow—and had a drink at a bar sticking out into the Pacific. "Do you like my brother?" one said.

A surprising number of people speak as if the South—or at least South Carolina—is eclipsed by the North, a poor cousin to the Northeast. RT always goes for losers; maybe that's why he likes the South. As Richard Burton said of someone he knew well in the theater, I'm in love with myself, but I don't know whether it's reciprocated.

Maddeningly, the Ansaphone system is working only intermittently. But I did get one nice message while I was away from Boston—*Chicago Tribune* is publishing my China reforms piece. Good to get my name back in the paper on China stuff after the long hiatus of being an Australia-hand.

In between work in the Charleston library, I thought about how not to let myself be unhappy through the unsatisfactory tie with Edward, and I came up four points. Put work first. Will myself to be happy. Slow down. Accept my own separateness as an individual human being, and that of others.

April 4, 1989, Boston

Lunch with Pam at Saint Botolph. She is wildly biased on politics, but otherwise, good fun. She thinks that if I had a steady lover who was also a writer, the gap between private life and public would be less. She even implies that I would be more accepted in the Boston literary community, invited to things more often if that were the situation.

Tonight, Neal. I go all the way to South Carolina for Black sex, but it is here waiting for me.

April 7, 1989, Boston

In the colonoscopy, another polyp was removed. Dr. Taitlebaum did not volunteer that it was certainly benign. "I'm upset," she said when she came to my bedside after I had fully woken up, "I hoped there wouldn't be one."

I was spaced out with the intravenous Demerol and Valium. That afternoon Mike came by. When Jodi called, I invited him around too. The three of us lay on the bed watching a sex movie. I'm not sure I would have mixed these two if I had not been heavily sedated. Then Reggie came in and fucked me—with a condom. This once again was something I might not have invited—since the polyp that was removed was, Dr. Taitlebaum told me, just inside the anus—if I wasn't still spaced out.

April 9, 1989

John Cage[332] music at Kirkland House today. I find it interesting. But Persian scholar Richard Frye stalked out with the comment that, in Iran, music like that appeared in the 1970s and led to the Khomeini fascist revolution! To me, the performance was festive rather than commanding. It plays upon your mind, hardly communicates to your mind.

Afterwards, lunch with Cage, and when he said sounds and noises are the same, I asked him if all the sounds he uses are pre-existent in nature or whether he creates them. He said every sound is new. He reached across to the chair between us, moved it, and said that sound is just made fresh at that moment. I wondered what would happen if, as a writer, I put letters together and made up words. He said why not? I rejoined that I would feel I was failing to communicate. He reckons communication has got a lot to do with the receiver. Strange.

Robert Rauschenberg[333] once gave Cage a completely blank canvas, four plain squares put together. Cage tells me it's the most wonderful thing he's ever been given. He has made it into something of his own; it changes with the light, with dust, with time and position in his house. "It has enormously enriched me."

April 11, 1989

The colonoscopy done by the demur Dr. Greta Taitlebaum is benign. A large polyp, but not cancerous, was removed. It is not inconceivable that it could go cancerous but not suddenly—polyps start out benign, and there is time "to nip them in the bud."

Apparently, I did ruffle Edward's feathers. "I had the same conversation with Larry last night." This remark gave me the shivers. Larry is, I think, the one who "lives with a lover" but sees Edward sometimes as he is "not satisfied" with his lover. So I'm in a category with Larry! All I want, I said, is sincerity and to see you every month or so.

April 12, 1989

Got the Dazu revision and the Cooktown article off to Nancy Sharkey at *The New York Times* as requested. Also, a version of the *World Monitor* article on Chinese reforms to *Actualité* in Montreal and two pieces to *Insight* syndication in Toronto. If tomorrow I can finalize the article for *Memories* on "Looking Back on Mao," shorter pieces will all be done prior to facing the Orient.

Greg N came in, a spark ignited, we made furious love. Then he went off to get some jewelry from a friend who lives nearby. Afterwards, Chris came in. He watched TV as I worked in my study, but I joined him for a while, fucking him as he watched his "ladies" on a video.

---

[332] John Cage (1912-1992), major American composer of post-War avant-garde music.
[333] Robert Rauschenberg (1925-2008), American painter and sculptor.

April 13, 1989

Just as I settle down to work, Michael comes in. He's in a frisky mood. For what seemed an eternity, we lay there, me pumping my prick against his balls. Then he grabbed the two cocks, lying on his back, oiled them, and stroked them till we both came. I went back to work, and he watched movies until it was time for me to play squash with Sergei. Both of us were still smeared in baby oil and Michael's cum.

April 14, 1989, Boston YMCA

The dancer's huge Black dick drove me crazy. He stared at the head of my now-exploding cock. The solid white guy suddenly got up from next to the dancer and went out. I moved beside the dancer and put a hand to his ass. Then the light went out, and the white guy came back in—he'd only gone out to switch it off.

Things intensified. As the white guy sucked the dancer's tits, I moved behind the dancer and got my cock between his magnificent legs. I think the white guy felt the dancer was mainly his, but the dancer seemed to like my attention to his ass.

Still, this was late 80s safe sex. Almost no one was even grabbing someone else's cock in the room, and I didn't get inside the dancer. Soon everyone was sitting down politely jerking off. The dancer came with groans. It was hard for me to prevent myself coming, but I did—I was heading home to see Stu.

April 16, 1989

I am in good shape to get away to the Orient via California tomorrow. Have printed out another draft of the Early 60s chapter of *COMM*, sent articles to *Boston Globe* and *LAT*, and cleared my correspondence box of everything urgent. I even found time last night—having missed Ann and Justin's party for Marilyn French [334] because of misreading the invitation—to phone a few people. Mum sounded down, self-pitying, and weak. She cheered up only when I assured her I would come again this summer.

Li-li said she will miss me (only three weeks!). Terrible weather here. It will be a pleasure to get to California and the *Ocean Pearl* [335] under the sunny skies of the China coast.

Greg N comes in to get his air ticket. He looks tired. I have to rush down to the Y to put some copies of disks into my locker, and when I get back, he's jerked off watching *Sex Messengers*." I feel disappointed. Yet 20 minutes later, we are making love, and in the end, he comes a second time. He is nervous about his California trip, meeting me there on my way back from Asia.

April 19, 1989 San Rafael

In San Francisco, impressive to see the Oriental newsboys, handsome, proud. I hope it was all right to leave Foell with that China article; if China events move fast, *World*

---

[334] Marilyn French (1929-2009), Feminist writer. Her most famous book was *The Women's Room* (1977).
[335] The 480-passenger cruise ship was the first non-Chinese vessel to navigate the Yangzi River.

Monitor might go with it half-baked (he doesn't like the term half-cocked). Good to see Chunyi again.

The Los Angeles Times seems quite excited by my column they are running this week; the *Toledo Blade* also. The two lectures at the genteel college here also went well—good to see all these people fired up reading one of my books.

I try the whirlpool in this Courtyard Marriot. GTO avoid having wet shorts in my luggage, I went in the nude—delicious feeling.

In late April, Terrill returned to China for another lecture cruise on the Pearl of Scandinavia. *At Beijing University, he saw evidence of the nascent democracy movement.*

Taipei

A dream flight last night. When had I last got an answer to a call button in coach? The trick may be to treat a long coach trip as a bus trip and expect nothing.

In my red tracksuit from South Carolina, I go to the President Sauna and luxuriate in the hot pool. A perfect recovery after a 14-hour flight. In the pool, vaguely familiar faces; is that not Rupert, the dancer, who I fucked when I was just getting TB years ago? Good news from Julia at *Sawasdee* magazine: she wants the Sichuan food article. If she takes Dazu, she will need slides, she says.

April 22, 1989, Hong Kong

Reading *Deng*—a depressing book as to quality, and I will have to say so in my review. The English language is clearly in decline here. A meeting in the Shangri-La Hotel with Henry that did not rise above the cordial.

April 26, 1989, Beijing

I ask a cabbie about the meetings the students have been holding; he simply replies, *mei you yong,* "no use." He goes on, "After two thousand years of feudalism, with Mao just like emperor Qin Shihuang,[336] and a hundred years of reform, with Deng Xiaoping just like Li Hongzhang,[337] how can the students change much in a few months?"

My Jiang Qing bio[338] is either sold out (common) or not stocked; my *Mao* I cannot find sign of it ever having been stocked.

April 29, 1989, Qingdao

My lecture on Jiang Qing is evidently a triumph—lots of women come up on deck later to say they want to read all about her.

Thirty-five Chinese officials invite themselves on board for lunch; envy leaps out from their faces as they tour the ship after the feast. A handsome Turkish sailor gets me

---

[336] Qin Shihuang (259 -210 BCE), unifier and first emperor of China.

[337] Li Hongzhang (1823-1901), pro-modern Chinese politician and general, described as "the yellow Bismarck."

[338] *Madam Mao: The White-Boned Demon.* Both this biography and his biography of Mao had just been published in Chinese translations.

into a mutual jerk-off session, though by the end I am thinking of a certain Black man in Boston.

April 30, 1989, Shanghai

This city looks better than a decade ago. Half close your eyes, and you could be in a backward part of Japan. On board the ship, I spend a lovely quiet morning on *China in our Time*. On land, I try to phone Greg N once more—again, not home. Back on board, the skies are gray, the sea rises.

May 2, 1989, Nanjing

In the lobby of the hotel, a box with the unexpected message, "Help the Needy." What needy, in the Communist paradise of China? The Party sees to all, does it not?

Good news from *The New York Times*—they love the Dazu article and are rushing it into production. The collective editing is effective and unusual and recalls Communist China or a Catholic seminary.

At the Jinling Hotel, breakfast for 300, a grotesque concept, and a grotesque spectacle. Then as the tour departs for the environs of Nanjing, peace. I think it is the condescension of leaders and guides which wears people out on tours. Will the Pearl run aground once more in the Yangzi?

Here am I, a difficult writer, trying to pretend I am a hail fellow well met, ordinary guy—it is more of a strain than being a difficult writer. I stay personally enigmatic to the passengers. What you say is more interesting if you hold back much. Some women passengers, knowing little, speculate that I was once involved with Jiang Qing!

May 4, 1989, South China Sea

Met a friendly travel editor at the *Sunday Times* of London, and maybe I have sold him the Dazu story.

The trip has been wonderful—only the weather disappointed me; one hour of sun, at 6 PM, just like Melbourne! The Filipino cabin boys would have been a disappointment had I now known in advance not to expect anything from them. A few hundred dollars in book sales.

Will Greg N be in San Francisco to link up with me on my return flight from Hong Kong? Today I went shopping in Amoy with the passengers, receiving compliments for my lectures. Then a movie, sauna, and a glass of champagne as I look back on the last day on Chinese soil of this pleasant cruise.

May 6, 1989, San Francisco

I check into a run-down hotel in an interesting neighborhood and meet a guy, half Dutch and half Indonesian. The whites, who make up 90%, are less attractive than at the Boston Y.

I meet Greg N at the airport and he looks great. We pop round a few bars—Badlands, Phoenix, among them—and go home to bed at 3 AM.

In the morning, we have sex, but, after the cruise, I do not feel physically well-tuned and it reduces my sexual edge, both in giving and receiving. Not to speak of the truly crumby room we were in, which looked even worse in the morning than the night before.

A nice walk around Fisherman's Wharf and the Hologram. Then lunch with Shen and his wife—an interesting foursome. Greg is fascinated by the Chinese cigarettes. Later, Greg does not feel well, even after we move to a nicer hotel on Market Street. He makes phone calls back to Boston with premature judgments about San Francisco. As he sleeps, I go for a drink at Blue and Gold and then Cable's Reef. Meet a Laotian. I like Asian men, especially the sounds they make when having sex. "Come to my boat," he says. I want to—then he discovers I write and is scared.

May 7, 1989, San Francisco

Greg N is not well, so I am a lot on my own. At a seedy cinema, I get turned on by the maneuvers. Tried for a 3-together jerkoff scene, but when that did not materialize, a double Black jerkoff scene at the back did—both handsome, lovely skin, one with fantastic chest, neck, nipples.

In the back room, Number 2 sucks my tits, then I start "fucking" him from behind. The die seemed to be cast for coming as he sucked, kissed, or tit-sucked Number 1, who meanwhile pulled down my red pants and played with my ass. Everything you could want.

My dick got grabbed, the guy was trying to fuck me. Too dark, so the combination moved to where there was more light. Now, total passion as Number 2's little blue shorts came down. I think he wanted Number 1 to fuck him, but I did instead. I looked at Number 1 as I screwed Number 2, and as he returned the gaze and grabbed my ass, I shot in torrents. Running through my mind: will Greg still be feeling ill, or will he want it; should I spend my orgasm here, or save it. Too late.

May 10, 1989, Boston

This "love" thing—I seem to care about him as much as I care about myself. When he comes into my house, I brighten; when he phones, I am pleased. Fascinating about love is the degree to which we love being loved; you get excited by someone in part because that person likes you so much.

He told me what he likes about me: intellect, we fit together in sex, I am Australian, older and don't do dumb things, candid, I pay attention to him. What he likes much less: wine, I get difficult when no sex, obsessiveness, possessiveness.

I have learned things from Edward: that I have an addictive streak, learned sex techniques, especially fucking, how to enjoy the present moment and that I tend to dramatize everything.

Sexually, I don't think I have taught him much, despite my extra experience—except to smear each other in honey and cream and lick it off.

I cannot work out the mixture of solicitude and naked selfishness in his approach to me. He seems to steer certain situations away from threesomes yet seize on them if the third person is unavailable to him other than through me. I said to him, if you pick up a white guy, just disappear with him; if it is a Black guy, bring him here—I may watch, or if everyone wants, I may join in. At squash, I win 3-2 over Nat. Edward and Steven quarrel. "He paid no attention to me; went to sleep as I talked."

Laurent came in and said he had been trying to call. After a long phone talk with Shen in the Midwest, I confided to Laurent that Edward wanted him, but Laurent said he was here only to study. The clocks do not always chime in synchronization.

May 13, 1989

Got the last of the books off to passengers from the *Pearl,* who paid for copies of my works by mail—all signed and inscribed.

It is good to be back at the bench press, and the arms show some results. Yet it is puzzling that the stomach is so little affected—these days—either by excessive eating (as on the *Pearl*) or by cutting back (since my return); only lying on the sloping board really flattens my stomach, but it is such a pain to do.

May 16, 1989

The *Nightline* producer calls to say thanks for last night. Unusual. I think one reason was he felt the balance of the show, as between Orville and me, had tipped too far into Orville's lap. The thank-you was a kind of apology. No problem; having a little credit with Ted at *Nightline* is no bad thing.

"The man you want, Greg N, is being checked for trouble. Please try your affair later." Dream?

May 18, 1989

After several false starts, Charles S and I got together, and the delay was worth it. We did everything, amazingly so for a first meeting. In the course of it, he said most of the things one could ever wish someone to say: "You're amazing; I love you; I can't believe this; don't stop, please don't stop!"

May 19, 1989

The days fly by with everything made tense and hectic by the Chinese crisis.[339] I put the *World Monitor* piece on the reforms to bed—again—and then began a round of interviews: *Nightline*, Canadian radio, TV's *One Norway Street*. All the while, the line that comes over from most commentators disturbs me. Few are clear that the political systemic issue is basic: a CP [Communist party] is a CP, and democracy is something else.

---

[339] On April 15, Chinese had students began pro-democracy demonstrations in Beijing's Tiananmen Square. By May, the protests had spread to several hundred other Chinese cities.

Tonight, all seemed to be quieting down, and Neal came in. We were together in the shower when NPR rang from Washington. Could I go on the air live with Noah Adams in four minutes?

I did, and the producer called back ten minutes later—by then, Neal and I were in bed—to say it was the best segment they have had all week.

May 20, 1989

Another half day goes on Chinese events, phone calls from friends in China, devouring the news, giving background to the media.

These are lovely spring days when Boston sparkles and the phone at last stops.

Reggie comes in and my cock just goes crazy. I shot big all over the green sheets. Reggie, after a year of marriage, has taken on a mature, almost noble look. He says of Cedrik, "He needs convincing that some men are attracted—not to other men—but to women. He thought the whole world was gay."

At Ramone's place, the gorgeous James looks at me intently when, listening to Joan Sutherland singing, I say, "Ah, my countryman." Then he pronounces: "Yes, the chin, I see it."

May 22, 1989

I was upstairs with Wyatt when Laurent comes in. A little later, the doorbell rings. I am busy on the phone, so the others let in Brian, of all people. It turns out he and Wyatt had met. There was a funny look in Laurent's eye when I introduced him to Brian. To my amazement, Brian, who is strictly into Steven, came on to me on the back deck. Mass Ave was crowded, and Laurent was in the living room, but still, this horny Georgian pulled out my dick and began sucking it.

I did an NPR Interview while Laurent slept next door in my bed. Then, after Laurent went to work, a threesome developed between Wyatt, Brian, and me. But I had to interrupt to do a *White-Boned Demon* interview. Only after Wyatt left did Brian and I really get it on—great fun.

May 23, 1989

Final, final version of reforms piece for *World Monitor* off to Earl Foell—has any piece ever gone through so much for so little? Tagore's words are fine: "Your idol is shattered in the dust to prove that God's dust is greater than your idol." In that transcendence, there is freedom.

May 24, 1989

Edward is here, and after we go to bed, I just can't sleep for excitement. When are we going to do it, I keep wondering. We had embraced when he came to bed, and my roaring cock pushed against his lovely tummy and thighs. He held me and went to go to sleep within an embrace—this isn't an easy position for me to sleep in.

"I have an infection," he said gently when, as passion stirred in both of us, I went to suck him. For a moment, I thought he meant the HIV virus, but he meant the current problem—some infection in the urinary tract, it seems. So we avoided some things. But after putting on a condom, he screwed me delightfully.

Breakfast at Thornton's, a favorite of his, as we talked about his hope to go to California and study psychology. I went over to *World Monitor*. When I got back, I found, not one, but two men in my bed. That morning at 7:30, when Edward and I were making love for the second time, the buzzer rang, but I did not answer it. At the time, I murmured to Edward that it was probably Michael. Of course, his curiosity being insatiable, he would have liked me to invite Mike up, but we were in full swing, and I didn't.

Mike, it turned out, came back later, while I was over at Earl's, and Edward buzzed him in and said, "Ross will be back soon." They had not had time to do anything—"I never even saw his cock," Edward lamented afterwards.

May 25, 1989, Boston

Who should come in but Laurent! He gave Mike a quick, disapproving glance. Edward was leaving for his Fenway appointment about the same time as Laurent was off to class. "Can you drive me?" Edward asked gaily. As they drove, Edward got Laurent's phone number. So enmity has turned to warmth. Poor Laurent is so horny, I think, that he'd fuck a dog.

May 27, 1989

I am with Reggie when Tara, producer for Ted Koppel at ABC phones to ask "a bizarre question." Could I go to China next week and help Ted do a prime-time special on the current events in the Middle Kingdom? Reggie is in the lobby, itching for something or other. I told Tara I would think about it. She said Ted would phone me in half an hour to pin it down. Reggie said he wanted me to type out his résumé there and then.

I told Koppel I would do it. I am to go down to DC on Memorial Day for a conference with him to go through the plan. So much for my long weekend. And can I do for Ted what he expects me to do? He has all the video, he said. He wants me to probe the background to how and why it all happened.

June 1, 1989

Arrived exhausted at Logan only to find the United Airlines nonstop to San Francisco is delayed by hours. Perhaps I will not go out on the town tonight in SF—perhaps it may be best to stay at an airport hotel.

Terrill arrived in Beijing on the evening of June 3.

June 3, 1989, Beijing

Three days ago, a Chinese diplomat at the New York PRC Consulate said, "It's all over and everything is returning to normal." Three evenings later, Beijing airport is not normal. Customs officials ignored my luggage and declaration form. My flight from Tokyo was the last international flight into Beijing for the night, next day, and beyond. Outside the terminal, many taxis, few passengers. One cabbie, with eyes averted, asked an outrageous 180 yuan to take me into the city. "It's complicated and dangerous to drive into that part of Beijing," said a second driver, asking 220 yuan after we had begun the trip.

Bumping down dusty ill-lit lanes, we were on a checkerboard of trial and error as passersby leaned toward the taxi window with advice on which streets were tractable. Cream and red-painted public buses were parked to block military vehicles. Students in red or blue headbands were speaking to the crowds about corruption and the need for democracy, and arguing to nearby troops that the army should not advance to Tiananmen.

"Don't go into the streets. In particular, don't go near Tiananmen Square," said the Chinese language taxi radio as we neared the Palace Hotel, where I had a reservation. "Citizens of Beijing, stay in your homes." It was ten o'clock in the evening. I headed for the square.

"There is war!" said a pedicab driver, as he quoted a fare five times the norm to pedal me from the Palace Hotel to Tiananmen Square. "I could be arrested."

As we rolled down Beijing's leading shopping street of Wang Fu Jing, the air was turbulent with shouts and sirens. When the pedicab reached Chang An Avenue and the Beijing Hotel, my driver had to stop in the face of a huge, agitated crowd facing west toward Tiananmen.

I have come upon an extraordinary cat-and-mouse game between the Chinese military and a citizenry with anti-government emotions on the boil. Armies were inching toward the city for days, but as they advanced, they were resisted by tens of thousands of people. The city was full of damaged military vehicles stopped by the cunning of the populace.

Later

It is not yet midnight and still possible to go into Tiananmen Square in my pedicab. Through rising coils of smoke, I make out the giant portrait of Mao that hangs at Tiananmen (the Gate itself). As I draw near it, the tall white student-erected statue of the Goddess of Democracy, its surface looking as smooth as marshmallow, looms from the south. My pedicab whirs between Mao and the goddess.

As I moved around on foot or in my pedicab, the student radio, *Voice of the Hunger Strikers*, speaks of democracy and determination to attain it. "Democracy is something everyone builds gradually on a proper foundation," rebuts the government radio from near the Great Hall of the People. "Tiananmen Square is a sacred place."

Students and workers draw close on their bicycles to chat. "What do you think of our movement?" "Please take care of yourself." It is part of the camaraderie of these hours that people share information with cheerfulness and good humor, and the foreigner is welcomed.

"Have you heard the one about Li Peng?" says a rakish young man in a straw hat, and I motioned my driver to speed up so I could listen. "'Premier Li,' says this citizen, 'how come we ordinary folk haven't benefitted from all the foreign money that floats around China?' And Li Peng says, 'The people have received things: we've imported tear gas specially for you.'"

Soldiers were jogging into the eastern fringe of the square past the Museum of the Chinese Revolution. "Go home, we don't need you," a young man cried to a row of troops. "We are all Chinese," a girl shouted in an appeal against the use of force.

My driver sighs with relief as he swings into Wang Fu Jing. "Were the Martin Luther King demonstrations like that?" he asks as we find ourselves in a more normal street setting. "I suppose they were in a way," I say, groping a little.

"Did you have as many people in the streets as we saw here tonight?" he inquires.

"About the same."

He jerks his head sharply sideways to look at me. "You know, mister, we shall overcome too." We turn into Goldfish Lane. "You know, I carried the students for free," the driver says as he pockets his large fee for our dangerous foray. "Didn't charge them a penny." Why was that?

"Because they're doing something," he goes on.

Terrill went to his hotel, scribbled down some notes, then returned to the streets.

Leaving the hotel lobby, as I head back toward the streets, a green-uniformed concierge says to me: "If they kill the students, I will attack them myself." A fresh pedicab driver, making good business out of danger, uses the same argument to bargain with me, but with extra resonance. "It's war," he says. "War or civil war, I could be killed."

Angrier, now, were the confrontations between regular troops gathering at the square and agitated crowds backing up the students' last-ditch struggle from Chang An Avenue and other streets east of the square. On all sides were shouts, smoke, and cursing of soldiers. Rocks, bottles, and chunks of flagstone were being thrown toward the massed troops. I could not hope to enter the square again.

"Stand on the bicycle seat and you'll get a better snapshot," cried a bystander as I readied my camera to photograph wrecked buses and smoke puffing irreverently around the Mao portrait and the Goddess of Democracy.

From the west, a move—or was it just a threat of one?—by the soldiers who now seemed installed in Tiananmen Square sent people scurrying.

"They're going to shoot," someone called out, and all of us flew eastward, bumping each other as we turned and ran, my pedicab driver maneuvering his vehicle in the new direction as best he could. The flagstones beneath our feet were littered with the debris of street fighting.

T T T T T T....T T T T T T....T T T T T T. For years, that sound for me in China meant firecrackers, but tonight it meant gunshots. The firing was close, offensive, terrifying. Deng Xiaoping's soldiers were firing on unarmed crowds in the streets of

Beijing for the first time since the revolution in 1949. "Tell the world our government has gone mad," a woman cried to me, tears running down her face.

A near-festival atmosphere ended as fifty meters ahead, on Chang An Avenue, gunfire rang out and people at the front of the crowd fell down. We surged back, turned around, and fled helter-skelter to the east. Where the crowd had made contact with the troops, to the west, the Gate of Heavenly Peace had become a gate of tumult.

My pedicab driver and I argued. "If you stop, it's dangerous," he gasped. "You look suspicious. Let's keep moving." Hot, shocked, nervous, I objected, "But I want to talk to people!" I would instruct the driver to pedal me deeper into the crowd, keeping to the darker edges of Qian Men Wai. Then shots would crackle, cries of horror and alarm would rise from the front of the crowd, and impatiently I would urge him to turn around and flee, grabbing his waist in my eagerness to have him whip us to safety.

Incredulity spread across central Beijing like a whirlwind. Sustained crackles of gunfire close by made me retreat north along Zheng Yi (Righteousness) Street. About 4 AM, I reached the Beijing Hotel. "Two young people fell dead at my feet," a woman screamed. Holding her spectacles in her hand and looking upwards from the pavement, she begged me: "Please tell the truth about our land!"

I took an elevator to the seventeenth floor, hoping to view Chang An Avenue and Tiananmen from on high, but a white-jacketed man at the service desk stopped me from stepping onto his balcony.

"There's nothing to see," he said in the familiar style of a Chinese government gatekeeper. It was the first time all night, starting with Beijing airport, that I met a hand of authority.

Picking at random a lower floor, the twelfth, I found a guest room open and peered inside. Four Hong Kong businessmen were on the balcony. They were speaking emotionally in Cantonese. I crept into the room. So preoccupied were the quartet with the scene below on Chang An Avenue that I remained unnoticed beside a bed near the window. Beneath us, the front entrance of the hotel was barricaded with buses, minibuses, and trucks.

"Excuse me," I said, "could I watch with you from the balcony for a moment?" One Hong Kong businessman replied, "As long as you're not from the press." Another burst into English out of mental turmoil: "It's the last straw! China is finished!"

Since my third pedicab driver had abandoned me, I found myself walking slowly north on Wang Fu Jing toward the Palace Hotel. Despite the presence of troops, citizens clustered to report news on the night's events, quiz each other, and offer ever-ready analysis. Not for years had Beijing people known such a sense of participation in news as it was made. The resulting feeling of citizenship did a little to mitigate the tragedy that engulfed Beijing.

A hubbub arose near the green-roofed Capital Hospital. Ambulances came and went, exhausted nurses and doctors mopped their brows as they moved along the verandas, and tense crowds pressed toward the hospital gates seeking news of family or friends. Near the Wang Fu Jing department store, fifty soldiers standing by two trucks stared at me. These dark-skinned, round-faced young men obviously were not from Beijing, and not northerners. Buses and trucks barricaded the Palace Hotel's doors. "It is for your protection," a flustered hotel manager said. "The trouble in the streets could overflow in here."

Just before 5 AM, I fell into bed, 30 odd hours after leaving Boston, and on the pillow was a chocolate mint and a card from the Palace Hotel management with a quotation from Shakespeare's Macbeth: "Sleep that knits up the ravel'd sleeve of care, the death of each day's life, balm of hurt minds, great nature's second course..."

June 4, 1989

I awoke to the sound of gunfire and the sight of black smoke rising above parts of the city. On foot, reaching a lane by Capital Hospital on the way to Tiananmen, I came upon knots of people dissecting the night's bloody events with an openness that still made the foreigner welcome.

A shocked populace amidst the wreckage of street warfare was asking itself how and when China would recover from the night's trauma. An older man said an era was ending, and the Communist dynasty dating from 1949 had run its course.

The lobby of the Beijing Hotel resembled scenes of a civilization submerged by the flow of lava from a volcano. On the café tables, half-eaten sandwiches, full ashtrays, and dishes of ice cream turned to liquid bespoke the rude intrusions of the night. Chairs were strewn or piled high, and the bar, restaurants, and shops were dark. I went up to the seventh-floor restaurant in the old wing of the hotel to view Tiananmen. "There will be no lunch," a waitress said with impeccable logic, "because there are no people."

From the restaurant balcony, I saw a phalanx of tanks in the square, looking like even-toothed, murky-green dragons, with a row of soldiers in front of them facing Chang An Avenue. Between Tiananmen and the Beijing Hotel, a further 15 tanks were arrayed on Chang An. A teenager beside me cut through the analyses of his elders, "We have no guns; that's the curse of it. If only the people had guns!"

As people talked angrily in random groups, the Chinese words for "warlord" and "crazy" recurred. I asked a woman who said she had been in the vanguard of the crowd exactly what had just happened in broad daylight. "People shouted insults at the soldiers," she replied, "and some threw rocks at them. The soldiers opened fire and shot at us, at first at our feet, and then higher up. Some people were killed."

As smoke curled into the sky that afternoon, I left the Beijing Hotel, torn with emotions, and went to the Catholic cathedral, Nan Tang, southwest of Tiananmen Square. Mass was over, there were few people in and around the sanctuary, and the cathedral compound was a welcome place of retreat. I found a youth sitting in meditation within the gray stone walls of the compound.

Zhu Yasheng was a 16-year-old middle school student, who had marched with other Christians behind a banner that read, "THE LORD LOVES YOU, LONG LIVE DEMOCRACY." Zhu's father was a master chef for senior government leaders, his mother worked in the Communist Party secretariat of Beijing city, and no one else in the family—only Yasheng—was a Catholic. I asked why he had become a Catholic. He gave a smile that suggested both innocence and passion, and replied, "Because in China there is nothing you can believe in."

Over the next week, Terrill talked to ordinary Chinese citizens about what had happened. Many felt that any meaningful reform had been stalled. One friend told him, "There are only two ways out for people like us: go abroad or go into business." On June 9, Deng Xiaoping announced that the "counter-revolution" had been crushed.

"Beijing had seen three epochs within the span of three weeks," Terrill later wrote. "A festival of Jeffersonian freedom in late May; guns Molotov cocktails, bleeding bodies, and the wail of ambulance sirens on June 3 and after; and now, Orwellian repression.... My Chinese friends' dismay, fear, and dashed hopes pulled me away from my role as a 'China watcher' and put me beside them as I had not felt before."

Later that month, Terrill left Beijing and flew to southern China for some R & R.

June 18, 1989, Canton

At Shamian,[340] where I stay in a new hotel, wrought iron fences, shuttered windows that stretch outwards. Streets are lined with trees, and there are little side gardens too. On park benches, little notices: "Please don't sleep here"—but people do. The fact that the bench is too short for an adult to sleep is probably significant, an encouragement to adherence to the law. Window frames in faded green, stone in faded mustard. Battlements which announce an extra dimension of confidence to the building, a statement of projection into the world, like that of empire across the globe—facing out, defiant in a way.

Little food shops, now TV College of Good, a mixture of nondescript blocks, tall white oblong of White Swan Hotel. Ugly blue corrugated iron half shelters for bikes. A tree labeled *ficus lacor*.

Small shops take names from hotels—White Swan this and that. A kid wears "Thailand" on his T-shirt; does he know what or who it is? Absolute confusion of styles, parts look like Macao. No

architectural harmony. There are still, as there were when I first saw Shamian, many service organizations, for shipping, trade, links with the world. Far more consumer places than before: nightclubs, cafés, inns. Among the people, there is more drinking than before.

Family planning notice, another to congratulate everyone on May Day. Here's a building with a real turret and a dunce-cap-type roof at the corners. Opposite is the Guangdong Navigation Institute in a building like a small-town motel. Another tree, *ficus retusa*.

Girls with sunshades, boys in parks reading manuals about making money or getting out of the country. One mansion is being repainted in a brilliant lipstick pink— destined to be a club or restaurant. Badminton courts have grown up around the tennis courts, to blend the Chinese with the foreign, all surrounded by gum trees. Kids play on a huge cannon pointed out over the Pearl.

---

[340] Shamian, literally "sandy surface," is an island off the mainland of Guangzhou (Canton), China, important during the European colonial period and now the location of several hotels, restaurants and tourist sites.

A branch of Beneton by the hotel, and Adidas sporting clothes are the rage. Broad hats against the sun on men and women alike—a certain class and age in the case of the men.

Yang and Feng came by at lunchtime. I had expected Yang alone. Also, they were an hour late, which pissed me off. But the reason for the latter problem was that both guys keep their watches on Hong Kong time! An index of their sense of exile in their own country. The reason for the former I knew intellectually, but again and again, one tries to deal with Chinese as individuals—often to be disappointed.

But in this case, the outcome was fine. We ate—they ordered Italian dishes, everything Western: pizza, milk, coffee, spaghetti. While I watched them eat, I spawned the idea of asking them—Feng mainly—if he would help me with my book by being interviewed about gay life in China. They talked interestingly, and with courage. After that was over, I noticed we had no cigarettes and asked Feng if he would mind going downstairs to buy some. He fell into this trap. While he was away, I drew near to Yang and embraced him.

The physical nearness, the holding itself, seemed like a defense against the anomie that comes from living under a dictatorship. Of course, you're never really free of the fear of being raided, at least listened to, so in the end, you do feel inhibited even as you feel the joy of the intimacy. We sucked each other's tits. He didn't really know how to work them; he just stuck his mouththere and left it.

Then he went to the bathroom. By the time he came back, I was lying on the bed, and he came straight over and began to stroke my body. He opened my pants and was just tickling my balls when Feng arrived back with the God-damned cigarettes. I embraced Feng, too, to keep things balanced. Something had been established with Yang—and Feng.

I walked around Shamian. It is more recognizable than the Dong Fang area as compared with 20 years ago—mainly because of the layout and the atmosphere those British buildings give, and because you can't pull down more than so many trees. I would hardly have recognized the Dong Fang, so much built around it, new and jazzier signs on it, shops and cafes in the Hong Kong style nestle around it.

The Chinese must be the rudest people in the world. How refreshing it would be to get an apology sometimes, when a mistake is made, something goes wrong, or a regrettable incident occurs. How nice it would be for someone to hold the door other than when they are paid to do so. In Shijiazhuang what I encountered, and have seen in other places, is highly-organized lawlessness.

By late June, Terrill was back in Boston.

June 25, 1989. Boston

This virus is making rather slow progress through my system. I should get more rest, but the enticements of *The Australians* manuscript and Black flesh are hard to resist. In the street, I pass the little Black guy I sometimes see cruising at Northeastern. In the nature of things, we don't speak—let alone know each other's names—but today something made me glance at this guy (instead of glancing away) as we passed in

Huntington Avenue. He was looking straight at me, and he was beaming! Amazing—why? Out went his arm to my shoulder as he continued his broad smile.

I had never seen him smile before, and he looks nice when he smiles. "I saw you on *Nightline*." You were perfect—just perfect."

Wonderful sex with Danny this afternoon. "I want to come today, too," he said with a smile as we climbed into bed. I noticed that fucking him seemed to get him nice and randy for his own orgasm.

Bad news about his girlfriend. She was raped by a gang. They hit her in the face with a hammer. Two days in hospital. Danny comments: "You know, some guys don't know how to approach a girl. They end up hitting her 'cos they don't know how to talk to her."

July 2, 1989

A golden day with Edward. We took a boat to Nantasket beach, lay in the sun, swam, talk of many things. "There are more beautiful men in the world than beautiful women," he remarked as we walked along the foreshore. He really does take delight in swimming, seeing a new place. On board the boat, he had brought on watermelon and doughnuts for us to eat. In the early evening, we dined at a seafood restaurant. Then took the boat home, showered, went to bed early, made long and delicious love.

For the first time, he smeared me with honey—tits, cock, asshole—and licked it off. His tongue went far inside me, hungrily, obsessively, and then he began to fuck me, upside down, sideways,

front-ways, until I sat on him for the last bout. Afterwards, he labeled the honey jar so that only I would eat from it. "Because I put my finger in it after my finger had been up your asshole." Later he went alone to see *Batman* as I went happily to sleep.

July 3, 1989

Edward slept late, and I woke him up just as Li-li arrived for lunch and a session with a draft of part of *COMM*. The China events deeply stirred Li-li. "Never have I followed world news as much as these past weeks." Before my brother Peter arrived, Edward made the bed, tidied up the videos, set the little room straight. He wanted Peter to have a good impression. I was touched by this.

July 4, 1989

A warm feeling inside about being in America for July 4, after having been in China for June 4!

At 5 AM, I continued work on my memos for tomorrow in NY. An outline for *National Geographic* in case McCarry wants to go ahead with an article now rather than wait for the total coverage of "Chinese Youth" that we originally envisaged. And a book outline for Simon & Schuster, to give Fred a chance to bite on that, as an alternative to ploughing the Massacre material into *COMM*.

Back home, Cornell comes by. I wasn't planning anything, yet the Wild Thing crept up on me. We showered. Suddenly he began rimming me, the deepest, strongest, wildest tongue lashing my asshole can remember. Soon I came in his mouth. Cornell mentioned that last week his "ex-boyfriend Frank" fucked him, and it hurt terribly, and he bled. Frank said, "It will take a week for you to recover."

July 5, 1989, New York

Barbara came in to see me at the Harvard Club, and we talked over the China material ready for lunch with Fred. I gave her the new outline for a "Massacre" piece for *National Geographic*. I also showed her the outline for a book on the subject, but, like Fred, she leans strongly to ploughing the stuff into *COMM*.

In pouring rain, we went over to the Sea Grill. Over dishes of absurd price, we heard Fred say that *COMM*, now, will not only be a successful seller but a book likely to win a prize. "Your career is poised for that, I think. We would expect to be putting this up for a Pulitzer." Barbara seems to rise three inches in her Queen Anne chair.

After I told the story of my trip to Hebei and the huge sales of my *Mao* in Chinese, Fred made a very welcome suggestion. When *COMM* is coming out, he said, perhaps Simon & Schuster should at the same time bring out a trade paperback of both *The White-Boned Demon* and *Mao*. I gobbled up the suggestion, though, when the time comes, I think I will urge a twin edition, pruned of the notes, and mass paperback.

Fred was quite smitten by my TV appearances from China—quoting what I'd said on the *Today Show*. I remarked that it would be nice if *we* could choose the timing of my appearances on *Today*. "Ah, it will be different next time," Fred said with a gleam in his eye.

Zhou Yiliang[341] came to see me at the Harvard Club. At his age, he must experience fear, dismay, amazement at the Communist Party he trusted and served for so many years.

Afterwards, I was too tired to venture into any of my usual haunts or to phone friends. In the muggy, rainy early evening, I went to La Guardia. Once again, my shuttle flight was plagued with mechanical problems and substantially delayed.

July 7, 1989

Long talk on the phone with Edward—his answering machine has been playing up again, and he doesn't always get my messages. He has been depressed for two days—despite sex with two new people.

At night he calls again to say the roses arrived. His mother took receipt of them. She saw the card and nodded in approval at the birthday greeting: "Happy Birthday to a Wonderful Person, Whose Days are a Blessing to Many. 30 down, 60 more to come—Roscoe."

---

[341] Zhou Yiliang (1913–2001), prominent Chinese historian. His memoir, *Just a Scholar: The Memoirs of Zhou Yiliang*, was published posthumously in 2014.

The doorbell rings and it's "Alan." I thought from the voice, and from the fact that I know only one Alan, that it was "NY Alan." While I was still talking to Edward, in comes this unfamiliar lean, dark guy. He said we met last winter on Westland Avenue. I guess I am a taste that takes a few months to mature. We had a very nice time indeed. He nearly bit my tits off, which is

just what I felt like.

The summer gets to me: this morning I went to bed with José, the Salvadoran I met yesterday at the showers, this afternoon with Johnny, the straight guy from Missouri, and, in between times, played around with a big Black guy I met at the YMCA in mid-afternoon. I am glad I saved my orgasm up for Alan—long and abundant.

July 9, 1989

I can't call it a first—perhaps a third—but it was daring and fun: sex amidst the books on the third floor of the Dodge Library. And with someone I already know!

It was Junior, and both of us had entered the library minutes after its noon-time opening. Almost empty. He was concentrating hard on his economics text when I came up on him. Soon he had a hand up my wide-legged blue shorts. I had no underpants on, so he soon had my cock in that strong black paw. I began to massage his neck and shoulders. He wondered perhaps if we should stop. So did I—but we didn't. I moved in between the shelves, pulled down my blue shorts, and beckoned him. He walked over, his huge dick making a wreckage of his gray pants.

In the afternoon, Neal calls and it turns out to be a great visit. He wanted a shower; this he had, together with me. In the shower, I found out he wanted something else; I all but fucked him under the water, but he said at one point, how about we move to the bed. It was an excellent idea. I could hardly believe that, not only was I screwing the famous macho, Neal, but that he was wiggling his ass to get more of my "white Australian dick."

July 10, 1989

A bit of sex with Wyatt before and after he does some errands for me. His legs look better since I watched Edward fuck him.

Barbara calls to say she "loves" chapter two of *COMM*—the part on 1964. 3ock indeed. We got into a threesome—the third guy didn't turn me on—and given its limits, it was very exciting. The guy had dark, brooding eyes. His balls were as big and magnificent as his dick.

July 11, 1989

Lunch with David Zweig[342] at Dolphin. David said our ABC program was "really excellent." I still haven't seen it, and he finds it strange that I haven't. It's the same with

---

[342] David Zweig (1950 -), Canadian-born China expert.

something I've written; once it's published, I have no desire (for months at least) to read it.

Went to see Dr. Westbrook, Susy's replacement, during her maternity leave, at HCHP.[343] Many tests, and she gives me an antibiotic for my throat and some white mixture for my stomach.

She thinks I have a virus from China. "You're not fifty," she said when she came into the room. "You *can't* be fifty!" And later she said it was great to meet a famous author. Gee, I should be charging her for the meeting.

Late at night, a long talk with Edward on the phone. He has received his birthday watch and likes it very much. Tonight, he went to a group therapy session which makes him feel better. He told the group he felt "confused, angry," and somehow, in ways I do not fully understand, they made him feel better.

He asked me what I am going to do for my birthday, and we tentatively decided to get together the weekend afterwards, August 26-27. He said, "I love you," and the words tingled down my tired spine. And he said that old phrase which I love so much, "What am I going to do with you!" It not only made my day; it will make my week, my month.

July 12, 1989

I do a CSM Radio program with Pat Bodner. I had a headache, and also the questions were not terribly sharp. The result—except where we got into a historical view, how things differ from 25 years ago—was probably rather ordinary.

I loved the sight of Alan in his khaki shorts. It was like meeting a guy by the river in a south Georgian township. This turned me on, and soon he was sucking me beautifully. He has a terrible cough; I wonder if mine came from him last week—I noticed it then, but thought nothing of it at the time.

Mark comes in to borrow my fan and sucks me off for a while. He has improved enormously at that particular act. I still get very turned on by his eyes. He wants me to fuck him again, and I think I will—given the right opportunity.

Wonderful sex with Greg N, it went on and on, as I like, and when I came, it was an orgasm that did not want to end. I remarked—in a sub-conscious quote from Edward, I suppose—that the second burst of cum had gone as far as Chicago. "More like LA, I'd say," said Greg with a lovely smile.

We dined at Thai Cuisine—very nice—and when we got back, the doorbell rang and it was Reggie. Hardly had he got in when he said to me, "Can I see you alone for a moment?" Greg felt he should leave, said goodbye, and was off. In the study, Reggie simply handed over the jewelry and soon after went downstairs to join Caroline, who was waiting in the car. I realize Greg may be hurt; certainly it is unlikely he realized that Reggie had only drawn me aside alone in order to give me the stuff.

Greg shows a stoicism about his illness and other matters, which is not the same as Chinese stoicism. The Chinese are stoical as part of a total worldview, a deep and convinced view of life itself. Greg's stoicism is sectional; he is aware that things are not

---

[343] Harvard Community Health Plan.

the same for him as for white Americans—expectations are less, he has to put up with more.

July 13, 1989

The thought has persisted that my scratchy throat could be VD, so I went to the City Hospital clinic. Large crowd, understaffed due to recent budget cutbacks. One woman was there with her two kids!

Fat Mike came in and nearly wrenched my dick off. At first, he pulled out a condom and said, "Put this on, I want to suck you." I declined. He is working now as a landscape gardener.

The CBS *48 Hours* program on Revolution comes over, and it is hosted by Dan Rather. This perhaps explains why I was first invited to be interviewed, and then disinvited. Rather does not go for me. If so, that looks like twice he vetoed me during the recent China events. The first time was when Bill Whittaker, the Tokyo bureau guy, interviewed me with great fanfare at the Palace Hotel for the Evening News. It never got used.

D came in for magnificent sucking of my tits, then my cock—without coming. Later I dined alone at Legal Seafoods, and passing through Park Square, I saw Danny— at the same spot where we first met that summer evening almost a year ago. I have grown fond of him.

July 14, 1989

Lovely weather for the 200th birthday of the French Revolution. The world in general seems to have a tinge of excitement. And closer to home, I have even started writing a few pages on the recent China events.

So Greg N did feel a chill on Wednesday night at Reggie's behavior. How careful one has to be of one's proud lions. I must not forget that Reggie and I have known each for some six years, and that he naturally assumes a special role at my place.

Mac seems to think it unlikely that *National Geographic* will go ahead with a separate story on the Chinese crisis—all because they do not have pictures taken by their own photographers. So I may have to sit on my material until *COMM* comes out. Could this perhaps be a good thing?

Good can come even out of an unpromising venture. I was upstairs playing squash with Stanley Jenkins—a charitable act on my part—when a guy in a yellow T-shirt, passing me on the staircase, smiled broadly and said hello. I felt the same way about him as he evidently did about me. I had to hurry Wyatt—who was doing odd jobs for me— out of the place to get ready for Scott. He's a dancer.

(Just before he left, Wyatt mentioned to me that Glen, his older white friend, hasn't been well "again." Rashes. "He gets it now and then." I asked if he was positive to the HIV virus. He has been for nine months. So).

Dancer Scott tears off my clothes and, in general, takes the initiative. He sucks my tits, kisses the tongue off me, then sucks my cock. He asks to fuck me, which initially turns out to be an oblique request for me to fuck him. I keep him waiting quite a long time. Eventually, I fucked him in a number of positions.

He gets to the point where he really does want to do it to me. This rich Black boy says, "Gee, I want to get inside you!" (Not, "fuck you.") But I am hopelessly sore with effects of my illness, so it does not continue very long.

July 15, 1989

Gu told me that he had asked Mingming why he didn't defect. "Because my daughter is in China," the young diplomat replied. While I was away in China, Gu organized a drive for a "mutiny" against the Beijing government. He now thinks he cannot go back soon. Last week, his 7-year-old daughter arrived from China and was full of the government's line about the wonderful soldiers. "I had to argue with her," said Gu.

He asks eagerly if I am going to write a book on the spring events in China. He himself is switching PhD topics from China's international economic dealings with Taiwan and Hong Kong to the recent crisis.

Magnificent time in bed with Hank. I realize anew that there are very few people ever who I have been with in a sustained way that are as handsome as this guy. If you single out his cock, I guess it is the loveliest I have ever regularly had. Calvin would push him, Reggie, too—but Hank's is far bigger than Reggie's and also a bit bigger than Luther's. In looks, Hank is well ahead of Luther, not really ahead of Reggie.

July 18, 1989

This virus is making rather slow progress through my system. I should get more rest, but the enticements of my *The Australians* manuscript and Black flesh are hard to resist. In the street, I pass the little Black guy I sometimes see cruising at Northeastern. In the nature of things, we don't speak—let alone know each other's names—but today something made me glance at this guy (instead of glancing away) as we passed in Huntington Avenue. He was looking straight at me, and he was beaming! Amazing— why? Out went his arm to my shoulder as he continued his broad smile. I had never seen him smile before, and he looks nice when he smiles. "I saw you on Nightline. You were perfect—just perfect."

Wonderful sex with Danny this afternoon. "I want to come today, too," he said with a smile as we climbed into bed. I noticed that fucking him seemed to get him nice and randy for his own orgasm. Bad news about his girlfriend. She was raped by a gang. They hit her in the face with a hammer. Two days in hospital. Danny comments: "You know, some guys don't know how to approach a girl. They end up hitting her cos they don't know how to talk to her."

July 20, 1989

The Harvard talk goes well; even I could tell that without listening to opinions. The most interesting questions were not from Harvard regulars. Don Price asked how I could say that the only alternative to Leninism was political pluralism, when I also said that there are two variants of authoritarianism—Leninist and non-Leninist. Could not communism turn into South Korea-type non-Leninist authoritarianism?

The answer is that the successor regime to Leninism, based on all historical experience, would seem to have to be, not another authoritarianism, but something brought about by a tremendous

Ruction—given a Communist government's ability to repress uprisings—and thus likely to be the more hopeful genus of political pluralism.

July 21, 1989

A wonderful time with Charles S this noon. Deep, deep rimming. He is so soft and charming in his preparation of my asshole, that by the time he began to fuck me in the doggy position, I really wanted it. Watching it in the mirror added to our frenzy. It seems Charles really likes me. He spoke of his friend, Earl, who is moving in with him next week. "If Earl had not been there at that time, it would have been you." I told him a little about Edward. "He's crazy to leave you here alone—I wouldn't dare risk it," he said touchingly.

So Charles knows Hank. One night they met at a party, he and Earl took Hank home, a threesome ensued.

It happened again. Greg N called about 8 PM. "I'm horny." But I had to say no. Soon I have both Danny and Neal at the window, borrowing this, calling out that. There is too much traffic in and out of here on the part of my Black acquaintances, I think.

July 22, 1989

Fourth game of squash in four days and it feels marvelous. I lost to Alan this afternoon, narrowly, in part because I was physically tired. But that is so much better than being stiff and unpracticed.

While I was taking a call, Reggie showered and was all ready for me. I played a trick on him but scared the hell out of him. "I'm worried there's something wrong with my balls," I said. "They've suddenly gone hard." He felt in my pants. A look of deep anxiety came over him as he felt the cold hard mass behind my zipper.

"Did you call the doctor?" He did not even want—dare—to look inside my pants. I smiled and kissed him. I had put Li-li's Chinese mental health balls down my pants.

He went to work on my tits, and soon he had me where he wanted me—legs up. How brilliantly did he work my asshole with his fingers! Soon his dick was in there. God, he pumped me. "Do you want to put a condom on, or just stop there?" I asked, gasping. But he was about to come, swooning and going on. All sorts of things ensued, accompanied throughout by the Daddy-Son talk. We did everything close to the mirror to double the visual pleasure. I eventually came as he did three things to me simultaneously (the darling guy): a finger up my asshole, mouth on one tit, big Black hand stroking my throbbing prick. I sprayed his neck and face and chest.

July 24, 1989

Sent off a handsome bible to Li Liyong in Beijing, despite some misgivings over the diplomacy of the situation.

A nice time with Tony O last night. We saw the movie *When Harry Met Sally* at Copley Place, then ate at Legal Seafoods. Today he met an Irish guy from Woburn at his favorite spot in Cambridge, the bird sanctuary. Still, he seems ambivalent about his boyfriend, complaining all the time, yet sticking with him.

July 26, 1989

Dr. Westbrook decides to X-ray my lungs. She also gets on my case a little over drinking 3/4 bottle of wine each evening. "That's an awful lot," she says with the air of one who knows little of wine, and one who would probably consider one glass too much.

Cleveland came in and it was old times. I will always associate him with the Roberts Club at the Y, where we met. He is a cheerful, peaceful character who enjoys things and says so. He played with my Australian koala bear—naked, in bed—and I took a nice snap of him. In the end, I fucked him and came nicely. He beamed. "It didn't hurt much at all," he said. "I never come," he said, when I asked him if he didn't want me to keep on jerking him off.

July 27, 1989

I got into Neal but didn't stay long or go very deep. Perhaps I should have let him wiggle me in as he did last time. Otherwise, as tonight, he seems to resist when I push. Perhaps after Cleveland last night, I wasn't imaginative enough—but the orgasm was fantastically good. Neal was in a wonderful mood. He seems to accept perfectly the new policy—he called on the dot and, on leaving, said gaily, "See you next Thursday."

July 29, 1989

The doorbell rings, and a voice says, "Danny," but it doesn't sound like Danny. Anyway, the guy is reasonably nice, so I offer him a beer and we chat. Turns out Neal mentioned my name to him.

Julius says—on the phone from Walpole—that he'd been "doing research" in the prison library. I was curious as to the topic. "This guy came, see, and he says he's in for attempted murder," Julius says. "But we think he might be a rapist. So I went to look up the case—he is a rapist."

"What difference does it make?"

"Well, everyone hates a rapist. A rapist gets stabbed, beaten, burned out. So this guy is just pretendin' to be in for murder; he's really in for rape."

Julius says his mulatto friend is a fairly open homosexual. "Sometimes, he embarrasses me—grabbing my dick and that." In the previous prison, Julius remembers a case of a gay guy who, the others said, flirted with them and then held back. "Six of them did a train on him—he needed 18 stitches in his asshole."

July 31, 1989

Caroline is ill—so there was time to shower first, etc. Reggie's body is even more beautiful than ever. He left about 2:30 AM after watching a movie while I began to go to sleep.

In the morning, he had gone to church—mainly to please his old school friend, the pastor who handled Reggie and Caroline's wedding. It was the pastor's first day at his new church. How many people in the congregation, I wondered. Only fifteen.

One moment Reggie is talking about fucking and rimming; the next, he says, "You know our pastor talked in tongues this morning."

Am getting a package off to the UK on *COMM* tonight. A revised outline together with two draft chapters. We will see if the sleepy Abner can do something with it.

Barbara calls to say Fred is very pleased with the draft chapter I showed him (the one on the early 1960s). "It's some of the best writing Ross has done," Fred told Barbara. Good! That means I have a green light to go ahead with the blend of memoir and history that I have used so far.

August 1, 1989

Just as something important is happening in China, I sense that something important also is happening, or should, in my life: the end of addiction.

Earl talks to me about more pieces for *World Monitor*—I guess the July issue piece was judged a great success.

A dream last night: A curvaceous Boadicea kneels down on the sidewalk in Huntington Ave, puts her Black mouth across me, and sucks like a vacuum cleaner. Behind me, a cloud of young men materialize. Voices from within their midst spur the woman on, urge me to thrust my cock further into her throat. One young Black guy pulls at my pants. Another finishes the job and hauls them to my ankles. "Fuck me, someone," I cry out, surprised at myself. "Anyone who doesn't have AIDS, fuck me!"

August 2, 1989

At last, a start on the chapter I am simply calling, at the moment, "Late 1960s."

A letter from Edward about our times together at the coming of his birthday. "Your return from China was the biggest satisfaction," he wrote, "though I always knew you would. The meals, the beach, the roses, meeting Li-li, etc. made for an unprecedented birthday. Words cannot describe what I feel. With love—Edward."

August 3, 1989

I won a good 3-2 at squash over Jim and then took a shower in the general locker room. A guy seems to shoot a lightning glance at me. Why does he come back into the shower room a second time, where I still was, when he had seemed to have been finished? He is wearing trunks, but when wet they readily reveal a lovely cock. Then, did I see a wink? He is with two other guys and evidently, he cannot speak to me.

I put my number on a piece of paper, he grabs it. I am hardly home when he calls. Says his name is Harry. He has waited around in the hope of meeting me straight away. "Now," he said when I proposed meeting tomorrow. I walk back to the Y, and he is sitting in his parked car.

The first question takes me aback a bit—have you got a condom at home?—as I saw in the shower that his handsome, cut cock is very big. But, apprehensive as I was about getting screwed by this huge tool, I reassured him that I had condoms. On my deck, his bulging cock set me alight. Does he want a drink? No, he says, he just wants to take his clothes off. "I come quick," he grunted.

I licked and sucked his balls—he lay on his back like an insect. He groaned and said he had never had his balls sucked before. He gets so excited that there isn't time for much more before he shoots a Laurent-like stream, but very white, and the smell of it entrances me almost as much as his lustful enjoyment of the moment. We shower together. Can I teach him to suck?

He asks if I meet people at the Y; what is he getting at? "I can take lessons," he says disarmingly; "I can watch you to see how to do it." Why does he say, at least four times, that my cock is big, when his is far bigger? An extraordinary man I may never forget.

—END OF VOLUME 1—

About the Author and Editor

Ross Terrill, Author

A world-renowned China specialist and former Associate in Research at Harvard's Fairbank Center for Chinese Studies, Ross Terrill is the author of more than a dozen books. Raised in rural Australia, he graduated in history and political science from the University of Melbourne in 1962 and served in the Australian Army. He took a Ph.D. in political science at Harvard in 1970, where his thesis on the philosophy of R. H. Tawney was awarded the Sumner Prize and was later published by Harvard University Press as *Socialism as Fellowship*.

While teaching at Harvard on political thought, Chinese politics, and international affairs, Terrill wrote *800,000,000: The Real China, The Future of China: After Mao, Flowers on an Iron Tree: Five Cities of China*, and the original edition of *Mao*, his acclaimed biography of the Chinese leader. As a contributing editor of *The Atlantic Monthly* he won the National Magazine Award for Reporting Excellence and the George Polk Memorial Award for Outstanding Magazine Reporting for writings on China. In 1979 he became an American citizen.

Terrill is a many-time contributor to the *New York Times* and other newspapers, including *Newsday, Chicago Tribune, Los Angeles Times, Miami Herald*, and *Washington Post*. In addition to the *Atlantic Monthly*, he has written for *Foreign Affairs, New Republic, National Geographic, World Monitor* and other magazines. More recent books he has written include *The White-Boned Demon: A Biography of Madame Mao* and *The Australians*.

Terrill has moved within a triangle of academia, journalistic writing, and public life, testifying numerous times before committees of the United States Congress. He has been a special commentator for CBS News, the *Today Show*, ABC's *Nightline, Firing Line* and—often from China—on NPR's *All Things Considered*.

Terrill has visited China almost every year for many years and within China his *Mao* in Chinese translation has sold more than 1.5 million copies. He spent the month of June, 1989 in Beijing, including the climactic night of June 3-4 in Tiananmen Square.

Recently, he has been visiting professor at the University of Texas at Austin and at Monash University in Australia. Terrill's *The New Chinese Empire* won the *Los Angeles Times* Book Prize. In 2020, he published his memoir, *From Australian Bush to Tiananmen Square*.

Terrill lives in Boston.

Philip Gambone, Editor

Philip Gambone has been writing and publishing fiction and nonfiction since the 1980s. His five books include a collection of short stories, a novel, a book of interviews with gay fiction writers, and a collection of profiles of prominent LGBTQ Americans. His most recent book, *As Far As I Can Tell: Finding My Father in World War II* (Rattling Good Yarns Press, 2020), is a memoir about a gay son tracing the route his father made across Europe during that war. It was named one of the Best Books of 2020 by The Boston Globe.

Printed in the USA
CPSIA information can be obtained
at www.ICGtesting.com
LVHW090846220224
772532LV00003B/180

9 781955 826181